Human Behavior in Organizations
Third Edition

J. Clifton Williams

H.R. Gibson Professor of Management
Baylor University

George P. Huber

Fondren Foundation Centennial Chaired
Professor of Business
University of Texas at Austin

Published by

G78 **SOUTH-WESTERN PUBLISHING CO.**

CINCINNATI   WEST CHICAGO, IL   DALLAS   PELHAM MANOR, NY   LIVERMORE, CA

Copyright © 1986
by South-Western Publishing Co.
Cincinnati, Ohio

ISBN: 0-538-07780-8
Library of Congress Catalog Card Number: 85-50614

1 2 3 4 5 6 7 8 K 1 0 9 8 7 6

Printed in the United States of America

Our goal in writing *Human Behavior in Organizations,* third edition, is to help the reader become successful in predicting, understanding, and influencing behavior in organizations.

Of course, every reader has already acquired a good deal of knowledge about human behavior through years of personal experience. So why write this book? One reason is that a significant portion of what most people think they know about human behavior is erroneous. Another reason is that, for a person who has had thousands of personal experiences, careful reading of this book will provide a far more intensive learning opportunity (in terms of information acquired per unit of time) than would an equivalent number of additional hours of personal experience.

A third reason for studying organizational behavior is that a primary purpose of education is less to teach facts than it is to teach how to acquire facts. Thus in this book we examine not only facts but concepts and frameworks that will enable the reader to convert future experiences into useful knowledge.

Organizational behavior, the subject of this book, has become established as a discipline in its own right. This is not to say that all contributors to the field view its scope and content in exactly the same way. Essentially, however, organizational behavior is that aspect of management that focuses on predicting, understanding, and influencing human behavior in organizations.

Building on the bedrock belief that there is nothing so practical as a good theory, organizational behavior is deeply grounded in research, especially in the research of the behavioral sciences of industrial/organizational psychology and industrial sociology. Organizational behavior, a uniquely interdisciplinary field, is committed to the formulation of sound, empirically tested theory and to the application of that theory in organizations. It is concerned with human personality and behavior— but always within the context of organizational life. A major goal of organizational behavior is, therefore, a thorough melding of individual and group psychology with organization theory. Studiously avoiding quick and easy solutions to problems, it offers a variety of theories, models, and strategies through which thinking managers can find their own solutions in specific situations.

Anyone with an interest in relating more effectively to others in a work environment should find this book interesting and valuable. It is, however, written primarily for undergraduate students in colleges and universities. It may also be used by managers and advanced supervisors in development courses or programs of self-study. Although the organizational behavior course in most colleges and universities follows the introductory course and elaborates on the human aspects of management, an introductory course is not a prerequisite for understanding this book.

This third edition of *Human Behavior in Organizations* differs from the second primarily in four ways. First, the entire book has been updated to reflect recent research and changes in the organizational, social, and economic environments within which organizations and their members function. Second, in keeping with changing organizational practices, a chapter on participation in organizations has been added. This chapter contains many practical guidelines for gaining and managing participation on both day-to-day and more formal bases. Third, again in keeping with changing organizational practices, a good deal of readily applied material has been added to the chapters on motivation and decision making. Finally, the chapters on leadership have been slightly altered to achieve a better balance; the content of the second edition's chapter on effective discipline has been merged into this edition's chapter on the first line supervisor; and material concerning the important role of managers in creating organizational culture has been added to the chapter on managerial effectiveness.

To make *Human Behavior in Organizations*, third edition, interesting and to facilitate learning, each chapter begins with a thought stimulator—a quotation or point of view to arouse interest, perhaps at times even to antagonize for the purpose of generating thoughtful consideration of the content to follow. Objectives are stated in the chapter introductions, and each chapter ends with a list of *Important Terms and Concepts* to help students focus on the most relevant content. The *Suggested Readings*, articles and books related to the chapter, will be of special interest to those who wish to investigate the subject matter in greater depth. The use of the end-of-chapter *Study and Discussion Questions* and *Critical Incidents* (short cases) is continued in this revision.

We particularly appreciate the contributions to this third edition made by the following reviewers: Gerald Biberman, University of Scranton; Margaret Fenn, University of Washington; William Hahn, Savannah State College; John Hartley, Rochester Institute of Technology.

The result of all of this is, we hope, a useful and readable book. Part One presents the key foundations of the book with two chapters. Chapter 1 contains an introduction that motivates students by making clear why it is important to study organizational behavior. This chapter puts the field into perspective by describing the historical predecessors of organizational behavior, such as scientific management, and then goes on to describe the modern-day field. Chapter 2 provides unusual and highly relevant material on the goals of organizations and managers, including material on managerial ethics and corporate social responsibility. The intention is not to indoctrinate the students with any belief but rather to lend perspective to some of the forces that shape human behavior in organizations.

Part Two examines the relationships between individuals and organizations. Chapter 3 discusses the impact of both individual differences and job characteristics on behavior in organizations and explains Theories X, Y, and Z. Chapter 4 describes how needs affect organizational behavior and the strengths and weaknesses of the important need theories of Maslow and Herzberg. Practical guidance for motivating people is provided in Chapter 5, and the advice is based on sound research and theory. Topics include analyzing motivational problems, money as a motivator, and expectancy theory.

Part Three of the book moves on to the nature of groups and their important roles in organizations. Chapter 6 gives a thorough introduction to the dynamics of informal groups, stressing key variables such as cohesiveness, leadership, and internal control mechanisms. Practical analyses focus on how to deal with hostile groups and the types of informal work groups that develop in unionized organizations. The problems of disadvantaged groups are dealt with in Chapter 7. Statistical data on the changing status of racial minorities, women, and maladjusted employees, combined with an objective discussion of discrimination and reverse discrimination, provide the student with a useful perspective for understanding the problems of disadvantaged work force members. Chapter 8 provides in-depth understanding of the nature and role of unions in modern organizations and society. Of particular interest is the section describing the effects of unions on the behavior of both managers and employees. Conflict and stress are natural consequences of the competing forces and changing conditions found in modern organizations. Chapter 9 explains the organizational and individual conditions leading to conflict and stress and then describes proven approaches for minimizing their undesirable outcomes.

Organizational structures and processes are addressed in Part Four. Chapter 10 provides the student with a practical understanding of classical, neoclassical, and modern organization theory. A unique and important feature is the description, from contrasting classical and neoclassical viewpoints, of key organizational design concepts such as span of management, line and staff, and authority and responsibility. Chapter 11 is an explanation of how the organization's structure and processes, such as its communication, control, and reward systems, affect managerial behavior and performance. This unusual subject matter will be viewed by students as realistic and relevant to the work environment many of them expect to experience. An important and uncommon feature of Chapter 12 is its stress on the mistakes commonly made by decision makers. In this way the chapter retains the book's behavioral emphasis. The chapter goes on to describe proven approaches for overcoming mistakes and is thus prescriptive at the same time that it is descriptive. Chapter 13 describes the nature and causes of communication problems and then gives research-based but practical guidance on how to improve communication in organizations. The chapter is more practical and concrete than the communication chapter found in most textbooks. Besides addressing the expected topics of change, resistance to change, and organizational development, Chapter 14 examines the important topic of management development in depth.

Part Five deals with the important subject of leadership in organizations. Chapter 15 takes a modern approach to the subject of authority and power, explaining in addition the alternative forms of influence that pervade modern organizations. Chapter 16 presents in an understandable way the important leadership concepts and theories. Blake and Mouton's Managerial Grid®, Fiedler's contingency approach, and House's path-goal approach are each described. The chapter also introduces related material that is treated in greater depth in later chapters, such as participation and management by objectives. Chapter 17 takes the unusual step of looking at managers as individuals rather than as a class of position holders. Personal characteristics such as emotional maturity, problem-solving skills, and varying motivations provide concreteness and realism. A unique feature of the chapter is the discussion of the leader's role in creating organizational culture. No book on human behavior in organizations could be considered complete without a strong chapter on that key figure, the first line supervisor. Besides thoroughly addressing the topics of the supervisor's role conflicts, responsibility, and authority imbalance, Chapter 18 sensibly treats the subjects of supervisory role design and effective disciplinary action. Participation has become a key practice and behavior in organizational life. Chapter 19 provides research-based guidelines for gaining the benefits of participation on both an everyday basis and in more structured group meetings and gives a more practical and thorough treatment of this subject than any other text. Finally, Chapter 20 provides a thorough and objective treatment of goal-setting and management by objectives. The material is research-based but is described in a clear and useful way with many practical suggestions for using these important techniques.

The writing of a book on a subject as broad as human behavior in organizations necessarily requires continual decisions about what to include. We believe this book contains the best of what is known about the interrelated cluster of subjects that make up the discipline of organizational behavior. Extraneous detail and lengthy illustrations that would likely detract from relevant facts and concepts have deliberately been omitted. It is our hope that, as in the case of the successful first and second editions, *Human Behavior in Organizations*, third edition, will meet the needs of serious students of organizational behavior both in the classroom and in the real world of management and organizations.

J. Clifton Williams

George P. Huber

CONTENTS

PART FOUR

Organizational Structure and Process

PART FIVE

Leadership in Organizations

FOUNDATIONS OF ORGANIZATIONAL BEHAVIOR

1 Organizational Behavior in Perspective
2 The Goals and Values of Organizations and Managers

The two chapters of Part 1 lay the foundation for the remaining chapters. They describe the historical and methodological context from which organizational behavior (OB) emerged as a more or less distinguishable field of study within the discipline of management.

Part of the difficulty in tracing the development of OB, or even in stating confidently that it is a subdiscipline of management, arises from the fact that it is in the fullest sense an interdisciplinary field with historical roots in psychology, sociology, and anthropology as well as management. OB has drawn liberally from both the content and methods of these behavioral sciences, and they continue to contribute to OB theory and application.

OB is philosophical as well as scientific; it has a long-standing commitment to certain humanistic values. Those values are difficult to define because the personal values and perceptions of professionals in the field differ, but they exist nonetheless. OB is concerned with profits, with efficiency, with productivity; but from its beginnings it has also been concerned with the worth of the employee as a person rather than merely as one through whom organizational goals are achieved. It is because of this orientation that an early chapter on the goals and values of organizations and managers is included. All that is said in this book about how to understand and influence people may justifiably appear to be manipulative and exploitive unless placed within a value context—a frame of reference in which concerns for people and productivity are maturely integrated.

Organizational Behavior in Perspective

It is important to recognize that every student already has a good deal of knowledge about human behavior, acquired through a fifth of a century or more of personal experience. So why formally study organizational behavior? One reason is that a significant portion of what we think we have learned from experience is much less correct than we believe it is. This is easily demonstrated in a number of ways, one of which is to ask three people the best way to handle a particular behavioral problem and then to observe their disagreement.

There is much evidence to demonstrate that people frequently mislearn from experience. Their conclusions about human behavior are based on limited experience, and this "knowledge" is usually ill-suited to any management situation. In contrast, the knowledge obtained by studying what scientists have concluded about behavior in organizations is based on thousands of carefully studied "experiences."

Another reason to study organizational behavior is that for a person who has already been exposed to thousands of personal learning experiences, formal study provides a far more intensive learning opportunity. In terms of the amount of knowledge acquired during a given period of time, much more can be learned through study than through an equivalent number of additional hours of personal experience.

A third reason for formally studying organizational behavior is that the primary purpose of post-secondary education is less to teach facts than it is to teach concepts. In this book, therefore, we will examine not only "facts" but also concepts that will make us far more effective in converting future experiences into useful knowledge.

Throughout recorded history leaders have recognized the need to understand human behavior and to develop leadership and other interpersonal skills. Thus, the needs of today's managers for effective methods of coping with the human aspects of their work are essentially the same as those of past leaders. The uniqueness of the modern approach lies in the extent of our accumulated knowledge and, perhaps more importantly, in our improved methods for collecting and analyzing data and making practical applications.

The prescientific approach to studying and teaching human relations in organizations was wasteful and inefficient because of its dependence on trial-and-error learning and its acceptance of theories that had not been systematically tested. Our modern approach—the organizational behavior (OB) approach—is not totally scientific. Nevertheless, because of its deep commitment to scientific methods, its progress has been impressive and its future is promising. The objectives of Chapter 1, an introduction to the field of organizational behavior, are

TO UNDERSTAND:

1. The definition of organizational behavior

2. The relevance of organizational behavior

3. The historical background of organizational behavior

4. The influences of the behavioral sciences on organizational behavior

THE FIELD OF ORGANIZATIONAL BEHAVIOR

Organizational behavior (OB) is a field of management that is primarily concerned with understanding, predicting, and influencing human behavior in organizations. Specifically, OB attempts to understand individuals in formal organizations as a basis for meeting individual needs and achieving organizational objectives.

This definition of OB contains concepts that may need clarification. In fact, the term *organizational behavior* is itself somewhat ambiguous. Do organizations behave or is it really individual behavior with which OB is concerned? These are relevant questions. Their answers provide an appropriate introduction to the field of organizational behavior.

The table of contents of this book suggests that OB is indeed concerned with the behavior of individuals—especially with how individuals are motivated and led. Individuals do not, however, behave identically in various situations, and appropriate behavior in one situation may be inappropriate in another. People are accustomed to being members of organizations—as family members, students, members of social or religious groups, and so on—but each type of organization is unique and worthy of special study. Organizational behavior is concerned primarily with the workplace—mostly with business organizations—although much of what we know about human behavior in profit-making firms applies equally to educational, governmental, religious, and other formal organizations.

The more deeply we study people in organizations, the more obvious it becomes that individual behavior cannot be understood apart from the many interacting aspects of the individual's environment, including the actions of other people and groups. The behavior of individuals is also related to characteristics of the formal organizations of which they are members: for example, the organization's size, complexity, levels of management, purpose, goals, technologies, policies, and styles of management. All the personal behaviors, actions of informal groups, and formal organizational characteristics interact to form a whole organism: a more or less unified social system in which changes in one part have an impact on the other parts. It is all these variables—the behavior and performance of individuals, groups, and formal organizational units—that comprise the subject of organizational behavior.

The concern of the OB field with understanding, predicting, and influencing behavior implies, first of all, that the field contains a body of research and theory devoted to this purpose. OB takes seriously its task of achieving depth of understanding and providing generalizations that managers can use to anticipate the effects of certain actions and thereby avoid the costly mistakes of trial-and-error learning.

Practical-minded business students sometimes become impatient with theory and want to get on with the task of learning how to manage as though theories have no practical value. It is noteworthy, however, that even the practical seminars that are currently offered for the training of practicing supervisors are filled with theories that have evolved within the field of organizational behavior. Understanding these theories and principles provides the depth of education needed for creative thinking and problem solving in the human relations area.

The field of organizational behavior is committed to helping managers more effectively achieve organizational objectives. However, the cooperative efforts of employees and managers that are required to reach those objectives can be achieved only if the organization contributes to the satisfaction of its members' needs. Thus, one of the main themes running through the subject matter of OB—leadership, goal setting, decision making, communicating, and so on—is motivation. Both the understanding and the influencing aspects of OB are concerned with human motivation, a subject in which most of us have an interest and some intuitive knowledge.

HISTORICAL FOUNDATIONS

Organizational behavior began as a part of general management and has only recently become a distinct field of study. The body of research, theory, and application associated with a growing concern for people in the workplace emerged as the field of organizational behavior when a significant number of researchers adopted the methods of the behavioral sciences.

Evidence that leaders have long been aware of the importance of human relations is common in the ancient writings of the Greeks, Romans, Persians, Phoenicians, Egyptians, and Hebrews. Although a scientific approach to management did not exist, many of civilization's early leaders and scholars were astute observers of human nature, and their thoughts exerted a strong influence on subsequent leaders. Prior to 2000 B.C., one book of instruction for Egyptian leaders included the following suggestion for communicating with subordinates:

> If thou art one to whom petition is made, be calm as thou listenest to what the petitioner has to say. Do not rebuff him before . . . he has said that for which he came. . . . It is not (necessary) that everything about which he has petitioned should come to pass, (but) a good hearing is soothing to the heart.[1]

This 4,000-year-old advice sounds surprisingly like some of that found in modern organizational behavior books. Although the field of OB tries to avoid the pitfalls of blindly following traditional wisdom, not all the advice OB has to offer is the result of direct scientific tests. Experimental data must be interpreted; modern experts, like those whom we study in histories, must make judgments based on an accumulation of sometimes conflicting data, and they must finally express their views.

Every generation of students and scholars builds on the experiences and conclusions of past generations, and many of the insights that each generation experiences have been experienced in various forms for centuries. The actions of Moses, for example, in preparing for and leading the exodus from Egypt, showed deep insights into methods of organizing people and delegating tasks. Democratic leadership was pioneered by the ancient Greeks; and several centuries before Christ, captains of merchant ships understood how to reduce fatigue and boredom by using music to pace their oarsmen and motivate them to work in smooth, rhythmical movements.

The Merchants of Venice

The detailed business records of the fifteenth century Italian merchants provide rich insights into the concepts of organizational behavior of that day. We know, for example, that workers who made oars were paid by the piece, that unskilled laborers were paid day wages, and that close supervision was considered necessary for high productivity. Strict attention was given to timekeeping and quality control. Apprenticeship programs within crafts were commonplace then as now, and examinations were sometimes a prerequisite for employment in the crafts. The records of that day show that managers conducted semiannual performance appraisals using a committee approach. They even had "wine breaks" much like our twentieth century coffee breaks and for the same reasons.[2]

Niccolo Machiavelli

An impoverished Florentine aristocrat, Niccolo Machiavelli held diplomatic posts in Florence from around 1498 to 1512 that required travel to other Italian city states and to cities in several European countries. Because Machiavelli was highly educated, skilled in the writing of documents, and politically astute, his services as a diplomat and advisor to rulers and bureaucrats were much in demand. Ironically, he was relatively unsuccessful in managing his own career, and after being exiled from Florence when a change in power occurred he spent much of his time writing. He is best known for *The Prince*, a short condensation of *The Discourses on the First Ten Books of Titus Livius*,[3] in which Machiavelli advises the young Medici princes on how to gain power and how to rule.

Machiavelli's advice was shocking, then as now, because he abandoned all attempts to ground it in conventional morality. Instead he based his views on empirical observations of how effective power holders gain and use power. For this reason, many professors of management insist that their students understand Machiavelli's writings. Richard Calhoon gives the following reasons for the continuing validity of Machiavelli's contribution, particularly his insights into leadership:

1. He was scientific in that he provided an orderly and logical analysis of his empirical observations.

2. The multitude of city-states and kingdoms that he studied, and the conditions of flux in which they existed, provided a laboratory for study that was unique in history.

3. His exile, after years of political involvement, provided an unusual time for reflection and insight.

4. He effectively used historical analogy, comparing the events that occurred in the Renaissance world with events that occurred in earlier civilizations. By this means he maintained perspective and gained insights that have continued to be relevant.[4]

Modern writers in the OB field whose humanistic values strongly influence their views of leadership reject the manipulative, exploitive, and devious aspects of Machiavellian leadership (or Machiavellianism), but few deny Machiavelli's brilliance and the breadth of his continuing influence since his early sixteenth century advice in *The Prince*.

The Early Industrial Era

The philosophy and attitudes that nurtured the development of capitalism, as well as the values expressed in capitalism, profoundly influenced the history of management including what we now call organizational behavior. Max Weber, a German sociologist, noted that the acceptance of capitalism was based on its relationship to the Protestant work ethic.[5] As described by Weber, the **Protestant work ethic** is an interpretation of Calvinistic theology which made the accumulation of wealth not merely acceptable but an obligation. Work is a calling, not a curse; productivity and thrift are Christian virtues. Persons who are lazy and do not invest their resources wisely are sinful because they fail to utilize and develop their God-given talents.[6] Those who can work and do not should not be allowed to eat.[7] In a culture strongly influenced by Christian theology, the Protestant ethic was a strong motivator. For many people it remains so; for others it does not. To the extent that the Protestant work ethic is followed today—and it certainly is not universally followed—it needs to be considered in all analyses of motivational problems and opportunities.

An account of the individuals who influenced the field of OB would be incomplete without reference to Adam Smith, although he is known primarily as an advocate of laissez-faire capitalism.[8] His philosophy had a monumental influence on the values and attitudes of managers and consequently on their treatment of employees. Writers infrequently note his generous contributions to the development of efficient production methods to which were added in 1832 the contributions of Charles Babbage, a British mathematician best known for his creative ideas on mechanical computers.[9] Both Smith and Babbage were strong advocates of the **division of labor**—the division of jobs into a number of narrow specialties requiring different levels of skill, difficulty, and responsibility. This early emphasis on efficient methods set the stage for the classical theories of management of the twentieth century in which concern for productivity greatly overshadowed concern for employees.

Scientific Management

A benchmark in the history of OB was established in 1911 when Frederick W. Taylor published his *Principles of Management*.[10] Taylor, an engineer, is best known for his emphasis on scientific work methods to replace the old rule-of-thumb approach that grew out of the philosophies of Smith and Babbage. Taylor insisted on a strict division of work between management and labor, leaving few decisions to workers about how to perform their jobs. Research, rather than the workers, would decide how the work should be done down to the smallest movement.[11]

Taylor's efficiency methods extend into every aspect of the workplace: the layout of machines, the flow of work, the systematic training of workers, and even the cost evaluation of every aspect of the work process. Taylor's ideas on the need for efficiency were not new, but his scientific methods were. The idea of scientifically studying jobs—the use of time and motion studies, for example—was revolutionary, and it rapidly influenced the entire industrialized world.

The focus of **scientific management** was on increasing production, but Taylor's management philosophy ran deeper than his efficiency methods suggest. He strongly advocated high wages—wages that firms could not afford to pay without high productivity. He believed that optimal productivity could be achieved only through the cooperative efforts of management and labor; each person contributes in the area of his or her highest potential, and everyone shares in the resulting wealth. Only recently has Taylor received the credit he deserves for his genuine concern for people. For the most part, his emphasis on efficiency obscured his conviction that everyone should benefit from the wealth created through scientific management. The clouding of Taylor's concern for people occurred because management too frequently seized the opportunity to increase productivity and profits, using scientific methods to justify increased demands for worker productivity, without increasing wages and improving working conditions.

Today, as in the early years of Taylor's influence, workers associate industrial engineering with management's efforts to increase production without increasing wages. They naturally resent both. Before methods to enhance efficiency are applied, employees pace themselves and select their own work methods; afterward the work is usually more monotonous and more tiring because of its faster pace. Jobs consisting of very few, narrowly defined tasks generally require low intelligence and skill. Therefore, they require little training and can be held by people of very limited ability. However, because the workers contribute so little to each item of production, they don't identify with the final product and, therefore, take little pride in it. Thus, despite the fact that methods to enhance efficiency reduce costs and therefore greatly benefit consumers, owners, and workers, they are a mixed blessing. These methods solve many problems, but they also create many problems.

Industrial Psychology

The contributions of Taylor soon dominated management thought, providing a reference point from which many others were to show creative, constructive thinking. Notable among these was Hugo Munsterberg, a German born and educated psychologist who headed an experimental psychology laboratory at Harvard University. Deviating from traditional laboratory research, Munsterberg expanded the role of psychology to include problems of (1) selecting personnel whose abilities match their work, (2) determining the psychological conditions that contribute to productivity, (3) and producing employee attitudes that are favorable to organizational life.

Since 1913, when Munsterberg's *Psychology and Industrial Efficiency* was published, **industrial** (or organizational) **psychology** has developed as a respected subdiscipline within the field of general psychology.[12] Industrial psychologists regularly contribute to the literature of organizational behavior in virtually every area. Their contribution is especially important in subjects such as motivation, power, leadership, and decision making in which an understanding of psychological theory is helpful. Industrial psychologists have also contributed significantly to OB in terms of research methods and the development of such data-collecting instruments as psychological tests, attitude inventories, structured interviews, and rating scales.

Principles of Management

When the full impact of Taylor's scientific management hit Europe and America, it so captured the attention of managers that outstanding contributions to managerial thinking by the successful French executive Henri Fayol were almost overlooked. In his 1916 *General and Industrial*

Management, Fayol was concerned with broad concepts of management—concepts viewed from the executive suite rather than from the bottom of the organization where efficiency experts were involved with the molecular movements of factory workers. Fayol was concerned with such managerial functions as organizing, planning, commanding, coordinating, and controlling.[13] He believed there were certain universal **principles of management** within each of these functions that could be discovered and taught to others. To Fayol, management was a field in itself, separate and distinct from such business fields as accounting, finance, or production engineering. This idea is, of course, well accepted now.

Fayol was the first to propose a comprehensive administrative theory of general management, but a number of other theorists were also advancing universally applicable principles of management and in this way attempting to contribute to administrative theory. In America, James Mooney and Allan Reiley published a principles of management (or administrative theory) book in 1931;[14] in 1937, Luther Gulick and Lyndall Urwick edited a similar publication that had a broad impact on management thought and practice.[15]

As we might expect, the advocates of universal principles were not in complete agreement. However, the principles they most often agreed upon and emphasized were the **division of labor** (each employee performing a specialized function); **coordination** (the harmonious integration of the different aspects of an organization); **span of control** (the number of subordinates reporting to one manager or supervisor); **hierarchy** (the vertical arrangement of function and authority); and **subordination** (the submission of persons within the hierarchy to institutional authority). Urwick proposed 29 principles, a considerably larger number than his fellow classicists advocated. Although this was far fewer than the number of variables considered by later theorists, it was a recognition that many different variables contribute to an organization's effectiveness.

The importance of principles of management to the field of organizational behavior can hardly be overemphasized. However, most present-day OB theorists question the practicality of searching for universal principles; they seek instead to discover the nature of the situations where different principles and guidelines apply.

Bureaucratic Theory

The contributors to scientific management, industrial psychology, and administrative theory did not concern themselves with the matter of overall organizational structure. (**Structure** is broadly conceived to include such qualities as the organization's policies and systems as well as the positions and relationships shown on organization charts.) This conceptual void was subsequently filled with bureaucratic theory, a system of thought associated primarily with Max Weber, a German sociologist whose complete writings on bureaucracy were first translated into English in 1947.

Weber was especially concerned with the structure of the management hierarchy. While Taylor was preoccupied with the details of a laborer's work, Weber studied the total organization, how it was constructed, and the relationships between its structure and effectiveness. He made unique contributions to our understanding of what he called *organizational office* (the managerial position) and how offices serve as the basic building blocks of the organization's structure. Although current thought criticizes many aspects of bureaucratic theory, Weber's ideal organizational structure and his rational approach to achieving objectives still serve as a point of departure from which we adapt to allow for the uniqueness of individuals—to allow for human characteristics that prevent organizations from functioning as rationally and impersonally as Weber believed they should.

Today, organizational structure is dealt with most thoroughly in **organization theory** (OT), a management subdiscipline that deals with the organization as an entity, with its environment, technology, structure, and apparent strategies rather than with the individuals and informal groups that operate within the organization. OT is generally thought of as taking a macro view of organizations, while OB, with its focus on individual and group behavior within organizations, is thought of as taking a micro view. Even though structure is a principal variable in OT, it is also important to OB in that it comprises a major part of the environment within which the organization's members function. Modern organization theory recognizes that bureaucracy is not always the best form of organization; it remains, however, the most common form.

The Human Relations Movement

Although a number of authors and managers throughout history—especially during the early part of the twentieth century—emphasized the importance of fair and considerate treatment of employees, practicing managers often regarded workers as little more than a necessary cost of production. Productivity was the goal of management, and people were a means to that end. Efficiency was a supreme value; to the extent that the personal needs of employees conflicted with efficiency goals, employees were expected to conform. In many ways this task-oriented, authoritarian approach to management was effective, but it caused the dissatisfaction that led many employees to unionize in order to protect their interests. It also provoked strong protests from humanitarians who were concerned with the plight of workers. Finally, a series of events and research studies produced a strong ideological reaction and a **human relations movement** developed that emphasized concern for the needs of people. So avid did the supporters of that movement become that they often minimized the legitimate needs of organizations for productivity; and in their zeal to provide new, nonauthoritarian forms of leadership, they failed to acknowledge the role of legitimate organizational authority.

The Hawthorne Studies. Of all the early influences on the human relations movement, the greatest was a series of studies conducted at Western Electric's Hawthorne plant near Chicago. Initiated in 1924 by the National Research Council of the Academy of Sciences, the Hawthorne research gained stature in 1927 when Elton Mayo and other members of the Harvard Business School were invited to participate. Although the results of the original studies were first published in the *Personnel Journal*,[16] their full impact was not felt until the studies were terminated and Elton Mayo published *The Human Problems of an Industrial Civilization* in 1933.[17] The studies were further described in 1939 by Roethlisberger and Dickson in *Management and the Worker*.[18]

Nature and Conclusions. The first stage of the Hawthorne studies occurred in the relay assembly test room to which five women assemblers of telephone relays were transferred from the factory floor. Over a period of two years, the productivity, attitudes, and behavior of these women were observed under a variety of conditions such as variations in the physical environment, work hours, rest pauses, and nature of the supervision. In this and subsequent studies, many environmental factors such as lighting, temperature, and humidity were studied for their possible effects on such variables as fatigue and boredom.

Although subsequent studies used more thorough methods, the conclusions drawn from the relay assembly room experiments established the framework within which later conclusions were made. The results were totally unexpected. At the end of two years the women's output increased by about 30 percent, but the increase was apparently unrelated to changes in working conditions. An increase in lighting, for example, increased productivity, but a decrease in lighting also increased productivity. The researchers concluded—and subsequent research did not change these conclusions—that the increase in productivity was due to changes in attitudes and motivation because of friendly supervision and to a cooperative, nonthreatening work environment.[19,20]

These and other conclusions of the Hawthorne studies led many researchers and managers to question traditional concepts about the value of financial incentives, competition, and authoritarian management. The Hawthorne studies established once and for all the social nature of employees: that employees informally organize themselves into informal groups through which personal needs are satisfied. So impressed were the managers of the Hawthorne plant with the importance of a friendly, conflict-free workplace that they established a formal company program that permitted employees to discuss personal or work-related problems with a counselor who could understand their needs, be supportive, and help them find solutions.

The Lasting Influence. Many researchers today reject the idea that a noncompetitive, conflict-free work environment is ideal, and all recognize that happy workers are not always productive. Critics of the Hawthorne studies note that by current standards the research was unscientific and that the conclusions reached do not necessarily follow from the data.[21] Nevertheless, the impact of the Hawthorne studies was dramatic. It set the pace for the research of the 1940s and 1950s that emphasized the worth of the individual and the influence of informal groups in organizations. Reflecting the personal values of the researchers, studies conducted during the human relations era expressed a preference for appealing to the inner needs of the individual rather than exercising external control to maintain productivity. A reaction against traditional leadership methods, the studies showed a strong bias against authoritarian leadership.

The Movement's Crest and Decline. From the 1930s through the 1950s a large number of articles and books were published that may logically be classified as literature of the human relations period. A major contribution was made by the psychologist Kurt Lewin at the Research Center for Group Dynamics at the Massachusetts Institute of Technology. Lewin later moved to the University of Michigan where he and his associates contributed generously to the literature on democratic leadership during the heyday of the human relations movement.[22,23] Researchers from the University of Michigan's Survey Research Center added to the understanding of employee attitudes and behavior and in recent years have been identified with an applied area of OB called organization development (to be discussed in Chapter 14).

One of the most significant works in the history of organizational behavior was *The Functions of the Executive* by Chester I. Barnard.[24] Although he was strongly influenced by Elton Mayo and his associates, Barnard's 1938 writings reflected a uniqueness arising from his executive experiences, including his tenure as president of New Jersey Bell Telephone Company. Barnard's philosophy of management, like Mayo's, emphasized deliberate, purposeful cooperation among employees and managers. One of the concepts with which Barnard is most often identified is the **acceptance theory** of leadership—the idea that a manager's right to influence subordinates (the manager's authority) is ultimately derived from subordinates rather than from higher levels of management. Acceptance theory, perhaps more than any other concept, captured the spirit of the entire human relations movement.

During the 1950s, human relations training for supervisors and managers virtually became a fad. To be a progressive manager was to be well versed in the ways of the human relations writers, especially to be people oriented and to reject authoritarian leadership methods. This viewpoint is still held in high esteem, but not in the same sense that it was then. During the late 1950s and 1960s, researchers began moving away from the human relations viewpoint as a dogma, philosophy, and system of values and began emphasizing objective investigation using the research methods of the behavioral sciences. It was inevitable that this approach would make some of the ideas that had become faddish during the human relations movement appear simplistic and biased. However, the best of the human relations movement was retained; for example, the notion that employers should show genuine concern for the needs of their employees and must respect the power of informal groups. But no belief about how to manage now lies beyond the critical scrutiny of the OB researcher, and the idea that there are human relations principles that apply in all situations (for example, the idea that participative leadership is always best) is highly suspect. The OB view of effective human relations is tough minded, sophisticated, skeptical, and above all empirically based.

The training programs initiated by the human relations movement are still being conducted—programs that teach practicing managers how to relate to people, lead, motivate, and so on. Such courses are also taught in many colleges, but the term **human relations**, in current usage, is not identified directly with the human relations movement. The content of current human relations courses is taken from the field of OB rather than from the ideology of the human relations movement. The content also tends to consist of the more applied aspects of OB, although many such courses include a substantial amount of theory and at the college level may be indistinguishable from OB courses.

Thus, the human relations movement, as such, has lost its identity. From one perspective it became a fad and then passed from existence. From another, it matured or evolved into the field of organizational behavior. The problem with the latter view is that many other streams of thought also contributed significantly to what is now called organizational behavior.

OB AND THE BEHAVIORAL SCIENCES

The most distinctive feature of the field of organizational behavior is its commitment to the same rigorous and systematic methods of fact finding that characterize the behavioral sciences of psychology, sociology, and anthropology. OB is an interdisciplinary field that seeks to conduct valid research about people in organizations.

The term **behavioral science** was popularized in the 1950s and 1960s as it became obvious that several of the disciplines that study people have much in common including their research methods, much of their subject matter, and many of the researchers themselves. Not only do researchers in the field of organizational behavior draw on the research findings of psychologists, sociologists, and anthropologists, but behavioral scientists publish OB literature and occasionally teach OB courses.

Behavioral Science Disciplines

The discipline of **psychology**, typically defined as the science of individual behavior, has contributed more to OB than other behavioral sciences. Psychologists began conducting systematic, controlled experiments in 1879 when Wilhelm Wundt established the first experimental laboratory in Leipzig, Germany. Since that time psychology has developed into a number of special-purpose fields, two of which have had an especially strong impact on the field of organizational behavior. Industrial (or organizational) psychology and social psychology are both closely related to OB and, with respect to some topics, are indistinguishable from it.

Industrial psychologists and OB specialists from the management discipline are quite different, their interests tend to merge at the research level, and often they do identical work as professors and/or consultants and researchers. OB courses, which are taught in departments of management, place greater emphasis on management applications and less on research than do industrial psychology courses; some industrial psychology courses deal with aspects of personnel and human resource work normally omitted from OB courses. Otherwise OB and industrial psychology courses are alike.

Because **social psychology** is the study of individual behavior within groups, the discipline makes direct applications to the OB field, especially in the area of group dynamics. Social psychology is interdisciplinary, bridging the gap between psychology and sociology. It is so interdisciplinary, in fact, that academic courses in social psychology are often taught in both psychology and sociology departments.

Sociology is the science of society—an academic discipline that studies social behavior, focusing attention on groups, organizations, and societies rather than individuals. **Industrial sociology** is the branch of the discipline that concentrates on group behavior in business and industrial organizations. It obviously overlaps greatly with the management field of OB and contributes directly to it.

Anthropology, literally the science of man, is a broad discipline that studies the origins and development of all human cultures and how those cultures have functioned in the past and continue to function in the present. Its contributions to OB have for the most part been indirect—through its influence on psychology and sociology. Anthropology helps us gain perspective and avoid generalizations that are distorted by a narrow viewpoint. For example, cultural anthropologists made it obvious that what many psychologists of the early twentieth century thought were instincts—inborn behavior patterns—were not that at all, but rather were learned, culture-specific behaviors. Competitiveness is a good example of a culture-specific behavior. In some subcultures that place high value on cooperation, competition is virtually nonexistent. Recently, management consultants and organizational scientists have taken a special interest in organizational culture, a subject clearly central to anthropology.[25,26]

Behavioral Science Methods

Sciences, including the behavioral sciences, qualify as sciences because of their methods. The data with which behavioral scientists work are often extremely difficult to measure and analyze, but a variety of respectable instruments, research designs, and techniques for analysis have been developed and successfully tested and used and others are continuing to evolve. Some of the research designs employed in the OB field are quite complex, so complex that one needs a thorough background in statistics and psychological measurement to decide whether the conclusions of a published article are valid and where to apply them. Generally speaking, it is the role of textbooks and survey articles to pull together the literature on a given subject and to interpret it within the context of all the relevant research on that particular subject. The authors of textbooks do not always agree, but most will point out the areas where disagreements exist.

This book does not teach research methods. It does, however, emphasize the importance of being critical about how the information in the field is gathered and analyzed. Certainly students have a right to expect the data from which conclusions in the field of OB are drawn to be **empirical**. Such conclusions are based on objective research and systematically accumulated experience rather than just armchair philosophy or common sense reasoning. OB research studies should be **replicable** (that is, repeated studies should produce the same results), and the methods used should be open for all to evaluate. In good research, definitions are precise and the data collection is unbiased. Where these guidelines are followed, as recommended, a field of study can accumulate a useful and theoretically sound body of knowledge. Organizational behavior is achieving precisely that. Its content provides students of management with the most thorough and practical body of information now available about how to understand and relate to people in the workplace.

IMPORTANT TERMS AND CONCEPTS

At the end of each chapter your attention is called to some important terms and concepts with the suggestion that you carefully define each. These are not, of course, all the important terms and concepts. A search for others, and for names with whom important concepts can be associated, will help you learn and remember the chapter content.

organizational behavior	organization theory
Protestant work ethic	human relations movement
division of labor	acceptance theory
scientific management	human relations
industrial psychology	behavioral science
principles of management	psychology
division of labor	social psychology
coordination	sociology
span of control	industrial sociology
hierarchy	anthropology
subordination	empirical
structure	replicable

STUDY AND DISCUSSION QUESTIONS

1. Whose behavior is studied in the field of organizational behavior? Explain your response.

2. In what ways does the modern field of organizational behavior differ from the observations of organizational behavior made throughout history?

3. What factors contributed to Machiavelli's ability to make observations that are still relevant? In what sense do his experiences suggest that students of organizational behavior should have some understanding of the historical foundations of the field?

4. Why is it important to formally study OB rather than to learn about behavior in organizations only from experience?

5. In what ways do OB and OT complement one another?

6. In what sense have the applications of scientific management created an image that poorly reflects Frederick W. Taylor's true motivation?

7. Explain the Protestant work ethic. Do you think that it affects the work behavior of today's professional employees? nonprofessional employees? self-employed persons?

8. From the content of this chapter, which major factors do you think contributed to the decline of the human relations movement?

9. What is misleading about the idea that the human relations movement matured and evolved into the field of OB?

10. What are the main similarities between industrial psychologists and specialists in OB?

11. What criteria would you use to determine whether information taught in an OB course is based on the methods of the behavioral sciences?

REFERENCES

1. George, Claude S., Jr. *The History of Management Thought.* Englewood Cliffs, N.J.: Prentice-Hall, Inc., 1968, p. 6.
2. George. *The History of Management Thought*, p. 37.
3. Machiavelli, Niccolo. *The Prince and Other Discourses*, trans. Luigi Ricci. New York: Random House, Inc., 1950.
4. Calhoon, Richard P. "Niccolo Machiavelli and the Twentieth Century Administrator," *Academy of Management Journal*, Vol. 12, No. 2, June, 1969, p. 208.
5. Weber, Max. *The Protestant Ethic and the Spirit of Capitalism*, trans. Talcott Parsons. London: George Allen and Unwin Ltd., 1930.
6. Matt. 25:14-30.

7. Thess. 3:6-12.

8. Smith, Adam. *An Inquiry into the Nature and Causes of the Wealth of Nations.* Vol. 1, London: A. Strahan and T. Cadell, 1793, pp. 7-8.

9. Babbage, Charles. *On the Economy of Machinery and Manufactures.* London: Charles Knight, 1832, pp. iv-v.

10. Taylor, Frederick W. *Principles of Management.* New York: Harper & Brothers, 1911.

11. Taylor. *Principles of Management,* pp. 36-37.

12. Munsterberg, Hugo. *Psychology and Industrial Efficiency.* Boston: Houghton Mifflin Company, 1913.

13. Fayol, Henri. *General and Industrial Management,* trans. Constance Storrs. London: Sir Isaac Pitman & Sons, Ltd., 1949, p.97.

14. Mooney, James D., and Allan C. Reiley. *Onward Industry!* New York: Harper & Row Publishers, Inc., 1931.

15. Gulick, Luther, and Lyndall Urwick, eds. *Papers on the Science of Administration.* New York: Institute of Public Administration, 1937.

16. Pennock, George A. "Industrial Research at Hawthorne," *Personnel Journal,* Vol. 8, February, 1930, pp. 296-313.

17. Mayo, Elton. *The Human Problems of an Industrial Civilization.* New York: Macmillan Publishing Co., Inc., 1934.

18. Roethlisberger, F. J., and W. J. Dickson. *Management and the Worker.* Cambridge, Mass.: Harvard University Press, 1939.

19. Pennock. "Industrial Research at Hawthorne," pp. 296-313.

20. Roethlisberger and Dickson. *Management and the Worker,* p. 160.

21. Carey, Alex. "The Hawthorne Studies: A Radical Criticism," *The American Sociological Review,* Vol. 32, No. 3, June, 1967, pp. 403-416.

22. Lewin, Kurt, Ronald Lippit, and Ralph K. White. "Patterns of Aggressive Behavior in Experimentally Created 'Social Climates,'" *Journal of Social Psychology,* Vol. 10, May, 1939, pp. 271-299.

23. French, J. R. P. "Retraining the Autocratic Leader," *Journal of Abnormal and Social Psychology,* Vol. 39, June, 1944, pp. 224-237.

24. Barnard, Chester I. *The Functions of the Executive.* Cambridge, Mass.: Harvard University Press, 1938.

25. Peters, Thomas J., and Robert H. Waterman, Jr. *In Search of Excellence: Lessons from America's Best-Run Companies.* New York: Harper & Row Publishers, Inc., 1982.

26. *Administrative Science Quarterly,* Vol. 28, No. 3, September, 1983, pp. 331-495.

SUGGESTED READINGS

Cummings, Larry L. "Toward Organizational Behavior," *The Academy of Management Review,* Vol. 3, No. 1, January, 1978, pp. 90-98.

Deal, Terrence E., and Alan A. Kennedy. *Corporate Cultures: The Rites and Rituals of Corporate Life.* Reading, Mass.: Addison-Wesley Publishing Co., 1982.

Dubin, Robert, ed. *Handbook of Work, Organization, and Society.* Skokie, Ill.: Rand McNally & Company, 1976.

Dunnette, Marvin D., ed. *Handbook of Industrial and Organizational Psychology.* Chicago: Rand McNally College Publishing Company, 1976.

Greenwood, R. G., A. A. Boulton, and Regina A. Greenwood. "Hawthorne A Half Century Later: Relay Assembly Participants Remember," *Journal of Management,* Vol. 9, No. 2, Fall/Winter, 1983, pp. 217-231.

Landsberger, Henry A. *Hawthorne Revisited.* Ithaca, N.Y.: Cornell University Press, 1958.

Mowday, Richard T., and Richard M. Steers, eds. *Research in Organizations: Issues and Controversies.* Santa Monica, Calif.: Goodyear Publishing Company, Inc., 1979.

Shapiro, H. J., and Mahmoud A. Wahba. "Frederick W. Taylor—62 Years Later," *Personnel Journal,* Vol. 53, No. 8, August, 1974, pp. 574-578.

Wren, Daniel A. *The Evolution of Management Thought.* New York: The Ronald Press Company, 1972.

2

The Goals and Values of Organizations and Managers

In answer to the question, "How do you define the social impact of a corporation?" Dr. Ruben F. Mettler, chairman and chief executive officer of TRW, Inc., expressed the corporate policy: A meaningful definition requires looking at the three levels at which TRW should have a positive impact on society:

"The first level concerns the basic performance of the company as an economic unit. How many jobs does it provide? Is its productivity increasing? Is it profitable enough to pay employees and shareholders fairly? What is the quality of its goods and services? Does it provide stability and growth in employment? What is its contribution to the economy of the countries in which it operates? Clearly TRW's primary social impact lies in our success as an economic institution efficiently producing quality products to fill society's needs.

"The next level concerns the quality of the conduct of our internal affairs. For example, are we ensuring equal employment and advancement opportunity for all? Is there job satisfaction? Do we provide proper health protection and safety devices and adequate pollution control? Is our advertising truthful?

"The third level concerns the additional things we do in relating to our external environment. This includes charitable and cultural contribution programs, youth projects, urban action programs, assistance to educational institutions, employees' participation in community affairs, and our good government program. TRW focuses its activities in these areas in communities where we have plants because we can have the most meaningful impact there.

"It would be a mistake to think that any one or two of these levels fully defines our corporate impact, and hence our responsibilities at all three levels. The corporate constituents that we're concerned about—shareholder, employee, customer, government, community, general public—have a particular interest at each level.

"For example, shareholders are not just interested in their return on investment—a part of the first level. They want to be sure that our activities at the second level and third level will not adversely affect that investment. Employees are interested in more than their paycheck. They want to be treated fairly and to enjoy equal rights and opportunities. They want to be proud of their company's outside activities and to participate in them.

"We are determined to meet the needs and expectations of each of our constituents at each of these three levels. That's how I believe TRW will be measured and judged on its impact and its responsibilities to society."[1]

Dr. Mettler's statement of TRW policy reflects the view that managers are continually faced with the task of making decisions involving value judgments—implicit or explicit judgments based on the decision maker's beliefs about what is right and wrong. For example, managers make numerous decisions about prices, profits, growth, and layoffs, most of which involve people. And when people are involved in managerial decisions, value judgments must be made.

As the TRW policy statement implies, the value judgments of managers touch many groups—employees, shareholders, customers, governments, local communities, and the general public—whose concepts of corporate responsibility have expanded in recent years to include the prevention and solution of major social and environmental problems such as inflation, unemployment, the conservation of natural resources, and pollution of the nation's waterways and atmosphere. Thus, the ethical and social responsibilities of management relate to virtually every aspect of organizational life.

No attempt is made in this chapter to catalog and provide easy answers to the ethical questions managers face. Certainly no easy answers exist. The considerably less ambitious objectives of this chapter are

TO UNDERSTAND:

1. The major concepts of corporate social responsibility

2. The goals of profit-making organizations

3. Values as a basis for decision making

4. Some means of making managerial decisions more ethical

PERSPECTIVES ON CORPORATE SOCIAL RESPONSIBILITY

Managers, scholars, politicians, judges, environmentalists, consumer advocates, and other interested groups and individuals view corporate responsibility differently. There is, however, a growing consensus that profit-making organizations must adhere to social values more closely in the future than they have in the past.

Several events and circumstances during the 1960s and 1970s brought to attention the need for greater responsiveness of business to the needs of society as a whole. Prominent among these was the failure of President Johnson's Great Society programs to decrease crime, poverty, urban blight, and related social problems to a significant degree. Disillusionment with the ability of government to solve society's problems turned increasing attention to private business both as a cause of social problems and as a potential cure for society's ills.

Business as a Cause of Social Problems

A number of prominent social issues reflect the continuing unrest left over from the late 1960s. Among these are the emphases on environmentalism and consumer protection that have found expression in several highly vocal pressure groups. Consumer advocates such as Ralph Nader, and other social critics, have correctly pointed out a number of existing business practices which are either irresponsible or not in the public interest; but these same critics often have been guilty themselves of overzealousness, overreaction, and scapegoating.

The many blue-chip companies that have confessed their sins or been otherwise exposed give credibility to the critics of business, but too often these critics see only the bad side of managerial behavior. When people are chronically frustrated and unable to deal effectively with their problems, they commonly single out a scapegoat upon which to vent their feelings. But good scapegoats are hard to find, and well-informed people are not easily fooled into believing that an innocent bystander is a villain in disguise. Business, unfortunately, has not been just an innocent bystander, and so with the help of various consumer advocates and social critics, both business and capitalism have on occasion fallen under heavy criticism. At least some of the criticisms have been justified while others have not.

For example, it is inexcusable for industries to have dumped their untreated wastes into the nation's streams and rivers (as, indeed, cities and other public institutions have also done in disposing of sewage). The cement plant, oil refinery, or steel mill that unceasingly belches its pollutants into the atmosphere and the coal company that mars the countryside and fails to provide safe working conditions for its employees create a negative image that generalizes to all industry. When high-pressure marketing attempts insult the public with television advertisements that deceive rather than inform, it should be expected that an increasingly well-educated populace would question the motives and integrity of business leaders.

The Classical View of Corporate Responsibility

The **classical view** of corporate responsibility was accepted by both business and society during the nineteenth and early twentieth centuries. Following Adam Smith's belief that an "invisible hand" works to direct events for the public good,[2] management's sole responsibility was seen as maximizing profits, constrained only by the limits of the law.

In the classical view, the primary mechanisms within which the public good is preserved are inherent in the free market system. The organization must produce the best possible goods and services at the lowest possible price. If low efficiency or commitment to other goals interferes with this process, the competitive marketplace rewards the efficient and punishes the inefficient, thereby protecting the public. From this viewpoint, morality lies within the workings of a competitive market rather than within an individual manager. To tamper with the system (with price controls or supports, for example) is, by definition, to compromise the best interests of society.

The most influential modern advocate of the classical viewpoint is the 1976 Nobel prize-winning economist Milton Friedman:

> In a free enterprise, private property system, a corporate executive is an employee of the owners of the business. He has direct responsibility to his employers. That responsibility is to conduct the business in accord with their desires, which generally will be to make as much money as possible while conforming to the basic rules of society. . . . Insofar as his actions in accord with his "social responsibility" reduce returns to stockholders, he is spending their money. Insofar as his actions raise the price to customers, he is spending the customers' money. Insofar as his actions lower the wages of some employees, he is spending their money.[3]

Generally the classical view has held to the **caveat emptor**—let the buyer beware—philosophy in the sales area. The buyer's protection results from the seller's desire to survive in a competitive market. It is the seller's self-interest rather than altruism that protects the customer.

The classical view of corporate responsibility does not rely on the morals of business owners and managers. Instead it relies primarily upon an impersonal force—the dynamism of a free, competitive market—to protect society. Unfortunately, because of international cartels, oligopolies, and monopolistic labor unions, competition and pricing do not function as the classical view implies. In an environment of imperfect competition, the system provides inadequate protection for the public.

A stronger concept of individual and corporate responsibility is not, however, inconsistent with a belief in the virtues of a competitive market, to the extent that competition exists. In fact, if past generations of managers had been more moral, law abiding, and responsive to society's needs, the factors which limit free market competition would be fewer and the benefits of free market conditions would be better realized in today's economy.

The Accountability Concept

The **accountability concept** of corporate responsibility emphasizes the belief that private businesses receive their charters—their right to operate and make a profit—from society and are therefore accountable to society for their behavior.[4]

While this concept may not be new, the belief that businesses are accountable to society for their behavior is new. For example, one result of the production of goods has been contamination of the nation's atmosphere and waterways. Today society expects businesses to help remedy this situation by investing in pollution abatement facilities. Business is also expected to respect society's aesthetic values by preserving the country's natural beauty and to protect employees by treating them fairly and taking reasonable measures to protect their health. In like fashion, a business has an obligation to consider the safety and other needs of its customers. None of these obligations diminishes the necessity for the firm to be efficient in production and competitive in pricing. Management's objective of increasing the wealth of the owners is unchanged and may even be made easier to achieve in the long run because of the firm's sense of responsibility.

The idea that management is accountable to anyone except the shareholders is repugnant to advocates of the classical view. Yet, even during the nineteenth century, child labor laws, the Interstate Commerce Act of 1887, and other actions of government expressed society's conviction that uncontrolled maximization of profits should not be the only goal of management. In recent years, numerous laws have been passed to express society's concept of corporate responsibility and to limit managerial freedom in areas where abuses have most often occurred. Through the passage of laws, society demonstrates that business is ultimately accountable to society for its actions.

Businesses as Instruments of Society

A third view of corporate responsibility greatly extends the accountability concept. It holds that because businesses receive their charters from society, they should be viewed as instruments for the attainment of societal goals.[5] For example, during wars a nation's government frequently makes decisions for business that are considered to be in the nation's best interest.[6] During economic crises it is not uncommon for governments to impose wage and price controls on businesses. During (and after) periods of social change, government units in the United States have used rewards and penalties to persuade businesses to hire veterans, youths, females, racial minorities, the handicapped, and to subcontract work to small businesses or to businesses owned by females or members of racial minorities. Many people judge the rightness or wrongness of using businesses as instruments for achieving societal goals on the basis of whether the particular goal is one that they personally support.

The business-as-an-instrument-of-society perspective can be adopted by individual managers as well as governments. Such managers do not deny the importance of profits, but they believe that concern for people is more important than making money and they behave accordingly. In relating to customers, **caveat emptor** is replaced with **caveat venditor** (that is, let the seller beware). Managers who operate within this philosophy take actions that go far beyond what is normally expected of them in society. (They do more than avoid polluting the environment or discriminating against minority groups.) Such managers believe that the firm should actively assume responsibility for curing society's ills without reference to who caused them.

The view of a quality-of-life manager, described as a humanist rather than a materialist, is that a worker's value as an employee cannot be separated from the worker's value as an individual. This manager's philosophy is that "we hire the whole person and all of that person's problems." The quality-of-life manager's view about minority groups is that members of these groups need support and help whenever necessary. This manager's political values dictate that government and politicians are necessary contributors to the quality of life; rather than resist government, the quality-of-life manager believes that business and government must cooperate to solve society's problems.

This view of social responsibility differs from both the classical and accountability viewpoints we have discussed. The contribution of business to the solution of social problems is not limited to meeting obligations incurred while concentrating on the profit-making objective of the business. Contributions toward solving social problems, such as inflation, unemployment, poverty, crime, and depletion of natural resources, are not considered side ventures. They are accepted, along with making a profit, as primary organizational objectives. The quality-of-life manager agrees that profit is essential for the firm, but profits in and of themselves are not the end objectives of the firm.

This altruistic viewpoint proposes that the lofty ideals to which many managers aspire should be guiding principles of the firms for which they work. The viewpoint is commonly criticized on the following two grounds.[7]

1. Traditionally, business organizations have had as their primary mission in our society the delivery of goods and services that maximally serve the needs of society's consumers. Can a quality-of-life firm keep the quality of its offerings as high as possible and its costs and prices as low as possible if it diverts its financial and human resources to the solving of societal problems rather than the serving of its customers?

2. Similarly, our society believes that societal (consumer) needs are best served by firms faced with competition and thus has created laws barring price fixing, mergers that reduce competition, and so forth. Can a quality-of-life firm survive in competition with a different type of firm whose managers are not obliged to divert their company's resources to tasks not directly serving the market in which it competes?

There are no clear answers to these questions, but the remainder of the chapter offers insights that can help avoid answers that deal too lightly with the complex issues involved.

THE MULTIPLE GOALS OF BUSINESSES

All organizations have multiple objectives. The primary objective of a business is to make a profit for its investors. This does not, however, mean that profit making is the only objective of a business or that managers necessarily seek to make as much profit as they possibly can. In practice, effective managers perform a spectacular juggling act in order to meet the increasing demands of employees, government, consumers, and the general public while still earning a satisfactory return for the firm's stockholders.

People invest their money in businesses in order to make a profit, and they hold business managers accountable for making a profit that is satisfactory. This does not, however, mean that profit making is the only goal of a business or that managers necessarily seek to make as much profit as they possibly can. To the contrary, employees, government, consumers, and the general public place a variety of demands on businesses, and managers must respond to these demands on behalf of investors. The need to respond to the demands of these constituencies causes business to have, in effect, multiple goals.

While giving lip service to the idea that profit-making organizations have multiple goals, designers of corporate financial decision models typically assume that managers attempt to maximize shareholder wealth. Some advocates of increased social responsibility, on the other hand, admit that profits and corporate growth are important but act as though profit is a dirty word, an unworthy goal of a truly moral person or organization. The daily lives of operating managers exemplify a pragmatic middle ground. One executive expressed this concept of the executive role:

> Corporate executives are really "middlemen" in that they strive to bring a fair return to the owners. In addition, they see that employees are compensated properly and treated fairly, that customers get the product/service they paid for and the price is fair, that the product really is of use to society, and that the company's image reflects all this and a true concern for the welfare of society. This, in the long run, is in the best interest of the company.[8]

This quotation reflects the attempts of operating managers to integrate their diverse goals and to seek more satisfactory long-term solutions rather than maximum short-term profits.

The Tainted Image of Profits

To one who favors government ownership of a nation's productive resources, profits are associated with the heartless bourgeois capitalist whose selfishness leads to a two-class society in which workers suffer in order to make the rich richer. To the employee whose already meager paycheck is eroded by inflation, corporate profits may be viewed as funds that should have been allocated for wages. To the avid sportsperson-environmentalist who catches fish that cannot be eaten because of chemical wastes or to the embittered victim of a preventable industrial accident, profits may symbolize management's irresponsibility—its failure to pay its way in society. To these individuals, profits—and perhaps even the private enterprise system—may be seen as an evil without socially redeemable qualities. It is difficult for such persons to see how managers in profit-making organizations could possibly be morally sensitive and socially responsible persons.

During the rise of capitalism in America most people had some commitment to the Protestant ethic, a system of values associated with Calvinistic theology. John Calvin saw Christianity as supporting individual responsibility, reward based on merit, and the accumulation of wealth through hard work, productivity, and frugality. This doctrine, equally applicable to the industrialist, farmer, and factory worker, involved no conflict between morality and profit making, and persons who are still committed to it see no need to abandon the profit motive in order to make business socially responsible. Leon Keyserling, former chairman of the Council of Economic Advisors, once expressed this point of view as follows:

> The system has evolved and will continue to do so. Most well-informed people in 1900 or even in 1928 would have called what we welcome today socialism rather than capitalism. But looking backward I would say instead that we have been progressing, and still are, toward a more socially minded society rather than toward socialism, that being a system where the major instruments of production and distribution are in public hands, not guided by the profit motive as we employ it.
>
> Our system has many blemishes, and our virtue consists in recognizing them. But I am convinced that during the past four decades we have made an unparalleled record of progress—economic, social, and what might be called civil. And we have done this under our free institutions with remarkably little turmoil and upheaval by historic tests. We should aim to improve the system, not abandon it.[9]

It should be expected that persons who believe in improving rather than abandoning the system will view social responsibility differently from those who are convinced that capitalism is inherently immoral and therefore inconsistent with social responsibility.

Social Responsibility as a Supportive Goal

From society's point of view, the purpose of private business is to provide efficiently the goods and services needed by its people. Society's decision to encourage the formation of private business is an expression of a belief that the private enterprise system will more nearly meet the people's needs than will an alternative system.

Society's purpose in permitting private enterprise should not, however, be confused with the motivation of a business investor. In a capitalistic system, profit making or, more precisely, increasing investor wealth is generally regarded as the primary purpose of a business firm (though not the *only* purpose, as indicated earlier). This concept of relatively limited purpose may, as illustrated by Milton Friedman's position, be interpreted to mean that business should not concern itself with social responsibility goals. A less extreme position would make profit the primary goal of business and would subordinate social responsibility to it only if the two should come into conflict.

Primary and Supportive Goals. Limited purpose is inherent in the nature of all organizations. Academic, religious, governmental, service, and social organizations, like business organizations, are formed with a primary purpose in mind. Schools are not criticized because they fail to provide the community with police and fire protection, nor is Alcoholics Anonymous condemned because it fails to teach reading and mathematics. Like these institutions, a business is formed for a limited purpose, and if it is accepted that this purpose is honorable and serves a valuable function in society, the business should be judged only on the basis of whether it fulfills that purpose in an ethical and honorable way.

Like most organizations, a business has many **supportive goals** (goals which are important in achieving the firm's primary objective and expressing the personal values of its managers and stockholders). Its primary goal, however, is to provide goods and services in order to make a reasonable profit for its stockholders. If the business cannot make a profit, it ceases to exist. A firm's supportive goals may include treating its employees with fairness and dignity, supplying its customers with superior products, providing safe working conditions, and protecting the environment.

To a point, the concept of supportive goals is not difficult for managers to accept because such goals are consistent with their self-interests, at least in the long run. A serious question arises, though, when businesses are called upon to help solve social problems to which they have not contributed directly. Even assuming that the long-term interests of firms are served when they make direct contributions to social programs, serving the public good in this way helps firms that do not contribute as much as it helps those that do. The fact that contributors and free riders benefit on an essentially equal basis tends to diminish the motivation of managers to set goals that are not business related.

Unfortunately, there is no evidence that corporate executives are more altruistic than anyone else.[10,11]

The crucial question relating to corporate responsibility is not whether profit is the firm's primary goal. It is: What happens when the primary goal cannot be reached without sacrificing one or more supportive goals?

Sacrificing Supportive Goals. To some managers and policy-making investors, making a profit is more than the primary goal of the organization. It is the central value from which all other values derive their meaning. Profit can be the primary reason for forming the organization and the primary objective in its operation without undermining the personal values of its decision makers. Some managers, for example, are willing to fail in business rather than allow employees to work under conditions which adversely affect their health or lie to prospective customers in order to sell a product. For these persons profits are highly desirable—they are necessary for the organization's survival—but they are not a substitute for a more comprehensive value system and are not necessary for the managers' survival as worthwhile human beings.

To managers for whom making a profit is a central value, everything is subordinated to the profit motive. Their credo is: Make a profit. Make it responsibly if you can, but make a profit! If they cannot provide safe working conditions and still make a profit, safety standards are lowered. If they cannot make a profit without selling a shoddy product, quality standards are lowered. If a choice must be made between profits or fair wages, profits have first priority. These are clearly examples of social irresponsibility. Note, however, that they are not a necessary corollary of making profits the primary goal of the business. Rather, they result from placing profit making in the center of one's value system and making all other values peripheral or subordinate to it.

Some managers, like some government officials, educators, and members of the clergy, are morally bankrupt. Their values reflect a concern only for personal gain regardless of who gets hurt. Some organizations encourage unethical conduct and social irresponsibility by rewarding managers for contributions to short-term profits without reference to how the profits are made. This, too, reflects the values of individuals—the owners or policy-making executives—rather than the values of business per se. Such behavior does not have to exist in profit-making organizations, and in the long run this behavior may not only detract from profits but may bring about harsh reactions and controls on all businesses from societal overreaction to these activities.

Not-for-Profit Business Activities. In an affluent society, especially where monopolistic or oligopolistic companies can fulfill their various obligations and still make adequate profits, some managers express their personal values by supporting social projects which are, in the short run at least, altruistic in nature. The firm may, for example, sponsor a minority business, build an unprofitable plant in a ghetto, or support a sports program in an area with a high crime rate.

Although there have been instances of monumental losses from such activities, leading to questions about management's responsibility to stockholders, these activities exemplify attempts at social responsibility beyond tokenism and minimal obligation. Notable among companies whose social-action programs have led to serious problems is Boise Cascade Corporation. Its promotion of a minority enterprise in the heavy construction industry resulted in a pretax loss of about $40 million, and the price of the corporation's stock dropped 60 points.[12] Other large companies which have made significant investments in social-action programs are International Business Machines Corp., The Chase Manhattan Bank, Xerox Corp., Eli Lilly and Company, and The Coca-Cola Company.

Assuming stockholder support, such corporate programs may be justified by the assumption that management can be more effective than government, individuals, or nonprofit organizations in solving certain kinds of social problems—for example, alcoholism, drug addiction, and emotional problems of employees. Or it can be argued that business is failing society by engaging in such activities—that it can serve society best by paying more taxes or lowering prices, increasing dividends and wages if the situation warrants, or investing funds in the expansion of efficient business enterprises which are needed by society. Some critics of business believe that for corporations to retain earnings for the purpose of engaging in socially oriented activities which do not directly benefit stockholders is to increase corporate power and influence unjustifiably in areas where corporations lack both expertise and a mandate from society.

Although companies continue to engage in public interest projects, most often in charities and education, there is growing evidence that they are increasingly expressing a preference for social projects with special consequences for business.[13,14] Consistent with this trend, the results of a public opinion survey suggest that

> . . . corporate managers should be most concerned with social responsibility in doing the things that business was designed to do—producing quality products and services and attempting to alleviate negative consequences that the firm's behavior might have had on the public, consequences such as pollution, inflation, minority hiring, or human resources on the job. Respondents in this study generally did not believe business should be involved in social problems, such as education, support of charities, or decay of the cities not directly related to business.[15]

A BASIS FOR SOCIALLY RESPONSIBLE BEHAVIOR

Managers generally agree that socially responsible behavior is desirable but disagree about what behaviors are socially responsible. There is no uniform code of ethics or social responsibility to guide managerial behavior.

The term **social responsibility** has been used throughout this chapter without being defined. As a matter of fact, it is best defined operationally: in terms of the behaviors that set socially responsible managers apart from those who are irresponsible. But who is able to make such judgments? Whose criteria are objectively right? Who can decide what is right for others?

Davis and Blomstrom define **social responsibility** as the obligation of decision makers "to take actions which protect and improve the welfare of society as a whole along with their own interests."[16] Gordon Fitch defines corporate social responsibility as "the serious attempt to solve social problems caused wholly or in part by the corporation."[17] The differences between these two definitions are indicative of the even more varied views that exist among managers. Fitch's definition, the more conservative of the two, is more likely to be acceptable to a majority of managers.

In the following discussion, some of the criteria for evaluating right and wrong in the arena of business are considered. Call it business ethics, social responsibility, or business morality, the question remains: Upon what basis should managers make decisions which involve value judgments?

Increasing Expectations

Not many years ago, few people took seriously the problem of environmental pollution. There were no antipollution laws and no Environmental Protection Agency. By discharging raw sewage into rivers and lakes and burning refuse at city dumps, local governments joined industry as a full partner in polluting the environment. At the same time, the public demanded large, powerful automobiles whose engines were a major source of smog and a drain on the world's already short oil reserves.

The pollution problem became intense before people became concerned enough to do something about it. Then, almost overnight, industrial polluters became villains, and an indignant society stood aghast that managers could be so selfish and immoral. This, of course, is just one of many examples of how conditions and expectations (values or standards) change.

Especially since World War II expectations have increased dramatically concerning the treatment of the physically and mentally disabled, minorities, women, the aging, and other disadvantaged groups. During the 1970s we saw an emphasis on safety standards, truth-in-lending, advertising, and a concern about wasting fuel and other natural resources. In the 1980s we have seen an increasing concern about water pollution and toxic wastes. In these and other areas, society continues to formulate ever higher expectations regarding business behavior.

The freedoms enjoyed by Americans permit socially destructive practices to continue unabated long after they have become serious problems. Those same freedoms, however, eventually lead to an exposure of socially irresponsible behavior and to action to prevent its continuation. That action ordinarily takes the form of legislation. In some cases society expects both government and business to do the impossible—to solve society's problems free of charge. In the real world, however, nothing is free. Zero-defect quality control in the auto industry means higher prices, and stricter standards on emission control lead to smaller automobiles.

The cost of pollution controls is passed on to the customer in the form of higher prices. In some cases, the closing of pollution-emitting plants and investment in antipollution devices rather than expansion of productive capacity lead to increased unemployment. Pay increases that are greater than productivity increases combine with other factors to create inflation. Stringent rules regarding the mining and use of coal are desirable, but they also lead to increased fuel prices and continued dependence on oil and natural gas. As these facts indicate, the issues of social responsibility often involve trade-offs and are seldom clear-cut matters of moral versus immoral behavior.

Legality as a Standard of Conduct

It was once popular to say that morals cannot be legislated, but this statement is not altogether true. Laws that reflect a strong sentiment within the population and involve appropriate penalties for failure to comply are often imposed on persons who do not initially support them. Laws that receive vigorous enforcement can be singularly successful in changing behavior and subsequently modifying attitudes until they are congruent with the behavior that the laws require. Thus, a law such as the Occupational Safety and Health Act, which is deeply resented by some managers because parts of it are regarded as unrealistic and harsh, is eventually accepted and its standards internalized.

Almost every aspect of business is controlled by laws, rulings of quasi-judicial bodies such as the National Labor Relations Board, numerous state and federal agencies, executive orders, as well as court rulings. Literally thousands of thou-shalt-nots, expressed both in sweeping generalizations and in minute details, specify appropriate managerial conduct with reference to employees, customers, competitors, suppliers, stockholders, the government, energy, the environment, and other business-related areas. The extent to which laws regulating business proliferate reflects (1) skepticism concerning the ability of managers to act responsibly on their own; (2) a growing conviction that the controls associated with a free market are in themselves inadequate to protect the public; (3) a high level of dependence upon government to solve social problems; and (4) a widespread preference for the security of government controls over the freedom they inevitably destroy.

Another factor in the proliferation of laws, as sociologist Etzioni points out, is strictly political:

> . . . a good part of the laws passed are not meant to be implemented, at least not systematically and effectively. Passing laws is part of the make-believe or theater of politics, in which politicians try to placate two (or more) opposing camps. They give one faction the law (saying, in effect, "You see, I took care of it") while the other faction more or less retains the freedom to pursue activities which violate the law. It's a politician's way of eating his cake and having it.[18]

Whatever the reasons for the passage of laws, it is a favorite national pastime that has a monumental impact on business. Public dissatisfaction with the mild penalties that courts have assessed against irresponsible corporate executives is now being felt. Thus, executives increasingly risk criminal prosecution for their company's failure to comply with government regulations and for other violations of the law.[19]

The Law as an Equalizer. One positive aspect of laws relating to business behavior is that they serve as an equalizer among companies, some of which are not inclined to be socially responsible. However much the critics of business may want to cry "rationalization for irresponsibility," it is extremely difficult for one company to install costly antipollution devices while its competitors continue to pollute. And a large user of steel, for example, cannot buy expensive steel to support a socially minded supplier while its competitors buy the same grade of steel for less.

Problems in Legislating Morality. By equalizing the rules of the game, legislation modifies the free enterprise system by constructing a baseline of morality and responsibility. There is, of course, a point at which government controls become so extensive that the positive aspects of a free market cannot be realized, and it is the fear of many that we are rapidly approaching such a point. Another limitation in the legislation of morality is that managers may take the position that the minimum requirements specified by the law are all the morality that is needed.

Business morality can be legislated, but the legalistic approach has its drawbacks. There can never be enough laws to cover every situation. Neither can there be enough officials to police all the laws—unless most managers endorse them and conscientiously try to obey them. There is ample evidence to show that managers as a whole are motivated to behave responsibly, but it remains to be seen whether the sheer number of laws will cause a significant number of managers to feel overcontrolled and to react negatively by observing the letter of the law while violating its spirit.

Professional and Organizational Codes

Most professions have codes of ethics by which the behavior of their own members is guided. These are usually taken seriously since failure to comply may result in expulsion from the organization and in professional ruin. For example, an industrial psychologist whose membership in the American Psychological Association is lost because of unethical conduct will subsequently face the withdrawal of certification and licensing which are necessary to practice in his or her state. Although such codes directly apply only to the profession's members, they indirectly affect all members of the business community with whom the professionals work.

The Influence of Public Accountants. One profession having a significant impact upon the ethical behavior of managers is accounting. Certified public accountants (CPAs) not only impose their own ethical codes upon business but are also responsible, along with attorneys, for helping managers understand and obey the law.

The American Institute of Certified Public Accountants is explicit in stating its rules of conduct and insistent that those rules be followed.[20] Its rules of conduct are stated in the following areas:

1. Independence (avoidance of conflict-of-interest situations)
2. Personal integrity and objectivity

3. Professional competence with reference to work undertaken

4. Compliance with the Institute's auditing standards

5. Use of accepted accounting principles

6. Making forecasts of future transactions

7. Confidential client information

8. Payment of contingent fees

9. Offers of employment to a public accountant

10. Acts which discredit the profession

11. Soliciting and advertising personal services

12. Payment or acceptance of commissions

13. Engaging in incompatible occupations

14. Nature of a public accountant's practice and firm name

The standards expressed in items 4 and 5, in particular, place substantial demands upon the client to maintain adequate records and to conduct financial affairs in such a way that an audit can be performed and the firm's true condition discovered and noted in the audit report. There is a real sense in which public accountants serve as a firm's conscience in the financial area. Managers continually ask "what will our auditors say about this?" and they often seek an opinion before deciding upon a course of action.

International Business Machines Corp. Many organizations publish their own codes of conduct and are diligent in enforcing them. Notable among these is IBM whose *Business Conduct Guidelines* is an 84-page booklet that all managers must review each year. They must also certify that they understand it and will comply with it. Any violation is cause for dismissal from the company.

The IBM booklet provides guidelines for employee behavior relating to customers, suppliers, and competitors as well as to IBM itself. Among the specific guidelines and prohibitions are statements dealing with gifts and entertainment, marketing practices, tying up a source of supply, engaging in illegal activity, and a variety of statements concerning an employee's obligations to the company. One part of IBM's guidelines deals with a 1956 Consent Decree in which the firm agreed, in response to an antitrust action by the United States government, to avoid specific practices which were allegedly monopolistic. It is especially important that

IBM managers be aware of the Consent Decree because of its far-reaching implications for dealing with customers and competitors as well as with the federal government.

Organizational codes of ethics, statements of philosophy and behavior, or guidelines for conduct are not always structured in such a way that they will really influence organizational behavior. Unlike the IBM code, some are intended to be only window dressing—something to help convince government or the public that a firm's intentions and behavior are honorable.

Enlightened Self-Interest

It can be argued that organizations should promote socially responsible behavior because it is good business.[21,22] It pays to be honest with customers and to provide them with a quality product just as it pays to be generous with employees and to avoid further deterioration of the environment. Farsighted managers can see that certain very costly forms of socially responsible behavior may not pay off immediately but may actually be necessary for survival a few years hence. Questionnaire responses from 144 major corporations showed enlightened self-interest to be the most important motive for social performance in the areas of urban, consumer, and environmental affairs.[23]

It is important for managers to recognize that ethical or socially responsible behavior is better for business than are the alternatives to it. Part of being a morally sensitive person is knowing why a particular action is desirable rather than doing it out of fear, obligation, or blind obedience. On the other hand, it would appear somewhat insensitive to behave morally (say, by providing a safe work environment) only because of a belief that it will bring a good return on the investment. A logical corollary of the latter is that one should be morally responsible only when there is reason to believe that it will pay.

There is a more sophisticated version of enlightened self-interest (sometimes called intelligent selfishness). It is based on two distinctions. The first is between *self-interest* and *selfishness*. Everyone is motivated by self-interest. "I want to be a kind, generous, and compassionate person" expresses a desire to enhance oneself by acquiring some of the most noble qualities of which humans are capable. This is an expression of self-interest but not selfishness. Selfish people put their immediate interests ahead of others. Morally sensitive people have learned that it is in their own best interest to be unselfish—to be genuinely concerned for others. Out of such a commitment and experience emerge such virtues as compassion and mercy.

The second distinction is between **intrinsic** and **extrinsic payoffs**. To say that it pays to be socially responsible can mean that being socially responsible has an intrinsic payoff (meaning that the satisfaction from performing the act is itself the payoff). Or it may have an extrinsic payoff such as higher profits and other measurable consequences. There is satisfaction in being a moral person and dealing with other people honestly, fairly, and generously. It should not be assumed that all managers who verbalize their commitment to social responsibility in terms of enlightened self-interest or intelligent selfishness are necessarily selfish or expect an external payoff, even in the long run. Some, at least, seem to use such terms to camouflage a deeper value system—a religious belief, for example, which they have been unable to express in terms that seem appropriate in the tough, unsentimental world of business.

Social and Economic Philosophy

As with any occupational group, there are managers who have no particular social or economic philosophy but who are, instead, pragmatists. At the other extreme are managers who are greatly guided by moral and religious beliefs. In between, perhaps, are those whose behavior is strongly influenced by other belief systems. There are managers, for example, who believe strongly in allowing the law of supply and demand to determine wages and prices whenever possible. They believe in minimal government control, in a pay-as-you-go policy of government spending, and in other values associated with a conservative philosophy. Such managers are apt to place a high value on efficiency and to think that the benefits of free competition outweigh its shortcomings. Most managers tend to support this philosophy.

Managers of a more liberal persuasion are less likely to be concerned about deficit spending and to fear that government encroachment on the free market will destroy the system. They welcome government controls and have a deep appreciation for the buffering effect of government action upon the boom-and-bust swings of a free market. They minimize the positive contributions of our system of imperfect competition and are more impressed with the human suffering that results from unsuccessful businesses and other conditions in the competitive market. Efficiency is valued "but not as much as people," meaning that efficiency is not viewed as highly as is the well-being of people. The rights of the individual are believed to be endangered by the self-serving interests of big business. When the organization is pitted against an individual, the natural inclination of many people is to identify with the underdog.

Belief systems such as these provide individuals with a philosophical predisposition to evaluate people, situations, and events in a set way. At the extremes, such prejudice distorts perception and judgment to such an extent that a given situation cannot be evaluated on its merits. Extreme prounion or antiunion philosophies, for example, can lead to distortions of fact so that prejudice becomes the major determinant of whether an observer sees good or evil in the workplace.

A Matter of Conscience

Critics of competitive, profit-oriented business focus upon its lack of warmth, compassion, and genuine concern for people. It has been argued that problems of business morality can be solved only by managers with a deep commitment to a system of humanitarian values from which these qualities emanate. Such a moral value system—a relatively permanent system of beliefs and attitudes concerning the worth and treatment of people—would enable a manager to follow the lead of conscience rather than be guided by pragmatic or utilitarian motives. Such a conscience begins to develop in childhood experiences, in the home and school, and is not likely to be the product of a college course in business ethics.[24]

The Personal Values of Managers. During the 1960s and 1970s society emphasized as never before the social responsibilities of managers as well as their personal **ethics** (their standards of moral judgment and conduct). A 1972 study, repeating a study conducted in 1966, indicated that the value systems of managers change slowly, not a surprising result since the values of people in general are slow to change.[25] The managers in these studies placed highest importance on the company, customers, ability, high productivity, profit maximization, organizational efficiency, and achievement, although employees, subordinates, and co-workers also ranked high among the values that influence their daily decisions. Religion, trust, honor, employee welfare, loyalty, and dignity ranked high; while social welfare, compassion, government, and liberalism were relegated to positions of secondary importance.

It appears from these studies that the value systems of American managers are more achievement and task oriented than oriented toward people, as such. Managers do, nevertheless, regard people as highly important—especially those within their own companies and, more specifically, their own subordinates. A 1976 update of the 1961 views of *Harvard Business Review* readers indicates strong support for profit maximization among American executives, but that support is tempered by a modified view of their ethical and social responsibilities.

Those critics who continue to characterize the American business executive as a power-hungry, profit-bound individualist, indifferent to the needs of society, should be put on notice that they are now dealing with a straw man of their own making.[26]

Managers are, however, by the very nature of their jobs, committed to thinking of people at work in terms of their contributions at work rather than in terms of their value in general. Thus, rationality in organizational decision making is a more functional value within the manager's work environment than compassion and concern for solving the ills of society.

The values held by managers probably account for their being managers rather than social workers, members of the clergy, scientists, or college professors. Their values may also account for their ability to function in an environment that is highly demanding and potentially stress provoking. Managers believe that the production of goods and services for a profit is important in and of itself. In this regard they are like other professionals in that they probably cannot perform well without a belief in what they are doing.

Pseudomorality. There is a point of view that portrays managers without compassion because they sometimes make decisions that bring frustration and suffering to people. Managers fire employees, for example, and they close plants on which people depend for a livelihood. This point of view shows a lack of insight into managerial attitudes and responsibilities. Such decisions are usually made only after much agonizing and often after great expense to the company due to procrastination while seeking a less painful course of action.

Managers who lack the courage to make unpleasant managerial decisions often convince themselves that they are motivated by compassion and goodness. Thus, we apply the term **pseudomorality** (false morality). Consider this real-life example:

Too late to save the largest employer in a small city from bankruptcy, a management consultant was called in to talk with Charlene Reitz, the company's founder-president. In the course of the investigation it was discovered that the financial vice-president, Raymon Kelly, had for years caused the company's most effective managers to resign because of his harsh, domineering personality. Kelly was a bright, powerful man. No one, including Reitz, was willing to have a head-on confrontation with him.

Reitz had often considered replacing Kelly; but when it came to actually taking the step, she reminded herself of his years of faithful service, especially how he had worked long hours at low pay when the company was small. She also had to consider the fact that Janice Kelly, Raymon's wife and her good friend, had been supportive during times when she was ready to give up on the business.

When all the facts were out and Reitz was able to face the truth, she frankly admitted that she had known for a long time that Kelly was destroying the company but was unable to face the unpleasantness of replacing him. In order to avoid facing the fact of her own lack of courage, she had rationalized her behavior in terms of compassion and goodness. As a result, 150 employees would soon be out of work.

Examples of pseudomorality occur more often than most managers are willing to admit. Since hard decisions provoke hostility and create insecurity, it is not surprising that they are avoided and rationalized. Neither is it surprising that the depth of character often demanded of managers who make difficult business decisions is viewed as lack of compassion.

Everybody Is Doing It

One of the weakest foundations for a code of moral behavior is to play follow the leader—to see what others are doing and follow suit. In contrast to pacesetting managers whose behavior is constrained by deep religious convictions or a moral philosophy, some managers look primarily to common practice for a clue to right and wrong conduct.

If everybody is doing it, bribing the officials of foreign governments to buy a firm's products or misrepresenting the quality of a product can be rationalized as just another cost of doing business. Concerning product quality, one manufacturer expressed this position:

> I don't like selling a product that's designed to self-destruct in 18 months, but if I build-in quality, I can't compete on price. My competitors and customers are setting the pace, and I can't change until they do.

A close look at this firm's competitors revealed that some were, in fact, charging more and building a quality product. Actually making products of varying quality levels is not in itself unethical as long as consumer safety is not involved and consumers know what they are buying. There is, however, a fundamental weakness in any ethical code based primarily on what others are doing. It is at best amoral.

MAKING ORGANIZATIONS MORAL

A high level of morality in organizations—with all its implications for the behavior of managers within and outside the firm—does not happen by chance. It is a result of planning, commitment, goal setting, and the selection of managers with depth of character.

History has shown that when organizations fail in their responsibility to society the freedom to control their own destiny erodes. Laws passed to demand specific action impose increasingly narrow constraints within which managers retain the freedom to make decisions. Unions, the press, special-interest groups, and the general public emerge as cohesive forces to oppose real or imagined abuses of power. If there were no other reason for business organizations to initiate internal reforms, the threat of external controls should be enough. The following recommendations are given for making organizations moral.

1. *Management Selection and Development.* Companies that elect to make high profits and at the same time achieve social responsibility must select and develop managers with character, broad education, and professional competence.[27] An organization must make certain that its managers are informed concerning a wide range of social and economic issues in the firm's environment. Breadth of perspective should be sought and generously rewarded.

2. *Organizational Goals and Standards.* Organizations that are serious about becoming and remaining moral should define what they mean by morality. This definition can be expressed both in codes of ethics and in corporate goals. The goals may take the form of self-structured affirmative action programs relating to discrimination, the environment, employee relations, and other areas relating directly to the company. Goals may also involve whatever contribution the firm chooses to make regarding broad social issues such as crime, poverty, inflation, unemployment, and the need for more responsible government.

3. *Involvement of the Total Organization.* Rather than delegate the task to a few environmental or social responsibility specialists, managers at all levels should be made aware of their individual responsibility to enact the organization's goals and standards. They should be shown that a corporate social contribution can be developed within the context of the profit system—"not as a peripheral and purely philanthropic or moral exercise."[28] This means that the organization's goals

must be made a part of the goals of each manager and find fulfillment in every aspect of organizational life.

4. *A Corporate Social Audit.* As a means of satisfying themselves and society of their own morality, companies should make periodic audits of their performance in relation to their goals and objectives.[29] Contributions may be measured, for example, in terms of dollars spent to abate pollution, to improve safety on the job, and to support community projects. They may also be measured in terms of time spent by managers and employees in community affairs.

5. *Rewarding Desired Behavior.* The organization's motivational systems must be structured to reward socially responsible behavior as well as contributions to profit.

6. *Professionalization of Management.* For many years, writers in the field of management have indicated a need for the professionalization of management in the sense that medicine, law, and accounting are professions. This can be accomplished only if a substantial number of business organizations give their support to the development of competence criteria and a code of ethics against which to evaluate the qualifications and conduct of managers. Businesses will also need to initiate a professional organization to assume responsibility for the certification of managers. Such an organization will have an impact only as companies favor certified managers in selection and promotion and as its ethics committee becomes known for excluding incompetent or unethical managers from membership. This change is not likely to occur any time soon, but it is a worthy ideal.

7. *Training.* New employees should be thoroughly trained in the organization's view of its social responsibilities. This should be clearly stated in written form and readily available to employees.

IMPORTANT TERMS AND CONCEPTS

classical view	social responsibility
caveat emptor	intrinsic payoff
accountability concept	extrinsic payoff
caveat venditor	ethics
supportive goals	pseudomorality

STUDY AND DISCUSSION QUESTIONS

1. How does a competitive free enterprise system purport to protect society? Evaluate this position.

2. What are the major differences between the accountability and quality-of-life concepts of corporate social responsibility? Do you agree with one or the other of these? Why?

3. Some people view capitalists as unconcerned about human needs. What sort of moral philosophy might a person hold that would support capitalism? Is this moral philosophy consistent with a genuine concern for human welfare? How?

4. Contrast the purpose of business from the points of view of society and the investor. Does this distinction imply that the investor places no value on society's purpose?

5. What are the arguments against profit-making firms investing strictly in projects that will benefit society? Evaluate.

6. Professional (hired) managers who invest corporate funds in non-profit projects (for example, an antipoverty project in a ghetto of a distant city) are often hailed as expressing the highest form of social responsibility. What moral or ethical conflicts might such activities involve?

7. This chapter has not focused on possible differences between the goals and values of a manager and the manager's employer. How should managers deal with these differences? How should employers?

8. In view of the many statutory laws, government regulations, and court decisions that are designed to control the behavior of managers, what, if anything, is wrong with the position that "if it's legal, it's ethical"?

9. Evaluate this statement: Morals cannot be legislated.

10. How do professional codes of ethics influence the behavior of managers?

11. Explain and evaluate the following statement in light of the content of this chapter: In my role as a manager, my motivation for involvement in solving social problems is intelligent selfishness.

WHOSE WELFARE COUNTS THE MOST?

Omni, Inc., has been quite successful in buying and making profitable again small to medium-sized companies that were failing. Recently, after months of study, debate, and negotiation, Omni purchased the Aldo Company, a meatpacking and sausage-making company with a plant in each of three small, midwestern towns. At the time of purchase, one of Aldo's plants was making a small profit; one was incurring a small but gradually increasing loss, and Aldo's Smithville plant was incurring a significant and growing loss.

Largely by introducing more effective management practices, John Ryan, Omni's vice-president of operations, increased the profitability of the already profitable plant and stabilized the level of losses at the two unprofitable plants. He and Sandra Schumacher, Omni's vice-president of finance, agreed that the major remaining problem in the two unprofitable plants was that the machinery was old and in some instances was technologically obsolete.

The two vice-presidents also agreed that the least profitable plant, the Smithville plant, was by itself not salable, not even to the plant employees. Schumacher felt that the best course of action was to close the plant, take the corporate income tax write-off, and use the money to upgrade the equipment in the other unprofitable plant. Ryan, who had worked closely with the employees of the plants, was very concerned about the effect of the plant closing on Smithville. He made the following argument to Omni's Executive Committee:

> The plant is the largest employer in Smithville. The effects of closing it would be disastrous. Many of the plant's former employees would be forced to leave the town to find work, many of the small businesses would not have enough customers to survive, and property values would fall. I just don't see how we can justify turning our backs on the town

and our employees this way. I believe that with a large enough investment in new equipment we can make the plant profitable, save the employees and the townspeople from some real hardships, and in the process make Omni look like a hero. I admit that I would not recommend
buying the plant if it were for sale, but I believe we have an obligation
here. We are the only hope that the employees and their families have.
If we fail to act in their interest, there will be some real suffering.

Schumacher disagreed. Her statement to the Executive Committee
was just as emotional as Ryan's:

> Omni is not in business to save towns. I personally know that a
> good many of our retired employees rely almost exclusively on their
> dividends from Omni stock for their livelihood. There is no way that
> they or the other stockholders who own Omni should have their money
> spent to solve Smithville's problems. We thought we could turn the
> Smithville plant around with little additional investment. We found we
> were wrong. At this point I think we have better uses for Omni's fi-
> nancial resources, not the least of which would be to upgrade the ma-
> chinery in the other two Aldo plants so that they don't end up like the
> Smithville plant. Or we could increase our dividends this year and re-
> ward the people who have entrusted us with their savings and to whom
> we are responsible.

1. What are the key issues in this situation?

2. What are four alternative actions that Omni might reasonably take?

3. What are the long-run and short-run advantages and disadvantages of
   these actions?

4. Which action do you recommend?

REFERENCES

1. Hay, Robert D., and Edmund R. Gray, eds. *Business and Society: Cases
and Text.* Cincinnati: South-Western Publishing Co., 1981, pp. 34–36.
　2. Smith, Adam. *An Inquiry into the Nature and Causes of the Wealth
of Nations* (1776), ed. Edwin Cannan. New York: Modern Library, Random House,
Inc., 1937, p. 423.

3. Friedman, Milton. "Does Business Have a Social Responsibility?" *Bank Administration*, April, 1971, pp. 13–14.

4. Dalton, Dan R., and Richard A. Cosier. "The Four Faces of Social Responsibility," *Business Horizons*, Vol. 25, No. 3, May/June, 1982, pp. 19–27.

5. Spitzer, Carlton E. "Can Business Take Up the Social Slack?" *Business and Society Review*, No. 42, Summer, 1982, pp. 16–17.

6. Hah, Chong-do, and Robert M. Lindquist. "The 1952 Steel Seizure Revisited: A Systematic Study in Presidential Decision Making," *Administrative Science Quarterly*, Vol. 20, No. 4, Dec., 1975, pp. 587–605.

7. Weidenbaum, Murray L. "The True Obligation of the Business Firm to Society," *Management Review*, Vol. 70, No. 9, September, 1981, pp. 21–22.

8. Edmons, Charles P. III, and John H. Hand. "What Are the Real Long-Run Objectives of Business?" *Business Horizons*, Vol. 19, No. 6, December, 1976, p. 79.

9. Keyserling, Leon H. et al. "A System Worth Improving" in "The Future of Capitalism—a Symposium," *Business and Society/Innovation*, Vol. 10, Summer, 1974, pp. 14–15.

10. Keim, Gerald D. "Corporate Social Responsibility: An Assessment of the Enlightened Self-Interest Model," *Academy of Management Review*, Vol. 3, No. 1, January, 1978, pp. 32–39.

11. Keim, Gerald D. "Managerial Behavior and the Social Responsibility Debate: Goals Versus Constraints," *Academy of Management Journal*, Vol. 21, No. 1, March, 1978, p. 67.

12. Hay. *Business and Society: Cases and Text*, p. 14.

13. Fernstrom, Meredith M. "Corporate Responsibility: A Marketing Opportunity," *Management Review*, Vol. 22, No. 2, February, 1983, pp. 54–55.

14. Lehr, Lewis W. "Enlightened Self-Interest," *The Wall Street Journal*, September 7, 1982, p. 17.

15. Grunig, James E. "A New Measure of Public Opinions on Corporate Social Responsibility," *Academy of Management Journal*, Vol. 22, No. 4, December, 1979, p. 761.

16. Davis, Keith, and Robert L. Blomstrom. *Concepts and Policy Issues: Environment and Responsibility*, 4th ed. New York: McGraw-Hill Book Company, 1980, p. 6.

17. Fitch, Gordon H. "Achieving Corporate Social Responsibility," *Academy of Management Review*, Vol. 1, No. 1, January, 1976, p. 38.

18. Etzioni, Amitai. "There Oughta Be a Law—Or Should There Be?" *Business and Society Review/Innovation*, No. 8, Winter, 1973-74, pp. 10–11.

19. McAdams, Tony, and Robert C. Miljus. "Growing Criminal Liability of Executives," *Harvard Business Review*, Vol. 55, No. 2, March-April, 1977, pp. 36–40.

20. "Restatement of the Code of Professional Ethics," a booklet published for its members by the American Institute of Certified Public Accountants, effective March 1, 1973 (amended March, 1979).

21. Fernstrom. "Corporate Responsibility: A Marketing Opportunity," pp. 54–55.

22. Wall, Wendy L. "Helping Hands," *The Wall Street Journal*, June 21, 1984, p. 1.

23. Buehler, Vernon M., and Y. K. Shetty. "Motivations for Corporate Social Action," *Academy of Management Journal*, Vol. 17, No. 1, December, 1974, p. 769.

24. Miller, Mary Susan, and Edward A. Miller. "It's Too Late for Ethics Courses in Business Schools," *Business and Society Review*, No. 17, Spring, 1976, pp. 39–42.

25. Lusk, Edward J., and Bruce L. Oliver. "American Managers' Personal Value Systems—Revisited," *Academy of Management Journal*, Vol. 17, No. 3, September, 1974, pp. 549–554.

26. Brenner, Steven N., and Earl A. Molander. "Is the Ethics of Business Changing?" *Harvard Business Review*, Vol. 55, No. 1, January-February, 1977, pp. 68–69.

27. Andrews, Kenneth R. "Can the Best Corporations Be Made Moral?" *Harvard Business Review*, Vol. 51, No. 3, May-June, 1973, p. 63.

28. Gunness, Robert C. "Social Responsibility: The Art of the Possible," in *Corporate Social Policy*, eds. Robert L. Heilbroner and Paul London. Reading, Mass.: Addison-Wesley Publishing Co., 1975, p. 26.

29. Carroll, Archie B., and George V. Beiler. "Landmarks in the Evolution of the Social Audit," *Academy of Management Journal*, Vol. 18, No. 3, September, 1975, pp. 589–599.

SUGGESTED READINGS

Cochran, Philip L., and Robert A. Wood. "Corporate Social Responsibility and Financial Performance," *Academy of Management Journal*, Vol. 27, No. 1, March, 1984, pp. 42–56.

Corson, John J., and George A. Steiner. *Measuring Business Social Performance: The Corporate Social Audit*. New York: Committee for Economic Development, 1974.

Curtiss, Ellen T., and Philip A. Untersee, eds. *Corporate Responsibilities and Opportunities to 1990*. Lexington, Mass.: Lexington Books, 1979.

Fritzsche, David J., and Helmut Becker. "Linking Management Behavior to Ethical Philosophy—An Empirical Investigation," *Academy of Management Journal*, Vol. 27, No. 1, March, 1984, pp. 166–175.

Gervitz, Don. *Business Plan for America*. New York: Putnam Publishing Co., 1984.

Hargreaves, John, and Jan Dauman. *Business Survival and Social Change: A Practical Guide to Responsibility and Partnership*. New York: John Wiley & Sons, Inc., 1975.

Leone, Robert A. "The Real Costs of Regulation," *Harvard Business Review*, Vol. 55, No. 6, November-December, 1977, pp. 57–66.

Lerbinger, O. "How Far Toward The Social Audit?" *Public Relations Review*, Vol. 1, No. 1, January, 1975, pp. 38–52.

Richardson, Elliot L. *Corporate Responsibility, to Whom and for What?* University Park, Md.: College of Business Administration, Pennsylvania State University, 1981.

Schmidt, Warren H., and Barry Z. Pozner. *Managerial Values in Perspective.* New York: American Management Association, 1983.

Shapiro, Irving S. *America's Third Revolution: Public Interest and the Private Role.* New York: Harper & Row Publishing, Inc., 1984.

THE INDIVIDUAL IN ORGANIZATIONS

It is obvious from the preceding chapters that organizational behavior is concerned primarily with individuals and interpersonal relations, rather than with finance, accounting, production, or other aspects of management. Thus, it has much in common with the discipline of psychology. Unlike psychology, however, OB is always concerned with individual behavior and relationships among people in an organizational setting— usually in business and industrial organizations. For that reason, in Chapters 3, 4, and 5, where personality and motivation are discussed, attention is concentrated on those human qualities and motivational concepts that are of most interest to managers. Chapters 4 and 5 discuss concepts of human motivation that are most likely to help managers increase production, improve employee satisfaction, decrease employee turnover, handle grievances and disciplinary problems, and so on.

A study of organizational behavior can logically begin with a discussion of either organizations or individuals. Since functioning organizations are made up of people and can be understood only in the light of what we know about people, we first explore individual differences and the nature of human needs and motives. Nevertheless, human behavior cannot be understood apart from the environment in which it occurs. Therefore, in discussing either individuals or organizations, we constantly allude to one or the other in order to more effectively place the individual in a context that is meaningful to managers.

3

Personality and Performance in Organizations

As my hands press the plane forward, a smooth shaving curls up from the keen edge, filling the air with the tangy scent of fresh cut pine.

There is a soothing rhythm to the strokes of the plane and a delightful uniqueness in each spiraled shaving.

My chisel and mallet seek some more organic form hidden within a block of Hawaiian koa wood. The power saw that cut the block is no respecter of the flowing lines of light and dark that mark the pattern of growth. Sometimes, when my efforts at seeking the lifelines in the wood succeed, the form seems to take on a liveliness reminiscent of the forces that shaped the once tall and supple tree.

Now, as I seek to shape my life in more flexible, natural ways, the schools and offices that claimed so many of my years seem like a buzz saw that cut me into blocks irrespective of the life forms hidden within.

There are so many joys in my new vocation I wonder that I did not find it sooner. Perhaps my life had to be cut into blocks in order for me to know that was not the form I sought. Yet there are connections, too. The enjoyment I once got from organizing ideas and programs and peace marches I now find in planning the sequence of tasks and gathering materials to build a table. It is satisfying to see my hands transforming boards and glue into functional and even beautiful objects.

I now find myself with a set of useful skills that contribute to a sense of identity based on concrete work and achievements. These skills and the work I can produce give meaning to my life, meaning that is tangible, self-renewing, and growing—and very personal. To the extent that my craft becomes art my individuality is expressed through work that others can use and enjoy.[1]

As the excerpt that begins this chapter shows, work is potentially a pleasurable, self-fulfilling experience; and when it is, it is also self-motivating. Such fulfillment must, however, remain an ideal toward which we strive, since most people are employed in organizations whose objectives, technologies, and structures necessarily limit individual freedom and thereby limit satisfaction. The freedom of the managers who control organizations is limited—by the effectiveness of competitors, by laws and government regulations, union contracts, customer preferences, suppliers, available technologies, and so forth. Many managers are unable, regardless of their desires, to design jobs in such a way that all employees can find maximum fulfillment in their work.

Yet improvements can be made. There are ways of designing jobs and relating to subordinates that are more likely than others to stimulate satisfaction and intrinsic motivation. Managers who know what these are will be more effective in creating satisfying and productive work environments than managers who do not. We begin an exploration of these possibilities by looking at the assumptions managers make about people in the workplace. The specific objectives of Chapter 3 are

TO UNDERSTAND:

1. Three well-known views about managing

2. Some work-related differences among people

3. The nature of employee alienation

4. Some ways to make jobs more interesting

HUMANIZING ORGANIZATIONAL LIFE

An irreversible emphasis upon the human aspects of organizations that began during World War I and that made giant strides during the 1930s gained new impetus during the 1970s. What began as a human relations movement is today most often expressed in terms of the humanization of work or *quality of work life (QWL)*. It is increasingly a fact of industrial life that fair, equitable, and humane treatment of employees is more than just good business or a moral obligation. Employees have learned to expect it. To an increasing extent, it is a legal requirement.

During the first quarter of the twentieth century the power of the organization was formidable when compared with that of the individual employee or even with the fledgling unions which were beginning to gain strength. Although specific managers then, as now, demonstrated a degree of concern for the individual, employees generally were regarded as economic units or articles of commerce. The primary concern of the organization was efficiency. Labor was abundant. Employees who were dissatisfied with their treatment were free to leave, but often there was no place to go.

The most significant improvements in the treatment of employees began during times of great change within society as a whole: the Great Depression of the 1930s, World War II, the postwar economic expansion, and finally the emergence of a generation that has known only prosperity. Associated with these times, the human relations movement, the proliferation of laws, labor shortages, and the power of unions encouraged management to think seriously about employee motivation and satisfaction.

We now take for granted the first dramatic improvements made in the workplace—rest breaks, a 40-hour workweek, paid vacations—along with a number of employee benefits. Many of the gains made by employees occurred as a result of union power. Management was, in effect, forced to make certain concessions, either to avoid conflict with unionized employees or to avoid unionization altogether. Thus, employees often paid a high price for their gains and partly for that reason did not think that their employers had "given" them anything. Furthermore, their successes motivated them to seek even more ambitious objectives.

Managers who thought employees would be grateful as a result of an added employee benefit or pay raise soon learned that their expectations were naive. Motivation was not that simple; employees were complicated. They would not necessarily work harder when paid more, and a gain once made soon acquired the status of a right. Management would have to face the fact of continually increasing expectations and demands from employees as well as government, customers, and the general public.

A Sense of History

When an organization attempts to motivate employees to be more productive or cooperative, the response may be unexpected because of attitudes developed as a result of earlier experiences. The point is sometimes made that, because the basic physiological needs (food, shelter, and the like) of most workers are satisfied today, these needs no longer serve as motivators. In one sense, this is a valid statement, but it fails to take into consideration the importance of memory and the anticipation of future events.

There are still people in the work force, many of whom are in high-level positions, whose childhood memories of the Depression of the 1930s are vivid. These memories influence both present perceptions and future expectations. Employees are influenced by abuses suffered under previous employers and even by events, such as the Depression or anti-union violence, which were related to them by their parents and grandparents. Personality may be objectively conceived as a stream of consciousness flowing in the present; but subjectively we experience ourselves as liberated from the bonds of time—free to relive the past and project ourselves into the future.

Theories X and Y

Innumerable statements can be made about human nature, but they do not all have a direct bearing on how people should be dealt with in the work environment. The late Douglas McGregor did an excellent job of conceptualizing some of the assumptions about human nature that are relevant to organizational behavior.[2] He grouped and labeled one set of assumptions as **Theory X**, the classical or traditional view, and another as **Theory Y**, a progressive view upon which he believed an enlightened model for human relations in organizations could be developed.

Theory X. This theory holds that the average person inherently dislikes work, is innately lazy, irresponsible, self-centered, and security oriented and consequently is indifferent to the needs of the organization. Because of these characteristics, most people must be threatened, coerced, and controlled. In fact, most people prefer to be directed and controlled. They seek security above all, prefer to avoid responsibility, and both want and need external control in the work situation. Because people are basically gullible and immature, management should experience little difficulty in using a highly directive and manipulative style of supervision.

Theory Y. Experience has shown that Theory X assumptions result in a great deal of difficulty for management, although these assumptions remain popular with some managers. McGregor's Theory Y makes the opposite assumptions. People do not inherently dislike work and are not inherently lazy. Rather, they have learned to dislike work, to be lazy, and to be irresponsible because of the nature of their work and supervision. They have a high capacity for developing an intrinsic interest in their work, for committing themselves to organizational objectives, and for working productively with a minimum of external controls.

Critique. Theory Y represents a far more realistic set of assumptions about human nature. It provides the optimism about people that managers must possess if they are to win the cooperation and enthusiastic support of employees in achieving organizational goals. Increasingly managers who make Theory X assumptions meet extreme resistance and cannot function effectively.

Two points should be made with reference to these theories. First, Theory Y people are said to have the potential or capacity for the responsible behavior and attitudes described. However, potential must be developed, and it is questionable that a favorable work environment can always accomplish this feat, at least at a cost an organization can afford. Can employees whose backgrounds and choices have predisposed them to Theory X behavior change to such an extent that their behavior follows the Theory Y model? Employees do not enter the organization as a blank page upon which an enlightened management is free to write a new program that conforms to some organizational ideal. The implicit assumption of infinite educability and plasticity is misleading, and it may reflect a lack of respect for the individual's autonomy and right to individuality.

The second point in evaluating McGregor's X and Y classifications concerns his assumptions about the average person. One must ask, "Average on what dimensions?" Are we talking about intelligence? education? experience? Average is a statistical concept; and the average person is a nonexistent, hypothetical construct. When we make assumptions about the average person, at best we are referring to most people, and in doing so we must recognize that there are exceptions.

The notion that people are innately or inherently lazy and irresponsible is in no sense defensible, but it is an indisputable fact that some people have developed these qualities and strongly resist change. The assumptions made about the nature of most people tend to exert a controlling influence on the management styles adopted, and Theory Y provides a worthy foundation for a manager's general leadership pattern. One cannot, however, afford to ignore individual differences. For practical purposes some employees do fit the Theory X model, and the supervisor who blindly attempts to lead them with Theory Y assumptions will probably fail. If the characteristics McGregor described in his X/Y dichotomy are normally distributed throughout the population, we should expect most people to possess a mixture of the two descriptions with a few people at the extremes who are accurately described by the X and Y characteristics.

Use of the Concept. A practical application of the Theory X and Y concept is as a tool for diagnosing and changing managerial behavior. If a manager tends to instruct subordinates in great detail about how to do their work and tends to monitor them closely and to punish those who deviate at all, then this manager is behaving as if Theory X applies. If the manager is confronted with this fact but does not believe that Theory X describes the employees, this could cause the manager to rethink the way he or she manages. In addition, if the manager is reminded that (1) people tend to behave according to how they see themselves; and (2) people frequently adopt the view of themselves that others have of them, then the manager may choose to try managing as if Theory Y applied. This would allow the manager to see if the workers will respond by behaving more like Theory Y employees.

Viewed in this way, we can see why the terms Theory X and Theory Y are sometimes used as descriptions of employees and of managers, and even of organizations, in addition to being used as labels for sets of assumptions about human nature.

Theory Z

Especially in the 1980s, business leaders in the United States have become interested in Japanese management practices. One of the foremost authorities on the subject, Professor William G. Ouchi, has used the term **Theory Z** to refer to a group of employee-focused management practices that are commonly found in Japanese companies.[3] Theory Z practices include the following:

1. *Lifetime employment.* This varies with the ability of the company to provide lifetime employment, but the (generally unwritten) commitment to attempt to provide continuous employment is much greater in Theory Z companies. Similarly, the employee commitment to stay with the company is much greater.

2. *Slow evaluation and promotion.* This practice follows to a degree from the extensive training that Theory Z companies invest in their employees and is in keeping with Japanese cultural values. The practice is not well suited to the high need for achievement that characterizes many employees in the United States and is therefore not as frequently found in the American firms that are otherwise characterized by Theory Z practices.

3. *Supervisory style that implies a high level of trust.* The ability to trust others to do their job well follows in part from the extensive training and slower promotion that take place in Theory Z companies and that in turn lead to the higher skill and knowledge levels that

justify confidence in a person's ability. It also follows from the practices of extensive evaluation and lifetime employment that tend to ensure a commonality of goals.

4. *Participative decision making.* The focus of this practice is not only to acquire a broader base of information and commitment for the individual decision but also to disseminate organizational values and to signal the cooperative intent of the firm.

5. *Nonspecialized career paths.* This practice produces higher levels of company-specific knowledge that in turn leads to high levels of cooperation and coordination among individuals and functional units. It also helps make participative decision making more practical since employees tend to have had a more common set of experiences than would be the case if they were all specialists.

As Professor Ouchi makes clear in his book, these and other Theory Z practices are not found in all Japanese firms, and they are found in some firms in the United States. It appears that more American firms are attempting to adopt Theory Z, but other forces in the United States such as rapid technological change are making it difficult to implement some Theory Z practices. Theory Z gained high visibility at a time when American companies in several industries were under siege from intense Japanese competition and when American industrialists were struggling desperately to discover what the Japanese were doing right. Although increasing skepticism exists about the wholesale importation of Japanese management practices, Ouchi's Theory Z has strongly influenced American industrialists to rethink their own management practices.

It is important to understand that Theories X and Y are basically views or assumptions about people while Theory Z is a description of a set of management practices. On the other hand, managers who hold Theory X views will tend to adopt practices different from those of managers who hold Theory Y views. Similarly, Theory Z management practices are based on assumptions about people, their abilities and attitudes, and how these abilities and attitudes can be shaped by a particular work environment.

The Challenge to Management

The decades from 1965 to 1985 produced dramatic social changes that required a significant accommodation on the part of managers. The riots of the 1960s; the challenges to authority associated with increased emphasis on independent thinking and accentuated by the Vietnamese

War; and the rising demands of a variety of minority groups (which collectively constitute a majority of Americans) combined to challenge a way of life and a style of management. Traditional concepts of morality have changed, the stabilizing influence of the family has diminished, and the motivating influence of the Protestant work ethic has increasingly been called into question.

There are growing expectations today that one's work should be interesting and fulfilling in addition to providing security and affluence. There are also expectations, backed by force of law, that all discrimination on the basis of race, ethnic background, religion, sex, and age should be immediately ended; and that the workplace should be free from all conditions that might be dangerous to employees.

In the days when Frederick W. Taylor's revolutionary ideas made their first impression, it was fashionable to study the possible effects of break periods or the impact on productivity of reducing the 60-hour workweek. Today the fashionable topic is how jobs can be redesigned—enriched or enlarged—to increase employee satisfaction; and some management authors believe that in today's society employees have a right to intrinsically satisfying work.

Needless to say, the challenge to management is impressive. Only progressive and efficient organizations can survive, and only sophisticated and knowledgeable managers can succeed. Managers must have more than technical knowledge and an intuitive grasp of what is required to organize and lead effectively. They must become aware of the subtleties of formal organizations, informal group processes, authority, power, and communication within an organizational setting. They can no longer be content with uncreative, intuitive decision making at a time when their competitors are using more sophisticated methods. Managers must gain a deep understanding of human behavior as it is expressed in an organizational setting. In the final analysis, modern-day organizations are made up of individuals who are more frequently demanding to be viewed as individuals rather than as economic units in an impersonal bureaucracy.

PEOPLE AS INDIVIDUALS

Theory X does not describe all people. Nor does Theory Y. People differ. Managers who do not recognize this fact and manage accordingly will mismanage their work relationships and be less effective.

Each of us possesses a relatively stable set of characteristics called a **personality**. Although the most observable differences among people are physical—size and facial features, for example—certain personality differences are of greater importance in organizations. In the next few pages we discuss abilities, perceptions, beliefs, preferences, and attitudes. These aspects of personality significantly affect human behavior in organizations.

Differences in Ability

If there is any one characteristic of people that is universally valid and important, it is that they differ in their abilities.[4] To say that all persons are created equal is a statement of human rights under the law; it communicates nothing at all about human nature. As a matter of fact, people differ greatly in intelligence, aptitudes, physical strength, manual dexterity, knowledge, skill, interests, personality traits, motivation, and many other attributes that potentially influence behavior and productivity.

Figure 3-1 shows the distribution of mental ability (general intelligence expressed in terms of IQ) throughout the population. Notice that mental ability essentially follows a normal probability or bell-shaped curve. There are few persons with an extremely low or extremely high IQ, and the number of persons with a given IQ increases toward the center of the distribution (that is, toward the average IQ of 100). Simple as the observation may seem, it is significant that most people are average and therefore cannot be expected to perform well in very complex and demanding jobs—for example, in some scientific and professional posi-

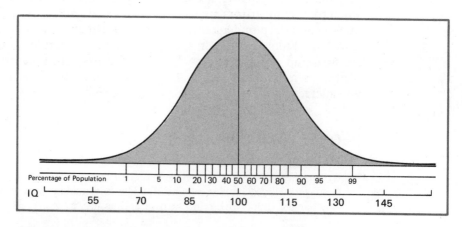

FIGURE 3-1   The Distribution of Mental Ability Throughout the Population

tions. Persons who are average in mental ability may, however, have outstanding potential in a variety of other areas.

Individual differences in mental ability have broad implications for organizational behavior. For example, we should expect an assembly line worker with an IQ of 128 to be bored and dissatisfied. In fact, we might hypothesize that all efforts to make assembly line work meaningful and interesting will be wasted on this particular individual. The reaction of a worker with an IQ of 90 or 100 (average) should be more favorable, and the person with borderline or subnormal intelligence may find the routine assembly line job extremely challenging. For some people this type of job is even too complex to be performed without provoking unacceptable stress. Obviously people are suited for greatly differing types of work—a fortunate circumstance since job demands vary widely.

Most abilities are distributed throughout the population in a pattern similar to that of mental ability, and many of them influence performance on the job. There is, of course, no one-to-one relationship between ability and productivity. Differences in motivation, experience, and work habits may result in many persons with high native potential performing below the level of others whose aptitudes are marginal for the task in question.

Differences in Perception

Our senses of seeing, hearing, smelling, and so forth, when impacted by stimuli such as light, sound, or fragrance, provide us with **sensations**. Meaningless as raw sensory data, when interpreted these sensations are transformed into **perceptions**. Perceptions, then, are only partly based on external stimuli; they are also a result of the knowledge gained from previous experiences. Since we have all had different previous experiences, we have different perceptions of the same "facts" that our senses bring to us.

Variability in perception can have very important effects in organizations and elsewhere. Herbert Simon, the Nobel prize-winning economist, and his associate Dewitt Dearborn, demonstrated this with a "classic" experiment. Twenty-three executives, all enrolled in an executive training program, were asked to read a case widely used in instruction in business schools. The case, Castengo Steel Company, contained a wealth of descriptive material about the company and its industry and the recent history of both with little evaluation. It was deliberately written to hold closely to concrete facts and to leave as much as possible of the burden of interpretation to the reader.

The executives appeared at a class session to discuss the case. Before the discussion began, the executives were asked by the instructor to write a brief statement about what they considered to be the most important problem facing the company—the problem a new company president should deal with first. Prior to this session, the group had discussed other cases while being reminded from time to time by the instructor that they were to assume the role of the top executive of the company in considering its problems.

The executives were in the range usually called "middle management." In terms of departmental affiliation, they fell into four groups:

1. Sales: Five product managers or assistant product managers and one field sales supervisor.

2. Production: Three department superintendents, one assistant factory manager, and one construction engineer.

3. Accounting: An assistant chief accountant and three accounting supervisors (for a budget division and two factory departments).

4. Miscellaneous: Two members of the legal department, two in research and development, and one each from public relations, industrial relations, medical, and purchasing.

The researchers compared (1) the executives who mentioned "sales," "marketing," or "distribution" with those who did not; (2) the executives who mentioned "clarifying the organization" or some equivalent with those who did not; (3) the executives who mentioned "human relations," "employee relations," or "teamwork" with those who did not. The data are summarized in Figure 3-2. We quote some of the researchers' findings:

The difference between the percentages of sales executives (83%) and other executives (29%) who mentioned sales as the most important problem is significant at the 5 percent level. Three of the five nonsales executives, moreover, who mentioned sales were in the accounting department, and all of these were in positions that involved analysis of product profitability. This accounting activity was, in fact, receiving considerable emphasis in the company at the time of the case discussion and the accounting executives had frequent and close contacts with the product managers in the sales department. If we combine sales and accounting executives, we find that 8 out of 10 of these mentioned sales as the most important problem; while only 2 of the remaining 13 executives did.

Organization problems (other than marketing organization) were mentioned by four out of five production executives, the two executives in research and development, and the factory physician, but by only one

Department	Total number of executives	Number who mentioned		
		Sales	"Clarify organization"	Human relations
Sales	6	5	1	0
Production	5	1	4	0
Accounting	4	3	0	0
Miscellaneous	8	1	3	3
Totals	23	10	8	3

FIGURE 3-2 Summary of the Castengo Steel Company Case Study

sales executive and no accounting executives. The difference between the percentage for production executives (80%) and other executives (22%) is also significant at the 5 percent level. Examination of the Castengo case shows that the main issue discussed in the case that relates to manufacturing is the problem of poorly defined relations among the factory manager, the metallurgist, and the company president. The presence of the metallurgist in the situation may help to explain the sensitivity of the two research and development executives (both of whom were concerned with metallurgy) to this particular problem area.

It is easy to conjecture why the public relations, industrial relations, and medical executives should all have mentioned some aspect of human relations, and why one of the two legal department executives should have mentioned the board of directors.

We have presented data on the selective perceptions of industrial executives exposed to case material that support the hypothesis that each executive will perceive those aspects of a situation that relate specifically to the activities and goals of his department. Since the situation is one in which the executives were motivated to look at the problem from a company-wide rather than a departmental viewpoint, the data indicate further that the criteria of selection have become internalized.[5]

Differences in Beliefs, Preferences, and Attitudes

Just as our experiences cause us to have different perceptions, they also cause us to have different beliefs, preferences, and attitudes. These beliefs, preferences, and attitudes have considerable impact on our work behavior. One very important belief concerns the location of the factors that determine outcomes, or what is often referred to as the **locus of control**.[6]

Locus of Control. Some people are characterized by a belief in **high internal control**. They believe that their actions have a major effect on the events that affect their lives. They tend to be initiators and prefer to be responsible for results. In contrast are those people who believe in **low internal control**. These people believe that the actions of other people are the principal determinants of the events that impact their lives. In addition, they see luck as playing a major role in whatever happens in their lives. Clearly our belief about the locus of control affects how hard we try to achieve goals, how we view the performance of subordinates, how we deal with defeat, and what kind of jobs we prefer. This last thought brings us to the matter of preferences.

Bureaucratic Orientation. Organizations, in both the private and public sectors, are bureaucracies. The classic description of bureaucracies and their advantages over other organizational forms was made by the German sociologist Max Weber. On the basis of his observations of a variety of industrial organizations, Weber portrayed the ideal organizational form, a bureaucracy, as possessing the following properties:

1. Specialization and division of labor, with clearly defined responsibility and authority for each position in the organization.

2. Positions arranged in a hierarchy, with each position under the supervision of a higher one.

3. A formal set of rules to ensure coordination of effort across organizational units and uniformity of action across time and across units.

4. Impersonal relationships. Weber felt that the ideal official should be characterized by "a spirit of formalistic impersonality, without hatred or passion, and hence without affection or enthusiasm."[7]

Clearly bureaucracies provide a working environment different from organizations that are less formalized. Many people prefer to work in such an environment. These people are said to have a **bureaucratic orientation**.[8] Specifically, they tend to have the following personality characteristics:

1. An acceptance of authority as a basis for action, such as persuasiveness or expertise.

2. A preference for well-defined and enforced rules and procedures.

3. A preference for impersonal, formal relationships, especially between people from different organizational levels.

Attitudes. Closely related to the concept of belief is the concept of attitude. An **attitude** is a predisposition to evaluate an object in a favorable or unfavorable manner. The attitude object may be, for example, a person, group, religion, process, or form of government. Attitudes involve both feelings and beliefs. Thus, a business owner who has negative attitudes toward unions may believe that they are bad for business, for the nation, for management, and for the union members. These beliefs are accompanied by strong feelings, and the interaction of the two provides a component of personality that is highly resistant to change. Once the attitude is formed, this manager may be blinded to any conceivable good in unions because everything unions do is interpreted through that attitude. Similarly, a coal miner with a long history of working for low wages under dangerous conditions has learned to view managers as ruthless exploiters. As a result, any statement made by a manager is viewed with skepticism, regardless of how true it may be. Managers who believe that people are inherently lazy and selfish will naturally interpret the behavior of others through that filter and consequently will have no difficulty finding reinforcing evidence for such a viewpoint.

Differing Needs

Employees cannot be treated as though their needs are all alike. Everyone has certain primary needs (the needs for food, rest, self-respect, and the approval of others, for example). Even these needs vary greatly in intensity. As a person goes about satisfying them, new needs emerge, such as the needs for power, achievement, recognition, and the need to engage in certain interesting activities. These are learned secondary needs. As such, they may be strong in one person and virtually nonexistent in another.

Chapters 4 and 5 describe in some detail the nature and function of human needs and their relationship to motivation. For now, the important point is that human needs vary greatly from person to person, a fact that makes generalizations difficult.

Constraints of Attitude and Perception

The fact that one's environment strongly influences behavior is indisputable. The person whose early background consistently provides rewards for hard work and responsible behavior will probably perform more acceptably on the job than one whose history is characterized by rewards for antisocial behavior and opposition to the established order. There is no doubt that human behavior, like that of lower animals, is to a significant extent conditioned by its consequences (reward and punishment). This does not, however, necessarily lead to the conclusion that humans have no freedom or autonomy.

Freedom of Choice. A number of prominent psychologists have taken the stance that human freedom is an illusion—that the choices an individual appears to make are totally determined by the impact of events upon and within the individual. Like the billiard ball that comes to rest at a specific spot on the table because of its velocity and the position of the other balls with which it comes in contact, human choices are thought to be totally determined. This assumption is somewhat outdated and is one that many people do not accept.

Most people perceive themselves as having a degree of genuine autonomy or control over their own destinies—an important fact since perceptions of reality influence behavior. Furthermore, most people seem to have the need to exert some control over their destinies, including their destinies in the workplace. Consistent with this need, many people find greater job satisfaction when they have an opportunity to initiate and make decisions about how their work is done. It is interesting to note that even people who are somewhat irresponsible on the job accept the idea that they cause their own problems and they should be held responsible. In fact, people sometimes believe so strongly that they are responsible for their own behavior that they develop intense feelings of guilt as a result of failure to measure up to their own expectations. The fact that people develop such feelings indicates a deep belief in their own freedom of choice, a belief that is expressed behaviorally even by persons who argue that freedom of choice is only an illusion. That people hold others responsible for their actions is further evidence that, for practical purposes, people are committed to a lofty view of humanity which states that individuals have a capacity for choosing between alternatives and for assuming responsibility for their behavior. Organizations cannot function optimally without these pragmatic assumptions.[9]

Levels of Freedom. Practically speaking, some people have more freedom than others: for example, two sales representatives with equal ability have an opportunity to make a sale. The one who believes the sale is possible is free to attempt it. The other, believing that the probability of making the sale is zero, is consequently bound by that belief. Subjectively, to attempt the sale would be pure folly. This dimension of freedom, or lack of it, may also be seen in the simple task of cutting a pie. There are many conceivable ways of cutting it, but the person who assumes that pie slices must be wedge shaped is limited by that assumption.

To varying degrees everyone loses freedom through limitations posed by past experience, ignorance, prejudices, beliefs, assumptions, attitudes, opportunities, and the like. Some employees and managers feel boxed in, while others in the same environment experience the exhilarating freedom that comes from an awareness that many courses of action are available. Objective observers can clearly see that in many cases the constraints lie within an individual's self-perception and perception of the external environment rather than in a real lack of ability or opportunity.

ORGANIZATIONAL NEEDS AND DEMANDS

An organization can survive and achieve its objectives only through the application of efficient processes and methods. Historically a primary means of achieving efficiency has been a division of labor which has deprived large numbers of employees of the opportunity to engage in work that is intrinsically satisfying. To provide employees with meaningful work is perhaps the greatest challenge currently being presented to management. It has yet to be demonstrated, however, that the feat is possible or that a significant investment in making all jobs intrinsically satisfying is worthwhile.

An organization is formed when the specific and limited objectives of its founders can be achieved only through the cooperative efforts of a group of individuals. Organizations make possible efficiencies that individuals cannot achieve and consequently enable their members to earn more than each could earn working alone. As organizations grow, their efficiency may be increased by the use of highly specialized machines, simplified work methods, and specialized personnel. Thus, one employee may do nothing but routinely enter insurance claims data into a computer; another performs the simple operations that combine two parts of a carburetor; still another checks for errors in the compilation of telephone directory information. The resulting problems of boredom and indifference constitute one of the major problems of industrial life.

Closely related to this problem is the fact that organizational life requires that the organization's members conform to a broad spectrum of behavioral expectations. The rules, regulations, work standards, and social norms that collectively define acceptable performance are often experienced by employees as unacceptably restrictive and by observers of organizational behavior as promoting immaturity and irresponsibility.

We look now at a few of the many demands organizations make on their members and at member reactions to these demands.

The Nature of Work

The scientist, artist, manager, or engineer whose fascinating work has become an obsession may indefinitely postpone vacations and voluntarily work long hours with little concern for external rewards. In contrast, the bright but bored accounts payable clerk watches the clock in eager anticipation of the moment the workday yields to the leisure time activity of working in the garden or engaging in an energy-consuming and fatiguing activity. We commonly speak of "mothers who work" as though mothers who use their day rearing a family do not work. Obviously the term *work* is an ambiguous one.

The concept of work lends itself to a variety of interpretations. To the ancient Greeks, it was a curse. To the early Hebrews, it was a form of punishment resulting from the sinful nature of humanity. To Marxists, work is an opportunity for the oppressed worker to escape the tyranny of capitalistic oppression and joyously participate in building an improved material environment. To many people, work is an opportunity to serve God and humanity, to utilize their natural talents, and to fulfill their vocation or calling to service.

In practice, the meaning of work is uniquely personal, depending upon one's philosophy, opportunities, specific work situation, and a variety of other factors that influence perceptual processes. One definition includes several aspects of work and avoids the popular notions that work is paid employment or activity engaged in from necessity rather than for pleasure. This definition is that work is "an activity that produces something of value for other people."[10] Although organizational behavior deals primarily with work for which one is paid, the pay received is by no means restricted to money. Furthermore, the notion that work is somehow intrinsically distasteful may itself be the main curse of work in organizations.

Instrumental and Intrinsic Aspects of Work

Most employees do not work primarily for pleasure. Their work is an instrument for the achievement of certain valued objectives. It is, for example, a means of earning money and providing for security and leisure time. However, this does not mean that work is only a means to an end. In fact, research studies indicate most employees would continue to work even if they should inherit enough money to make work unnecessary. The intrinsic or noninstrumental reasons for continuing to work vary greatly with groups and individuals. Blue-collar workers, many of whom are instrumentally oriented, would continue to work primarily to keep occupied, while white-collar employees are more likely to be motivated by interest and accomplishment.[11]

For many employees work provides a sense of identity. The employee who says with pride "I work for IBM" is saying, "If you want to know who I am, just think of the well-established qualities of my employer and note the kinds of people IBM employs." Another employee, who identifies more with a prestigious vocational field than with an organization, responds to questions about employment with "I am a tool-and-die maker" or "I'm an engineer." In contrast, to be both unemployed and to have no trade or profession, especially if one has no income, is subjectively to be a nobody. This can be an ego-crushing experience, as many of those out of work report.

People whose services are in demand perceive themselves to be worth something. The belief that one is worthwhile is somehow validated in work. People who can look with pride upon something they have produced (a painting, a house, a manufactured product, or an idea) are rewarded by the identification. One of the major problems encountered in assembly line manufacturing is that employees perform such a minor operation on the product that they are unable to identify with the finished product. Such work can only be instrumental and is consequently less rewarding than some other types of work.

The Division of Labor

The manufacturing methods used before the industrial revolution had some definite advantages. Artisans who made an entire pair of shoes had a personal investment in the product and could justifiably feel pride in the fruits of their labor. On the other hand, a shoemaker could produce very few shoes and was consequently destined to be poor, at least when compared with the modern factory worker. Factory workers today enjoy luxuries that could be afforded only by the very rich in earlier times.

The efficiency of the factory system was greatly increased by the division of work into small, simple jobs (a process sometimes referred to as **job simplification**). In 1832 Charles Babbage extolled the virtues of the division of labor, outlining its advantages as follows:

1. The reduction of learning time. (In contrast to the years an apprentice must serve, an assembly line worker can reach peak performance within a few hours.)

2. A reduction in wasted materials during learning.

3. The small amount of time lost when employees are moved from one job to another or when they change occupations.

4. The specialized and simple tools that can often be used.

5. The high level of skill acquired by the frequent repetition of the same process by an individual.

6. The stimulation an employee receives to think of new tools and processes to perform the specialized function assigned.[12]

These and other benefits that were believed to be inherent in the division of labor were expressed in the work of Frederick W. Taylor. Taylor advocated the scientific study of all jobs in order to maximize labor efficiency. Through time and motion studies, jobs were reduced to the fewest and simplest movements, and wherever possible Taylor's piece rate system of payment was installed as a means of encouraging workers to produce at their peak. Although organizations continue to utilize many of the efficiency methods advocated by Taylor, they are aware that these methods often lead to negative attitudes and counterproductive behavior. For example, creative ideas about how to improve production (point 6) are often intentionally hidden from management, and even employees who are paid incentive wages sometimes restrict production.

Employee Alienation

In recent years much has been written about **employee alienation**. This term refers to an estrangement from the organization and indifference, if not outright disdain, toward work. Presumably this alienation results from the dull, fragmented jobs which are a product of the division of labor and from the impersonality of large, bureaucratic organizations. Studies consistently show that the problem is worse among young, well-educated employees who are less tolerant than their elders of these dehumanizing conditions.

The Extent of the Problem. There is no agreement concerning the extent of the alienation problem. A tendency exists for behavioral scientists, as well as other observers, to interpret data through their preconceived viewpoints. To some extent, what one sees is a function of the particular industry, organization, and work group studied. For example, automobile assembly line workers might be expected to experience more alienation than comparable employees in new industries such as electronics. In the latter, a high degree of sensitivity to the needs of employees often has been expressed in the formulation of organizational policy. Generally speaking, assembly line and machine-tending jobs are viewed as more boring than most others, although some white-collar jobs (data entry operations and routine office support, for example) may run a close second.

Based on Bureau of Labor Statistics data concerning jobs with assembly line or operative features, James O'Toole and his associates have concluded that the problem is less restricted than popularly believed:

> It is clear that classically alienating jobs (such as on the assembly line) that allow the worker no control over the conditions of work and that seriously affect his mental and physical functioning off the job probably comprise less than 2 percent of the jobs in America. But a growing number of white-collar jobs have much in common with the jobs of auto workers and steelworkers. Indeed, discontent with the intrinsic factors of work has spread even to those with managerial status.[13]

One of the difficulties in determining the extent of dissatisfaction is that the techniques used to survey workers are sometimes inadequate. For example, a Gallup poll asks only, "Is your work satisfying?" Nevertheless, there has been considerable research on the subject, leading George Strauss to this position:

> Very briefly, my thesis is as follows: most workers report satisfaction with their work, and there is no evidence of rising dissatisfaction. Although the typical worker reacts positively to having more challenging work, he has learned to cope with a lack of challenge (sometimes at a considerable psychic cost); blue-collar workers at least tend to focus their lives away from their jobs and to give higher priority to economic benefits and adequate working conditions than to intrinsic job challenge. As a consequence, they are motivated to produce only a "fair day's work" (whatever this may be in local context). Job design schemes, such as job enrichment, offer hope of increasing satisfaction and productivity in some cases, although perhaps their main advantage lies in providing a more flexible work force, in improving communication among workers, and in increasing the supply of "amenities" on the job.[14]

Other conclusions concerning long-term trends in employee satisfaction are more pessimistic. On the basis of the quit rate of employees (Bureau of Labor Statistics data), Dennis Organ concluded that job satisfaction was relatively unchanged from 1947 to 1976, although it improved somewhat until the early 1960s followed by a decline through the 1970s.[15] Further conclusions are based on the responses of 175,000 employees in 159 companies for whom Opinion Research Corporation conducted attitude studies from 1950 to 1978. That research supports the idea that employee discontent is increasing and shows that employees are also expecting more from their jobs now than in the past.[16]

To some extent the growing discontent of American workers may be a function of an increase in the number of young employees, since they tend to be more discontented than older employees. It may also be a direct result of a general increase in expectations. If employees believe they have a right to interesting work, that expectation alone is sufficient to cause dissatisfaction. It remains to be seen how real or serious the decline in job satisfaction is and whether growing expectations that all work should be made satisfying is creating unrealistic expectations.

Routine versus Boring Work. Many jobs require employees to perform the same work hour after hour. Assembly line and machine-tending jobs are obvious examples, but even managerial jobs involve routine: e.g., answering correspondence, preparing and reviewing reports, and attending meetings. Routine, however, is not in itself necessarily boring and dissatisfying. It may be dull in the sense that it allows for little or no variety or autonomy, but not all employees are concerned with these qualities. Boredom is a psychological condition that results in part from one's environment and in part from the attitudes and perceptions of the individual.

Consider what occurs in the classroom. The lectures of one professor are highly interesting and even motivating and exhilarating to one student while to another they are boring and uninteresting. What is boring, subjectively speaking, is a matter of perception, and the qualities that induce boredom are as often brought to the classroom by the student as by the lecturer. In this regard, it is equally important that people with a high need for self-expression, autonomy, and creativity not be placed on routine jobs and that routine-loving people not be placed in jobs that require responses to irregular problems. It is significant that most organizations appear to have as much difficulty finding employees who are willing to tackle challenging jobs as they have in solving the problem of too much routine.

Adaptation to Routine. Employees have an amazing capacity to adapt to routine jobs. Of course, some adapt more easily than others, and some never adapt. It would indeed be surprising if an uneducated employee whose intelligence and aspirations are low had as much trouble adapting to a routine job as the mentally alert, ambitious individual who was forced to drop out of college because of financial problems. Naturally, adaptation is easier for people who are properly placed. It is, in fact, preferable to transfer a misplaced individual to a more suitable position rather than to demand the psychological change required for adaptation.

For many employees and managers work is a central value. It is a means of self-expression and an opportunity for personal development and ego satisfaction. In contrast, employees on routine jobs often accept their employment solely as a means to an end. Work is something one does to provide a livelihood, security, and retirement benefits. Meaning is found not in the work itself but in the fact that one is responsibly working, providing for the needs of one's family, and making a contribution to society. The factory worker may not enjoy working as such; this becomes a serious problem only to the person who has been led to believe that all work should be intrinsically satisfying. This is easiest to believe when prosperity reigns and an affluent work force continually hears the critics of industrial organizations, including some prominent behavioral scientists, complain about the demeaning nature of factory jobs. In times of economic downturn it is less credible that all jobs can and should be made interesting—in 1979–1980, for example, when obsolete steel mills were permanently closing and automobile companies were laying off masses of employees. During such times employees are preoccupied with holding a job and avoiding the decline in real earnings caused by inflation. Chrysler Corporation employees, for example, accepted a labor contract significantly less favorable than industry rates as a means of keeping the firm from bankruptcy. Concerns about unemployment make demands for interesting work seem irrelevant.

Workers use a variety of techniques to avoid the pain of excessive boredom. The most common is daydreaming about the "really important" activities that take place away from work such as time spent with family, recreation, and vacations. As another boredom-reducing device, workers contrive various games involving creative ways of performing tasks: getting ahead and then resting or unofficially trading off tasks with a co-worker. There are other less desirable forms of adaptation too, such as loafing, engaging in antiemployer activity, chronic complaining, absenteeism, and frequently changing employers. The more poorly matched an employee is to the job, the higher the probability that adjustment techniques will be undesirable.

The Trouble with Adaptation. Organizations can survive and attain their objectives only because their members are willing to adapt to some extent to organizational demands. The managerial task of efficiently turning out a product or service requires that a certain degree of individuality be sacrificed in order to achieve organizational objectives. There are major differences in perceptions of what this aspect of organizational life does to or for its members.

From one perspective, organizations require their members to behave in ways that promote or perpetuate immaturity. Chris Argyris has for a number of years called attention to those aspects of organizations that tend to reward dependence, submissiveness, the development of few rather than many abilities, and the development of a short time perspective. As employees accept inducements to behave rationally— that is, rationally in terms of organizational goals and rules—they develop submissiveness before the power of the organization. As this continues over time, they begin to suppress or deny their self-actualizing tendencies and to define responsibility and maturity in terms of their ability to conform to organizational demands. Individuals who cannot make the adaptation to the norms of this immature subculture become extremely frustrated and cannot function harmoniously within the system.[17]

MAKING JOBS MORE INTERESTING

The selecting and organizing of tasks to make them suitable for one person to perform is called job design.[18,19] Job design is not a new idea, as evidenced by the work of Charles Babbage and Fredrick W. Taylor. What is new is the idea that jobs should be designed for the purpose of making employees more satisfied rather than solely for the purpose of making them more efficient.

Four approaches have been used to help make jobs more interesting: (1) job rotation, (2) job enlargement, (3) job enrichment, and (4) sociotechnical systems design.

Job Rotation

Job rotation refers to the practice of moving the employee from job to job. For example, in a fast-food restaurant an employee may work as a cook for two days a week, as an order taker two days, and as a cleanup person the fifth day of the week. The payoff from job rotation follows from the fact that when a person starts each "new" job there is some degree of stimulation, and this stimulation causes the work to be less boring than it otherwise would be. Job rotation on a short-term basis, such as in the restaurant example, is primarily for making the overall employment situation more interesting. Job rotation on a long-term basis, as when a junior manager is given a series of six-month assignments, is generally for the purpose of preparing the employee for a higher level position.

Job Enlargement and Job Enrichment

Job rotation does not affect the content of a particular job. **Job enlargement** does. Job enlargement refers to the practice of adding tasks to those that are already part of a job. The resulting *task variety* causes the employee to acquire and use a greater variety of skills, and this in turn results in greater satisfaction for many workers. If all of the tasks associated with some larger work module are included in the job, we create *task identity*, such as when one person assembles an entire product and can identify with that product. If the larger work module is also viewed by the worker as having value, we create *task significance*. Like task variety, task identity and task significance make jobs more satisfying for most people.

Other job features, such as including tasks that provide *feedback* about work quality or including *goal setting* as a formal part of the employee's job, also contribute to job interest. This process of including tasks of a managerial nature in a job is called **job enrichment**.

Effects of Computers

Computers are impacting the workplace in several important ways. One way, of course, is when they actually take over the computational or information retrieval tasks formerly performed by humans. Examples are when they compute weekly take-home pay or when they "look up" references for someone. Computers can also be used as part of a mechanism, as in a robot, and accomplish physical work like spray painting an automobile.

Another way that computers affect the workplace is by increasing the variety of tasks that people perform for themselves. For example, many professionals now use word processors to do typing that previously they gave to a typist. At a recent meeting, a vice-president of a steel company described how he used a computer to obtain answers to questions that he previously would have asked of employees.[20] Most of the tasks that computers now allow people to do for themselves involve skills of a lower level than the average skill used in the person's job. Thus the result is increased efficiency and autonomy but not necessarily increased job satisfaction.

A Focus on Individual Differences

There is no doubt that the conditions Argyris described that reward dependence, submissiveness, the development of few rather than many abilities, and the development of a short time perspective do exist in some organizations. It is probable that most researchers and practitioners would regard his position as an overgeneralization, but it does make a point. Specifically, it focuses attention on the need to provide meaningful work whenever possible and to organize and manage so that the employees' uniqueness, maturity, and sense of responsibility are respected, preserved, and developed.

On the other hand, a number of facts about organizations and the individual seem to run counter to the lofty view of people and the pessimistic view of organizations that Argyris presents.

1. Even among traditional organizations there are vast individual differences in the nature of the work and the leadership patterns employed. Thus, the tendency to stereotype organizations is hazardous.

2. Most organizations actively promote the personal worth and development of their members. The constantly changing social and economic environment increasingly requires organizational members to adapt and acquire new skills and knowledge.

3. Contrary to the view that organizations promote or perpetuate irresponsibility and conformity, studies of successful managers suggest that, even with all the organizational support provided (such as organizational structure, formal authority, and policy and procedure), managers have about all the responsibility they can handle and neither reward submissive and irresponsible subordinates nor perceive themselves to be rewarded by such behavior. In a very real sense the nurturing and protective structure provided by the organization is what enables a manager to withstand the tremendous pressure of work without collapsing from a psychic overload.

4. The justification for a movement to make work at all levels more intrinsically rewarding does not require that most workers be dissatisfied. The facts rather consistently show that most workers adapt remarkably well to their work—so much so that one of the major

problems with job enrichment programs is overcoming employees' resistance to changing from the routine to which they have become accustomed. Managers should be able to enrich certain jobs without seriously undermining efficiency while at the same time being thankful for the many employees who do not seriously object to routine.

5. Organizations with large numbers of jobs that are difficult to enrich without unacceptably sacrificing efficiency have options for improving job satisfaction. Managers can relate to subordinates in a manner that increases their self-esteem and satisfies other important needs. Many possibilities exist for easing problems of routine work through the use of flexible work schedules and employing more workers for fewer hours per week or day.[21]

6. Management should continually evaluate the benefits to the employee and the organization of improving job satisfaction, since improved satisfaction may not increase productivity. There is even evidence that job satisfaction may have less influence on absenteeism and turnover than do some other factors such as employee perception of fair treatment.[22]

Many writers focus attention of the virtues of autonomy, creativity, freedom, and responsibility in the workplace. However, the rewards of job security, routine duties, and protection from excessive demands are highly valued by a significant number of employees. Consideration of individual differences among people suggests that if all routine jobs were made significantly more challenging (where this is taken to mean more complex and thus requiring more ability) a great many more people would be condemned to the welfare rolls. The following conclusion, drawn by Reif and Luthans, is noteworthy:

> The introduction of a job enrichment program may have a negative impact on some workers and result in feelings of inadequacy, fear of failure, and a concern for dependency. For these employees, low level competency, security, and relative independence are more important than the opportunity for greater responsibility and personal growth in enriched jobs.[23]

Socio-Technical Systems Design

In order to carry out more complex tasks, it is often necessary for groups of people to work together. The idea of allowing the work group to organize itself and to determine the procedures that it will use to accomplish its overall task is called the **socio-technical approach**.[24,25] It is concerned with integrating the technological system and the social system. Some of the projects described in the next few paragraphs have employed the socio-technical approach.

Diversity of Application

Several companies have attempted to make routine jobs more challenging—both in the factory and in the office. The companies include the American Telephone and Telegraph Co.; Xerox Corp.; Donnelly Mirrors Inc.; Texas Instruments Incorporated; Motorola Inc.; Corning Glass Works; Maytag Co.; The Prudential Insurance Co. of America; General Foods Corp.; and Merrill Lynch, Pierce, Fenner & Smith Incorporated. In many cases, they have performed enrichment experiments in a single location and on a very limited basis. In Europe, job enrichment experimentation has taken place in such well-known companies as Saab, Volvo, and Fiat.

The enrichment projects themselves have varied greatly. Some involved little more than placing two or more simple, routine tasks in a series (for example, a telephone directory assembler both entering items and proofreading for errors). Other projects have added responsibility; sometimes they may even have too much added responsibility. Janitors personally order needed supplies. Machine service employees are given authority to decide on expenses, to make work schedules, and to order their own supplies. Teams of workers are allowed to set production goals and solve production problems. Employees are rotated from assembly line to bench work, and the fractionated tasks of processing a stock certificate are combined into a single job.

Generally speaking, only successful cases have been reported in published literature. In many cases quality and quantity of work and also morale improved while absenteeism, turnover, and wasted materials were significantly reduced. However, the results are still inconclusive. There is little doubt that attention and concern on the part of management are capable of producing temporarily favorable results (an outcome called the **Hawthorne Effect**). In many cases, however, costs as well as productivity increased. At times the employees and their unions resist the changes, preferring instead to suffer the boredom and opt for shorter hours. In some instances, profitable and lasting improvements have been made, but the results are not so conclusive as to convince skeptics of the general applicability of job enrichment.

IMPORTANT TERMS AND CONCEPTS

Theory X   bureaucratic orientation
Theory Y   attitude
Theory Z   job simplification
personality   employee alienation
sensations   job rotation
perceptions   job enlargement
locus of control   job enrichment
high internal control   socio-technical approach
low internal control   Hawthorne Effect

STUDY AND DISCUSSION QUESTIONS

1. Consider the organization with which you are most familiar. What proportion of its members would you estimate to be most accurately described with Theory X? If you had the authority, what strategies would you use if you wanted more of them to be described by Theory Y? What proportion would you be able to move from Theory X group to the Theory Y group? What would be the payoffs to the organization?

2. How do Theory Z practices increase organizational productivity? How do they decrease it?

3. What are some of the implications for management of the fact that most human abilities are normally distributed throughout the population?

4. What are some characteristics of organizations that lead to the kind of differences in perception observed in the Dearborn and Simon study?

5. If you wanted to reduce differences in perception among your subordinates, what would you do?

6. Weber's concept of an ideal organization is appealing. In what ways would you expect the nature of people to prevent bureaucracies from functioning as well as Weber envisioned?

7. Why, in general terms, do organizations break complex jobs down into simple ones and require that their employees conform to a broad spectrum of standards and norms?

8. Evaluate this statement: Employees have a right to work that is interesting and fulfilling.

9. What is the most enjoyable job you have ever had? Where did it stand in terms of job simplification? job enlargement or job enrichment? socio-technical systems design? How would you have wanted to change it on any of these dimensions?

10. What could your instructor do to enlarge your "job" as a student in this course? (Think in terms of task variety, task identity, task significance, feedback, and goal setting.)

CRITICAL INCIDENT

CHANGE IN THE WORKPLACE

Throughout the 15 years since Frank Simmons founded his firm it has been highly profitable, and he has enjoyed friendly relationships with his employees. The firm produces a single item, a technically sophisticated ditching machine designed to dig trenches for small pipelines and cables. It is sold to rental companies and building contractors. Sales of the ditcher have been brisk since its introduction because of a superior hydraulic system that makes the machine resistant to breakdowns and easy for inexperienced persons to operate.

The ditcher is produced on an assembly line modeled after those in the automobile industry. Since each employee performs only minor operations as the partially assembled machine moves along at a fixed pace, the skill needed to perform a given job with high proficiency can be acquired within a few hours. The jobs were designed with such skill that lost motion was minimized and production costs were low. Although assembly line employees are paid an hourly wage, part of their weekly pay is based on the total number of units produced. Motivation to keep the line moving is high, and when for any reason the line stops everyone exerts maximum effort to get it moving again.

Although Simmons knows there has been some grumbling about the routine, sometimes boring nature of the work, he also knows that his employees have a strong identification with the company. They are required to work hard, but they are well paid and enjoy an enviable package of employee benefits. Absenteeism and employee turnover are low, grievances are within acceptable limits, disciplinary problems are few.

Simmons is convinced that one reason for the company's success is its progressive management. Employees are treated fairly, and managers are well trained in participative leadership methods. Although supervisors rely heavily on the job design work of industrial engineers, they involve subordinates in decision making and problem solving whenever possible. They make an honest effort to relate to their subordinates as individuals. Consistent with his history of staying abreast of current thinking in management, Simmons attends seminars on job enrichment and reads extensively on subjects he thinks are applicable to his situation. He is particularly impressed with what he hears about a new Volvo automobile assembly factory that did not adopt traditional assembly line methods. He believes that some of Volvo's methods can be useful in his own plant.

After extensively researching job enrichment possibilities, Simmons and his engineers have developed a new production method that appears to be efficient and able to reduce the routine involved in traditional methods. In the new system, the ditchers are constructed on low, flat, electrically powered platforms that will be moved from one work station to another. At each station a small team of employees will assume responsibility for a particular aspect of the assembly such as the electrical system, hydraulic system, or power track. Since the work will be more interesting and intrinsically motivating than it was previously, the incentive pay system will be unnecessary. To further emphasize individual responsibility and autonomy, employees will no longer be required to punch time cards. Quality control inspectors will be eliminated since each team will be held responsible for turning out a superior product.

The design of the production system has been completed, but Simmons is apprehensive about implementing it. Since the plant has only one assembly line he will have to close it for conversion to the new methods. The costs will be enormous, and he is unsure of all the implications of the change.

1. What risks are involved in the change?

2. Under the most optimistic assumptions you feel justified in making, what benefits will the company receive?

3. How do you expect the employees to react to the change?

4. If you were a management consultant to whom Simmons came for advice, what would you tell him?

REFERENCES

1. Mosher, Craig. "Woodworker," *The Humanist*, January-February, 1975, pp. 36–37.

2. McGregor, Douglas. *The Human Side of Enterprise*. New York: McGraw-Hill Book Co., 1960.

3. Ouchi, William G. *Theory Z: How American Business Can Meet the Japanese Challenge*. Reading, Mass.: Addison-Wesley Publishing Co., 1981.

4. Mischel, Walter. *Introduction to Personality*, 2d ed. New York: Holt, Rinehardt, and Winston, 1976.

5. Dearborn, Dewitt C., and Herbert A. Simon. "Selective Perception: A Note on the Departmental Identifications of Executives," *Sociometry*, Vol. 21, June, 1958, pp. 140–144.

6. Anderson, Carl R., and Craig E. Schneier. "Locus of Control, Leader Behavior and Leader Performance Among Management Students," *Academy of Management Journal*, Vol. 21, No. 4, December, 1978, pp. 690–698.

7. Weber, Max. *The Theory of Social and Economic Organization*, ed. Talcott Parsons, trans. A. M. Henderson. New York: Oxford University Press, Inc., 1947, p. 340.

8. Gordon, L. V. "Measurement of Bureaucratic Orientation," *Personnel Psychology*, Vol. 23, 1970, pp. 1–11.

9. Tyler, Leona. *Individuality: Human Possibilities and Personal Choice in the Psychological Development of Men and Women*. San Francisco: Jossey-Bass, Inc., Publishers, 1978, p. 274.

10. O'Toole, James, ed. *Homo Faber, Work in America—A Report of a Special Task Force to the Secretary of Health, Education, and Welfare*. Cambridge: The M.I.T. Press, 1973, p. 2.

11. Strauss, George. "Job Satisfaction, Motivation, and Job Redesign," *Organizational Behavior: Research and Issues*, eds. George Strauss et al. Madison: Industrial Relations Research Association, 1974, p. 28.

12. Babbage, Charles. *On the Economy of Machinery and Manufactures*. London: Charles Knight, 1832, pp. 169–176.

13. O'Toole. *Homo Faber, Work in America*, p. 9.

14. Strauss. "Job Satisfaction, Motivation, and Job Redesign," p. 20.

15. Organ, Dennis W. "Inferences about Trends in Labor Force Satisfaction: A Causal-Corelational Analysis," *Academy of Management Journal*, Vol. 20, No. 4, December, 1977, pp. 510–519.

16. Cooper, M. R. et al. "Changing Employee Values: Deepening Discontent?" *Harvard Business Review*, Vol. 57, No. 1, January-February, 1979, pp. 118–125.

17. Argyris, Chris. "Personality vs. Organization," *Organizational Dynamics*, Vol. 3, No. 2, Fall, 1974, p. 217.

18. Dunham, R. "Job Design and Redesign," ed. Steven Kerr. *Organizational Behavior*, Columbus, Ohio: Grid Publishing Co., 1979.

19. Hackman, J. R., and G. R. Oldham. *Work Redesign*. Reading, Mass.: Addison-Wesley Publishing Co., 1980.

20. Huber, Jacque, R. "A Senior Executive's Perspectives on Decision Support Systems." Paper presented at the Fourth International Conference on Decision Support Systems, Dallas, April 3, 1984.

21. Best, Fred. "Preferences on Worklife Scheduling and Work-Leisure Tradeoffs," *Monthly Labor Review*, Vol. 101, No. 6, June, 1978, pp. 31–37.

22. Dittrich, John E., and Michael R. Carrell. "Organizational Equity Perceptions, Employee Job Satisfaction and Departmental Absence and Turnover Rates," *Organizational Behavior and Human Performance*, Vol. 24, No. 1, August, 1979, pp. 29–39.

23. Reif, William E., and Fred Luthans. "Does Job Enrichment Really Pay Off?" *California Management Review*, Vol. XV, No. 1, 1972, pp. 30–37.

24. Gyllenhammar, Pehr G. *People at Work*. Reading, Mass.: Addison-Wesley Publishing Co., 1977.

25. Cummings, Thomas G. "Self-Regulating Work Groups: A Socio-Technical Synthesis," *Academy of Management Review*, Vol. 3, No. 3, July, 1978, pp. 625–634.

SUGGESTED READINGS

Alber, Antone F. "The Real Cost of Job Enrichment," *Business Horizons*, Vol. 22, No. 1, February, 1979, pp. 60–72.

Aldag, Ramon J., and Arthur P. Brief. *Task Design and Employee Motivation*. Glenview, Ill.: Scott, Foresman and Company, 1978.

Cattell, Raymond B., and Ralph M. Dreger. *Handbook of Modern Personality Theory*. New York: John Wiley & Sons, Inc., 1977.

Ivancevich, John M. "High and Low Task Stimulation Jobs: A Causal Analysis of Performance-Satisfaction Relationships," *Academy of Management Journal*, Vol. 22, No. 2, June, 1979, pp. 206–222.

March, J. G., and H. A. Simon. *Organizations*. New York: John Wiley & Sons, Inc., 1958. See Chapter 4.

Pierce, Jon L., and Randall B. Dunham. "Task Design: A Literature Review," *Academy of Management Review*, Vol. 1, No. 4, October, 1976, pp. 83–97.

Staines, Graham L., and Robert P. Quinn. "American Workers Evaluate the Quality of Their Jobs," *Monthly Labor Review*, Vol. 102, No. 1, January, 1979, pp. 3–12.

Weiss, Andrew. "Simple Truths of Japanese Manufacturing," *Harvard Business Review*, Vol. 62, No. 4, July-August, 1984, pp. 119–125.

4

Understanding Human Needs

. . . Systematic research into the motivation of people at work had a late start, partly because the sources of other people's behavior were thought to be so self-evident that research hardly seemed necessary. It is already clear, however, that we are not nearly as knowledgeable about the reasons why people behave as they do as we once thought we were. Research results indicate that many traditional ideas about motivation are too simple, or too pessimistic, or both.

Motivation, as we commonly use the term, is our speculation about someone else's purpose, and we usually expect to find that purpose in some immediate and obvious goal such as money or security or prestige. Yet the particular goals that people seem to be striving for often turn out, on analysis, to be the instruments for attaining another more fundamental goal. Thus, wealth, safety, status, and all the other kinds of goals that supposedly "cause" behavior are only paraphernalia for attaining the ultimate purpose of any individual, which is to be himself.

The ultimate motivation is to make the self-concept real: to live in a manner that is appropriate to one's preferred role, to be treated in a manner that corresponds to one's preferred rank, and to be rewarded in a manner that reflects one's estimate of his own abilities. Thus, we are all in perpetual pursuit of whatever we regard as our deserved role, trying to make our subjective ideas about ourselves into objective truths. When our experiences seem to be confirming those ideas, we are likely to feel that life is good and the world itself is just; but when we are denied the kinds of experiences to which we feel entitled, we are likely to suspect that something is drastically wrong with the world.[1]

The insights conveyed in this statement are as true today as they were when they were written. We are still learning about human needs and their effect on motivation. Nevertheless, we have learned a great deal in the intervening two decades. Many managers are aware of this new knowledge and use it to have a positive effect on the lives of those with whom they work. Others remain uninformed and therefore less able to cope with workplace variables they do not understand.

This chapter describes concepts that will aid managers in understanding and positively affecting the attitudes and behaviors of their employees and associates.

Chapter 3 emphasized **job satisfaction**—the degree to which employees favorably view their work—and the efforts of managers to make work more satisfying by redesigning jobs. **Motivation**, the main subject of Chapter 4, is related to satisfaction. But unlike job satisfaction, which primarily is concerned with attitudes, motivation deals with the inner needs, drives, impulses, or intentions that cause a person to behave a certain way. As Gellerman suggests in the introduction to this chapter, motivation is a complex matter that we too often take for granted as though life's everyday experiences make us experts on the subject.

If an organization is to function effectively, it must somehow find ways of involving people in its objectives. It must solicit a type of individual commitment that will ensure a good deal of effort with relatively little supervision and control. To achieve this, managers need a conceptual framework through which to understand the behavior of others, predict the consequences of alternative courses of action, and inspire cooperative effort. That is why the study of motivation is important to managers.

The objectives of Chapter 4, the first of two chapters on motivation, are

TO UNDERSTAND:

1. The role of needs in employee motivation

2. The theories of Maslow and Herzberg

3. How interests motivate

4. Unconscious motivation

5. The motivation behind defensive and abnormal behavior

INTRODUCTION TO MOTIVATION

The ability to understand why people behave as they do and the ability to motivate people to behave in a specific manner are two interrelated qualities that are important to managerial effectiveness. Fortunately they are qualities which a manager can acquire.

Motivation in organizations is a complex subject and should not be treated as if it were otherwise. At the same time a manager need not understand the intricate details of each motivation theory in order to make use of its practical contributions. A certain amount of theory is necessary to integrate and systematize what we know about the subject. A knowledge of motivation theory provides a framework for drawing generalizations and for analyzing novel motivation problems. However, the manager who becomes too involved in theorizing may lose the ability to make practical applications of the theory.

In practice, a manager applies an understanding of motivation theory primarily in two ways. The first is highly intuitive—a half-conscious awareness of why someone reacts in a particular manner or how the individual will react to being treated in a specific way. People differ greatly in their sensitivity to the needs and motives of others, and these differences are a product of learning experiences that date back to infancy. Fortunately the fact that we have been students of motivation throughout our lives simplifies the task of learning objective concepts and facts in this area. On the other hand, objectifying and pressing into conceptual form the "feel" we have for why people behave as they do tends to educate the intuition and to sharpen and sensitize the judgment processes that are so critically important in everyday relationships with people.

The second application of motivational theory is cognitive and objective. We are confronted with the task of understanding the motives behind specific behaviors. For example, why is no one in the department willing to accept a promotion to supervisor? Why do first line supervisors refuse to enforce the work rules? Why does the productivity in two comparable plants differ significantly? Since such problems do not require instant action, a manager has time to employ an objective, rational analysis through the use of a motivational model that provides a systematic framework for thinking critically and avoiding too limited a perspective. Chapter 5 includes such a model. Its use will serve to further educate the intuition, to increase a manager's ability to understand why others behave as they do, and to motivate in situations where instant action is required.

UNDERSTANDING HUMAN NEEDS

Human motivation can best be understood in terms of the needs we have in common and the different means by which these needs are satisfied. When a **need** (a physical or psychological deprivation) is aroused, an individual develops a *drive* toward a *goal* or *incentive* (that which is perceived as capable of satisfying the need or removing the deprivation). This process by which behavior is energized is called **motivation**.

Everyone has needs that must be satisfied if life is to be sustained. For purposes of discussion these needs may be grouped into two general categories—physiological and psychological—although few psychologists would attempt to draw hard and fast lines between the two. Because a person functions as a whole, as an integrated unit, our classifications for purposes of understanding are somewhat artificial. Nevertheless, we have no acceptable alternative to an analytical approach which focuses on one dimension at a time as if it were not an integral part of the whole.

Physiological Needs

The physiological needs for air, water, food, and rest are concerned with the preservation of life. Because the physiological needs are part of a life support system, we have no difficulty in understanding their purpose and the implications of failure to satisfy them. Our motivation to satisfy them can at times become acutely intense and prolonged.

Although we recognize the ultimate end served by our physiological needs, the immediate motivation for their satisfaction does not require this awareness. The immediate motive is typically a desire to remove or avoid pain or to experience pleasure. Although pain is subjectively experienced as undesirable, no rational person would want to eliminate the ability to experience it, as pain is the automatic alarm system by which we learn that a physiological need is not being satisfied and is one of the compelling forces that motivates us into action.

Psychological Needs

The definition of psychological needs is complex, and experts are by no means consistent in their approach to the task. Freudians link psychological needs to primitive biological urges of a sexual nature. Behaviorists do not discuss needs at all but instead focus on how the environment reinforces behavior. A third general point of view is usually called an *organismic-holistic* point of view.[2]

Organismic-holistic psychology stresses the idea that an individual functions as a whole and is simultaneously influenced by a number of factors, including physiological needs, the need for maintaining and enhancing one's self-image, and one's perception of a given situation. From this point of view we are all motivated for self-preservation and enhancement; but for this statement to make sense, it must be kept in mind that in the organismic-holistic view the *self* includes all that one is. Beginning with the physical body and self-image, the self is extended, in a sense, to include everything and everybody with which a person identifies, such as family, friends, school, profession, religion, and possessions. You can experience in a personal way just how much a part of you these outside identifications are when someone puts the first dent in the fender of your new car, attacks your school, or makes derogatory remarks about your family.

Three observations may be made with reference to the relationship between the physical, social, and psychological selves depicted in Figure 4-1:

1. Everyone has a need for self-preservation and enhancement. When it appears that this is not so, it is usually because we have failed to analyze carefully enough the true motives behind overtly self-destructive behavior. For example, a highly successful computer salesperson made a series of blunders during the final stages of negotiating the biggest sale of her career. The sale failed to materialize, and the salesperson's career was seriously jeopardized. She later realized that

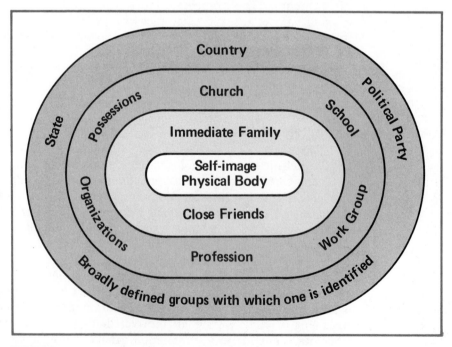

FIGURE 4-1   Possible Dimensions of the Self

she had unconsciously caused her own failure because she felt guilty about this sale and previous sales during which she had sold computer hardware to customers who really did not need it. Through the overtly self-destructive behavior, this salesperson was attempting to maintain self-respect.

2. Psychological needs are highly social in nature. Our self-image is strongly influenced by the feedback we get from others, and our inner standards are largely learned from others for whom we have respect and upon whom we depend. As a result, our need for self-esteem is closely intertwined with a need for belonging or being accepted by others.

3. We are continually involved (consciously and unconsciously) in a process of matching our inner standards with our behavior, as we perceive it. When we fail to live up to our expectations (an inner standard is not met), our attention is drawn to this fact by an alarm reaction, expressed in the form of irritation, tension, apprehensiveness, anxiety, fear, or guilt feelings. These varieties of pain, like physical pain, warn us of real or imagined danger. We are then motivated to perform in a manner which will remove the pain and restore an inner sense of security, self-acceptance, and equilibrium.

Primary and Secondary Needs

We all have certain physiological and psychological needs, and everyone strives for self-preservation and enhancement in the broad sense in which the self has been defined. An awareness of these basic needs enables us to understand similarities in the motivation and subsequent behavior of people. We begin to understand motivation at this point, but it is only a small beginning. Analyzing the differences among people is much more difficult, as we began to see in Chapter 3.

In order to understand how motivation differs from person to person, it is practical to make a distinction between primary and secondary needs. The **primary needs** include the physiological needs and also the basic psychological needs for self-esteem, self-respect, and self-acceptance (or whatever related terms one prefers to use to describe the need to preserve and enhance the social-psychological self). The **secondary needs** are derived from the primary needs and contribute to their satisfaction. They are learned standards a person has internalized and a set of self-expectations that have become highly important. In one sense they are wants and goals that have become central to one's values because their acquisition is critical to maintaining an adequate self-image.

Although there are theoretically as many secondary needs as there are means by which the primary needs are satisfied, only four are described here: power, achievement, affiliation, and autonomy. All these needs are very common to Americans. They are to some extent culturally determined in that they are rewarded in most subcultures of American life.

The Need for Power.[3] In this context *power* (or *social power*) is the ability to influence the behavior of others. Persons with a high need for power have learned that acquiring power is an effective means of self-preservation and enhancement. The manager with a high need for power is willing to take risks involved in competing with others in order to gain power and make optimal use of it. Such a person is motivated to strive for promotions, often with great intensity. Eye-to-eye confrontations, showdowns, and involvement in organizational politics are often a part of the power seeker's life-style; and, although the role is a dangerous one, the payoff from playing the power game and winning is perceived by the players as being worth the risk.

The Need for Achievement.[4] Persons with a *high need for achievement* play solitaire rather than poker. They have learned to satisfy their primary needs by means of a game in which the product itself symbolizes their contribution. Although achievement involves an element of competition, it avoids the head-on clashes involved in power seeking. Sometimes extreme introverts, who carefully avoid the power game, are able to gain considerable power through the low-risk game that allows them to gain the status of a recognized authority in a special field.

Individuals with a high need for achievement and a low need for power often choose staff positions such as accounting or engineering, while those with a high need for power prefer positions in sales or line management. Thus, the type of secondary needs one develops is logically related to vocational choice as well as to behavior on the job.

The Need for Affiliation. Many people find greater need satisfaction in being loved than in being powerful or in achieving. They prefer to avoid power because people with power must often make decisions that alienate others. Those with a high *need for affiliation* care very much what others think about them, and acceptance by others is the primary clue that is used to demonstrate their own acceptability. Their first priority is to belong, to be accepted, and they are motivated to behave accordingly.

Extremely high needs for power and affiliation in a given individual are somewhat incompatible. On the other hand, people with a high affiliation need may achieve in many situations and in the process actually increase rather than decrease their feelings of belonging. Achievement and power are compatible needs, although the presence of one does not necessarily indicate the presence of the other.

The Need for Autonomy.[5] Persons with a high need for *autonomy* have learned to satisfy their primary psychological needs by being independent, self-directed, and relatively free from the controlling influence of others. Like other secondary needs, the need for autonomy is not universal; some people, in fact, have high dependency needs and constantly seek out persons who will make their decisions and take care of them. Nevertheless, a need for autonomy is strong in many people, especially in countries like the United States where great value is placed on freedom and individuality.

Managers often have a strong need for autonomy, a need that is sometimes blocked by the controlling authority of superiors and organizational constraints such as policies and rules. Promoters, entrepreneurs, salespersons, professors, and physicians may find greater fulfillment of their need for autonomy than managers, although managerial power does lead to autonomy in many positions. Technicians and crafts persons usually enjoy more autonomy than unskilled workers. Although the latter may achieve a form of autonomy through union power or seniority rights, they may have little or no choice about how their work is performed. As we discuss in Chapter 19, participative management, which is designed to give every employee and manager as much decision-making power as possible, contributes directly to satisfying the need for autonomy.

SECONDARY NEEDS AS STANDARDS

Employees enter the workplace with greatly varying self-expectations. Some have extremely high standards, demanding of themselves outstanding performance regardless of external controls and incentives. Others, whose performance standards are low, feel comfortable doing as little work as possible. Thus, a manager's potential for motivating subordinates is to some extent limited by the selection process.

Implied and stated throughout this chapter is the idea that needs constitute a set of standards against which an individual constantly makes a self-evaluation. When we are relatively successful in meeting our needs, we feel safe, satisfied with ourselves, and contented. When we perceive that a need is not being met, we are motivated to behave in ways we believe will lead to need satisfaction. Figure 4-2 graphically expresses this relationship between needs, expressed as internalized standards, and motivation. At a given point in time (A) we are engaged in a sequence of activities that is intended to satisfy a variety of needs (that is, to meet the standards we have accepted for ourselves). At point B we become aware (through insight, fear, apprehensiveness, guilt, shame, and so on) that a standard or aspiration is not being met and that we are not moving steadily and directly toward C. In effect, we become aware that a need is not being satisfied, that our actual or anticipated performance (D) is falling short of our self-expectations (C). The unpleasantness of this experience and the desire to restore the pleasurable equilibrium that exists when we are on target is the triggering mechanism (stimulation or motivation) to do whatever is required to get back on target (to move from D to C). As long as a discrepancy exists between C and D, a motivational basis for improved performance exists. An example will clarify this concept.

Leon Diaz, a senior business major, began interviewing, along with his classmates, in the late fall of the year before he was to graduate in June. Because he had been a good student, he expected to be able to choose among several attractive job offers. His need level (C) was established. By February it was becoming painfully obvious that his friends were receiving job offers and he was not; that is, he became aware (B) that his actual performance (D) was below his standard or expectation

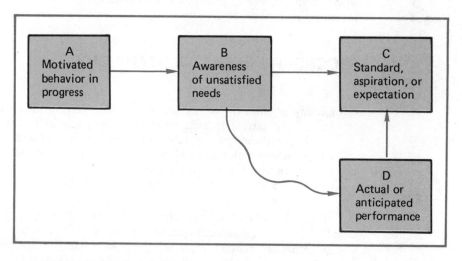

FIGURE 4-2   Standards as Motivators

(C). As his awareness of the situation grew, his anxiety mounted and the intensity of his need was expressed in two ways: (1) a preoccupation with the difference between his expected and actual behavior (C>D); and (2) a tendency to have doubts about his own potential (a direct threat to his self-image which occurred as he compared himself with his successful peers—another C>D discrepancy). As a result, he was motivated to act in order to remove the discrepancy and threat. Not knowing what to do, he sought the advice of a friendly management professor who suggested that Leon trim his hair and beard and replace his running shoes with more conventional footwear. Although he had long since given up such a traditional appearance, his need for employment proved to be stronger than his need to be like a small group of friends with whom he had begun to identify. As a result, the interviewers were able to see him for the outstanding prospect he really was (C=D), his anxiety disappeared, and his faltering self-confidence was restored.

One strategy by which people maintain a favorable self-concept (or at least avoid intense feelings of guilt, shame, anxiety, and the like) is to refuse to commit themselves firmly to any demanding standards. Being late for work, turning in low-quality work, and being reprimanded for breaking rules do no damage to the self-image of persons who see nothing wrong with such behavior. Others bring to the job high and firm self-expectations and are receptive to the challenges of their supervisors to perform at levels consistent with their highest potential.

The internalized standards by which we judge ourselves are expressed in many different forms. For example:

1. Self-perception of abilities (I have superior intelligence).

2. Work standards (I do only what is required to get by).

3. Moral or ethical standards (I don't lie or steal).

4. Aspirations (I intend to become a company executive).

5. Interests (I work only to support my fishing hobby).

6. Status (I am not required to punch the time clock).

7. Goals (I plan to get an outstanding performance rating this year).

Theoretically anyone can be motivated to perform acceptably, but it should be obvious that in some cases the costs to the organization would be prohibitive. Persons with demanding and deeply internalized work standards are more productive, require less supervision, and are more likely to have attitudes that contribute to a positive work environment than persons whose standards are average or low.

THE CONCEPT OF NEED HIERARCHY

> Human needs are insatiable. As one need is reasonably well satisfied, an individual's aspirations and expectations are raised and a new level of need arises. For several years it was generally assumed that the hierarchy formed by the emergence of new and higher level needs was common to all people, but such a viewpoint has now been discredited.

One point of view which has stimulated considerable thought and research on human needs was proposed by the prominent psychologist Abraham Maslow.[6] The major aspects of his contribution are as follows:

1. Within a given individual there are great differences in the motivational force of different needs. What motivates at one point in time may have no motivational potential at another. This is true for two reasons: (1) certain needs develop only after others are satisfied, and (2) a satisfied need is not a motivator.

2. Human needs may be classified along a scale of priority which constitutes a **need hierarchy**. Lower level needs are satisfied first; higher level needs develop only as lower level needs are reasonably well satisfied. As lower level needs are satisfied, the emerging, higher level needs take precedence as motivators. This does not mean that needs on the different levels cannot motivate at the same time, but there is at any given time a level of needs within the hierarchy that is uniquely active. This **activation/gratification proposition** is so termed because needs become active and thus become motivators only as lower level needs are gratified and lose their motivational force. In its usual form, this theory presupposes that we all have the same relatively stable need hierarchy.

3. The **deprivation/domination proposition** states that the greater the deprivation of a need, the stronger its motivational force will be. The implication is that a person tends to become preoccupied with the need that is least well satisfied; the need caused by the greatest deficiency dominates all others.

Maslow's Need Hierarchy

The need hierarchy shown in Figure 4-3 was viewed by Maslow as applying to people in general. Moving from the lowest level to the highest, it is described as follows:

1. *Physiological needs.* These are the needs mentioned earlier in this chapter—food, water, rest, and so on.

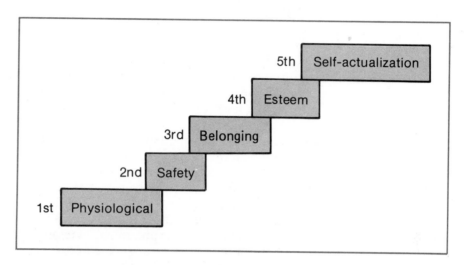

FIGURE 4-3 Maslow's Need Hierarchy

2. *Safety needs.* These are concerned with protection from danger and threats. The drive to achieve economic and job security would logically be included in this category (for example, seniority provisions and pension plans). Maslow also suggested that the desire for savings accounts and various forms of insurance would also be calculated to satisfy needs at this level.

3. *Belonging or social needs.* Included here are the need for acceptance by others and the need for love, affection, and friendship (the affiliation needs mentioned earlier).

4. *Esteem needs.* This level moves beyond merely being accepted and refers to a need to be held in high esteem by others and by oneself. Maslow speaks of the need for a "firmly based self-esteem" in that one's esteem is based on real capacity, achievement, and the respect of others. At times he appears to equate the esteem needs with self-respect.

5. *Self-actualization.* Once the lower level needs have been reasonably well satisfied a new discontent develops. This is expressed as a need to do what one is best suited for, to achieve at the level of one's highest potential, to become everything one is capable of becoming. So complex and open-ended is this need that it seems safe to say that human needs for self-actualization are insatiable.

Critique of Maslow's Theory

For years after Maslow's theory was published it was accepted more or less uncritically, probably because it focuses our attention upon some important truths about human needs. It does, however, contain some serious flaws, not the least of which is the fact that it has not withstood rigorous testing. We look now at the pros and cons of the theory.

Questionable Concepts. Maslow developed his theory on the basis of clinical observations rather than rigorous experimentation, and in spite of the great amount of attention it has received there has been no convincing experimentation to support it. In fairness to Maslow, it should be understood that he was often critical of his own theory and periodically altered it over several decades. Nevertheless, the theory has received a high degree of acceptance and must therefore be carefully evaluated. On the basis of the research conducted over the past 25 years, the following conclusions appear to be justified:

1. Maslow's concept of need and definitions of the specific needs are vague. Thus, we find ourselves discussing belonging or esteem needs without really knowing what these terms mean. Furthermore, no studies identify Maslow's five need categories as uncorrelated or independent factors. Note that power and autonomy needs, both of which are important in the workplace, are not included in Maslow's hierarchy.

2. Although it may be generally true that satisfied needs do not motivate, the meaning of satisfaction is unclear. At the physiological level it is evident that one is not motivated to eat, for example, immediately after a big meal. But humans have memory and the ability to anticipate the future when hunger will again occur. How then can it be said that even these needs are ever satisfied completely?

   At the higher levels the problem is even more complex; and, although specific needs emerge as uniquely active at certain times, it has yet to be demonstrated that the lower level (so-called satisfied) needs cease to motivate. The executive, for instance, whose self-actualization needs are strong, may still be motivated to act out of a need for esteem, belonging, and safety.

3. Research does not support the activation/gratification proposition. For this part of the theory to be valid, an increase in need satisfaction on a given level (safety, for example) must cause the strength of that need to decrease and result in an increase in the importance of the

next higher level need (belonging). This process continues up the hierarchy in lock-step fashion. Presumably at the top level (self-actualization), a reversal occurs, and need satisfaction results in increased rather than decreased motivation.[7]

It is not surprising that research fails to support the activation/gratification proposition, since it fails to support the existence of a universal five-step hierarchy. Some evidence has been found for a two-step hierarchy: step one including the physiological and safety needs and step two including the remaining three levels in no particular order.[8,9] It has not been satisfactorily established, however, that even a two-step hierarchy exists that applies to everybody.

4. There is little support for the deprivation/domination proposition. Some research evidence, in fact, indicates that the opposite may sometimes be true—that a high level of satisfaction may strengthen a need rather than diminish it.[10] For example, success in meeting one's primary needs through popularity and acceptance may actually strengthen the need to belong; likewise, success in acquiring power may create a desire for more power. Perhaps this is how strong secondary needs develop; they are reinforced by success (satisfaction) and thus continue to grow.

Applications. The vagueness with which Maslow's theory is stated makes proving or disproving it almost impossible, although hard evidence gives it little support. The lack of support for Maslow's theory does not mean, however, that it is useless. The thought and research that it has stimulated have significantly increased our understanding of needs in particular and motivational theory in general.

Three practical applications of Maslow's theory are especially noteworthy. First, even though there is no one hierarchy that applies to everyone, hierarchies do exist within individuals, and our ability to motivate an individual depends in part on our awareness of his or her need hierarchy. Second, Maslow's proposition about how needs become active may not be valid, but we do know that within certain individuals some needs are more active than others. We should, therefore, make our motivational appeals to active needs. We should not expect, for example, that a group of highly paid employees will be motivated to increase production in anticipation of a modest pay increase; they may, however, respond to a challenging task or to the recognition they expect to accompany outstanding performance. Finally, closely related to the second point, what we learn from Maslow should alert us to expect shifts and changes in needs. We should, therefore, vary our motivational appeals, tailoring them to individuals as much as possible.

HERZBERG'S TWO-FACTOR THEORY

Herzberg's two-factor theory has been valuable in stimulating research and concern for making work itself more rewarding. Although its usefulness as a workable motivational theory is quite limited, it continues to be highly influential in focusing the attention of management on the intrinsic aspects of work.

In recent years many research studies and publications have been stimulated by the **two-factor theory** proposed by Frederick Herzberg. This theory should not be confused with the two-step hierarchy previously discussed. Herzberg based his original theory on two sets of data—a review of published literature on job attitudes and a series of interviews with 200 engineers and accountants in the Pittsburgh area.[11,12] In the interviews employees were asked to think of times when they felt particularly good and of times when they felt particularly bad about their jobs. They were then asked to describe the conditions leading up to these feelings. The result was that the employees tended to cite different conditions as leading to their good and bad feelings. For example, interesting work was associated with good feelings, but lack of it was not ordinarily associated with bad feelings; low status was associated with bad feelings, but high status was not associated with good feelings.

Herzberg concluded that many of the factors that managers have traditionally believed to be motivators, such as pay and the nature of supervision, do not really motivate at all. The two-factor idea is that the job factors which are generally regarded as motivators should actually be divided into two groups: one consisting of *motivational factors*, or what he called *satisfiers*, and the other consisting of *maintenance factors*, or *dissatisfiers*.

The motivating factors are intrinsic or job content factors. They occur at the time the work is performed and make it rewarding in and of itself. Job maintenance factors, on the other hand, are extrinsic or job context factors. They are part of the work environment but not of the work itself. As Herzberg continued to elaborate on his two-factor theory, he referred to intrinsic and extrinsic factors as **motivators** and **hygiene factors** respectively and to the theory as the **motivation-hygiene theory**.[13] Figure 4-4 is intended to clarify Herzberg's sometimes confusing terminology. It also presents a list of satisfiers and dissatisfiers as classified by his research.

TWO-FACTOR THEORY (Motivation-Hygiene Theory)	
FACTORS Motivation Factors Job Content (Intrinsic) Factors Satisfiers	**FACTORS** Maintenance (Hygiene) Factors Job Context (Extrinsic) Factors Dissatisfiers
EXAMPLES Achievement Recognition Advancement Responsibility The work itself Growth possibilities	**EXAMPLES** Company policy and administration Supervision Peer relations Relations with subordinates Status Pay Job security Working conditions

FIGURE 4-4 Herzberg's Terms and Factor Classifications

Critique

One of the most controversial aspects of the two-factor theory is the proposition that job satisfaction and dissatisfaction are not two ends of a continuum but rather are two separate and distinct variables; that is, the presence of job content factors is satisfying and motivational, but the absence of such factors is not the cause of dissatisfaction. The presence of job context factors is not motivational, but their absence causes dissatisfaction. Since motivation and maintenance factors are viewed by Herzberg as qualitatively different variables, and since pay is a maintenance factor, we would have to conclude that pay is not a motivator. Aside from the fact that this contradicts a mountain of evidence, such a conclusion is unsatisfactory in that it is a perfect example of all-or-nothing, either-or thinking about human motivation. The hundreds of research studies and systematic observations about motivation simply do not support this type of thought, and there is a question about whether Herzberg's own research supports the idea that a given factor should always be placed in one classification or the other.

Few theories have received more attention than the two-factor theory, and there is still not complete agreement concerning its value. However, the research evidence against it appears to have the edge, particularly since it was generated through the use of a wide variety of methodologies. Evidence for the theory, collected primarily by Herzberg's original method, has been widely criticized as being an artifact of the method itself. After a thorough critique of the published literature, Campbell and his associates had this to say:

> The most meaningful conclusion that we can draw is that the two-factor theory has now served its purpose and should be altered or respectfully laid aside. Theories are never true or false but exhibit only varying degrees of usefulness. The Herzberg theory has stimulated a great deal of argument and considerable research activity. On these grounds it has been useful. However, on the basis of the data that it has generated, it also seems to be an oversimplification. Repeated factor analytic studies of job attitudes have failed to demonstrate the existence of two independent factors corresponding to motivators and hygienes.[14]

Applications

It may seem foolish to discuss applications of an invalid theory, but this is not necessarily so. As a matter of fact, many inadequate theories have produced valid and useful concepts—concepts that often become parts of other theories and hypotheses for subsequent testing.

Herzberg's two-factor theory has been especially useful in focusing attention on the importance of job content factors, particularly in view of their relevance to job enrichment and job satisfaction. We now recognize that many jobs can and should be enriched and that doing so may increase job satisfaction. We also know, however, that employees can have job satisfaction without being productive and that managers can increase satisfaction without motivating valuable behavior. In equating satisfiers and motivators, Herzberg confused traditional terminology and made a correct distinction between job satisfaction and motivation. Keep in mind that his terminology is uniquely his and that it is nontraditional.

Both research and logic indicate that, contrary to Herzberg's theory, the factors he studied—recognition, pay, status, and so on—sometimes motivate and sometimes cause dissatisfaction, depending on the individual and the situation. This flaw in Herzberg's overall theory does not, however, prevent the concept of the dissatisfier from being valid and useful. Most of us have had experiences in which failure to receive an expected reward—a respectable raise, for example—caused dissatisfaction, when to have received it would not have made us any more valuable to our employers. Thus, we intuitively validate the dissatisfier concept. It is, therefore, meaningful in specific situations, with specific individuals, to ask whether a factor we hope will motivate will actually do so, and if it does not motivate, whether its absence will cause dissatisfaction. A further question arises: If the factor does not motivate but does result either in job satisfaction or dissatisfaction, will that result significantly affect the organization? When applied in this way, the dissatisfier classification has definite value.

INTERESTS AS MOTIVATORS

> High intrinsic interest in one's work will, under certain conditions, result in an increased motivation to produce. It may also motivate an individual to accept employment or to remain on a job, to think creatively, and to identify with the goals and objectives of the organization.

When a student says "I am interested in management," the meaning is quite unclear. This may simply mean "I want to become a manager" or "I want to study management." The statement could mean "I am motivated (by what, I don't know) to enter the field of management." Perhaps this interest in management stems from parental pressure, from a knowledge that top managers earn high salaries, or from the student's strong identification with a particular professor of management.

On the other hand, "I am interested in management" may imply an intrinsic satisfaction in doing what managers do—that is, an interest in the work itself. Most of us have had work experience that did not seem like work at all because of the intensity of our interest in it. Time passed quickly, concentration was strong, and despite all the effort exerted, the work was pleasurable. Interests, in this sense, are an important form of motivation. They are, in fact, an ideal form of motivation for both the organization and the employee. An organization reaps the benefits of high productivity, creativity, initiative, and few human resource problems; and the employee is compensated with a pleasurable work experience in addition to regular forms of pay.

The Nature and Intensity of Interests

Since interests are learned, interest in a particular subject or type of work varies greatly from person to person, depending on the nature and degree of one's past exposure to it. Some people have relatively shallow interests or no interests at all while other people are virtually consumed by interest in their hobbies, studies, work, and other activities. To some

extent whether something is interesting is related to the activity or object in question (such as a job or hobby); however, this is just as often
a function of a person's attitudes, curiosity, and intellectual ambitious-
ness. Those with generally low interest levels probably will not respond
as favorably to what management regards as interesting work as will
others with high interest levels. However, interests are to some degree
motivators for everyone; and management should carefully consider individual differences in interests when making selection, placement, and
promotion decisions. Certainly it is not, as was once thought, an advantage only to the employees for their work to be interesting. The managerial goals of high motivation and job satisfaction are both supported
when employees are intrinsically interested in their work.

One way to understand interests is in terms of needs. For example,
think for a moment of an individual you know who has developed a deep
and lasting interest in music. He or she is constantly drawn to it and
feels that not to be able to hear, compose, or play music is to suffer a
void that cannot be filled by any other activity. Once a person learns
through continued experience to associate a deep satisfaction with a particular activity, a need is created for that activity, and the individual
who can satisfy such a need through work is doubly rewarded.

When Interests Motivate

Interests do not always motivate. Some people are strongly motivated to be highly productive because of characteristics within themselves that have little to do with the type of work they are doing or the
environmental factors surrounding the job. They have set high expectations for themselves and have internalized high work standards; and
since they typically do their best because of other needs, interests have
little effect on their productivity. On the other hand, people with low
work standards often do well only in areas where interest is high. This
is exemplified by the fact that some students with high ability consistently make good grades in courses they enjoy while their grades in other
courses may be consistently lower.

We should not conclude that attempts to match interests with work
and to make work more interesting are of value only for those employees
with poor work habits. Motives for accepting a job, for being productive,
and for leaving that job may be quite different. Aside from what interesting work does to enable an employee to satisfy needs for self-fulfill-
ment or self-actualization, an organization needs the creativity, emotional involvement, and loyalty that are typically found in employees
who are interested in their work. For the person who is already exerting

maximum effort to produce, interesting work may provide motivation for other behaviors that are valued by the organization. Productivity is important in all jobs, but it is certainly not the only activity toward which motivated behavior in organizations must be directed.

INTERNALIZED MOTIVATION

Employees who believe in and identify with the organization—its purpose, its people, its policies, and its goals—serve both themselves and the organization better than employees who are motivated principally by incentives to produce and a fear of doing otherwise.

It has long been recognized that reward and punishment leave something to be desired as motivators. Employees do work for extrinsic rewards, such as money, and at specific times and under certain circumstances their efforts are motivated by a fear of being punished, but these alone are relatively poor motivators. If other motivators are not operative alongside these, employees may slow down or stop working altogether when external controls are absent; and, unless rewards are strategically planned, employees may never produce beyond minimum requirements.

Harry Levinson refers to the assumption that people can be successfully motivated by reward and punishment as the "great jackass fallacy."[15] The image that comes to mind when one thinks of the reward-punishment approach is that of the jackass being lured forward by a carrot or driven from behind by fear of a stick. If carrot-and-stick motivation dominates a manager's thinking, subordinates will not be treated with the dignity and respect they deserve and often demand.

It is generally accepted by those who understand human motivation that some degree of **internalization** of organizational standards and goals by members of the group is necessary for the organization to function effectively. If employees do not accept the idea that a rule or regulation is meaningful and just, no amount of external control will be adequate to produce the desired behavior. The analogy of law enforcement is applicable here. The police officer serves an important function in apprehending lawbreakers and making citizens fear punishment should they decide to become offenders. But the critical determiner of whether laws will be obeyed is the citizen's belief in and commitment to the law. This has been clearly demonstrated in situations where a law has not had general public support. National prohibition of the sale of alcoholic beverages failed miserably, as have attempts to enforce speed laws when the people involved have not really believed in them. The best controls are internal. Whether or not the existence of strong internal controls negates the usefulness of reward and punishment as motivators is an interesting and debatable question. Most scholars believe that reward and punishment can be useful supplements to internal controls. Others believe that using pay as a reward offsets the motivational potential of intrinsic motivation from job enrichment.[16,17]

Indoctrination

The process of introducing internalization is sometimes referred to as **indoctrination**. Through this process, people who are expected to behave in a certain way are somehow led to believe that they should behave in that way. When we internalize an organization's standards and values, we accept them as our own. Then if we fail to live up to these standards by being late for work or by making a costly mistake we become harsh critics of ourselves.

Internalized work standards become a part of one's own value system. Failure to live up to these standards becomes an occasion for remorse or regret, and outstanding performance with reference to them is a cause of pride and satisfaction. It is only when an organization's goals and standards have to some extent been internalized that employees have a basis for believing that their work has meaning—that it makes a worthwhile contribution. Thus, indoctrination serves the employee as well as the organization.

The Internalization Process

The first day of employment workers are provided information concerning rules, regulations, policies, procedures, and performance expectations; and, if their attitudes toward work are reasonably mature, they willingly accept a broad spectrum of such standards. In effect, they agree to sacrifice certain personal freedoms and to conform to specified organizational norms in return for pay and other forms of compensation.[18] In time employees become aware of more subtle and covert expectations and must choose whether to internalize them, to conform because of possible rewards and punishments, or to refuse to conform and live with the consequences.

To some extent internalization is a form of "social role taking." An employee with a work history has developed a general image of the role or behavior expectations of an accountant, supervisor, or chief executive, for example. Most employees accept the fact that organizations cannot survive without the predictability and control that result from the sacrifice of a certain degree of individuality that accompanies the internalization of job expectations. On the other hand, effective managers are sensitive to the need of employees on all levels to remain unique, self-respecting individuals who have not sold their souls along with their skills, efforts, and perhaps their loyalty.

UNCONSCIOUS MOTIVATION

> Most of us desire at one time or other to understand our own motives. On the other hand, we also desire to maintain a favorable self-image. This means that often we will be considerably biased, both in drawing conclusions about our own motives and in reporting to others why we behave as we do.

Since the early 1930s, a popular method of research on the importance of various motivational factors has been self-report.[19,20] This typically involves asking workers to rank the importance of various factors as work motivators. As mentioned earlier, Herzberg's original research was based on data obtained from the interview, which is one form of self-report technique. This has been a valuable and, at times, valid approach to understanding motivation, but a note of caution should always be involved in its use. The truth is that much motivation is unconscious, and to the extent that it is unconscious people cannot possibly describe their own motives. Some motives are hidden from consciousness by a desire to look good to ourselves and others. Furthermore, our motivations are often so complex that we are unable to sort them out.

High ability workers who restrict production because they fear rejection by peers may not be sufficiently objective to admit their dependence on peer approval. In fact, they may not even be aware that they are performing below their potential. Employees who are frequently absent from work because of minor illnesses may have little if any insight into the fact that their excessive absences may be due to a sympathy-getting syndrome developed during childhood. Even rational and objective employees may be hard pressed to communicate accurately whether they are more motivated by money, security, or interesting work, when all three are motivational; and their answers to questions about motivation may change with general economic conditions and other job-related variables.

The fact that we are unaware of many of our own motives is not all bad. The many defense reactions by which we psychologically protect ourselves from reality are, to a point, quite valuable. It is also true that preoccupation with our own mental processes may result in diminished attention to the needs of others and to those aspects of our work that require intense concentration. At any rate, it follows that at times we are much more capable of understanding the motives of others than we are our own.

DEFENSIVE AND ABNORMAL BEHAVIOR

Defensive and abnormal reactions are motivated behaviors and are understandable within the context of our need for self-preservation and enhancement. The manager who is naive about these behaviors will be unable to understand and rationally react to a significant aspect of organizational life.

During the past twenty years major changes have been made in the treatment of persons with serious personality problems. With the discovery of tranquilizing drugs it became possible to remove large numbers of seriously ill people from mental institutions and return them to their home environments and to useful, productive work. People who in years past would have required hospitalization now receive outpatient treatment and continue to work, often without awareness on the part of their supervisors of the nature and seriousness of their problems.

Several large companies now cope with problems of alcoholism and drug use as though they are routine medical problems; and, where specialists are available in this area, managers should take full advantage of the opportunity to make referrals. However, most problems resulting from defensive and abnormal behavior on the job, problems such as excessive tardiness or absenteeism, inability to relate effectively to other people, withdrawal, alcoholism, or drug addiction must be dealt with by line managers as they occur. This means that managers must have greater than average insight. Fortunately the problems we have mentioned can be understood within the general frame of reference already established.

Barriers to Need Satisfaction

We begin by considering what happens when individuals are chronically unable to view themselves as acceptable and worthwhile. To understand what chronic inability to meet one's needs involves, consider the case of George, a young man who flunked out of college and began working as a machinist's helper.

Because of early parental influence George developed an aspiration to become a lawyer, and during his teen years this aspiration was a continual source of satisfaction and recognition. He developed a strong need to become a lawyer.

Unfortunately some barriers stood between George and a successful legal career. To begin with, he had a *personal barrier* to need satisfaction: He lacked the mental ability to pass his law courses. Because of this deficiency he faced a major *environmental barrier*: a group of bright, highly motivated young law students with whom he had to compete for grades. George could see no way out. He was trapped. He could not meet his need, but neither could he get it out of his system. His aspiration to become a lawyer had become a significant part of his self-identity, and to give it up would require the ego-crushing admission that he and others had long overrated his potential.

George's problem was compounded by the fact that his parents could not accept the truth either. They had too often gained status with their friends by boasting about their son's brilliant future. George was acutely aware of their disappointment and was constantly reminded of their insistence that his leaving school would be temporary and that he would return and complete his education after a brief period of adjustment. Unfortunately he was unable to face his problem head-on and solve it in a healthy, direct, realistic manner. Instead he found it necessary to make some internal adjustments that involved self-deception and reality distortion. Some of the many alternatives open to him are discussed in the following section.

Defensive Behavior

When relatively direct attempts to overcome barriers and meet needs are unsuccessful and the need itself cannot be modified, a psychological adjustment must be made. The most common adjustment is to employ one or more **defensive reactions**. These are ways of thinking which are calculated to cushion the blow to the self and thereby enable a person to maintain a favorable self-image. A few of the most common defense reactions are:

1. **Rationalization**: a form of self-deception in which a socially acceptable justification is developed to avoid having to face an unacceptable view of oneself. For example, an executive fails because of poor business decisions, but insists that the cause of failure was an unfavorable economy.

2. **Flight into fantasy**: inappropriate daydreaming. A management trainee who is frustrated by low status and unchallenging work daydreams about a future in the executive suite rather than creatively working to make such a future a reality.

3. **Projection**: unconsciously rejecting an unacceptable thought, such as a desire or impulse, by blaming it on someone else. The executive who has ceased to be promoted because of nonperformance may project his or her failure onto superiors by believing that they block opportunities and favor other candidates.

4. **Aggression**: destructively attacking the real or imaginary source of frustration. This may be expressed verbally in slander and gossip or physically in such behaviors as sabotage or fighting.

5. **Scapegoating**: behaving aggressively toward someone who cannot fight back as a substitute for aggression toward the source of one's frustration. A supervisor who is angry at his or her superior takes it out on subordinates or family.

6. **Overcompensation**: as a means of handling inadequacy in one area, exaggerated and inappropriate behavior is expressed in another. For example, an individual who feels ill at ease with people may talk too much and too loudly in a vain attempt to gain social acceptance. On a less extreme level called *compensation,* students who flunk out of school make up for feelings of shame by intensively applying themselves in a substitute career. Various forms of such a substitution can be wholesome forms of defense, except when they involve giving up too soon on a worthwhile initial objective or lowering too quickly one's self-expectations when the going gets rough.

7. **Repression**: blotting out of consciousness certain ideas, memories, and so on that cause conflict and tend to lower self-esteem. This is exemplified by supervisors who selectively forget their own errors and blunders, refuse to accept constructive criticisms of superiors, and thus are unable to make the behavioral changes required for effective performance.

8. **Reaction formation**: a pendulum swing in the opposite direction from one's true desires or impulses as a means of maintaining self-control or self-respect. A highly ambitious manager whose career is stymied accepts defeat and becomes extremely critical of working hard and playing the upward mobility game.

9. **Withdrawal**: physically and/or psychologically pulling away from people and conflict. This is exemplified by the shy individual whose protection is to be excessively quiet or by the manager whose reaction to departmental conflict is to avoid becoming involved—to act as though the conflict were nonexistent.

Defense reactions such as these clearly are motivated, goal-directed behaviors, and the goal is still self-preservation and enhancement. We all use defense reactions at times, and when not used excessively or for too long a time these reactions are helpful and effective in achieving short-term need satisfaction.

Neurotic and Psychotic Behavior

Sometimes a person who is unable to maintain a favorable self-image with the limited use of defense reactions resorts to chronic dependency upon them. They are used like alcohol or drugs to provide escape from reality. This means of escape often increases the problem and contributes to a spiral of decreasing effectiveness that is typically viewed as abnormal behavior.

Abnormal behavior can best be understood as an exaggeration or extension of so-called normal behavior. The mentally ill person has a chronic inability to adjust: either to find need satisfaction directly or to accept altered or modified standards of self-judgment. As a result, such a person may exhibit one or many behaviors that others recognize as being unhealthy (symptoms of the defense reactions just described, such as suspicion, illogical thinking, and so on).

When people become mentally ill it is not because a foreign substance, such as bacteria, has entered their psyches. Rather, in their desperate attempts to find self-acceptance they have resorted to extreme, costly, and inefficient defenses for coping with their personal problems. Lay people are often unable or unwilling to diagnose a person as abnormal, but professional psychologists and psychiatrists can detect certain clusters or syndromes of unhealthy behaviors which they classify as a type of neurosis or psychosis.

A **neurosis** is, relatively speaking, a mild personality disorder—one that lacks gross personality disorganization. Even before the discovery of tranquilizers, neurotics seldom had to be hospitalized and were often found in the work environment. They include, for example, people with phobias, high anxiety levels, and a preoccupation with imaginary illnesses, as well as people who are excessively perfectionist or given to constant worrying and mild depression. A **psychosis** is a severe personality disorder in which the defenses employed are so extreme that an individual loses touch with reality (through hallucinations, delusions, and extreme withdrawal, for example).

Since today only chronically ill psychotics and occasionally neurotics are hospitalized, managers must relate to large numbers of people who would be totally incapacitated except for their continued medication. They are people with problems and are thus a problem for their supervisors. They are often the people with whom the supervisor has the most direct contact: the chronic absentee, the troublemaker, the low producer, and the individual who has difficulty relating to others. At this point we are concerned primarily with understanding their motivation.

IMPORTANT TERMS AND CONCEPTS

job satisfaction
motivation
need
primary needs
secondary needs
need hierarchy
activation/gratification proposition
deprivation/domination proposition
two-factor theory
motivators
hygiene factors
motivation-hygiene theory
internalization
indoctrination

defensive reactions
rationalization
flight into fantasy
projection
aggression
scapegoating
overcompensation
repression
reaction formation
withdrawal
abnormal behavior
neurosis
psychosis

STUDY AND DISCUSSION QUESTIONS

1. Why is it valuable for managers, who are of necessity concerned with practical problems, to study motivation rather than rely on their intuitive ability?

2. Why is it unnecessary for an individual to understand the underlying purpose of a need in order to be motivated to satisfy it?

3. What is meant by the *self* in the organismic-holistic view? What is misleading about saying that our most basic need is for *self-preservation* as the term is popularly used?

4. In what sense do the needs of people differ? How did these differences occur?

5. Three of the many needs in which people differ are the needs for power, achievement, and affiliation. Assign a rating of 1 (low), 2 (average), or 3 (high) to the degree of each of these needs you would expect to find in these individuals: (a) a sensitive, submissive career records clerk; (b) an unsociable professor who has authored five books; (c) an insensitive and overbearing line supervisor.

6. In what sense is a need an inner standard against which self-evaluation takes place? What are the signals by which we may become aware that a standard has not been met?

7. Evaluate Maslow's theory. How can managers use it?

8. Evaluate the motivation-hygiene theory. What are its practical uses in management?

9. How does Herzberg confuse job satisfaction and motivation as these terms are usually defined? Is a distinction between the two important? Explain.

10. Under what circumstances do interests motivate employees to be more productive?

11. Why should we be suspicious of a study in which employees are asked to rank the following in order of their importance as motivators: money, security, good supervision, a comfortable work environment, and friendly co-workers?

12. Describe the meaning and importance of *internalized motivation* as the term is used in this chapter.

13. What is abnormal behavior? Why does a manager need to understand the motivation behind it?

CRITICAL INCIDENT

CHANGING STANDARDS

Mrs. Rudd was the 50-year-old supervisor of 45 workers engaged in the assembly and testing of tape recorders. Most of the people who worked for her were women who, like Mrs. Rudd, had little work experience other than their years with the electronic equipment manufacturer for whom they currently worked. Seven years ago, after serving as an hourly worker for eight years and then as an assistant supervisor for six months, Mrs. Rudd had been promoted to supervisor of the day shift.

For the past several years, demand for the company's tape recorders had been going up. Mrs. Rudd had been given more employees to meet this demand, but when the demand took a sudden spurt four months ago a night shift was started. Ms. Joske, a 23-year-old technical school graduate who had worked as an assistant supervisor under Mrs. Rudd for six months, was made supervisor of the night shift.

Local union rules gave senior employees the right of first refusal for the transfer to the night shift, and as a result only ten of the day shift employees transferred, all of these employees having less than five years of seniority. Rudd and Joske were then each allotted another ten employees from the large number of applicants who responded to advertisements in the newspaper and to postings on the company bulletin boards.

Both shifts were on the same piece-rate incentive system. After just three months, Ms. Joske's night shift employees were averaging 30 percent above "standard," while Mrs. Rudd's day shift employees were still averaging 10 percent above, as they had for several years. Ms. Haney, the production supervisor and a former design engineer for the company, brought this fact to Mrs. Rudd's attention several times, and then told her:

> I don't know why your people aren't producing, but clearly they aren't. Demand for our products is going up, and very soon we're going to hire another dozen employees. Most will end up on the night shift. After that, if the productivity gap between the two shifts is still present, the company will have to take some action. I'm not saying that this means that you'll be replaced, or that any of your people will be transferred, but something must be done. I'd like to avoid anything drastic, and I'm asking you to bring me a plan sometime next week for increasing your shift's productivity. Maybe we should publicize the relative production of the two shifts or of the individuals in them.

Rudd was hurt, angry, and a bit dejected. She confided the following to her old friend and new assistant supervisor Marge Hernan:

> I don't know why Ms. Haney is so worked up. Even though Joske took ten of the young hotshots, the day shift is still producing as well as it ever did. We have a stable, loyal, and congenial group of workers on the day shift. Who knows how long the night shift hotshots will last? I expect them to burn out or be at each other's throats sooner or later. Anyway, what does Ms. Haney think I can do to get 35 people, many my age, to suddenly change the way they work? I wish I was back in the union—then I'd tell Haney off!

1. What needs appear to be related to the behavior of the people in this case?

2. What motivational problems are likely to be involved in this situation?

3. How should Rudd handle the situation?

4. How should Haney handle the situation?

REFERENCES

1. Gellerman, Saul W. *Motivation and Productivity.* New York: American Management Association, Inc., 1963, p. 190.

2. Cartwright, Desmond S. *Introduction to Personality.* Skokie: Rand McNally & Company, 1974, pp. 13–70.

3. McClelland, David C., and David H. Burnham. "Power is the Great Motivator," *Harvard Business Review*, Vol. 54, No. 2, March-April, 1976, pp. 100–110.

4. Atkinson, J. W., and N. T. Feather, eds. *A Theory of Achievement Motivation.* New York: John Wiley & Sons, Inc., 1966.

5. Harrell, Thomas, and Bernard Alpert. "The Need for Autonomy among Managers," *Academy of Management Review*, Vol. 4, No. 2, April, 1979, pp. 259–266.

6. Maslow, Abraham H. *Motivation and Personality*, 2d ed. New York: Harper & Row Publishers, Inc., 1970.

7. Maslow, Abraham H. *Toward A Psychology of Being*, 2d ed. Princeton, N. J.: Van Nostrand Reinhold Company, 1968, p. 30.

8. Wahba, Mahmoud A., and Lawrence G. Birdwell. "Maslow Reconsidered: A Review of Research on the Need Hierarchy Theory," *Organizational Behavior and Human Performance*, Vol. 15, No. 2, April, 1976, pp. 212–239.

9. Hall, D. T., and K. E. Nougaim. "An Examination of Maslow's Need Hierarchy in an Organizational Setting," *Organizational Behavior and Human Performance*, Vol. 3, No. 1, February, 1968, p. 12.

10. Dachler, H. P., and C. L. Hulin. "A Reconsideration of the Relationship Between Satisfaction and Judged Importance of Environmental and Job Characteristics," *Organizational Behavior and Human Performance*, Vol. 4, No. 4, March, 1969, pp. 252–262.

11. Herzberg, F. et al. *Job Attitudes: A Review of Research and Opinion.* Pittsburgh: Psychological Service of Pittsburgh, 1957.

12. Herzberg, F., B. Mausner, and B. Snyderman. *The Motivation to Work*, 2d ed. New York: John Wiley & Sons, Inc., 1959.

13. Herzberg, F. *Work and the Nature of Man.* Cleveland: World Publishing Company, 1966.

14. Campbell, John P. et al. *Managerial Behavior, Performance, and Effectiveness.* New York: McGraw-Hill Book Company, 1970, p. 381.

15. Levinson, Harry. "Asinine Attitudes toward Motivation," *Harvard Business Review*, January-February, 1973, pp. 70–76.

16. DeCharms, R. *Personal Causation: The Internal Affective Determinants of Behavior.* New York: Academic Press, Inc., 1968, p. 328.

17. Pritchard, Robert D., K. M. Campbell, and D. J. Campbell. "Effects of Extrinsic Financial Rewards on Intrinsic Motivation," *Journal of Applied Psychology,* Vol. 62, No. 1, February, 1977, pp. 9–15.

18. March, J. G., and H. A. Simon. *Organizations.* New York: John Wiley & Sons, 1958. See Chapter 4.

19. Lawler, Edward E., III. *Pay and Organizational Effectiveness: A Psychological View.* New York: McGraw-Hill Book Company, 1971, p. 28.

20. Herzberg. *Work and The Nature of Man,* pp. 40–42.

SUGGESTED READINGS

Gorn, Gerald J., and Rabindra N. Kanungo. "Job Involvement and Motivation: Are Intrinsically Motivated Managers More Job Involved?" *Organizational Behavior and Human Performance,* Vol. 26, No. 2, October, 1980, pp. 265–277.

Green, Charles N. "The Satisfaction-Performance Controversy," *Business Horizons,* October, 1972, pp. 31–41.

Moch, Michael K. "Job Involvement, Internal Motivation, and Employees' Integration into Networks of Work Relationships," *Organizational Behavior and Human Performance,* Vol. 25, No. 1, February, 1980, pp. 15–31.

Newstrom, John W. et al. "Motivating the Public Employee: Fact vs. Fiction," *Public Personnel Management,* January-February, 1976, pp. 67–72.

Reif, William E. "Intrinsic versus Extrinsic Rewards: Resolving the Controversy," *Human Resource Management,* Summer, 1975, pp. 2–10.

Reitz, H. Joseph, and Linda N. Jewell. "Sex, Locus of Control, and Job Involvement: A Six-Country Investigation," *Academy of Management Journal,* Vol. 22, No. 1, March, 1979, pp. 72–80.

Slocum, J., P. Topichak, and D. Kuhn. "A Cross-Cultural Study of Need Satisfaction and Need Importance for Operative Employees," *Personnel Psychology,* Fall, 1971, pp. 435–445.

Steers, Richard M., and Lyman W. Porter. *Motivation and Work Behavior.* New York: McGraw-Hill Book Company, 1983.

5

Motivation: Key to Achievement and Productivity

> A machine that works at only 20 to 30 percent of its capacity is repaired or discarded. An employee who misses one out of every three workdays is quickly terminated. Yet studies show that certain workers can perform at 20 to 30 percent of their ability without being fired and that average employees work at only two thirds of their capacity. Creating a climate which will inspire people to achieve above these levels—ideally, to the fullest extent of their capabilities—is a problem shared by anyone who directly or indirectly has a responsibility for the efforts of others or a concern that they reach their full potential.[1]
>
> The achievement of the people who work with or for you is determined by three factors: (1) motivation, (2) ability, and (3) resources. You as a manager or co-worker have, in general, relatively little opportunity to increase people's ability or resources. While, in the long run, selection and training might lead to greater ability in the people around you, most employees are already in place when you arrive, and most are already trained to such a level that additional training would yield minimal returns. Similarly, most organizations do not allow lack of resources to interfere with productivity; if they do, prior decisions to withhold resources are made at a high management level and for good reasons. What you have to work with therefore is motivation: a factor that is hardly ever at its maximum level and that can be greatly influenced by your actions. If you are ineffective in diagnosing causes of low motivation or in creating positive motivation, your presence will have little positive impact in the achievement of those around you.

Because managers must achieve organizational objectives through the efforts of others, they are not content with merely understanding what motivates people to behave as they do. Managers must go beyond just understanding their subordinates and must influence their subordinates' behavior.

Some persons are uncomfortable learning techniques of motivating others. These people think that learning to motivate is synonymous with learning to *manipulate* others by controlling their thoughts and behavior for selfish ends through crafty, illusive methods. Manipulation is, of course, generally considered to be immoral. In addition to this it has other major drawbacks. Manipulators are usually found out, and the resulting distrust undermines their efforts. Employees can sometimes be deceived for a short time, but most employees are too insightful for manipulation to be effective in the long run. Managers who manipulate are not likely to be effective motivators. Effective motivators are usually characterized by integrity and straightforward behavior. They are sometimes tough, but they are seldom crafty, as the motivational techniques described in this chapter show. The objectives of this chapter are

TO UNDERSTAND:

1. How perceptions of fairness and fear affect motivation

2. How money and competition motivate

3. How expectations affect motivation

4. How positive reinforcement motivates

5. How to analyze and solve a motivational problem

EQUITY IN THE WORKPLACE

Employees are most highly motivated to contribute to the organization when they view their inputs of time, effort, loyalty, and cooperation as favorable relative to the various forms of compensation they receive in exchange. Employee perceptions of the fairness of this exchange are strongly influenced by the compensation they believe other employees are receiving.

Imagine a situation where you receive your largest raise ever—larger than expected and unquestionably fair when judged by the income and raises of managers in other organizations. It is obvious that your colleagues are satisfied with their raises; and you are satisfied also until you discover that the other managers on your level—employees who are very much like yourself in terms of background, experience, productivity, and so on—received considerably more. Under such circumstances you would naturally wonder why you were discriminated against. Were you disliked? Was your performance perceived as substandard? Why the inequitable exchange? Such experiences provide the basis for our understanding of work motivation within the **equity exchange model** or **equity theory**.

Although the equity exchange model continues to be tested and refined, it may be generally stated as follows:

1. In judging whether pay (or any other form of compensation) is fair, employees do not use an absolute standard of comparison. Fairness is always in the eye of the beholder, and ordinarily employees compare their pay (the outcome of their work) with that of specific *reference persons* whose *inputs* (to the organization) they perceive to be comparable to their own.[2]

2. Inequity exists when an employee perceives that the ratio of his or her outcomes to inputs and the ratio of his or her reference persons' outcomes to inputs are unequal.[3]

3. Perceived inequity in either direction creates a state of disequilibrium or tension that a person is motivated to remove.

4. The behavior motivated by perceived inequity depends on a number of factors such as perceived direction of the inequity, attitudes, and the availability of alternatives. Extremely alienated employees may passively accept perceived underpayment; it may motivate passivity (because they see no way to remove the inequity), or it may motivate them to leave the organization. At a higher level of involvement, employees may react to perceived underpayment by absenteeism, reducing productivity, lowering quality, or requesting raises, each of which is intended to restore an inner equilibrium or perception of equity. Perceived overpayment may lead to increased productivity, improved quality, and other means of reducing the inequity.[4]

5. Perceived inequity in the direction of underpayment is greater than perceived inequity in the direction of overpayment. That is, overpayment is easy to accept without developing a motivating tension, but perceived underpayment is intolerable and is a powerful motivator. Overpayment—when it can be recognized—is easy to rationalize away.

Perceptual Aspects of Equity

Many interacting factors contribute to an employee's perception of his or her contribution to the organization. The most obvious contributions are skill, education, experience, and effort; but such inputs as length of time on the job, appearance, cooperativeness, loyalty, and even friendliness and charisma may also be perceived as contributions. Any quality a person values is likely to be viewed by that person as a relevant input, whether or not it objectively makes a contribution to the organization or is perceived to do so by management.

The complexity of the perceptions involved in an exchange is increased by a variety of subjective, often inaccurate judgments. One employee, for instance, places low value on another employee's superior academic background and thus perceives their employer to be unfair in heavily weighting education in a promotion decision. Evaluations of pay are distorted because, in the absence of factual information, estimates of what others earn are usually exaggerated. Persons with an excessively strong personal need for money, status, security, or recognition may, because of the strength of this need, perceive generous amounts of these forms of compensation as small and inadequate. Similarly, perception is distorted because people see what they expect to see. Employees who distrust their employer, for example, expect unfair managerial decisions and tend to view them as unfair regardless of the facts. These points are not intended to express pessimism about management's ability to be perceived as fair. They do suggest that (1) managers should be aware of factors that distort employee perceptions of fairness and (2) they should make a deliberate effort not only to be fair but to be perceived as being fair by employees.

Evaluation and Implications for Management

Since equity theory is in a state of continual evolution, it is hard to determine exactly what all its propositions are. Research does, however, give some support for the most common statements of the theory.[5,6] Like most theories it is not a complete explanation—several aspects of motivation are not included. It is useful, however, as one of several ways to capture part of what we know about the subject.

Managers should apply equity theory when establishing pay systems—especially when deciding how much secrecy should be involved. Equity theory indicates that employees need some facts in order to avoid overestimating how much others are earning. Managers should realize that employees' distrust of managerial decisions—and their resulting fear that personnel decisions are unfair—have often led employees to prefer across-the-board raises and seniority-based promotions to outcomes based on merit. In many situations employees discourage outstanding performers, thereby forcing roughly equal output in exchange for roughly equal pay. Some organizations could have avoided this employee behavior had they been more sensitive to the motivational implications of perceptions of fairness.

As shown in Figure 5-1, employees have more to contribute to the exchange we have discussed than a fair day's work, and management has

Some Organizational Contributions to the Exchange	Some Employee Contributions to the Exchange
Financial compensation	Loyalty
Security	Cooperation
Social relationships	Problem-solving behavior
Fair treatment	Support of goals
Responsibility	Dependability
Growth opportunities	Initiative
Status and power	Creativity
Safe working conditions	Productivity

FIGURE 5-1   Some Factors in the Organization-Employee Exchange

more to offer than a fair day's pay. Managers who value good human relations recognize the advantage of avoiding adversarial relationships where the parties to the exchange constantly bargain to minimize their own contribution while compelling the other to contribute as much as possible. A positive approach is better. Progressive managers unilaterally contribute as much as possible—for example, praise, recognition, and other behaviors that increase subordinates' self-esteem—on the assumption that such an approach will both motivate favorable employee outputs and improve job satisfaction. Equity theory supports managerial actions that create an inequity that employees can remove only by increasing their contribution to the organization, especially where favorable employee relations minimize the likelihood that the inequity will be removed by rationalization.

FEAR MOTIVATION

The use of fear to motivate is generally unproductive as a motivational style. It debases and demotivates the employee and creates unnecessary problems for management. On the other hand, some degree of fear motivation is always present in healthy individuals as a defense against the temptation to behave inappropriately when other potential motivators are ineffective. Thus, fear motivation is not all bad.

Classical organization theory resulted in a style of management that relied heavily on coercion or the fear of punishment for motivating employees. This approach is still very much alive although it is increasingly ineffective. It has serious shortcomings, the most obvious of which is the fact that no one likes to be motivated by fear. To the extent that a manager is able to get compliance with an order by threatening a subordinate, coercive motivation has been successful, but in a deeper sense it may have failed.

Problems with Fear Motivation

The subordinate who complies because of fear resents the tactic. Especially if coercion is the supervisor's typical motivational style, the subordinate is likely to build up hostility and express it in hidden ways that are seriously damaging to the organization and the supervisor. Resentment may be expressed in the form of marginal productivity or behavior designed to arouse the resentment and hostility of other employees. Unhealthy as these actions are, they may not be as serious as the resulting absence of positive attitudes and behavior. Where coercive motivation is extensively applied, initiative, loyalty, and creative problem solving are greatly diminished. The organizational environment may be rich in other potential motivators, but fear and its resulting hostility reduce their effectiveness.

When Fear Is Useful

We noted earlier that a given behavior, especially a complex behavior such as sustaining a high level of productivity, is seldom the result of a single motive. Fear probably operates as one of these motives for most employees in most organizations. To suggest that fear may have some positive value is not inconsistent with the proposition that the constant use of fear motivation is undesirable.

Confident, self-actualizing individuals are not devoid of all fear. In fact, strange as it may seem, even highly successful managers are often characterized by a fear of failure. They are not basically fearful people; they are not dominated or debilitated by fear. Rather, they sometimes fear failure because they constantly accept challenges that tax their abilities to the utmost. Successful managers recognize the risks involved in the kind of behavior required of them and know that there is always a possibility of failure. The fear is a warning signal and a defense against carelessness in a dangerous environment. In general, such fear is healthy, similar to fear of crossing a busy intersection before the light changes. It reflects an awareness of real danger and provides a healthy motivation for avoiding unnecessary risk taking.

Fear is also an appropriate motivator when other motivators are insufficient for curtailing misbehaviors. The ideal motivation for an employee to refrain from stealing, for example, is conscience or respect for the organization. However, if only fear of punishment can control the employee's behavior, then fear has served a useful purpose for both the organization and the potential offender.

Fear as a motivational force may produce either positive or negative results. It is never absent as a potential motivator, but ideally it comes into play only as a last resort when positive forms of motivation have failed.

MONEY AS A MOTIVATOR

Money is a symbol that represents different things to different people. Because of this and other factors, some people will be more highly motivated than others to work for money, but for practically every employee making money is one motive for working. Usually it is an important one.

Some researchers have failed to make the important distinction between motivation to work for money and motivation to work harder in order to earn more money. Others have arrived at the indefensible conclusion that money either is not a motivator or is not an important motivator. Still other researchers have proceeded with little apparent recognition of the fact that money is often just one of many motives that interact in a complex way to produce a given behavior. If money had the same meaning to everyone, it would be easy to draw generalizations about it. However, because of its different symbolic meanings and its almost unlimited potential as a medium of exchange, the conditions under which money motivates vary greatly.[7]

The Meaning of Money

To the very poor, money symbolizes immediate satisfaction of the basic needs for food, health care, clothing, and shelter. Most employed Americans do not function at this level, however, and for them the symbolism becomes more complex. At higher economic levels money may symbolize security, status, power, or prestige or it may highlight the fact that a person is a winner in the tricky and complicated game of business. To some it is an indicator of value or worth. More than we may wish to admit, the statement that a person is worth a million dollars may reflect the depth to which materialism is a part of our basic value system. Clearly, money's reward strength necessarily relates to its unique meanings for a given individual.

Changes in the Need for Money

Those who belittle the potential of money to motivate sometimes point to the fact that most employed persons in this country have their basic needs met reasonably well, and thus the motivational value of money is reduced or nonexistent. Although there is some truth to be found in this idea, it overlooks the fact that the reason these needs are satisfied is because people are motivated to work and earn money for a variety of reasons besides the satisfaction of their basic needs.

Although the motivational value of money may change after a person's basic needs have been reasonably well satisfied, human beings have a way of continually redefining their needs. At one point in time, satisfying the need for food is viewed as having the staples needed to avoid hunger. At another time, it means being able to buy a balanced diet of precooked foods and high-protein beef. Still later it may mean the ability to afford frequent dining out in expensive restaurants. The necessities of dental care change imperceptibly from the ability to get an aching tooth filled to being able to afford an orthodontist. Even after the necessities of life are satisfied, money will continue to motivate an individual who associates money with the acquisition of such qualities as power, recognition, prestige, belonging, and love. Such associations are easily formed in our culture.

Whether money will motivate is to some degree a matter of the amount of money involved and the amount an individual is already earning. Generally speaking, the more people earn, the more they must receive to be motivated to work harder or longer. For example, the clerk who earns $7,000 a year may be motivated by the prospect of earning an 8 percent raise, or $560. To an executive who is earning $70,000 the prospect of a $560 raise would be considered an insult. A comparable percentage increase is more acceptable, although many top executives require a pay increase of 25 to 30 percent as an inducement to change companies.

Money often ceases to motivate because an individual has reached a **comfort level**. Admittedly, inflation, media advertising, and built-in product obsolescence make this an unlikely prospect for most people who work for a living, but such people do exist. Reaching a comfort level is typically associated with having the opportunity to live within one's income by controlling wants and spending in order to gain a degree of independence and freedom.

Needs in Conflict

One of the important determinants of whether money will motivate is the price one must pay to earn it. That price is not simply a matter of the fatigue and effort involved. An even more serious consideration may be the prospect of a conflict between satisfaction of different needs. The employee who is paid on a piecework basis must weigh carefully whether the needs satisfied with increased earnings will offset being rejected by peers as a rate buster. Even if the financial payoff is sufficient to make the sacrifice of peer support worthwhile, an internal conflict that partially neutralizes the motivational impact of money is created within the worker.

At times value conflicts reduce the attractiveness of money. For example, a salesperson may refuse to misrepresent a product, or a certified public accountant may sacrifice a client rather than compromise principles. In another case, making more money conflicts with health needs. Some employees refuse to take certain accident risks or to continue working under intense pressures when stress is affecting their health. The behavior required to earn more may also conflict with a need for love and self-respect when, for example, continual travel disrupts family life. In other situations, increased effort simply interferes with leisure-time activities, and the employee's response is to reject overtime work or a promotion into management.

A Symbol of Success

For top executives the motivational value of money often lies primarily in its ability to symbolize success. For executives who have acquired personal wealth through stock options and private investments, for example, even a substantial raise may have little practical value other than to increase income taxes. Yet, even under these circumstances, a raise does communicate appreciation for continuing peak performance. Failure to receive a raise, especially if executives in a comparable position get one, may subjectively be viewed as a pay cut. Under such conditions, money may very well fit Herzberg's description of a dissatisfier in which a raise does not motivate increased effort, but failure to get it causes dissatisfaction. On the other hand, if raises contribute to sustaining a high level of effort, it can hardly be said that money has no motivational impact.

The Probability of a Payoff

Money will motivate increased effort only if employees believe that working harder or producing more will result in more money. Unfortunately many compensation systems reward performance and nonperformance equally. The typical end-of-year bonus, in particular, is notably unrelated to behavior in the minds of those who receive it.

Money motivates best when it is received immediately after the behavior it purports to reward. For example, one manager of direct sales representatives in Colombia, South America, pays the representatives at the close of every day just to make sure they see clearly the relationship between behavior and reward. The practice would not be feasible today, but there was a time when, as a means of keeping motivation high for work that was both difficult and boring, sewing machine operators were paid in coin when each bundle of garments was turned in. Attempts to motivate managers by rewarding them on the basis of performance are often ineffective. Failure results partly because it is difficult for top management to be perceived as fair in their judgments about performance and pay. In addition, especially at the top of the management pyramid, there is often little relationship between performance and pay.[8] The problem is complicated by the fact that effectiveness, as measured by profits, is partially dependent on economic and market factors that are unrelated to manager motivation. Furthermore, the managers of some companies are so motivated that neither money nor any other payoff can increase their efforts.

COMPETITION

Because the performance of others provides employees with a measure of success where more objective measures are lacking, spontaneous competition between employees is one of the important motivational forces within organizations. Competition that is deliberately promoted by management may be effective under certain circumstances, but it should be used with caution and combined with other forms of motivation that are less likely to be viewed as manipulative and cause destructive conflict.

In a capitalistic, private enterprise system, competition is by definition national policy. In the United States, antitrust laws have been passed to preserve competition on the assumption that competition among companies is in the public interest. Under competition, managers are highly motivated to produce better products and services at the lowest possible cost to the consumer. Anyone who has experienced or studied the abuses of power under monopoly has little difficulty accepting the idea that competition is good. Yet it is easy to see that competition leaves behind it a continuous line of casualties. When marginal and inefficient companies fail, their owners and employees are hurt, sometimes seriously. Another problem of competition among organizations is that it leads to monopoly unless it is carefully regulated. Competition within organizations has comparable advantages and disadvantages.

The Nature of Competition

The urge to compete is by no means universal although it is highly promoted in our culture. It is a secondary need, a learned means of satisfying more basic needs. Since all kinds of games reward the winner, most children learn to enjoy competition, and this enjoyment continues into adulthood. Obviously some people compete in athletics, some in street fighting, and others in producing goods or services. We learn to compete in areas where we are most likely to succeed, and it is therefore not surprising that some people learn not to compete at all.

Competition always exists as a motivator within organizations. Where one potential job opening exists and there are several contenders, it is inevitable that a certain degree of competition will develop. Motivation to compete, like motivation for money, has many facets and offers many forms of potential need satisfaction. In competing for a promotion, an obvious dimension of the competitive urge is the lure of money, power, and prestige. Competition gives many people a sense of goal direction that both increases achievement and provides a satisfying sense of purpose. There is also a game aspect to competition within and among organizations. Playing the game is fun, and the prospect of winning reduces boredom and makes fatigue more acceptable. This effect is observed in the willingness of athletes to exert extreme effort and often to endure pain in order to win.

Successfully competing with worthy opponents is ego enhancing. It contributes to a sense of self-worth, and most of us learn early in life not to be seriously hurt if we invest heavily in winning and then lose. In many situations it is all but impossible to find acceptable measurements for performance other than comparison with other people; and for persons who perceive themselves to be outstanding performers, being rated high within a respected peer group may provide a better norm than would an absolute standard.

For the great mass of average performers in any area who perceive themselves to be as good as the next person, the desire to avoid being classified at the bottom rung of the ladder may also provide a degree of competitive motivation. Competition does not always involve a drive to be number one. The level to which one aspires depends upon past experience—upon the goals one has learned to perceive as realistic to pursue in relation to other people.

Competition Within Work Groups

A distinction should be made between the more or less spontaneous, natural competition that develops in a work environment and competition promoted by management. Attempts to stimulate competition as a means of increasing productivity are usually unsuccessful among blue-collar workers and white-collar workers who are on relatively routine jobs (such as office support personnel, data entry employees, or members of a word processing center). Employees who too obviously demonstrate their superiority and desire to win the favor of superiors are rejected by their peers and pressured to behave in ways that will not make their fellow employees appear mediocre by comparison.

Attempts to stimulate competition among employees (as contrasted to line or staff management) are challenged by two limitations within the work environment. The first, described in Chapter 3, involves the fact that abilities are typically distributed throughout the work group in such a way that most employees are just average. This means that the few whose outstanding abilities enable them to stand head and shoulders above the others under competitive conditions can be successfully discouraged from competing by the other group members.

The second limitation on competition is inherent in the fact that in many situations employees are rewarded for seniority rather than merit. Under such circumstances competition benefits only the organization. Employees will not ordinarily compete just to please management, especially when doing so may result in peer rejection and punishment.

Competition Among Salespeople

Sales managers have learned to be relatively successful with competition motivation, mainly for two reasons. First, they tend to recruit people who are likely to have competitive natures—people who have learned to satisfy their individual needs through competition. Secondly, the sales situation can usually be structured to provide an opportunity for individuals to be directly rewarded for their effort and ingenuity (this is why it is appropriate to recruit competitive people). Most sales contests are set up so that everybody can win something. The salesperson who loses a contest but earns increased commissions is not left with the feeling of having been manipulated into working only for the good of the company.

However, competition among salespeople often has negative side effects. Salespeople sometimes promote low profit but easy-to-sell items, lie to and exert undue pressure on customers to buy unneeded merchandise, and otherwise engage in behavior that may hurt long-term sales. In the heat of a sales contest they may also engage in behavior that undermines the success of a competing salesperson (stealing leads, for example) or increases sales at the expense of the organization (for example, by excessive price cutting or by orally committing the company to perform unusual warranty services).

Although people outside the sales field are often critical of techniques used to increase competition (such as offering a weekend resort vacation for two to salespeople who meet their quotas), some rather unusual methods are accepted and even welcomed by commissioned salespeople. They know from experience how difficult it is to stay motivated when prospective customers are saying no. Contests generate enthusiasm and excitement because they are associated with high sales. When properly conducted, they increase commissions, decrease boredom, and, for the winners, add a material bonus along with status and prestige. Sales executives are in general agreement that compensation is the most important element in sales motivation, but the method of compensation determines whether motivation or sales will increase.[9]

Competition Among Managers

Highly competitive managers, like salespeople, are not beyond putting their own interests above the interests of the organization. They sometimes withhold information in order to make a competing manager look bad, even when the competitor is an immediate superior. They may start unflattering rumors or otherwise behave in ways designed to destroy competitors rather than defeat them in fair competition.

An organization cannot function efficiently when its resources are wasted on internal conflict, and competition among managers often creates undesirable conflict along with valuable motivation. One of the important functions of a manager is to serve as a mediator between competing subordinate managers. Managers must prevent competition among subordinates from becoming destructive and must also guard against the possibility that destructive competition will be rewarded within the organization. The objective is not to eliminate competition among managers but to keep competition within reasonable limits and to make sure it does not prevent competitors within the organization from cooperating to achieve organizational goals.

Competition Between Groups

Some of the destructiveness of competition among people is diminished when competition is switched from individuals to groups. It is commonly observed that when one work group is challenged by another, group cohesiveness and cooperation, as well as motivation, increase. Often the advantages of intragroup cooperation outweigh any disadvantages that might result from intergroup competition.

Competition between groups is most effective when it arises, (or appears to arise), spontaneously. A manager may create conditions that will lead to competition by posting group production records, for example, but caution must be exercised in overtly encouraging competition. If a manager's behavior is viewed as an attempt to get something for nothing, this strategy may backfire and significantly decrease motivation.

THE EXPECTANCY MODEL OF MOTIVATION

At the present time there is no motivation model which effectively combines our existing knowledge into a comprehensive motivation theory. Expectancy models are no exception, but they do provide the most promising framework yet developed for evolving such a theory.

Expectancy theory is typically associated with the work of Vroom[10] and Porter and Lawler[11], although the basic theory was developed in the 1930s, primarily by psychologists E. C. Tolman and Kurt Lewin.

Predicting Effort

Basically, in the work context, expectancy theory states that a person's work effort depends on three factors:

1. the perceived probability that a given level of effort will lead to a particular level of performance,

2. the perceived probability that the particular level of performance will lead to a particular outcome, and

3. the psychological value of the outcome.

Of course, in a complex work environment, effort could lead to a number of intermediate outcomes besides performance, and each intermediate outcome could lead to a variety of other outcomes. For example, high performance alone can lead to more income, less peer acceptance, higher esteem in the eyes of management, and so forth.

To see how expectancy theory explains effort, consider, as an example, a salesperson's decision about how much effort she should exert during the first six months after taking a new job in life insurance sales. Expectancy theory says that in making her decision she would consider the probabilities that a high level of effort would lead to various **first-level outcomes**, such as high sales and reduced social life. These perceived probabilities between effort level and other first-level outcomes (such as performance) are called **expectancies**. As a probability, the magnitude of an expectancy ranges between zero or total disbelief and 1.0 or certainty as shown in Figure 5-2.

Total Disbelief	Subjective Probability of Occurrence							Certainty	
0 .10 .20	.30	.40	.50	.60	.70	.80	.90	1.00	

FIGURE 5-2 Expectancy: Perceived Probability of an Outcome

The theory goes on to say that this salesperson would also consider the probabilities that first-level outcomes (such as high sales) would lead to various intermediate or **second-level outcomes** (such as high commissions and expanded sales territories). Second-level outcomes are the consequences that follow from attaining particular first-level outcomes. Perceived probabilities that link the two types of outcomes are called **instrumentalities**, because the first-level outcomes are instrumental in obtaining the second-level outcomes. Instrumentalities also range, of course, between zero and one.

The psychological values of the second-level outcomes are called **valences**. Valences can be very positive (1.0), very negative (−1.0), or somewhere in between, as shown in Figure 5-3. An example expectancy theory model is shown in Figure 5-4 on page 130.

Strong dislike for the outcome		Indifference toward the outcome		Strong preference for the outcome	
−1.00 −.75	−.50	−.25	0 .25	.50	.75 1.00

FIGURE 5-3 Valence: Psychological Value of the Outcome

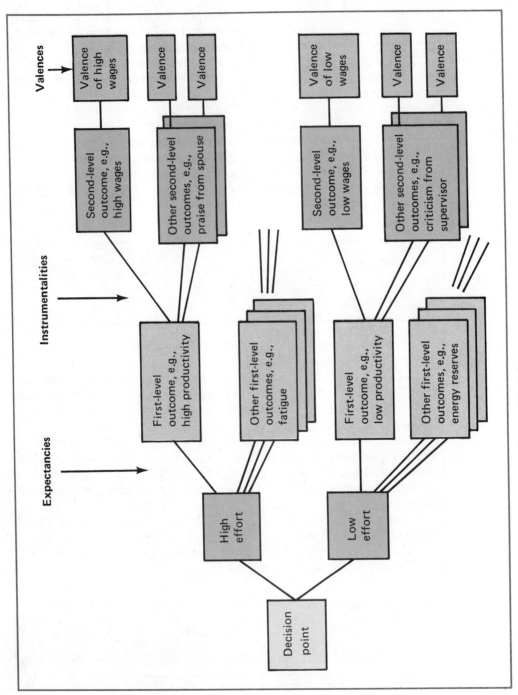

FIGURE 5-4 An Example Expectancy Theory Model

Because it focuses on valences, instrumentalities, and expectancies, expectancy theory is sometimes called **VIE theory**. Sometimes the product of these three factors is called **motivational force**. Thus considering for the moment only one first-level outcome and one second-level outcome,

$$\text{motivational force} = \text{(valence) times (instrumentality) times (expectancy)}$$

$$= \text{VIE}$$

Clearly, if any one factor is very low, the motivational force (and resulting effort) would be low, no matter how large the other two factors are.

Expectancy Theory as a Tool

One use of expectancy theory for managers is as a diagnostic tool. When faced with the need to motivate a subordinate, managers should ask themselves if they have done all that they can to maximize the expectancies, the instrumentalities, and the valences. This is not a trivial undertaking. For example, valences of second-level outcomes depend on the employee's particular needs, and managers would be wise if they got to know their employees well enough that they understand what kind of outcomes particular employees are likely to value highly. If a particular employee appreciates recognition, then by earlier actions or current statements the manager would want to make clear to the employee that high achievement would be publicly recognized, thus maximizing instrumentality and highlighting the valence.

Continuing with the use of expectancy theory as a tool, the manager should attempt to create a work situation where effort has a high probability of leading to helpful first-level outcomes; then the manager should attempt to make this fact very clear to the employee. The manager should also, of course, attempt to ensure that all likely first-level outcomes have high probabilities of leading to second-level outcomes that have positive valences and that have low probabilities of leading to outcomes that have negative valences.

MOTIVATION AS REINFORCEMENT

The reinforcement approach to motivation follows the behavioristic model of ignoring what takes place within the mind while concentrating on the process of reinforcing desirable behaviors. Often viewed by nonbehaviorists as simplistic, reinforcement theory has much to offer that is practical and theoretically sound.

Reinforcement theory (also called *contingency theory*) is an approach to understanding and modifying human behavior that is based upon reinforcement principles of learning. In its most elementary form, reinforcement refers to the positive or negative consequences that follow a behavior and determine, to some extent at least, whether the behavior will be repeated. Reinforcement theory is closely identified with behaviorist B. F. Skinner, although a large number of other people have been responsible for developing its principles and applications.

Reinforcement theory has much in common with the expectancy model just described. They are alike in that both stress the importance of the relationship between a behavior and its consequences (the reward or punishment that follows it). A major difference between the two is that expectancy theory deals with such internal processes as perception, evaluation, and subjective probability, while reinforcement theory attempts to avoid reference to internal psychological processes in order to focus only on behavior. In fact, behaviorists prefer not to use the word *motivation*. They think instead in terms of modifying behavior. The founder of the behaviorist school of psychology, John B. Watson (1878–1958), and his modern-day followers believe that only behavior, as contrasted with subjective experience, can be scientifically studied.

Behavioral Principles

Reinforcement theory is based on a few simple principles of learning that are treated in a straightforward, noncontroversial manner in practically any introductory textbook in psychology. They have no necessary connection with **philosophical behaviorism**, which is the philosophy that advocates that society should mold its members very precisely to fit its needs. As Perry London suggests, we would do well to separate the technology involved in working with human behavior from behaviorism as such.[12]

The following behavioral principles form the basis for the reinforcement model of motivation.[13]

1. Reinforced behavior tends to be repeated. A reinforcement is any consequence that increases the likelihood that a specific behavior will occur in the future. (For example, praise following a behavior increases the likelihood that the behavior will be repeated.)

2. Reward is more effective than punishment in motivating a person to perform in a particular way.[14] Punishment is to be avoided whenever possible.

3. An important form of reinforcement is feedback on performance. Even the simple feedback that comes from knowing that a supervisor is aware of a behavior may positively reinforce it. On the other hand, when desirable behaviors are consistently ignored they eventually cease to occur.

4. For fastest results, a reward should follow as soon as possible after the occurrence of the behavior one seeks to reinforce.

5. A clear distinction should be made between a need for training and a need for motivation. These two problems are often confused so that attempts to motivate fail because an employee needs training or training is unsuccessful because of weak motivation.

6. Desired performance should be clearly defined and stated. It is only when the behavioral objectives are made explicit and concrete that they can be measured and rewarded.[15,16]

7. Reward should be given for movement toward the desired target behavior. Rewarding so-called successive approximations provides assurance that an individual will continue to move in the right direction. Behavior modification technology often provides for graduated schedules of reinforcement by which people move from wherever they are (their **baseline behavior**) to target behavior.

Evaluation

It is inevitable that a behavior will be followed by consequences which will, to some extent, determine whether it will be repeated. Behavior theory proposes that it is better to analyze and control the consequences of a behavior than to leave them to chance. Making the consequences known is not manipulative. To the contrary, this provides the employee with an optimal opportunity to make deliberate choices between explicitly defined alternatives.

Managers often behave like a parent who encourages a child to have tantrums by showing an excessive amount of attention when such behavior occurs and by giving in to these demands. The everyday, unplanned patterns of reinforcement, which are as common in organizations as in parent-child relationships, are expressed in the example of a manager who could not motivate subordinates to turn in their reports on time. The manager needed the reports on the fifteenth of the month

in order to have a report prepared by the twentieth. When bribes, scold-
ing, reasoning, and threatening failed to work, the consequences of turning in reports late and on time were analyzed. The manager found that
subordinates who were on time had been punished by having their reports sent back for corrections and additions. Subordinates who turned
their reports in on time were never rewarded because they were perceived as doing only what they were paid for and expected to do.

The reinforcement model of motivation takes many forms and has
much to offer a manager who is concerned with understanding and influencing behavior. People with a bias against philosophical behaviorism
would do well to lay aside any feelings that might prevent their taking
advantage of the potential contributions of reinforcement motivation
theory. The point cannot be made too strongly that we do in fact continually reinforce behavior. What could be more intelligent than understanding and rationally controlling the reinforcement processes within
an organization?

HOW TO ANALYZE A MOTIVATION PROBLEM

One of the major problems in analyzing a motivational problem is understanding the many variables within the individuals involved. A practical alternative is to deal with the problem as behaviorally as possible,
emphasizing primarily the consequences of behaviors and how they can
be altered in order to positively reinforce desired behaviors.

A **motivation problem** exists within an organization when there is
a discrepancy between expected and achieved results due to lack of effort
rather than to lack of ability, training, or other factors. For example, the
motivational problem may be expressed in terms of the failure of employees to obey a specific safety rule (smoking in a restricted area only),
failure to perform certain supervisory practices (handling disciplinary
problems in private), or failure to follow a procedure (checking a customer's credit balance before every shipment). A **performance problem**
exists anytime an employee's behavior falls short of expectations, but
such a problem may not be caused by low motivation. The determination of whether nonperformance results from low motivation is a matter
of rejecting at least four other possible causes of the substandard behavior:

1. *A problem of communication.* In this case failure to perform is caused
   by the employee's misperception of what is expected.

2. *A problem of ability.* The person in question lacks the physical or

mental ability to perform according to expectations and is therefore untrainable.

3. *A problem of training.* In this case performance will be inadequate regardless of motivational level until training occurs.

4. *A problem of opportunity.* The employee knows what to do and how to do it but is held back by environmental conditions (for example, inadequate tools, obsolete methods, being paced by the performance of others or by market conditions).

Once it has been established that the problem is due to low motivation, further analysis is required. We begin with the simple proposition that the substandard behavior persists because it is more rewarding than any alternative behavior currently available to the individual in question. From management's point of view it may seem totally irrational for the employee to persist in a behavior that is in direct opposition to the preferences of management. It should be noted, however, that understanding motives requires that we get into the other person's shoes and see a situation from that unique vantage point. What is rational to a manager may not appear rational to a subordinate because the two are interpreting the facts from entirely different points of view.

Guidelines for Analysis

A convenient way to analyze the motivation for a particular behavior is to examine its consequences as much as possible from the viewpoint of the person whose behavior we are studying. A format for visualizing the problem is presented in Figure 5-5 (the case analyzed in this table will be presented later). First let us take a look at some of the basic principles or guidelines to be used in our motivation analysis (since each of these principles has already been considered in some detail, little additional detail is presented here):

1. Rewarded behaviors tend to be repeated, and behaviors that are not rewarded (or that are punished) are not repeated.

2. For a factor (such as the work itself, pay, praise, or a promotion) to serve as a motivator, the individual we hope to motivate must *believe* it will satisfy an active need. The higher the subjective probability of each of the following, the greater the likelihood that a factor will be a motivator: (a) that the expected performance standard can be reached; (b) that the hoped-for reward will be forthcoming; (c) that the reward will satisfy an active need.

RELATIVELY LOW MOTIVATIONAL VALUE	BALANCE OF CONSEQUENCES TABLE		RELATIVELY HIGH MOTIVATIONAL VALUE
	Effect of the Consequences		
O	Organizational	Personal	P
	Timing of the Consequences		
D	Delayed	Immediate	I
	Probability of the Consequences		
G	Gamble	Certain	C
	Perceived Importance of the Consequences		
1	1 (low) through 5 (high)		5
	A. Supervisors Enforce the Rules		
	Possible Positive Consequences		
D-G	Recognition by management		P 3
D-G	Receiving a promotion or raise		P 3
O-D-G-2	Increased productivity		
O-D-G	Improvement in accident rate		4
	Possible Negative Consequences		
	Conflict with subordinates		P-I-C-5
	An increase in work load		P-I-C-5
O	Increased trouble with the union		P-I-C-5
O- G-2	Decreased productivity		I
O- G-2	Reduction in quality of product		I
	Increase in peer pressure		P-I-C-5
	B. Supervisors Do Not Enforce the Rules		
	Possible Positive Consequences		
	Good relations with workers		P-I-C-5
	Comfortable work load		P-I-C-5
	No difficulty with peers		P-I-C-5
	Possible Negative Consequences		
-2	Pressure from higher management		P-I-C
O-D-G-1	High dollar cost to the company		
O-D-G	Less than optimal accident rate		4

Sources: The basic idea for this table came from the lecture and discussion content of a University of Michigan seminar in "The Management of Behavior Change," James V. McConnell, senior seminar leader. The perceived importance of the consequences factor is an expression of one dimension of cognitive expectancy theory.

FIGURE 5-5 Balance of Consequences Table

3. Generally speaking, rewarding desirable behavior is a more effective motivator of high performance than punishing undesirable behavior.

4. A given behavior (whether it is good or bad) is more strongly reinforced when the reward or punishment follows *immediately* than when it is *delayed*.

5. The motivational value of a promised—or anticipated—reward or punishment is higher when it is *certain* to occur than when its occurrence is subjectively viewed as a *gamble*.

6. The motivational value of a reward or punishment is higher when it affects the individual *personally* than when it has an effect only on the *organization* of which the individual is a part. For example, a quality control inspector who must personally assume responsibility for a returned product will be more highly motivated to avoid the shipment of defective merchandise than will the inspector who knows the defective merchandise will merely be traced back to the quality control department.

7. Motivation to perform in a specified manner will be higher when the standard in question has been internalized than when the individual is only being extrinsically rewarded.

A Motivation Problem

We will now analyze a typical problem in management behavior from a formal motivational viewpoint. Consider the case of a general superintendent of an automobile parts remanufacturer who had a problem getting his supervisors to enforce the work rules. For example, workers were allowed to use the grinder without wearing their goggles; one worker punched the time clock for another who left work early; and contrary to company policy, frequent personal calls were made on company telephones during working hours. The supervisors knew the rules and had the authority and interpersonal skills needed to enforce them. They knew what they should do, but they were not motivated to do it.

After proceeding through the steps to determine that the problem was one of motivation rather than communication, ability, training, or opportunity, the analysis began by seeking the answers to seven strategic questions.

1. Have the expected performance standards been internalized? If not, why not? The apparent answer to this question was no. In this particular case the reason seemed to lie in the fact that the organization

had a history of (1) always making rules and never modifying or discarding them when they became obsolete and (2) not enforcing the rules once they were made. This tended to communicate the idea that rules were relatively unimportant. The president and other top officials set the pace for this lax behavior.

2. What are the positive and negative consequences of enforcing the rules? (In what ways is the desired behavior rewarded and punished?) The answers to this and the following five questions are expressed in the Balance of Consequences Table presented in Figure 5-5.

3. What are the positive and negative consequences of not enforcing the rules? (In what ways is the undesirable behavior rewarded and punished?)

4. Is each of the positive and negative consequences perceived as having *personal* application or as merely having beneficial or harmful effects on the *organization* (P or O)?

5. Is each of the positive and negative consequences of enforcing and not enforcing the rules perceived (by the supervisors whose behavior we want to change) as being *immediate* or *delayed* (I or D)?

6. How important is each of the positive or negative consequences as a need satisfier to this specific group of supervisors? This is expressed in the Balance of Consequences Table on a scale of *one* (of little importance) to *five* (of great importance insofar as the analyst is able to determine).

7. Is each of the positive and negative consequences perceived as being *certain* to occur or to some degree a *gamble* (C or G)?

The judgments expressed in the Balance of Consequences Table are valid and useful only to the extent that they represent the point of view and subjective probability estimates of the supervisors whose motives are being analyzed. Assuming the investigation has been objective so that the judgments do in fact represent the supervisor's viewpoint, we can now see what the data mean.

The supervisors perceive their present behavior to be more rewarding than the behavior their superiors prefer. Notice, in particular, that the perceived negative consequences of enforcing the rules are highly motivational (four of the six consequences are rated P-I-C-5, personal-immediate-certain-highly important), while the perceived negative consequences are not motivational (all consequences are perceived as being delayed and a gamble). On the other hand, note that the positive consequences of not enforcing the rules, compared with the positive consequences of enforcement, strongly indicate that nonenforcement is more rewarding. (All three consequences of not enforcing the rules are rated P-I-C-5, which indicates the highest possible motivation.)

The supervisors do place a high value on promotions and raises (shown by the rating of P, personal, and 5 in importance in the right column beside these factors), but the motivational value of the factor is minimal because a promotion or raise would not be received immediately and might not be received at all (as indicated by the D-G, delayed-gamble, in the left column). In other words, one supervisor is saying the following:

> I would very much like to have a raise or promotion, but the probability that the enforcement of the work rules will lead to either is quite low. And even if I should get a raise or a promotion in exchange for my cooperation, it would be so long in coming that I really can't get excited about it.

This illustrates a point made in the discussion of VIE theory; namely, that when valence, instrumentality, or expectancy is low, motivation will be low. The prospect of winning a million dollars in a lottery would be extremely motivational to some people, but not to the person who thinks that the probability of winning it is nil.

When we look at the negative consequences of nonenforcement, it becomes obvious that the supervisors know they will receive pressure from their superiors (the P-I-C in the right column), but they are not greatly disturbed about it (the 2 rating on importance in the left column). The supervisors obviously do not think that they will be seriously hurt by any punitive action management might take. On the other hand, they would be deeply concerned by what they believe to be the certain consequences of enforcing the rules (indicated by the four P-I-C-5 ratings given to such factors as conflict with subordinates and an increase in work load).

Once an accurate analysis has been made, motivating the desired behavior is essentially a matter of altering the consequences. In the case just presented, several steps may be taken. First, a committee of supervisors may be established to work with human resource specialists in revising the rules to make sure all are relevant and accepted as such by the supervisors. The supervisors would then be informed of the importance of enforcement and the changed policy of top management. Since all supervisors and workers are made aware of what is taking place and the seriousness with which the move is being taken by management, group pressures can be made to work for rather than against enforcement; and to the extent that hostility results from the enforcement, top management, rather than the supervisors, can be the major recipient. "Rules enforcement" may be added to the semiannual supervisor performance appraisal scale as a means of stressing the fact that enforcement is more rewarding than nonenforcement. As a last resort, one or more supervisors who refuse to cooperate can be suspended or discharged. These actions will tip the balance of consequences in the direction of compliance.

This type of analysis has many applications despite its lack of quantitative precision. The alternative to such a model is typically fuzzy thinking that fails to consider many important variables. Although some important dimensions of motivation are omitted or incompletely dealt with here, it is at least a start in the direction of scientifically analyzing a motivation problem. An analysis of this type capitalizes on an important principle used in decision theory; namely, that a complex decision is easier to make when it is broken down into a number of parts and each part is analyzed individually before arriving at a final conclusion.

CONSTRAINTS ON MOTIVATION

Motivating subordinates to produce at their highest potential, one of a supervisor's major concerns, is often blocked by organizational constraints that require lock-step behavior. Procedures, controls, and technology intended to optimize productivity often destroy a supervisor's ability to motivate subordinates to perform above the lowest acceptable level.

One of the most obvious motivational constraints results from the necessity for making personnel decisions on the basis of seniority. If workers with the capacity for outstanding productivity know that seniority rather than merit will be the sole criterion for promotions, their motivation for peak production may be undermined. The same can be said for situations in which raises are based on negotiated contracts or length of service rather than performance. Treating unequally performing people as though they were performing equally tends to motivate everyone to perform at as nearly the same level as possible—often at the lowest acceptable level.

In many work environments productivity is determined more by the technology than by the employees who apply it. An operator who primarily monitors instruments for deviations from standards in the production of petroleum products may have little to do with the rate of productivity and may work at or near capacity only when a breakdown occurs. Assembly line workers are often paced by a conveyor belt and the productivity of others on the line. An office worker who performs at a level that permits completion of specific tasks within a specified time may have nothing to do once the tasks are finished. In situations such as these, conditions outside the individual are the controlling elements in productivity. In such cases, attempts to increase productivity are more apt to be made by engineers and job analysts than by managers, and a manager's role as a motivator may only be to keep workers on the job, cooperative, and willing to apply the minimal effort required of them.

In some large business and government organizations, motivation for excellence is squelched by the effect of an inordinate number of guidelines, policies, rules, and regulations that define both what is to be done and how. The achievement of outstanding performance requires that individuals have some degree of autonomy and freedom to choose between alternatives. In the absence of such freedom, employee motivation consists mostly of willingness to conform.

In situations where technology and organizational controls are the primary determinants of productivity, an acceptable level of performance is often maintained even when motivation to perform is low and attitudes toward the organization are negative. In a sense, the structured environment provides an alternative to employee motivation. Experience has shown that large numbers of persons are capable of functioning throughout a lifetime in such an environment. However, the highly structured environment has the potential both for degrading personality and exercising a stultifying effect on the organization.

IMPORTANT TERMS AND CONCEPTS

equity exchange model
equity theory
comfort level
expectancy theory

first-level outcomes
expectancies
second-level outcomes
instrumentalities

valences   philosophical behaviorism
VIE theory   baseline behavior
motivational force   motivation problem
reinforcement theory   performance problem

STUDY AND DISCUSSION QUESTIONS

1. Why do employees place so much emphasis on what others receive in judging the fairness of their own earnings? What alternatives are available?

2. What factors make it difficult for employees to evaluate whether a given personnel decision is equitable?

3. Why is a reward generally a better motivator than punishment? Under what circumstances might punishment be better?

4. Defend this statement: It is unrealistic to believe that all fear motivation can or should be eliminated from an organization.

5. In recent years many knowledgeable persons have questioned the motivating power of money. Why do you think this is so? What do you think of such a position?

6. Under what conditions do you think money will motivate a highly paid executive to work harder?

7. Why do most people in our culture enjoy competition?

8. Under what circumstances does competition motivate best?

9. Contrast and evaluate the reinforcement and expectancy models of motivation.

10. Because of your expertise as a management consultant, you have been asked to advise an organization on how to more effectively motivate its assembly line employees. Their output is paced by a conveyor belt; they are paid and promoted on the basis of a collective bargaining agreement. What possibilities remain for developing an effective motivational system?

MOTIVATION AT THE TAYLOR CORPORATION

The Taylor Corporation, a wholesale hardware distributor, has an office force of about 80 employees. The employees are of all ages, and they work together in a single large room. Their work consists mostly of processing orders and following up on back orders and lost or late shipments. Once an employee learns the work, it becomes routine and requires little decision making. Therefore, few employees find the work mentally challenging.

Recognizing that many companies have problems with their office employees, management has established policies that it believes will maintain high satisfaction and motivation. The employees are paid monthly salaries rather than hourly rates, and no one is required to punch a time clock. The pay, which includes an end-of-year bonus based on the overall profits of the company, is 10 percent above the going rate in that geographic area; employee benefits are better than most, and the work environment is pleasant. Lighting and acoustics are ideal; and to break up the large work expanse and provide a basis for the formation of informal, friendly relationships among employees, attractive free-standing partitions define the work areas of the office's six departments. Recent attitude surveys showed that employee satisfaction is high. Although the work is somewhat routine, the employees expressed approval of their employer, compensation, supervision, employee benefits, and other major aspects of their employment.

In spite of the favorable level of employee satisfaction, two problems—tardiness and a high rate of paid sick leave—plague the managers. They have counseled numerous employees about these problems and at times have warned of possible disciplinary action, but the problems persist. During the past year, two employees whose abuses far exceeded those of the group were fired after repeated warnings. On two occasions the office manager met with the entire group and explained that because of absenteeism and tardiness an unnecessarily large number of employees are required, a condition that obviously lowers profits and end-of-year bonuses. The manager also appealed to the employees' loyalty to the company and to their sense of fairness. Management had hoped that peer pressure would be exerted on the worst offenders, leading to a solution to the problems, but for some reason that did not occur. Top level managers know that something must be done, but they are not sure what.

1. Analyze the motivational factors involved, using the model presented in Figure 5-5 on page 136. Why do the employees not respond to the appeals of management?

2. How would you solve the problem?

REFERENCES

1. Scanlan, Burt, K. "Creating a Climate for Achievement," *Business Horizons*, Vol. 24, No. 2, March-April, 1981, pp. 5–9.

2. Martin, Joanne. "The Fairness of Earnings Differentials: An Experimental Study of the Perceptions of Blue-Collar Workers," *The Journal of Human Resources*, Vol. XVII, No. 1, Winter, 1982, pp. 110–121.

3. Adams, Stacy J. "Inequity in Social Exchange," ed. Leonard Berkowitz. *Advances in Experimental and Social Psychology*, New York: Academic Press, Inc., 1965, p. 280.

4. Gould, Sam. "An Equity-Exchange Model of Organizational Involvement," *Academy of Management Review*, Vol. 4, No. 1, January, 1979, pp. 53–62.

5. Campbell, John P., and Robert Pritchard. "Motivation Theory in Industrial and Organizational Psychology," ed. Marvin D. Dunnette. *Handbook of Industrial and Organizational Psychology*, Chicago: Rand McNally College Publishing Co., 1976, pp. 104–109.

6. Carrell, Michael R., and John E. Dittrich. "Equity Theory: The Recent Literature, Methodological Considerations, and New Directions," *Academy of Management Review*, Vol. 3, No. 2, April, 1978, pp. 202–210.

7. Lawler, E. E. III. *Pay and Organization Development*. Reading, Mass.: Addison-Wesley Publishing Co., 1981.

8. Baker, John C. "Are Executives Overpaid? Readers Respond," *Harvard Business Review*, Vol. 56, No. 4, July-August, 1978, pp. 54–66.

9. Steinbrink, John P. "How to Pay Your Sales Force," *Harvard Business Review*, Vol. 56, No. 4, July-August, 1978, pp. 111–122.

10. Vroom, V. H. *Work and Motivation*. New York: John Wiley & Sons, Inc., 1964.

11. Porter, L. W., and E. E. Lawler III. *Managerial Attitudes and Performance*. Homewood, Ill.: Richard D. Irwin, Inc., 1968.

12. London, Perry. "The End of Ideology in Behavior Modification," *American Psychologist*, Vol. 27, 1972, pp. 913–920.

13. Schneier, Craig E. "Behavior Modification in Management: A Review and Critique," *Academy of Management Journal*, Vol. 17, No. 3, 1974, pp. 528–548.

14. Hamner, Clay W. "Reinforcement Theory and Contingency Management in Organizational Settings," eds. H. L. Tosi and C. W. Hamner. *Organizational Behavior and Management: A Contingency Approach*, Chicago: St. Clair Press, 1974.

15. Wiard, Harry. "Why Manage Behavior: A Case for Positive Reinforcement," *Human Resources Management*, Vol. 2, No. 2, 1972, pp. 15–20.

16. Babb, Harold W., and D. G. Kopp. "Applications of Behavior Modification in Organizations: A Review and Critique," *Academy of Management Review*, Vol. 3, No. 2, April, 1978, pp. 281–292.

SUGGESTED READINGS

Andrews, I. R. "Wage Inequity and Job Performance," *Journal of Applied Psychology*, January, 1967, pp. 39–45.

Campbell, John P., and Robert D. Prichard. "Motivation Theory in Industrial Organizational Psychology," ed. Marvin D. Dunnette. *Handbook of Industrial and Organizational Psychology*, Skokie, Ill.: Rand McNally & Company, 1976, p. 64.

Dyer, Lee, and D. S. Schwab. "Personnel/Human Resource Management Research," eds. Thomas A. Kochan, D. J. B. Mitchell, and Lee Dyer. *Industrial Research in the 1970s: Review and Appraisal*, Madison, Wis.: Industrial Relations Research Association, pp. 187–220.

Goodman, Paul S. "Social Comparison Processes in Organizations," eds. Barry M. Staw, and Gerald R. Salancik. *New Directions in Organizational Behavior*, Chicago: St. Clair Press, 1979, pp. 97–132.

Hamner, Clay W., and Ellen P. Hamner. "Behavior Modification on the Bottom Line," *Organizational Dynamics*, Spring, 1976, pp. 2–21.

House, Robert J., H. Jack Shapiro, and Mahmoud A. Wahba. "Expectancy Theory as a Predictor of Work Behavior and Attitude: A Reevaluation of Empirical Evidence," *Decision Sciences*, December, 1974, pp. 54–77.

Kerr, Steven. "On the Folly of Rewarding A, While Hoping for B," *Academy of Management Journal*, Vol. 18, No. 4, August, 1975, pp. 769–783.

Lawler, Edward E. III. *Motivation in Work Organizations*. Monterey, Calif.: Brooks/Cole Publishing Company, 1973.

Lawler, Edward E. III. *Pay and Organizational Development*. Reading, Mass.: Addison-Wesley Publishing Co., 1981.

Matsui, Tamao, and Toshitake Terai. "A Cross-Cultural Study of the Validity of the Expectancy Theory of Work Motivation," *Journal of Applied Psychology*, April, 1975, pp. 263–265.

Mitchell, Terence R. "Motivation: New Directions for Theory, Research, and Practice," *Academy of Management Review*, Vol. 7, No. 1, 1982, pp. 80–88.

Stahl, M., and A. Harrell. "Modeling Effort Decisions with Behavioral Decision Theory: Toward an Individual Differences Model of Expectancy Theory," *Organizational Behavior and Human Performance*, Vol. 27, 1981, pp. 303–325.

GROUPS AND INTERPERSONAL INFLUENCE

Classical writers on management theory and practice did not understand the dynamics of informal groups. From their perspective management always dealt with individuals. That was a gross oversimplification, of course, and one that often led managers to underestimate group influence on employee behavior. Drawing on insights that began to emerge during the human relations era, Chapter 6 discusses the nature of informal groups and their relationship to management. Through its discussion of individual motivation for participating in groups, the leadership of informal groups, group cohesiveness, and group norms and controls, Chapter 6 provides a background one needs to understand groups of all sorts.

Chapter 7 is concerned with disadvantaged groups in organizations, particularly minorities, women, retired and elderly people, and persons with emotional problems. In recent years minorities and women have organized formal groups to promote their interests, greatly increasing their power and influence. In addition they often form highly cohesive informal groups and relate powerfully to other power blocks that pose a threat to their organizational success. Employees approaching retirement are less likely than minorities and women to form cohesive groups, but as their numbers swell they collectively constitute an increasingly powerful influence on organizational life. Although persons with emotional problems are not inclined toward cohesive group activity, they also exert a growing influence on organizational behavior.

Chapter 8 is about unions—why and how they develop, their tactics for gaining and maintaining power, and their relationships with management. Recently unions have fallen on hard times, contrary to the impression sometimes given by their awesome power acts. Nevertheless, they strongly influence organizational behavior in both unionized companies and those that are trying to avoid unionization.

Chapter 9 deals with the conflict that develops among groups and individuals—conflict that creates both beneficial and destructive stress. Conflict and stress play a positive role in preventing lethargy, stimulating excitement, and maintaining a vigorous and challenging organizational climate. Excessive conflict and stress can, of course, drive employees into defensive, self-serving, ego-enhancing groups, increasing employee turnover, decreasing efficient movement toward organizational objectives, and causing problems of physical and emotional health.

6

The Dynamics of Informal Groups

From birth onward, people need other people. Not only must we depend on others for survival, but within the context of that dependency we identify with others, imitate their behavior, draw upon their strengths, internalize their attitudes, and use feedback from them to evaluate our own adequacy. We are all in varying degrees creations of society. It is not surprising, therefore, that employees exhibit an irresistible urge to seek the supportive relationships of groups, and that the great majority of employees belong to one or more informal groups at their place of work.

For reasons that we will discuss in this chapter, informal groups are prevalent in the workplace and have a tremendous influence over the behavior of employees. Managers who do not recognize this fact are destined to have less influence over the performance of their subordinates and to have generally poor personal relationships with their co-workers. This chapter will help you to understand how informal groups function and, as a consequence, will put you in a better position to deal with this extremely important aspect of organizational life.

Classical management theory had no place for informal groups—for any spontaneous, unplanned, and unpredictable activity within the formal organization. It did not deny the existence of informal groups; they were just irrelevant. There was no need for them in an impersonal, scientifically structured organization. That omission is understandable in view of the fact that during the early decades of this century, when most of the classical views were formulated, behavioral scientists were still discussing the *group mind* and the *herd instinct*—concepts that contributed nothing to an understanding of informal group behavior. The Hawthorne studies, published and widely discussed throughout the 1930s, marked a turning point in management's awareness of the role informal groups play in organizations. These and subsequent studies on groups left no doubt about the importance of group dynamics and the social nature of workers.

In contrast, later researchers and scholars were deeply impressed with the small, informal groups or subcultures that spontaneously emerge among the members of formal organizations. Such groups do not appear on organizational charts, but they strongly influence organizational effectiveness. They have their own leaders, more or less definable memberships, and powerful means of controlling members' behavior—not always for the good of the formal organization.

Although these spontaneously emerging groups are most often referred to as **informal groups**, they are also called *primary groups, informal organizations*, and *shadow organizations*. Whatever they are called, stating that a collection of individuals constitutes a **group** implies that members have developed interdependencies; to some degree they identify with one another, influence one another's behavior, and contribute to mutual need satisfaction. Because the combined resources and power of group members greatly exceed the sum of their individual resources and power, informal groups exert a strong influence on organizational life. For this reason managers should encourage the positive aspects of informal groups and, whenever possible, work to channel this influence into the organization. The chapter's objectives are

TO UNDERSTAND:

1. How informal groups develop
2. The nature of informal group leadership
3. How informal groups influence and control employee behavior
4. How informal groups relate to formal organizations

THE NATURE OF INFORMAL GROUPS

> Informal groups develop in order to meet a variety of individual needs that are not met by the formal organization. Their presence is not, however, an indication that the formal organization is inadequate or deficient since informal groups exist in all organizations.

Most of us belong to several groups. This is equally true of the employed and unemployed. Outside our work, families constitute a major type of informal group. Some family groups are small and loosely held together. Others are large and clannish, sometimes including distant relatives who are, nevertheless, quite close psychologically. Sharing a common name, ancestry, and values provides a bond that is far stronger than the lines of formal organization. Most common are the many family groups held together by bonds of love, religion, and mutual dependency.

Other informal groups are based on common interests such as bridge, golf, drama, music, running, yoga, aviation, gardening, or intellectual pursuits. Friendship groups have sometimes developed among neighbors who would have had little in common had not the location of their homes or apartments brought them together. As we shall see, family groups, social groups, and friendship groups have much in common with the informal groups found in work situations.

Autonomy Within Structure

A formal organization structures the behavior of its members. They enter the organization with a wide diversity of interests, goals, attitudes, and other personal attributes that would lead to utter chaos if no behavioral guidelines were provided. Accordingly, an organization provides job descriptions, goals, policies, and procedures to structure member activities. These reduce individual autonomy and promote purposeful, cooperative behavior.

In spite of the structure provided by formal organizations, much discretion is left to the individual. Even a detailed job description leaves undefined much of an employee's life within the organization. New employees are immediately presented with subtle clues and direct communication about differences between the picture presented by management and the way organizational life really is. The informal communication process itself is one of the major undefined areas of organizational behavior, and yet without it many organizations could not function. It provides a source of coordination that is vital to the smooth functioning of an organization.

Informal groups among blue-collar personnel are sometimes viewed as relatively autonomous subcultures that are often alien to the decorum expected of white-collar employees. For example, the hazing of lower status employees and the practical jokes and prankish physical contact that are sometimes characteristic of the blue-collar culture are often taboo in the white-collar culture.

The freedom of action that permits the development of informal groups may have both positive and negative consequences for an organization. On the positive side, it allows employees to express their individuality, to be known and accepted by others for the unique persons they are, and to find a degree of freedom from the routine that may characterize their work. However, when the organization is perceived as the enemy, the autonomy becomes destructive, and the sometimes awesome power of informal groups is used to undermine the achievement of formal goals.

Informal Groups and Upward Mobility Patterns

The nature of informal groups, at either the employee or the management level, is influenced by the upward mobility patterns within an organization.[1] Different types of groups are likely to develop under conditions of (1) promotion on the basis of merit, (2) promotion on the basis of seniority, and (3) no possibilities for promotion.

The most significant factor in each of these three conditions is the **reference groups** whose standards are used to evaluate one's own attitudes, abilities, and performance. Employees who perceive themselves as having a good chance of being promoted into the supervisory ranks, like managers who anticipate a series of promotions, are more sensitive to the attitudes and opinions of their immediate superiors than are employees who see little possibility for upward mobility. Upwardly mobile managers are more likely to be in competition with their peers than in collusion with them.

Where promotion opportunities are nonexistent or promotions are based primarily on seniority, competition between peers is minimized and identification with peers is high. Close friendships can develop under these circumstances; and since promotions are not related to performance, the need to make a favorable impression on one's superiors is minimal.

Where no upward mobility is possible, employees are motivated to form groups that often conflict with the needs and goals of the organization. Since there is no motivation toward promotion, the group's responsiveness to superiors is low. Group pressures may be strong to "make progress" by such devices as restricting production, increasing power, and resisting upward movement of lower status groups.

Groups with no promotion opportunities often focus their attention on social rewards as though the work were merely a necessary evil, unworthy of serious emotional involvement. This defensive reaction makes the routine and relative meaninglessness of a job more acceptable psychologically. Group attention is focused on important personal interests such as sports, hobbies, family, and other concerns unrelated to work.

Need Satisfaction in Informal Groups

Because individual needs vary greatly and are satisfied in unique ways, it is not possible to list all the human needs that are satisfied at least to some degree in informal groups. However, research has identified a number of areas where informal groups meet the needs of their members.

Companionship. Group affiliation provides an opportunity for close association with others which in itself is a source of satisfaction. It enables an individual to avoid the pain of loneliness and the ego-crushing experience of rejection. Group affiliation also gives one a sense of belonging—of being a person rather than a number or an article of commerce.

Reassurance and Support. There is power in numbers. Just knowing that one other person is supportive may give an individual the courage to express a conviction or take a stand on an important issue. The support of a unified group often serves to greatly reduce fear, anxiety, and apprehensiveness. The group often provides the self-confidence an employee or manager needs to face challenging work situations. Without support, the organizational environment can be unbearably frustrating and threatening.

Reduction of Tension. This is, of course, closely related to reassurance and support, but it is not identical. Informal groups often contribute to a reduction of internal tension through humor and horseplay that prevent members from taking themselves and their work too seriously. Tension is also reduced through **catharsis**, the process by which merely talking about a problem or source of irritation makes one feel better. Catharsis takes place, for example, when an employee who is hostile toward a superior finds emotional release by talking to a peer. When repressed, hostile feelings may accumulate and result in irrational behavior over which one has little control.

Sense of Identity. A group gives its members a sense of personal identity—a sense of being somebody. The size and impersonal quality of formal organizations often give rise to the feeling that personal identity is lost. If, however, one feels a strong identity with an informal group, personal identity is maintained even within the context of a large organization. It is especially ego enhancing to be identified with a high prestige group—for example, a group recognized for high productivity, possession of unusual skills, or power to deal effectively with management.

Improved Communications. Informal groups are sometimes developed around a person who has access to information that contributes to group security. Secretive managers keep subordinates ignorant concerning actions that affect their welfare and may thereby invite formation of informal groups to fill the void.

Reduction of Boredom. The point was made in an earlier chapter that routine work is not necessarily boring work. Interest or boredom depends on the individual and the work situation. In many work groups, boredom is minimized by group interaction. Most of us have had experiences in which doing nothing—waiting for a plane, for instance—was far from boring because of the opportunity it provided us to be with someone with whom we have an emotional bond or common interest. When an assembly of individuals becomes a group, just being together, especially where conversation is possible, becomes an end in itself. As long as the work does not seriously interfere with group interaction the likelihood that it will be perceived as boring is minimal.

INFORMAL GROUP LEADERSHIP

Informal group leaders emerge in response to the needs of the group, and their leadership is accepted because of the contribution they make to the achievement of group goals.

Informal group leaders are not appointed or elected as they are in formal organizations. In fact, group members may not be fully aware that leader-follower relationships exist. In some cases an informal leader emerges spontaneously, depending on the needs of the moment, and when the specific needs are satisfied the leader may again become indistinguishable from other group members. Because leadership needs change, the most appropriate leader in one situation may be unqualified to lead in another.

We will now examine some of the major roles played by informal group leaders. Although one person may play all the different roles, it is probable that leadership will be rotated among the membership.

The Representative to Management

The individual who serves as a representative to management is ordinarily talented in two important areas: courage and communication skills. The role may be played by the diplomat who enjoys good relations with management or by an aggressive, power-oriented type who simply is unconcerned about being liked by management. The former is often viewed by management as having potential for a supervisory position. The latter may become a union steward or in the absence of union protection may find it necessary to change employment frequently.

The Technical Expert

Individuals with expertise (an unusually high level of knowledge or skill) are particularly influential in groups whose work is somewhat technical and involves problem solving. Mechanics, electricians, and plumbers, as well as engineers, research scientists, and accountants are often in need of expert leadership. An individual with little potential to be either a representative to management or a supervisor may play this role. It requires a minimum of courage, leadership ability, or human relations skills.

The Information Source

Certain individuals are looked to for leadership because they are well informed about matters relating to the well-being of the group. They may have access to inside information through friends or relatives within the company; or they may be avid readers of outside publications that provide insights into trends within the industry and/or a specific organization (such as plant closings, anticipated expansions, acquisitions, or development of new product lines).

The Enforcer

At times members refuse to conform to group norms and must be disciplined. This may require gentle persuasion of a verbal nature or the use of force. Whether the use of force would be considered would depend on the nature of the group and the degree of nonconformance. At any rate, certain group members are better prepared to play this role than others and thus emerge at their own initiative or at the urging of the group to assume the leadership role needed on such an occasion. Some of the techniques used are discussed in the next major section of this chapter. Although this role may not always be a pleasant one—for certain people it would be extremely unpleasant—it can be rewarding. The leader in this situation is recognized as having certain talents and is thereby accorded a position of prestige within the group.

The Tension Reducer

Sometimes this person is a comic whose puns lighten the conversation or whose jokes are always new to the group. At other times the tension reducer is a philosopher or human relations expert who helps the group interpret situations in such a way that tension is minimized. The role sometimes calls for a compromiser who can take opposing points of view held by group members and make them compatible. This can be an important leadership function, especially if friction between members threatens to destroy the group or reduce its effectiveness. In a large apparel company, one manager's career was greatly enhanced by her skill in reducing conflict among her fellow managers. On one occasion she received a promotion solely because no one else could relate without conflict to a majority of the managers to be supervised in the new position.

The Crisis Manager

Groups are sometimes threatened from without—for example, by organizational plans that require higher production standards, new job skills, or mass layoffs. In such cases the group leader who emerges may or may not be the type of individual who assumes leadership under normal circumstances. Perhaps the role calls for a bright tactical strategist, an individual with insight into the thinking of management, or an individual who is able to persuade the group to accept the inevitable without taking action that would cause irreparable damage to the group.

As implied earlier, it is possible for an informal group to have a single leader, but this would be unusual. Because of dominant personality characteristics or unusual charisma, group members may perceive a specific individual to be the leader of the group. Even under these circumstances, however, other members may lead on specific occasions.

Implications for Management

Much of what is known about informal group leadership can serve as a model for managers who aspire to become outstanding leaders. Without attempting to eliminate informal groups, it makes sense for supervisors to behave in such a way that strong, informal leadership is unnecessary.

First line supervisors should realize that on occasions they must represent subordinates who feel oppressed by the actions or policies of higher managers. Depending on the human relations skills of a supervisor, playing the role of an advocate for subordinates may involve a high level of risk. If subordinates have a legitimate complaint, however, such action is called for. It should be noted that risk is also involved in abdicating this role and leaving it to an informal leader.

First line supervisors are in a strategic position to provide subordinates with information. Yet many supervisors, following the lead of their superiors, keep employees ignorant as to what is going on in the organization. Management sometimes provides so little information about job performance that a new employee must depend on peers to learn job duties during the first few days of employment. It is difficult to over-emphasize the critical nature of the first week on the job.

Management should invest heavily in orienting the new employee to the physical and psychological environment and to the work itself. Many organizations have elaborate induction training programs that relieve the first line supervisor of much of the burden of getting new employees oriented favorably toward the organization. In fact, some induction programs provide a psychological and biographical profile of supervisors to give new employees the feeling that they know their supervisors personally. Such programs reflect an awareness of the needs of employees and demonstrate management's concern for satisfying those needs. It is only by doing so that managers can lead in the best sense of the word and reduce the individual employee's excessive dependency on peer groups.

CONTROLS IN INFORMAL GROUPS

Three important, interrelated characteristics of informal groups are their inclination to establish standards of acceptable member behavior, their ability to detect deviations from such standards, and their power to demand conformity to them. So effective is the control of a group over its membership that it often renders the power of management ineffective.

All cultures have norms or standards with which members are expected to comply and against which the behavior of members is evaluated. These behavioral expectations are expressed in a variety of forms, such as mores, religious values, ethical standards, rules of etiquette and decorum, laws, policies, and procedures. They necessarily relate to only a small segment of the range of possible behaviors, but within a given subculture such standards define the rules for belonging. They specify the behaviors that are relevant to group survival and enhancement and leave other possible behaviors to the discretion of the individual or the guidelines of some other group of which that individual is a member.

Group Norms

In informal groups these behavior expectations are called **norms**. More than any other aspect of group life they serve to define the nature of the group. They express the collective values of its membership and provide guidelines that ensure the successful achievement of its goals, as shown in the following examples.

Group A consists of 15 employees who work in a chemical plant. The nature of their jobs provides little chance for promotion. They rotate over three shifts and are primarily involved in loading ships with pelletized fertilizer. The following norms are of central importance to this group:

1. One employee shall not exert so much effort that other employees appear to be unproductive by comparison.

2. When an employee is unable to perform well, because of a hangover or fatigue, others will cover for that individual; however, abuse of the sick-day privilege will not be tolerated.

3. Employees will not discuss with management anything derogatory about another group member.

4. Employees will not express favorable attitudes toward management and the company in general.

The norms of Group A stand in stark contrast to those of Group B. Group B consists of 11 people in an information processing center of the same plant in which the Group A employees work. Each looks forward to promotion into a higher position. Promotion decisions are usually made on the combined basis of seniority, competence, and ability to adopt a managerial perspective. Group B reflects a need for nondestructive internal competition. The following are among its most obvious norms:

1. Taking the initiative with executives in order to be selected is taboo.

2. It is never permissible to make remarks or stimulate rumors that may interfere with a peer's promotion, even though the remarks or rumors are true.

3. Poor productivity and poor quality work from anyone capable of high performance is unacceptable, since it reflects negatively on the group.

4. An employee does not recommend friends or acquaintances to fill vacancies unless they fit the model required to maintain the favorable image the group enjoys.

The norms of informal groups tend to evolve as the collection of individuals becomes a group.[2] They are not always rational or functional since they may be perpetuated by habit and tradition long after their usefulness has passed. As a result of past labor strife, for example, group members sometimes maintain norms against communicating freely with management even though such communication could allay fears, remove distrust, and provide a cooperative spirit of mutual benefit.

How Norms Are Communicated

The communication systems that operate within informal groups are most impressive. Employees with previous work experience have some insight into norms typically held by groups in their type of work and geographic area. Nevertheless, norms vary somewhat from one situation to another, and new employees are therefore sensitive to cues concerning acceptable and unacceptable behavior. The normal insecurity experienced by new employees provides high motivation for mapping the environment; that is, making rapid and sensitive observations that will serve as a sound basis for behavior.

New employees are typically given help in detecting group norms. Conversations are staged—half consciously in many cases—to educate the new employee, and fellow employees volunteer advice about appropriate behavior. If the new employee conforms to the norms, acceptance into the group tends to follow. If the employee does not conform, warnings are often given. If information and warnings fail to get conformity, a group member may directly challenge the new employee's deviant behavior.

Modifying Deviant Behavior

Not all norms are equally important to a group. For example, inappropriate dress may not elicit the same response as passing along inside information to management or exceeding a work quota. Groups tend to have **crucial norms** which, when violated, threaten the survival or well-being of the group and **peripheral norms** that are viewed as less important. In other words there are felony and misdemeanor violations from a group perspective. The penalty to be paid usually corresponds to the seriousness of the offense.

A number of possible actions can be taken by a group to reduce or eliminate nonconforming behavior:

1. *Unfriendliness or the cold shoulder treatment.* This is strong enough action to get results with sensitive individuals who have a strong need for acceptance. Others, however, will not even be aware of it.

2. *Verbal expressions of hostility and criticism.* This approach leaves no doubt about the feelings of the group. It may or may not get the results desired.

3. *Ridicule.* This may involve assigning the offender an undesirable nickname and/or continually making the offender the butt of jokes and pranks.

4. *Spreading unflattering gossip about the offender.* This can be a very damaging type of aggression—strong enough to cause the offender to be discharged or to resign.

5. *Harassment.* This may take many forms: The offender's time card may be punched early and then placed behind another card where it cannot be easily found; or the individual's lunch box may be hidden. On one occasion, a pair of expensive calipers was placed in an employee's lunch box, and the plant guards were notified of the theft.

6. *Disruption of work.* Even where an employee works in relative independence of others, it is possible for peers to interfere with the offender's productivity. Defective raw materials or tools may be selectively issued to the offender; misleading information may be supplied; reports are sometimes lost or held up; or the individual's schedule might be disrupted by forced waiting periods or the deliberate mistakes of others. The last two examples have been observed at the management level. One tactic, where inspectors collude with production workers, is the practice of switching product identification so that substandard production is attributed to the offender. It is difficult for a worker to succeed against these odds.

7. *Overt intimidation and threats.* The offender becomes the object of painful physical hazing with the stated or implied threat that it could become even more serious. This threat may be veiled as humor or harmless horseplay, but the message is clearly communicated. At times the message is more strongly emphasized through destruction of the offender's property such as a slashed tire or seat cover, a dented fender, or a scratch on a new paint job. In some circumstances the offender's children are intimidated by the children of the other employees. This adds a vicious dimension to the pressure of the group.

8. *Physical violence.* Violent events are often associated with attempts to unionize a plant or with strikebreaking by management, although the motivation for such actions is usually fomented in informal groups rather than formal organizations. Again, the theme is the same: Individuals are punished for refusal to conform to crucial group norms. Antiquated and immoral as such tactics may appear, they are, nevertheless, still in vogue. For example, in recent memory strikebreakers have been ambushed and killed, labor leaders murdered, and nonstrikers threatened and assaulted.

Naturally, the degree to which the group will inflict punishment on a nonconformist depends on the personal values of the group members; certainly not all groups would consider violence as a solution to nonconformist behavior. The emphasis here has been upon punishment as a means of enforcing group norms. Positive reinforcement is, of course, also used. Individuals who comply with group norms are rewarded by being accepted, protected, and provided with a high degree of support in meeting the demands of the formal organization. The combined positive and negative reinforcements are sufficient to gain the conformity of most employees in a work group.

Group Influence on Attitudes, Beliefs, and Perceptions

Where group pressures for conformity are strong, group members are highly motivated to remove the dissonance between what they feel and believe and the way they are required to behave. For example, employees who have high potential for rapid promotion but are compelled to support a seniority-based promotion policy are placed in a psychologically untenable position. On the one hand, they know that their best interests are served by freedom to compete and earn promotions. On the other hand, they know that group structure makes this course of action impossible. A common way of dealing with the conflict is through rationalization.

The rationalization process gets abundant support from the group, since much of the employee's information is filtered through the attitudes and biases of the group and since expression of contrary attitudes brings immediate condemnation. Psychology has in recent years made the point that behavioral changes lead to attitude changes in order to bring about a consistency between the two.[3] Informal groups are masterful at changing both, and their members develop perceptual filters which admit into consciousness only selected "facts" that reinforce existing attitudes and beliefs.

GROUP COHESIVENESS

Informal groups differ greatly in their ability to agree upon goals, maintain control over members, and achieve long-term objectives. The single, most important contribution to group effectiveness is group cohesiveness.

Cohesiveness is defined as unity of purpose and action. It is an expression of the degree to which group members are committed to common goals, to a set of norms for the guidance of behavior, and to one another as individuals. As a group's cohesiveness increases, its members assume increased responsibility for results. Individuals who are low in motivation become more highly motivated when placed in situations fostering group motivation for success.[4] Whether this motivation will benefit the organization depends, of course, on the group's orientation toward the formal organization. Group success may be defined in terms of high productivity or effectiveness in restricting productivity, depending on the predominant attitudes, beliefs, and perceptions of the group.

Determinants of Cohesiveness

Cohesiveness is determined by a number of factors. Because these factors interact with one another and with many aspects of the formal organization, their isolation for analysis is naturally somewhat incomplete. Nevertheless, it is practical to abstract a few causes of group cohesiveness. Nine of these are especially important.

1. Homogeneity

2. Group size

3. Opportunities to communicate

4. Group isolation

5. External threat

6. Group success

7. Individual mobility

8. Membership in other groups

9. Availability of effective leadership

Homogeneity. The homogeneity of a group depends on the similarity of member characteristics and interests. For example, a group of individuals with the same racial or ethnic background and the same socioeconomic status is likely to be more cohesive than a group whose members differ widely in these characteristics.

Cohesiveness is increased most when the common attributes of group members are particularly relevant to group purposes and goals. Thus, in a work group whose primary goal is improving the economic status of its members, a common need for more money may contribute more to group unity than would a similarity in sex, race, religion, or type of work.

Several studies support the general hypothesis that homogeneous groups have a higher degree of both job satisfaction and cohesiveness. On the other hand, homogeneous groups are less effective in problem solving than are those with greater diversity of membership.[5] Thus, group homogeneity is a mixed blessing for the group and for the formal organization of which it is a part.

Group Size. Everything else being equal, small groups are more likely to be cohesive than are large ones. The larger a group becomes, the more heterogeneous are its members, and the fewer common views they hold. As in the case of formal organizations, large groups become impersonal. When it is difficult for members to know one another well, large groups tend to break up and produce small, homogeneous groups. Group members are attracted to others with similar interests, attitudes, values, and abilities, and this interpersonal attraction is strongest among a very few individuals who know one another well.

Opportunities to Communicate. Groups in which members can communicate freely are apt to be more cohesive than groups in situations where face-to-face communication is difficult. For example, sewing machine operators endure a high noise level and have a requirement for intense concentration in their jobs; these factors minimize conversation except during break periods. In many factories noise levels are so high that they cause hearing damage. These situations contrast with offices where employees are physically close to one another in a quiet environment performing work requiring personal interaction. When employees are required to converse in order to do their work, they are ordinarily free to discuss the personal matters that increase cohesiveness.

Group Isolation. The conditions just discussed show how an environmental situation may decrease cohesiveness by isolating group members from one another. In contrast, isolation of one group from other groups increases internal cohesiveness. This effect is demonstrated by a situation where a company moved into a new building designed for closer personal relationships. In the old building, most white-collar employees worked in one large room. Because there were no partitions to delineate the different departments, departmental identification was weak, and loosely structured informal groups cut across departmental lines. As soon as the departments were separated, cohesive cliques began to form along departmental lines. This proved to be a mixed blessing. Morale and intradepartmental teamwork improved, but conflict among departments increased.

External Threat. Members of a threatened group typically band together for survival. A classic example of this on an international level occurred in the 1950s and 1960s when the leaders of Communist China unified a country that for centuries had been ruled by provincial warlords. Their primary tactic was to convince the citizens that the country was in imminent danger of attack by the United States. More recently the same strategy has been used in China with Russia cast in the role of the enemy.

Within business organizations management is often perceived as a source of threat to nonmanagement workers. In industries, specific companies, or geographic localities with a history of labor-management conflict, a pervasive spirit of distrust and group paranoia make it easy to interpret a wide range of management behaviors as threatening. The filtering process through which group leaders interpret and screen management communications is often designed to maintain the perception of external threat and consequently to maintain a high degree of group cohesiveness.

Group Success. Since everyone likes to be identified with a winner, group success contributes to cohesiveness. When group members perceive a group to be unusually successful, they take pride in it, draw personal strength from its power and status, and go to great lengths to maintain the group's prestige. When the prestige results from management's recognition of high productivity, outstanding product quality, a low accident rate, or other behavior valued by the organization, this success-based cohesion serves to increase productivity motivation. Unfortunately group success may also be defined in terms of behavior that is detrimental to the organization, such as restricting production, reducing the effective authority of a supervisor, or breaking rules.

Individual Mobility. Where employee turnover is high because of resignations, discharges, transfers, or promotions, group cohesiveness is difficult to maintain. Leadership and membership roles are difficult to establish, and the impact of new members prevents the crystallization of group norms. Without a relatively stable membership and identifiable norms, what might normally be a close group is little more than a collection of psychologically isolated individuals.

Membership in Other Groups. Membership in several groups reduces the influence or control that any single group is able to exert on an individual. The most cohesive and effective work groups are composed of members for whom the group occupies a central life position. They value the group's goals and have a strong, sometimes narrow commitment to their group's achievements. The following individuals illustrate this point.

> Following in his father's footsteps, Mason Clark has worked on a General Motors Corp. assembly line all his adult life and cannot imagine doing anything else. He has few social contacts outside work and spends most of his leisure time gardening, working in his shop, and watching television. He is married, and his one child, age 21, is no longer living at home. He is a member of no organizations other than the United Auto Workers union, and his greatest ambition is to save enough money to take an early retirement. Although his work is routine and not especially challenging, it is Mason's one major contact with people, and he identifies strongly with the union and a small group of workers with whom he has been associated for several years.
>
> In contrast, Judy Akira is an engineer who has been employed by Texas Instruments Incorporated (TI) for five years. Although she identifies with TI and her local work group, she thinks of herself first of all as an engineer and only secondarily as an engineer working for TI. She has deep commitments to her large family, with whom she spends a great deal of time. She is active in her church; she coaches a Little League baseball team and is on a local boy's club board of directors. She has broad interests and takes pride in the fact that she has taken a number of correspondence and evening courses in electronics, mathematics, and other subjects related to her field. She perceives herself to be a professional and enjoys associating with fellow engineers in local, state, and national associations. Judy is enthusiastic about the many groups with which she is associated, but she is not controlled by any of them.

College-educated, white-collar employees often have more group contacts than do blue-collar employees. For this reason they may be less likely than blue-collar employees to develop deep commitments to informal groups in the work situation. White-collar employees also tend to be more competitive with one another and to identify more readily with the goals and norms of the formal organization.

Availability of Effective Leadership. On many occasions a group is unified primarily by the impact of a dominant, charismatic personality. Although groups are typically led by different members at different times, one member may be so outstanding that practically all members identify with that individual. To a significant degree, the cement that provides group solidarity in such a situation is the one person rather than a network of interdependencies. In other situations potential leaders influence members in different directions and none is capable of unifying the factions.

Dealing With Hostile Groups

Factors affecting group cohesiveness have practical applications when dealing with groups that are hostile to management. On some occasions management must reduce the solidarity of a group that opposes a managerial policy. The first step is usually to determine why the group opposes rather than supports this policy. It may be that management should deal directly with some underlying problems rather than treat symptoms by attempting to reduce the power of an informal group.

Even after management has done everything possible to eliminate the causes of group hostility, the remaining negative attitudes may still justify steps to reduce the group's effectiveness. Such action should be carried out as unobtrusively as possible to prevent further group solidification in response to the external threat. How can this be done? The answers may be found by reviewing the factors that make for cohesiveness. One or several of the following actions may be appropriate, although such actions may be costly both in terms of money and morale:

1. Increase the rate of turnover within the group through transfers, layoffs, or whatever means are feasible.

2. Remove undesirable leaders and transfer into the department employees known to be capable of influencing the group in a positive way. (One large organization has found that individuals who are misplaced in a work group because they are overqualified are a nuisance at the employee level but perform admirably in supervisory, inspection, and other skill-based positions.)

3. Modify the physical environment to reduce the level of interaction among group members and/or to dilute group solidarity by increasing member interaction with other groups.

4. Train first line supervisors in leadership techniques, increase communication from management, improve the organization's motiva-

tional systems, handle employee grievances as early as possible, and take other constructive steps to reduce threats to the group and to encourage individual employees to identify with the formal organization.

Hostile groups do not develop without cause. Unless the cause is discovered and rationally treated, management's efforts to cope with group hostility will probably fail. Unfortunately managers are sometimes so hostile and defensive themselves that they are blinded to the possibility that the group hostility may have arisen from their own actions. In diagnosing such problems it helps to determine whether hostile feelings are widespread or are restricted to a local plant, department, work shift, or to the subordinates of one manager. Consideration should also be given to what changes may have occurred prior to the development of the hostility and to whether the hostility may be a result of industry-wide problems such as low wages or a long history of labor-management strife.

The presence of hostile work groups is not unusual, and the situation cannot always be corrected. Regardless of whether the groups are within the employee or managerial ranks, success is most likely when management takes a diagnostic approach (using an attitude survey, for example) and then systematically proceeds to solve the underlying problems.

FORMAL-INFORMAL GROUP RELATIONS

Informal groups are not always supportive of the formal organizations, but their development is inevitable and, all things considered, they are a positive force in organizational life.

Managers who have experienced frustration with hostile employee groups sometimes conclude that the ideal situation would be a total elimination of informal groups. Aside from the fact that destruction of informal groups would be impossible, it certainly would be unprofitable. Informal groups sometimes pose serious problems for the organization; they typically prevent the organization from being as rational as it would be without them. But it is precisely at this point that informal groups make their greatest contribution by introducing into the workplace warmth, humanity, and an opportunity for individual expression.

Informal groups provide a source of emotionality and concern that at times stands in stark contrast to the tough-minded personnel decisions that managers are required to make. Given the problems of employee motivation and morale that have resulted from job dilution, many jobs would be intolerable without the psychological support provided by informal groups.

Figure 6-1 shows some of the advantages and disadvantages of informal groups. In some instances similar behaviors are listed on both sides. Some informal groups resist management policies and goals while others actively support them. In fact, a group may resist the leadership of management at one time and actively support it at another. The apparent contradictions are resolved in part by the fact that the positive or negative impact of a group's behavior is contingent upon a large number of variables—for example, management actions or labor-management history—which are inherent in the nature of informal groups.

To maintain their identity and solidarity, groups enforce their norms and thus reduce individual freedom. On the other hand, they provide

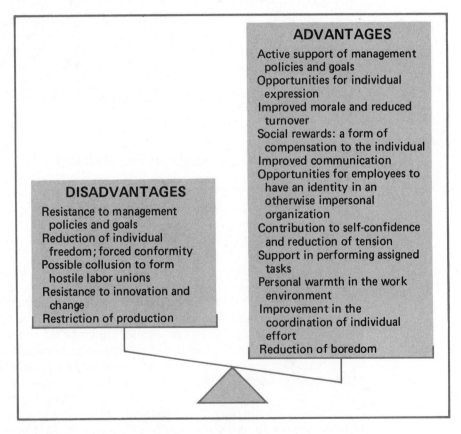

ADVANTAGES

Active support of management policies and goals
Opportunities for individual expression
Improved morale and reduced turnover
Social rewards: a form of compensation to the individual
Improved communication
Opportunities for employees to have an identity in an otherwise impersonal organization
Contribution to self-confidence and reduction of tension
Support in performing assigned tasks
Personal warmth in the work environment
Improvement in the coordination of individual effort
Reduction of boredom

DISADVANTAGES

Resistance to management policies and goals
Reduction of individual freedom; forced conformity
Possible collusion to form hostile labor unions
Resistance to innovation and change
Restriction of production

FIGURE 6-1 The Advantages of Informal Groups Outweigh the Disadvantages

opportunities for individual expression. Both of these conditions may occur in a given group, whether its sentiments and behavior favor or oppose the organization. Both the members of a group and the organization pay a price for the benefits that result from group action. The point of Figure 6-1 is simply that formal organizations benefit from their informal groups.

Formalizing Informal Groups

Hostile employee groups often form the nucleus of labor unions. When a group that opposes management policies and practices develops strong leadership, effectively enforces norms, and demonstrates a high degree of cohesiveness, the next logical step is to organize officially and to form alliances with like-minded groups in other organizations. This step is facilitated by the aggressive organizing tactics of many unions.

Since most managers prefer to deal directly with their employees rather than experience the loss of control that results from dealing with a union intermediary, they sometimes employ aggressive and irrational tactics to suppress informal groups. Although union-management relations are more appropriately the subject of Chapter 8, one word of caution is in order at this point: poorly planned, aggressive attempts to destroy informal groups often increase group hostility and cohesiveness. The best way to deal with such groups is to (1) diagnose and treat the cause of the group's alienation and hostility and (2) unobtrusively employ some of the techniques described earlier for weakening group cohesion. The objective should not be to destroy the group but to have it work for rather than against the organization.

Types of Informal Work Groups in Unionized Organizations

One of the most thorough studies of the nature of informal groups in the work environment was conducted by Leonard Sayles during the mid-1950s. He examined 300 work groups in 30 industrial plants and from his observations developed a classification system based primarily on the relationship of the informal group to the formal organization. The four classifications observed by Sayles are:

1. Apathetic groups

2. Erratic groups

3. Strategic groups

4. Conservative groups[6]

Apathetic Groups. Of all the groups studied, the ones Sayles classified as apathetic are the least likely to express grievances or engage in collective action to influence management or the union. These groups usually consist of relatively low-paid individuals whose work requires a minimum of teamwork. Group cohesion is low, and internal jealousies and bickering are commonplace. Leadership is widely dispersed over several members. Although there is little unity of action, there is much suppressed discontent.

Erratic Groups. The dominant characteristic of this type of group is inconsistency. Although such groups may overlook serious problems for a long period of time, a minor grievance may suddenly trigger a wildcat strike or major protest. Because of their explosiveness and irrationality, erratic groups are generally regarded by management as dangerous to the organization. In spite of their centralized leadership, the pressure tactics of erratic groups tend to be poorly controlled. The jobs of employees in these groups usually require a high degree of interaction. The employees typically do essentially the same kinds of work (assembly work, for example). Relationships with management may change rapidly from excellent to extremely poor and back again.

Strategic Groups. These groups consist of employees at a higher level than those in the two previous groups. Members tend to be union regulars. Their pressure tactics are consistent, highly organized, goal directed, and oriented toward crucial rather than trivial issues. The groups are highly cohesive, and their activities are strictly in the interest of the membership. Their productivity is ordinarily acceptable to management.

Conservative Groups. These groups consist of the most skilled and independent plant employees—machine maintenance crews, for example. Their abilities are in short supply, they are well paid, and their productivity is usually acceptable to management. They seldom act without warning, typically are not union activists, and evidence little internal conflict. Members occupy the enviable position of being able to work elsewhere if management does not comply with their demands. As a result, they are usually treated very well. Because of their independence, they have few grievances. As often as not, it is management that has a grievance to express. Most highly skilled groups value their freedom and autonomy to the point that they sometimes attempt to write their own rules rather than respond graciously to the desires of their superiors.

IMPORTANT TERMS AND CONCEPTS

informal groups	norms
group	crucial norms
reference groups	peripheral norms
catharsis	cohesiveness

STUDY AND DISCUSSION QUESTIONS

1. The statements are made in this chapter that (1) informal groups develop in order to meet a variety of individual needs that are not met by the formal organization and (2) their presence does not indicate that the formal organization is inadequate or deficient. How can both of these statements be true?

2. Why are groups that are composed of employees with no opportunities for promotion more likely to oppose the formal organization than are upwardly mobile employees?

3. In what ways do informal groups contribute to the reduction of tension within individual group members?

4. What problems of communication are involved in labeling certain types of work as boring? How do these relate to informal groups?

5. Why will a group accept the leadership of an individual who has no organizational authority or other formal right to play the leader role?

6. In view of the thoroughness with which a group is able to detect and punish deviations from norms, how can one build a case for the idea that informal groups provide an opportunity for individual expression that is not allowed by formal groups?

7. The point is made that homogeneous groups are less effective in problem solving than are those with greater diversity of membership. What logical explanation would you give for this research finding?

8. When a group is threatened from without, cohesion is often increased as a defensive measure. How should this affect managerial action to decrease the cohesiveness of an antimanagement group?

9. Under what circumstances is it advisable for management to structure the work environment so that the formation of informal groups is encouraged?

10. Why is it inevitable that informal groups will develop in formal organizations?

CRITICAL INCIDENT

THE LONELY SUPERVISOR

During his four years of college, Ed Wagner had been active in the social life of his dormitory and as an officer in the student government association. He planned to build on his social skills and his degree in industrial technology to advance in his chosen career of manufacturing management.

Shortly after graduation, Ed accepted a job offer as a supervisor with Electrical Systems Corporation, a manufacturer of custom-specified electrical switches, controls, and other electrical devices used by aircraft, long-haul trucks, boats, and other products where cheaper standard components were not always suitable. He was particularly attracted to the job because, as he explained to his wife Lynda:

> The production scheduling department, using data from our own experience and a knowledge of our equipment and people, estimates how many days or weeks it will take to produce an order. This serves as a standard. These estimates are within plus or minus 10 percent for nine of every ten orders. I think I'm going to be a good manager, and by beating these forecasts I'll be able to prove that to myself and to upper management.

Ed had two weeks of apprenticeship and on-the-job training during which time he got to know the company's other five production supervisors and many of the people who would later work under him. Then on a Friday afternoon Ed was given a small order to fill. The job was estimated to take 23 workdays from its release to its completion.

Instead of doing the planning for the job on Monday, Ed did it on the weekend. This, and the earnestness and enthusiasm that he conveyed and that his subordinates responded to (although with some chuckling about "helping out this new kid"), caused the order to be completed the fourth Friday after he'd received it which was three days earlier than forecasted. Ed was excited, encouraged, and eager to see how this accomplishment would be received.

On Monday evening, when Lynda returned from her calls as an insurance adjuster, she expected an enthusiastic report. Instead Ed was quiet and thoughtful, and in response to her questions he described the day's events as follows:

> Well, when I got in, I found a note saying that Mr. Mendoza, the production superintendent, wanted to see me. He was really complimentary. Mrs. Jason, the production scheduling manager, was with him, and she was complimentary too, although she kidded me that I was making work for her people since they would have to begin revising the standard times used to estimate production runs.
>
> What I found a bit strange was the reactions of the other five supervisors, especially Pete who is sort of a spokesperson for the supervisors. He was friendly at lunch like he usually is, but he said during a moment of silence when everyone could hear that he hoped Mr. Mendoza wouldn't expect everyone to work on weekends. None of the other supervisors said a thing about the matter; actually they didn't talk much at all. They've been with the company for some years and maybe they don't like my beating the estimate on my first assignment.
>
> The only other comment I heard all day was when I heard Jim, one of my least enthusiastic workers, tell some fellow in the coffee line that the crew hadn't minded helping me get off to a good start, but that they'd agreed that they were going to get back to normal on the next job.

1. What group norms are present in this incident?

2. What informal group leadership roles are present?

3. If some of the work-crew members decided to continue working beyond what had been "normal," what actions do you think the others might take to force them to conform?

4. What actions might Ed take to continue his high level of accomplishment but at the same time maintain an agreeable relationship with the other supervisors?

5. What actions could Mr. Mendoza take to help Ed with this problem?

6. What actions might Ed take to maintain the high level of productivity that his work crew has exhibited?

REFERENCES

1. Tichy, Noel. "An Analysis of Clique Formation and Structure in Organizations," *Administrative Science Quarterly*, Vol. 18, June, 1973, pp. 194–208.

2. Feldman, Daniel C. "The Development and Enforcement of Group Norms," *Academy of Management Review*, Vol. 9, No. 1, January, 1984, pp. 47–53.

3. Schneier, Craig E. "Behavior Modification in Management: A Review and Critique," *Academy of Management Journal*, Vol. 17, No. 3, September, 1974, pp. 528–548.

4. Zander, Alvin F. "Productivity and Group Success: Team Spirit vs. the Individual Achiever," *Psychology Today*, Vol. 8, No. 6, November, 1974, pp. 64–68.

5. Huber, George P. *Managerial Decision Making*. Glenview, Ill.: Scott, Foresman and Company, 1980, pp. 172–173.

6. Sayles, Leonard R. *Behavior of Industrial Work Groups: Prediction and Control*. New York: John Wiley & Sons, Inc., 1958, pp. 7–40.

SUGGESTED READINGS

Cummings, Larry, George P. Huber, and E. Arendt. "The Effects of Size and Spatial Arrangements on Group Decision Making," *Academy of Management Journal*, Vol. 17, No. 3, September, 1974, pp. 460–475.

Cummings, Thomas G. "Self-Regulating Work Groups: A Socio-Technical Synthesis," *Academy of Management Review*, Vol. 3, No. 3, July, 1978, pp. 625–634.

DiMarco, Nicholas. "Life-Style, Work Group Structure, Compatibility, and Job Satisfaction," *Academy of Management Journal*, Vol. 18, No. 2, June, 1975, pp. 313–322.

Heinen, J. Stephen, and Eugene Jacobson. "A Model of Task Group Development in Complex Organizations and a Strategy of Implementation," *Academy of Management Review*, Vol. 1, No. 5, October, 1976, pp. 98–112.

Jackson, J. *Norms and Roles: Studies in Systematic Social Psychology*. New York: Holt, Rinehart & Winston, 1976.

Janis, Irving L. *Victims of Groupthink; A Psychological Study of Foreign-Policy Decisions and Fiascoes*. Boston: Houghton Mifflin Company, 1972.

Meyers, David G., and Helmut Lamm. "The Group Polarization Phenomena," *Psychological Bulletin*, Vol. 83, No. 4, July, 1976, pp. 602–627.

Shaw, Marvin E. *Group Dynamics: The Psychology of Small Group Behavior*, 3rd edition. New York: McGraw-Hill Book Company, 1981.

Varca, Philip E., and Jodie C. Levy. "Individual Differences in Response to Unfavorable Group Feedback," *Organizational Behavior and Human Performance*, Vol. 33, No. 1, February, 1984, pp. 100–111.

Zander, Alvin. "The Psychology of Group Processes," *Annual Review of Psychology*, Vol. 30, 1979, pp. 417–451.

7

Relating to Disadvantaged Groups

> *A woman finds that society has certain preconceived notions about her personality. So-called feminine traits are expected in her regardless of what she is really like, and her job is assigned on the basis, partly, of an imaginary person, not her real self. She is supposed to be* submissive, passive, *and* dependent *in contrast to men who are* assertive, independently responsible, *and* full of initiative. *Women are reputed to be* diligent, *especially at* routines, *rather than* imaginative *like men. They are* selfless and devoted, *rather than* ambitious *like men. They are* sensitive *to the feelings of others rather than cooly* objective, *like men, and their own feelings are also more sensitive than those of* rational, thinking *men. These sex differences in personality are often perceived regardless of actual behavior.*
>
> *The reason for reviewing these beliefs about women is not to discuss whether on the average they are realistic or not. The important point is, rather, that the judgments are made of individuals not on the basis of their own behavior but because of traits rightly or wrongly attributed to the group in which they belong. Even when stereotypes represent real average differences, they are seldom valid bases for judging one individual and their use causes all members of the group to be viewed as coming from the same tight mold.[1]*
>
> *Managers who are less effective in dealing with disadvantaged groups will not be able to obtain full cooperation and performance from some of their employees and associates. Nor will they be fully effective in their dealings with customers, union officials, government officials, or other resource controllers. They will lose out, in the long run, to those managers who are effective in dealing with both advantaged and disadvantaged groups.*

As Jane Torrey indicates in the quotation which opens this chapter, women as a group are at a disadvantage in the workplace. This is true despite the fact that women graduates are sometimes offered higher salaries than men with comparable abilities as companies attempt to remedy the effects of past discrimination. On occasion women are also given preference in promotions for the same reason, but even these apparent advantages sometimes create problems for women. Especially troublesome are problems arising from suspicions that women have been hired or promoted in order to meet government demands and not because of their competence. Thus women, like some other groups discussed in this chapter, continue to be members of a **disadvantaged group**—a group that is to some degree a victim of prejudice and discrimination in the workplace.

Collectively members of disadvantaged groups constitute a majority of the nation's work force. Of the four groups discussed in this chapter—minorities, women, the aging, and the emotionally maladjusted—the first three have special legal protection against discrimination. Although these groups overlap and interact, they are treated as separate groups for purposes of discussion. Difficulties are obviously compounded for persons who are members of more than one disadvantaged group. One way to profit from this chapter is to step into the shoes of disadvantaged persons and try to feel as well as understand the problems they face.

Managers ignore the unique characteristics of disadvantaged groups at their own peril. Group members remain individuals, but they can be best understood by persons who recognize the needs, values, and norms of the groups with which they identify. Nevertheless, as Jane Torrey points out in the introductory quotation, even valid group stereotypes are not a sound basis for judging an individual. The problems presented by disadvantaged groups are important and complex.

In this chapter we look at several aspects of disadvantaged groups that have proved to be important to managers. The chapter objectives are

TO UNDERSTAND:

1. The work implications of prejudice and discrimination

2. Some needs and problems of minority employees

3. The special needs and problems of working women

4. Problems associated with the aging

5. What managers need to know about emotional maladjustment

PREJUDICE AND DISCRIMINATION

Since **discrimination** involves the act of making distinctions and recognizing differences, it is a necessary aspect of managerial decision making. Thus, a manager cannot avoid discriminating but should discriminate on the basis of criteria that are relevant to the achievement of organizational objectives, are fair, and show a respect for human rights.

A serious indictment against management is the lack of employee confidence that its personnel decisions are impartial. The strength of unionism can be traced, in part, to the fact that managerial decisions about personnel often involve prejudice, ignorance, and seeming disregard for rationality, objectivity, and individual rights. At no point did classical theory prove to be more idealistic and naive than in its assumption that managers would make unbiased decisions about people merely because that is the rational thing to do. The insistence of some employee groups upon the seniority rule as a criterion for personnel decisions reflects their lack of confidence in management's ability or willingness not to discriminate on the basis of inappropriate criteria such as race or sex.

Prejudice in Decision Making

To say that a personnel decision shows **prejudice** implies that the decision maker's negative attitudes toward an individual or group results in unfair discrimination. Extensive prejudice against minority groups such as blacks, Hispanics, Catholics, and Jews is common in our society and has been harmful both to individual victims and to society as a whole.

Prejudice is not, of course, the exclusive property of majority groups. Some members of minority groups have developed bitter and hostile feelings because of their perceived unfair treatment at the hands of the majority. There is, for example, intense prejudice among some people toward men, whites, Protestants, Democrats, and other majority groups. Special attention, including legal protection, is given to minorities because of their relative inability to protect themselves against unfair discrimination by a prejudiced and self-serving majority.

Although social and legal constraints often force prejudiced people to control their actions, these external persuaders receive internal support from the values and standards of many decision makers. At times managers with strong prejudices toward particular groups or individuals will bend over backwards to behave consistently with their own values and contrary to their prejudices. Therefore, prejudice does not necessarily result in unfair discrimination.

Legal constraints inhibit unfair discrimination against minority groups, the handicapped, women, and the aging, but unfair discrimination in personnel decisions cannot be controlled primarily by this means. There are so many subtle forms of unfair discrimination that the problem is never completely solved where large numbers of managers are internally motivated by prejudice. The motivation needed to contain discrimination can arise from a variety of sources such as humanistic values, a genuine concern and compassion for people, and/or economic self-interest. Economic self-interest in particular requires that management fully utilize the talents of all people, regardless of their sex, race, age or other attributes, and that management should focus on what disadvantaged people can do rather than on what they cannot do.

Fair and Unfair Discrimination

The term *discrimination* is commonly used to imply unfair discrimination. This tends to obscure the fact that managers must constantly discriminate (differentiate or make distinctions) in their decisions about people. Since discriminating is an integral part of all decision making, it is inevitable that even relatively unprejudiced managers will at times discriminate unfairly. Decisions are never completely objective, standards of acceptable behavior constantly change, and value judgments concerning fairness differ from person to person and within a given person over time. Society has, on several occasions, expressed its values in ways that have resulted in charges that management is unfairly discriminating. An example of this concerns affirmative action programs for hiring and promoting members of disadvantaged groups. In this case, society's need to make restitution for past wrongs is given priority over the long-accepted right of an individual to be evaluated on the basis of qualifications and past performance.

Returning veterans have also received preferential treatment in hiring and promotions, and some companies contract with unions to discriminate in favor of union members when hiring new employees. It is common practice, particularly in unionized companies, to discriminate in favor of employees with seniority, even if this leads to promoting a poorly qualified employee and passing over a better qualified employee. During the recession of the mid-1970s, discriminating on the basis of seniority led to mass layoffs of minority group members. This occurred because in recent years organizations had responded to government pressure to employ and promote an increasing number of minority employees, and the last to be hired were the first to be laid off.

Both government pressures for hiring and promoting members of minority and disadvantaged groups and union pressures for making seniority the main criterion in personnel decisions discourage management support for many of the programs others have devised for eliminating unfair discrimination. Managers are often caught between pressures to hire or promote minority members, even if they are not the best-qualified candidates, and the need to maintain a competitive position in the marketplace. What appears as indifference to the need to achieve balances in the work force may simply be management's quest for survival. For a business to survive, its managers must place a high value on efficiency and productivity as well as individual needs. This is not a justification for unfair discrimination, but it is a partial explanation for its occurrence.

The point of these examples is that the problems of eliminating unfair discrimination necessarily involve value judgments and biased perceptions. In order to understand the content of this chapter, it is important that we remain aware of the unique perspective from which each of us views the problems involved and that we be cautious in judging the motives, morals, and behavior of others in this complex area.

Legal Protection Against Discrimination

The freedom marches, riots, and civil rights legislation of the 1960s marked a major turning point in the discrimination against disadvantaged groups. Although the political and social influence of blacks was the major force in calling attention to the plight of these groups, the effect was beneficial to all. Title VII of the Civil Rights Act of 1964, the "Equal Employment Opportunity" section, forbids discrimination on the basis of race, color, religion, sex, or national origin in all aspects of organizational life. The Equal Employment Opportunity Commission (**EEOC**) was created to administer and ensure compliance with the Act. Section 703A states that:

> It shall be an unlawful employment practice for an employer (1) to fail or refuse to hire or to discharge any individual or otherwise to discriminate against any individual with respect to his compensation, terms, conditions, or privileges of employment because of such individual's race, color, religion, sex, or national origin; or (2) to limit, segregate or classify his employees in any way which would deprive or tend to deprive any individual of employment opportunities or otherwise advertently affect his status as an employee because of such individual's race, color, religion, sex, or national origin.[2]

The EEOC vigorously enforced the Civil Rights Act by making full use of its powers to negotiate with companies, unions, and employment agencies to correct specific acts of discrimination and require the development of affirmative action programs to eliminate discriminatory practices. The EEOC, on a number of occasions, filed suit in the federal courts against private employers who would not respond to less drastic measures.

The March, 1971, Supreme Court decision in the case of *Griggs v Duke Power Company* strengthened the 1964 Act by requiring companies to prove that their selection procedures do not tend to discriminate.

This decision established the illegality of selection tests or employment standards that discriminate even though there is no intent to discriminate.

The case of the *United States v Georgia Power Company* (1973) further established that any employment requirement, a high school diploma in this instance, must assess the qualifications of applicants for specific jobs rather than for general employment by the organization. These decisions have led to intensive efforts to validate selection standards, especially psychological tests. If selection criteria are not correlated with on-the-job performance, and because of this unfairly screen out members of a protected group, they are clearly illegal.

The Civil Rights Act of 1964 was landmark legislation for the protection of disadvantaged groups; but a number of other laws, amendments, court decisions, executive orders, and policies of government agencies have also strengthened legal efforts to eliminate unfair discrimination.

Affirmative Action Programs

The Labor Department's Office of Federal Contract Compliance (OFCC) and the EEOC have required many organizations to evaluate opportunities for disadvantaged groups and to specify detailed plans to guarantee equal opportunities for employment and promotions. Such **affirmative action programs** include definite schedules for recruiting, hiring, and promoting members of disadvantaged groups. The programs may also include commitments to hiring and promoting based upon the populations of the different disadvantaged groups in the locality. If, for example, a company is located in an area where 30 percent of the population is Spanish American and only 5 percent of its employees are from this group, discrimination is presumed to exist.

Although hiring and promoting on such a basis has merit in many cases, it is sometimes irrational and causes undue hardship on organizations. This is especially true if the personnel needed by the organization are not available locally. When an organization which is located in an area populated by unskilled workers requires large numbers of skilled and professional personnel, the problem cannot always be solved according to a timetable acceptable to the EEOC or OFCC.

Serious questions have arisen about the legality of affirmative action programs that discriminate against one group in order to make amends for past discrimination against another. This **negative discrimination** or **reverse discrimination** was tested in two Supreme Court decisions, the first concerning Allen Bakke, an applicant to the University of California Medical School at Davis in the fall of 1972.[3] Denied admission because of minority quota admissions of less qualified students, Bakke was finally granted admission when the Supreme Court ruled that rigid quotas, based solely on race or ethnic background, were illegal. Closely related was the case of Brian Weber, who in 1977 was denied admission to a company training program because of an affirmative action program jointly developed by the union and the Kaiser Aluminum and Chemical Corporation.[4] The Supreme Court ruled in favor of this affirmative action program, seemingly establishing once and for all the principle of affirmative action.

Managers often believe that the administrators of the law are not sensitive to organizational needs and that they possess a zeal that interferes with good judgment and effective management. Some government administrators and members of disadvantaged groups, on the other hand, are convinced that any request by an organization for more time is necessarily an excuse to continue discrimination. Depending upon the individuals involved, governmental efforts to eliminate unfair discrimination may result either in a cooperative government-business partnership to solve a common problem or a bitter struggle between adversaries who appear to have no common interests.

NEEDS AND PROBLEMS OF MINORITY EMPLOYEES

The moral and social climate in America is more favorable than at any time in the past for eliminating discrimination against minority employees and for providing an organizational climate that will meet their needs for growth and self-esteem. There remain, however, formidable barriers to the achievement of these objectives. Both organizations and minority employees must recognize these and cooperatively develop plans for overcoming them.

Accurate generalizations about minorities are difficult to make because of the great differences among minority groups and the individuals within them. The problems of a religious minority are different from the problems of a racial minority, and both are different from the problems of minorities based on national origin. Some of these distinctions will now be explained.

The Changing Pattern of Discrimination

Discrimination against minority groups has persisted throughout history. Strong, pervasive prejudice against Jews and blacks in particular has existed for centuries. Both of these groups have maintained their unique identities in contrast to other groups that have been assimilated into the general population. For many groups, such as the Irish, Polish, Slovaks, and Chinese, prejudice and discrimination have centered primarily upon a recent immigrant status and concomitant characteristics of poverty, low skill levels, poor education, and culture-based characteristics that set group members apart as different and therefore "inferior."

Many European immigrant groups had the further disadvantage in Protestant America of being Catholic. As their ethnic group status increased, however, and their members gained the freedom to become assimilated into the general population at will, prejudice against Catholics declined. The nation's level of general education and traditions of religious freedom have also reduced religious prejudice. The election of John Kennedy to the presidency attests to this fact, as did Jimmy Carter's capture of a substantial Catholic vote in 1976. This does not mean that religious prejudice in America has ceased, but in most organizations its influence is minimal and as likely to operate in one direction as the other.

Spanish-Speaking Americans. The influx of unskilled Puerto Ricans into metropolitan areas such as New York City has tended to push other ethnic and racial groups up the status ladder. The social status of Spanish Americans in states such as New Mexico, Texas, Arizona, California, and Colorado is also suffering at the present time. This is, in part, due to the large numbers of illegal immigrants who dilute the favorable image that millions of skilled, well-educated Spanish Americans have earned for themselves. The national policy that has in effect allowed employers to hire illegal immigrants from Mexico provided a needed source of unskilled labor at relatively low rates while doing serious damage to Spanish Americans who have tried to remove the stigma of second-class citizenship.

Immediately following the communist revolution in Cuba, more than a half million Cubans migrated to the United States to escape the Fidel Castro regime. Since they represented the skilled and educated citizens of Cuba, they avoided many of the problems faced by the masses of boat people (including some criminals) that Castro allowed to migrate to the United States in 1980. The acceptance of the first wave of Cuban refugees into the work force shows that problems associated with inadequate education, lack of earning potential, and consequent inability to adopt a middle-class life-style may be as much a cause of discrimination as ethnic background. Both prejudice and discrimination against other immigrant groups have diminished as they have gained educational and economic equality with the general population.

At least in recent times, people of Spanish heritage have been financially better off than blacks (see Figure 7-1), but they commonly perceive themselves to be more disadvantaged. Many Spanish-speaking Americans are strongly linked to a foreign culture, have language problems, and are Catholics. People of Spanish heritage often make distinctions among themselves of which outsiders are generally unaware. For example, those with light colored skin, reflecting a Spanish or Anglo rather than an Indian ancestry, generally consider themselves superior. Such within-group distinctions are present in all disadvantaged groups, further increasing the disadvantage of various subgroups.

Median Family Income	Total Population	White	Black	Spanish Heritage
1978	$17,640	$18,368	$10,869	$12,566
1982	$23,433	$24,603	$13,599	$16,228

Source: *Current Population Reports.* "Money Income and Poverty Status of Families and Persons in the United States: 1978," Bureau of the Census, November, 1979, and *Current Population Reports*, "Money Income and Poverty Status of Families and Persons in the United States: 1982," Bureau of the Census, March, 1983.

FIGURE 7-1   Median Family Incomes of Whites, Blacks, and Persons of Spanish Heritage

American Indians. Although American Indians constitute a relatively small portion of the total work force, their numbers are growing and their problems are increasingly gaining national attention. They are at a definite disadvantage in the workplace because of social and cultural characteristics related to reservation life that make difficult an adjustment to the fast pace and regimentation of urban industrial life.

The present status of American Indians in the work force and their impact on organizational behavior can be understood only in the light of their history. When the reservation system was begun in 1871, the federal government attempted to assimilate Indians into the general population. Certain tribal rituals, customs, and dress were forbidden, and Indian children were forced to attend special English-language boarding schools. These measures, as well as attempts to teach adult males to farm on plots of family land, were generally unsuccessful. The ensuing apathy and the pessimism associated with their military defeat set the stage for unique adaptation problems in the years that followed.

After more than 40 years of intensive efforts to assimilate Indians into the mainstream of American life, the Bureau of Indian Affairs (BIA) reversed its policy. The Indian Reorganization Act of 1934 provided for tribal self-government and financial aid for education, agriculture, and industrial development. Tribes were encouraged to retain their own identities, religions, and cultures; but administrative and legal controls prevented the tribes from achieving anything like complete self-rule. This policy continued in effect, with some improvement in the general status of reservation life, until 1947 when the BIA began an organized effort to relocate Indians to urban centers where employment was available. Although BIA relocation programs have not been a phenomenal success, many large cities, such as Chicago, Minneapolis, Cleveland, Dallas, Denver, Los Angeles, San Francisco, Oklahoma City, and Seattle, have a significant number of citizens who identify themselves as American Indians and maintain close relationships with other Indians on and off reservations. Between 1950 and 1970 the Indian population of Minneapolis (Hennepin County) increased from 426 to about 10,000.[5] These growth figures were characteristic of the Indian populations of many large cities in the West and Midwest.

Employers need to be aware that American Indians identify strongly with their ethnic group long after they have adjusted to urban life and work. They seek the supportive social relationships of other Indians and often hold to many of their ancestral traditions and beliefs long after they appear to have been assimilated into the general population. In fact, in recent years a strong nationwide movement has emerged to develop a common bond between Indians of all tribes and to improve their well-being by encouraging ethnic pride and discouraging loss of identity through assimilation. Since problems of identity and self-esteem have long contributed to the disadvantaged condition of American Indians, the unity movement may serve to improve their general status and consequently to improve their employment situation.

The many problems that have plagued American Indians, not the least of which is prejudice carried over from frontier days, should not obscure the facts that an increasing number are successful vocationally and that large numbers of individuals have none of the characteristics that place the group at a disadvantage in the workplace. Because they have as a group been disadvantaged in terms of receiving formal education, the fact is often overlooked that they are not disadvantaged in terms of intelligence. The latter provides a note of optimism for their educational and economic future.

Blacks in the Work Force. Over 12 percent of the population of the United States identify themselves as blacks. As shown in Figure 7-2, the majority hold blue-collar and service jobs. They have experienced a relatively low level of participation in business careers, perhaps because opportunities for success in managerial positions have been minimal. A somewhat greater number have been successful in the professions, especially as teachers and clergy. Until recently discrimination within unions has been a serious barrier to the upward mobility of blacks within the blue-collar ranks. These and other factors have forced blacks into the least desirable, least secure, and lowest paid jobs in the labor market. When compared with other minority groups over a long period of time, blacks have suffered the highest rates of unemployment and have been subjected to the greatest cultural and educational handicaps because of poverty.

Occupation	Total	White	Black	Hispanic Origin
Total: Number (thousands)	108,162	92,434	10,020	5,708
Percentage	100.0	100.0	100.0	100.0
White-collar workers:				
Managerial and professional specialty	23.6	24.6	14.3	11.7
Technical, sales, and administrative support (including clerical)	30.8	31.5	25.3	25.8
Blue-collar workers:				
Precision production, craft, and repair (includes mechanics, construction, etc.)	12.4	12.8	9.0	14.0
Operators, fabricators, laborers	15.9	15.1	23.7	24.1
Farming, Forestry, & Fishing	3.7	3.8	2.8	6.7
Service	13.6	12.2	24.9	17.7

Source: *Employment and Earnings.* U.S. Department of Labor, Bureau of Labor Statistics, Vol. 31, No. 7, July, 1984.

FIGURE 7-2 Employment of White, Black, and Spanish-Speaking Workers by Occupational Group: Percentage, 1984

The Civil Rights Act of 1964 and other legislation have greatly increased the number of job opportunities for blacks. Various branches of government and large numbers of companies aggressively recruit blacks and provide training opportunities to ensure their promotability. In spite of these efforts and the outstanding success of many individuals, the problem of fully assimilating blacks into the work force is far from being solved. Following are some of the major problems and their implications:

1. Racial prejudice remains a barrier. This is offset to a degree, however, by the sincere efforts of large numbers of decision makers who are committed to compensating for past discrimination.

2. Education and training problems cannot be overcome immediately, in part because there are still relatively few blacks receiving the type of formal education required to compete successfully for promotions within management.

3. Blacks and other minority employees are often skeptical about whether extensive educational and vocational preparation will pay off. They have learned through experience to doubt that the golden age of opportunity has finally arrived. Thus, an understandable problem of motivation slows their progress in gaining equality in education and in the workplace.[6]

4. The road to success is often so rough that it is not considered worth the effort.[7] Even the white, Protestant, Anglo-Saxon male with an outstanding education and many cultural advantages often decides that the price of becoming a successful manager is too high. The stresses and personal risks in management are sufficiently high that many people find it difficult to stay motivated to succeed, unless they have their share of advantages.

The success of blacks in management and many other professions is slow because it must follow educational preparation. There are, however, numerous reasons for optimism. Educational opportunities for blacks have improved enormously since 1964, and more high-level opportunities are now available. Networking among black professionals is yielding sizable career benefits.[8] The success of blacks in the entertainment field and in college and professional sports has helped to reduce prejudice; and, especially at the college level, school integration may be having the same effect. Nevertheless, many blacks continue to be pessimistic about their vocational futures. Such attitudes are reinforced by the high level of unemployment among blacks, especially among teenagers, even during times of relatively high employment for the national work force.

Asian Americans. The Asian-American population consists mostly of Japanese, Chinese, Asian Indians, and Filipinos to which a number of Vietnamese and other Southeast Asians were added during the 1970s. Although prejudice still exists, Asian Americans as a group have been more successful than other minority groups in making a place for themselves and minimizing the minority stigma.

Asian Americans have placed a high value on education, a fact which accounts to a significant degree for their enviable position among minorities. In fact, the average educational level of both Chinese- and Japanese-American men exceeds that of white men. Although the influence of social and cultural characteristics can never be ruled out in accounting for the relatively high status of Asian Americans in the United States, their emphasis on education is unquestionably a major factor. It is doubtful that any minority group can compete favorably for skilled, technical, and managerial positions when an educational barrier exists. If white males cannot compete favorably for such positions without an education, it is unlikely that minorities can do so.

Relating to Minority Employees

A manager's effectiveness in relating to minority groups depends on many factors such as the ability to empathize and the presence of genuine concern for the needs of others. These qualities are not sufficient, however, to ensure good relations with minority employees. Some degree of sophistication in understanding their special problems is helpful. The following generalizations are particularly important.

Recognizing Individual Differences. A university professor of Japanese ancestry mistook a Japanese student for Chinese, made a remark about the Chinese student, and was corrected by a colleague. The somewhat embarrassed professor retorted, "Frankly, all these Orientals look alike to me!" Since the professor was himself an Oriental, his remark was humorous; however, it is related here to accent the common tendency to stereotype minority groups—to expect all members of a minority group to be alike.

Allowing for Personal Defensiveness. Experiences of early childhood and adolescence are critical in shaping attitudes, perceptions, and personal identities. James Farmer, the son of the registrar and professor of religion and philosophy at Rust College, a black Methodist school in Holly Springs, Mississippi, tells a gripping story of an unforgettable event that occurred a few blocks from Rust College when he was a child. James watched through the screen door of a drugstore as a white boy enjoyed a drink at the soda fountain. The dialogue between James and his mother continued:

> "But I told you you can't get a Coke in there," she said. "Why can't I?" I asked again. Her answer was the same. "You just can't." I then inquired with complete puzzlement, "Well, why can he?" Her answer thundered in my ears. "He's white."
>
> We walked home in silence under the pitiless glare of the Mississippi sun. Once we were home she threw herself across the bed and wept. I walked out on the front porch and sat on the steps alone with my three-and-a-half-year-old thoughts.[9]

Although this specific experience would not likely happen today, many variations of it do occur; and regardless of when such an experience takes place, the memory of it is likely to remain vivid. Members of minority groups cannot be understood without an awareness of this fact.

Minority members who have suffered discrimination often harbor feelings of resentment and hostility which they express in damaging ways. Managers cannot allow unlimited expression of these feelings—most managers will not tolerate a physical attack or a verbal attack that becomes abusive. On the other hand, a mature manager can learn to absorb some hostility and to accept some defensiveness without responding in kind. A smart-aleck remark or injection of sarcasm into a question need not be taken personally by a manager.

With reference to the feelings just described, a note of caution is in order. People who have been discriminated against often have feelings of hostility and resentment, but not all people who have been discriminated against necessarily have such feelings. We need to avoid misinterpretations of behavior that occur because we project into minority employees the feelings we expect them to have.

Accepting Rather than Tolerating. An American Indian whose attitudes concerning punctuality have been conditioned by years of reservation life or a black whose vocabulary and diction bear the stamp of an impoverished ghetto background can be *tolerated* as "one of them" or *accepted* as a unique human being of infinite worth and potential. Some managers have an unfortunate knack for being judgmental and harshly critical of subordinates who are different from themselves. Others project a warmth—a touch of genuine human compassion—that makes subordinates want to do their best, to perform responsibly, and to communicate openly.

Managers should assume that, in the final analysis, their attitudes toward minorities will be known. It is extremely difficult for managers with deep prejudice toward minority employees to sustain good relations over an extended period of time. Where prejudice exists, attitude changes are clearly in order.

THE CHANGING ROLE OF WOMEN

> Employment opportunities for women are increasing at all levels, but equality with men in opportunities and pay will not soon be achieved. The growing number of women with the motivation and ability to compete favorably with men is handicapped by cultural stereotypes. These are, in part, based on the behavior and attitudes of other women who prefer the traditional wife-mother role.

Title VII of the Civil Rights Act prohibits discrimination on the basis of sex, and a series of court decisions and EEOC rulings have demonstrated that the Act is indeed capable of causing some changes in the status of working women. Even past inequities have to some degree been corrected by actions of the EEOC and the Wage and Hour Division of the Department of Labor. It is impressive, for example, that the New York Telephone Co. agreed, within a specified period, to give up to 57 percent of future vacancies in middle management to women; that PPG Industries paid $11.1 million to 371 women against whom it had allegedly discriminated; and that Delta Air Lines, Inc., agreed to pay one thousand women and minorities $1 million in back pay because of discrimination. American Telephone & Telegraph Co. paid $15 million in back pay to women employees and agreed to provide fifty thousand higher paying jobs for women within a 15-month period. Also notable is the issue of equal pay for comparable jobs for employees of the State of Washington.[10] This issue is still pending in the courts.

Such actions do not tell the whole story. Barriers to the elimination of sex discrimination are deeply embedded in the attitudes and values of men and women alike. Back pay and affirmative action programs are a positive step toward removing discrimination, but alone they are insufficient to achieve the goal.

The Present Status of Working Women

Women make up an increasing proportion of the total work force. From 1950 to 1984 the proportion of the work force composed of women increased from 29 to 43 percent, and the latter represents over 50 million women (about 54 percent of all women over 16 years of age). Not only are more women in the labor force today than in the past, they tend to be different from the women of a few decades ago in many respects. For one, they marry later, have fewer children, divorce in greater numbers (but also remarry more often), are better educated, and maintain separate households much more often than in the past.

As shown in Figure 7-3, the increase in working women is not restricted to a given marital status. Women will continue to make up a high percentage of the work force in the foreseeable future. The increasing number of women in professional schools suggests that a larger proportion of women will increasingly view their work in terms of a career and will become progressively more competitive with men for challenging, high-paying positions.

Total (thousands)	41,364
Married, spouse present	21,897
Widowed, divorced or separated	8,185
Single (never married)	11,282

Source: *Employment and Earnings*, DOL, BLS, Vol. 31, No. 7, July, 1984.

FIGURE 7-3 Women at Work in Nonagricultural Industries by Marital Status

Occupational Segregation

The annual income of both women and men continues to increase, but the gap between the two remains relatively constant. In 1984 the weekly earnings of women were 64.5 percent of men's earnings, up just slightly from the 1967 figure of 62 percent. Women in professional and managerial jobs fared somewhat better. Their earnings were about 68 percent of what men earned.[11]

Although many factors contribute to this difference in earnings, the most influential is **occupational segregation**, the tendency for certain jobs to be occupied by men and others by women. Over 80 percent of all elementary school teachers, librarians, bookkeepers, cashiers, registered nurses, bank tellers, secretaries, telephone operators, and typists are women. In contrast, women comprise only a small percentage of all managers and a lower percentage still of top-level executives. In some high-level positions the participation of women has increased since the passage of the Civil Rights Act in 1964, but these increases do not raise their total participation to high levels. For example, women accountants have increased from about 18 to 38 percent, physicians from about 8 to 13 percent, and managers from about 15 to 27 percent.[12,13] It is important to recognize that the percentage of new female entrants into a higher paying occupation is often much higher than the overall percentage of women in that occupation. For example, while the percentage of practicing female physicians is 13 percent, the percentage of new female entrants into medical schools is over 30 percent.[14]

Another contributor to the overall lower average earnings of women is the fact that some relatively low-paying jobs have been traditionally filled by women. Some of the stereotypes about women (to be discussed later) are partly responsible for this along with the large supply of people prepared for these jobs in terms of a supply to demand ratio. This situation has led to the wages for many occupations being less than the work itself seems to justify. This situation led to passage of the Equal Pay Act with its concept of **comparable worth** or equal pay for equal work.[15] Implementation of this concept will no doubt lead to relative increases in the earnings of women. Progress in this area is being affected by the actions of a variety of interest groups and by the complexities of defining comparable worth.[16,17]

Women in Management

Under pressure from the EEOC, other government agencies, and in accord with specific company policies, an increasing number of women are filling managerial positions. For some women, the pursuit of careers in management and other professions is accompanied by special motivational problems. Jobs in management, law, medicine, and other fields at the upper end of the employment spectrum require extensive educational preparation, and a high level of success on the job usually requires intense effort and persistence. For many women who have the option of staying out of the labor force and pursuing the wife-mother role, the price of career success in these fields offsets its benefits. Although the rewards of vocational success are high, the high price of that success becomes a critical factor in a woman's continuing decisions to persist in the struggle for success rather than accept what may be a less demanding life-style.

Public accounting, for example, requires frequent travel because auditors must examine the books and operations of clients that may be located far from their firm's office. It also can involve long stretches of grueling overtime when the firms enter their busy season, after the close of the financial year and before the audited financial reports are issued.

"For years I worked 60 to 70 hours a week," recalls Mary H. Mead, the first woman partner in the medium-sized accounting firm of Seidman and Seidman. "I don't know how I'd have taken care of a family."[18]

Many men, of course, also reject the rigorous life-style required for managerial success, preferring instead less demanding staff positions. The homemaker role that is open to many women provides an option—one that often becomes more attractive as business stresses mount.

Judith Laws makes the cogent point that the failure of women to enter stressful and demanding career fields is partly a result of their low expectation of being successful.[19] Applying expectancy theory she notes that if a woman places a high value on becoming a manager but perceives the probability of success to be low, her motivation to acquire the education and endure the rigors of the competitive environment will be low. As women come to realize that their chances of success have increased, more will prepare for and succeed in the field of management.

Stereotypes About Women

Much discrimination against women at work is a result of conventional notions about women that either are false or apply to only a limited subgroup. We look now at three examples of such stereotypes.

1. *Women work only to provide short-term, supplementary income.* A sequel is that women will not remain on the job long enough to justify an investment in training for a difficult, high-paying job. Although these generalizations apply to some women, they certainly are not valid for all. An increasing proportion of women now head households and work out of economic necessity. In addition, an increasing proportion regard their work as career oriented and have no plans to quit regardless of economic necessity or family situation.

2. *Women are less concerned than men about getting ahead on the job.* Research indicates that women are as interested as men in having a job where the chances of getting ahead are good. It seems likely that increasing opportunities for advancement will lead to increased aspirations.

3. *Women prefer jobs that are not intellectually demanding.* Research shows that more women than men perceive themselves to be in jobs that are intellectually undemanding. When this factor is held constant, however, no differences are found between the sexes in preference for intellectually demanding work.

The research and writing on the subject are not altogether effective in debunking these and other stereotypes about women in the work force; and, in some instances, stereotypes that managers have for years used as a basis for discriminating against women are reinforced by surveys of women's attitudes about women in careers. These problems will be greatly diminished by the increasing amount of research on the role and status of working women that does not treat women as a homogeneous group since the averaging effect in such research will always produce misleading results. Large numbers of women have traditional attitudes about women in the workplace, and when the attitudes and behavior of this group are combined with the attitudes and behavior of career-oriented women, the resulting "averages" reinforce the attitudes of managers who consciously or unconsciously try to prevent women from gaining equality with men. It is irrelevant how other women feel or think when it comes to deciding whether a particular woman will be effective in a given position.

The notion that research about women as a group may detract from our understanding of the potential role of career women is well expressed by researchers Reif, Newstrom, and Monczka. They conclude that

> . . . decisions made about women on the basis of their sex, without considering such individual factors as background, education, experience, personality, and potential, are likely to be wrong. It appears that many of the stereotypes of women are not representative of women who hold or aspire to responsible positions in business. Moreover, the supposed sex differences in personality, abilities, and attitudes about work for the most part have not been based upon empirical observations of women managers but have resulted from judgments about traits that have been rightly or wrongly attributed to women in general.[20]

Just as traditional attitudes about the role of women in society should not influence the decisions of managers or of women interested in pursuing a career, neither should current attitudes about the desirability of having an increased number of career-oriented women in the work force influence the decisions of women interested in undertaking traditional roles. Women who choose to be mothers and wives should not feel that the role they have chosen is an inferior one. Morality and the law demand that career women be given every opportunity to succeed without sex discrimination, but this should not interfere with the freedom of other women to choose with dignity an entirely different life-style.

OPPORTUNITIES AND PROBLEMS OF AGING

Employees with the good fortune of living long enough to grow old have many problems in common; individuals differ greatly in the skill with which such problems are faced. Research and experience have provided satisfactory solutions to most problems of aging, but unfortunately many employees wait until they are too old to begin searching for them.

In contrast to many Asian countries, the United States has always placed a premium on youth. It started with the earliest explorers and colonists who needed strength, vitality, and physical endurance to survive and conquer a new land. It continues today because of (1) the human energy demands of competitive organizations, (2) the learning demands of the knowledge explosion, and (3) the adaptability demands of rapid change in all aspects of society. It is noteworthy, however, that it is usually the older people in organizations who have the most interesting jobs and the greatest power. Aging poses some serious problems and disadvantages, but it also brings some unique satisfactions and opportunities.

Special Problems of Aging

Some of the problems of aging occur whether or not one is employed. The most common of these are

1. Coping with an increasing number of physical infirmities
2. Adapting to a decline in physical strength
3. Adjusting to becoming elderly
4. Facing the deaths of family members and friends
5. Having to face the implications of one's own death
6. Meeting the financial and social needs of advancing years
7. Accepting a growing dependency upon other people

Unfortunately the youth orientation of our culture encourages people to deny that they are getting old and thus to be poorly prepared for it. The millions of middle-aged people who have viewed old people as a worthless burden on society face the dilemma of either having to change their perception of old people or accept a negative view of themselves as they grow old. The latter commonly occurs and is a major pathology of aging.

Actually the organizational problems faced by declining abilities are fewer than one might imagine. Barring sudden physical problems such as a stroke that can affect thought processes, employees whose work is primarily mental need not experience a noticeable decline in mental ability before age 65. Fortunately the physical abilities of employees who do manual work usually decline even more slowly than those of persons who do only mental work. Because of health problems, a few manual workers must be transferred to less strenuous jobs (job reassignment), but older employees usually have the experience and seniority to claim such jobs anyway. In some cases, *job redesign* is necessary to enable a person with an age-related handicap to continue to perform (for example, by removing from a job functions that require heavy lifting or rapid movements). Generally speaking, older workers perform about as well as younger ones, have a much lower rate of turnover, are more safety conscious, and of course have a broader base of experience on which to draw in the performance of their jobs.

Age Discrimination

Older employees who lose their jobs often have problems finding suitable employment. Many employers are reluctant to hire employees over age 40 because (1) the employers question whether the necessary investment in training will pay off; (2) they are unwilling to pay the increased cost of insurance premiums; and/or (3) they want to avoid problems relating to pension plans and policies of promotion on the basis of seniority.

To protect individuals between the ages of 40 and 65, the Age Discrimination in Employment Act of 1967 prohibits discrimination in compensation, terms, conditions, or privileges of employment because of age.[21] The Employee Retirement Income Security Act of 1974 gives further protection to aging employees by reducing the likelihood that older employees will lose their jobs because an organization wants to avoid paying their retirement benefits. Such laws cannot eliminate the hardships faced by older employees who must begin new jobs that do not make use of their prior training and experience. On January 1, 1979, an amendment to the Age Discrimination in Employment Act extended its protection against age discrimination and prohibited mandatory retirement before the age of 70 for most jobs. With the passing of that law, older workers became a uniquely protected group.

Problems of Retirement

Prior to 1979 most companies required retirement at age 65. Supporters of compulsory retirement point out that it (1) avoids a number of the problems inherent in making separate decisions about each individual; (2) requires older employees to move out and give young employees an opportunity for promotions; (3) enables management to be more effective in human resource planning; and (4) is fair in that everyone is treated alike. There is, however, strong sentiment in some organizations for abolishing mandatory retirement specifically because it does treat everybody alike when in fact people are quite different. Some are capable of many years of outstanding service after age 65 or 70, while others probably should retire earlier.

One of the advantages of compulsory retirement is that it does not imply that the retiree has become inadequate. It thus enables an employee to retire with dignity. Many companies have developed preretirement programs to help employees prepare both psychologically and financially for retirement. Especially for individuals who have centered their lives around their work, have become dependent upon their formal status and power for self-esteem, and have few outside interests, retirement can be psychologically devastating. It may even lead to an early death. On the other hand, if begun early and taken seriously, preretirement planning will usually help one avoid such reactions.

Although a sizable number of organizations have instituted flexible retirement policies (gradual retirement by extending vacations, for example), it is unlikely that there will be a rush to plans that remove mandatory requirements. The stronger movement is in the direction of providing opportunities for voluntary early retirement. Notable among such programs are those of the federal government and the major automobile manufacturers. Both allow voluntary retirement with full retirement benefits for employees with 30 years of service. To qualify, government employees must be 55 years of age, but employees of automobile companies may be any age as long as they have fulfilled their 30 years of employment.

Very few legislators resisted the amendment to forbid compulsory retirement before age 70. One reason for the meager resistance was a belief that social security payments would be reduced if more persons continued to earn wages for an additional five years, thus providing relief to a federal program in serious trouble. In addition, large numbers of influential elderly legislators, government employees, and jurists had for many years advocated the change. Nevertheless, there is strong evidence that since the social security program and most retirement programs are designed for retirement at age 65, the prohibition against forced retirement at 65 has done little to change the number of actual retirements at that time. Some persons—especially those whose work is intrinsically satisfying—will continue to work after age 65.

PERSONALITY MALADJUSTMENT IN ORGANIZATIONS

One of the largest disadvantaged groups is made up of people with emotional problems. Their cost to organizations through employee turnover, absenteeism, substandard production, labor-management strife, and disciplinary problems is enormous. Yet most organizations make no special provisions for understanding and relating to them.

Approximately 10 percent of the general population suffers from some form of emotional problem that is serious enough to interfere with performance on the job, and many of these have compounded their problem through alcoholism or drug addiction. In addition to this group are the increasing number of people who are either sociopathic, in that they have an underdeveloped conscience, or who for other reasons have adopted an antisocial or criminal life-style. Although many of these people are institutionalized, most of them at sometime or other are part of the work force and more often than not create problems for management.

Recognizing Emotional Problems

Employees with emotional problems are beset by a chronic inability to find need satisfaction. The emotionally maladjusted have had difficulty coping with their environmental frustrations and internal conflicts, and the symptoms they exhibit represent the inadequate means they have adopted as coping devices which we discussed in Chapter 4.

Managers legitimately become involved in the personal problems of subordinates when those problems interfere with their work. Although it is not the humane or economically feasible thing to do, managers commonly treat the unacceptable behavior of an emotionally maladjusted person as if it were just another disciplinary problem. For this reason, it is important (1) that the symptoms of maladjustment be recognized, (2) that employees' emotional problems be considered in personnel decisions, and (3) that employees with serious problems be referred to someone who can give them professional help. Figure 7-4 lists some of the common symptoms of emotional maladjustment. It is especially important in detecting emotional problems that managers take notice of changes in behavior as well as the presence of combinations of the symptoms listed. It should be obvious that most of the behaviors listed in Figure 7-4 are not necessarily in themselves abnormal. It is the nature of their onset, the degree to which they are present, the combinations in which they occur, and their negative effects in the workplace that provide a basis for viewing these behaviors as symptoms of emotional problems.

Alcoholism and Drug Abuse

Although in recent years the use of a variety of drugs ranging from amphetamines to heroin has become a serious problem, the excessive use of alcohol continues to be more prevalent and more costly in terms of economic loss and destruction of lives. During the 1970s the average annual consumption of alcohol per person ranged from 2.63 to 2.69 gallons for ages 14 years old and older. This is the highest consumption since 1850 and has predictably resulted in serious personal and social problems. Various estimates of problem drinkers, including alcoholics,

Emotional problems may be indicated by combinations of the following when such behaviors are excessive, have an acute onset, or noticeably increase over a period of time.

Irresponsibility	Absenteeism	Aggressiveness
Indifference or apathy	Tardiness	Irrationality
Forgetfulness	Low productivity	Poor judgment
Defensiveness	Errors and mistakes	Withdrawal
Procrastination	Constant complaints	Heavy drinking
Irritability	Preoccupation with	Use of narcotics
Daydreaming	health problems	Fearfulness
Memory lapses	Bizarre behavior	Perfectionism
Self-criticism	Criticism of others	Suspiciousness
Shyness	Inferiority feelings	Guilt feelings
Indecisiveness	Inability to concentrate	Chronic rule-
Inappropriate emotions	Unpredictable behavior	breaking
Self-preoccupation	Rapid personality changes	Excuse making

FIGURE 7-4 Possible Symptoms of Emotional Problems

range from 9.3 to 10 million adults with an additional 3.3 million problem drinkers among youths in the 14 to 17 age range.

Excessive drinking and drug abuse significantly affect organizational behavior, particularly in the areas of reduced productivity, absenteeism, accidents, and employee turnover. For example, the National Council on Alcoholism states that the alcoholic employee is absent three times as much as the average employee, involved in four to six times as many off-the-job accidents and two to four times as many on-the-job accidents, and makes sickness and accident benefit claims at a rate three times greater than the average employee.[22] A 1983 estimate of the U.S. Senate Finance Committee estimated the economic cost of alcoholism to be $120 billion annually.[23] Statistics on the economic consequences of drug abuse are not as well-founded as those on alcoholism, but it appears to have many of the same underlying causes and consequences as does alcohol abuse.

Although the American Medical Association and most professionals in the health sciences regard alcoholism as an illness, it must also be considered as a symptom of underlying emotional problems—as one of many inadequate means of coping with internal conflict. It provides a common avenue of escaping from present stressors and past emotional problems. Unfortunately it offers no solutions and itself creates problems.

Managing Maladjusted Employees

Most employees who are dismissed from their jobs have the ability to perform adequately but for personality-related reasons do not do so. Even when managers are fully aware of underlying emotional problems, they cannot tolerate inadequate performance indefinitely without adversely affecting co-workers, customers and clients, stockholders, and themselves.

Noting the seriousness of the problem, a number of companies have developed in-house programs to provide help for maladjusted employees, including alcoholics and drug addicts. Such programs result both from a growing sense of social responsibility and management's awareness that the dollar loss in productivity warrants an investment in this area. Whether or not their organization provides services of this kind, managers should use their authority to persuade maladjusted employees to get professional help instead of treating their unacceptable performance as a run-of-the-mill disciplinary problem.

Virtually every community has resources for helping people with emotional problems. Managers should become acquainted with those resources and develop skill in making referrals. Among those individuals and organizations most capable of providing help are ministers, priests, rabbis, psychologists, psychiatrists, social workers, family physicians, and organizations such as Alcoholics Anonymous, community mental health centers, and detoxification centers. Experience has demonstrated that most employees will accept a referral and profit from treatment when motivated by a desire to maintain their employment and good standing with their employers.

IMPORTANT TERMS AND CONCEPTS

disadvantaged group   negative discrimination
discrimination   reverse discrimination
prejudice   occupational segregation
EEOC   comparable worth
affirmative action programs

STUDY AND DISCUSSION QUESTIONS

1. A solution to the problem of unfair discrimination in employment decisions depends upon what factors?

2. What evidence supports the belief that affirmative action programs will be an organizational fact of life for years to come?

3. Upon what factors are the prejudice and discrimination against immigrant groups most likely to be based?

4. What are the major problems presently faced by blacks as they attempt to gain equal standing with the majority of the work force?

5. Assuming that it is wise to avoid stereotypes and relate to members of ethnic and racial groups as individuals, of what value to a manager is understanding subculture norms and attitudes?

6. What factors could cause the gap between the average pay of men and women to increase at a time when the status of women is obviously improving?

7. How can expectancy theory be used to explain the motivation of women to prepare educationally for management careers?

8. Statistical studies have often failed to debunk stereotypes about

women that have caused unfair discrimination. What change in research methodology would improve this situation?

9. What are the pros and cons of compulsory retirement?

10. Why is it important for managers to know when disciplinary problems are a result of the offender's emotional maladjustment?

CRITICAL INCIDENT

THE HOSTILE IRISHMAN

Advancement to master machinist was slow in the Dayton Machine Tool Company because employee turnover was low and promotions were dependent on job openings and seniority. The line of progression led from helper to third class, to second class, to first class, and finally to master. The number of jobs at each level was relatively fixed by tradition with a large number of helpers and few masters (a total of eight). The company's reputation for fairness and excellent treatment of its employees was unusually good. There had never been any serious union-management problems in the unionized plant.

In March of 1979 Dayton entered into an agreement with the EEOC to increase the number of minority employees hired and promoted. Because the union itself was in trouble due to years of discrimination against minorities, it reluctantly supported the agreement in spite of its implications for setting aside the seniority promotion rule.

At the time of this incident Jim McBride had been employed by Dayton for 27 years and planned to take early retirement at age 60, which was three years away. Many years earlier, recognizing that his long-term opportunities were better in a technical area, McBride had taken a cut in pay from his warehousing job to begin at the bottom as a machinist's helper. After 15 years he had become a first-class machinist with three years in grade and was next in line for master.

Juan Salinas, a 33-year-old native Puerto Rican, had been employed by Dayton for six years and had been promoted to first class at an accelerated pace in conformity with the affirmative action plan. Although he had been a first-class machinist for only 11 months and had not learned certain tasks related to die and model making, Salinas rather than McBride was promoted when a master machinist retired unexpectedly.

McBride was taken by surprise when the announcement was made. At first he was merely disappointed, but he then became upset over the possibility that he would retire before making master machinist. This would result in less retirement pay than he had anticipated. Finally, he became intensely hostile, and with the support of his union steward he took his case to management. At one point in the bargaining, he made this impassioned plea:

> Why me? Why discriminate against me? I took a cut in pay to become a machinist's helper and in 15 years of total dedication to my work I have earned this promotion. Don't talk to me about minorities. I have never discriminated against a minority. In fact, in the Irish ghetto where I grew up, I always thought I was one. Salinas is an individual just like I am, except that he is a young man with 6 years of experience and I'm a not-so-young man with 15 years experience. You're promoting an individual, not a minority group, and you're doing it at my expense. Don't old Irish Catholics have some rights too?

1. What are the arguments for and against the promotion of Salinas over McBride?

2. How should the current problem be resolved? Why?

3. What additional information is needed in order to answer Question 2?

REFERENCES

1. Torrey, Jane W. "A Psychologist's Look at Women," *Journal of Contemporary Business*, Vol. 2, Summer, 1973, p. 26.
2. *Civil Rights Act, 1964, Title VII, Section 703A.*
3. "Regents of the University of California Petition v Allan Bakke," *United States Supreme Court Reports, Lawyers' Edition*, Vol. 57, No. 2, August 18, 1978, p. 750.
4. "Decisions Announced June 27, 1979." *The United States Law Week*, Vol. 47, No. 50, June 27, 1979, p. 4,853.
5. Bahr, Howard M. "An End to Invisibility," *Native Americans Today: Sociological Perspectives*, eds. Howard M. Bahr, Bruce A. Chadwick, and Robert C. Day. New York: Harper & Row Publishers, Inc., 1972, p. 408.
6. Bhagat, Rabi S. "Black-White Ethnic Differences in Identification with the Work Ethic: Some Implications for Organizational Integration," *Academy of*

Management Review, Vol. 4, No. 3, June, 1979, pp. 381–391.

7. Westcott, Diane Nilsen. "Blacks in the 1970's: Did They Scale the Job Ladder?" *Monthly Labor Review*, Vol. 105, No. 6, June, 1982, pp. 29–37.

8. *The Wall Street Journal*, October 12, 1984.

9. Farmer, James. "The Shock of Black Recognition," *Minorities, A Text with Readings in Intergroup Relations*, ed. Eugene Griesman. Hinsdale, Ill.: Dryden Press, 1975, p. 239.

10. Siniscalco, Gary R., and Cynthia L. Remmers. "A Symposium: Comparable Worth," *Employee Relations Law Journal*, Vol. 10, No. 1, Summer, 1984, pp. 5–29.

11. *Employment and Earnings*. U.S. Department of Labor, Bureau of Labor Statistics, Vol. 31, No. 7, July, 1984.

12. Vetter, Betty M., Eleanor L. Babco, and Susan Jensen-Fisher. *Professional Women and Minorities—A Manpower Resource Service*, 3rd ed. Washington, D.C.: Scientific Manpower Commission, 1982.

13. Garfinkle, Stuart H. "Occupations of Women and Black Workers," *Monthly Labor Review*, Vol. 98, No. 11, November, 1975, p. 28.

14. *The Cincinnati Enquirer*, September 28, 1984.

15. Siniscalco, Gary R., and Cynthia L. Remmers. "Nonjudicial Developments in Comparable Worth," *Employee Relations Law Journal*, Vol. 10, No. 2, Autumn, 1984, pp. 223–240.

16. Thomas, Clarence. "Pay Equity and Comparable Worth," *Labor Law Journal*, Vol. 34, No. 1, January, 1983, pp. 3–12.

17. Mahoney, Thomas A. "Approaches to the Definition of Comparable Worth," *Academy of Management Review*, Vol. 8, No. 1, January, 1983, pp. 14–22.

18. Rankin, Deborah. "Women Accountants Are Scarcely Adding Up," *Business and Society Review*, No. 25, Spring, 1978, pp. 59–61.

19. Laws, Judith Long. "Psychological Dimensions of Women's Work Force Participation," *Sloan Management Review*, Vol. 5, Spring, 1974, p. 49.

20. Reif, William E., John W. Newstrom, and Robert M. Monczka. "Exploding Some Myths about Women Managers," *California Management Review*, Vol. 17, Summer, 1975, p. 78.

21. *The Age Discrimination in Employment Act of 1967*. U.S. Code Congressional and Administrative News, pp. 2,213–2,228.

22. Tersine, Richard J., and James Hazeldine. "Alcoholism: A Productivity Hangover," *Business Horizons*, Vol. 25, No. 6, November/December, 1982.

23. *Christian Science Monitor*, September 21, 1983.

SUGGESTED READINGS

Adams, Jerome, Robert W. Rice, and Debra Instone. "Follower Attitudes Toward Women and Judgments Concerning Performance by Female and Male Leaders," *Academy of Management Journal*, Vol. 27, No. 3, 1984, pp. 636–643.

America, Richard F., and Bernard E. Anderson. "Moving Ahead: Black Managers in American Business," *MBA*, December, 1978/January, 1979, pp. 40–49.

Brookmire, David A. "Designing and Implementing Your Company's Affirmative Action Program," *Personnel Journal*, April, 1970, pp. 232–237.

Burke, Ronald J., and Tamara Weir. "Readying the Sexes for Women in Management," *Business Horizons*, Vol. 20, No. 6, June, 1977, pp. 30–35.

Camisa, Kenneth P. "How Alcoholism Treatment Pays For Itself," *Advanced Management Journal*, Vol. 47, No. 1, Winter, 1982, pp. 53–56.

Colburn, David R., and George E. Pozzetta, eds. *America and the New Ethnicity*. Port Washington, N.Y.: Kennikat Press Corporation, 1979.

Cooper, Elizabeth A., and Gerald V. Barrett. "Equal Pay and Gender: Implications of Court Cases for Personnel Practices," *Academy of Management Review*, Vol. 9, No. 1, January, 1984, pp. 84–94.

Fairhurst, Gail Theus, and B. Kay Snaverly. "Majority and Token Minority Group Relationships: Power Acquisition and Communication," *Academy of Management Review*, Vol. 8, No. 2, April, 1983, pp. 292–300.

Feldman, Daniel C. "The Development and Enforcement of Group Norms," *Academy of Management Review*, Vol. 9, No. 1, January, 1984, pp. 47–53.

Heilman, Madeline E. "Information as a Deterrent against Sex Discrimination: The Effects of Applicant Sex and Information Type on Preliminary Employment Decisions," *Organizational Behavior and Human Performance*, Vol. 33, 1984, pp. 174–186.

Krumboltz, Helen B., and Johanna Shapiro. "Counseling Women in Behavioral Self-Direction," *The Personnel and Guidance Journal*, Vol. 57, No. 8, April, 1979, pp. 415–418.

Larwood, Laurie, Marion M. Wood, and Sheila Davis Inderlied. "Training Women for Management: New Problems, New Solutions," *Academy of Management Review*, Vol. 3, No. 3, July, 1978, pp. 584–593.

O'Brien, John, and Denise Gubbay. "Training to Integrate the Multi-Racial," *Personnel Management*, January, 1979, pp. 20–23.

8

Union Influences on Organizational Behavior

Managers of unionized organizations, ever mindful of union sentiments and power, seldom make organizational decisions without anticipating how the union will react. Union members, unlike employees in non-unionized organizations, recognize that they are indeed powerful, and they value their ability to confront management collectively. They also value the security that results from their influence on managerial policies and the autonomy that a demand for their services alone could never produce. Thus, unionized organizations differ dramatically from others. The emotional and political climates of the two are different in part because union members have dual loyalties that are often put to the test during contract negotiations. At such times union and management employees become acutely aware that they have conflicting as well as common objectives—that they are both competitors and co-operating determiners of organizational success.

In passing the National Labor Relations Act of 1935, Congress attempted to equalize the power between an employer and a single employee. The Act created an atmosphere conducive to the growth of unions and officially endorsed collective bargaining, a system its supporters hoped would become a mature form of industrial democracy. It created a source of legitimate power in organizations that challenged the authority of management and called for major adaptations in managerial style. The Act and the union growth it spawned also contributed to the creation of a large class of middle-income consumers and enthusiastic supporters of a competitive private enterprise system.

Current views of organizational behavior emphasize that the effectiveness of managerial practice is contingent upon the environment in which managers operate. A union's influence may preclude the use of merit raises and promotions to reward high performance. In doing so, it poses challenging problems for managers who prefer to take a personal and individualized approach to employee motivation. All kinds of decisions—concerning work rules, styles of leadership, location of plants, even choice of technology—are influenced by unions.

Managers who understand the role of unions in the workplace, who understand the structure and procedures of the union with which they are faced, and who have given some thought to how good relations with the union can work to everyone's advantage, are less frustrated and are more effective than are those managers who have not applied themselves to these tasks.

Between 1935 and 1945 union membership quadrupled. In the 1940s union membership included over one third of the nonfarm labor force in the United States. That compares with less than one fifth in 1984. Between 1976 and 1984 even the absolute number of union members declined slightly despite extensive union organizing efforts and significant membership increases in the public sector. Membership during that period as a percentage of the total work force was the lowest since the late 1930s.

Although unions are facing difficulties, they are still one of the most powerful forces in the United States and a major influence on organizational life. Union influence on organizations is in fact more pronounced than the total number of union members might suggest. In some organizations, the union is virtually a partner—usually an unwelcomed partner—in managing the enterprise.

Many organizations, both large and small, have no unions. Even in such organizations, however, the impact of unions is felt. The managers of nonunion companies are aware that their policies and procedures are constantly being compared with those of unionized companies. They may use high wages, liberal fringe benefits, and even participation in decision making to avoid the loss of control associated with unionism.

This chapter discusses the nature of unions and their role in organizations. Specifically the objectives of Chapter 8 are

TO UNDERSTAND:

1. The history of the development of unions

2. Trends in union membership

3. Why employees join unions

4. Union strategies for gaining power and influencing organizations

5. Some alternatives to collective bargaining

UNION PHILOSOPHY AND DEVELOPMENT

The growth of labor unions in America has, for the most part, been motivated by the desire of employees to influence decisions that affect their welfare. The labor movement essentially has been oriented toward the use of power to achieve economic advantages rather than to promote a political philosophy.

An individual is at a distinct disadvantage when dealing with a large corporation. This was especially true prior to the human relations movement when authoritarian management was commonplace and employees were typically regarded as expendable articles of commerce rather than as persons. The resulting imbalance in bargaining power and the abuses suffered by workers at the hands of unenlightened, arbitrary managers led to formation of unions as early as the Colonial Period.

Unions in an Affluent Society

The intense commitment of many union members is not altogether explainable in terms of present working conditions. Large numbers of union members make more than $20,000 a year plus extensive economic supplements (fringe benefits). They often live in the suburbs, own at least two automobiles, send their children to college, and enjoy more leisure time than the managers for whom they work. Top union leaders are usually well-paid executives supported by a professional staff of attorneys, accountants, and economists and bear no resemblance to the traditional image of a proletariat or downtrodden working class.

This is not to say that everything is going well for unions. They are having serious problems maintaining their membership and their influence. Nevertheless, unionism in America is far from dead. There are at least three reasons for this. First, unionism is seen as the goose that laid the golden egg. The union is perceived as being the cause of worker strength and prosperity and is thus worthy of preservation and expansion. Second, human needs and wants are insatiable. Employees always desire higher income, better working conditions, more interesting work, and greater autonomy and security. Finally, the employment experiences of parents and grandparents are not altogether forgotten, especially those that were bitter and traumatic. Such memories are passed from one generation to another and interact with present dissatisfactions to cause distrust of management and loyalty to the union.

Early Growth of Unions

Small **craft unions** of the Colonial Period were primarily fraternal societies of skilled workers such as stonemasons, shoemakers, and carpenters. They existed as self-help organizations concerned with training apprentices and with the general enhancement of their membership. But local fraternities of craftspersons had little potential for influencing powerful employers. Labor historians often cite the Philadelphia cordwainers (shoemakers) formed in 1792 as the earliest union in the United States. It was not until 1850 that such local associations began to form national unions. In that year a national union of photographers was formed followed by the stonecutters union in 1853 and the hat-finishers union in 1854. Within two decades, over 30 such national unions had been formed.

Early Amalgamation of Unions

Once national unions were formed they combined into still larger units. The first effective amalgamation was the Knights of Labor, organized in 1869. This organization, spearheaded by the garment workers, welcomed existing craft unions as well as other skilled and unskilled labor. By 1886 a peak membership of 703,000 was achieved. The diversity of membership, the impact of several unsuccessful strikes, and unfavorable public opinion, however, led to this union's rapid demise.

The decline of the Knights of Labor was accompanied by the formation of the American Federation of Labor (AFL) in 1886. This loosely knit group of craft unions (25 at the beginning) avoided affiliation with **industrial unions**, that is unions made up primarily of unskilled and semiskilled employees. Under the strong leadership of Samuel Gompers, the AFL grew rapidly as an association of the labor elite.

The Congress of Industrial Organizations (CIO) was organized in 1936 to meet the needs of the rapidly expanding unions in the mass production industries. The organization was headed by John L. Lewis, the powerful president of the United Mine Workers, and was supported by other labor leaders who disagreed with the exclusivist policies of the AFL. The CIO became aggressive in unionizing the mass production industries. Unlike the AFL, the CIO welcomed all employees, including minorities, and became active in local, state, and national politics. In 1955 the two groups merged to form the AFL-CIO. Bureau of Labor Statistics data published in 1984 indicated that AFL-CIO membership totaled about 14.7 million.[1] A few large unions, such as the International Brotherhood of Teamsters, Warehousemen, and Helpers of America and the United Auto Workers, have withdrawn from the AFL-CIO. Such unions are classified as independents.

Figure 8-1 shows the structure of the AFL-CIO. Ultimate authority rests with the elected delegates at the biennial convention. The number of delegates from each union is based on paid-up memberships. The executive branch of the organization consists of the elected president, secretary-treasurer, and 33 vice-presidents. Supporting these executives are large staffs (concerned with such activities as accounting, civil rights, education, legislation, and public relations) and standing committees (such as civil rights, ethical practices, political affairs, education, and safety).

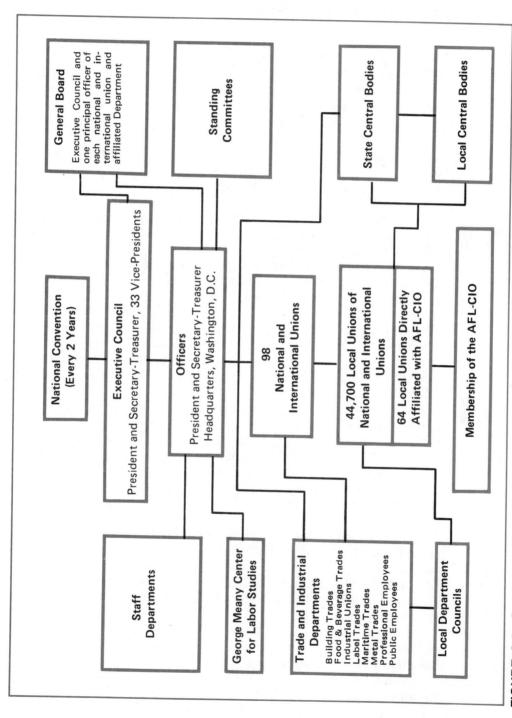

FIGURE 8-1 Structure of the AFL-CIO (1983)

Trends in Union Membership

Union membership among workers in the United States increased greatly between 1935 and 1945 from less than 16 percent to more than 36 percent. This dramatic spurt can be accounted for by three factors. The first was the 1935 passage of the National Labor Relations Act (Wagner Act) which guaranteed the right of collective bargaining. This was strategically followed by the formation of the CIO, with its aggressive tactics for organizing the masses of semiskilled and unskilled workers. Finally, union growth received new impetus because of the labor shortage and consequent increase in labor power during World War II.

Since 1965 unions have made significant gains among white-collar, professional, farm, and government employees. None of these was considered fertile ground for union expansion as long as large numbers of industrial workers remained outside the union and these groups were small. Since the most significant increase in the work force now lies in the service areas consisting of white-collar, professional, and government employees, it is understandable that these areas are now selected as prime targets for unionization drives.

In spite of union efforts and successes in obtaining members from these nontraditional sources, since the end of World War II the number of union members has declined relative to the size of the total labor force to less than 20 percent in 1984.[2] This has occurred for a number of reasons, not the least of which is the expansion of jobs for white-collar employees not traditionally associated with the labor movement. The programmers, systems analysts, data entry clerks, computer operators, and technicians of the computer industry are examples of such personnel. Although many employees in these positions become union members, others identify closely with management and shy away from union membership. A second reason for the relative decline in union membership is that the absolute number of jobs in heavily unionized industries such as steel and automobiles has declined.

White-Collar and Professional Employees. As the number of white-collar and professional employees increases, other changes occur that stimulate employee discontent. Historically white-collar workers have identified closely with management. However, when hundreds of data entry clerks and other clerical and administrative support personnel are assembled to perform routine tasks in a giant, impersonal organization (so-called white-collar factories), they feel much in common with the masses of blue-collar machine tenders and assembly line workers. Under such conditions, unions become attractive.

Within the last fifteen to twenty years, public school teachers have shown an interest in collective bargaining. The current generation of public school teachers is unwilling to tolerate low pay, arbitrary decisions by administrators and boards of education, heavy teaching loads, and abuses by students. During the 1970s two rival groups, the American Federation of Teachers and the National Education Association, spent millions of dollars recruiting members, often in competition with one another. So successful have these unions been in New York, where the two unions have merged, that virtually all public school teachers are union members.[3] A merger of the two unions at the national level would produce the largest independent union in the nation. The desperation of unionized teachers has been shown in the same willingness to strike that has characterized some of the more effective unions (that is, effective in terms of achieving their demands).

Statistics on the growth or decline of unions are somewhat confusing because about three million members of employee associations are not included in government statistics related to union membership. These employee associations, most of which are state organizations, expanded rapidly during the 1970s while many unions, especially in manufacturing, were losing members. In only two years, from 1974 to 1976, the National Education Association gained 400,000 members; and this union has now grown to 1,600,800 members, partly by mergers that increase its membership but do not increase the total number of organized employees. In recent years, mergers have become an important means by which union power and effectiveness are increased. The trend shows no signs of abating.[4]

Government Employees. The impressive success of organizing drives among public service employees is due in no small part to the late President Kennedy's Executive Order 10988, issued in January, 1962. It required recognition of and collective bargaining with certified associations of federal employees. Since 1962 the organization of employees at all levels of government has increased rapidly in spite of legislation limiting the right of government employees to strike.

With the important exception of President Reagan's handling of the air-traffic controller's strike in 1983, no-strike legislation has proved ineffective in curbing strikes by public service employees.[5] Strikes by garbage collectors, police officers, and fire fighters in major cities across the nation have demonstrated the inability or unwillingness of public officials to deal effectively with this type of illegal behavior. When striking employees report in sick and union leaders disavow any connection with the strike, politically minded officials are reluctant to deal boldly with the situation. Occasionally illegally striking public-service employees are jailed for violating a back-to-work court order only to be pardoned as part of a settlement to end the strike. This unwillingness on the part of public officials to act firmly and to stick by their actions constitutes one of the most serious problems with public-service unions and one that arouses antiunion sentiment.

Resistance to Unionization. In spite of government efforts to promote unionism, organizing efforts have encountered problems. Prior to passage of the Norris-La Guardia Act in 1932 unionism was contained by the use of court injunctions to stop strikes and by the requirement that employees sign the despised **yellow dog contract**, a commitment not to join a union. During this period it was also common for employees to be fired for union activity.

After passage of the 1932 and 1935 legislation (Norris-La Guardia and Wagner Acts), it appeared that unions would have freedom for unlimited organizing activity. This growth, in turn, was expected to provide the political power unions needed to consolidate their gains. A serious problem arose, however, when public opinion turned against unions immediately after World War II (1946). A few unions were communist dominated while others were controlled by racketeers, and voters feared that unions were becoming too strong. A number of nationwide strikes reflected the immaturity of the labor movement and showed contempt for public welfare and the national economy. This resulted in the passage of the Taft-Hartley Act (Labor-Management Relations Act) in 1947. This legislation spelled out a number of unfair practices on the part of labor and permitted states to pass right-to-work laws which prohibited dismissal of individuals for refusal to join unions. The Taft-Hartley Act also outlawed the **closed shop** in which only union members are eligible for employment. These and other provisions of the Act expressed some of the public's antagonism toward union power and recognized the belief that big unions as well as big business can destroy individual rights.

Concern over the power and abuses of unions was again expressed in the Landrum-Griffin Act (the Labor-Management Reporting and Disclosure Act of 1959). The Act was designed primarily to protect the rights of union members from the union itself. It includes a bill of rights for union members, requires extensive reporting by both unions and employers, and contains safeguards for democratic government within the union. Although the Act significantly improved the quality of unionism in America, its protection of individual rights also tended to restrict union power.

Regional Differences in Union Membership

The percentage of nonagricultural employees who belong to unions varies greatly from state to state. As shown in Figure 8-2, the heaviest concentration of union employees is in the industrialized eastern and midwestern states and the western seaboard states. Union membership

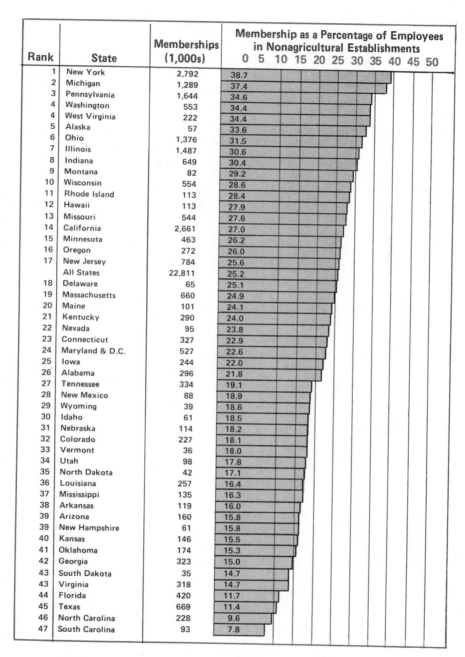

Rank	State	Memberships (1,000s)	Membership as a Percentage of Employees in Nonagricultural Establishments
1	New York	2,792	38.7
2	Michigan	1,289	37.4
3	Pennsylvania	1,644	34.6
4	Washington	553	34.4
4	West Virginia	222	34.4
5	Alaska	57	33.6
6	Ohio	1,376	31.5
7	Illinois	1,487	30.6
8	Indiana	649	30.4
9	Montana	82	29.2
10	Wisconsin	554	28.6
11	Rhode Island	113	28.4
12	Hawaii	113	27.9
13	Missouri	544	27.6
14	California	2,661	27.0
15	Minnesota	463	26.2
16	Oregon	272	26.0
17	New Jersey	784	25.6
	All States	22,811	25.2
18	Delaware	65	25.1
19	Massachusetts	660	24.9
20	Maine	101	24.1
21	Kentucky	290	24.0
22	Nevada	95	23.8
23	Connecticut	327	22.9
24	Maryland & D.C.	527	22.6
25	Iowa	244	22.0
26	Alabama	296	21.8
27	Tennessee	334	19.1
28	New Mexico	88	18.9
29	Wyoming	39	18.6
30	Idaho	61	18.5
31	Nebraska	114	18.2
32	Colorado	227	18.1
33	Vermont	36	18.0
34	Utah	98	17.8
35	North Dakota	42	17.1
36	Louisiana	257	16.4
37	Mississippi	135	16.3
38	Arkansas	119	16.0
39	Arizona	160	15.8
39	New Hampshire	61	15.8
40	Kansas	146	15.5
41	Oklahoma	174	15.3
42	Georgia	323	15.0
43	South Dakota	35	14.7
43	Virginia	318	14.7
44	Florida	420	11.7
45	Texas	669	11.4
46	North Carolina	228	9.6
47	South Carolina	93	7.8

Source: U.S. Bureau of the Census, *Statistical Abstract of the United States: 1984*, 104th edition, p. 440.

FIGURE 8-2 Distribution of Union and Employee Association Memberships by State, 1980

is lowest in the South and Southwest. It is also notable that states with the lowest percentage of union members are also those with right-to-work laws. Although right-to-work laws tend to weaken unions and make organizing difficult, such laws are not the major reason for the relatively low level of union activity in most of these states. As a matter of fact, it was the low level of unionization (lack of union power) that made passage of the laws possible.

Several factors contribute to the weakness of union activity in certain states. One is the paucity of large, labor-intensive industries in these states—a condition which is changing. Conservative attitudes, commitment to the Protestant work ethic, and retention of the dream that it is still possible to achieve financial independence also appear to be more prevalent in these areas. Many employees who are only one or two generations removed from the independence of farm life contrast sharply with employees in industrial centers whose industrial labor ancestry goes back to the sweatshops of the American colonies and Europe.

Personal Decisions Regarding Union Membership

We look now at the motivation of employees for joining unions. Managers have little control over the environmental factors that affect unionization on a national level. Managers do, however, influence organizational behavior and consequently need to understand employee motives for union activity.

Why Employees Join Unions. Because differences exist between unions, situations, and individuals, employees join unions for many different reasons. During the early years of the nineteenth century, pay and working conditions were intolerable by today's standards. Adults were forced out of the job market by employers who hired children for a few cents a day to work under adverse physical and psychological conditions. A 60-hour workweek was the rule, and some employees worked as long as 12 hours a day, 7 days a week. The work was difficult and often dangerous. There was little job security, and supervisory styles were commonly dictatorial and arbitrary. By comparison, employees receiving the minimum wage today are well off. It is interesting to note, however, that the underlying reasons for joining unions have not changed greatly. Some of the most common of these follow:

1. *Desire for security and protection.* The individual who stands alone against the organization may still feel insecure and powerless. Most employees are afraid that absolute power will be misused, and managers often behave in ways that increase the suspicion and distrust

of subordinates. Collective action continues to be a means of countering organizational power.

2. *Desire for more money and better working conditions.* Employees who earn $10 an hour today may feel the need for money just as employees of the 1930s who earned $1 a day did. A 40-hour workweek is good, but a shorter workweek and longer vacations are desirable. The elimination of the back-breaking labor from most jobs was admirable, but today's employees have no memory of the nineteenth century sweatshops or construction labor gangs, and their expectations have increased. Employers today are often called on to provide work that is interesting, challenging, and well paying. The point is sometimes made that more money is no longer the primary objective of unions. Indeed, an increasing amount of bargaining time is spent on other matters such as the nature of the work, supervisory practices, and guaranteed employment. Guaranteed employment has taken an added importance in view of the increasing use of robots, computers, and other laborsaving devices.

3. *Social pressures.* Nowhere are informal group pressures more overtly expressed than in the techniques used by unions to enlist and hold members. Since union-management problems deal with vital economic, social, and family issues, feelings become intense. Employees who refuse to join existing unions must often bear the brunt of frustration-generated hostility. When unions are successful in achieving their objectives, nonunion members are resented because they receive the benefit of union efforts without paying the price for it. When unions are unsuccessful, nonunion employees are perceived as being partially to blame because they have withheld their financial and personal support.

4. *The absence of an alternative.* Many labor contracts require a new employee to join a union within a short time after employment. Such a provision is legal in all states except those with right-to-work laws. In organizations with a **union shop** every employee is required to join the union within a specified time or be dismissed. Although it is illegal for a company to contract with a union to hire only union members, it is not an unusual practice, especially in the building trades.

Only a few employees join unions for philosophical reasons. That minority believes in the economic and social benefits of unionism for society in general. The vast majority of union members are motivated by practical concerns rather than by philosophical beliefs.[6] Significant numbers of union members are political conservatives whose values actively support private enterprise and a capitalistic economy. Most employees, union and nonunion alike, believe that a competitive system is the principal cause of the unique affluence of the United States.

Why Employees Do Not Join Unions. The decline in union employees as a percentage of the total work force indicates that considerable numbers of employees choose not to belong to unions. Again, their reasons differ greatly:

1. *Desire to bargain on the basis of personal contributions.* Individuals in the work force who obviously lack the motivation to join unions include the self-employed and professional managers—although many such persons belong to employer and professional associations for motives similar to those of union members. Managers employed to represent the organization tend to be individualists and to prefer bargaining with the organization on the basis of personal contributions rather than collective power.

2. *Low status of union members.* Employees may refuse to join because of the perceived low status of union members and a preference for identification with management or a professional group. Secretaries and engineers have traditionally fallen into this category. Many employees, even those who earn less pay than union members, want to avoid what they perceive to be a low status that society places on working with one's hands and to enjoy the high status of doing more intellectual work.

3. *Limiting of opportunities.* For some employees union membership is perceived as limiting the opportunities for advancement. These employees prefer performance evaluation to seniority rules. Such views are most likely to be held by ambitious, self-confident individuals who have no distrust of management and who perceive themselves as having a high probability of success.

4. *Costs seen as greater than benefits.* Some employees avoid union membership because they see in it no real benefits. They identify with the organization that employs them and believe that they are treated fairly. Additionally, they want to avoid the payment of union dues and the control unions exert upon their membership. They are aware that the formation of a union could lead to costly strikes, pressures to restrict production, and other actions that could be economically destructive. Such individuals are most likely to work in organizations that already outperform many unionized companies in terms of pay, fringe benefits, and other forms of compensation. In such organizations, warm, personal relationships with management are a valued

aspect of the workplace that would probably be disrupted by unionization.

5. *Fear of management reprisals.* Employees of nonunionized companies often fear management reprisals for union involvement. The Wagner Act makes it an unfair labor practice for management to discriminate against an employee for union activity; such discrimination is, nevertheless, a common practice in some companies. Ordinarily managers disguise their actions, for example, by making working conditions so unpleasant that the subordinate prefers resignation to the harassment. Nonunion employers, usually with the help of sympathetic employees, have powerful means at their disposal for influencing the behavior of employees who actively promote unionization. In the emotionally charged atmosphere surrounding a union representation election, both management and unions resort to pressure tactics that would otherwise not be considered acceptable.

STRATEGIES FOR UNION SECURITY

The power and effectiveness of unions depend on their ability to represent legitimately a united membership in bargaining with management. One of the major tasks of union leadership is to establish and maintain this legitimacy.

The right of a union to speak for all or part of an employee group must be established before meaningful collective bargaining is possible. Once the employee group and management accept the initial right of a union to serve as the bargaining agent, the union customarily bargains for agreements that will further strengthen its leadership position and protect its membership from erosion by apathy, turnover, or management action. The strategies by which the union's right and ability to represent a group of employees are maintained are called **union security agreements**. The most common of these are the

1. Exclusive bargaining agent

2. Closed shop

3. Union shop

4. Modified union shop

5. Preferential shop

6. Agency shop

7. Maintenance of membership

8. Check-off

The Exclusive Bargaining Agent

In spite of the power of unions in America and a national policy that encourages collective bargaining, virtually all companies prefer to deal with their employees as individuals. And as long as they conform to the law in their efforts to discourage the formation of unions, this **open shop** arrangement is perfectly legal.[7] An organization with an open shop makes no collective agreements and recognizes no unions even though many of its employees may be union members.

The most elementary form of union security is the organization's recognition of a union as the **exclusive bargaining agent**. This means that the company recognizes the right of a union to represent a specified group of employees in collective bargaining without regard to whether all the employees are union members. In heavily unionized geographical areas or industries, recognition may occur without government involvement. If the company insists on maintaining an open shop, however, the union, in order to be recognized by the company, must engage in a membership campaign and subsequently win an election supervised by the National Labor Relations Board. Figure 8-3 briefly describes the election procedure.

Representation elections may be held under a variety of circumstances, the basic criterion being that "a substantial number of employees" desires to bargain collectively with an unwilling employer. The request that a representation election be held may come from a single employee (when there is evidence that an unfair management practice has discouraged the free signing of authorization cards) or a group of employees. The election request may also be made by an existing labor union that management has refused to accept as an exclusive bargaining agent or as a bargaining agent for its own members. Ordinarily the immediate goal of union organizers is to get as many employees as possible to sign authorization cards. These are 3 by 5 inch cards on which employees specify their name, employer, work unit, job title, address, and phone number. An employee's signature indicates a desire for a certification election but does not bind that individual to vote for certification. An employer may also request an election. This would normally occur in order to demonstrate, with a strategically timed election, that most employees do not desire union representation.[8]

YOUR GOVERNMENT CONDUCTS AN ELECTION
For You - on the job

General Information

Prior to any election conducted by the NLRB there will be posted at the place of your work a Notice of Election issued by the NLRB to inform you of:

- The date, hours, and place of the election

- The payroll period for voter eligibility

- A description of the voting unit of employees

- General rules as to conduct of elections

There is a sample ballot on the Notice of Election which, except for color, is a reproduction of the ballot you will receive when you vote.

You should read the Notice of Election so that you will be familiar with the ballot.

The Voting Place

In the voting place will be a table, a voting booth, and a ballot box. At the table there will be observers for the Union and the Employer and a representative of the NLRB, each of whom will be wearing an official badge. The observers' badges will have ''Observer'' on them. The NLRB representative will wear an "Agent" badge.

The Agent is in charge of the election. If you have questions, talk only with him.

The Voting Procedure

1 Go to the voting table, standing in line if necessary.

2 Give your name and your clock number, if you have one, to the observers. The observers will find your name on the voting list and tell the Agent your name has been found. If any questions are asked, talk only with the Agent. Do not argue with the observers.

3 After your name has been checked off, go to the Agent and he will give you a ballot.

4 Go into the vacant voting booth. Mark the ballot with one X only. **Do not sign the ballot.** Fold the ballot to hide the mark and leave the voting booth taking your ballot with you.

5 Put your ballot in the ballot box yourself. Do not let anyone else touch it.

6 Leave the polling place.

You will notice that only the Agent handled the blank ballots and only you handled your marked ballot. Once your marked ballot is in the ballot box it becomes mixed with all other ballots in the box and cannot be identified. No one can determine how you have voted.

Challenged Ballots

Questions sometimes arise about eligibility of certain persons. Any observer or the NLRB representative can challenge an individual's right to vote. This challenge, however, must be for good cause and not for personal reasons; for example, a name may not appear on the eligibility list because of a clerical error.

If your vote is challenged, take your ballot into the booth, mark it, fold it to keep the mark secret, and return to the voting table. The Agent will give you a challenged ballot envelope on the stub of which are written your name and clock number and the reason for the challenge. You put the ballot in the envelope. You seal the envelope, and you deposit it in the ballot box.

You will note that while your name is on the stub of the envelope it is not on the ballot. **Secrecy** of your vote is maintained because if challenged ballots must be counted and if later investigation reveals challenged voters are eligible to vote, the stub containing the name and clock number of the individual voter is first torn off and discarded. All challenged ballot envelopes are then mixed together. . . .

Source: Information brochure prepared by the National Labor Relations Board.

FIGURE 8-3 General Information Concerning NLRB Supervised Elections

The Closed Shop

Under the closed shop only union members may be hired, and only members in good standing may be retained by the organization. Although the closed shop is prohibited by the Taft-Hartley Act, it is still practiced in industries where union hiring halls are the exclusive source of employees (for example, in the maritime and construction industries). Because employees who are expelled from the union automatically lose their jobs, this arrangement gives the union an inordinate amount of control over the individual employee and consequently over the organization.

The Union Shop

In a union shop, nonunion individuals may be employed, but they are required to join the union after a specified probationary period, usually no longer than a few weeks. Like the closed shop, this form of agreement gives the union a high degree of control over the labor force. Although the union shop is legal under federal law, it has been the prime target of state right-to-work laws. The assumption of right-to-work laws is that a person has a right to gainful employment without being forced to join a union.

The Modified Union Shop

Under the **modified union shop** specified categories of individuals are exempted from having to join the union. Examples of employees not covered by the agreement are those who have religious objections to union membership, those who are employed on a temporary or part-time basis, or those who were employed prior to a certain date.

The Preferential Shop

Under the **preferential shop**, the company agrees to discriminate in favor of union members at the time of employment. This strengthens the union by reducing the likelihood of membership attrition through separations, retirements, and death. Companies object to such an agreement because of their preference for hiring on the basis of qualifications to perform.

The Agency Shop

The **agency shop** does not require union membership, but it requires both members and nonmembers to pay union dues. The goal is to overcome the objection of certain employees to joining a union and at the same time to prevent nonunion members from being **free riders**. A free rider enjoys the advantages of union membership gained in collective bargaining without paying for them.

Maintenance of Membership

As a hedge against loss of union members, the maintenance of membership agreement states that employees who are union members or who join the union after a specified date must maintain their membership in good standing for the remainder of the contract period. Employees who desire to drop their membership are given a period of about two weeks to do so before the agreement takes effect.

The Checkoff

One of the most serious problems encountered by early unions was the collection of dues. This problem was solved by negotiating for the **checkoff**, a contract agreement by which union dues are deducted from paychecks by the employer and remitted to the union. Ordinarily the checkoff requires each individual's authorization, but this is a routine matter.

Presently most contracts provide for the checkoff. It often benefits management in that the organization can avoid discharging employees merely because of nonpayment of union dues. (This would be a problem, for example, under a union shop agreement.)

INDUSTRIAL DEMOCRACY AND THE RIGHT TO MANAGE

Industrial democracy in the United States has been expressed through relatively free, two-party collective bargaining. Although managerial decisions under collective bargaining are often dictated or influenced by union power, collective bargaining is more effective than some alternative systems in protecting management's right to manage.

Although the concept of industrial democracy has been expressed in many ways, essentially it is the notion that democracy should be extended from the political to the industrial arena—that workers should participate in the governing of industry.[9] In America it finds expression primarily in government-endorsed collective bargaining. Employees influence organizational decisions through their elected union representatives who negotiate with management on issues affecting employee welfare. Industrial democracy has also found expression in a variety of participative techniques that do not involve unions. Furthermore, in a number of unionized companies (General Motors Corp., Chrysler Corp., The Bendix Corporation, Rockwell International Corp., TRW Inc., Ford Motor Co., and Safeway Stores, Inc.), labor-management committees have been established to create avenues for cooperation in order to increase profits, prevent the loss of jobs, meet aggressive competition, and solve a variety of common problems.[10,11]

Industrial Democracy Versus Industrial Warfare

The ground rules for the participation of employees in the governing of industrial organizations are expressed in a number of laws, the most prominent of which are the Wagner Act (1935) and the Taft-Hartley Act (1947). These, however, constitute only a small portion of the total body of statutory and common law governing collective bargaining and labor relations. Several hundred labor laws are enacted each year at the state level alone. The continuing flood of labor laws relates to all aspects of labor relations, such as wages, hours, safety, and discrimination in selection, promotion, and compensation.

Government is clearly a third party in the daily decision making and control of industrial organizations. Still, collective bargaining remains an important means by which industrial democracy is achieved. By law, the two parties are forced to discuss their differences and attempt to arrive at rational solutions. At times, government serves as a mediator to keep constructive negotiations moving. In some instances, especially in disputes over employee grievances, third party arbitrators are used by mutual consent of labor and management to make binding decisions and thus to moderate the conflict.

In the final analysis, however, the possibility always exists that the differences between labor and management will be settled by a contest of power. The power of management lies primarily in its access to the economic resources of the organization. It can offer raises, fringe benefits, changes in working conditions, job security, and other sources of need satisfaction. Management also has a potential for using the **lockout** for closing down operations, usually as a means of gaining an advantage in timing when a strike is expected. By using the lockout, however, management inflicts injury upon itself as well as the union.

The union's power lies in its ability to withhold strategic human resources. Although the strike is the most common means of achieving this end, the union may also use other tactics such as the **slowdown** (a deliberate reduction in productivity) or the **boycott** (an effort to influence union members and others to refuse to use the company's products). In a few instances, the union has bargained by promising to increase productivity, but this approach is unusual.

Although the managers of many organizations, including a number of the corporate giants, appear to have accepted the collective bargaining approach in theory as well as practice, acceptance is by no means universal. Resistance has been particularly strong from owner-managers who view the system as an infringement upon their property rights as well as their right to manage. Conscientious employers who believe that they manage fairly and have good employee relations resent what they consider to be the alienation of their employees by the union. They dislike the split loyalties of union members and the imposition of a system that interferes with an employer's ability to relate to employees as individuals. Nevertheless, like the hundreds of federal, state, and municipal laws that regulate employee relations, union power is a reality with which managers must deal.

The Right to Manage

By the very nature of collective bargaining, management is called upon to take action that would not be taken if management had a free choice in the matter. This continually exposes the raw nerve endings around the question of management's *right to manage;* that is, management's right to make the decisions that it believes are necessary for efficient and effective operation of the enterprise. Given the erosion of management decision-making power because of government controls (through legislation, rulings of government agencies, judicial decisions, and the endless rulings of quasi-judicial bodies such as the National Labor Relations Board), management is particularly sensitive to what it perceives to be encroachments upon its right to manage.

Legislation does not specifically limit the subject matter to be dealt with in collective bargaining. In practice such matters as wages, hours, vacations, union security, and fringe benefits are the most common grist for the bargaining mill. But, as a union's power increases, so does its perception of its rights and legitimate interests. For example, who decides whether new automated equipment shall be installed? Management's primary concerns are for economic survival, efficiency, and profits; from management's point of view this question should clearly be answered by management. The union, on the other hand, believes that a need to protect the jobs of its members gives it a right to influence the decision. Such conflicts can hopefully be resolved through the give-and-take required for good-faith collective bargaining. Certainly that was the intent of the labor legislation which provided the guidelines for the bargaining process. Nevertheless, the element of power is ever present in collective bargaining, and at times a test of power must be made to settle the dispute. It would be naive to assume that the most powerful of the two parties is always right in a strict moral sense; however, from a pragmatic viewpoint the system works, and satisfactory alternatives to it are difficult to find.

One advantage of the formal arm's-length bargaining practiced in the United States is that it maintains a high degree of management autonomy in decision making compared with the alternative systems found in several European countries. Since practices in other countries often become trends in this country, it is important that students of organizational behavior be aware of what others are doing. It also helps us to put our own practices in perspective and thus evaluate them more objectively.

In Sweden, where about 90 percent of the blue-collar workers and half the white-collar workers are union members, the influence of unions on organizational decisions is considerably stronger than in the United States. Historically Sweden's labor relations functioned under a right-to-manage concept which included the provision that management's interpretation in any rules disagreement would prevail unless the matter was taken to the labor court by the union or employee. A 1975 law virtually eliminated management's right to manage and gave employees the right of first interpretation, with management having to appeal to the labor court.[12] As labor power in Sweden continues to grow, it is increasingly difficult for management to implement decisions of any sort without employee consultation. The effects on productivity and the survival of the private enterprise system are yet to be determined.

After a quarter century of experience with labor representatives on boards of directors, West Germany enacted a new **codetermination** law that went into effect on July 1, 1976. It provides that every corporation employing more than two thousand persons will be required to establish a supervisory board (roughly equivalent to a board of directors in the United States) divided equally between representatives of shareholders and workers.[13] This means that workers essentially have an equal voice with management in making policy decisions and that the owner's representatives have, for practical purposes, lost the right to manage. Not unexpectedly, native West German and foreign-owned companies immediately began to seek loopholes to avoid the effects of codetermination. Some changed their corporate structures to partnerships, while others pared the number of employees to below the two thousand level. Still others transferred part of their operations to a foreign parent organization.

Although European experience has not borne out the worst predictions for codetermination, neither United States labor nor management has shown a serious interest in it. Even with all its theoretical and practical complications, collective bargaining is preferred because management still maintains the right to manage, relatively speaking; and union leaders, who really do not want the responsibilities of managing the company, are free to represent the interests of their constituents. The recent appointments of UAW presidents Douglas Fraser and Owen Bieber to the Chrysler board of directors, and similar appointments of union officers to the boards of other corporations in the United States, may indicate a reversal of this position.

Union Cooperation Under Stress

The economic downturn in the early 1980s combined with major changes in the nation's economic structure created a crisis atmosphere for managers and union members in the manufacturing sector. In many instances competition from foreign companies with lower labor costs caused management to demand that high wage rates be reduced in the form of **givebacks**—actual reductions in wages or changes in agreements for planned future increases. Faced with agreeing to these demands or losing jobs to foreign competition, many union leaders and members chose to accept the idea of givebacks in exchange for job security. In other instances employers demanded and obtained reductions in wages in return for the promise to continue operating plants and retail outlets that otherwise would have been unprofitable, even though faced with only domestic competition.

A second form of increased union cooperation resulting from the stress of the economic situation was agreeing to changes in work rules and other working conditions that would lead to increased quality or lower labor costs. It remains to be seen, after the crisis atmosphere passes, whether the idea that "what's good for the company is good for the workers" is actually made valid by managerial action and continues to be endorsed by union leaders.[14,15]

THE NATURE AND PURPOSE OF STRIKES

In the short run, strikes are damaging to the national economy, the employer, the striking employees, and the general public. In a sense, collective bargaining has failed when a strike occurs. Alternatives to the strike are becoming increasingly important because of the growing power of unions in the public sector.

Occasional strikes are necessary to make management respect the strike threat. At least management must perceive that a strike is always possible. Yet the strike itself is commonly a destructive weapon. Employees often suffer irrecoverable wage losses during a strike. Mortgage foreclosures, changes in family plans, mounting debts, and a variety of other environmental and psychological problems make strikes a serious matter. As a result, there is strong motivation for mature union leaders to bargain, compromise, and avoid a strike.

Other major costs involved in strikes are not directly related to the dispute in question. A major strike affects suppliers, subcontractors, customers, local retailers, and at times even the national economy. A strike by one union often prevents members of other unions from working, either because of the latter's respect for the strikers' picket line or the interrelationships in their work. These many and complex interdependencies make a strike everybody's business.

Causes of Strikes

Press releases about strikes usually oversimplify their causes. Typically one cause is assumed; for example, a dispute over wages, working conditions, or job security. As a general rule, however, the causes are multiple, and the most publicized issue may be the least significant. Wages are often the primary focus of attention even when the more fundamental problem is a matter of pride and ego defensiveness—for example, a determination on the part of management and the union to hold to prior proclamations about a minimally acceptable settlement.

Even when a settlement is satisfactory to both employees and management, the local union is sometimes forced to strike in support of the national organization. In still other situations, the principal barrier to a settlement lies within the union. Two types of intraunion problems cause the greatest difficulty: (1) **jurisdictional disputes** (that is, disputes over the range of jobs for which a union claims the exclusive right to represent a group of employees) and (2) political problems of the union leadership.

The basic political problem is expressed in the following quotation from a labor relations director in the rubber industry:

> I had done everything I knew to back the union away from their absurd wage demands, but a strike seemed inevitable. Finally, I decided to have a beer and a private conversation with the chief union negotiator. When he was certain the talk would be confidential, he confessed that his constituency was accusing him of being too easy at the bargaining table. He had to give the image of a tough, aggressive negotiator or lose out in the next election. We decided to keep up the charade until the last possible moment and then settle on a figure we both knew was reasonable. I welcomed the opportunity to help shore up his position. His successor could have been a lot worse to deal with.

Since the strike, or threat of it, is the union's major source of power, the fact is often overlooked that management may actually provoke a strike to serve its own purposes. For example, management may take a position that is sure to result in a strike when it believes that a strike will weaken union leadership. Some strikes are also precipitated by a management refusal to engage in good-faith collective bargaining. From the union's viewpoint all strikes are forced by management, a valid position only if we assume that management should always accede to union demands.

Strike Effectiveness

No objective criteria exist by which a union can consistently evaluate the effectiveness of a strike by determining whether union objectives have been achieved. By the very nature of the bargaining process the union's initial demands may be quite different from what it actually hopes to achieve, and what it originally hoped to achieve may prove to be too high or low as the bargaining progresses. In a given strike a union's objectives may be highly complex so that trade-offs between them are possible. For example, the union may be simultaneously bargaining for higher wages, better economic supplements, changes to make jobs more interesting, and the settlement of a large number of grievances in single plants or smaller work units. Evaluating the success of a strike when these union demands are achieved in varying degrees is necessarily a subjective matter. In fact, occasionally an outside observer might feel that a strike is a failure because the union's economic gains seem small compared with the cost of the strike; however, at the same time union leaders and members may feel quite successful because of a psychological gain (for example, an increase in the ability of union leaders and members to present a united front rather than collapse under the stresses involved in a strike). This accounts in part for the fact that both parties can feel successful after a hard-fought bargaining session.

Both union and company leaders have a high capacity for rationalizing. A favorite management rationalization centers around its ability to pass along increased labor costs to the customer. Capitulation is justified because it avoids a strike, while little consideration is given to its effects on the economy, international competition, and other important, long-term factors.

Strike Timing and Targeting. The effectiveness of a strike is often related to its timing. For example, an auto union prefers to strike at a time when it is strategically important for the manufacturer to produce an innovative model ahead of a competitor or take advantage of a surge in consumer buying. Ideally for the union, the time for a strike threat is when inventories of high demand items are low. If inventories are excessive the threat of a strike may have zero impact. Management may be indifferent or may even welcome the strike if the alternative is a layoff until inventories are reduced. In either case there is a work stoppage, but the strike is more likely to deplete union funds and to reflect negatively upon union leaders while only management is blamed for a layoff.

Management also may be indifferent to a strike threat when chances for negotiating a favorable contract are high. This occurs when unemployment is high, when other recently negotiated contracts have been favorable to management, or when the union appears to be weakened because of internal conflict.

Unions sometimes target their strikes. For example, auto unions tend to strike plants that are producing the fast-selling or most profitable lines of cars. In this way they can have a large impact on the employer without putting an equivalent proportion of union members out of work.

Union and Management Propaganda and Escalation. Before and during a strike, both union and management propaganda is abundant. There are charges and countercharges, trial balloons to probe the opponent's expectations and defenses, and biased announcements from both sides concerning profits and losses. Both union leaders and management are concerned with the degree of support employees are willing to give them. They are also concerned about public opinion and the likelihood of government involvement. Both parties are prone to bluff with the skill of professional gamblers. In recent history, court decisions have increased management's willingness to enter the propaganda arena with a growing confidence that free speech is a two-way street.

It is important to note that statistics do not support the idea that violence is a frequently used tactic by either labor or management. There are thousands of peacefully negotiated contracts every year with very few incidents of violence. When violence does occur, however, it is widely publicized, while peacefully negotiated contracts get little attention.

Arbitration as an Alternative to Strikes

One alternative to the disruptive effect of strikes is the use of third-party binding arbitration: Although approximately 95 percent of the labor-management agreements in the private sector provide for binding arbitration of grievances,[16] arbitration to resolve an impasse in negotiations for the basic contract has not been accepted in the private sector.

Critics of compulsory arbitration voice two major objections. First, neither labor nor management likes the idea of having an outsider make the critical decisions about their respective rights and responsibilities which normally are made at the bargaining table. The second objection centers around what former Secretary of Labor W. Willard Wirtz called the "narcotic effect."[17] Wirtz contended that a legal requirement that labor disputes be arbitrated would promote a narcotic effect in the sense of providing an easy, habit-forming release from the difficult task of responsible bargaining. At the present, there is little evidence either to support or deny this belief.

One approach which has recently received an increasing amount of attention is called **final offer arbitration**. Its purpose is to provide an alternative to strikes while avoiding the possible narcotic effect of traditional arbitration. In final offer arbitration, the arbitrator has only the authority to decide which of the final offers is most fair and realistic. Once the judgment is made it becomes binding on both parties. Its value over traditional arbitration lies in its purported ability to motivate both parties to make realistic offers rather than to adhere rigidly to absurd demands in the expectation of a down-the-middle compromise. Though perhaps less painful than the effects of a strike, final offer arbitration provides definite penalties for failure to bargain responsibly. Experience to date tentatively suggests that this approach is somewhat more effective than traditional arbitration.[18] This would especially be true where parties to the dispute are reasonably sophisticated in bargaining techniques and have the sensitivity to anticipate the standards by which the arbitrator's judgment will be made.

EFFECTS OF UNIONS ON BEHAVIOR

The presence of a union in an organization has important effects on the behavior of both managers and workers. Most of these effects follow from the limitations that union contracts put on management's prerogatives.

Limiting the Variety of Tasks

The variety of tasks carried out by an individual worker is generally smaller in a unionized organization. The union's reasons for restricting the variety of tasks include ensuring that workers are not required to do work that they are not qualified to do and ensuring that specialists' jobs are not eliminated by having other workers perform the specialized tasks. For example, contracts that restrict machine operators from making machine adjustments or carrying out maintenance duties, when not actively engaged in operating the machine, create and protect jobs for maintenance personnel.

Such contracts restrict the behavior of managers and workers alike. While they protect workers in terms of both safety and employment, jobs with little variety tend to be less interesting. In addition, any unnecessary employment that follows from excessive task specialization can put a firm at such a competitive disadvantage that it may not survive or may be forced to lay off workers.

Limiting the Amount of Work

Most union contracts restrict the amount of work that a worker can be asked to do in a given period of time. Often this is accomplished by requiring the employer to pay premium wages for work beyond 40 hours per week or work done on Saturdays or Sundays. Such premium payments are sometimes provided by nonunionized employers as well.

The union's goals in restricting the amount of work done by a worker include increasing the number of workers employed and also ensuring that employees have leisure time, are not unduly fatigued, and obtain high incomes.

Restricting the amount of work affects workers' on-the-job behavior by reducing fatigue, and it affects off-the-job behavior by providing more opportunities to pursue hobbies or family interests. It also affects management's behavior by requiring more work-force planning in order to avoid paying premium wages.

Limiting Management's Discretion in Setting Wages

Most union contracts call for wages to be determined in part by seniority. This practice prevents management from paying higher wages to "favorite" employees or requiring unreasonable performance in order to obtain high wages. It also limits the ability of management to pay higher wages to employees who are more productive.

Limiting management's discretion in setting wages affects the behavior of workers by removing one incentive to be productive. It also removes an incentive to compete with other workers in terms of either productivity or sychophantic behavior.

Limiting Management's Ability to Punish Workers

Without union restriction (or other legalistic restrictions such as civil service rules), the fairness of punishment is determined by the ethics and judgment of supervisors and by the ability of workers to retaliate for unfair punishment. These factors of ethics, judgment, and opportunity for retaliation vary among individuals and situations in sometimes capricious ways. In order to protect workers from unfair punishment, union contracts almost invariably call for due process and grievance procedures.

These contract features obviously reduce the range of management's behavior. In contrast, they tend to increase the range of worker behavior. For example, they permit a worker to complain of unfair treatment without fear of reprisal.

An important effect of unions is that they cause workers' loyalties to be divided between the union and the employer, thus creating tension. They also tend to create an adversarial environment in the workplace as the union and management compete for workers' loyalties. In the eyes of many, these tensions are on balance preferable to the tensions resulting from unfair treatment received by some workers and the worker anxiety associated with the imbalance of power between an employer and an individual worker.

IMPORTANT TERMS AND CONCEPTS

craft unions
industrial unions
yellow dog contract
closed shop
union shop
union security agreements
open shop
exclusive bargaining agent
modified union shop
preferential shop

agency shop
free riders
checkoff
lockout
slowdown
boycott
codetermination
givebacks
jurisdictional disputes
final offer arbitration

STUDY AND DISCUSSION QUESTIONS

1. In what ways do unions influence the policies and practices of organizations that have no unions?

2. Members often have a strong identification with the union even though their standard of living is relatively high and many of the management abuses that led to the rise of unions have been eliminated. What accounts for the continuing strength of this identification?

3. Develop a profile for each of two employees based on the following information: The first employee prefers to work for a nonunion company and the second employee does not. Include probable backgrounds, attitudes, values, personality characteristics, and so forth.

4. Explain how each of the following might contribute to the decline in union popularity and membership: (a) relatively full employment nationwide, (b) the movement of industry to the Sun Belt, (c) growth of high technology industries, and (d) increasing numbers of college educated employees.

5. Describe the managerial behaviors that are most likely to encourage unionization.

6. In view of the prounion legislation of 1932 and 1935, what accounts for the fact that unionism began to level off soon after the end of World War II?

7. Recently a nonunion manufacturer, with plants in five countries, employed a national consulting firm to make a site study. The critical question was: Where should we locate our new plant in order to find personnel who will most likely fit into a nonunion organization with a participative management structure? Where would you suppose they might locate? Why?

8. Why do unions place such a high value on union security agreements?

9. What is meant by *industrial democracy*?

10. Neither labor nor management in the United States has shown an interest in a West German type of labor-management collaboration. Why?

11. Describe and evaluate final offer arbitration.

CRITICAL INCIDENT

A MOVE TO THE SUN BELT

General Tire and Rubber Company seriously considered following the lead of its competitors, The Goodyear Tire and Rubber Company, The B. F. Goodrich Co., and Firestone Tire and Rubber Co., by moving its inefficient Akron, Ohio, plant to the Sun Belt, where economic and labor conditions were more attractive.[19] General Tire's expansion into the Sun Belt states during the 1940s had made the firm's executives acutely aware of the advantages of relocating the Akron plant, although it would mean that over two thousand skilled employees would lose their jobs and that valued relationships with suppliers would be disrupted.

General Tire president Jerry O'Neil decided to explore the possibilities of building a new facility in Akron before concluding that the exodus was inevitable, even though the likelihood of staying there appeared remote. To offset the benefits of the move, the firm would have to negotiate a revolutionary new contract with its union, the powerful United Rubber, Coal, Linoleum and Plastic Workers of America (URW), which in 1976 had hastened the flight of jobs from the Akron area with a 141-day strike.

The contract required to keep General Tire in Akron would involve changes of practices that the labor movement had fought for decades—changes such as the following:

1. The abolition of the rigid seniority system that required recently hired employees to be laid off first even though it caused chaos and inefficiency when older employees moved into jobs for which they were untrained or had obsolete skills.

2. Modification of inefficient work rules that unnecessarily restricted production (for example, requiring that an electrician be called in just to replace a light bulb).

3. Giving percentage wage increases rather than across-the-board raises of a fixed amount per hour and giving merit raises to more productive employees.

4. A pay cut of 50 cents per hour, to be phased in during the first nine months of the new contract (a change that would be even more difficult to make because of double-digit inflation).

Nate Trachsel, president of URW Local 9 of the Akron area, considered the alternatives and decided to negotiate—in effect for a new $100 million plant in the Akron area rather than face another in a long series of moves from that increasingly unattractive industrial area.

As Trachsel recalls, "All you had to do was pick up the newspaper to see that things were bad in Akron." One reason, it seemed clear to him, was: "Labor was missing the boat. We were spending too much time saying 'here is what we demand' rather than trying to develop a cooperative atmosphere between the two parties."[20]

After prolonged bargaining and compromising, an agreement was reached and subsequently ratified by an 845-to-5 vote of the union membership. Under the new agreement, ambitious workers could earn more than others, the practice of bumping was reduced, work rules were liberalized, and employees took a 36 cents an hour pay cut. Since, however, an agreement was also made to move from a six- to an eight-hour shift (a condition existing since the job shortage days of the 1930s Depression), all employees, especially those ambitious enough to increase their productivity, would earn more than their previous take-home pay. The new contract would improve the plant's production efficiency at a time when national productivity was steadily decreasing.

1. Why have such cooperative agreements between employers and unions been almost nonexistent?

2. What conditions are necessary for the development of an agreement such as that worked out at General Tire in Akron?

3. What national and international changes have taken place in recent years to produce a need for significant changes in union and management relations?

REFERENCES

1. Akey, Denise S., ed. *National Organizations of the U.S.* Vol. 1, Part 2 of *Encyclopedia of Associations: 1984*, 18th edition. Detroit: Gale Research Company, 1984, p. 1,530.
2. *The Wall Street Journal*, December 29, 1983, p. 13.
3. "A 'Teacher's War' That's Costing Millions," *U.S. News & World Report*, April, 1976, p. 90.
4. "Why Unions Are Going the Merger Route," *U.S. News & World Report*, June 4, 1979, pp. 61–62.
5. Northrup, Herbert R. "The Rise and Demise of PATCO," *Industrial and Labor Relations Review*, Vol. 37, No. 2, January, 1984, p. 167.
6. Berger, Chris J., Craig A. Olson, and John W. Boudreau. "Effects of Unions on Job Satisfaction: The Role of Work-Related Values and Perceived Rewards," *Organizational Behavior and Human Performance*, Vol. 32, 1983, pp. 289–324.
7. National Labor Relations Board. *A Guide to Basic Law and Procedures under the National Labor Relations Act*. Washington: U.S. Government Printing Office, 1978.
8. Sloane, Arthur A., and Fred Witney. *Labor Relations*. Englewood Cliffs, N.J.: Prentice-Hall, Inc., 1981, p. 113.
9. Derber, Milton. *The American Idea of Industrial Democracy: 1865–1965*. Urbana, Ill.: University of Illinois Press, 1970.
10. Bratt, William L. Jr., and Edgar Weinberg. "Labor-Management Cooperation Today," *Harvard Business Review*, Vol. 89, No. 4, January-February, 1978, pp. 96–102.
11. Main, Jeremy. "Ford's Drive for Quality," *Fortune*, April 18, 1983, p. 62.
12. Fay, Nancy, and Herman Gadon. "Worker Participation: Contrasts in Three Countries," *Harvard Business Review*, Vol. 54, No. 3, May-June, 1976, pp. 71–83.
13. "When Workers Help Call the Tune in Management," *U.S. News & World Report*, Vol. 80, No. 19, May 10, 1976, pp. 83–85.
14. Mills, D. Quinn. "Reforming the U.S. System of Collective Bargaining," *Monthly Labor Review*, Vol. 106, No. 1, March, 1983, pp. 18–22.
15. "Why the UAW May Go Back to Old-Style Bargaining," *Businessweek*, March 12, 1984, p. 98.
16. Cohen, Sanford, and Christian Eaby. "The Gardner-Denver Decision and Labor Arbitration," *Labor Law Journal*, Vol. 27, No. 1, January, 1976, p. 18.

17. Wheeler, Hoyt N. "Compulsory Arbitration: A 'Narcotic Effect'?" *Industrial Relations*, Vol. 14, No. 1, February, 1975, pp. 117–120.

18. Feuille, Peter. "Final Offer Arbitration and the Chilling Effect," *Industrial Relations*, Vol. 14, No. 3, October, 1975, pp. 302–310.

19. Armbrister, Trevor. "Revolution at the Bargaining Table," *Reader's Digest*, February, 1980, pp. 144–148.

20. Armbrister. "Revolution at the Bargaining Table," p. 146.

SUGGESTED READINGS

Bass, Barnard, and Charles Mitchell. "Influences on the Felt Need for Collective Bargaining by Business and Science Professionals," *Journal of Applied Psychology*, Vol. 61, No. 6, June, 1976, pp. 770–773.

Beal, Edwin F., and James P. Begin. *The Practice of Collective Bargaining*, 6th ed. Homewood, Ill.: Richard D. Irwin, Inc., 1982.

Cohen, Sanford. "Does Public Employee Unionism Diminish Democracy?" *Industrial and Labor Relations Review*, Vol. 32, No. 2, January, 1979, pp. 189–195.

Feldacker, Bruce S. *Labor Guide to Labor Law*, 2d ed. Reston, Va.: Reston Publishing Co., Inc., 1983.

Freeman, Richard B., and James L. Medoff. *What Do Unions Do?* New York: Basic Books, 1984.

Hammer, L. H. "Relationship between Local Union Characteristics and Worker Behavior and Attitudes," *Academy of Management Journal*, Vol. 21, No. 4, December, 1978, pp. 560–577.

Holden, Lawrence T., Jr. "Final Offer Arbitration in Massachusetts: One Year Later," *The Arbitration Journal*, Vol. 31, No. 1, March, 1976, pp. 26-33.

Jacoby, Sanford M. "The Future of Industrial Relations in the United States," *California Management Review*, Vol. XXVI, No. 4, Summer, 1984, pp. 90–94.

Kochan, Thomas A. *Collective Bargaining and Industrial Relations: From Theory to Policy and Practice.* Homewood, Ill.: Richard D. Irwin, Inc., 1980.

Mills, D. Quinn. "Reforming the U.S. System of Collective Bargaining," *Monthly Labor Review*, Vol. 106, No. 1, March, 1983, pp. 18–22.

9

Managing Conflict and Stress

The executive position is well known for its complex and persistent demands. The buck stops here *and* if you can't stand the heat, get out of the kitchen *symbolize the popular image of the chief executive's position, and the assumption is typically made that the temperature rises as managers ascend the organizational ladder. The constant pressure for profits, the uncertainty of the organizational environment, the never ending demands of unions, the long hours associated with excessive work loads—everyone knows that such job factors ultimately transform healthy, optimistic college recruits into harassed, chain-smoking, ulcer-ridden, self-sacrificing executives. Or do they?*

That's a popular myth, but it is only a myth. Research increasingly supports the idea that white-collar nonexecutives experience more stress than executives do and that blue-collar employees are more likely than either to react negatively to job-related stressors.

The executive's position is ambiguous and its demands unending, but those are the very job characteristics that give certain managers the flexibility and autonomy they need to achieve and find personal fulfillment. These managers are the **internals** *who believe they have control over their environment and set out to make their own luck; they stand in contrast to* **externals** *who believe they are controlled and have no influence over their own destinies. The ability of the internals to face their responsibilities and at the same time have a relatively low stress level is associated with the devices they use for coping with stress. Because such managers are flexible, believe they can influence their environments, and take a problem-solving rather than an emotional approach, they are not threatened by difficult problems. The less potential managers or employees realistically have for controlling their own organizational destinies, the lower the probability that such a positive perceptual set will prevent occupational stress. Especially vulnerable are employees who are locked into jobs that poorly fit their abilities and interests and that are inflexibly designed and closely controlled.[1,2]*

Managers can do a great deal to control the level of stress on themselves and their subordinates and associates, but most managers do not know how. Those who do are happier and healthier and have a more positive impact on the people around them.

An organization can achieve its objectives only if its members co-operate and coordinate their efforts toward a common end. For this to occur, everyone must subordinate a degree of individuality and personal freedom to the organization. Such behavior is not achieved, however, without a struggle. Thus, while organizations require cooperative effort, this does not prevent conflict within and between individual employees.

Previous chapters have dealt with many of the conflicts between individuals and between groups. In this chapter, attention is focused primarily on the individual, with particular emphasis on the practical means by which employees and managers reduce the inner tension and stress associated with work. First, however, we examine the nature of organizational conflict, since this is the context within which individual stress is experienced.

The objectives of this chapter are

TO UNDERSTAND:

1. The nature of organizational conflict
2. The nature of personal stress
3. The causes of job-related stress
4. The creative management of stress

CONFLICT WITHIN ORGANIZATIONS

Conflict is both a disruptive force within an organization and a primary source of individual stress. Yet it can also be a stimulus for creativity and innovation and improved communications. The organization's goal should be to control conflict rather than to eliminate it.

Traditional organization theorists assumed that conflict within organizations was a sickness to be treated with rational principles of organization and a heady dose of formal authority. Human relations theorists agreed that conflict is pathological but believed that it could be eliminated through mutual understanding, improved communications, and a shared awareness that conflict is unnecessary. Neither of these positions is satisfying to modern theorists.

The Inevitability of Conflict

It would be comforting to believe that people are entirely rational and good, but it would not be true. As a matter of fact, all people are a blend of good and bad, rational and irrational, selfish and unselfish. Therefore, it is realistic to assume that unless human nature changes significantly conflict cannot be eliminated. Experience shows, however, that conflict can be contained sufficiently to minimize its destructive effects.

Although organizational conflict occurs in countries with different political and economic philosophies, the United States is unique in its acceptance and institutionalization of conflict as a way of life. This is expressed in four important ways. First, every possible means is taken to protect the rights and freedom of the individual, including a strong adversary system of jurisprudence. Secondly, the use of collective bargaining has, since the 1930s, been promoted by law. Third, the competition between organizations, long institutionalized through antitrust legislation, tends also to legitimize and promote competition between individuals. Finally, our entire system of government, from the election of officials to debate over legislation, is based on the assumption that the benefits of controlled conflict more than offset its disadvantages.

Sources of Organizational Conflict

Since managers must engage in continual combat with competitors, parties to lawsuits, union representatives, and a host of others encountered in operating the firm, it is understandable that a combative lifestyle is also expressed in manager-to-manager relations within the organization. The same competitive spirit that motivates managers to make enormous personal sacrifices for the organization also motivates a sometimes destructive struggle for power. Where the pace is set at the top for cutthroat competition, managers and employees at lower levels have no difficulty justifying their own similar behavior.

Although power struggles within management are an important source of organizational conflict, they are only one of many. Prominent among other sources of conflict are the following:

1. *Line and Staff Competition.* The growth of highly specialized, creative, well-educated staff poses unique problems for line managers. Faced with a growing dependence on staff, line managers must adjust to a reduction in organizational power and prestige. Conflict in most

organizations persists between line and staff because it is virtually impossible to define precisely the responsibility and authority relationships between the two.

2. *Functional Interdependence.* Conflicts between an organization's functional units, such as sales, accounting, and manufacturing, are commonplace. The sales department is at odds with manufacturing because quality is too low or prices are too high to meet the competition. Accounting is viewed as exercising excessive control over budgets, and the sales department is perceived as a culprit because of its free spending. Although departments are separated on the basis of function, they can never function as completely autonomous units. They must somehow resist the constant urge to view the organization in terms of their narrow self-interests.

3. *Labor-Management Polarization.* This is one of the most common sources of organizational conflict. Its implications have already been discussed in Chapter 8.

4. *Organization-Individual Disagreements.* From one perspective, the conflict between the organization and the individual centers around the individual's failure to fulfill the organization's expectations regarding productivity or compliance with rules. From another, the conflict is often seen as resulting from excessive organizational demands. Such conflict may be overt or hidden from view, depending on the perception each side has of the power of the other.

5. *Disagreement over Goals.* Conflict among managers is often caused by the fact that there is poor agreement over goals. One manager makes decisions as though the organization's primary goal were immediate profits, while another acts as though long-term growth were more important. Perhaps an even more common source of conflict is the clash of the personal goals of managers and employees with the goals of the organization.

6. *Overlapping or Ambiguous Responsibilities.* Organizations constantly change in response to personnel turnover, expansion or contraction, the adoption of new policies, changes in the external environment, and so forth. As a result, it is impossible to establish job responsibilities once and for all. When a change occurs, one person reaches out to assume more responsibility, another retrenches, and still another tentatively assumes responsibility for certain functions without knowing definitely who should be performing them. Thus, the stage is set for conflict.

7. *Bottlenecks in the Flow of Work.* Line supervisors in manufacturing must meet production deadlines, but they are dependent upon pro-

duction schedulers, warehousing, shipping, and others for effective performance. A bottleneck at any point can prevent the line supervisors from being effective and is quite naturally an occasion for interpersonal conflict.

8. *Personality Clashes.* Individual differences in such personal qualities as values, attitudes, abilities, and personality traits are often the cause of conflict. Two managers may learn to despise each other thoroughly for reasons totally unrelated to their work, but their performance on the job may suffer because of it. Manager A believes, for example, that Manager B blocked a promotion. As a result, information that B needs for optimal effectiveness is withheld.

Positive Contributions of Conflict

The negative implications of conflict are obvious. Both the individuals involved and the organizations for which they work are usually hurt by it. In recent years, however, both operating managers and organization theorists have discovered positive aspects of conflict. For example, in a study conducted for the American Management Association, executives noted the following positive outcomes of conflict in their companies:

1. Better ideas were produced.

2. People were forced to search for new approaches.

3. Long-standing problems surfaced and were dealt with.

4. People were forced to clarify their views.

5. The tension stimulated interest and creativity.

6. People had a chance to test their capacities.[3]

These outcomes of conflict within organizations are similar to those experienced externally. For example, legislation regulating pension funds, safety on the job, pollution of the environment, or consumer protection may be frustrating and costly, but it still motivates managers to do what is needed. It is not uncommon for an economic recession or the aggressiveness of a competitor to stimulate improvement in an organization's efficiency.

Conflict within organizations, like external conflict, serves as an energizer. Like an electric shock or an injection of adrenaline, it attacks the foundations of complacency and mobilizes the resources required to meet the adversary. Although conflict within organizations is in many ways analogous to a civil war, if it is maintained within bounds its impact in most organizations is less destructive than the lethargy that exists where little conflict is present.

THE NATURE OF STRESS

> Stress is an exceedingly complex concept that does not lend itself to a simple definition. It can best be understood in terms of the internal and external conditions necessary for its arousal and the symptoms by which it is identified. Its identifiable symptoms are both psychological and physiological.

It is not the situation but one's perception of it that determines whether it will be stressful. Thus, Larry Jones, a recent university graduate in an entry-level management position, viewed his job as extremely taxing and wondered whether he would be able to perform adequately in it. Within two months the job's appearance began to change. Although the work itself was at least as demanding as it first seemed to be, Larry discovered that his superiors were tolerant of his initial ineptness and realized it would take several months for him to reach the proficiency level of his predecessor. Although his job remained a challenge, he was soon able to work without the apprehension and physical tension he had felt earlier. In time he became confident that his performance was acceptable, but because of his high level of stress-related motivation he was able to perform at the peak of his ability during a critical time in his career.

Stress is a very imprecise term in the literature of the behavioral sciences. Joseph McGrath, a respected researcher and theorist, prefers to think in terms of the conditions necessary for stress rather than give it a straightforward definition:

> So there is a potential for stress when an environmental situation is perceived as presenting a demand that threatens to exceed the person's capabilities and resources for meeting it, under conditions where he expects a substantial differential in the rewards and costs from meeting the demand versus not meeting it.[4]

As this statement implies, stress occurs in response to an environmental demand upon an individual, but the degree of stress experienced is imperfectly correlated with that demand. It is the "stressee's" perception of the demand rather than the demand itself that determines the degree of stress experienced. That perception is greatly influenced by the individual's self-perceived abilities and overall self-confidence.

The latter part of McGrath's statement indicates that one precondition for stress is that the individual be motivated to perform in a specific situation. For example, a student who is taking an examination on which failure appears likely will experience stress only if the outcome is regarded as important. Or a manager, faced with high employee turnover, may experience stress if superiors expect turnover to be reduced; however, this manager may experience little stress if superiors view high turnover as inevitable.

McGrath gives meaning to stress in terms of the conditions necessary for its arousal. In a later section of this chapter, a further interpretation of stress is given in terms of its symptoms. Within the context of these conditions and symptoms, **stress** may be defined as a psychological and physical reaction to prolonged internal and/or environmental conditions in which an individual's adaptive capabilities are overextended. Stress is one (among many) of a person's adaptive reactions to threat. One may or may not be fully conscious that a threat exists. Even when such awareness is present, the source of the threat may not be known. Since some stress is necessary for life, the word *stress* normally connotes *excessive stress*.

That the perceived threat may be internal—that is, from within the person rather than in the external environment—is seen in the fact that barriers to need satisfaction are often psychological. The two major classes of such barriers are (1) **personal barriers**, in which one's own lack of ability, motivation, or education, for example, prevents need satisfaction and (2) **conflict barriers**, in which one's inability to decide between alternatives becomes a problem. An example of a conflict barrier would be making a choice between the status quo and accepting a promotion that necessitates leaving a preferred geographical area. The notion that the threat must be experienced over a prolonged (but undefined) period of time differentiates stress from short-term emotional states such as momentary fear reactions.

THE SYMPTOMS OF STRESS

Situationally induced stress provides the psychological and physical energy needed for peak performance. When the stress-producing factor cannot be overcome and stress becomes chronic, its effects are mentally and physically destructive.

When one perceives an element in the environment to be threatening or unusually challenging, the brain sends instructions to the endocrine glands to prepare for an emergency. Hormones produced by the pituitary, adrenal cortex, and other glands trigger a series of responses that release the adaptive energies of the body. Under normal conditions the body responds with more physical strength, greater speed, prolonged endurance, deeper concentration, a sharper intellect—whatever the situation demands. But the emergency preparation is not intended to last indefinitely. If the **stressor**, the stress-producing factor, is not eliminated, the body's emergency reaction itself becomes a problem.

The General Adaptation Syndrome

Hans Selye, the world's foremost authority on stress, was the first to describe systematically the changes through which the body passes to deal with a perceived threat. He described what he called the **General Adaptation Syndrome** (G A S), an adaptive response which occurs in three phases: A, an alarm reaction; B, the stage of resistance; and C, the stage of exhaustion.[5]

The alarm reaction is the preparation for emergency action, commonly referred to as preparation for *fight* or *flight* (for aggressive action to meet the threat or for the speed required for a hasty retreat). During this stage, the normal digestive functions slow down, but energy is made available through an increase in blood sugar. The heart beats faster and more strongly to improve the flow of energy resources and waste products, and the blood pressure rises to dilate the vessels and increase the flow of blood to the muscles. Rapid and deep breathing increases the oxygen needed for high energy production, and perspiration offsets the rising body temperature generated by the high activity level. These reactions stand in sharp contrast to the state of internal equilibrium which exists under conditions of relaxation and security.

If the stressor (for example, a financial crisis within the firm) is removed, an internal state of equilibrium or homeostasis is restored. If the perceived threat continues, the body often develops an increased resistance to it. In effect, one's potential for stress is raised, but it takes a toll in use of the body's adaptational resources. In this *stage of resistance* the characteristics of the alarm reaction disappear and bodily functions return to normal.

If the stressor is removed, the body's natural resistance to stress has performed its function. Equilibrium is thereby restored. If, on the other hand, the stressor persists, the individual continues into the irreversible *stage of exhaustion* where the signs of the alarm reaction reappear, the body's adaptive energies are depleted, and the life span is shortened. A wide range of diseases such as ulcers, heart ailments, and high blood pressure are in some instances directly traceable to stress.[6] Many other diseases fail to respond to normal treatment because stress has greatly diminished the body's natural defenses.

Detecting Signs of Unhealthy Stress

Symptoms of unhealthy stress in others may or may not be obvious. Neither do we always recognize them in ourselves. We often move in imperceptible increments from one stage to another, with our standards of normalcy shifting with changes in bodily condition. Thus, a manager whose stymied career results in perpetual stress may forget how it felt to be free from apprehension, tension, and a burning stomach. It is a good day when there is no pain and when life is tolerable without tranquilizers.

Another barrier to objectively diagnosing one's own stress level arises when the stage of resistance is mistaken for equilibrium. The ambitious, hard-driving manager, noting that the original symptoms of stress are gone, is tempted to assume additional stress-producing responsibilities during this stage rather than use the time wisely to reduce the stressors.

The physiological and psychological symptoms of stress occur in many combinations and degrees—enough to make self-diagnoses quite hazardous. Figure 9-1 lists some common symptoms of stress. Applying the checklist to oneself will not provide a professionally respectable analysis of one's stress level, but it should give an insight into the nature of stress.

THE CAUSES OF STRESS

The causes of stress are found within the environment, the individual, and the interaction between the two. The stress experienced by a given individual is seldom traceable to a single source.[7,8]

In exploring the causes of stress it is important that a clear distinction be made between stress and the stressor (the source of the stress). It is confusing and technically incorrect to speak of a "stressful situation" as though anyone placed in that situation would experience stress. For purposes of analysis and understanding, stressors are divided into two classes: Those that lie within the individual and those that are a part of the external environment.

SYMPTOM	DESCRIBES POORLY					DESCRIBES WELL
Constant fatigue	☐	☐	☐	☐	☐	☐
Low energy level	☐	☐	☐	☐	☐	☐
Recurring headaches	☐	☐	☐	☐	☐	☐
Gastrointestinal disorders	☐	☐	☐	☐	☐	☐
Chronically bad breath	☐	☐	☐	☐	☐	☐
Sweaty hands or feet	☐	☐	☐	☐	☐	☐
Dizziness	☐	☐	☐	☐	☐	☐
High blood pressure	☐	☐	☐	☐	☐	☐
Pounding heart	☐	☐	☐	☐	☐	☐
Constant inner tension	☐	☐	☐	☐	☐	☐
Inability to sleep	☐	☐	☐	☐	☐	☐
Temper outbursts	☐	☐	☐	☐	☐	☐
Hyperventilation	☐	☐	☐	☐	☐	☐
Moodiness	☐	☐	☐	☐	☐	☐
Irritability and restlessness	☐	☐	☐	☐	☐	☐
Inability to concentrate	☐	☐	☐	☐	☐	☐
Increased aggression	☐	☐	☐	☐	☐	☐
Compulsive eating	☐	☐	☐	☐	☐	☐
Chronic worrying	☐	☐	☐	☐	☐	☐
Anxiety or apprehensiveness	☐	☐	☐	☐	☐	☐
Inability to relax	☐	☐	☐	☐	☐	☐
Growing feelings of inadequacy	☐	☐	☐	☐	☐	☐
Increase in defensiveness	☐	☐	☐	☐	☐	☐
Dependence upon tranquilizers	☐	☐	☐	☐	☐	☐
Excessive use of alcohol	☐	☐	☐	☐	☐	☐
Excessive smoking	☐	☐	☐	☐	☐	☐

FIGURE 9-1   Checklist of Symptoms of Stress

Internal Stimuli for Stress

The internal sources of stress are complex and difficult to isolate. Some sources are internal in that no external stimulus is needed to maintain the stress, some are internal in that they influence the perception of potential external stressors, and others are internal in that they determine an individual's threshold of resistance to potentially stress-producing stimuli. One's level of motivation is also a factor in the arousal of stress. Each of these internal influences on stress is considered separately, although they function in continual interaction.

Inner Conflicts. For many people stress is a constant companion regardless of how favorable or unfavorable external conditions may be. Nonspecific fears, anxiety, and guilt feelings maintain the body in a state of readiness for emergency action on a continuing basis. The environmental events that left their impact on the individual may even be repressed from memory, but they continue to activate the endocrine glands that in turn provoke the alarm reactions.

Perceptual Influences. Is the boss a menacing, threatening antagonist or a kind, considerate friend? Is there a constant danger of an arbitrary discharge or layoff? Does the future offer broad opportunities for personal advancement or no opportunities at all? The answers to these questions lie only partially outside oneself. Regardless of the facts, the potential of people and situations in the environment to provoke stress depends on perceptual processes that are uniquely individual.

Perception is influenced by a number of internal factors. Certainly people with inner conflicts sufficient to cause stress are more likely than self-confident people to perceive environmental conditions as threatening. Thus, perceptual distortion stimulates a circularity that is hard to break. Because the environment is presumed to be full of danger, evidences of danger are perceived everywhere. They are selectively perceived in exaggerated form.

The perception of a threat is also related to all dimensions of one's self-image. To people who see themselves as problem solvers, for example, a given problem may be welcomed as a friend, while others who question their own competence may view the problem as dangerous.

Perception is also a function of one's attitudes. This is reflected in the attitude of Susan Asano, a respected oil company executive, toward demotions.

> The company had for many years been divided into multistate regions, each with a vice-president for exploration, production, accounting, and the other major functions. For reasons of economy, however, the company had begun to combine regions leaving in each case a large number of competent managers faced with the choice of finding new jobs or taking a demotion. Although Asano was, in fact, one of the managers most likely to be offered a position after the reorganization, she did not perceive this and she became increasingly apprehensive as the decision date drew near.
>
> Asano's perception of her own standing within the company was inaccurate, but much of her problem stemmed from her attitude toward taking a demotion should that be necessary. She saw a demotion as a sign of failure, incompetence, and lack of good standing with one's superiors; and she seemed totally unable to see that a demotion can have different meanings depending on the circumstances. When she was able to see that a demotion in this situation was really no different from being outpaced by a worthy competitor in a race for a promotion, Asano's attitude changed and her rising stress level began to subside. She

got the new job, but she probably would not have had her stress gotten out of control and itself contributed to further perceptual distortion.

Thresholds of Stress. The threshold of stress is not independent of the two factors just discussed but is worth considering as a separate internal influence upon stress levels. We have already discussed the subject of **stress threshold** without calling it by name. People who have few internal conflicts and a minimum of perceptual distortion can withstand external conflict and pressure that weaker personalities would find intolerable. People who have high thresholds for stress have high levels of resistance to it.

Thresholds are related both to ego strength and self-confidence and to specific personality characteristics. If, for example, a stressor is applied to two individuals, the one with the least sensitivity and concern for others is less likely to experience stress. On many occasions, the tough-minded, task-oriented manager survives a business crisis unscathed, while a more sensitive but equally mature and competent colleague develops ulcers and high blood pressure.

Resistance to stress can be due to many other factors. Purely physiological differences in the functioning of the nervous system, glands, and body organs may influence stress levels. Under identical experiences of threat and tension, people differ in their predisposition, for example, to develop high blood pressure (which itself becomes a stressor and compounds the stress problem). On the psychological side, people differ in their repertoire of alternatives for coping with stressors. Personality flexibility is better than rigidity, for example. Such flexibility might manifest itself in the ability to rationalize, to blow off steam rather than to bottle up feelings, or to laugh at oneself and the stressful situation. All these and other behaviors (that could be detrimental if taken too far) provide resources that enable one to face pressure without stress.

Motivational Level. Persons who are ambitious and highly motivated to achieve are more likely to experience stress than are those who are content with their career status. Persons whose self-expectations exceed their abilities and opportunities are especially stress prone.

Lack of career success is cause for concern only if a manager's or an employee's aspirations exceed present or anticipated progress. The second-string professional quarterback will experience no stress from sitting on the bench year after year unless he is deeply motivated to get into the game. Environmental events become stressors only to the person who cares what happens.

Environmental Stressors

Environmental and internal conditions that lie beyond an individual's control are called **environmental stressors**. Such stressors can have a considerable impact on work performance and adjustment.[9] Dr. Thomas H. Holmes and his colleagues have developed a stress scale (Figure 9-2), measured in life change units (LCU), and have predicted that people whose LCU points exceed 300 run the risk of becoming seriously ill within the next two years. You may find it interesting to calculate your personal LCU rating or that of another person you know well.

Numerous aspects of organizational life are potential stressors. They are not, of course, stressors in and of themselves, but for specific individuals they play such a role. Since the controlling conditions have already been discussed, the potential stressors are discussed only briefly.

Organizational Structure. The extent to which the organizational structure influences stress levels depends on the compatability of members with the organization. The rigid structure and strict rules, procedures, policies, and controls of many bureaucracies are preferred by some people but make others feel grossly overcontrolled.

Events	Scale of Impact	Events	Scale of Impact
Death of spouse	100	Change in responsibilities at work	29
Divorce	73	Son or daughter leaving home	29
Marital separation	65	Trouble with in-laws	29
Jail term	63	Outstanding personal achievement	28
Death of close family member	63	Spouse begins or stops work	26
Personal injury or illness	53	Begin or end school	26
Marriage	50	Change in living conditions	25
Fired at work	47	Revision of personal habits	24
Marital reconciliation	45	Trouble with boss	23
Retirement	45	Change in work hours or conditions	20
Change in health of family member	44	Change in residence	20
Pregnancy	40	Change in schools	20
Sex difficulties	39	Change in recreation	19
Gain of new family member	39	Change in church activities	19
Business readjustment	39	Change in social activities	18
Change in financial state	38	Mortgage or loan less than $10,000	17
Death of close friend	37	Change in sleeping habits	16
Change to different line of work	36	Change in number of family get-togethers	15
Change in number of arguments with spouse	35	Change in eating habits	15
Mortgage over $10,000	31	Vacation	13
Foreclosure of mortgage or loan	30	Christmas	12
		Minor violations of the law	11

Source: T. S. Holmes and T. H. Holmes, *Journal of Psychosomatic Research*, Vol. 14, June, 1970, pp. 121–132.

FIGURE 9-2 Holmes Scale of Stress Values

Ivancevich and Donnelly studied 295 sales representatives in tall, medium, and flat organizations. (Tall organizations have many levels of management with relatively few subordinates reporting to each manager; flat organizations have few levels, and each manager has many subordinates.) They found that sales representatives in flat organizations experience lower amounts of "anxiety-stress" than those in medium or tall organizations. To the extent that individual autonomy is a desired quality in the workplace, this finding will probably generalize to other types of employees and other organizations.[10]

Leadership. Although managers have less potential today than in the past for intimidating subordinates and otherwise contributing to stress, managerial behavior is the most critical stressor for many employees. The irresistible urge of some managers to misuse power and the negative reaction of many people to authority combine to make any position of organizational leadership a potential source of threat.

Monotony. Especially at the employee level, monotony is likely to be a stressor. Even employees who find variety and autonomy stress provoking also find monotony frustrating. Monotony is especially likely to be a stressor for managers and others who expect intrinsic satisfaction from their work.

A Blocked Career. One of the most common career crises occurs when managers with high aspirations realize that their upward mobility has stopped. Another occurs when one's employment is threatened by personality clashes, company financial problems, or any other factor which appears beyond the individual's control.

Excessive Responsibility. When organization members fail to perform according to their own expectations or the perceived expectations of their superiors, stress often results. It is interesting to note that the stress-producing effect of this condition may be independent of actual performance. Low producers with low self-expectations may experience no stress, while superior producers with demanding standards are stressed to the breaking point. Excessive responsibility may also result from an inadequate grant of formal authority or other resources.

Task Load. In some situations, no single task demands too much, but the combination of tasks imposes an excessive work load. Time pressures are intense, and there is no letup. For managers, especially, this situation may involve long hours of work with little time off for vacations.

Ambiguous Demands. Although some people need more structure than others, everyone needs a general idea of performance expectations. Frustration results when employees get no feedback on performance or discover that management is using performance criteria which are arbitrary, irrelevant to organizational goals, and constantly changing.

Value Conflicts. The organization sometimes requires behavior that a member cannot perform with a clear conscience. A manager may, for example, be called upon to give kickbacks or to misinform customers about a product.

Interpersonal Conflicts. Having to work day after day with another person who is irritating, aggressive, or repulsive because of personal habits may be highly stress provoking.

Family Crises. Problems relating to marriage, children, health, finances, and other aspects of personal life may cause stress which affects job performance.[11] These problems sometimes combine with on-the-job stressors to produce a stress pattern that is extremely difficult to reverse.

One of the most troublesome aspects of stressors is the fact that two or more may combine to produce an effect which is greater than the sum of the parts. This is illustrated by the case of a mature but overworked financial manager who had to be hospitalized for so-called nervous exhaustion when he discovered that his daughter was on drugs

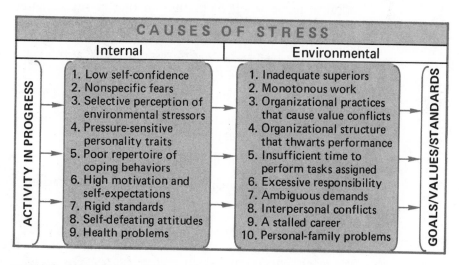

FIGURE 9-3 Some Interacting Causes of Stress

and his wife was unfaithful. Not everyone will break under a combination of intense pressures, but there is a point of frustration at which everyone will experience stress and some deterioration of performance.

THE CREATIVE MANAGEMENT OF STRESS

Since the causes of stress lie both within individuals and their environments, there is no way management can eliminate all organizational factors that trigger undesirable stress. Management can, however, minimize stress, and individuals can control their stress-provoking reactions to the organization.[12]

In most organizations, management assumes that reading the signs of excessive stress and adjusting intelligently are strictly personal matters. Although an increasing number of companies underwrite periodic physical examinations for their managers, any effort to monitor stress levels routinely is presumed to constitute an invasion of privacy. Accordingly, stress reduction is viewed as a personal matter, and most suggestions for the management of stress are made with this fact in mind.

Modifying the Organizational Environment

There are many opportunities for managers to modify the organization to reduce their own stress or that of subordinates. Examples of such actions are

1. Clarifying task assignments, responsibility, authority, and criteria for performance evaluation.
2. Introducing consideration for people into one's leadership style.
3. Delegating more effectively and increasing individual autonomy where the situation warrants it.
4. Clarifying goals and decision criteria.
5. Setting and enforcing policies for mandatory vacations and reasonable working hours.

Too often managers and employees alike assume that organizational changes affecting their welfare can be initiated only by their superiors. As a result, they submissively endure excessive work loads, vague goals, inadequate decision criteria, and similar stressors, when even the slightest initiative to propose solutions would eliminate the stressors.

Escape Techniques

Most people are creative in discovering ways to reduce stress, but their techniques are not always constructive. For example, one escape device is the reduction of one's level of aspiration to the point that productivity becomes unusually low. Other escapes are excessive daydreaming, television watching, and alcohol or drug use. Even overeating is sometimes linked to unconscious attempts to reduce stress. An otherwise wholesome escape becomes destructive when its side effects cause problems (as heavy drinking usually does) or when the amount of time spent in the diversion prevents one from directly facing the stress-producing problem (for example, watching television all evening when selected reading might help remove a stressor problem).

Among the many healthy ways of escaping work pressures and reducing stress are the development of hobbies, direct participation in sports, involvement in civic or religious activities, relaxing with family or friends, and other activities that provide a diversion from work-related problems. As long as a person can set aside time for these activities and approach them in such a way that they themselves do not cause stress, they may contribute significantly to solving the stress problem. These are escape techniques only in the sense that they provide relief from work-related stressors. Labeling them in this way is not meant to imply that they are of intrinsically less value or importance than work, although ambitious managers often behave as though they are.

The Frontal Attack

Stress is sometimes experienced because an individual is unwilling to face and solve a problem directly. While one overworked, underpaid bookkeeper, for example, nurses an ulcer and complains about lack of opportunity, another attends night school to prepare for a career in accounting. At times such a direct confrontation is the ideal way—the only way—to eliminate the source of stress.

The feeling of being boxed-in may characterize the person who insists on having both the comforts of a secure position and the benefits of risk taking. But since the stress associated with a stagnant, no-opportunity situation cannot always be managed by a psychological adaptation, bold action may be needed.

When Calvin Janis was discharged from his four-year tour in the Navy, he took advantage of his military background to gain entry into a civil service career and for ten long, monotonous years worked in a job he considered a waste of the taxpayer's money. One day he awoke to the appalling fact that he had become a clock-watcher whose one goal in life was to retire. Rather than live with the frustration, he left his lucrative civil service job, borrowed the money to go into business for himself, and launched what turned out to be a highly successful career in appliance sales. His business was not without its problems, but they were not the type that produced an unhealthy level of stress.

A frontal attack on the cause of stress sometimes requires a person to play less and work more. Hard work does not in itself cause stress, but one's reaction to failure or inadequate performance often does. It is well to keep in mind the fact that one must usually pay a price for reducing stress to acceptable levels. Students, for example, should not overlook the obvious fact that an ideal way to avoid the stress surrounding examinations is to pay the price of more studying. One might also cope by lowering aspiration levels (for example, making Cs rather than Bs). The immediate price to be paid in this case is lower than that of a frontal attack, but in later years that price may prove to be exorbitant.

Value Clarification

Many people, including some successful managers, have never reflected on their total life situation long enough to decide what is important. As a result, they attempt to achieve career success while neglecting other aspects of their lives such as family, religion, health, and recreation. The stress generated by the neglect in these areas is carried over to the job and effectiveness on the job is thereby undermined.

People with this problem should become introspective long enough to decide what their values really are. In many instances, the value clarification process is less a matter of developing a philosophy than of setting priorities. It may, for example, involve a decision to reject a promotion and preserve one's health or to limit time spent in a career so that more time may be spent in recreation and family activities. Value clarification may lead to the conclusion: I will not sacrifice my personal integrity by engaging in what I consider to be immoral or unethical behavior—even if it means changing jobs. To establish value priorities and to express them in the use of one's time may, for some individuals, be the only way to reduce stress to a healthy level.

The concept of value clarification has numerous applications on the job. Many of the ambiguities in managerial positions are removed when managers take the time to decide what is really important. Managers often waste time on trivia because they are not sure how to distinguish it from what really matters. Managers who decide that their most important problem is, for example, improving the company's cash flow position or improving product quality, know where to concentrate their efforts and invest their resources. Such decision making decreases uncertainty and thereby decreases stress.

Value and time priorities are always closely associated, and both involve decision making. None of the techniques yet devised for helping people reduce stress has much chance of success when priority decisions have not been made. Until such decisions have been made, stress-reduction techniques may have the effect of treating symptoms while the disease continues to spread.

Perceptual Adaptation

Some situations that provoke stress cannot be significantly changed. In the best of companies, for example, managers must weather prolonged periods of recession, the onslaught of a tough competitor, or a crisis caused by an unfortunate decision. This may result in months or years of difficult decisions, long hours of work, and intense pressures from investors, lending institutions, and others. Some managers simply walk away from these situations, but others persist and learn to cope without undue stress.

Some managers who function effectively in such situations have developed creative perceptual sets which prevent excessive stress. These are learned ways of interpreting situations and events. They may comprise frames of reference that allow people to face problems at a level that is not psychologically destructive. Two examples will show how this is accomplished. Except for their names, following are some descriptions of managers with whom the author has worked in management development.

> Linda Hansen's progress in management had been phenomenal; but because her position was valued so highly and her pay was so exceptional, she became apprehensive when making routine decisions. Quite simply, she was afraid she would make a poor decision that could stall her career or cause her to lose her job.
>
> Her fear subsided and her ability to make decisions improved when she stopped thinking of losing her job as the end of a brilliant career. Her altered perception was something like this:
>
> "My security is not based on my success in this particular company but upon my competence and ability to perform. I will give this company all I have to offer. To be sure my effectiveness here is not impaired, I will maintain my contacts within the industry and will always have somewhere else I can go—probably with a promotion. If I get fired, it will not be the end of the world. Good managers get fired every day,

and I have never heard of one who failed to get another job. Making money has never been a problem for me, so all this company can really give me is a rewarding state of mind. If, in fact, the state of mind it gives is one of fear and insecurity, I don't want to work here. I will not trade my self-esteem and sense of well-being for a job, here or anywhere else."

The unhealthy stress experienced by Linda Hansen was removed by a change in perception because the perceptual set through which she had previously viewed her situation was the cause of her difficulty. Had her stress been caused primarily by something else such as a long-standing psychological problem, the perceptual change would not have been so effective.

A slightly different type of situation, involving an inexperienced supervisor, shows how a change in perception, combined with efforts to change the situation, reduced stress:

After only 18 months on the job, Sara Diaz was promoted to office manager. In this capacity, she supervised 8 men and 12 women, several of whom had been candidates for the same promotion. Except for a lack of supervisory experience, she was eminently qualified for the job, and her performance was excellent. She was, however, plagued by a high level of stress. Although the added responsibility was a stressor, it was less so than Sara's inability to accept the fact that two of her subordinates deeply resented her promotion and on occasion negatively influenced the attitudes of other employees toward her. Actually her effectiveness was not in jeopardy, but she could not accept the fact that some subordinates disliked her.

Sara's stress began to subside when she learned to perceive the problem in a different way. Her new perceptual set was: "I don't have to be liked by everyone to be effective. I am not, after all, in a popularity contest. It is enough that I do my job well and am respected. Also, I don't have to be liked by everyone in order to see myself as worthy of being liked. I especially do not have to be liked by people whose attitudes are biased by jealousy. Actually their hostility is not directed toward me so much as toward anyone who might be in my position. Part of my job is to absorb such hostility. It is all in a day's work."

Another approach Sara Diaz used to reduce stress emerged from an insight she expressed this way: "I have been under pressure because I've been working in a hostile, threatening environment; but I created part of that environment by getting promoted and part of it by my perception of others' reactions to that event. I have expected everyone to be hostile, and as a result I have seen hostility where it did not really exist."

Sara's solution was designed to reverse the situation: "Without regard for what anyone else says or does, I am going to be the most effective, likable, considerate supervisor in the company. Although being liked is not critically important, I am going to expect that sooner or later everyone will like me and I am going to act as if they already do. It would be foolish for me to feel uncomfortable in such a warm, friendly environment." As one might expect, her expectation became a self-fulfilling prophecy. Her stress subsided, and her interpersonal relations continually improved.

The technique of **perceptual adaptation** in order to reduce stress has merit only when it does not lead to excessive wishful thinking and escape from the real world. Nevertheless, any situation can be interpreted in many ways, and managers need the flexibility provided by a repertoire of possible interpretations. Accordingly, there is virtue in learning the ways in which effective, stress-resistant managers view their worlds.

The Medication Approach

Tranquilizers are commonly used to reduce stress. If they are taken under the guidance of a competent physician, they can be of benefit in helping to weather a crisis or maintain composure while dealing constructively with a stressor. They should not, however, be viewed as substitutes for coping with the causes of the stress. Because tranquilizers tend to suppress the symptoms of stress and therefore create a false and dangerous illusion of well-being, they should not be considered a long-term solution to the stress problem.

Biofeedback

Whether the task is learning to operate a machine, to conduct an employment interview, or to maintain an inner tranquility in the presence of potential stressors, feedback on performance is essential. What situations, behaviors, and thought patterns cause a person to become tense and exhibit the bodily changes of the alarm reaction? The question is difficult to answer because the initial bodily changes are often imperceptible. By the time one finally becomes aware of the cumulative effect of many stressors, the symptoms cannot be linked to their specific causes. Immediate feedback is needed to establish this association.

Biofeedback is a process through which the bodily changes under stress are magnified and presented to an individual in such a way that the relationship between stressors and stress can be understood. Any number of bodily responses such as those involving muscle tension, skin temperature, perspiration, blood pressure, and heart rate can be monitored simultaneously in a laboratory setting, and research concerning changes in such bodily responses is extensive. Numerous experiments show that through feedback these responses, once considered totally involuntary or automatic, can be consciously controlled.[13,14]

An electronic apparatus called the **electromyograph** provides feedback on the electrical activity (tension) within the muscles and is now available at a reasonable cost. Electrodes placed on the head, for example, provide impulses that are fed back as sound beeps. As tension decreases, the beeps occur less frequently. As an individual gains insight into the thought processes and physical actions that reduce tension, the beeps occur so infrequently that the apparatus must be reset and the process repeated until the desired level of tension reduction is achieved.

Less complicated but equally reliable biofeedback instruments reflect changes in skin temperature. Under stress conditions, the smooth muscles surrounding the blood vessels near the skin surface contract causing a decrease in blood vessel diameter and a constricted blood flow. The reduced capillary blood flow to the skin surface causes skin temperature to drop. Since skin temperature is highly correlated with other bodily responses of the stress syndrome, thermal biofeedback is used to enable persons to raise their skin temperature and thus to reduce stress. Under constant room conditions of about 72 degrees Fahrenheit, fingertip temperatures vary from below 70 degrees Fahrenheit for persons with high stress to above 95 degrees Fahrenheit for persons who are extremely relaxed.

After a few hours' use of the feedback device—sometimes daily periods of fifteen to thirty minutes over a two-week span are sufficient— a person learns how to relax without using a biofeedback instrument. Once the relaxation technique has been mastered, a busy manager can pause occasionally for short relaxation periods—three to five minutes in length—to prevent an accumulation of tension and to reinforce the need to relax.

Biofeedback is definitely useful in controlling the negative physiological effects of stress, especially when the technique is administered by a skilled professional. Its value for this purpose cannot be overemphasized. The technique does not, however, deal with the causes of stress as effectively as it might. In a sense it treats only symptoms, but in many situations this may be sufficient.

Meditation Techniques

Writers and practitioners of **transcendental meditation** (TM) have popularized a variety of meditation techniques that are capable of reducing stress. Although such techniques were originally associated with Far Eastern religions such as Zen Buddhism,[15] many have now lost their ideology. The meditative techniques were developed to help the deeply religious person withdraw from external stimuli into increasingly deeper levels of concentration upon deities or purifying thoughts. Today emphasis is most likely to be upon escape from the harmful effects of external pressures and the achievement of a stressless, if not blissful, state of inner harmony.

Shapiro and Zifferblatt make the point that from research on biofeedback, meditation, and self-control a new model or paradigm of the individual is emerging within the scientific community:

> This paradigm conceptualizes the healthy person as an individual who can pilot his or her own existential fate in the here-and-now environment and who can have far greater self-regulatory control over his or her own body than heretofore imagined. Concomitant with this new paradigm is an attempt to develop and improve techniques by which people can self-observe their behavior, change it (if desired), and then continually modify and monitor it according to their needs.[16]

The scientific research mentioned by these authors points to the conclusion that there is nothing inherently religious or mysterious in TM in spite of the language and thought forms with which it is usually combined. The essential elements of TM are readily available apart from their traditional religious use to anyone concerned with avoiding the damaging effects of stress.

Herbert Benson, Harvard University professor of medicine, describes for the readers of the *Harvard Business Review* the essential features of TM in what he calls the "relaxation response."[17,18] Roughly, the technique involves the following:

1. The meditation place should be quiet. Freedom from all types of distractions is important.

2. The meditator repeats a single-syllable word such as *one*, in a low, gentle tone. This focus upon a single point is a kind of autohypnotic technique for narrowing concentration and releasing oneself from external concerns. (In TM this word is called a **mantra** and would be the name of a deity or some other word with special meaning. It should be a smooth, mellifluous word with many Ms, Ys, and vowels, and no one but the meditator should know what mantra he or she is using.)

3. The meditator assumes a passive, relaxed attitude and avoids any attempt to force a response.

4. The meditator's position should be as comfortable as possible: no tight clothes, arms and legs supported, and so forth.

5. Guidelines are provided for progressively relaxing each part of the body and for breathing in a specified manner. (The breathing exercise is apparently an adaptation from Zen meditation.)

Benson recommends practicing the relaxation response for about 20 minutes at a sitting. The research on such techniques leaves little doubt that they are effective in controlling the physiological effects of stress. They are superior to biofeedback in requiring no mechanical instruments and to medication in avoiding undesirable side effects and the possible development of a dependency. TM techniques are healthy, natural, self-control methods; and, although it has not been fully demonstrated, it is possible that they have a lasting, integrative effect upon one's personality.

IMPORTANT TERMS AND CONCEPTS

internals	stress threshold
externals	environmental stressors
stress	perceptual adaptation
personal barriers	biofeedback
conflict barriers	electromyograph
stressor	transcendental meditation
General Adaptation Syndrome	mantra

STUDY AND DISCUSSION QUESTIONS

1. Why is it reasonable to expect that conflict within organizations cannot be eliminated?

2. Evaluate the following statement: Although conflict within organizations is in many ways analogous to a civil war, its impact in most organizations is positive.

3. In what sense is it misleading to think of environmental factors as causes of stress?

4. What physiological changes occur in the alarm phase of the General Adaptation Syndrome? How is each change adaptive or purposeful?

5. What are the relationships between perception and stress?

6. What personality characteristics or traits are likely to contribute to a high threshold of resistance to stress?

7. It was observed by a new chief executive of the XYZ Company that stress levels within most of the company's managers were extremely high. What hypotheses with regard to possible causes should be tested?

8. What kinds of escape from work stressors are healthful and constructive?

9. Evaluate the merits of tranquilizers for reducing stress.

10. Compare the relative merits of biofeedback and transcendental meditation in reducing stress.

11. How does thermal biofeedback help a person reduce stress?

CRITICAL INCIDENT

SYLVIA'S STRESS

When she entered college, Sylvia Carnes decided to major in management. Although she was confident about her decision, she knew that her mother had mixed feelings. Her mother wanted what was best for Sylvia and knew that her own role as a mother had been very satisfying. She was less sure of the satisfaction to be obtained from a managerial career.

After graduation Sylvia began her career as a management trainee for a major manufacturer of soap products. The company only employs the most outstanding graduates—as, indeed, Sylvia is—but this causes intense competition for promotion. After three years on the job, Sylvia's progress has been mediocre. Sylvia's personal life has been equally unsatisfactory. At times she has considered marrying the man to whom she has long been engaged. Sylvia is, however, cautious about marrying because she sees that her career progress may depend on geographic moves that could interfere with the locally focused career of her fiancé.

Sylvia's work group is highly informal. Her immediate superior, Vernon Katona, follows the lead of higher management in using an informal, participative leadership style, but Sylvia is never at ease around him. When he criticizes her work or gives her directions, he reminds her of her bossy stepfather whom she thoroughly disliked.

The product development team of which Sylvia is a member works diligently, and there never seems to be a time when anyone feels that the pressure is off. Because there are always several projects going at once, it is difficult to attain a feeling of completion and closure. Actually the production schedules are not too demanding, the pay and other incentives within the company are outstanding, and the employees seem to perform at their peak with a minimum of supervision.

Sylvia finds her work interesting and challenging, but the work pressures are almost too much for her. She sometimes goes home so tired that she sleeps for ten hours without feeling completely rested. She suffers from recurring tension headaches which prevent her from participating in many recreational activities which she might otherwise enjoy. She and her fiancé spend several hours a week together, but the relationship is not what she hoped it might be. Sylvia vacillates between thinking (1) that she should yield to her fiancé's insistence that they marry; (2) that she should forget marriage altogether; (3) that she should combine marriage and a career; and (4) that, regardless of what she does about marriage, she should change jobs.

1. What are the probable sources of Sylvia's stress?

2. What actions would be likely to relieve the stress?

3. What further information do you need to answer the previous two questions with confidence?

REFERENCES

1. Anderson, Carl R. et al. "Managerial Response to Environmentally Induced Stress," *Academy of Management Journal*, Vol. 20, No. 2, June, 1977, pp. 260–272.

2. Fletcher, Ben et al. "Exploding the Myth of Executive Stress," *Personnel Management*, May, 1979, pp. 30–35.

3. Schmidt, Warren H. "Conflict: A Powerful Process for (Good or Bad) Change," *Management Review*, Vol. 63, December, 1974, p. 5.

4. McGrath, Joseph E. "Stress and Behavior in Organizations," ed. Marvin D. Dunnette. *Handbook of Industrial and Organizational Psychology*. Chicago: Rand McNally College Publishing Company, 1976, p. 1,352.

5. Selye, Hans. "The General Adaptation Syndrome and the Diseases of Adaptation," *Journal of Clinical Endocrinology*, Vol. 2, 1946, pp. 117–230.

6. Friedman, Meyer, and Ray H. Rosenman. *Type A Behavior and Your Heart*. New York: Alfred A. Knopf, Inc., 1974.

7. Parasuraman, Saroj, and Joseph Alutto. "Sources and Outcomes of Stress in Organizational Settings," *Academy of Management Journal*, Vol. 27, No. 2, June, 1984, pp. 330–350.

8. Gaines, Jeannie, and John M. Jermier. "Emotional Exhaustion in a High Stress Organization," *Academy of Management Journal*, Vol. 26, No. 4, 1983, pp. 567–586.

9. Bhagat, Rabi S. "Effects of Stressful Life Events on Individual Performance Effectiveness and Work Adjustment Processes within Organizational Settings: A Research Model," *Academy of Management Review*, Vol. 8, No. 4, October, 1983, pp. 660–671.

10. Ivancevich, John M., and James H. Donnelly, Jr. "Relation of Organizational Structure to Job Satisfaction, Anxiety-Stress, and Performance," *Administrative Science Quarterly*, Vol. 20, June, 1975, pp. 272–280.

11. Bhagat. "Effects of Stressful Life Events," pp. 660–671.

12. Benson, Herbert, and Robert L. Allen. "How Much Stress Is Too Much?" *Harvard Business Review*, Vol. 58, No. 4-6, September-October, 1980, pp. 86–92.

13. Lazarus, Richard S. "A Cognitively Oriented Psychologist Looks at Biofeedback," *The American Psychologist*, May, 1975, pp. 553–561.

14. Schwartz, Gary E. "Biofeedback as Therapy: Some Theoretical and Practical Issues," *The American Psychologist*, August, 1973, pp. 666–673.

15. Shapiro, Duane H., Jr., and Steven M. Zifferblatt. "Zen Meditation and Behavioral Self-Control," *The American Psychologist*, July, 1976, pp. 519–532.

16. Shapiro and Zifferblatt. "Zen Meditation and Behavioral Self-Control," p. 519.

17. Benson, Herbert. "Your Innate Asset for Combating Stress," *Harvard Business Review*, Vol. 52, No. 4, July-August, 1974, pp. 49–60.

18. Peters, Ruanne K., and Herbert Benson. "Time Out from Tension," *Harvard Business Review*, Vol. 56, No. 1, January-February, 1978, pp. 120–124.

SUGGESTED READINGS

Blanchard, W. B., and L. H. Epstein. *A Biofeedback Primer*. Menlo Park, Calif.: Addison-Wesley Publishing Co., 1978.

Butler, F., ed. *Biofeedback: A Survey of the Literature*. New York: Plenum Publishing Corporation, 1978.

Carrington, P. *Freedom in Meditation*. Gordon City, N.Y.: Anchor Press, 1977.

Cooper, Cary, and Derek Torrington. "Strategies for Relieving Stress at Work," *Personnel Management*, Vol. 11, No. 6, June, 1979, pp. 28–31.

Gupta, Nina, and Terry A. Beehr. "Job Stress and Employee Behaviors," *Organizational Behavior and Human Performance*, Vol. 23, No. 3, June, 1979, pp. 373–385.

Ivancevich, John M., and Michael T. Matteson. *Stress and Work: A Managerial Perspective*. Glenview, Ill.: Scott, Foresman and Company, 1980.

Jacobson, Edmond. *You Must Relax*. New York: McGraw-Hill Book Company, 1978.

Parker, Donald F., and Thomas A. DeCotiis. "Organizational Determinants of Job Stress," *Organizational Behavior and Human Performance*, Vol. 32, October, 1983, pp. 160–177.

Sheane, Derek. "When and How to Intervene in Conflict," *Personnel Management*, Vol. 2, No. 2, November, 1979, pp. 32–36.

ORGANIZATIONAL STRUCTURE AND PROCESS

The effectiveness of individual managers and employees is determined by their personal characteristics and the groups with which they identify. It is also determined by the organizational environment in which they function—by such factors as organizational structure, the management philosophy to which the organization is committed, and the network through which organizational members communicate with one another and their various publics. Part 4 is about that environment.

Chapter 10 begins with a discussion of the three major aspects of classical organization theory: bureaucratic theory, scientific management, and administrative theory. The classical views of how an organization should be structured and managed are then contrasted with the neoclassical views stimulated by the human relations movement. The chapter concludes with a discussion of modern organization theory.

Chapter 11 is concerned with aspects of organizational structure and process on which managerial effectiveness depends. Managers, for example, must have identifiable expectations; they necessarily function within the constraints of position descriptions and an unwritten role. To further facilitate their work, managers structure systems of motivation, status, communication, and personnel practices. Furthermore, they create systems of control and formal processes for the distribution of authority. In complex organizations managers could not function well without these structuring systems.

Chapter 12 discusses decision making in organizations, a process that depends both on unique individual skills and on the organizational structure that provides decision makers with standards and guidelines. Chapter 13 discusses the nature of communication in organizations. Chapter 14 is concerned with how organizations and managers adapt to continual changes—in the marketplace, in legislation, technology, cultural and social values, and concepts of management.

10

Evolving Views of Organizations

Either as students or as working adults, most of us spend a good deal of our lives participating in organizations or dealing with organizations as consumers or providers of goods or services. Whatever the form of our interaction with organizations, we find them important because they control resources we need. We also find many of them interesting due to their complexity and due to the fact that at any one moment we generally see only a small part of what we know to be a much larger whole.

All people, but especially managers, are more effective in dealing with an organization when they understand how it functions, what its structure is, and what its processes are. This chapter provides perspectives, concepts, and terminology that can be used to analyze organizations and to predict some of what we might find beyond whatever portions of the organization we are able to observe.

Organizations develop because individuals cannot meet their needs and fulfill their aspirations without cooperative effort. From the simple task of lifting a log in the construction of a cabin to the complex task of building a space shuttle, some degree of organized behavior is necessary. In the former case, the advantage of organized behavior may lie only in the fact that two people have more lifting capacity than one. In the latter case, organization involves a large number of specialists interacting to produce a whole that is infinitely greater than the sum of its parts. Whether the objective of an organization is to make a profit, to provide services, or to provide pleasure for its members, the underlying assumption is that the value of the outputs (such as products, services, and salaries) will somehow exceed that of the inputs (for example, money, raw materials, and human effort). The universal compulsion of people to organize attests to the validity of this assumption.

All aspects of organizational behavior—leadership, decision making, motivation, and communication—interact with and are influenced by the formal organization in which they occur. Our understanding of these relationships is incomplete, but we do know that organizational behavior cannot be understood apart from the environment in which it occurs. For this reason, we look now at some of the characteristics of formal organization. The objectives of this chapter are

TO UNDERSTAND:

1. Classical/mechanistic organization
2. Neoclassical influences on organizations
3. Modern concepts of organization
4. Relationships and interactions among differing views

INTRODUCTION TO ORGANIZATION THEORY

There is nothing more practical than a good theory. Because of the many variables involved in organizational life, it is especially important that practicing managers possess theoretical frames of reference within which specific events may be given meaning and predictions made. All managers operate from a theoretical base. It is important that this theory be made explicit and that it meet the standards of logical thinking and empirical testing.

The enormous variation in the size, purpose, and complexity of organizations makes generalization difficult. Statements made about an organization such as General Motors may not apply to a small nonunion research and consulting firm and vice versa. Yet generalizations must be made if our understanding of organizations is to progress. A suitable place to begin is with a statement about the nature of formal organizations.

Formal Organizations

A **formal organization** is a rationally structured system of interrelated activities, processes, and technologies within which human efforts are coordinated to achieve specific objectives.

First of all we must differentiate between formal organizations, such as we are accustomed to observing in business, schools, hospitals, and government and **informal organizations**, which spontaneously develop whenever people interact closely for a period of time. Informal organization exists in cliques, gangs, and cooperative work groups. As discussed in Chapter 6, these informal groups often develop a high degree of structure, including leadership patterns and enforceable standards of acceptable behavior. Because of the overlapping memberships of formal and informal organizations, the latter play a significant role in the life of the formal organization. Unless otherwise specified, however, the term *organization* should be understood to mean formal organization.

Organizations are *rationally structured* in that such elements as the allocation of work, lines of authority, and policies and procedures are designed to fulfill the organization's ultimate purpose and achieve its short-term goals. The organization is a *system* in that all its parts—its structure, activities, processes, and technologies—are interdependent. A change in one area potentially affects all other areas. Finally, organizations do not exist without people, and only through coordinated human effort can organizations achieve their objectives.

Formal organizations are structured in two related ways.[1] First, **structural dimensions** such as size, span of control, and number of management levels define the physical aspects of the environment in which behavior occurs. Second, the **structuring dimensions**, which include the goals, strategies, policies, rules, and similar variables, prescribe and restrict the behavior of an organization's members. When combined, the structural and structuring dimension make up the formal organization structure. In this chapter the distinction between the two dimensions is minimized, but it is helpful in understanding the basic anatomy of organizations.

Organization Theory

Generally speaking, a **theory** is a systematic statement of the interrelated principles and concepts that explain a specific set of observations. For example, motivation theory explains such behaviors as an employee's accident proneness, low productivity, aggressiveness, or general insecurity. Theory is intended to give meaning to or to show the relationship between otherwise unexplainable facts. It subsequently provides a basis for prediction and control.

Organization theory attempts to explain how organizations function and to predict the result that a given change will have on organizational effectiveness. One might ask, for example, what effect the involvement of employees in managerial decision making might have upon productivity and profit. Under ideal conditions organization theory would enable a manager to predict that in a given situation one organizational structure would produce good results while another would not. Unfortunately many aspects of organization theory are not yet developed to the point that accurate prediction is possible.

It will soon become apparent that organization theorists are highly selective in the subject matter they discuss. Actually there is no single theory that deals effectively with all aspects of organizational life, nor is such a theory anticipated. Organization theory is fragmented. A given theorist focuses upon an area viewed as most important, most interesting, or most in need of investigation. Nevertheless, the twentieth century has produced a rich and exciting body of organization theory, much of which has far-reaching implications for the practicing manager as well as for the researcher whose primary concern is understanding.

Organization theory has gone through two stages—the *classical* stage and the *neoclassical* stage. Many of the concepts and terms of these stages are in use today, and it is therefore important to understand them. Modern organization theory is superseding the two earliest stages and is much more useful in prediction and control. Nevertheless, it builds on what has gone before and in some instances is most easily appreciated when contrasted with the classical and neoclassical theories. In this chapter we will examine all three theories.

CLASSICAL ORGANIZATION THEORY

Most organizations are strongly influenced by classical theory. Some of its assumptions are questionable and many of its principles are deficient; its assertions are too sweeping, and its application has often led to undesirable results. It is, nevertheless, a brilliant expression of organization theory and a standard of reference which cannot be ignored or considered insignificant by either the theorist or practicing manager.

Classical organization theory represents a relatively well-defined body of concepts and principles that were formulated during the first half of the twentieth century and were predominant in the thought and practice of managers during most of that period. Three streams of thought converged to produce classical theory: (1) bureaucratic theory, (2) scientific management, and (3) administrative theory (or principles of management).

Classical organization theory is concerned with only rationally structured organizations. We should not overlook the fact that rationally structured organizations have historically been the exception rather than the rule. Even today entire nations are organized around families or individuals rather than around the structures and principles most likely to meet national and individual needs. Some third-world dictatorships are examples of this. Many small businesses follow nonrational models as well. They are developed around their owner's personality and begin to assume more rational dimensions only when they get too large for the owner to personally manage.

Bureaucracies are in direct contrast to personalistic organizations. Bureaucracies are the most rationalistic type of organization and were first presented as a formal organizational type by Max Weber, a pioneer in sociology, who viewed them as ideal organizational structures.[2] Five of the important characteristics of bureaucracies follow:

1. *Specialization and division of labor.* Bureaucracies contain units each with "A specified sphere of competence. This involves (a) a sphere of obligations to perform functions which has been marked off as part of a systematic division of labour (b) the provision of the incumbent with the necessary authority . . . [and requires] (c) that the necessary means of compulsion are clearly defined and their use is subject to definite conditions."[3] This statement acknowledges the historically perceived importance of having the authority and power to carry out assigned duties. It also recognizes that managers must know the precise limits of their scope of authority so as not to infringe upon that of others.

2. *Positions arranged in a hierarchy.* Weber stated, "The organization of offices follows the principle of hierarchy; that is, each lower office is under the control and supervision of a higher one."[4]

3. *A system of abstract rules.* Weber felt a need for "a continuous organization of official functions bound by rules."[5] A rational approach to organization requires a set of formal rules to ensure uniformity and coordination of effort. It also provides the continuity and stability that Weber thought were so important. Rules persist, whereas personnel may frequently change.

4. *Impersonal relationships.* Weber believed that the ideal official should exhibit "a spirit of formalistic impersonality, without hatred or passion, and hence without affection or enthusiasm."[6] Once again, Weber was speaking from the viewpoint of ideal rationality and not of realistic implementation. He felt that in order for bureaucrats to make completely rational decisions they must avoid emotional attachment to subordinates and clients or customers.

5. *Employment based on technical qualifications.* Organizational members are protected against arbitrary dismissal, and promotions are made according to seniority and/or achievement.

In total, it must be remembered that Weber's bureaucracy was intended to be an ideal construct: No real-world organization exactly follows this model, and Weber realized this.

Robert Presthus notes that Weber's analysis could not possibly have considered the ideological climate of contemporary America such as our emphasis on individual rights, the demands of minorities and women, and our changing attitudes about authority, merit compensation, and work.

> . . . Weber deals almost exclusively with the formal, manifest characteristics of bureaucracy, and gives little attention to their unanticipated consequences, either favorable or unfavorable. This orientation is explained in part by the social context in which he lived and wrote; namely, Germany at the turn of the century, with its patent class stratification, its patriarchal family structure, its extreme respect for authority, and its highly disciplined military and governmental bureaucracy.[7]

In popular usage, the term *bureaucracy* is associated with large, inefficient organizations whose members spend more time muddling through an endless maze of red tape than achieving organizational objectives. A *bureaucrat*, an official of such an organization, is perceived as a nameless, robotlike individual whose primary concerns are job security, clockwatching, retirement, and a slavish obedience to unnecessary rules.

There is much evidence to justify the popular use of these terms, but they are not what Weber had in mind; and the Weberian definitions continue to be meaningful in the literature of organization theory. A **bureaucrat** is one of the managers or administrators above the worker level but below the decision-making level. Accordingly, the **bureaucracy** refers to a group of in-between functionaries (middle and lower level managers) who carry out policy rather than make it (Figure 10-1); and a *bureaucratic organization* is one that is structured along hierarchical lines with employees at the bottom, bureaucrats in the middle, and executive leadership at the top.

Weber emphasized the functional superiority of bureaucracy over any other form of organization. "Precision, speed, unambiguity, knowledge of the files, continuity, discretion, strict subordination, reduction of friction and of material and personal costs—these are raised to the optimum in strictly bureaucratic administration."[8] Weber's bureaucracy eliminates "from offical business love, hatred, and all purely personal, irrational, and emotional elements which escape calculation."[9]

Weber was concerned primarily with organizational structure, especially as it relates to the management hierarchy. In contrast, Frederick W. Taylor, usually referred to as the father of scientific management,

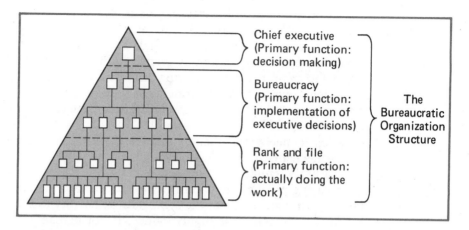

FIGURE 10-1   Weber's Concept of Bureaucratic Structure

was preoccupied with the everyday operational efficiency of an organization, primarily at the employee level. He was particularly impressed with the fact that many employees performed far below their potential, either because of low motivation or because methods and tools were inefficient. Taylor emphasized standard practices (all employees doing a job the same way—the most efficient way); standards of performance (a specified level of productivity per hour or day); breaking complex jobs down into simple, routine ones (job simplification or job dilution); and the development of specialized tools to increase the efficiency of operators.

Although his emphasis was primarily on the needs of the organization for productive efficiency, Taylor was not, as he has sometimes been pictured, an advocate of a heartless exploitation of the individual. Quite to the contrary, he viewed increased efficiency as beneficial to the employee by providing increased income through greater productivity. In spite of inequities and problems along the way, this is exactly what has occurred. No better example can be cited than automobile assemblers whose earnings have exceeded those of many managers in small and inefficient organizations.

Because of his involvement in such molecular functions as time and motion studies, Taylor's contribution to organizational theory was less impressive than Weber's. That cannot be said of the contributions of persons identified with administrative theory (principles of management). Although their approach was similar to Weber's, the two streams of thought developed somewhat independently, especially during the first quarter of the twentieth century. One of the early expressions of organizational principles was made by James Mooney and Allan Reiley.[10] Later a publication by Luther Gulick and Lyndall Urwick[11] and the translation of a book written by French industrialist Henri Fayol[12] continued the trend toward specifying universal principles of the ideal organization. Several of these principles, such as division of labor, unity of command, and hierarchical structure, are discussed later in this chapter.

When conceived as a composite viewpoint, classical organizations have a **mechanistic structure**.[13] They break jobs down into highly specialized units, emphasize the technical rather than the human aspects of increasing production, and firmly posit decision making and authoritative control at the top of the organization. Loyalty to the organization and to one's superiors is highly valued, if not demanded. **Local expertise**—knowledge, skill, and experience obtained within the organization—is often valued more highly than creativity and **cosmopolitan expertise**, the professional expertise that is generally recognized across organizations.

A constantly recurring theme in classical theory is the search for *universals*—guidelines and principles that are applicable to all organizations. Because of this emphasis, classical theory tends to be somewhat mechanical, inflexible, and conservative. In its purest form, it tends to appeal to people with a need for clear-cut and rigid categories. It does not account for a great mass of important data dealing with such subjects as the behavior of informal groups and human values, attitudes, and needs. Nevertheless, classical theory provided the foundation and point of departure for later theories.

NEOCLASSICAL ORGANIZATION THEORY

Neoclassical organization theory evolved as a reaction to the deficiencies in classical theory. Building upon the classical foundation, neoclassical theory incorporated the findings of behavioral scientists, particularly those identified with the human relations movement. Accordingly, neoclassical theory was a step in the direction of humanizing organizations and correcting some deficiencies in classical theory.

The contributions made by classical theory were enormous. Much of what Weber and the other classicists wrote continues to occupy a central position in organization theory. But classical theory had shortcomings which became painfully obvious with experience and with the enlightenment that resulted from behavioral science research.

The most serious flaw in classical theory arose from its assumptions about human nature, especially the simplistic notion that the motivation to work can be understood primarily in economic terms. Running a close second in the list of classical theories challenged by behavioral research was the indefensible position that organization principles can be regarded as universal—that is, applicable to all organizations. The latter assumption gave classical theory a rigid, mechanical dimension that blinded its proponents to a great many facets of organizational behavior.

It is important to recognize that at the time classical theory was set forth, many of the assumptions were much more valid than they now appear. The needs and aspirations of workers were more closely linked to monetary rewards, and organizations did not exist in the variety that they do now. This latter fact caused the idea of universal organization principles to be much more credible than is the case today when one can find an exception to almost any general statement about how organizations are or should be designed.

The Human Relations Movement

To the extent that neoclassical theory can be identified with **the human relations movement**, it may be seen as a reaction to the so-called pathologies of classical theory. Although reformers sought to build upon rather than to destroy classical theory, they were of a different persuasion from the classicists. If classicists were at times undesirably tough-minded, authoritarian, and task oriented, human relationists, at the opposite extreme, were unrealistically people oriented. They have often been accused of being concerned only with making employees happy, as if that would inevitably result in high productivity or as if productivity were unimportant. To the extent that this allegation is true, the movement was naive, blinded in part by its praiseworthy humanitarian values and its sometimes overzealous desire to save the individual from the organization.

Although the origin of the human relations movement is generally associated with the Hawthorne experiments,[14] it is the hundreds of research studies and articles that followed during the 1940s and 1950s that constitute the most significant content of the movement.[15] Although much of the research employed relatively unsophisticated designs and dealt with minute fragments of organizational life, the overall effect was to produce a body of information that contributed significantly to the development of organization theory.

The human relations researchers included psychologists, sociologists, anthropologists, political scientists, professors of management, and practicing managers. Their subject matter was broad, but a few areas stand out. Heavy emphasis was placed on the study of informal groups, employee satisfaction, group decision making, and leadership styles. Although the findings of psychologists on the nature of perception and motivation were introduced into management literature, the focus of the human relations movement was upon the group rather than the individual and upon democratic rather than autocratic leadership. Relatively little attention was given to organizational structure.

The Neoclassicist

Classical theorists are easy to identify. One is, however, on less stable ground in labeling a writer or researcher as a human relationist or neoclassicist, the latter being the broader category. Many who were identified with the human relations movement have become more sophisticated and no longer accept the thinking associated with the human relations movement of the 1950s.

Although neoclassical theory is sometimes equated with human relations theory, this view is not altogether justified. Contributions to neoclassical theory were made by a diverse collection of individuals. Many researchers were behavioral scientists and managers searching for increased understanding while having little concern for or identification with the value-oriented, humanistic applications that characterized the human relations movement. The industrial sociologists often fell into this category.

The human relations movement has given way to the more sophisticated discipline of organizational behavior. The latter deals with the same subject matter as human relations, essentially the content of this book, but is more concerned with research, understanding, and theory development. Today, the term *human relations* is avoided by many writers who do not wish to be labeled as do-gooders having the best of intentions but with little depth of understanding. A minority influence gave the term this negative connotation; nevertheless, *human relations theory* is being replaced by the term *organizational behavior*. The best of the human relations theory is now classified as neoclassical.

Problems Addressed by Neoclassical Theory

The deficiencies of classical theory are the primary subject matter of neoclassical theory, although they are often dealt with indirectly and in piecemeal fashion. These deficiencies are sometimes called the pathologies (illnesses) of bureaucracy. Seven of the more commonly observed pathologies of bureaucratic organizations are briefly described in the sections that follow.

Overconformity. An organization's survival depends upon the willingness of its members to sacrifice a degree of individuality and to conform to certain behavioral norms. But conformity can be taken too far, limiting creativity and individual growth and at times rewarding immature behavior. Where willingness to conform becomes a standard by which behavior is evaluated, managers throughout the hierarchy sometimes become carbon copies of top management in attitudes, beliefs, and behavior.

Obscured Goals. Following an organization's rules, policies, and procedures to the letter may become so important to its members that they lose sight of the organization's reason for existence. This may often be observed in government agencies where employees sometimes appear to be more intent on complying with rules than with meeting the needs of the public. The problem is much in evidence in business as well.

Uncontrolled Growth. Organizational units have a tendency to proliferate beyond what can be justified on the basis of increased productivity. Ambitious managers sometimes strive for bigger budgets, more employees, and expanded operations with little appreciation for their effect on overall productivity and profit.

Rigidity. The many stabilizing elements within organizations—lines of authority, position descriptions, policies, work rules, traditions, vested interests—make adaptation to environmental change difficult. Thus, in the mid-1970s a large restaurant still refused to accept credit cards, and internal resistance to change prevented a department store chain from adopting discount marketing methods which could have enabled it to avoid bankruptcy.

Specialization Problems. Specialists pose some unique problems in that the development of expertise in one area leads to a neglect of others and often to conflict-producing tunnel vision. The brilliant accountant who perceives all the company's problems from a balance sheet perspective may thereby be hindered in understanding the problems of marketing or manufacturing. To maximize the benefits of specialization is often to increase problems of communication and coordination. Other problems arising from task specialization (making simple, routine jobs out of complex jobs) were discussed in Chapter 3. The efficiencies gained are accompanied by problems of boredom and minimal utilization of human ability.

Loss of Motivation. The more an organization is routinized through rules and standards, the fewer are the opportunities for exercising initiative and exerting maximum effort. Seniority provisions and other measures that are taken to make jobs secure are often accompanied by a loss of motivation for personal growth and increased productivity. Especially in stable, noncompetitive organizations whose personnel feel secure, motivation for high productivity may be replaced by a Parkinson's law mentality in which the "work expands to fill the time available for its completion."[16]

Subordination of Human Needs. The standardization and impersonal treatment in large bureaucracies often give members the feeling that they are expendable components of a big, heartless machine. In many profit-making organizations, productivity and profit goals are predominant. Managers are sometimes encouraged to put career goals above all others (such as maintaining one's family and health), and employees are treated only as economic units. Because of the limited purpose of organizations, people may be perceived only in terms of their contribution to organizational objectives, with little concern shown for their intrinsic value.

CLASSICAL VIEWS AND NEOCLASSICAL RESPONSES

> Classical theory is concerned with organization structure and with how the services of people can best be utilized. While recognizing the value and necessity of structure, neoclassical theory introduces a real concern for the individual and a conviction that the value of people must not be sacrificed on the altar of organizational principles and objectives.

Seven important classical principles, or pillars of organization, are briefly discussed in this section with the neoclassical response to each. Generally speaking, the classical position may be stated more categorically and precisely than the response. The neoclassical response represents a great many voices, but they are generally characterized by a desire to improve the welfare of employees, to humanize the workplace, and to incorporate the research findings of the behavioral sciences into organization theory.

Division of Labor

From one point of view the **division of labor** refers to task specialization: the practice of making small, simple jobs out of large, complex ones. Thus, instead of a tailor making an entire suit, each of many semi-skilled workers performs a specialized function. One lays out patterns, another cuts the material, while still another sews collars or stitches buttonholes. Professional and technical specialization also is a form of division of labor. Specialists—accountants, engineers, or machinists—perform within a relatively narrow but valuable area of expertise. Professional specialization contrasts with task specialization in which workers are valued for high productivity on work that requires a minimum of knowledge.

Classical Position. To the classicist, task specialization is a means of gaining maximum production efficiency and reducing costs at the work level. But Taylor was an advocate of functional task specialization at the managerial level as well, a practice he termed **functional management**. Under such a scheme, one person would handle timekeeping, another machine repair, another product quality, and so forth. As we shall see later, the increased use of professional and technical specialists has to a great extent diluted management jobs, particularly at the supervisory level.

Neoclassical Response. The division of labor is accepted by neoclassicists, but its dehumanizing effects are emphasized. Employees in excessively specialized jobs often exhibit boredom, indifference, negative attitudes, low motivation, and immature behavior. This means that, apart from any value judgments about the dehumanizing impact of unchallenging jobs, the efficiencies gained by job specialization are partially offset by negative side effects.

At the professional level specialization creates poor communication and coordination. The language of the specialist is often difficult for others to understand, and specialization brings about a perceptual distortion and a tendency to protect one's area of interest. For example, the sales department in one company was in constant conflict with the accounting department over the fact that sales were lost because high standards of customer credit were maintained. Neither seemed able to understand and respond to the needs of the other.

Hierarchical Structure

The positions and jobs of bureaucratic organizations are arranged in a **hierarchical structure**, meaning that they are scaled from highest to lowest on the basis of authority, status, and breadth of responsibility.

Classical Position. From the classical viewpoint the building blocks of organizations are jobs or positions. (Weber called the bureaucratic positions *offices*, a term that is still used extensively, especially in government.) The duties of each position are clearly defined, and the authority relationships among positions are specified. Thus, all members of the hierarchy are aware of their own positions in relation to superiors, peers, and subordinates.

Because the attributes of a position (responsibilities, authority, and the like) are relatively stable regardless of who occupies the position, the organization has stability and resists pressures for change by the whims and personal goals of its members. Because authority relationships are clearly defined, the ability to command and get compliance is theoretically assured.

Neoclassical Response. The principle is sound to a point, but it is too simply stated. Neoclassicists attack the notion of authoritarian leadership, preferring democratic or participative leadership in which the role of formal authority is minimized. They also believe that the structure of the hierarchy should not be rigid. A position should to some degree reflect the characteristics of the person filling it, and the effects of the authority hierarchy should be softened by committee action and participative management programs. Finally, organizations are composed of people, not just positions. To minimize this fact is to subordinate people unnecessarily to the often unsympathetic demands of the organization.

Limited Span of Management

The optimum **span of management** (called *span of control* by classical theorists) refers to the number of subordinates a manager can supervise effectively. The appropriate size of the span was a hotly debated issue among classicists, but neoclassicists have refused to take it seriously. Classicists are perceived as asking the wrong questions and making invalid assumptions.

Classical Position. Classicists believed there was an ideal number of subordinates, but there was no general agreement on what the exact number should be. They believed, however, that the smaller the span of management, the better the control would be. Good control was perceived as tight control. Some believed that a manager's effectiveness would decline when the span exceeded five or six subordinates and that under certain circumstances a span of three might be ideal.

Neoclassical Response. Control took on new meaning for the neoclassicist. The ideal control was believed to be self-control rather than external control through authority. This being the case, the classical notion that a manager should supervise only a limited, specific number of subordinates required alteration. A number of variables affect the proper span of management. Among the more important are

1. The qualifications of the manager (for example, experience and leadership skills).
2. The nature of the technology (for example, routine assembly line versus a job shop operation in which the manufacturing methods change constantly).
3. The qualifications of subordinates (for example, skill level, self-discipline, and motivation to be productive).
4. The number of personal contacts the manager makes with subordinates and others. (One manager may have fewer personal contacts while supervising fifty relatively autonomous store managers or factory workers than another manager—for example, a company president—has in supervising four or five vice-presidents.)
5. The degree of staff support (for example, assistants, quality control inspectors, engineers, secretaries, and personnel specialists).
6. The number of nonsupervisory functions a manager performs (such as serving on committees, making reports, relating to customers, and handling correspondence).

Clearly the appropriate span of management depends upon many variables in the work environment; there can be no simple formula for deciding on the ideal span of management. The classical notion that there is one best span for all situations is without support. In one situation, such as a routine assembly operation, an acceptable span might be fifty. In another, where several employees require the manager's personal attention (a computer programming department, for example), a span of six or eight may be excessive. In all cases, the neoclassicist prefers the broadest possible span of management. This is consistent with a Theory Y view of employees and a conviction that self-discipline under general supervision is preferable to the external control of authoritarian leadership.

It is noteworthy that span of management has a direct bearing on the shape of the organization pyramid, as shown in Figure 10-2. The narrow span of the classicist results in a tall structure while the broad span of the neoclassicist results in a somewhat flatter structure. Neo-classicists prefer the flat, decentralized organizations because decision making occurs at the lowest possible level. Each member is given the greatest possible amount of autonomy, and the inner control that results from individual goal setting and personal commitment is maximized. This is consistent with a neoclassical preference for participative leadership and general rather than close supervision.

Unity of Command

Unity of command means that a given individual takes orders from only one superior.

Classical Position. Unity of command is universally applicable because the person who receives directions from more than one person is apt to get conflicting signals. This would disrupt the chain of command, reduce predictability, and place the subordinate in an untenable position.

Neoclassical Response. The principle is valid to a point, but it does not always apply in the rigid, mechanical fashion envisioned by the classicists. Some adaptation is necessary because of the influence of staff and the concept that authority should be related to competence. In practice,

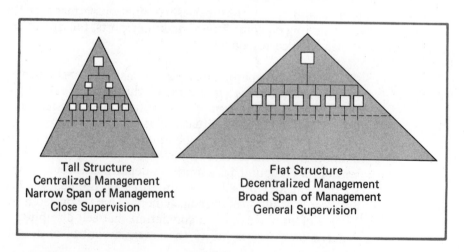

Tall Structure
Centralized Management
Narrow Span of Management
Close Supervision

Flat Structure
Decentralized Management
Broad Span of Management
General Supervision

FIGURE 10-2 Relationship Between Span of Management and Organization Structure and Function

the difference between accepting the advice of a staff expert and obeying the command of a line manager may be difficult to discern, and failure to take the expert's advice may be as disastrous as failure to accept the command. The more complex organizations become, the lower the probability that the unity of command principle can be applied in every situation.

Equal Responsibility and Authority

This principle states that the individual who is assigned a job should be delegated the authority needed to ensure its completion. An unstated assumption is that the use of authority is the primary means of achieving organizational objectives.

Classical Position. The logic of the classicist was simple: It would be irrational and unfair to expect managers without the appropriate authority to get results in terms of the job assigned. A manager assigned the job of manufacturing a product could hardly be expected to succeed without the authority to spend money, hire personnel and direct their activities, and utilize space, materials, and equipment—to take whatever action is necessary to achieve the assigned objective.

Neoclassical Response. Although neoclassicists accept the equal responsibility and authority principle, they understand that more is involved in achieving an objective than the exercise of formal authority. The classicist's statement of the principle seems to imply that the degree of authority and the ability to achieve the assigned objective are perfectly correlated. To the contrary, the exercise of authority may at times interfere with employee motivation and result in resistance and hostility. Leaders whose formal authority is minimal are sometimes better off for the lack of it because they are more inclined to use persuasion, suggestion, and other inoffensive types of influence while taking steps to win the enthusiastic support of subordinates. The point is also made that a manager may officially possess formal authority but lack the ability to exercise it. There are many kinds of authority, power, and influence, a fact not considered by the classicists.

This position does not deny the value of authority. Managers known to possess formal authority are less likely to have to use it than are managers whose authority is questionable. Formal authority is useful, but it should be used sparingly. It should be held in reserve and, except as a last resort, should be subordinated to leadership behavior, expertise, and cooperative goal seeking.

Line and Staff

Organizations are composed of two types of managers. **Line managers** are those who are in the central chain of command. Marketing and production are always considered as line departments because they contribute directly to the organization's primary objective. Line managers receive authority from above and delegate to lower echelons of the hierarchy. **Staff managers** include the specialists who advise and otherwise serve line managers but have no formal authority over the primary operations. Personnel, advertising, and purchasing are considered staff departments, and their leaders are classified as staff managers. (Actually in large organizations there is a chain of command within staff departments—a line within staff—but this is not what we mean by line organization.)

Classical Position. In classical theory, line and staff are easily distinguishable. Line operations pertain to the vertical structure of the organization (delegating, assuming responsibility, maintaining unity of command, and the like) and are called the *scalar process* (from the scale of authority and responsibility). In contrast, staff positions are related to the *functional process* and are a part of the horizontal growth of the organization.

Although staff personnel usually perform specialized functions such as accounting, engineering, and industrial relations, in some cases they are junior administrators who function in positions as assistants to line managers. Since staff personnel support the line organization in a service or advisory capacity, staff is subordinate to line.

Neoclassical Response. Concepts of line and staff were greatly altered by neoclassical thought. As organizations became more technical and complex, staff specialists came to play an increasingly important role in decision making. Even in the early part of this century when Taylor's impact was first felt, industrial engineers and other staff personnel were dictating production methods, rates, and related production matters. Yet classical theorists could find no place for staff in the decision structure because it conflicted with the unity of command principle.

Glenn Stahl, Robert Golembiewski, and others have pointed out that the classical concept of staff as advisors of and inferior to line is not only a questionable concept but actually was never totally accepted in practice.[17] There are numerous examples in the military where staff officers operate more as colleagues than as inferior aids or advisors. It was obvious to most observers that when Henry Kissinger was serving as a foreign affairs advisor to President Nixon he was actually more powerful than the secretary of state and often (even before Kissinger became secretary of state) was in a position to make foreign policy because of his expertise and proximity to the president.

This same phenomenon occurs in industry where personnel move freely between line and staff positions and where influential staff specialists unofficially speak with the authority of their line superiors. For example, an individual was a staff advisor for scientific affairs to the president of IBM one day and the next day was managing a factory (a line position). A top-level Conoco executive was assigned as an assistant to a division production vice-president because he was available and had the ability to solve problems. Within a short time, this staff assistant was promoted to the position of production vice-president in another division of the company. Such persons are never lacking in power merely because they occupy staff positions.

Obviously whether a staff manager is weak or powerful and influences or does not influence decisions cannot be totally predicated on the basis of line-staff identification. Thus, the unity of command problem must be solved in order to avoid excessive line-staff conflict. The neoclassical concept of authority helps to deal with this problem in two ways. First of all, the point is made that formal authority is not the only kind of authority or source of power. Power is also associated with expertise and personal qualities such as charisma and social dominance. Secondly, the dispersion of the decision-making function throughout the organization diminishes the problem somewhat. Staff, like line personnel, can make certain decisions and be held accountable for them. In fact, the neoclassicists are strong advocates of group problem solving in which expertise and formal authority become inextricably intertwined and awareness of line-staff distinctions is minimized. Staff managers have for several decades increased their power relative to line. Only in doing so was it possible for organizations to take advantage of the benefits of specialization (a principle which lies at the heart of classical theory), but the price paid in line-staff conflict has often been high.

Rationality

The principle of rationality has many dimensions, but essentially it means that the structure and function of organizations are goal directed and, for the most part, free of contamination by emotion and human sentiments.

Classical Position. Rationality finds many expressions in the bureaucratic organization. The positions and authority are logically planned according to the bureaucratic principles already discussed. Rules (policies, procedures, regulations, and standards) provide the guidelines for individual behavior. Jobs are simplified as required to maximize efficiency, and personnel decisions (such as selection, promotions, compensation, and disciplinary matters) are made on the basis of performance rather than personal bias.

Neoclassical Response. In principle the rationality concept is admirable and should not be abandoned. It does, however, produce some negative side effects that require attention. The classical approach tends to subordinate the individual to the organization in an unhealthy manner, requiring excessive conformity and destroying the individuality needed to stimulate change and high motivation. The use of rationality helps eliminate prejudice in personnel decisions, but it may also result in treating employees as though they were numbers or machines.

Classical rationality is at points irrational in that it fails to consider the importance of individual differences and to recognize the fact that all people are emotional as well as rational. Rationally, from the classicist's viewpoint, people should exert more effort in order to earn more money, but often this does not happen. This and many other expressions of the classicist's rationality principle sound rational but omit too many important facts about human nature to be workable. The classicist's illusion of rationality is often maintained only by thinking in rigid, oversimplified terms. The greater rationality of the neoclassicist is expressed in an attempt to take all of the data into consideration when making generalizations, especially the great mass of empirical data concerning the nature of individuals and groups.

MODERN ORGANIZATION THEORY

Modern organization theory is theory about organizations that has been developed through scientific study. Use of the word *modern* does not imply that neoclassical theory is out of date. In fact, the two coexist, interact, and in places are indistinguishable. Modern theory, however, is less encumbered by entanglements with classical theory, draws heavily on empirical research, tends to be less ideologically driven, and is more committed to an as yet unrealized integration of its components into a unified system.

Although the lines between neoclassical and modern theory are by no means tightly drawn, modern theory breaks more thoroughly with the rigid, mechanistic aspects of classical structure and is inclined to view organizations as living organisms which are constantly in the process of moving, changing, and adapting.

Modern organization theory is not entirely modern from a time perspective. Although modern theory generally dates back to the 1950s, Chester I. Barnard's 1938 definition of organizations had a distinctly modern ring to it, and Barnard is often viewed as a modern theorist. Setting the pace for modern theory, he defined organizations in terms of a system of consciously coordinated and interrelated personal activities and forces.[18] Yet Barnard had a significant influence on neoclassical theory, too. Because a number of writers are associated with both neoclassical and modern theory, it is impossible to pigeonhole individuals according to the two classifications. Even the concepts involved often defy classification.

A Systems Approach

Modern theory views an organization as a total system rather than concentrating on a single aspect of the system without regard for its relationship to the whole. The point is emphasized that all aspects of an organization are interrelated and that a change in one area affects all others. Thus, a change in executive personnel, promotion policy, methods of accounting, or quality control standards could have implications for apparently unrelated aspects of the organization. For example, promotion of an executive who is an advocate of automation may trigger labor unrest that may ultimately lead to a strike. A minor change in accounting procedures may force a change in record keeping that disrupts the sales force, and the transfer of an employee may upset the equilibrium of an informal work group of which management is not even aware.

As shown in Figure 10-3, there are many kinds of organizational *inputs* or resources of which the organization is composed. The unplanned inputs contribute to organizational irrationality and to undesirable outputs (for example, personal frustrations and losses rather than profits).

Of considerable importance in organization theory is the external environment: Congress passes an Occupational Safety and Health Act, OPEC nations raise the price of oil, and the economy falters with simultaneous inflation and recession. Modern theorists point out the importance of maintaining a dynamic equilibrium with the external environment and of regarding organization as an "open system" in continual interaction with a changing environment.[19] **Dynamic equilibrium** refers to a balance which the organization is able to maintain only by continually adapting, adjusting, or controlling.

Figure 10-3 shows some interrelated variables that influence organizational behavior. The systems approach to studying organizations focuses attention on the fact that, because these variables are always influencing one another, we can understand any given part (for example, decision making) only by understanding how it influences and is influenced by all the other continually changing parts (for example, the organization's objectives, policies, and communication systems, as well as environmental variables such as market conditions and government regulations).

Unfortunately the means of quantifying these interacting variables are not available. In addition, we know relatively little about how the variables affect one another, so it is difficult to develop a workable organization theory based on a total systems approach. Therefore, systems theory presently is more an ideal toward which to strive than a practical foundation for developing functional organization theory.

Contingency Theory

Contingency theory states that the effect (or effectiveness) of any action depends on the situation. For example, the effects of an incentive system based on group performance depends on whether the group mem-

Inputs	Transformation Variables in the Organization	Environmental Variables Affecting Output	Output
Money	Technology	Economic	Product Sales
Materials	Product mix	conditions	
Raw materials	Objectives	Market	Service
Subassemblies	Decisions	conditions	
Energy	Policies	Competition	Profit or Loss
Technology	Management	Cultural values	
Processes	Motivational	and attitudes	Dividends
Scientific	systems	Government	
discoveries	History and	requirements	Satisfactions
Personnel	traditions	World affairs	
Intelligence	Informal	War and peace	Frustrations
Aptitudes	group action	Trade barriers	
Expertise	Communication	Product demand	Personal growth
Attitudes	systems	Union relations	
Motives	Cooperation	Community relations	Wages and
Experience	and conflict	Labor supply	salaries

FIGURE 10-3 Organization as an Interactional System

bers' jobs are interdependent. However, its success also depends on how much the members value money versus a relaxed organizational atmosphere, the ability of the manufacturer to make a profit in an industry where technology is changing rapidly and unpredictably, and on whether the organization has a flexible or a rigid structure.

As can be seen, contingency theory focuses on the compatibility or equilibrium among various aspects of the organization, such as its reward system, workflow, and member value systems, or its environment and its structure. In this respect it is similar to the systems approach. It differs from the systems approach in that it is a research-based body of knowledge about the effects of incompatibility between specific variables rather than being a general approach or perspective.

Integrating Processes

Modern organization theory has given considerable attention to the linking processes by which the units of an organization are integrated into a dynamic, functioning whole. Three of these are decision making, organizational goals and objectives, and communication networks.

Decision making in an organizational context is the process through which organizational actions are selected. In many instances it involves allocating organizational resources. Clearly it is a process that links organizational units, either as participants in the decision process or as recipients of shared resources. We will examine decision making more thoroughly in Chapter 12.

Sometimes decision making involves selecting goals and objectives to be achieved by organizational members or larger organizational units. This process links organizational units, since most units depend upon other units to successfully carry out tasks that they themselves are not prepared to undertake. Thus the sales department depends upon the production and payroll departments to achieve their respective goals and objectives. Unless these goals and objectives are achieved, it will not be long before the sales department will not be able to function. Chapter 20 discusses organizational goals and objectives and their development in detail.

Organizational communications link organizational units in two ways. One is that they are the mechanism through which decision making units direct other units to take the actions decided upon. The second way that communications link various units is that they enable units with information to link to other units who need this information to carry out their tasks, such as communications from sales offices that tell the warehouse what to ship where. Communications are the subject of Chapter 13.

Organic and Mechanistic Structures

Because of the complexity of society and organizations, modern theorists tend to prefer *organic structures*—based on the qualities of living, adapting organisms—to the mechanistic structures of the classicists. **Organic structures**, most appropriate in rapidly changing environments, deemphasize the boundaries of narrowly specialized jobs because those constraints interfere with cooperative problem solving. Responsibility, authority, and control rest with all organizational members; lateral interactions between peers and between persons of different rank are encouraged; and consultation often replaces command. Professional expertise within the industry is more highly valued than local knowledge and blind loyalty to one's employer. Compliance with rules is subordinated to achieving organizational goals. Decision making is presumed to be appropriate at all organizational levels.

The modern emphasis on organic structures has by no means eliminated mechanistic structures, nor is it likely to do so. Mechanistic structures still exist in most organizations and are more appropriate than organic forms in business units such as large automobile manufacturing plants and the clerical processing departments of large insurance companies. Both structures are necessary and can harmoniously coexist in large organizations.

Matrix Organization

A variety of organization structures that differ from the bureaucratic model and violate classical principles of organization are included in modern theory. One of these is called the matrix organizational structure. A **matrix organization** is one where a program or project manager draws upon and has temporary authority over personnel from more permanent units, such as the engineering department or the legal staff. Upon completion of the program or project, the borrowed person returns to his or her home unit or is assigned to another program or project. It is often used when a new product must be developed, say a new aircraft, while maintaining production of existing models. Its most conspicuous feature is that there is dual authority; that is, both the manager of the project and the manager of the permanent units who "loaned" personnel to the project have authority over these personnel.

A matrix organization is often a temporary appendage to a traditional structure, although on major projects temporary could mean several years. The main advantage of a matrix organization is that an objective can be achieved without the expense and time required to develop a totally new organization. In many instances personnel can be drawn from throughout the parent organization without seriously impairing its efficiency. This is especially true of scientific and technical personnel whose work is creative and who lack the routine duties associated with line management.

Depending upon the task, the project manager may develop a large personal staff or may operate virtually alone except for the support received by members of the permanent organization. The matrix organization may consist of temporarily assigned staff members working at the project site or working in their usual job location such as a laboratory, shop, or office. Since one of the advantages of a matrix organization is that it maximizes use of existing facilities as well as personnel, some efficiency may be lost when employees are brought together in a central location. This is, however, necessary on some projects.

Some authorities argue that only when the matrix arrangement is permanent should it be referred to as a matrix organization, such as when the "project" is the ongoing marketing of the organization's services to a large government agency.[20] The example matrix organization structure shown in Figure 10-4 would be applicable whether the matrix organization was temporary or permanent.

Matrix organizations vary in other respects besides their permanency. For example, in some situations the employees who actually perform the project work are never assigned to the project manager. They continue to work under their usual supervisor while performing the tasks needed to complete the special project. They may, in fact, apply their

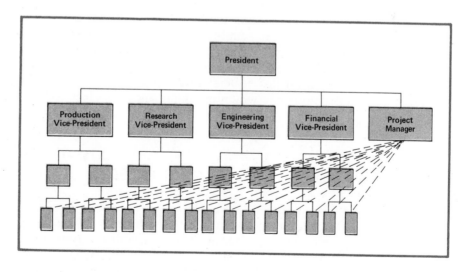

FIGURE 10-4 Matrix Organization Structure

expertise to two or more projects simultaneously. Since project managers work through the existing organization over which they exert no formal authority, one would expect innumerable conflicts to arise, as indeed they sometimes do. On the other hand, the matrix organization can be made to work effectively. There are a number of elements in its dynamics that make it work.

1. The project manager is known to have a high level of competence and the support of upper management.

2. The project manager has a responsibility to perform certain functions which are necessary to achieve the project objectives and has access to the resources (for example, money, people, materials, and space) needed to do the job.

3. A complex network of schedules and communication techniques is maintained to coordinate the work, reduce friction, and ensure the completion of the project.

4. The impact of formal authority that exists within more traditional organizations is softened because the organization places a high value on cooperation, expert judgment, committee action, and scientifically analyzed decisions.

Within matrix organizations, authority to make decisions follows from expertise rather than from formal position in a rigid hierarchy. Since authority of competence is equated with authority of position, matrix and other new organization designs are not new patches sewed onto old garments. They are genuine departures from classical structure. Bureaucratic designs are satisfactory for stable organizations (those with regularized production processes, stable product lines, low employee turnover, or fixed sales outlets), but they are often unable to cope with the complex problems which many organizations face today.

IMPORTANT TERMS AND CONCEPTS

formal organizations
informal organizations
structural dimensions
structuring dimensions

theory
classical organization theory
bureaucracies
bureaucrat

bureaucracy
mechanistic structure
local expertise
cosmopolitan expertise
neoclassical organization theory
the human relations movement
division of labor
functional management
hierarchical structure

span of management
unity of command
line managers
staff managers
modern organization theory
dynamic equilibrium
contingency theory
organic structure
matrix organization

STUDY AND DISCUSSION QUESTIONS

1. Describe the two main dimensions of organizational structure.

2. What problems occur in applying Weber's bureaucratic theory to the development and operation of American organization in the 1980s?

3. Contrast mechanistic and organic structures.

4. Why do practicing managers need to know organization theory?

5. What is the major difference between a formal and an informal organization?

6. What are the major differences between classical and neoclassical theory?

7. What problems are involved in the concept of universal principles of organization?

8. What are the two different ways in which the division of labor principle is expressed?

9. In what ways does the bureaucratic hierarchy contribute to the stability of an organization?

10. How have neoclassicists reacted to the span of management principle?

11. Evaluate the classical notion that staff is generally weak and inferior when compared with line management.

12. What are some of the advantages of working as a member of a matrix organization?

WHO'S IN CHARGE OF WHAT?

Ed Watt's first job after graduating from college with a major in management was in the personnel department of Casper Cleaning Compounds, a small but growing manufacturer of industrial detergents and other cleaning products.

The personnel department had been under some pressure from the company's president to do two things: "Get the federal health and safety inspectors off our backs and make this plant as safe a plant as there is in the city." Rose Steinway, the department manager, was also concerned about the plant's safety record. She gave Ed the task of reviewing the federal inspectors' reports, discussing with all first line supervisors the safety problems that they knew about and the ideas they had for dealing with the problems, and writing a draft report for her to use as input to her report to the company president. Ed felt good about having an important first assignment, and he felt that the assignment would help him to get to know people outside his department.

The only interview that did not go well was with Tim Connery, production supervisor of the abrasive compounds department. Tim gave Ed the impression that "getting the product out the door" was the overriding responsibility of the production department and that plant safety was the responsibility of the personnel department. This attitude seemed to crop up again some weeks later when Ed did a safety tour of all departments and saw one of Tim's employees not wearing a face mask while emptying a sack of silica abrasive. Since silica dust does not dissolve once in the lungs, this was a serious safety violation, and Ed was surprised when he saw it. He thought to himself, "I probably should go to Tim with this, but given his attitude, maybe I could save everyone some grief if I just ask this man if he knows that he is required to wear a face mask when exposing himself to silica dust." With some misgivings Ed did ask, and the man, Frank Carzin, replied that "the boss said I don't have to wear the mask on hot days."

After finishing his tour, Ed returned to the personnel department to find Rose waiting to meet with him. "Tim, we've got a problem," she said. "Frank Carzin told Tim Connery about your questioning him. Frank called me and said that he didn't want you or anyone from the personnel department talking to anyone in his department without first getting his permission. I really doubt that he's got the authority to enforce that. I'm either going to call him back after he's had a chance to cool down, or I'll call the general production manager to see what his views are about Tim's authority to keep staff people from doing their jobs and about Tim's telling employees that safety rules can be violated if they cause people to sweat. In the meanwhile, maybe you'd better not talk to individual employees about safety violations."

1. What classical principles of organization are at issue here?

2. How should Rose handle this situation?

3. What should the general production manager do if Rose calls him about Tim's statements to Frank, Ed, and her?

4. What should be done in the long run to avoid this type of conflict?

REFERENCES

1. Dalton, Dan R. et al. "Organization Structure and Performance: A Critical Review," *Academy of Management Review*, Vol. 5, No. 1, January, 1980, p. 61.

2. Weber, Max. *The Theory of Social and Economic Organization*, ed. Talcott Parsons, trans. A. M. Henderson. New York: Oxford University Press, Inc., 1947.

3. Weber. *The Theory of Social and Economic Organization*, p. 330.

4. Weber. *The Theory of Social and Economic Organization*, p. 331.

5. Weber. *The Theory of Social and Economic Organization*, p. 330.

6. Weber. *The Theory of Social and Economic Organization*, p. 340.

7. Presthus, Robert V. *The Organizational Society*. New York: St. Martin's Press, Inc., 1978, p. 4.

8. Gerth, H. H., and C. Wright Mills, eds. and trans. *From Max Weber: Essays in Sociology*. New York: Oxford University Press, Inc., 1946, p. 214.

9. Weber. *The Theory of Social and Economic Organization*, p. 8.

10. Mooney, James D., and Allan C. Reiley. *Onward Industry!* New York: Harper & Row Publishers, Inc., 1931.

11. Gulick, Luther, and Lyndall Urwick, eds. *Papers on the Science of Administration*. New York: Institute of Public Administration, 1937.

12. Fayol, Henri. *General and Industrial Management*, trans. Constance Storrs. London: Sir Isaac Pitman & Sons, Ltd., 1949. First published in France, 1916.

13. Burns, Tom, and G. M. Stalker. *The Management of Innovation*. London: Tavistock Publications, 1961, pp. 119–125.

14. Roethlisberger, Fritz J., and William J. Dickson. *Management and the Worker*. Cambridge, Mass.: Harvard University Press, 1939.

15. Gardner, Burleigh B., and David G. Moore. *Human Relations in Industry*. Homewood, Ill.: Richard D. Irwin, Inc., 1964.

16. Parkinson, C. Northcote. *Parkinson's Law, and Other Studies in Administration*. Boston: Houghton Mifflin Company, 1957.

17. Browne, Philip J., and Robert T. Golembiewski. "The Line-Staff Concept Revisited: An Empirical Study of Organizational Images," *Academy of Management Journal*, Vol. 17, No. 3, September, 1974, p. 407.

18. Barnard, Chester I. *The Functions of the Executive*. Cambridge, Mass.: Harvard University Press, 1938, p. 73.

19. Scott, W. Richard. *Organizations: Rational, Natural, and Open Systems*. Englewood Cliffs, N. J.: Prentice-Hall, Inc., 1981.

20. Duncan, Robert. "What is the Right Organization Structure? Decision Tree Analysis Provides the Answer," *Organizational Dynamics*, Winter, 1979, pp. 59–80.

SUGGESTED READINGS

Bobbitt, H. R., Jr., and Jeffrey D. Ford. "Decision-Maker Choice as a Determinant of Organizational Structure," *Academy of Management Review*, Vol. 5, No. 1, January, 1980, pp. 13–23.

Carper, William B., and W. E. Snizek. "The Nature and Types of Organizational Taxonomies: An Overview," *Academy of Management Review*, Vol. 5, No. 1, January, 1980, pp. 65–74.

Cascino, Anthony E. "How One Company 'Adopted' Matrix Management in a Crisis," *Management Review*, Vol. 68, No. 11, November, 1979, pp. 57–61.

Daft, Richard L. *Organization Theory and Design*. St. Paul: West Publishing Co., 1983.

Dewar, Robert D., and Donald P. Simet. "A Level Specific Prediction of Spans of Control Examining the Effects of Size, Technology, and Specialization," *Academy of Management Journal*, Vol. 24, No. 1, March, 1981, pp. 5–24.

Fry, Louis F. "The Maligned F. W. Taylor: A Reply to His Many Critics," *Academy of Management Review*, Vol. 1, No. 4, July, 1976, pp. 124–129.

Huber, George P. "The Nature and Design of Post-Industrial Organizations," *Management Science*, Vol. 30, No. 8, August, 1984, pp. 928–951.

Kast, Fremont E., and James E. Rosenzweig. "General Systems Theory: Applications for Organization and Management," *Academy of Management Journal*, Vol. 15, No. 4, December, 1972, p. 451.

Osborn, Richard N., J. G. Hunt, and L. W. Jauch. *Organization Theory: An Integrated Approach*. New York: John Wiley & Sons, Inc., 1980.

11

Organizational Contingencies and Managerial Effectiveness

> *When managers fail—when they are fired, demoted, or passed by when others receive promotions—people who are unaware of all the facts usually assume that the manager's failures are a result of inadequate performance. This assumption often is unjustified. It rests on a prior assumption that the organization has little if any influence on managerial performance. Insiders know that inadequate managerial performance may be due to inadequate opportunity to perform well—that managerial effectiveness is contingent not only on the personal characteristics and behavior of the managers themselves but also on the characteristics of the organization.*
>
> *Managers who know which organizational characteristics can affect their performance are in a better position to choose jobs wisely—to choose jobs in settings where they are more likely to succeed. They are also better able to determine which organizational features are interfering with their effectiveness and thus to take corrective action.*

In this chapter we examine some of the organizational characteristics that influence managerial effectiveness and success. Such an emphasis does not imply, however, that managers are victims of the organization and unable to influence its performance. Because of vast individual differences, an impenetrable barrier to one manager is a challenge to another. One converts the apparent barrier into an asset in reaching organizational goals and achieving personal success while others passively assume that their fate is determined by an all-powerful organization. Nevertheless, managerial effectiveness is determined by the organization as well as the individual.

Although there is no unified body of managerial theory to explain the endless interrelationships among environmental and managerial variables, rapidly expanding numbers of contingency studies are contributing a good deal of useful knowledge. Chapter 11 draws on some of these studies to discuss a few major variables that are generally accepted as having broad applications. The chapter objectives are

TO UNDERSTAND:

1. The difference between situational and contingency theories
2. The manager's need for identifiable expectations
3. The effects of supportive organizational systems
4. The contribution of controls to managerial effectiveness
5. The nature and importance of delegation
6. The stabilizing effect of the organization's status system

SITUATIONAL AND CONTINGENCY MANAGEMENT

The search for universal principles of management often leads to sweeping generalizations that cannot be defended because what works in one situation may not work in another. Contingency theory, the most recent trend in understanding organizational behavior, takes a diagnostic approach in an attempt to isolate certain characteristics of the organizational environment and make "if-then" statements: If a given characteristic is present, then a certain management practice will apply.

For the past two decades, it has been popular to talk in terms of *situational leadership* (or management). In its common usage, the term conveys the idea that a leadership approach that works well in one situation (for example, the presidency of a college fraternity) may be a total failure in another (for example, the management of a construction crew). When generalized, this concept carries the notion that the success of any given management practice in one situation is no assurance that it will succeed in another where conditions are different. Thus, organizational goal setting (management by objectives) has been highly successful in some companies and a miserable failure in many others.

The terms *situational management* and *contingency management* are often used interchangeably. However, Luthans has made a meaningful distinction between the two.[1] **Situational management** proposes that the organizational environment must be analyzed before choosing an appropriate course of action, but it does not attempt to identify the specific conditions under which a given management practice will succeed. **Contingency management** takes the same basic point of view but attempts to go a step further by specifying the relationship between managerial action (say, deciding on the most effective span of management) and other relevant variables (for example, a manager's leadership skills, the nature of the work, and the abilities of subordinates). As research provides new insights into such relationships, contingency management offers considerably more promise than the situational approach.

Contingency management is a middle ground between the view that there are universal principles of organization and management and the view that each organization is unique and that each situation must be analyzed separately. Contingency management does not involve a search for universal principles, but it does seek to draw generalizations within limited contexts. For example, Fiedler's research led him to conclude that task-oriented leaders perform best in situations that are very favorable or unfavorable, while people-oriented leaders perform best in situations of intermediate favorableness (as he defined these terms). This is a contingency if-then approach (if certain conditions exist, then a certain leadership style is best).[2] The situational approach merely states that the most appropriate style depends upon the situation. It does not attempt to specify the if-then conditions.

IDENTIFIABLE EXPECTATIONS

Managerial effectiveness is contingent upon a balance between two environmental extremes: (a) so little position structure that a manager is unable to identify critical job requirements and (b) so much structure that the position cannot be adapted to the unique qualifications of the manager who occupies it.

Position stability is a critical factor in making an organization predictable and thus making possible coordinated effort in achieving goals. Because positions remain stable as individuals flow through them, predictable behavior may continue in the face of high personnel turnover, rapid expansion, and other conditions that would otherwise result in chaos.

The Need to Know What Is Expected

Few management positions are so simple that the incumbents know exactly what is expected of them. A position description helps define expectations, but it is never complete. It represents only the general superstructure of the position. And just as the steel frame of a building shows little of its style, warmth, and uses, the position description only outlines what is expected of a manager. Like a highway map, which cannot show stoplights, rough roads, and washed-out bridges, the position description serves a general purpose but leaves much to the discretion of the user.

The structure provided by a position description is supplemented by supervisory directives, policies, and procedures (many of which are not expressed in writing), and by organizational goals and controls. All these contribute to managerial effectiveness. To the extent that managers know what is expected, they can behave rationally. They can also have reasonable expectations concerning the standards by which their performance will be assessed. In the absence of these conditions, even managers with outstanding potential may find it difficult to perform effectively.

The Managerial Role

As the term is used here, **role** refers to a set of behaviors that is generally regarded as appropriate for a given individual in a specific situation. Like the actor who adapts from one drama to another, we all play many roles, each requiring behavior that may be inappropriate elsewhere. Thus, a manager plays one role as a subordinate and quite another as a peer or superior. The role of parent must be played in one situation, and the role of manager or United Fund drive chairperson must be played in another. The confusion of these roles can be disastrous.

There is, of course, no simple book of rules to describe the many facets of the managerial role. Successful managers are sensitive to their environments, constantly observing and reading the subtle cues, hints, and innuendos by which the unwritten role expectations are communicated. This brief excerpt from a conversation between a newly appointed supervisor and the department superintendent illustrates the point that not all expectations are shown in position descriptions and policy manuals.

> *Supervisor:* Are you telling me I have to give up Tuesday night poker with the friends I've worked with for eight years?
> *Superintendent:* I am not saying that. I have no right to say who your friends should be or what you should do outside your work.
> *Supervisor:* But you're suggesting that I make a break with my friends. You think it's best.
> *Superintendent:* Let's put it this way. Some of the people working under your supervision are accusing you of favoritism toward your close

friends, and it's hurting your effectiveness. In addition, the other supervisors stop talking when you enter the room because they're afraid you will talk out of school. You may want me to tell you how to handle your personal affairs. I will just say this: I shouldn't have to tell you! To succeed in this job you're going to have to see and respond to some cues that you've elected to ignore. Your Tuesday night poker game is just a situation that you must evaluate differently now that you have this job.

In this illustration, the superintendent is finding it difficult to maintain the fiction that managers do not get involved in the private lives of their subordinates; and the newly appointed supervisor is having an understandable problem adapting to the managerial role. This is the characteristic effect of a broad spectrum of unwritten and often unstated expectations to which an effective and successful manager must respond. A manager may be expected to work long and irregular hours and to be supportive of certain attitudes held by higher level managers. Only managers who are aware of and responsive to such expectations will be likely to receive the support necessary to be effective and to be personally successful.

Autonomy and Flexibility

Although formal structure and role expectations may strongly support a manager's efforts to be effective, they can also be a hindrance. Two conditions must be present before they are likely to be supportive. First, structure and role expectations must be flexible enough to permit expression of the individuality involved in adapting position requirements to a manager's unique abilities and needs. Second, and closely related, is the condition that organizational standards and values must be relatively consistent with those held by the manager in question.

Most management positions change over time. Subordinates are selected who can perform well in areas in which the superior is weak or disinterested; new and challenging problems are sought out; and tasks are shifted, within limits, from one manager to another. Much of a position's potential for adaptation depends upon the initiative and motivation of its occupant.

On the basis of extensive research in a variety of companies, Henry Mintzberg and others have shown that what managers say they do varies greatly from what they actually do.[3,4] Following the classical view, they often say that they plan, organize, coordinate, and control. In reality, however, their work involves a variety of unrelenting, short-term, fragmented, and unplanned activities (lasting typically from a few seconds to 30 minutes) that are designed to meet the needs of the moment. Given this lack of rigid structure in most management positions, managers who are proficient in planning, organizing, and delegating have almost unlimited possibilities for shaping their jobs for an optimal match with their personal abilities and needs.

SUPPORTIVE ORGANIZATIONAL SYSTEMS

Organizations vary greatly in the extent to which they provide managerial support. Depending upon the favorableness of the environment, a manager's job may be easy or difficult, possible or impossible. In a highly favorable environment, a marginally qualified manager may perform well; in an unfavorable environment, a superbly qualified manager may fail miserably.

An endless number of organizational conditions interact to determine the favorableness of the manager's environment. In this section we look briefly at three conditions that prove to be important in most organizations. These are concerned with (1) motivational systems, (2) communication systems, and (3) personnel practices.

Motivational Systems

An organization's **motivational systems** consist of all the means by which the work-related behavior of its members is influenced. The most obvious of these have to do with financial compensation—programs and policies by which wages and salaries are used to reward desirable behavior. Other motivational forces are expressed in the extent to which promotions and recognition follow desirable behavior and the degree to which loyalty and interest in the work itself result in positive behavior. The various forms of punishment designed to discourage undesirable behavior are also part of the overall motivational system.

How do an organization's motivational systems relate to managerial effectiveness? Where motivation is generally high, even a manager with mediocre leadership ability may get acceptable results. The system itself gets results whether or not the manager is performing acceptably. However, where motivation is generally low because of organizational conditions over which the manager has no control, personal efforts to motivate subordinates may be unsuccessful.

The following comment from an attitude survey is a good example of a motivational stance that is difficult to overcome. This view was typical of those expressed by most employees in this newspaper composing room.

> I have worked for this company for over 20 years, and I know almost all there is to know about it. Management doesn't really care whether we live or die except that some of us might be hard to replace. Whether you do good work or bad work doesn't matter—you are paid the same either way. Whether you get promoted depends more on your willingness to play politics than on your ability to do the work. I'm not blaming my supervisor for this. My supervisor is a victim of the system, too, with good intentions that don't matter. I'm convinced that nothing will ever be any different until we unionize and run the show ourselves.

Effectiveness is also related to a manager's own motivation to perform. A certain degree of technical and human relations ability is required, but differences in managerial effectiveness are as often attributable to motivation as to ability. Simply stated, some organizations make it rewarding for a manager to perform at a high level while others are structured to reward mediocrity. Accordingly, some organizations find it exceedingly difficult to attract and hold managers with high potential.

Communication Systems

Chapter 13 discusses the process of communication in organizations. At this point our objective is only to show the relationship between an organization's communication systems and managerial effectiveness. Three closely interrelated aspects of the communications process demonstrate this relationship. They are (1) access to information, (2) feedback systems, and (3) written policies and procedures.

Access to Information. The most critical aspect of managerial effectiveness is the ability to make good decisions. This, in turn, is contingent upon the availability of information and the ability to communicate freely with other organizational members who can contribute useful facts or ideas.

Feedback Systems. Organizations have a variety of devices for obtaining feedback. Management reports concerning profits, productivity, quality, sales, employee turnover, and other aspects of organizational life provide valuable information on the extent to which managerial actions are effective. In addition, performance evaluations and attitude surveys may provide feedback on the basis of which a manager may adapt rather than continue an undesirable course of action. These opportunities for feedback are normally built into the fabric of the organization, and their potential for influencing managerial performance varies greatly from one organization to another.

Feedback devices necessarily involve many informal channels of communication that can make an environment either favorable or unfavorable to managerial effectiveness. In commenting on the poor performance of a departmental superintendent, a management consultant made the following observation:

> Mrs. Grossman is not altogether to blame for her plight. She made one big mistake, and it continues to haunt her. Because she resented the condescending treatment of her male peers, she became angry and overreacted by telling them she didn't need their help. But she does need it, and she is not getting it. She lacks the benefit of the exchanges that take place at coffee breaks and lunchtime where much of the really meaningful, work-related communication is taking place. In a real sense she is isolated from the organization. She does not know what is going on most of the time, and she is not getting the benefit of the special consideration the other supervisors are showing for one another's needs. There is no question about her competence, but she is out of the system and cannot perform well under such conditions.

Written Policies and Procedures. Many of the problems a manager faces have been faced before, perhaps with minor variations. It is customary for recurring problems to be dealt with by means of written policies and procedures. This leads to consistency of action and eliminates the frustration and time pressures that result from handling each problem as if it were an isolated event. It would, for example, be foolish to make every credit decision without reference to policies and procedures that capture past experiences and set forth guidelines for dealing with the request of a specific customer or prospect.

The development of policies and procedures is a decision-making process that establishes the limits within which future decisions are made. The manager who has the benefit of current, wisely developed policies and procedures uses these as criteria or standards for decision making. They define what a good decision consists of and thus make good decisions possible. In some organizations, small ones especially, most of the guidelines are locked in the brain of a chief executive. Since subordinate managers must guess at what these guidelines are, they are often forced to be either dependent decision avoiders or high-risk decision makers whose careers are in constant jeopardy.

Personnel Practices

Over a period of time an organization's personnel policies strongly influence its character and personality. Consider the impact of personnel selection. One organization exercises great care in selection in the conviction that each new employee is a valued individual with a unique contribution to make. Special attention is given to how each new employee will relate to existing personnel and to whether the individual's values, standards of behavior, and leadership style are compatible with those held by the organization.

Another organization pays little attention to selection in the expectation that turnover will be high under any circumstance. Employees who are productive and compatible will remain with the organization; those who are not will leave or be fired. These two approaches usually produce organizations with quite different temperaments. Some organizations consistently build upon personnel with outstanding potential in terms of the jobs and challenges available, while others are staffed primarily by personnel whose qualifications are marginal.

The implications for managerial effectiveness are obvious. Some managers have such outstanding talent working for them that they could hardly fail. Others are expected to get results with problem subordinates, and attempts to replace ineffective subordinates are met with resistance from other employees and managers. Effective management may be further thwarted by practices of nepotism, bias in giving promotions and raises, and a variety of other behaviors that sooner or later encourage the manager with high potential to find a job in a different organization rather than fight the system.

Theodore Levitt points out that the process by which a manager is selected is a critical element in managerial success. It is as though meticulous care in selection is required in order to give higher ranking managers the confidence and motivation they need to provide a new manager with the backing required for success. Commenting on the elaborate screening through which successful managers usually pass before employment, Levitt makes a subtle but important point:[5]

> The purpose was to determine whether his particular talents, competences, attitudes, styles, and personality were appropriate for the tasks and problems of the new situation he would enter. He turned out to be successful not alone for what he brought to the situation but for what his selectors saw in him as suitable for the situation. Those two things are not the same, though they may seem so at first.

Personnel policy influences managerial effectiveness in at least one other way—namely, the degree of staff support to which a manager has access. The quality of professional services in such areas as engineering, accounting, and human resources can sometimes make the difference between success and failure. They are specialized functions on which a manager may have a high degree of dependence but little control. They are often the critical determinants of managerial effectiveness.

Growth Opportunities. Organizations that provide little opportunity for managers to grow are unable to make optimal use of managerial talent. Managers are most effective when challenged to use their full potential. Although personal characteristics are important determinants of whether a manager's abilities will be developed and used, environmental constraints are also a factor.

The motivation for personal growth is closely linked to advancement opportunities, but other factors are also involved. The two interrelated questions concerning growth opportunity are (1) whether top management actively encourages management development and (2) whether managers who continually learn and develop new skills are subsequently rewarded for doing so. Affirmative answers to most of the checklist questions presented in Figure 11-1 indicate that an environment is favorable for growth.

Advancement Opportunities. Where advancement opportunities are perceived as few or nonexistent, managers typically (1) lose their motivation to grow, with a resulting loss of effectiveness or (2) are motivated to grow only in order to move on to greener pastures in another firm. In either case, the organization suffers.

The availability of advancement opportunities and the expectation of advancement are not the same thing; the latter is in many respects more important. Recently a senior engineer who was slated by her superiors to succeed the retiring production vice-president resigned, completely unaware that she was being considered for the post. In fact, she was afraid of being laid off because of the company's recent loss of contracts. The position she took actually paid less than the one she left, but it offered more stability and prospects for continual promotions.

Expectations for advancement are shaped by a number of factors in the work environment. The actual frequency with which openings occur is important, but for a given individual it may not be the most important factor in determining promotions. Professor Eugene Jennings, whose book *The Mobile Manager* provides some brilliant insights into the conditions which are correlated with upward mobility, notes that a manager must have both visibility and exposure in order to advance.[6]

Visibility is the opportunity to see one's superiors in action, to learn how they think and operate, and to become aware of what they value. **Exposure** is the ability to be seen by one's superiors and to demonstrate one's competence (or incompetence). To some extent these conditions are a function of the leadership style of high-level managers. Managers can influence their own visibility and exposure, but they do not have complete control over these conditions.

ORGANIZATIONAL CONTROLS

An organization is most effective when its members require a minimum of supervision because they are competent and goal oriented. Nevertheless, under optimal conditions of individual commitment and self-control, organizations need formal controls.

MANAGEMENT DEVELOPMENT PRACTICES	Yes	No
1. Definite expectations exist that managers shall continue to learn and develop new skills.	☐	☐
2. The organization requires annual goal setting for personal growth and follows up on progress made.	☐	☐
3. Released time is provided for special seminars and other forms of education and self-improvement.	☐	☐
4. Tuition and other expenses for work-related development activities are paid by the organization.	☐	☐
5. Development is encouraged by in-house seminars, lectures, behavior-modification projects, and related activities.	☐	☐
6. Managers are rewarded for developing subordinates.	☐	☐
7. Evidence of serious individual efforts to learn, mature, and develop skills is rewarded.	☐	☐
8. Managers are encouraged to coach subordinates for development purposes.	☐	☐
9. Programs of job rotation, designed to broaden managerial experience, are sponsored.	☐	☐
10. The organization makes every effort to utilize the highest level of talent developed by each manager.	☐	☐
11. To the extent that internally developed talent is available, promotions are made from within.	☐	☐
12. Managers are provided with all possible information concerning position openings, expected opportunities, and position requirements as an aid to long-range career planning and personal growth.	☐	☐

FIGURE 11-1 Checklist of Management Development Practices

The control function of organizations consists of the following:

1. *Establishing standards by which many aspects of organizational life are evaluated.* Most organizations have formal standards relating to spending, production, sales, product quality, safety, inventory, personnel selection, acceptable employee behavior, and so forth.

2. *Establishing feedback systems by which actual performance is compared with predetermined standards.* These are best exemplified by management reports that show, often on a daily basis, expected and actual performance. A manager whose budget report shows the amount allocated for a particular item, the amount spent to date, the amount committed but not spent, and the amount remaining, is provided with a practical basis for the control of expenditures.

3. *Taking appropriate action to ensure that substandard performance is improved and that standards will be met in the future.*

It is common practice to refer to the standards and feedback systems as *controls* although it should be obvious that they serve a control function only if managerial action is involved. They are not a substitute for supervision, but they minimize requirements for personal supervision. A correlate of this is the fact that self-control or self-management is possible only when the standards and expectations spelled out in formal controls are available as guidelines for behavior.

Controls and Managerial Effectiveness

The availability of effective control systems has a direct bearing both on managerial effectiveness and the success of the total enterprise. This can be seen in the case of a rapidly expanding manufacturing firm whose financial controls were inadequate. Its chief financial officer, an ultra-conservative major shareholder, was slow to change to the sophisticated types of financial controls required in this fast-paced and volatile organization. As a result, sales often outpaced production; a higher level of inventory was maintained for costly, slow moving items than for others that were fast moving and subject to wide fluctuations in demand; and the company experienced almost daily cash flow problems. Because of system inadequacies, a succession of office managers and accountants resigned or were discharged because of presumed incompetence, and for several years the company wavered on the brink of disaster.

Poor controls make unnecessary demands upon managers. They require that a manager spend an inordinate amount of time in direct supervisory relationships, and the excessively close supervision is resented. Subordinates do not always have favorable attitudes toward controls (toward demanding production and quality standards, for example), but at least the controls introduce an element of predictability into the environment. In reducing the amount of superior-subordinate contact, controls also reduce the subordinates' feelings of being controlled and personally dominated by a superior.

Problems Caused by Controls

Because rewards and penalties are associated with meeting the standards established in control systems, the standards often become ends in themselves. Knowing that their effectiveness will be evaluated against a set of standards, managers meet the standards, or appear to do so, at the organization's expense. Two brief examples illustrate this point.

> In one organization sales quotas were often met by forcefully selling merchandise customers did not need, selling merchandise to be shipped in a subsequent month, and selling merchandise with the understanding that it would be returned. This managerial behavior was designed to postpone the day of judgment on the assumption that by some means that day could be postponed indefinitely.
>
> In assembly-line manufacturing, where each of a large number of employees performs a minor operation on a product, the end of a work period normally leaves many production units on the line at various stages of completion. In one plant, for example, at the end of the day, approximately 60 incomplete inflatable life rafts are left in the plant—some almost completed and others just begun. At the end of the week, when a production report is due, the superintendent sometimes "bleeds the line." Instead of continuing to start new units until the end of the work period, employees at the beginning of the line are assigned to help those nearer the end so that when the time of accounting comes a maximum number of units will have been produced. Contrary to the expectations of superiors, however, there are few, if any, partially completed units on the floor, and the crash effort to meet a production quota has drastically reduced efficiency.

Some common abuses of controls can be avoided by minor changes in the system. Controls that reflect a basic distrust of and lack of consideration for people tend to invite abuses; and when top management evaluates performance only on the basis of results, with no consideration for how they are achieved, subordinate managers often behave irrationally to achieve the desired results.

THE DELEGATION PROCESS

> Delegation at higher levels of an organization is a primary determinant of a manager's opportunities to perform well. While a manager's success and effectiveness are not totally dependent upon the superior's willingness to delegate, they may be severely limited by it.

Delegation is the organizational process by which (1) a manager assigns specific duties to a subordinate, (2) the subordinate is provided with a grant of authority commensurate with the duties to be performed, (3) the subordinate assumes responsibility for satisfactorily performing the duties, and (4) the subordinate is held accountable for results.

Like most definitions, this is an oversimplification. For example, it seems to imply that only authority is necessary for satisfactory performance of the assigned duties. As we shall see, delegation is a highly complex and dynamic process involving a number of interacting variables. We say, for example, that managers should always be given authority to match the responsibility that they are expected to assume, but in practice there is no simple way to accomplish this. The amount of authority needed depends upon such factors as leadership style, attitudes of subordinates, the extent to which managers perceive themselves to have authority, and the extent to which managers possess the authority that comes from expertise and personality characteristics.

Extent of Delegation

Delegation occurs anytime a subordinate performs work for which that person's superior is ultimately responsible. It occurs, for instance, every time a secretary types a letter for a superior, even when little or no discretion exists for the secretary to influence the ultimate product.

The extent to which a subordinate is permitted to determine the means of task performance may vary from none to all. Some managers specify detailed means and supervise closely to see that results are accomplished by those means. Others specify the results to be achieved and leave the means to the discretion of the subordinate. Both qualify as delegation, but in the latter case the manager delegates more completely.

Clarifying the Levels of Delegation. A manager often begins by delegating only the most elementary aspects of a job, supervising closely to ensure effective completion. Then, as it becomes obvious that the subordinate is capable of assuming more responsibility, an increasing amount of work is delegated. Finally, the superior may feel confident in specifying only the results desired.

Some managers, for reasons to be discussed shortly, have extreme difficulty in allowing subordinates to make decisions and work on their own long after the subordinates are capable of doing so. Such managers do delegate, but they delegate much less than they could. This means that both they and their subordinates assume less responsibility than they are capable of assuming. Managers who refuse to delegate tasks for which great amounts of authority are required involve themselves in unnecessary detail and limit their contributions to the organization and their promotion potential. To achieve a high degree of success, a top-level manager must develop and supervise subordinate managers who possess a high level of authority and who will assume responsibility for important managerial functions.

A technique used by one management consultant, a specialist in management development, illustrates the problems of minimal delegation. The consultant makes use of a program, always with the full support of the chief executive, in which a study is performed to determine how the organization's managers actually spend their time. The duties performed are then classified according to predetermined standards to show whether they should be performed by a manager, a staff specialist, a clerk, a secretary, and so forth. Given the percentage of time spent in each type of activity, the manager's total job is evaluated on the basis of the average earnings of employees in each category. It is a shocking experience for $70,000-a-year executives to discover that much of their time is occupied with tasks that should be performed by $30,000-a-year assistants or $18,000-a-year secretaries. It is a strong incentive to delegate more completely and to use as much time as possible for performing managerial functions.

Since the aggregate amount of responsibility assumed in an organization is directly related to the extent of effective delegation, good management generally favors maximum delegation. This amount, however, may vary greatly over time. Since new personnel are continually entering an organization and experienced personnel theoretically are able to assume increasing responsibility, the amount of work a manager delegates is constantly in flux. This poses no serious problem as long as duties and authority are reasonably well defined at any given time.

Although duties and authority can never be perfectly defined, managers need to be aware of (1) when to take action solely on their own; (2) when to take action and inform their superiors of that action; (3) when to plan an action and inform their superiors of what will be done unless the superiors intervene; (4) when to ask their superiors for a decision; and (5) when to take no initiative unless specifically told to do so.

Awareness of when to act at each of these levels comes only from experience in a particular environment and is influenced greatly by the perception, sensitivity, management philosophy, self-confidence, and risk-taking tendency of the manager. One effective manager, an executive vice-president, has increased personal authority and responsibility by following this philosophy:

> When I'm not sure whether I have the authority to take a certain course of action—when it is really in a gray area—I assume I have it and take whatever action seems appropriate. If I later discover that I have overstepped my authority, I apologize. This has worked for me for 20 years. Someone has to interpret the gray area, and it may as well be me.

Another manager takes an entirely different approach:

> I'm careful not to make decisions in areas where I'm uncertain about my authority. I don't want the embarrassment of having to apologize or back down. When I'm not sure of where I stand, I ask for a clarification.

Everything else being equal, managers of the former type will grow in power and responsibility more rapidly than the latter. They stand a greater chance of losing their jobs, or having clashes with superiors, but their assertiveness will ordinarily lead to a rapid expansion of authority and responsibility. These cases demonstrate the fact that the subordinate as well as the superior defines the limits within which delegation will occur. Managers who complain that they lack authority to perform effectively sometimes lack it because they have not reached out to grasp it.

Upward Delegation. Managers who have difficulty in delegating often find themselves victims of upward delegation. This refers to the process by which subordinates bring problems to their superior for a decision instead of personally assuming responsibility and taking the risk involved in decision making. The superior sometimes may be critical of subordinates for not being able to make decisions while unconsciously the superior is encouraging the practice because it is ego enhancing.

A new manager who replaces one who delegated poorly can usually reverse the upward delegation process by turning the questions back on subordinates and gradually refusing to make the decisions that the subordinates should be making. Only if this is done can subordinates be held accountable for results.

Nondelegable Duties. Theoretically managers can delegate all the duties for which they are responsible, but in practice this is not possible. Most managers perform a variety of functions that are much like the work of their subordinates. They read and edit reports, for example. They answer correspondence, some of which may require minimal ability but cannot ordinarily be delegated (for example, answering a letter from an important customer). At times, even a chief executive, such as the President of the United States, must become involved in speech writing, entertaining, studying, and other activities that are not delegable.

It is important to note that responsibility can never be delegated. Managers remain accountable to higher levels of management for all the tasks they delegate to subordinates. The manager whose subordinates fail to produce cannot be absolved of responsibility by blaming the incompetence or low motivation of subordinates. This principle applies at all organizational levels.

Favorable Conditions for Delegation

Ineffective delegation occurs for a variety of reasons. Attempts to remedy the situation are usually unsuccessful unless the causes have been diagnosed and corrected. Figure 11-2 presents a checklist in which many of the causes of poor delegation are listed. Use of this instrument as a diagnostic tool will help ferret out possible causes that might otherwise go undiscovered.

THE ORGANIZATIONAL STATUS SYSTEM

Whenever people associate closely with one another over a period of time it is inevitable that status differences will be recognized. Most organizations take deliberate steps to establish and maintain a status system. Personnel on all levels tend to support it.

Status refers to the ranking or relative position of an individual within a group. Status is highly correlated with prestige and is based on the predominant values held by members of the reference group. Although society in general has certain values by which status is assigned, an individual may have high status in one group and low status in another. For example, an irresponsible, noncontributing member of a work group may have extremely low status on the job but high status with a group of friends because of athletic expertise.

CAUSES OF POOR DELEGATION	Yes	No
1. Subordinates lack the aptitude needed to do the work.	☐	☐
2. Subordinates are inadequately trained.	☐	☐
3. Managers have no confidence in subordinates.	☐	☐
4. Managers have misconceptions about delegation.	☐	☐
5. Managers are too cautious — afraid to take risks.	☐	☐
6. Higher ranking managers constantly interfere.	☐	☐
7. Managers feel more secure doing than delegating.	☐	☐
8. Managers enjoy doing and dislike supervising.	☐	☐
9. Managers are too intolerant of subordinates' mistakes.	☐	☐
10. Superior-subordinate working conditions are too close.	☐	☐
11. The organization has unclear goals and/or work standards.	☐	☐
12. The general organizational climate is one of distrust.	☐	☐
13. Managers do not know their subordinates' capabilities.	☐	☐
14. Systems for monitoring performance are inadequate.	☐	☐
15. Managers are too detail minded — have limited perspective.	☐	☐
16. Too little value is placed on developing subordinates.	☐	☐
17. Managers are afraid of losing power through delegation.	☐	☐
18. Organizational working conditions are unstable and chaotic.	☐	☐
19. Decision making is too concentrated at the top.	☐	☐
20. Managers want all the credit for themselves.	☐	☐
21. Planning for the purpose of delegating is poor.	☐	☐
22. Subordinates avoid responsibility by delegating upward.	☐	☐
23. It is organizational philosophy to supervise closely.	☐	☐
24. The organizational systems of motivation are inadequate.	☐	☐
25. Managers desire to keep subordinates dependent.	☐	☐
26. Subordinates lack the information needed to perform well.	☐	☐
27. Superiors fail to provide adequate back-up authority.	☐	☐

FIGURE 11-2 Checklist of Causes of Poor Delegation

The aggregate values, techniques, and symbols by which these relative rankings are established and maintained within an organization are called a **status system**. As we shall see, the status system plays a major role in making an organization orderly and in structuring relationships among people which make effective management possible.

Status Categories

Status can best be understood in terms of four general categories: objective, subjective, scalar, and functional.

Objective status refers to the ranking of people on the basis of generally accepted standards of evaluation. For example, in our society there is general agreement that physicians have higher status than nurses, that managers have higher status than nonmanagement workers, that skilled craftspersons have higher status than machine tenders, and so forth.

Subjective status refers to the perception of one's own status. An understandable bias often enters the picture when we rank ourselves. It is interesting to note that even the lowest employees on the objective scale can find some basis for viewing others as having lower status than themselves. The maintenance workers of one building perceive themselves as above those of another because of the physical quality of the building they work in or because of its occupants or because of cultural biases relating to such personal attributes as race, national origin, religion, age, or sex. For example, members of recently arrived immigrant groups are typically accorded a low status. Noncommissioned military officers often perform an interesting twist of logic by which they look with some disdain upon their commissioned superiors; and veteran construction workers sometimes elevate themselves by pointing up the inexperience and impractical "book learning" of the young, college-educated engineers and architects with whom they work.

Scalar status is based upon the formal organizational hierarchy. Thus, the president has higher status than the vice-president who in turn has higher status than managers at lower levels. Scalar status is perfectly correlated with formal authority.

Functional status is based upon the type of work one performs, without reference to formal authority within the organizational hierarchy. For instance, a research physicist has higher status than a bookkeeper. This is because of personal and work characteristics, not because the physicist has any organizational authority over the bookkeeper.

It is notable that one's status on the job, whether scalar or functional, tends to generalize to one's relationships with others outside work. The corporation president, CPA, attorney, or physician is accorded higher status than the supervisor, bookkeeper, secretary, or nurse, wherever they are. This generalization is a major reason why most personnel are highly motivated to seek and retain scalar and functional status in organizations.

Establishing and Maintaining the Status System

The most obvious means of establishing employee status is the use of titles. One's status may be elevated by this means even when duties and responsibilities remain the same. It is not uncommon, for instance, for the term *maintenance workers* to be used instead of *janitors*. The former title communicates higher status, especially to people outside the organization.

Unlike the military, the clergy, and educational institutions, business organizations have few ceremonies (such as parades, inaugurations, ordinations, and graduations) by which status is formally conveyed; but promoted employees are given recognition in company publications and the public news media, and a wide variety of status symbols separate the status levels. Among these are

1. Clothing: tie and suit rather than sport shirt or coveralls.

2. Office location: a large corner office with windows or, in some companies, a particular floor or proximity to a top executive.

3. Office furnishings: notable differences in quality of furniture, wall decorations, and carpeting.

4. Parking space: private, close, preferably with the name indicated.

5. Support in doing work: private secretaries, staff assistants, access to consultants.

6. Other privileges and **perquisites** (compensation other than wages or salary): use of company automobiles and aircraft, liberal expense accounts, freedom to set one's own work hours (or, at a lower level, freedom from having to punch a time clock), inclusion in certain social groups, access to inside information, permission to use first names, and related privileges which are not officially spelled out but which are highly visible to those within the company.

At the employee level, the status system flourishes, even in informal work groups. Insiders recognize status differences based upon seniority, the type of machine one operates, whether one's work is clean or dirty, whether one is willing to stand up to the boss, and a large number of other criteria, many of which are difficult for outsiders to detect. Generally speaking, at all organizational levels status differences are related to requirements of ability, education, training, and experience.

The system of status differences is vigorously defended because of its link with self-esteem, sense of identity, and personal security. A few companies have attempted to eliminate status differences because of the barriers they sometimes pose to free communication and good human relations; but what usually occurs is that obvious status symbols are simply replaced by more subtle ones. The observation that everyone is equal, but some are more equal than others, is still true.

Functions of the Status System

A status system serves both the individual and the organization. For the organization, its greatest contribution is probably the manner in which it helps to define levels of authority and competence. Everyone needs to know where formal authority lies and who has the competence to serve as an authority on a particular type of problem. Status differences indicate who has a right to issue commands or to give an opinion worthy of being held in high esteem. The status system also serves the organization because of its role as a motivator. "Status pay" is sometimes valued even more highly than financial compensation.

Both high status and low status serve a purpose for the individual. The person with high status is given recognition for ability, education, productivity, or another valued quality. Thus, it is advantageous to seek higher status at any organizational level. At times, however, it is also psychologically rewarding to claim low status. Thus, the laborer is protected from excessive demands by a right to say "you will have to ask my supervisor" or "I'm not paid to make decisions. I just do what I'm told." Likewise, the chief financial executive is protected by the disclaimer, "The question is really out of my field. I suggest that we call in a tax specialist for an opinion."

Employees have a need to attribute high status to those from whom commands are received. Recently promoted supervisors often have difficulty because their subordinates question the justification of someone so much like themselves telling them what to do. On the other hand, when we are able to view our superiors as outstanding and identify with them, we draw upon their status and thereby grow in self-esteem. A related phenomenon occurs when combat soldiers exaggerate and embellish tales of bravery about their superiors as a means of reducing fear and bolstering their own self-confidence.

Generally speaking, subordinates prefer to view their supervisors as superior and are usually willing to rationalize in order to maintain the illusion. For this reason, when they are forced to face the fact that a supervisor is incompetent, their reaction is often a pendulum swing to aggressiveness and hostility. Early studies referred to the status hierarchy as a "pecking order," a term drawn from the observation that chickens (and other animals, for that matter) establish definite superior-subordinate rankings.

IMPORTANT TERMS AND CONCEPTS

situational management	status
contingency management	status system
role	objective status
motivational systems	subjective status
visibility	scalar status
exposure	functional status
delegation	perquisites

STUDY AND DISCUSSION QUESTIONS

1. Many authorities believe that contingency management is superior to situational management as a framework for understanding organizational behavior. By what logic can this point of view be supported?

2. Think of an individual, perhaps someone you know well, who possesses all the personal qualifications you think would lead to success in management. What conditions within the organizational environment may cause such an individual to perform poorly?

3. What factors keep practicing managers from being able to read professional journals and to apply contingency research findings?

4. Why are the specific features of a managerial role not written out in an organization handbook or position description?

5. What conditions of organizational life support a manager's efforts to modify his or her position for a more favorable match between position demands and the individual's abilities?

6. In what sense does an organization's long-term approach to personnel selection influence the effectiveness of a given manager?

7. What did Levitt mean by his statement that a manager "turned out to be successful not alone for what he brought to the situation but for what his selectors saw in him as suitable for the situation?"

8. How does making a distinction between managerial effectiveness and managerial success contribute to an understanding of organizational behavior?

9. Based on the concepts discussed in this chapter, list several examples of organizational controls.

10. Why is it true that, within the work environment, self-control or self-management is possible only when the standards and expectations spelled out in formal controls are made known?

11. Under what circumstances would it be wise for a manager to delegate only the most elementary aspects of a job, supervising closely to ensure completion according to expectation?

12. Imagine an organization in which no status symbols are visible. What negative consequences might be expected?

13. Why might individuals with low status be motivated to preserve an organization's status system?

CRITICAL INCIDENT

A SMALL, FRIENDLY ORGANIZATION

When Larry Mills, an honor graduate in management and accounting, received his BBA degree, he received job offers from all five auditing firms with which he had interviewed. He accepted a position with a big-eight accounting firm where he worked for four years. Eminently successful, he was promoted to manager early in his third year. At the end of that year he received an offer from another company that he could not refuse.

His new employer was Dallas businessman Carl Graham whose investments included several oil-producing properties, a large cattle ranch, land developments, and minority interest in several businesses for which he had provided financial backing. At age 65, Graham was extremely active studying proposals for investments, buying and selling land, and managing his oil and ranch properties. Graham's purpose in bringing Mills into the business as general manager of Graham Investments, Inc., was to give himself freedom to travel and relax, luxuries he had denied himself throughout his challenging and successful career.

The plush corporate offices of Graham Investments, Inc., were in a suburban high rise owned by the corporation. The organization—small, simple, and familylike—included a CPA office manager, four bookkeepers, two secretaries, and a typist-receptionist. Three managers reported directly to Mills: Nelda Baines, the office manager; Monica Rivera, a properties manager who supervised a building maintenance crew; and Milton Wade, the ranch manager.

Although Rivera had an office in the corporate suite, she seldom occupied it. Wade lived on the ranch where Graham was a frequent visitor since he liked to check on his not-too-profitable, prize-winning cattle herd and discuss ranch business with his ranch manager.

Graham and Mills worked well together, although some aspects of Mills' job were frustrating. After two years Graham had still not taken a vacation; and, although everyone in the company technically reported to Mills, they also reported to Graham. Mills spent much of his time analyzing potential investments and taking care of closings when properties were bought and sold. He took his job seriously and showed a superior capacity to make profitable business decisions and to manage employees. Graham was totally satisfied with Mills' performance and paid him generously for it.

Mills, on the other hand, was frustrated with his job. A highly organized individual, he particularly disliked his inability to plan and control his personal life. He could never be sure when an important dinner engagement would have to be canceled because of a last-minute conference arranged by Graham; and because of Graham's informality and unpredictability, Mills had been unable to plan a vacation. Three concrete events demonstrate some of the problems and frustration Mills experienced.

For several weeks Mills had investigated the purchase of a large tract of ranchland with a high potential for oil and gas production. Because the undeveloped oil and gas resources were difficult to evaluate, the overall analysis was complicated, but finally the pieces of the puzzle fell into place: Mills was certain he had the makings of a uniquely profitable deal. But, before he could report his findings to Graham, Graham announced that he had been thinking about the purchase and had decided against it. Mills could scarcely understand his own reactions: extreme frustration, hostility, and the conviction that he was wasting his time and being treated like a personal servant. Yet he respected Graham and didn't question his right to decide against the purchase.

The second incident occurred when Mills developed a plan to make the ranch properties genuinely profitable only to have it rejected by Graham because he enjoyed the ranch as it was—inefficiency and all.

The third incident seemed trivial, but to Mills it was not. Mills gave Wade a substantial raise based on a study of the total compensation of comparable ranch managers, but Graham rescinded it because of considerations he did not share with Mills. Graham had used his influence to get university scholarships for three of Wade's children, saving Wade several thousands of dollars a year. Since Graham had given substantial gifts to the university, he considered the scholarships a part of Wade's compensation. Again, Mills could not deny Graham's right to decide as he had, but Mills still disliked the decision and seriously considered resigning. But where would he ever find another opportunity like this one? Resigning was not the answer.

1. Upon what basis is Graham Investments, Inc., organized?

2. Because of your expertise as a management consultant, Larry Mills seeks your advice. What should Mills do? How should he do it? Make specific recommendations for a reorganization of Graham Investments, Inc.

REFERENCES

1. Luthans, Fred. *Introduction to Management: A Contingency Approach.* New York: McGraw-Hill Book Company, 1976, p. 31.
2. Fiedler, Fred E. "Predicting the Effects of Leadership Training and Experience from the Contingency Model: A Clarification," *Journal of Applied Psychology*, Vol. 57, No. 2, 1973, p. 110.
3. Mintzberg, Henry. "The Manager's Job: Folklore and Fact," *Harvard Business Review*, Vol. 53, No. 4, July-August, 1975, pp. 49–61.
4. Kurke, Lance B., and Howard E. Aldrich. "Mintzberg Was Right! A Replication and Extension of 'The Nature of Managerial Work,'" *Management Science*, Vol. 29, No. 8, August, 1983, pp. 975–984.
5. Levitt, Theodore. "The Managerial Merry-Go-Round," *Harvard Business Review*, Vol. 52, No. 4, July-August, 1974, p. 121.
6. Jennings, Eugene Emerson. *The Mobile Manager.* New York: McGraw-Hill Book Company, 1967, pp. 30–34.

SUGGESTED READINGS

Dalton, Dan R. et al. "Organization Structure and Performance: A Critical Review," *Academy of Management Review*, January, 1980, pp. 49–64.
House, Robert J. "Role Conflict and Multiple Authority in Complex Organizations," *California Management Review*, Summer, 1970, pp. 53–60.
London, Manuel, and Stephen A. Stumpf. *Managing Careers.* Reading, Mass.: Addison-Wesley Publishing Co., 1982.

Lorsch, Jay W., and John J. Morse. *Organizations and Their Members: A Contingency Approach.* New York: Harper & Row Publishers, Inc., 1974.

Luthans, Fred, and Todd I. Stewart. "A General Contingency Theory of Management," *Academy of Management Review,* April, 1977, pp. 181–195.

Mintzberg, Henry. *The Nature of Managerial Work.* New York: Harper & Row Publishers, Inc., 1973.

Pavett, Cynthia M., and Alan W. Lau. "Managerial Work: The Influence of Hierarchical Level and Functional Specialty," *Academy of Management Journal,* Vol. 26, No. 1, March, 1983, pp. 170–177.

Raudsepp, Eugene. "Why Supervisors Don't Delegate," *Supervision,* Vol. 40, No. 5, May, 1979, pp. 12–15.

Rizzo, John R. et al. "Role Conflict and Ambiguity in Complex Organizations," *Administrative Science Quarterly,* June, 1975, pp. 272–280.

12

Managerial Decision Making: Nature and Process

Why study decision making? This is a good question to which there seem to be at least three good answers.

First, our lives are greatly affected by the decisions of other organizational members. If we understand more about how decisions are made, we are more likely to be able to predict decisions and therefore to plan our lives and work more effectively.

Second, if we understand how decisions are made, we are more likely to be effective in our attempts to influence decision makers.

Third, the quality and acceptability of our own decisions can have a considerable impact on our careers and job satisfaction and on the goal achievement of the organization, the people who work for us, and our co-workers. Thus it seems worthwhile to study decision making for the purpose of improving the quality of our decisions.

Of the many functions performed by managers, none contributes more directly to managerial effectiveness than decision making. Consequently, a manager's decision-making record is the principal basis for performance evaluation by superiors. Because managerial decisions reflect a manager's education, experience, and judgment, individual differences in decision-making ability are enormous.

Some managers can quickly make sound decisions in complex situations while others perform poorly under the most favorable conditions. This fact has led researchers to focus attention on the decision-making process—the techniques or methods by which decisions are made. While they have found no one *best* process for all decision makers, they have observed systematic differences in the way effective and ineffective managers decide. Managers who use this information can significantly improve their decisions. This chapter discusses some important aspects of decision making in organizations. To be specific, the chapter objectives are

TO UNDERSTAND:

1. The nature of managerial decisions

2. Common mistakes made in problem solving

3. Approaches for improving decision making

SOME DEFINITIONS TO SHARPEN OUR THINKING

A **problem** exists when there is a difference between an actual situation and a desired situation. Managers are continually faced with problems. When one of these differences becomes serious enough to demand action on our part we might call it an "active" problem. Fortunately, many problems, like volcanos, are inactive. Inactive problems certainly exist and can be referred to as problems, but they are not demanding of immediate managerial attention.

From our definition of what a problem is, we can see that to solve a problem a manager must change either the actual situation, the desired situation, or both. In many cases, changing the actual situation means increasing the level of our organization's performance. In other instances, the problem can be appropriately "solved" by changing the desired situation rather than the actual situation. For example, on a Friday afternoon we may have just 70 units of a product on hand but receive a customer order for 100 units. If we cannot quickly produce the 30 units without incurring unreasonable costs, we might solve the problem by asking the customer to accept 70 units now and the remaining 30 units next Wednesday (by which time we expect to have produced the desired product). Although there is a danger in using this approach, it is occasionally a very practical way to solve a problem.

Given that problems can be solved by changing either the actual or desired situation, we can define **problem solving** as the conscious process of reducing the difference between an actual situation and the desired situation. This leaves us with the need to define *decision making*. The term is sometimes used to describe the narrow set of activities involved in choosing one solution from a set of alternative solutions. On other occasions it is used to describe the broad set of activities involved in finding and implementing a course of action. In the first case, decision making is used in place of the narrower but less familiar term *choice making*. In the second case, it is used in place of the more encompassing but less specific term *problem solving*.

In our discussions we will use the terms choice making and problem solving to describe, respectively, the narrow and broad sets of activities that are sometimes referred to as decision making. We will use the term **decision making** to refer to an intermediate-sized set of activities that begin when a problem is being explored and end when an alternative has been chosen. Decision making is the process through which a course of action is chosen.

Figure 12-1 clarifies these distinctions. In this illustration we see that solving a problem may involve a great many activities, some of which take place after a decision has been made. On the other hand, making a choice from a given set of alternatives involves relatively few activities.

STEPS IN PROBLEM SOLVING	(CM)	(DM)	(PS)
1. Explore the nature of the problem. (Includes those activities dealing with problem identification, definition, and diagnosis.)		✓	✓
2. Generate alternative solutions. (Includes those activities dealing with generation of alternative solutions to the problem.)		✓	✓
3. Choose among alternative solutions. (Includes those activities dealing with evaluation and choice among alternative solutions.)	✓	✓	✓
4. Implement the chosen alternative. (Includes those activities dealing with implementation of the chosen solution.)			✓
5. Control the solution program. (Includes those activities dealing with maintaining, monitoring, and reviewing the implemented solution.)			✓

FIGURE 12-1   Activities Involved in Choice Making (CM), Decision Making (DM), and Problem Solving (PS)

As a final thought, we note that while we mean to define choice making as a process more limited in scope than decision making, we do not mean to distinguish a "choice" from a "decision." These two words both refer to the immediate outcome of the decision-making process.

THE NATURE OF MANAGERIAL DECISIONS

Managerial decisions are influenced by the manager's authority, formal education, experience, reason, and emotions. As organizations become more sophisticated, managers adopt methods of decision making that are more scientific and can withstand public scrutiny.

The quality of organizational decisions bears an interesting relationship to managerial authority. Few managers avoid the experience of having a good decision vetoed by a superior whose chosen course of action seems mediocre by comparison. The practice of obscuring the quality of decisions through the nonrational use of authority is one of the most common misuses of managerial power. As managerial authority has declined, however, managers have become increasingly aware of a need to defend their decisions on the basis of reason rather than power.

Traditional Decision Making

Decision making in most organizations differs greatly from the methods prescribed by decision theorists. Most managerial decisions are on-the-spot judgment calls that do not lend themselves to sophisticated methods. They are highly intuitive in nature, and neither the assumptions on which they are based, the alternatives from which a course of action is chosen, nor the criteria for the decision are clearly stated. Generally speaking, modern decision theorists stress the importance of making explicit the process by which decisions, especially major decisions, are made. This permits both the defense of a decision and the long-range improvement of a manager's decision-making capability.

Managers make many decisions by default or neglect. Reacting to problems referred to them by subordinates or superiors, they take action on the basis of habit or respond with an unthinking, mechanical application of policy. This contrasts sharply with decisions that are conscientiously made, after appropriate data collection and analysis, to solve or avoid specific problems. Since a manager's individual perception of a need for action is the occasion of initiative decisions, this kind of decision is avoided by mediocre, unaggressive managers.

Lindblom described an approach to decision making that maximizes personal security. Its rationale holds that the safest approach to change is to proceed in the direction one has traveled in the past while limiting the consideration of alternative action "to those policies that differ in relatively small degrees from policies presently in effect."[1] This commonly used approach is workable in a stable organization operating in a stable market. Its weaknesses surface, however, when the environment is characterized by novel situations and rapid change.

Another common approach to decision making is the "implicit favorite" model.[2] Following this model, the manager makes an implicit (not openly expressed) choice among alternatives and then continues to gather data until the implicit choice is confirmed. This often involves more rationalization than reasoning as the manager selectively perceives data that support the implicit decision and cause alternatives to appear weak by comparison.

Other people can often predict how a manager using the implicit favorite model will ultimately decide long before the decision is consciously made. This occurred, for example, when a firm's president and largest shareholder went through a prolonged, agonizing decision about promoting his son into the executive ranks. Other executives knew that the president's decision to consider his son for the position was, in effect, his decision to promote him. Since, however, fairness and objectivity demanded a comparison with other candidates, the charade had to be played out.

A third description of traditional decision making was made by Mintzberg and his associates.[3] They observed three distinct decision phases: identification, search, and selection. In the *identification phase*, opportunities, problems, and crises are recognized and diagnosed. In the *development phase*, the heart of decision making from Mintzberg's perspective, one or more solutions are developed—either through *search activity* for ready-made solutions or through a *design routine* for custom-made solutions. Ready-made solutions are preferred, of course, because they require less effort and expense. In the *selection phase*, which is intertwined with development, a number of choice steps or subdecisions lead to a solution. These subdecisions are entangled in a morass of creative thinking, critical analyses, and *authorization routines* (getting the approval of superiors) until the final decision is reached. Most decision theorists are convinced that a more systematic and orderly process would improve managerial decisions.

A Good Decision

Managers who cannot hide behind their formal authority must devise a means of justifying their decisions. One alternative is simply to evaluate decisions in terms of their results. Another is to evaluate them in terms of the methods or processes by which they are made.

Decisions and Results. The simplest characteristic of a good decision is that it works. Given management's current interest in managing by objectives, it is reasonable to emphasize the role of results in evaluating the quality of managerial decisions. From one perspective, a single criterion seems adequate: Decisions that produce good results are good decisions; those that produce poor results are not.

The results criterion has merit. Certainly good decision makers get better results than poor decision makers, on the average. It does not, however, follow that a manager whose achievements are outstanding has necessarily been a good decision maker. Good results may be due to such opportunity factors as having effective subordinates or operating in a favorable market environment.

The results criterion offers particular problems in evaluating a specific decision. Two investors buy stock on the same day. Investor A plays a hunch, invests all available funds in a single speculative stock, and immediately makes a fortune. Investor B meticulously studies the market, calculates the risks, diversifies purchases, and makes a reasonable profit. Which investor made the better decision? Which is the better decision maker? These questions can best be answered with another question: With whom would you prefer to trust your investment funds? It is rational to prefer the calculated risk taker to the gambler. Under the conditions stated, a poor decision may yield good results.

The Decision Process. Since managerial decisions are made about future events, they are made on the basis of incomplete information. Consequently, they involve risks. The possibility always exists that a good decision will have undesirable consequences. The automobile dealer who purchased a large stock of big automobiles just before the 1974 oil embargo could not possibly have anticipated the rush to small automobiles. The fact that unpredictable events affect the outcomes of decisions suggests that decisions may best be evaluated in terms of the process by which they are made. From this perspective, one should not be surprised that outstanding decision makers occasionally get poor results. They qualify as outstanding decision makers because of their approach to decision making; their superior overall results are a predictable consequence of that approach. One of the major purposes of this chapter is to describe methods that are most likely to yield good results.

Rationality in Decision Making

One criterion of a good decision is its **rationality**, the extent to which a chosen course of action is designed to achieve an objective in an efficient manner. Although rationality is an ideal to be sought, in practice the decision maker must be content to settle for something less, for a **bounded rationality**. Rationality is bounded or limited by such factors as (1) time and cost considerations in data collection and analysis; (2) only partial awareness of alternative solutions; (3) inadequate knowledge of the consequences of alternative solutions; (4) poorly defined goals; (5) conflicting and continually changing goals; and (6) human limitations in the areas of memory, reasoning, and objectivity.

One of the main barriers to rational decision making in organizations arises from the fact that managers must promote their own careers while making organizational decisions. This results in continual compromises and inconsistencies. Executives have personal needs that are not always consistent with the needs of their employers. They compete with one another for promotions, power, and prestige; they hold tenaciously to certain ideas to defend their self-image; and they otherwise behave irrationally when judged by organizational criteria. Thus, rationality can only be understood with reference to a point of view. Unfortunately for their employer, it is not unusual for executives to make organizational decisions of questionable rationality because they are behaving rationally in terms of enhancing their own careers.

Maximizing Behavior. In the classical economic model, business decision makers are presumed to behave rationally in that they *maximize* profit-making behavior; that is, they supposedly make business decisions that will produce the maximum amount of profit for the firm. When applied to an individual, this theory postulates the rational weighing of alternatives with decisions ultimately made in terms of maximizing self-interest.[4]

The notion that behavior is maximized either at the level of the firm or the individual is indefensible. It assumes, for example, clarity of objectives, complete awareness of alternatives and their consequences, and unlimited reasoning capacity. In effect, all the limitations on rationality listed earlier prevent decision makers from being maximizers in a classical sense.

Satisficing Behavior. Under the *bounded rationality* concept, decision makers may be seen as **satisficers** rather than maximizers; that is, they seek satisfactory rather than optimal solutions to problems. March and Simon distinguish the two as follows:

> An alternative is *optimal* if (1) there exists a set of criteria that permits all alternatives to be compared and (2) the alternative in question is preferred, by these criteria, to all other alternatives. An alternative is *satisfactory* if (1) there exists a set of criteria that describes minimally satisfactory alternatives and (2) the alternative in question meets or exceeds these criteria. . . .[5]

The task of searching for the optimal alternative is infinitely more difficult than finding a satisfactory alternative. Since managers always operate with limited resources, they are of necessity satisficers rather than maximizers.

The Use of Heuristics. Bounded by limitations of time, resources, and mental capacity, real-world decision makers use imperfect models, rules of thumb, or heuristics to reduce the elements of a decision into manageable, bite-size pieces. A **heuristic** is a technique or principle that permits limited data collection and analysis in decision making. Computers are often used to implement heuristics for arriving at usable, approximate solutions. Managers use relatively simple rules and criteria to reach conclusions in situations which are so complex that all the relevant variables could not possibly be considered. Recognizing that there are many other criteria which would ideally be considered, managers select a few important criteria and apply them to the most obvious alternatives.

The use of heuristics leaves the decision maker open to possible criticism. Why were the particular standards of evaluation used? Why were additional data not collected? Regardless of the methodology used, a manager's ultimate defense is as follows: "Given the available options and resources, the course of action I chose was, in my judgment, the best one." This ultimate right to decide does, of course, allow bias to enter the decision process. A manager may, for example, cite an unpredictable economy as a reason not to expand into a new market. The overriding decision criterion, however, may be a personal desire to avoid the stress, conflict, and hard work associated with the action. Nevertheless, there is no practical alternative to a heuristic approach for a decision maker with limited resources in an environment with changing and conflicting objectives.

Systems Constraints. Effective managerial decisions are never made in a vacuum. For example, a decision of the marketing department affects manufacturing, accounting, human resources, purchasing, and, in a sense, every function of the organization. Because of this, a high level of participation and coordination is necessary in making organizational decisions.

The constraints within which a decision maker must work are often political. Ideal alternatives are compromised to gain acceptance by superiors, peers, or subordinates. What appears to be an engineering and financial decision (for example, a change in machines or methods) turns out to be influenced more by union power than by technical or financial feasibility.

Since organizations are in continual interaction with the external environment, the consequences of business decisions are strongly influenced by external factors. Possible factors such as the following cannot be ignored:

1. A new technology makes our product obsolete.

2. Lending institutions refuse financing.

3. New competitors enter the market.

4. The government initiates antitrust proceedings or passes unfavorable legislation.

5. An international cartel restricts supplies.

The complexity of organizational decision making is steadily increasing. It is not surprising, therefore, that the process by which organizational decisions are made has gradually become less individualistic and personal.

Personal Influences on Managerial Decisions

Given the same set of facts, two decision makers often select alternative solutions that differ greatly. They perceive and evaluate the facts differently, based upon values, standards, and motives that are partially or wholly unconscious. The possibility of such biases influencing decisions can never be eliminated, but it can be reduced somewhat by making explicit each step of the decision process.

Although personal characteristics interact in complex ways to influence the decision process, it is possible to identify a number that affect decision quality. The following are among the most important of these characteristics.

1. *Intelligence.* Although superior intelligence is generally preferred, the kind of intelligence, as well as the amount, is important. For example, managers who are extremely high in abstract reasoning ability and low in practical judgment tend to become theoretical intellectualizers rather than practical problem solvers. Both analytical ability and practical judgment are significant contributors to decision quality.

2. *Cautiousness versus impulsiveness.* Managers who are unusually cautious may spend so much time gathering data that they miss important opportunities. They are risk avoiders who place a high value on safety. At the opposite extreme, impulsive decision makers become anxious when the loose ends of a complex problem are dangling. To avoid this anxiety, they decide too quickly. As a result, they spend much time rationalizing and attempting to hide or correct their mistakes.

3. *Risk taking.* The tendency to take high risks is not perfectly correlated with the cautiousness-impulsiveness continuum, although the two are related. Some managers are prone to take high risks, but only after calculating the success-failure probabilities. This tendency may result from a variety of motivations including (1) an extremely high level of aspiration, (2) a need for the thrill or excitement of taking chances, or (3) a naive optimism with reference to the probability of success.

4. *Optimism versus pessimism.* To some extent, optimism and pessimism are related to one's self-image. Decision makers who think poorly of their own abilities and have feelings of guilt and self-doubt are more likely than others to overestimate the probability of failure. The self-images of highly optimistic managers may be unrealistically positive because of an inability to accept self-criticism and because of a tendency to repress or rationalize away past failures. Tough-minded, mature managers attempt to calculate the actual risks rather than systematically vary in either direction. They tend to rely heavily on their own abilities and to have little use for the idea of luck.

5. *Ego defensiveness.* The decisions of managers who are constantly on the defensive suffer from lack of objectivity. Their perception and logic are distorted by a need to view themselves favorably.

6. *Dependence on others.* Managers with a strong need for the approval of others excessively weigh the reactions of others to their decisions.

The course of action selected may be successful in terms of the manager's personal goal of avoiding conflict but relatively unsuccessful in achieving organizational objectives. At the opposite extreme, some managers, insensitive to the needs and reactions of others, make decisions that may be logical but are unworkable because they cannot be implemented.

7. *Level of aspiration.* Good decisions are sometimes costly to the decision maker. They require hours of hard work and may involve a high level of personal tension and interpersonal conflict. Because of this, the manager whose self-expectations are relatively low may settle for a poor solution rather than pay the price required to find a good one.

8. *Decisiveness.* Since all decisions are made in terms of certain standards, it is important that a decision maker be committed to personal values and other standards such as goals, productivity expectations, and guidelines for effective management. Having made personal decisions in these areas, the manager is able to be decisive on the job; that is, to make decisions without undue hesitation. Decisiveness also depends on a manager's self-confidence and ability to face the consequences when poor decisions cannot be avoided.

9. *Creativity.* Although good decision makers are not always creative, creativity is an asset in generating alternative solutions. It is possible, however, for a manager to be too creative, to behave creatively when, for example, the situation calls for someone who can routinely implement a good decision rather than continually work at improving it.

In practice a given manager will be much stronger in some areas than in others. In certain situations decision quality can be maintained by delegation, use of participative techniques, and other devices which permit compensation for a manager's weakness.

COMMON MISTAKES IN PROBLEM SOLVING

Problem solving can be usefully thought of as consisting of the five-step process shown in Figure 12-1 on page 325. Due to the dynamic nature of most problem-solving environments and to the "learning" that causes some steps to be repeated, actual problem solving does not generally follow such a straightfoward path.

A good decision is one that is likely to solve the problem. This means that the solution must be workable, and its implementation must be controllable. In order to anticipate during Step 3 of the problem-solving process the mistakes that might be made in Steps 4 and 5, we will examine the mistakes made in these later steps as well as those commonly made in the earlier decision-making steps.

Step 1—Exploring the Nature of the Problem

Exploring the nature of the problem involves identifying, defining, and diagnosing the problem and its causes. When properly carried out, it helps us avoid solving the wrong problem or choosing a solution that doesn't deal with the real causes of the problem.

There are four tendencies that frequently interfere with adequate problem exploration:

1. *The tendency to define the problem in terms of a proposed solution.* For example, "the problem is that the public relations department is understaffed" focuses on one possible solution and reduces the likelihood that other solutions will be considered. The more basic problem may be that the organization needs but does not have a favorable public image. Viewed in this way, there are a number of possible solutions besides enlarging the public relations staff. Perhaps the department should use different public relations strategies. Perhaps it should hire a consultant to determine why the quality of public relations activities is not as high as the firm desires.

   Is the problem that "we have no mousetraps in the house" or that "we have mice in the house"? Which statement leads to an enduring solution? The danger in defining the problem as the lack of implementation of a particular solution is that it reduces or eliminates the search for other solutions that might be much more effective.

2. *The tendency to focus on narrow, lower order goals.* In identifying the desired situation, a manager may focus on narrow, lower order goals. More successful managers—or at least those managers who tend to move upward in their organizations—are those who keep in mind the need to achieve broader, higher order goals.

   Perhaps the most dramatic recognition of higher order goals was by the March of Dimes organization in the 1960s. After having contributed greatly to conquering polio, the March of Dimes organization chose not to disband but instead to raise funds for research directed toward overcoming birth defects. Clearly, the original goal had been achieved. It then became clear that *the* goal was really a higher order goal: to survive as an organization that served the needs of its members for either employment or the opportunity to provide altruistic service.

Is the goal "to build a cheaper mousetrap" or "to produce and sell profitably a product that gets rid of house pests"? Which statement better ensures the long-run survival of the firm? Achieving lower order goals is a means of achieving higher order goals. The more sophisticated manager views achievement of lower order goals as a means to achieve other ends rather than as an end in itself, and this manager defines problems accordingly.

3. *The tendency to diagnose the problem in terms of its symptoms.* For example, taking aspirin for tension headaches may be appropriate problem-solving behavior. But if the headaches are frequent, severe, and debilitating, it becomes appropriate to diagnose the causes so that the causes and not just the symptoms can be addressed.

Sometimes dealing with symptoms is appropriate. Often, however, the manager must dig deeper. How far we should go in probing through the layers of a problem varies from one situation to another. Each layer may be both the cause of a superficial problem and a symptom of a more basic problem. Most managers probably probe too little and hence spend much of their time fighting the repeatedly erupting symptoms of the same problem. We are all guilty, to some extent, of dealing with symptoms rather than causes. We recognize the fact only occasionally, as when we exclaim, "oh, not that again!" Thus, a third tendency that managers and other problem solvers exhibit in the problem-exploration step is that they tend to diagnose the problem only in terms of its symptoms rather than in terms of its causes.

We should note here that in many cases problems are identified and defined for us by others, such as our superiors or subordinates. This does not mean that problem exploration should not be a part of the problem-solving process. It simply highlights the fact that each step within the overall problem-solving process does not need to be carried out by the same individuals or groups.

4. *The tendency to move too quickly toward looking for solutions.* The fact is that some problem exploration occurs throughout the problem solving process, but the larger the proportion of the exploration activities that occur as a first step, the less backtracking will be required and the more likely it is that an appropriate solution will be found. People don't like problems. Problems create tension. To reduce the tension, people avoid adequately exploring the problem and move too rapidly toward seeking solutions—an unwise action in the long run, but it makes them feel better.

Step 2—Generating Alternative Solutions

The second step in the problem-solving process, generating alternative solutions, involves identifying items or actions that could reduce or eliminate the difference between the actual situation and the desired situation.

The effectiveness-reducing behavior frequently exhibited at this point in the problem-solving effort is *the tendency to slight the alternative-generation* process in favor of *proceeding to the alternative-evaluation* process. In other words, efforts to *generate* alternative solutions are not separated from efforts to *evaluate* the potential solutions already identified.

Many readers will recall having observed this tendency in problem-solving meetings where most of the meeting was devoted to arguing the merits of the first solution proposed rather than to identifying a set of alternative solutions to be considered. Because the tendency diverts the group members away from the solution-generation process, it reduces the opportunity for high-quality solutions to be identified or developed.

Old-fashioned *brainstorming*, with its instructions to participants not to criticize the ideas put forth, was an early attempt to deal with this tendency. More recently developed techniques are even more effective in both overcoming this tendency and generating high-quality solutions.[6] We will examine the most thoroughly proven of these techniques, the *Nominal Group Technique*, in Chapter 19. Here we simply note that people often rush through the alternative-generation process in order to move on to steps that more directly reduce the tension created by the problem. This shortchanging of the alternative-generation process is a shortsighted strategy that in most cases guarantees a solution of lesser quality.

Step 3—Choosing Among Alternative Solutions

The third step in the overall problem-solving process is choosing among the alternatives, or choice making. The following four tendencies interfere with good choice making.

1. *The tendency to overfocus on the cost of information.* The cost of information is generally immediate and assessable—for example, the cost of a long-distance phone call or the felt *cost* of living with the tension of an unmade decision while waiting for information to arrive. In contrast, the payoff from information is often in the future and not easily measured. As a result, some people subconsciously assign information costs as high and the payoffs as low and conse-

quently don't gather the information that is justified given the importance of the decision.

2. *The tendency not to obtain the same information about each alternative.* Many people, when they choose jobs, obtain different kinds of information about each job. Sometimes it is necessary to compare apples and oranges, but when it isn't, we should not. Relative to the cost of making a poor choice, the cost of obtaining comparable information is generally very, very small.

3. *The tendency to overreact to vivid information.* Many parents, when their children are seniors in high school, try to be helpful by seeing to it that their sons or daughters visit a few college campuses. As helpful as this seems, in some ways it is dangerous. The visiting teenager gets jostled in a cafeteria line, gets caught in the rain, likes the football stadium, sees an attractive member of the opposite sex, misses a train, or encounters other vivid facts. Such facts are much less relevant than are less vivid but more pertinent facts such as the test scores of the average student, the proportion of students who graduate, the number and quality of the faculty in the anticipated field of study, and so forth.

   All of us tend to overreact to vivid information, information such as scare stories about what might happen, or the occurrence of a missed shipment that caused unusual problems, and so forth.

4. *The tendency to choose the first-found alternative that seems to solve the problem.* In many cases, this is an efficient approach. However, it is greatly overused. It allows for no improvement in our overall situation across time whereas, in many cases, an improved situation can be developed if we make even a moderate effort to look beyond the conspicuous, off-the-shelf alternative. We should not "back in" to the decision not to search beyond the first acceptable alternative. We should instead consciously treat the question of whether to search for more alternatives as a decision, and we should force ourselves to consciously consider whether the expected benefits might outweigh the actual costs of the search.

Step 4—Implementing the Chosen Solution

This step involves planning and initiating the activities that must take place in order for the chosen solution to actually solve the problem. Inadequate managerial attention to the implementation step is one of the main reasons why good solutions frequently do not solve the problems they were intended to solve.

1. *The tendency not to ensure understanding of what needs to be done.*
   One important way to ensure understanding of what needs to be done
   is to involve the implementors in the choice-making step. When this
   is not possible, a strong and explicit attempt should be made to identify any misunderstanding, perhaps by having the implementors explain what they think needs to be done and why.

2. *The tendency not to ensure acceptance or motivation for what needs
   to be done.* An important approach to ensuring acceptance and motivation is to create involvement of the implementors in the choice-
   making step. Other efforts are to vividly describe the payoffs for effective implementation (for example, the problem will be solved) and
   to describe how completion of the various implementation tasks will
   lead to successful implementation.

Before leaving this discussion of implementation, we should note
again that, because the quality of a decision is a function of its potential
for implementation, experienced managers concern themselves with this
factor during their earlier decision-making efforts. Thus, although implementation is not part of the decision-making process, it still affects
this process.

Step 5—Controlling the Solution Program

In this step, the manager takes the actions necessary to see that
what actually happens is what was intended to happen. For example, if
we chose to use an incentive-bonus system to increase the performance
of our salespeople, controlling the solution program would mean maintaining records and disbursing bonuses in accord with what we intended
when we chose this solution. Controlling the solution would also mean
assessing whether or not the actual performance increase justifies the
cost of the incentive-bonus system.

This step is really the program administration step—the monitoring, supervising, and evaluating of a program that has survived implementation and is, we hope, an effective solution to the problem. The
word *control* indicates that, to ensure that this solution is solving the
problem, we should compare the actual goal achievement with the desired goal achievement. An effectiveness-reducing behavior often observed at this point is *the tendency not to provide in advance for the
information necessary to monitor the solution program.* As a result, a
less than satisfactory patchwork evaluation is the rule rather than the
exception.

Even a solution that has been carefully chosen and implemented can
encounter unforeseen conditions, conditions that cause it to be a less

effective solution than it was anticipated to be during the choice-making step. When comparison indicates a significant difference between the actual and desired situations, we have a "problem." The consequent problem-solving efforts would often be less costly if it were not for the second effectiveness-reducing behavior, *the tendency not to develop contingency plans in advance for problems that can be anticipated.*

IMPROVING DECISION MAKING

Given the importance of decision making, it is not surprising to find that a great deal of effort is being directed toward its systematic study and improvement. Much of this work is being carried out by scientists in universities, large corporations, and consulting firms. The results of their work form a valuable and important knowledge base for us to draw upon, particularly when these results are first screened for their managerial relevance and practicality.

Creative Search for Alternatives

Managers who practice choosing from among alternatives tend to make better decisions than those who evaluate isolated solutions on an accept-reject basis. Since acceptance or rejection of the most obvious solution is easier than creatively generating alternative solutions, the creative step in decision making is commonly omitted.

Creativity in decision making is the process of generating new and useful solutions to problems. A creative solution, like a creative work of art, involves more than novelty or uniqueness. Anyone can produce a one-of-a-kind painting, but not just anyone can produce an aesthetically appealing work of art. Anyone can offer solutions to management problems, but genuinely creative solutions require the decision maker to be disciplined, knowledgeable, and highly motivated.

Creativity and Personality. Creativity is deliberately defined as a process rather than as a personal attribute. It is, in one sense, a personal attribute, but there is good reason for conceptualizing creativity as a behavior. Thus, an individual *behaves creatively* in a particular situation rather than *being creative* as if it were a general personality characteristic. An artist, for example, may be exceptionally creative when painting or sculpturing but very uncreative when generating alternative solutions to a scientific or managerial problem.

Creativity, then, is situational. In order to be highly creative in solving a given problem, the decision maker needs depth of relevant background. By placing bits of information together in unique ways, novel and useful combinations emerge.

Managers are often so accustomed to operating within the constraints of goals, policies, rules, laws, and traditions that creative thinking appears strange and frustrating. They associate it with an uninhibited, Bohemian life-style more fitting for musicians and artists than for managers. This is an unfortunate perception since it often reduces motivation to be creative and raises questions about one's potential for it.

Actually everyone has the potential for behaving creatively. Individuals who are relatively uninhibited, open to new experiences, flexible and independent in their thinking, and committed to being creatively productive have an advantage over persons who lack these qualities. On the other hand, almost everyone with the motivation to do so can behave creatively for short periods of time. A variety of techniques have been developed to facilitate this behavior.

Techniques for Encouraging Creativity. One of the oldest and best known techniques for encouraging creative thought is **brainstorming**. Following this approach, a group of individuals apply a set of rules that encourage uninhibited free association about the problem at hand. No one is allowed to be critical, and group members are encouraged to draw upon the contributions of others in generating new ideas.

The enthusiasm, social stimulation, and permissive atmosphere of brainstorming is intended to stimulate the free flow of ideas, as indeed it does. In practice, however, the technique has its drawbacks. The ideas presented tend to direct group thinking into certain channels that inhibit the divergent thinking brainstorming purports to stimulate. Research indicates that, for the development of unique ideas and high quality ideas, the pooled efforts of individuals working in isolation is better than brainstorming.[7]

Another technique for stimulating creativity is called **synectics**.[8] This structured group approach is designed to force participants to deviate from usual modes of thinking. Under the guidance of an experienced leader, participants engage in role-playing exercises and various forms of fantasy designed to break down traditional ways of viewing problems. In one application of the technique, people with different backgrounds are locked in a room together until they find a novel solution. Although synectics is not as simple to use as brainstorming or individual creativity, it is a workable technique.

Breaking Creativity Barriers. The major barrier to creative thought is illustrated in Figure 12-2. Everyone has a characteristic way of viewing situations. These perceptual predispositions or *sets* are related to an in-

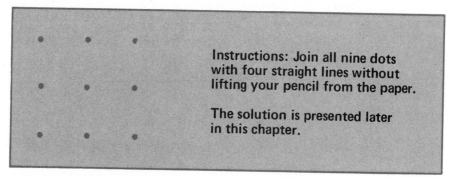

FIGURE 12-2 The Nine-Dot Problem

dividual's background, knowledge, experience, personality characteristics, attitudes, and intellectual abilities. Everyone is a victim of faulty assumptions and self-imposed constraints that restrict the freedom to form novel associations. It is common in approaching the nine-dot problem, for example, to assume that the lines cannot be extended beyond the limits of the dots. As long as this unanalyzed assumption controls one's thought processes, the problem cannot be solved.

The primary task of thinking creatively is to break the psychological barriers to free association. In the words of James L. Adams, the task is that of "conceptual blockbusting." He defines conceptual blocks as "mental walls which block the problem solver from correctly perceiving a problem or conceiving its solution."[9] The actions in the following list are helpful in breaking down these barriers and generating alternative solutions.

1. Postpone critical analysis of solutions until the creative step in problem solving is essentially completed.

2. Avoid dogmatic, all-or-nothing thinking.

3. Do not be inhibited by how others might react to a possible solution.

4. Allow time for ideas to incubate. Pressures of time tend to inhibit free association.

5. Analyze the assumptions on which previously developed alternatives are based. Create alternatives that might work under a variety of other assumptions even if such assumptions are unrealistic.

6. Think of solutions someone else might recommend, say, an engineer, accountant, politician, priest, or architect.

7. Discuss the problem with a variety of other people. Learn to see the problem from their viewpoint and to listen to their solutions.

8. Do not be too serious. Introduce humorous approaches to reduce tension and give a different perspective.

9. Discover how others have already solved the problem.

10. Imagine what an ideal solution would be like and work backward to possible means by which that end could have been achieved.

11. Work on other problems, then return to work on the focal decision problem in a different physical and psychological environment.

12. Keep a note pad accessible to jot down ideas that occur just before sleep, upon awaking from sleep, while traveling, and on other occasions which are not directly related to work.

13. Combine elements of different solutions, even when they are obviously absurd.

14. Brainstorm the problem with friends who know little about the problem as well as with experts in the problem area.

15. Reevaluate any negative attitudes about whether a good solution can be found. Think in terms of when, not whether, the problem will be solved.

Managers who recognize the importance of generating alternative solutions and who behave in the ways suggested above are, by definition, creative. They are behaving creatively at that time in the problem-solving process when such behavior is appropriate.

Critical Analysis of Alternatives

Just as the creative phase of decision making requires some analytical thinking, the critical analysis phase of necessity involves some creativity. It is generally advisable, however, to separate the two. Critical thinking inhibits creativity, and creativity may interfere with the tough-minded, analytical thinking required to determine which alternative yields the highest payoff.

Most of the literature of decision theory is concerned with critical analysis. It includes a wide assortment of models for determining which of several alternatives provides the best solution to a problem. A **model** is a simplified representation of reality and is designed to explain some part of it. Model building attempts to compensate for the limited ability of the human brain to cope with the massive data and the complex relationships involved in many decisions.

A simple decision model was suggested by Benjamin Franklin.[10] The decision maker draws a line down the center of a page and lists all the arguments for a course of action on one side and all those against it on the other. Then the evidence is evaluated. Items of equal weight on the two sides are systematically crossed off until one side is eliminated. This model is similar to modern decision models in that a major decision is broken down into a series of small, manageable ones.

Many of the models developed by decision theorists are too technical for use by the typical operating manager. They often require the expertise of a specialist in quantitative methods as well as the time to gather data and develop computer programs. In addition, many managerial decisions do not lend themselves to quantitative analysis. Both the data involved in management decisions and the evaluation criteria are often in the form of judgments and general impressions. In a recent promotion decision, for example, one criterion was that, "the new vice-president must possess attitudes and values that are compatible with those of the other members of the executive team." Such criteria and the data to which they are applied are better treated in open and rational conversation than in decision analysis models.

One approach to deciding among alternatives, which need not be highly complicated, involves the use of a payoff matrix. As shown in Figure 12-3, this is a technique for forecasting the payoff, or expected value to the organization, of each alternative under different conditions. In this illustration three *strategies* (alternative courses of action) are evaluated. The assumption is made that one of three *states of nature* (conditions which are beyond the decision maker's control) will occur. The probability of each state of nature is estimated. From the estimated profit under each condition, the expected payoff for each strategy is calculated.

The calculations shown in Figure 12-3 indicate that buying new machines will yield the highest profit. The decision maker may, however, want to apply criteria other than profitability. For example, it may be meaningful to ask whether the modest increase in potential profit is adequate to offset the personal effort required in making the transition to new machines and the 20 percent chance of a $20,000 reduction in profits (the difference between $100,000 and $80,000) if product demand stays constant. The use of quantitative data in this matrix in no way hinders the application of numerous other criteria.

Since the data used in analyses such as this involve several judgments of varying degree of accuracy, it may appear that the expected payoff values have a false and misleading appearance of accuracy. This

Strategies	STATES OF NATURE			Expected Payoff
	Product Demand Stays Constant	25% Increase in Demand	50% Increase in Demand	
S_1 Buy new machines	$ 80,000[1]	$130,000	$200,000	$151,500[2]
S_2 Modify old machines	90,000	135,000	170,000	141,750
S_3 Use old machines	100,000	130,000	160,000	137,500
Probability of occurrence	.20	.35	.45	1.00

[1] Estimated annual profit over a three-year period.
[2] Calculations of Expected Payoffs (EP) for each of three Strategies (S_s):

$$EP(S_1) = \$ \ 80,000(.20) + \$130,000(.35) + \$200,000(.45) = \$151,500$$
$$EP(S_2) = \quad 90,000(.20) + \quad 135,000(.35) + \quad 170,000(.45) = \$141,750$$
$$EP(S_3) = \quad 100,000(.20) + \quad 130,000(.35) + \quad 160,000(.45) = \$137,500$$

FIGURE 12-3 Application of the Payoff Matrix

is an ever-present danger of such a method. On the other hand, it is infinitely more rational to make each judgment explicit than to conceal it in a muddle of half-conscious assumptions.

It is inevitable, for example, that uncontrollable variables (in our example, the changes in market conditions) will influence the outcome of decisions. Decision makers need to be aware of such variables or at least aware of the fact that such variables are unknowns in the decision process. And, whether decision makers realize it or not, they inevitably apply probabilities to the states of nature they perceive to be present. Too often the probabilities that influence major decisions are vague expressions of optimism or pessimism such as "the chances are good that our market will improve next year" or "I see little chance of an improved market in the immediate future."

The requirement that probabilities be precisely estimated is an occasion for research, consultation, and systematic analysis. The outcome is necessarily in the form of an estimate; but at least it is a consciously made, informed estimate. At the worst, the decision maker becomes aware that a given decision is based on a gamble; and a meaningful note of caution is thus introduced into the decision process.

Many excellent publications are available to managers with an interest in learning how to use decision models. Although their greatest immediate value will be found in the solution of complex organizational problems, their principles should, in the long run, find expression in all sorts of managerial decisions.

Choosing a Solution and Taking Action

The skills and personal qualities needed to analyze data critically are often possessed by staff specialists who want no part of responsibility for taking action. Analysis is primarily an intellectual process, while choosing and taking action require courage and a willingness to take personal risks. Analysis of data can always be delegated, but decisions often cannot be.

It may appear that effective analysis is synonymous with choosing a solution. In practice, however, such thinking omits two important facts. First, since decisions concern future events, alternatives are seldom so clear that they eliminate the need for personal judgment. Secondly, since the decision maker must personally assume responsibility for the decision, the ultimate criteria are both organizational and personal. They are concerned with both the achievement of organizational goals and the manager's need for self-preservation and enhancement.

Implementation, Feedback, and Adaptation

Good decisions sometimes fail to produce good results because of poor implementation and follow-up. By the same token, mediocre decisions can get excellent results if a manager shows unusual ingenuity in implementation.

In one sense, choosing a solution and taking action is an irreversible process. What is done cannot be undone—or can it? Fortunately, as the implementation process unfolds and the future does or does not occur as predicted, adaptation is possible. New decisions are made that alter the original one and either prevent it from being a catastrophe or, if it proves to be effective, further enhance its effectiveness.

Some decisions are **absolute** in that, once action is taken, they cannot be reversed or significantly altered. A decision to sell often falls into this category, assuming, of course, that the decision is implemented. Other decisions are **adaptive**. They can be altered because their implementation is an unfolding process rather than a single, irrevocable event. Thus, a decision to enter a new market may at first involve buying and re-selling a product in a limited geographic area. Implementation may proceed gradually until the entire country is covered and the firm manufactures the products. Since the sequential nature of adaptive decisions greatly reduces risk, they are usually preferred to absolute decisions.

Sequential decisions may be expressed graphically by means of a decision tree,[11] as shown in Figure 12-4. By plotting the known alternatives in this fashion, a manager can simultaneously visualize both present and future decisions. By inserting probabilities and the financial implications of each alternative, the decision tree also serves the same purpose as the payoff matrix shown in Figure 12-3. Where quantitative data are not available, verbal descriptions of each outcome serve to clarify their implications.

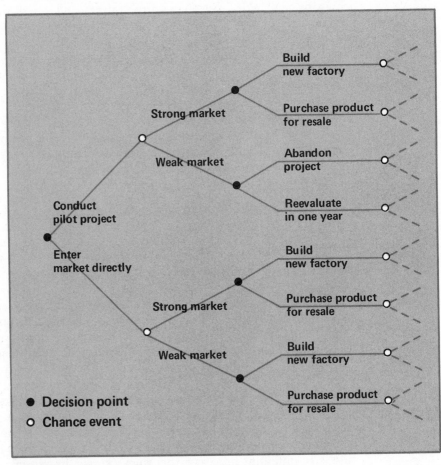

FIGURE 12-4 A Tree for Sequential Decisions

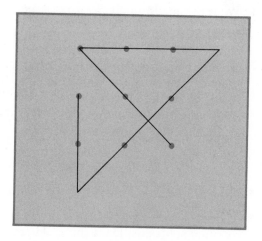

FIGURE 12-5 Solution to the Nine-Dot Problem

IMPORTANT TERMS AND CONCEPTS

problem   creativity
problem solving   brainstorming
decision making   synectics
rationality   model
bounded rationality   absolute decision
satisficers   adaptive decision
heuristic

STUDY AND DISCUSSION QUESTIONS

1. Describe some approaches you could use to avoid the mistakes commonly made when carrying out Step 1 in the problem-solving process (i.e., "exploring the nature of the problem").

2. In what sense does managerial authority obscure the quality of decisions?

3. How do managers benefit from making explicit the process by which their decisions are made?

4. What is the "implicit favorite" model of decision making?

5. Two store managers of a decentralized retail chain have an opportunity to invest in an item for resale during the Christmas season. Market conditions in the two areas are comparable. Manager A decides not to carry the item. Manager B decides to carry it and as a result earns the highest profit in the history of the company. Their superior ultimately concludes that A made the better decision. How could this conclusion be justified?

6. How does Mintzberg's description of how managers make decisions differ from how decision theorists say they should make decisions?

7. Why are results not the ideal measure of a good decision?

8. Herbert Simon observed that managers seek satisfactory rather than optimal solutions. Does this hold true even when managers use the best possible decision models? Explain.

9. How is a *problem* defined in this chapter? Can you think of problems in any area of life that cannot be defined in this way?

10. One way to solve a problem is to lower the standard or expectation. When is such action appropriate? Give examples.

11. What one factor is most likely to account for the great individual differences in creativity?

12. Why is *deciding* or *choosing* not the last step in a problem-solving effort?

CRITICAL INCIDENT

HASTY ACTIONS ON SLOW PROCESSING

Nancy Henry took a job with the National Heritage Insurance Company immediately after receiving her degree in business. After a month-long orientation and training program, she started work as a claims adjuster in the claims adjusting unit.

The adjusters receive the individual claims and the materials related to the claims from clerks in the adjacent claims processing unit, the work unit where incoming claims are recorded and where relevant information and forms are added to the claim before it is passed on to claims adjusting. Both claims processing and claims adjusting units have supervisors who report to the claims department manager.

It was the intention of both the claims department manager and Nancy that after six months of working as a claims adjuster, Nancy would become the supervisor of the claims adjusting unit.

Four months after starting work as a claims adjuster, Nancy was asked by the claims department manager if she would like to become the new supervisor of the claims processing unit, as the previous supervisor had unexpectedly announced that she was leaving. The manager, Loretta DuBois, explained that "I think you have more long-range managerial potential than anyone presently working for me; and, in addition, the average time for processing claims has been creeping upward, and I think some new ideas are needed."

Nancy was flattered by the confidence shown in her and felt it was important to appear career-oriented. She replied immediately that she would take the position. After a week of giving Nancy on-the-job training, the supervisor of the claims processing unit left and Nancy was in her first managerial position.

Increasing the rate at which claims are processed, Nancy felt, is a worthwhile, timely, visible goal. She decided to move quickly to attack the problem. An answer to the question of how to do this seemed to arrive in her office on the second day of her new job.

"Nancy, you know what you could do to make a real good impression with the people in this unit?" queried Sam Li, a long-time clerk who had worked with Nancy on several claims. "You could let people have a little more time off to take care of personal matters. Our previous supervisor was a real stickler for rules, and no one even dared take such leave unless it was an absolute emergency. Maybe you could be a bit more lenient about time off, and people would feel good about your taking over."

Nancy saw this "dissatisfaction" of the employees as an opportunity and let it be known that anyone who processed claims at a rate 10 percent higher during the next two months than in the previous two months could expect favorable responses if subsequently they asked to leave work an hour earlier for personal reasons.

1. What personal characteristics of the decision makers involved may have influenced their decisions?

2. Which of the common mistakes made in problem solving does Nancy seem to have made?

REFERENCES

1. Lindblom, Charles E. "The Science of 'Muddling Through,'" *Public Administration Review*, Vol. 19, Spring, 1959, pp. 79–88.

2. Soelberg, P. O. "Unprogrammed Decision Making," *Industrial Management Review*, Vol. 8, 1967, pp. 19–29.

3. Mintzberg, Henry, Duru Raisinghani, and Andre Theoret. "The Structure of 'Unstructured' Decision Processes," *Administrative Science Quarterly*, Vol. 21, No. 2, June, 1976, p. 252.

4. Huber, George P. *Managerial Decision Making*. Glenview, Ill.: Scott, Foresman and Company, 1980, p. 61. (Material in this chapter draws heavily from Chapter 2 of *Managerial Decision Making*.)

5. March, James G., and Herbert A. Simon. *Organizations*. New York: John Wiley & Sons, Inc., 1958, pp. 140–141.

6. VanGundy, Arthur B. *Techniques of Structured Problem Solving*. New York: Van Nostrand Reinhold Company, 1981, p. 268.

7. Huber. *Managerial Decision Making*, p. 195.

8. VanGundy. *Techniques of Structured Problem Solving*, p. 122.

9. Adams, James L. *Conceptual Blockbusting*. San Francisco: W. H. Freeman and Company, Publishers, 1974, p. 11.

10. Franklin, Benjamin. "Letter to Joseph Priestly" in *Mr. Franklin, A Selection from His Personal Letters*, eds. Leonard W. Labaree and J. Bell Whirfield, Jr. New Haven: Yale University Press, 1956, pp. 25–27.

11. Huber. *Managerial Decision Making*, p. 118.

SUGGESTED READINGS

Ford, Charles H. "Time to Redesign the Decision-Making Process," *Management Review*, Vol. 67, July, 1978, pp. 50–53.

Hellriegel, Don, and John W. Slocum, Jr. "Managerial Problem-Solving Styles," *Business Horizons*, December, 1975, pp. 29–37.

Isaack, Thomas S. "Intuition: An Ignored Dimension of Management," *Academy of Management Review*, October, 1978, pp. 917–921.

Janssen, C. T. L., and T. E. Daniel. "Applications and Implementation: A Decision Theory Example in Football," *Decision Sciences*, Vol. 15, No. 2, Spring, 1984, pp. 253–259.

Klein, Noreen M. "Utility and Decision Strategies: A Second Look at the Rational Decision Maker," *Organizational Behavior and Human Performance*, Vol. 31, No. 1, February, 1983, pp. 1–25.

Ulvila, Jacob, and Rex V. Brown. "Decision Analysis Comes of Age," *Harvard Business Review*, Vol. 60, No. 5, September-October, 1982, pp. 130–141.

Schwenk, Charles R., and Howard Thomas. "Effects of Conflicting Analyses on Managerial Decision Making: A Laboratory Experiment," *Decision Sciences*, Vol. 14, No. 4, Fall, 1983, pp. 467–482.

Simon, Herbert A. *The New Science of Management Decision*, rev. ed. Englewood Cliffs, N.J.: Prentice-Hall, Inc., 1977.

13

Understanding and Improving Communication in Organizations

Ineffective communications between people or groups are always significant because they produce destructive conflicts, poor coordination, dissatisfaction, and low productivity. Poor communication is costly both to the organization and to its members. Effective communication is essential for effective management.

The potential for communication to go awry is evident in the aggregate amount of time a manager spends in communicating: giving and receiving directives, participating in conferences, instructing subordinates, hearing grievances, disciplining, counseling, selling, observing, and reading and writing a wide variety of messages. A manager is constantly involved in some form of communication. As a consequence, a manager's success depends a great deal on his or her communication skills. Fortunately, increased insight into the communication process and increased skill in communicating are things that can be learned. Enhancing these insights and skills is the purpose of this chapter.

The subject of communication is illusive because it is intertwined with so many other subjects. Effective communication is, for example, an integral part of effective leadership, decision making, motivation, the management of organizational conflict, and other subjects with which the discipline of organizational behavior is concerned. Such subjects are the *content* of communication; they are concerned with communicating in order to achieve a particular objective in a particular situation. This chapter is concerned primarily with the *process* of communication— with how communication occurs in contrast to what is communicated. Implicit in this chapter is the assumption that a body of knowledge exists that can help managers communicate more effectively and thereby perform more successfully the many tasks in which communication is involved. The specific objectives of this chapter are

TO UNDERSTAND:

1. The nature of person-to-person communication

2. The nature of organizational communication

3. The barriers most likely to impede communication

4. Approaches to improving communication

THE NATURE OF PERSON-TO-PERSON COMMUNICATION

No single definition covers the range of behaviors studied in all areas where communication occurs, and there is no definition on which scholars in this field agree. **Communication** is here defined as the process by which messages are sent by one person and received by another.

The messages referred to in this definition may be expressed as bulletins, letters, memos, job descriptions, policy statements, telephone conversations, and other forms of verbal information. They may, in addition, include a broad spectrum of nonverbal data which are transmitted through such media as voice tone, facial expressions, gestures, and clothing. The implication of stating that the messages are sent *and* received is that communication must be achieved before it can be referred to as communication. A manager may, for example, make an important policy statement in the text of a newsletter article that nobody reads. In such a situation communication has only been attempted. Communication occurs only when the message is received.

Some definitions imply that communication occurs only when the sender is successful in transmitting an *intended* message. One difficulty with this qualification is that people are seldom totally effective in transmitting their intended meanings to others, and they often transmit messages to others when they have no intention of communicating at all (for example, through the way they walk). In practice we must often be content with transmitting a reasonable facsimile of the intended message—an approximation that is accurate enough to make a point or achieve a desired objective but which is short of perfection. As long as words, gestures, and other symbols are transmitted from one person to another, communication occurs, however far it may fall below an exact transmission of intended meaning. The goal of studying communication is to narrow the gap between the intended message and the message that is actually transmitted. The communication process is commonly thought of as including the five steps shown in Figure 13-1.

Encoding

Before a message can be transmitted from one person to another it must be **encoded**; that is, the intended message must be translated into a code or series of symbols (words, gestures, facial expressions, and so on) that represent the meaning the sender hopes to communicate. It should be noted, however, that only the symbols are transmitted. The meaning received depends upon the receiver's interpretation of those symbols.

Consider the case of a manager whose objective is to increase the productivity of subordinates by communicating dissatisfaction with their past performance. Encoding the message requires decisions not only about what will be said, but about how, when, and where it will be said. Encoding may also involve decisions about the expression or concealment of emotion. The manager may, for example, decide not to show frustration and to communicate in a matter-of-fact, unemotional manner. He

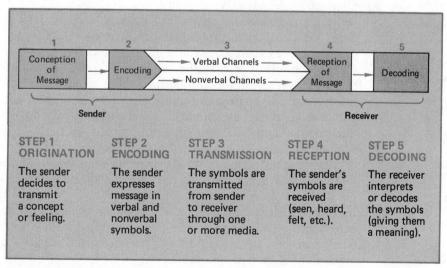

FIGURE 13-1 The Communication Process

or she may ultimately decide to talk with subordinates as individuals, tailoring the message to the unique circumstances of each and informally and privately communicating with each as the appropriate occasion arises.

Encoding may occur within the span of a few milliseconds, as when one person greets another with a "good morning" rather than with an alternative greeting. Regardless of the time required and the degree of conscious planning, the transmission of a message originates with encoding.

The Medium

As shown in Figure 13-1, various media provide the channels through which transmission occurs. The more important the message, the more likely managers are to give careful thought to media selection. Since the medium used (for example, a face-to-face interview in preference to a memorandum) often determines the success of a communication act, the selection process deserves serious consideration. Managers commonly fail, however, to give it the attention it deserves.

Decoding

The sender's symbols are sent through a sensory medium such as light or sound waves. When the symbols are received, they must be interpreted or **decoded**. Words and other symbols have multiple meanings, and there is no assurance that the intended meanings of the sender-encoder are identical to those of the receiver-decoder.

The more experiences the sender and receiver have had in common, the more likely it is that the sender's intended meaning will be communicated. When, for example, the sender speaks only Spanish and the receiver only English, a relatively primitive level of communication is probable. A similar experience occurs when college-educated, company-oriented managers attempt to communicate with employees whose education, attitudes, loyalties, and aspirations differ greatly from their own.

In order for people with different backgrounds to communicate, at least one must learn to speak the language of the other. In practice, this goes beyond the mastery of vocabulary. Managers who aspire to communicate with subordinates must learn how they think, feel, and characteristically respond in a variety of situations. By applying such knowledge, managers are usually able to predict with acceptable accuracy how a given message will be decoded.

Nonverbal Communication

Much of what a person communicates is transmitted nonverbally. People who are familiar with the sign language of the deaf or the early American Indians will recognize our ability to communicate without the use of words. What may not be so evident is the extent to which our own nonverbal language is actually used.[1,2] It is especially useful in expressing emotional states or reactions in contrast to complex ideas. Nonverbal communication may be classified as sign language, action language, and object language. A brief look at each type shows that our own culture is rich in nonverbal symbols of communication.

Sign Language. Any gesture that serves as a word substitute may be classified as **sign language**. Examples of common signs are head movements for yes or no and an outstretched arm with the palm forward for stop. As with all nonverbal messages, sign language must be interpreted in a specific context to be understood. Thus, outstretched arms and clenched fists can be a joyous victory sign for the winner of the Master's golf championship and a symbol of hostility and aggression from an angry mob in front of the White House. Similarly, a wave of the hand may say either hello or goodbye.

Action Language. All physical movements that convey a message but are not specifically used as word substitutes are classified as **action language**. For example, depending upon the context in which the actions occur, the way people walk, run, sit, eat, laugh, or embrace communicates something about them.

In a recent committee meeting, one member folded his arms and gradually pushed his chair away from the conference table. Everyone received the message: "If I can't have my way, I won't participate." Some actions, such as a predisposition to smile or to exhibit hand tremors and a cracking voice, communicate the presence of more lasting characteristics of the individual. The simultaneous transmission of verbal and nonverbal symbols is especially effective in giving the receiver the cues needed to decode accurately.

Object Language. An intentional or unintentional display of material things constitutes an **object language** through which one's identity, aspirations, attitudes, and motivation are communicated to others. One's clothes, automobiles, and office furniture often fall into this category. Similar to some forms of action language, they are a means through which personality and self-image are projected.

PERSONALITY FACTORS AND ENVIRONMENTAL INFLUENCES

Effective communication depends on personal characteristics and skills. These qualities can be expressed to the maximum, however, only if environmental conditions are optimal.

During the heyday of the human relations movement, the phrase "it's a communication problem" became a catchall explanation and a convenient scapegoat for the many difficult-to-solve problems arising in relationships between people. Conflict between individuals, for example, was often explained away as a communication problem as though real conflict were nonexistent and labeling would somehow result in a quick and easy solution. This period introduced a much-needed awareness of the importance of communication in organizations; but it was a shallow, faddish emphasis which was lacking in research support and a sound basis in communication theory. In contrast, in the past few decades, research into the nature of communication in organizations has been fruitful, and a steady stream of insights has resulted.[3] We look now at some of the personal and organizational qualities that determine the effectiveness of communication.

Regardless of the favorability of the organizational climate, individuals differ greatly in their ability to communicate. These differences are partly the result of variations in such skills as writing, counseling, interviewing, debating, and public speaking. One's vocabulary, grammar, style of delivery, and even spelling are related to communication skills. Yet these knowledge and skill factors are often less important than certain personality characteristics such as empathy, talkativeness, assertiveness, and character.

Empathy

People differ greatly in **empathy**, defined as awareness of the needs and motives of others. Problems caused by inadequate empathy are seen in the experience of Roger Green, an engineer with a major oil company.

Aptly described by his supervisor as having "the social sensitivity of a crowbar," Roger was repeatedly passed over for promotion into management. His technical competence, motivation, and dependability were unsurpassed, but he could not hear what others were trying to say. When Roger argued for a point of view, his position was based on facts—to a point. Unfortunately he never considered facts about others' feelings and personal needs. One of his superiors declared that Roger, "is a mechanical genius and a social idiot who communicates better with computers than with people." Although Roger's contribution to the company was outstanding, he was always assigned jobs that involved as little human contact as possible.

Few people have as much difficulty as Roger in understanding another person's frame of reference, and those who do are not likely to change significantly. People with greater natural empathy than Roger can improve their sensitivity by consciously attempting to understand how others think and feel.

In some cases, **sensitivity training** seems to improve empathy. This is a technique by which participants may become more empathic through self-disclosure, increased self-awareness, and awareness of how others feel and think. Sensitivity training has been strongly criticized because its effects are unpredictable, but it is one of the few techniques with a potential for improving the communication of the person with low empathy.

Talkativeness

It is difficult to communicate with people who refuse to talk, just as it is difficult to communicate with people who talk too much. Even in small classes, some students never say a word except in response to a direct question. Likewise, in business situations, a few quiet, withdrawn individuals attend conferences and committee meetings but speak only when forced to do so. Such persons often have more to contribute than many who talk freely, but their inability or reluctance to voluntarily communicate suppresses their potential contribution.

Usually quiet people are often poor communicators for another reason. Since communication is a two-way process, a good communicator motivates others to express themselves freely. But most people are inhibited in the presence of a person who talks very little. Free communication between two people has been described as a form of "mutual blackmail" in that self-disclosure develops in short, sequential steps until each understands the attitudes, beliefs, values, and needs of the other. In effect, people who refuse to disclose themselves to others fail to pay the price others demand for a full disclosure.

The importance of self-disclosure as an element in communication can hardly be overemphasized, particularly because it provides a basis for empathy. Also, the personal relationships that grow out of self-disclosure provide the channels through which informal communication among managers flows. Managers who are excluded from these channels may fail to receive the information needed to make sound decisions and take advantage of opportunities. The same holds for managers who cut themselves off from the informal, casual communication channels of subordinates.

Assertiveness

Individuals who are excessively assertive or domineering may undermine their effectiveness as communicators. It is, nevertheless, true that assertiveness is often required for good communication. At times, a manager must be persistent and argue forcefully for a point of view in order to exert a significant influence on the organization. The manner of presentation and the conviction with which one speaks are often more persuasive than the weight of facts and the strength of one's logic.

Character

During Lyndon B. Johnson's last year as president of the United States and in the period prior to the resignation of President Richard Nixon, the news media coined the term *credibility gap*. It occurs when people learn through experience that what an individual says is not trustworthy. Verbal fluency matters very little if trust is low. When trust is high, on the other hand, others will accept a message and attribute honorable motives to the sender. This holds even when the actual message is poorly expressed or contains information others do not want to hear.

The observation that actions speak louder than words is a forceful comment about communication. Actions tend to validate or repudiate one's words. Through their decisions, managers communicate something about their character, judgment, and dependability. The cumulative effect of such decisions is to provide a broad context within which messages are interpreted and evaluated. A manager should assume that deception will always be discovered and thus should behave so that others will assume that his or her words are truthful.

The maturity with which one treats information received from others is also related to trust. For example, employees who believe that supervisors can be trusted to respect confidences are often willing to share information which they would otherwise withhold. Some managers, like the king who killed the bearer of bad news, react so unpredictably to upward communication that subordinates learn to tell them only what they want to hear.

COMMUNICATION WITHIN ORGANIZATIONS

Organizations deliberately acquire and distribute information in order to carry out the critical functions of decision making and control. In many cases, this requires the processing of a large number of communications conveying information. Because a large number of communications may cause an overload on individuals and work groups, organizations are forced to seek efficiencies in their communication system.[4]

Processes Within Formal Organizational Communication Systems

Two processes that organizations use to increase the efficiency of their communication systems are *message routing* and *message summarizing*. Message routing causes any particular message to be distributed to relatively few organizational units. This selective distribution greatly reduces the communication load on the many organizational units having little or no use for the message and on the many intermediate units involved in transmitting the message. Message summarizing plays a similar role. It has as its purpose reducing the size of the message while at the same time faithfully reproducing its meaning. For example, large sets of numbers are replaced by averages, and multipage reports are replaced by appropriately derived recommendations or conclusions. Summarization can greatly reduce the work load on units having to process a message.

Messages vary considerably in their relevance, length, accuracy, timeliness, and other characteristics. As a consequence of this fact and the need to control their work load, the units responsible for routing and summarizing necessarily exercise some discretion in the way they handle messages. Such discretion allows two other processes to occur in parallel with summarizing and routing. These are *message delay* and *message modification*.

There is no value judgment or negativism implied in the use of the phrase message delay. Since the priority assignment given a message is a principal determinant of the time it will be delayed, and since making such assignments is necessarily (at least in part) a delegated and discretionary act, it is often difficult to make objective judgments about the excessiveness of individual delays. In any case, the sources of most delays are the same regardless of whether delays are considered to be excessive or routine.

Message modification refers to the distortion of message meaning. Its source may be either the abilities or the motivations of the sender or receiver. Modifications may be conscious or unconscious, well-intended or malicious. They range from the well-intended correction of minor errors to the extreme modification of substituting one message for another. Message modification differs from message summarization in that it distorts a message's meaning, whereas summarization does not.

Although these processes are often thought of as occurring in the context of a formal organization, they occur in informal organizations as well, as anyone's analysis of the "message board" in their own household will show.

Informal Communication

Informal communication includes all messages transmitted in the work setting other than those that are generated specifically to fulfill work-related assignments. These include, for example, a conversation between two supervisors about an unproductive employee, between two clerks about a better approach for posting an item, or among members of an informal work group concerning how to help one of their members cope with an emotional problem. The nature of such communication is nowhere described in the formal communication systems, but the organization could not survive without it.

One medium of informal communication is the **grapevine**, an unprogrammed communication channel that meanders through the organization carrying any and every type of information of interest to organizational members. Actually most large organizations are crisscrossed by several different grapevine channels with interconnecting links.

The individuals who comprise the links of a channel may have relatively little in common. A message originator may be an executive secretary whose sister is the best friend of the wife of a factory employee who acquires status from feeding information into an informal work group. Once a bit of information is received by a freely communicating informal group, it may fan out in several directions, for example, through members of a car pool in one case and through employees whose work is related in another.

The development of grapevines is inevitable. Although grapevines are neither good nor bad in themselves, the messages they carry are subject to distortion as messages transmitted from one human link to another become progressively more garbled. Their content is misinterpreted, abbreviated, embellished, and selectively transmitted in terms of what the sender believes the receiver wants or needs to know. Since the original message may be only partially true, it is not surprising that the grapevine is sometimes referred to as a rumor mill.

The grapevine is an undependable means of communication. In a given instance, many employees may be bypassed altogether. The grapevine commonly reinforces messages which are transmitted through formal announcements, bulletins, memos, newsletters, and other formal channels. Since the truth of its messages is highly correlated with the willingness of management to communicate openly and effectively through other means, the best way to guarantee the relative accuracy of the grapevine is to provide reliable information sources against which its messages can easily be checked.

Organizational Climate

Although the concept of organizational climate is somewhat nebulous, it is valuable in understanding several aspects of organizational behavior. **Organizational climate** is a set of attributes of a particular organization that are identifiable in the collective attitudes, perceptions, and expectations of its members. For instance, organizational climate is in part determined by how members perceive their organization's leadership, products, pay, employee benefits, discipline, policies, and goals. Definitive studies relating organizational climate and communication are few. There is reason to believe, however, that certain climates facilitate while others impede effective communication. We look now at two of the variables involved.

Openness and Trust. The human relations writers emphasized the importance of openness in communication. They advocated a participative approach to decision making and leadership which is possible only if information flows freely throughout the organization. The emphasis on openness of communication found expression during the 1930s in programs for counseling employees on personal as well as work-related problems. As the group dynamics movement developed, emphasis shifted to problem-solving groups in which authority, status, and other barriers to communication are minimized.

A climate that is favorable to open communication is not easily achieved. Employees who have long been accustomed to authoritarian leadership fear the negative consequences of openness, having learned through experience that their interests are best served through secretiveness. Why, for example, should an employee tell a supervisor about a better way to do a job when the supervisor may react by raising standards or with defensiveness or hostility because he or she did not think of it first? Even when management rewards openness, employees often act in terms of previously learned expectations and do not easily relinquish their resistance to open communication.

A climate favorable to openness must rest on a foundation of mutual trust;[5] but there are, unfortunately, substantial barriers to its development. Because efforts to develop open communication sometimes appear insincere, they have the effect of reducing trust levels. When, for example, supervisors who do not genuinely value the opinions of subordinates begin asking for them, their requests are met with suspicion. When information shared by employees results in managerial action of which the employees disapprove, secretiveness and distrust are reinforced. Yet such action is, at times, unavoidable.

Managers also have reservations about open communication. Certainly managers cannot always be open without creating unnecessary anxieties and, at times, getting employees involved in complicated management problems that will interfere with employee performance. In theory, it is difficult to argue with an openness policy, but in practice a degree of closed communication is necessary.

The Open-Door Policy. Top-level managers who favor open communication often establish a policy in which subordinates at all levels are invited to express their ideas and grievances directly, without going through the chain of command. Theoretically this open-door policy is the essence of egalitarian leadership and freedom of communication.

In practice, it is difficult to use an open-door policy effectively. It can be extremely time consuming. It tends to undermine the authority of bypassed managers and to create superior-subordinate conflict. In a sense, an open-door policy expresses a lack of confidence in the ability of subordinate managers to deal effectively with their subordinates. It clashes with the concept of delegation and implies that upward communication will be blocked unless bypassing occurs.

Yet an open-door policy appears to be a logical corollary of an open-communication philosophy. Why, after all, should it be inappropriate for any two organizational members to communicate freely with one another? An inconsistency between an open-door policy and open communication appears, however, when a bypassing employee assumes that the manager's door is open for closed or confidential conversations. Managers who invite lower level employees to express their attitudes and viewpoints cannot easily relate the conversation to the employees' immediate superiors without violating a confidence. This inconsistency often undermines an open-door policy over a period of time.

In practice, effective managers do not keep the door completely open. They ask the subordinate, "Have you talked this over with your immediate supervisor?" and they usually insist on that action. Consultation with one's immediate superior is a logical first step in a genuinely open system. Another way of keeping the door only partially open is for a manager to receive those who seek an audience but to avoid the encouragement inherent in an official open-door policy.

Managers must pay a price for openness. It can be highly threatening, and only mature organizations and individuals are likely to practice it over a long period of time. Yet, when the disadvantages of alternatives are considered, enlightened managers opt for openness as a general goal.

BREAKING THROUGH COMMUNICATION BARRIERS

Where the organizational climate is favorable for openness, management can improve communication by isolating and reducing the impact of specific barriers. Where the climate is unfavorable, reducing the impact of specific barriers is one means of improving it.

Individual efforts to improve communication are relatively unsuccessful if an organization is characterized by distrust and ego defensiveness. On the other hand, trust can be developed and ego defensiveness reduced. We look now at some means of achieving these ends and thereby improving communication.

Gatekeeping

A **gatekeeper** is a person who decides which items of information will be retained and which will be passed on in the communication chain. *Gatekeeping* is the process through which a gatekeeper obstructs the free flow of messages.

Perhaps the most obvious gatekeeping occurs between labor and management in conflict situations. Strong social pressures erect deliberate barriers to upward communication as employees of each informal group maintain close surveillance over the activities of one another. Rule breaking, loafing, theft, and sabotage, as well as positive contributions to the organization, are painstakingly concealed from management.

First line supervisors, caught between the demands of their superiors and subordinates, may carefully filter the information passed along to management lest they be suspected by superiors of being too close to their subordinates and by their subordinates of betraying a trust. In fact, managers at all levels become gatekeepers when open communication may jeopardize their careers or make them appear inept. If kept within reasonable bounds, these forms of gatekeeping need not be destructive. At any rate, their occurrence is inevitable.

A more subtle and sometimes unconscious form of gatekeeping is the message modification mentioned earlier. It occurs at every point in the transmission network. When information is evaluated and integrated, the resulting inferences and decisions are transmitted while at least part of the underlying information is withheld. Although this filtering may not represent a deliberate distortion, it nevertheless modifies the nature of the message as it is transmitted from one person to another. The message bears the imprint of the transmitter's perceptual process, judgment, and evaluation of what the receiver needs to know. In upward transmission, information unfavorable to the sender is often suppressed while favorable information is transmitted.

Although gatekeeping cannot be eliminated, it can be reduced. Once gatekeepers are discovered, specific steps can be taken to modify their behavior. In addition to directly confronting them, the superior can discourage such behavior by verifying their reports and developing alternative channels of communication. Formal techniques such as attitude surveys may be used to uncover the facts and increase the risk involved in deliberate gatekeeping.

The unconscious or semiconscious gatekeeping associated with minor forms of message modification is more difficult to eliminate. It is sometimes appropriate to transmit a written copy of the original message along with any necessary elaboration or special instructions. Formal management training may also be helpful. Managers who become aware of the common tendency toward unintentional distortion of communication can make improvements if they are motivated to do so.

Semantic Problems

The term **semantic** means having to do with meaning. There is a semantic difference, for example, between *bear* (to carry) and *bear* (an animal), although the spelling and sound of the words are the same. In communication the meaning of each word must be derived from its context.

Semantic problems are common in organizations. The terms *profit* and *efficiency* roll from the tongues of management with warmth and affection, but in the language of the rank and file they may carry a cold, impersonal message of potential wages unjustifiably withheld and speed-ups on the assembly line. Intellectually, the two groups may easily agree on a dictionary meaning; but in real-life communication, the words carry different emotional overtones for labor and management.

Because of the relatively common background of managers, they tend to communicate better with one another than with the rank and file. To communicate effectively with the latter they must be sensitive to the possibility of semantic problems and use words whose intended meaning will be understood. Fortunately, the many first line supervisors who are promoted from the ranks typically have little difficulty at this point, and it is they who communicate most directly with employees. Higher level managers are most likely to show their insensitivity in newsletters, bulletins, statements of rules, and in other written messages.

Communication is sometimes impaired by the specialists' use of insider language. The jargon and special terminology of accountants, engineers, and scientists impede communication with other specialists and with general management. Where technical concepts are involved, this problem is difficult to overcome. If the problem is primarily one of vocabulary, an awareness of the need to translate and the motivation to do so are usually sufficient to improve communication. If specialists are regularly evaluated and rewarded on the basis of this factor, communication problems become less frequent and less severe.

Another type of insider language is *slang*. Informal work groups develop their own words for tools, parts, processes, behaviors, and people. This language serves to identify group members and to brand outsiders. The use of slang is most characteristic of adolescents, and when used extensively by adults is often accompanied by evidences of adolescent immaturity and naivete. An example of this naivete is the notion that those who know the language are somehow superior to and more sophisticated than those who do not.

Because slang is deeply imbedded in the structure of informal groups, management usually makes no attempt to do anything about it. It seldom causes a serious communication problem at the employee level where it is most common. Within management it can be more serious. New managers and outside consultants are most likely to experience a problem because of it.

Status Differences

Significant differences in social status tend to inhibit upward communication. When a factory employee enters the walnut-paneled office of a well-dressed executive bulwarked behind a massive desk, it is not surprising that some degree of intimidation occurs. This is especially true if the walls are embellished with diplomas, awards, or other evidences of high status. After all, the symbols were carefully selected to show that the officeholder is important and powerful. The obvious way to reduce status barriers is to remove status symbols and emphasize similarities rather than differences between the personnel at different organizational levels.

It is noteworthy that status differences are not always a communication barrier. In fact, in downward communication, high status may be an asset. Employees, for example, generally prefer to take orders from someone they perceive to have high status rather than from their peers or from someone recently promoted from their own ranks. Since the status symbols exhibited by managers are also symbols of power, the possession of high status is an excellent means of attracting and holding attention. A casual remark by the company president may remain on the grapevine for months, while the same statement by a middle manager may never be heard.

Whether status differences are, on the whole, an asset or a liability depends to some degree on the dominant leadership style employed in the organization. An emphasis on status differences is more consistent with an authoritarian than with a participative style. Status differences are, therefore, less damaging in the authoritarian structure.

System Overload

The members of an organization, like electronic devices, have a limited capacity to receive and transmit messages. Air-traffic controllers in a large airport are a widely publicized example of persons whose capacity to communicate is sometimes stretched to the breaking point. Managers in large organizations sometimes have the same problem. They are often called upon to interact personally with large numbers of people and are bombarded with written correspondence, telephone calls, and a continuous stream of reports. Although skills commonly improve with practice under such circumstances, ability to communicate may deteriorate.

The capacity of computers to produce massive volumes of data often contributes more to communication problems than to solutions. Critically important information is lost in the volume of details. Managers who receive more messages than they can judiciously interpret must isolate the messages that are most important. In addition to consuming time, this process has a disorganizing effect on a manager's behavior. Also, the ever-present possibility that important messages will not be received produces frustration and stress.

In the case of line managers, system overload may be reduced by adding staff support or changing the nature of management positions in order to reduce the number of their communication contacts. Specialists in work efficiency techniques may also help managers in a variety of ways. Electronic devices for recording incoming messages or for dictating may be helpful in some instances. In most cases, however, a reduction in the flow of unnecessary information provides the most effective relief for system overload. The condensation of computerized operating reports, memoranda, and even important journal articles can be extremely helpful.

Communication specialists can provide a management team with valuable training in communication techniques. Managers can be taught, for example, when to dictate a memo and when to make a telephone call. They can learn a variety of time-saving techniques such as combining messages rather than interrupting another individual with a number of telephone calls. The mechanics of communicating may appear simplistic and unworthy of a manager's attention. In view of the time managers spend communicating and the cost of poor communication, however, training in this area is an unusually good investment.

Defensive Reactions

Defensiveness is among the most serious barriers to communication. Where the organizational climate is characterized by suspicion, cutthroat competition, and general insecurity, managers and employees alike are prone to filter what others say through their own fears and distrust.

An insecure employee whose supervisor says, "I suggest that in the future you set your alarm a little earlier," may incorrectly hear the supervisor say, "If you are late again for work, you will be discharged." Similarly, the supervisor who is congratulated by a superior for a job well done may react with the suspicion that the boss is preparing him or her for an undesirable assignment or for criticism for substandard performance elsewhere.

The causes of widespread defensiveness in organizations may be correctable by instituting changes in organizational policies. Management may, for example, change from a policy of secretiveness to deliberate sharing of information. Frequent occurrences of defensiveness that involve the same individuals are probably due to emotional immaturity. Messages directed to immature individuals must be carefully encoded to anticipate the defensive reaction and minimize distortion resulting from fear and suspicion.

IMPROVING COMMUNICATION

Effective managerial communication requires, in the long run, effective listening and effective speaking. These are skills that can be learned and must be consciously reviewed to be retained.

The major objectives of active listening are the improvement of learning effectiveness and communication skills. It is obvious, for example, that good listeners in the classroom learn more from lectures and discussions than do students whose listening skills are marginal. It may be less obvious that the feedback which results from listening is essential to good communication. It provides valuable insight into another person's general frame of reference and into that individual's intellectual and emotional reaction to a specific message. Effective listening, a major ingredient of empathic communication, is a skill in which people differ greatly. Fortunately it is one that can be improved.

Active versus Passive Listening

A degree of listening occurs as the passive, involuntary registration of auditory stimuli on consciousness. Hearing occurs because the listener is interested in what is being said or because there are no successfully competing stimuli in the form of external sounds or internal thoughts. In many situations, however, the competing stimuli are dominant, and we fail to receive relevant messages because of daydreaming or because attention is drawn to irrelevant stimuli in the environment.

Listening is most effective when one listens with a purpose. Contrast the common experience of being unable to remember a person's name immediately after being introduced with the recall of the entertainer who remembers the names of the individuals in a large audience after hearing each name only once. Effective listening begins with a motivation to hear, to understand, and to remember. Effective listening is not often a chance happening. It is, rather, the result of an intentional effort to concentrate.

Techniques of Active Listening

One difficulty in listening arises from the slowness of speech in comparison with listening. Pauses between words and phrases allow the listener time to get lost in the free association triggered by the speaker or by some irrelevant stimulus. This is most likely to occur when interest is low or when the speaker's subject is difficult to understand.

The following activities are recommended for improving concentration, effectively using the speaker's pauses, and consequently improving listening skills.

1. Be slow to brand any speaker as boring or uninteresting. These qualities are as often a function of the thought processes of the listener as of the content and delivery of the speech.

2. Determine to learn something when someone speaks.

3. Ask pertinent questions in order to influence the speaker toward interesting content.

4. Guard against a tendency to tune out the speaker when the content presented becomes difficult to understand. Counter with increased determination to learn and remember.

5. Make a game of self-examination after a conversation or speech to see how much of the content can be recalled.

6. Try to anticipate where the speaker is going. Establish and test hypotheses about the speaker's motives, values, and biases. Is the speaker attempting to persuade? to teach? to win friends? to entertain? to kill time?

7. Note the techniques used by the speaker. To what extent does the speaker rely on facts, on emotional appeal, on shock effect, or on authority?

8. Integrate what is being said with what the speaker has said before and with facts learned from other sources.

9. Evaluate the relevance of what is being said. Is it in any way practical? To what is it relevant? Should the content be classified as trivia?

10. Listen for intended meanings. Look behind the words and manner of presentation for what the speaker is attempting to communicate.

11. Be a responsive listener. Maintain eye contact with the speaker. Particularly in individual conversation use nods and facial expressions to let the speaker know that contact is being made.

12. Accept the challenge to become an expert at listening and remembering.

Learning to Use Brief but Influential Communications

Managers and the people they work with tend to be busy. At times they are very busy. Unfortunately, if they allow this condition to cause them to communicate ineffectively in order to save their own time and that of their listeners, they can end up busier than before—trying to repair the damage done by a faulty message. To avoid this, Arlene Yerys, a frequent lecturer and trainer in supervisory skills development, suggests the following three-step process:

1. *Describe the situation.* In other words, provide the other person with a picture of what's been happening. (Just because something is important to you doesn't mean the other person is even aware of the issue.) Effective description is specific and observable (like painting a picture); qualified (avoids absolute words like "always" and "never"); and nonevaluative (avoids judgmental words like "lazy" or "stupid"). Concrete and specific examples increase the other person's comprehension.

   Examples establish common ground: "When you come to our area, you demand your work in a loud voice. You never say 'please.' You label us as incompetent or lazy when your schedule is delayed. . . ." It's doubtful that the other person would like this type of news, but examples clarify the problem.

2. *Describe your reaction.* State your personal response to what is happening. You may describe your response in terms of a feeling like "annoyed," "upset," or "frustrated"—or with phrases like "take advantage of" or "concerned about." To the individual described as "rude," you might say, "Frankly, I am upset or embarrassed by your manner and remarks."

3. *Explain what you want.* Clarity is the key. For example, "we need more communication" is vague compared to "let's meet for 20 minutes on Tuesday and Thursday mornings to review what's happening."

   A statement to the "rude" individual may be: "I propose that you call us five minutes in advance so we can have your work ready when you get here. I would like you to eliminate the negative remarks, and if you have some suggestions on how we can be more effective, please speak to me personally."[6]

IMPORTANT TERMS AND CONCEPTS

communication   sensitivity training
encoded   informal communication
decoded   grapevine
sign language   organizational climate
action language   gatekeeper
object language   semantic
empathy

STUDY AND DISCUSSION QUESTIONS

1. In what sense is poor communication a motivation problem?

2. Some definitions involve the notion that communication occurs only when the *intended* meaning of the sender is transmitted to the receiver. In what sense is this notion inadequate?

3. Explain this statement: Only symbols, not meanings, are transferred from sender to receiver.

4. What is the difference between action language and object language?

5. Explain the relationship between empathy and ability to communicate.

6. Why do people who are unusually quiet sometimes have difficulty empathizing?

7. What is the primary relationship between character and the ability to communicate?

8. Why do managers need superior speaking and writing skills?

9. Even when a manager performs well, how may poor writing and speaking skills interfere with his or her success?

10. What changes are most likely to occur in the nature of the communication process as organizations grow?

11. Assuming it could be done, would it be advisable to eliminate the grapevine within an organization? Explain.

12. Be prepared to debate the pros and cons of the open-door policy. In organizing each position, it may be helpful to imagine how individuals at different organizational levels might feel when the open-door policy is operating.

13. Describe the nature of unintentional gatekeeping.

CRITICAL INCIDENT

BIG-TIME OPERATOR

When Al Lemanski took an early retirement from his position as a construction executive in Newark, he vowed he would never work another day. The son of a Boston factory employee, Lemanski had worked part-time as a construction laborer while in high school and college. Rising from a background of relative poverty, he amassed a sizable fortune through a series of construction and development projects. Within his company he had the reputation of being intelligent, honest, fair, and somewhat blunt in interpersonal relations. Although his decisions were often brilliant, and no one who knew him well found occasion to question his competence, his directness was sometimes inaccurately seen as a lack of concern for the feelings of others.

After two years of inactivity, Lemanski could no longer tolerate retirement. Several months of searching finally led him to purchase a large and prosperous wholesale and retail building materials yard near Houston. The yard's former owner was a mild-mannered, affable Mexican-American named "Sal" Salazar. Lemanski bought the company soon after Salazar suffered a severe heart attack. The employees were told only that the company had been bought by "a wealthy, retired executive from the northeast."

Between the time of Salazar's heart attack and Lemanski's arrival, the company was managed by Manuel Martinez, the yard superintendent and Salazar's lifelong friend. Although Martinez had met Lemanski while negotiations for the purchase were under way, the two had no opportunity to become well acquainted. Martinez was somewhat apprehensive about his future.

Two days after installing himself in Sal's old office and poring over the company records, Lemanski sent word for Martinez to come to the office. Although Martinez did not know what to expect, he vaguely felt that he was being called on the carpet. Sal would have casually talked in Manuel's office, a glass enclosure near the yard.

The conversation was relatively formal. Although the subject was not mentioned, Lemanski seemed to assume that Martinez would continue as yard superintendent. As was Lemanski's style, he wasted no time in speaking his mind. "As I see it, we have three problems that need attention immediately. Labor turnover is excessive, and returns for faulty materials are running too high. Also, we need to clean up the place, especially the customer pickup area."

The meeting was upsetting to Martinez. He had obviously lost a friend and acquired a boss. Although he felt it would be unwise to contest Lemanski's analysis, Martinez was furious by the time he left the room. He would not normally have taken lumberyard foreman Larry Bass into his confidence, but Bass was the first person he met, and he felt the need to get some things off his chest. Martinez began with "Who does that big-time operator think he is? On his first day aboard, he thinks he knows more about how to run the yard than I do. Well, let's hope he catches on quick how things work down here and in this business."

After a brief cooling-off period, Martinez regained his composure and wished he had not been so free in venting his feelings to Bass. The other foremen were sure to hear the story within the hour.

1. What communication problems are involved in this incident? Be specific in terms of the chapter content.

2. How could Lemanski have avoided the problem with Martinez?

3. Question 1 refers to the communication problems in this incident. Would it be just as accurate to call them human relations problems?

REFERENCES

1. Eisenberg, Abne M., and Ralph R. Smith, Jr. *Nonverbal Communication.* Indianapolis: The Bobbs-Merrill Co., Inc., 1971.
2. McCaskey, Michael B. "The Hidden Messages Managers Send," *Harvard Business Review,* Vol. 57, No. 6, November-December, 1979, pp. 135–148.
3. Porter, Lyman W., Linda L. Putnam, Karlene H. Roberts, and Fredric M. Jablin, eds. *Handbook of Organizational Communication.* Beverly Hills: Sage Publications, Inc., 1986.
4. Huber, George P. "Organizational Information Systems: Determinants of Their Performance and Behavior," *Management Science,* Vol. 28, No. 2, February, 1982, pp. 138–155.

5. Roberts, Karlene H., and Charles A. O'Reilly III. "Failures in Upward Communication: Three Possible Culprits," *Academy of Management Journal,* Vol. 17, No. 2, June, 1974, pp. 205–215.

6. Yerys, Arlene. "How to Get What You Want Through Influential Communication," *Management Review,* Vol. 71, No. 6, June, 1982, pp. 12–18.

SUGGESTED READINGS

Allen, Richard K. *Organizational Management through Communication.* New York: Harper & Row Publishers, Inc., 1977.

Farace, Richard V., Peter R. Monge, and Hamish M. Russell. *Communicating and Organizing.* Reading, Mass.: Addison-Wesley Publishing Co., 1977.

Feldman, Martha S., and James G. March. "Information in Organizations as Signal and Symbol," *Administrative Science Quarterly,* Vol. 26, No. 2, June, 1981, pp. 171–186.

McCaskey, Michael B. "The Hidden Messages Managers Send," *Harvard Business Review* , Vol. 57, No. 6, November-December, 1979, pp. 135–148.

O'Reilly, Charles A., III. "Variations in Decision Makers' Use of Information Sources: The Impact of Quality and Accessibility of Information," *Academy of Management Journal,* Vol. 25, No. 4, December, 1982, pp. 756–769.

Rosenblatt, Bernard S., Richard T. Cheatham, and James T. Watt. *Communication in Business.* Englewood Cliffs, N.J.: Prentice-Hall, Inc., 1977.

Rowe, Mary P., and Michael Baker. "Are You Hearing Enough Employee Concerns?" *Harvard Business Review,* Vol. 62, No. 3, May-June, 1984, pp. 127–135.

Wofford, Jerry C., Edwin A. Gerloff, and Robert C. Cummins. *Organizational Communication.* New York: McGraw-Hill Book Company, 1977.

14

Organizational Change and Management Development

A foreign visitor to downtown Boston asked a local seaman why American ships were built to last for such a short time. According to the visitor, "the sailor answered without hesitation that the art of navigation is making such rapid progress that the finest ship would become obsolete if it lasted beyond a few years. In these words, which fell accidentally from an uneducated man, I began to recognize the general and systematic idea upon which your great people direct all their concerns." The foreign visitor was Alexis de Tocqueville; the year was 1835; the observation about the rapidity of change is even more relevant today than it was then.

Futurists such as Alvin Toffler and John Naisbitt argue convincingly that the rate of change, almost imperceptible for millennia, continues to increase.[1,2] The most obvious changes have been in science and technology, with transportation catapulting within this century from the horse-drawn carriage to interplanetary travel, and with communication exploding from the simplest telegraph to color images beamed from Mars and Venus. But these highly visible changes represent only a small part of the changes that affect us. Many other changes are occurring in the very organizations in which we spend a large portion of our lives.[3]

After a 6,000-year history of authoritarian management, recent decades have witnessed a revolution in management's attitudes toward employees and employees' expectations of management. Employees, including managers, expect more of everything—pay, security, fringe benefits, vacations, retirement plans, work satisfaction, autonomy, consideration, and a larger voice in making decisions. Specialization is changing the meaning of authority as line managers necessarily defer to the expertise of their staff advisors. It is not surprising that a major aspect of managerial effectiveness is the manager's ability to change and to manage change.

How can managers become effective in coping with change? The process begins when they accept the fact that change is necessary, inevitable, and good. It is, of course, often frustrating and threatening as well. In fact, people who place a high value on avoiding risks or preserving the status quo probably should not become managers. Satisfaction in management will be highest for those who are challenged by risk taking, who view themselves as problem solvers, and who recognize that some of their worth to the organization is specifically due to their expertise in managing within a dynamic, ever-changing environment.

A major part of this chapter is concerned with the fact that managers themselves must constantly change or become obsolete. Effective managers learn to plan their own careers so as to take advantage of every possible opportunity for personal growth. They also develop skills needed to modify the organizational culture within which they work. The means by which such personal growth and organizational changes are brought about are discussed in this chapter. The four major objectives of this chapter are

TO UNDERSTAND:

1. The nature of change and resistance to change

2. The philosophy and goals of management development

3. How managers develop themselves and their subordinates

4. How organizational development (OD) is used to change organizations

THE NATURE OF CHANGE IN ORGANIZATIONS

One of the major challenges with which organizations are faced is the creation of an atmosphere in which rapid, appropriate change is possible. A delicate balance must be maintained between demands for continual change and the necessity for organizational stability.

In recent years the rate of change within society as a whole has accelerated rapidly. In many areas, changes that have occurred during the lifetime of our senior citizens are greater than those which occurred in all previously recorded history. Although technological advances are significant, they offer no greater challenge than changes in human attitudes and values. Such factors as the "knowledge explosion," decline of the Protestant work ethic, expectations of a shorter workweek, rejection of traditional sex roles, and growing expectations of affluence strain the adaptive capacities of organizations. These changes demand the sophisticated management of change.

Resistance to Change

Resistance to change often results in obsolete methods, machines, skills, and other factors that influence effectiveness. For this reason much attention is given to the subject, usually from the viewpoint of people who want to make organizational changes and who will fail only if resistance to change is encountered. As we should expect, therefore, resistance to change is usually discussed as an undesirable phenomenon— an organizational or individual deficiency to be overcome. Furthermore, those who write about resistance to change usually imply that employees consistently resist change, a viewpoint that may itself stimulate resistance.[4] Finally, of course, our everyday observations indicate that many managers are themselves resistant to change.

Employees often do resist change, but they are also agents of change and have been responsible for major changes in organizational behavior. Managers would do well to avoid the mind-set that employees always resist change and to begin to think of employees as potential change agents. Suggestion systems and other means of eliciting employee participation are based on the belief that employees can initiate beneficial change.

Benefits of Resistance.　Since organizations must constantly adapt in reaction to or in anticipation of environmental change, our emphasis is naturally on overcoming resistance to change. We look first, however, at the benefits of resistance.

1. Resistance forces the advocates of change to build a defensible case. Thus, ill-advised changes are sometimes avoided.

2. By limiting the degree of change, resistance provides a critical stabilizing influence. Particularly in organizations whose strategic decision makers are impulsive, conservative change resisters may provide the balance required for survival.

3. The anticipation of resistance to change forces management to think in terms of the effect of change on its employees. In doing so, management better satisfies individual needs and, therefore, is ultimately more effective in reaching organizational objectives.

Causes of Resistance. Employees, from executives on down, resist change for a variety of reasons some of which they may be totally unaware. Since motivations are complex, we should expect more than one cause of resistance to be involved in most cases. At any rate, success in gaining acceptance of change begins with diagnosing its causes. Diagnosing the causes reduces one of the most common mistakes managers make in instituting change: a tendency to use one approach—participation, manipulation, coercion, education, negotiation—rather than tailor the approach to the situation.[5] The most common causes of resistance to change are the following:

1. *Knowledge and skill obsolescence.* In some instances an organizational change makes obsolete the knowledge and skills acquired over a lifetime of experience. Thus, a bookkeeper whose security blanket is the mastery of a complex accounting system is understandably threatened by the change to a computerized system. An employee in a petroleum refinery takes immense pride in the years of experience and responsible service through which the status of senior still operator is reached. Then a change to a totally automated process makes worthless virtually every skill of the senior operator. And, because the new units are controlled by college-educated engineers, retraining and experience can never completely restore the status enjoyed by the operator of the old distillation unit.

2. *Economic loss.* The compensation level of employees and managers whose knowledge and skills have become obsolete is often maintained during a retraining period. Such a practice obviously reduces resistance to change. In many situations, however, retraining is impossible, and a demotion or loss of employment results. The mere possibility of such a loss is enough to cause some resistance. The cynicism employees often feel about change is expressed in an anecdote about suggestion systems. In response to an excellent suggestion the boss says, "Congratulations, Snodgrass, you have just won $25 for your suggestion. It has led to the elimination of five jobs, including your own."

3. *Ego defensiveness.* For five years Elaine Post, the executive vice-president of a plastics firm, was successful in overriding the recommendation of R & D specialists to convert to a vastly superior plastics extrusion process. Why was she so adamantly against it? First, it was not her idea. When the recommendation was initially made, moreover, she went out on a limb in opposition to it. Once

that action was taken, she was unable to see the facts objectively because she was afraid of losing face.

4. *Comfort with the status quo.* Change can be disrupting. A break in an established routine may force a person to think instead of daydream, to take risks rather than remain secure, and to work hard instead of loafing.

5. *Cautiousness and conservatism.* Because of personality characteristics, attitudes, and values, many people are predisposed to minimize risks and make changes slowly. Where strategic decision makers have these characteristics, an entire organization may be forced to follow their lead.

6. *Peer pressures.* Because peer cooperation is required for success in many jobs, even highly independent individuals are unable to withstand work-group pressures and support organizational change. For this reason obtaining group support for change is usually more effective than soliciting the support of isolated individuals.

7. *Lack of information.* When employees and managers who are affected by a change are ignorant concerning its purpose and implications, they are unlikely to support it. In the absence of information many people become suspicious and expect the worst to happen.

8. *Social displacement.* The social relationships that develop in the workplace are often more important to employees than commonly realized. Even where employees are fully protected against financial loss because of a change, resistance persists because it threatens to disrupt friendships through which a variety of personal needs are met.

9. *Limited perspective.* High-level managers become critical of subordinate managers when the latter protect their special interests (a specific department, for example) rather than support the whole organization. In one firm this was expressed in the resistance of the chief financial officer to developing computer programs to provide rapid feedback on budget expenditures. Without full awareness of his own motives, he resisted the change because it would limit the power that he and other members of the accounting department exerted through personal contacts in order to control spending.

10. *Too little time to adapt.* When frequent and rapid changes are made, those affected by them may experience an unhealthy level of stress. Under such circumstances resistance is one means of slowing the process until the changes are assimilated and a degree of equanimity is restored.

Traditional Approaches to Change

During the early part of this century, management's approach to change was simple and straightforward. Following classical organizational theory, changes were made by managerial decree with little concern for the response of subordinates. Because managers felt confident of their organizational power, they often misused it. This, in turn, brought aggressive challenges from labor and government. Change by decree is still practiced, but most managers have at least learned to be cautious in its use.

Propaganda is a traditional technique for motivating the acceptance of change. Employees who resist innovation are systematically confronted with rumors that the company will be closed or moved to a new location. They are bombarded with information supporting the change and pointing out the dire consequences of resistance. Propaganda may be supported by authoritative statements of consultants and other experts who appear to be objective. Although propaganda has been effective in some circumstances, it lacks the potential of open, two-way communication to establish trust and understanding. Propaganda may reduce resistance to change in the short run while increasing it over a long period of time.

Another power-oriented tactic used to support change is contrived personnel turnover. Employees or managers who resist change are discharged or encouraged to leave the organization. But this also may prove to be costly. Management's growing dissatisfaction with power tactics for instituting change and the positive influences of the human relations movement have encouraged experimentation with a variety of techniques for management of change.

The greatest challenges to a change-by-decree approach occurred in response to management's practice of unilaterally raising production standards as employees improved their skills and methods. Employees believed that they should reap the benefits of their efforts through either increased pay or shorter working hours. Management, on the other hand, was committed to increasing productive efficiency and maintaining competitive costs. In this situation the ability of employees to restrict production, to withhold information about methods improvement, and to undermine change efforts was a formidable barrier to change by decree. Such resistance helped to convince management that changes should be managed with more finesse and greater consideration for the needs and attitudes of those whose cooperation is needed to implement change.

During the 1940s and 1950s, the new look in change management was linked to an emphasis on participative management. Not surprisingly research studies demonstrated that employees who were given a voice in deciding on a change were less resistant to its implementation.

Some companies, applying their recently acquired knowledge of group dynamics, instituted programs through which employees participated in rule making and standard setting. Although many such efforts have been little more than crude attempts at manipulation, some have been successful. Even where participating employees do not significantly influence a given decision, they at least have an awareness that their voice has been heard. They also understand why management takes a particular course of action.

In the 1980s, employee participation was revived as a response to the need to improve quality and reduce costs. Ironically it was viewed by some as the application of a *Japanese* management technique![6]

Training managers in human relations skills, especially at the supervisory level, produced a significant impact upon the management of change. Since willingness to accept change is associated with the effectiveness of superior-subordinate relations, it is understandable that management development (or manager development) should be related to the task of producing change. Manager development is itself a change process which, ideally at least, facilitates other needed changes throughout the organization.

MANAGEMENT DEVELOPMENT: PHILOSOPHY AND GOALS

Programs of manager education, skills development, and attitude and behavior change are commonplace in modern organizations. The merits of specific programs in specific situations are justifiably called into question, but some form of continuing management development is a necessary part of organizational life.

Few operating managers or experts in organizational behavior question the importance of management development in principle, although development programs are seldom evaluated by objective methods. Many of the attempts at objective evaluation have been characterized by a misleading appearance of quantitative exactness and sophistication of experimental design. Nevertheless, experience with management development programs and both clinical and experimental evaluation of their effects have taught us much about the requirements for effectiveness.

Purposes of Management Development

The purposes of management development may be examined in terms of organizational objectives and the motivations of participants. First, the organization's primary concern is behavior change. The acquisition of knowledge (say, about electronic data processing), the modification of attitudes (developing favorable attitudes toward management by objectives, for example), or the acquisition of skills (such as how to negotiate a union contract) are all intended to change behavior. Specifically, the organization is concerned with behavior change that will make a manager more effective in working with or through others to achieve organizational goals.

Although managers typically support organizational goals and value development for its own sake, they have additional, uniquely personal motives for seeking development opportunities. Development opportunities are an expected form of compensation because they increase the probability that a manager will receive raises and promotions. Development provides a hedge against managerial obsolescence and contributes to the sense of security and independence managers experience when their services are in high demand. Opportunities for growth are sometimes more influential than salary in a manager's decision to accept or continue in a position. An organization must develop its managers in order to be effective in manager recruitment and avoid excessive management turnover.

Training versus Development

During the early days of the human relations movement, the terms *supervisory training* and *management training* were commonly used. They are still used to some extent, but they are not in vogue. Training tends to convey the notion of the acquisition of skills. For example, we train employees to assemble a unit of production or to operate a machine. Perhaps because of the use of the word in connection with animal training, it is implied that a trainer is a person who possesses superior knowledge and skills and is the thinking, active member of the team while the one being trained is being acted upon. In contrast, the term *management development* is intended to imply that the changes which occur involve a more active participation.

In large organizations, staff managers, usually human resource specialists, are assigned responsibility for making available a variety of management development programs. The availability of these programs does not, however, absolve line management of the responsibility for encouraging the development of subordinates, nor does it remove the ultimate responsibility of each manager for self-development. In the final analysis, all management development is self-development. It is not something one person can do for another.

Although line managers are responsible for encouraging management development, they do not, in a strict sense, develop their subordinates. All that line managers can do is to encourage self-development and to provide opportunities for it.

Some Generalizations About Management Development

Considering the great variety of management development programs and the even greater variety of development needs, it would be presumptuous to compile a set of management development principles. We can, however, draw some generalizations that cut across the different methods and provide criteria against which their merits can be assessed.

1. *Assessing development needs.* The ideal beginning of a development program is a complete audit of the objectives of the firm at all levels, the personnel needs over the next five to ten years, and the skill and ability of present personnel. The objective is to systematically define development needs as a basis for short- and long-term planning.[7]

2. *Providing feedback on performance.* Programs that provide knowledge of results are essential for meaningful change. A major reason managers fail to change is inadequate knowledge of the consequences of past behavior.

3. *Tailoring to the individual.* The development needs of managers differ greatly—so much so that a developmental program that is helpful to one manager may hurt another. Development programs should be matched with the carefully diagnosed needs of individual managers.

4. *Relating to the power structure.* What a manager learns will be of minimal value unless the reward structure of the organization is favorable to its implementation. Some managers, for example, learn to appreciate the virtues of participative leadership only to have all efforts to practice it undermined by their superiors. Supervisor rewards or punishments often have more to do with whether an act will be practiced than do the intrinsic merits of the act itself.

5. *Selection and development.* Selection and development are closely related functions in that selection limits development potential. Development dollars may be wasted on managers who are deficient in intelligence, general education, motivation to lead, emotional maturity, and other characteristics that are related to managerial effectiveness.

There are other limits within which management development may take place. Professor J. Sterling Livingston and others emphasize the importance of teaching managers to manage in ways that are consistent with their individual personalities: "One of the least rational acts of business organizations is that of hiring managers who have a high need to exercise authority and then teaching them that authoritative methods are wrong and that they should be consultative or participative."[8]

6. *Motivational factors in development.* A manager's motivation to develop into an effective manager may exert a more critical influence on development than the methods used. Livingston supports the notion that the *way* to manage can usually be found if there is a *will* to manage. The person who is lacking in this motivation will not invest the time, energy, and thought required to increase his or her managerial effectiveness.[9]

7. *A continuing activity.* Management development is never completed. Through on-the-job experience and formal development programs, a manager must continue to learn and change or accept the fact that obsolescence has begun.

What appears to be a need for management development may be a need for modifying the organization. The environment in which managers work may place such great demands on them that no amount of motivation or competence will enable them to perform adequately. This may be the case, for example, where a chief executive sets the pace with poor delegation, inconsistent policies, and poorly formulated goals. For this reason the development of managers is related to other forms of change within the organization. This theme is expanded later in this chapter under the topic of Organization Development (OD).

MANAGEMENT DEVELOPMENT METHODS

Since the needs of managers differ greatly, there is no one best development method. The effectiveness of a given method also depends on the skills and personality of the management development specialist applying it. These and other variables must be considered when deciding on the method to be used.

The brief descriptions of management development methods that are presented in this section are intended to present a summary of the salient features of each method and to provide resource guidelines for persons who are interested in studying the subject in greater depth. Since virtually every manager is charged with the responsibility of providing growth opportunities for subordinates, approaches for providing such opportunities is a subject about which all managers should develop some understanding.

On-the-Job Development Programs

Management development that occurs on the job is generally preferred to off-the-job methods.[10] The former can more readily be tailored to the needs of individuals, and it takes advantage of the sense of identification and authority relationships that exist between superior and subordinate. These and other benefits of on-the-job methods can be seen in the descriptions presented here.

Experience as a Developer of Managers. Is experience really the best teacher? Certainly it is not always the best. There are some attributes, however, that are likely to be developed only with experience. One of these is decision-making ability. Methods of gathering and analyzing data can be learned in formal courses and simulation exercises, but there is no substitute for making real-life decisions where the data are incomplete and the risks are high. Likewise, the development of poise and self-confidence in stress-provoking situations is unlikely to occur except through experience.

Not all experiences, on the other hand, are helpful. Some destroy self-confidence, teach ineffective leadership styles, and create attitudes and habits that thwart managerial effectiveness. Because on-the-job experience can be either good or bad and because it may or may not meet the needs of a specific manager, progressive organizations structure a manager's experience to provide optimal opportunities for self-development.

Job Rotation. A manager who has worked in one position for ten years may actually have only one year of experience ten times. Programmed job rotation occurs at the entry level where management trainees, ordinarily recent college graduates, are rotated through several short-term assignments. Some companies rotate middle managers in a similar way. A line manager, for example, may be transferred from the general management of plant A to the same position in plant B, to staff assistant to the president, to a trouble-shooting position in manufacturing, and then to a similar position in accounting. Companies that follow this practice recognize that a manager loses some effectiveness when a new job is begun, but these companies believe that this loss is offset by the development benefits. Moving costs and disruption of family life are further disadvantages, but job rotation is excellent for creating generalists having high potential for top management. Job rotation also develops an appreciation of the unique problems of different positions and contributes to a cross-fertilization of ideas. It greatly reduces the likelihood that a manager will stagnate in one job and habitually resist change.

Coaching. Many of the disadvantages of unplanned on-the-job experience can be overcome through coaching. The "coach," usually a manager's immediate superior, systematically provides feedback on performance, assists in planning for self-development, provides guidelines for goal setting, and counsels the subordinate on specific problems.

The effectiveness of coaching depends primarily on the skills of the coach and the amount of time and effort devoted to the task. The coaching process often falls short of the mark because it does not support strong relationships and contacts between a boss and subordinates. Among the most important reasons for this failure are that most line executives do not give enough time and thought to working with their juniors; the climate in business is not tolerant enough of mistakes and individual needs to learn; and rivalry between bosses and subordinates tends to be repressed instead of acknowledged.

Because a wide range of development techniques may be used in coaching, managers need special training to be effective. Motivation to develop subordinates must be strong, however, before the techniques will be consistently used. This means that the organization's reward systems should make the development of subordinates profitable.

Management Counseling. Some of the shortcomings of coaching, primarily a lack of time and expertise, are overcome by the use of outside consultants for the individualized development of managers. The specialist, often a professional industrial psychologist, performs a coaching function, as just described, but may also serve as an executive confidant. High-level managers, in particular, sometimes lead a lonely life and need an outsider with whom they can vent their feelings of frustration and confidentially discuss problems and proposed actions.

The roles of management counselors, who may spend from a half day a month to full time counseling the managers of an organization, vary significantly. Some, with a background in clinical or counseling psychology, inadvertently gravitate toward personal problems counseling, including marital counseling, and neglect their primary goal of management development. Management counselors with educational backgrounds in management or industrial psychology are more apt to avoid personal problems and concentrate on job-related problems.

One industrial psychologist, who serves as a management counselor in as many as 10 to 15 different companies simultaneously, makes use of an "inventory" to obtain descriptions of managers' behavior by subordinates, peers, superiors, and the managers themselves. Discrepancies between self-perceptions and the perceptions of others are used as a starting point for development. The manager with an unrealistic self-perception as an excellent delegator, for example, is given support in understanding delegation, in exploring the causes for his or her own failure to delegate, and in making the appropriate behavior modification.

Management counselors, like management coaches, use a variety of development techniques, including some which are described later in this chapter as OD interventions. Counselors with broad business experience may also play substantial roles as advisors on matters relating to selection, development, motivational systems, disciplinary problems, supervisory practices, morale, and other areas in which they are competent.

Questions of ethics sometimes arise when clients become increasingly dependent on the counselor's services rather than growing in self-reliance. Management counselors often accept positions in line management or management development within their client companies, posing interesting questions of ethics, especially when the consulting firm loses a client in the transaction.

The Critical Incidents Technique. During World War II and the following decade, extensive research was conducted on **the critical incidents technique**, a development technique in which managers are given continual feedback on "critical behaviors." Research is conducted to develop a list of positive and negative behaviors that are critical to the successful performance of a given job. On the supervisory level, for example, a negative critical behavior might be "Criticized the work of a subordinate in the presence of other employees." A positive behavior might be "Effectively involved subordinates in problem solving" or "Took the initiative to solve a long-standing problem."

After the instrument is developed, the superior systematically makes a record as critical behaviors are observed. Continual feedback then provides a basis for behavior change. Although this method is not widely used, its results have been impressive, and the principles on which it is based are sound. It takes place on the job and makes use of the organization's power structure. It provides regular feedback. The feedback deals with behavior. It provides for positive reinforcement of desirable behaviors as well as for discouragement of undesirable behaviors. Since the evaluation factor is built into the instrument, the manager need only observe and make a record of behavior rather than constantly make value judgments. In view of the current emphasis on behavior modification, the critical incidents method should increasingly be given high marks as a development method. Mintzberg and other researchers are increasingly calling attention to the actual behavior of managers and noting the wide discrepancy between what they do and what experts say they should do.[11,12] Use of the critical incidents technique can help remove this discrepancy.

This critical incidents technique is obviously different from the technique used at the end of the chapters of this textbook. The latter is an abbreviated form of case study. The former is basically a feedback device concerned with very specific, critical behaviors. Although both deal with incidents that are critical to managerial effectiveness, they are distinctly different techniques.

Special Projects. Managers are in a unique position to use special projects to develop their subordinates in areas of recognized deficiency. Two diverse examples will show the nature and purpose of this technique. In the first situation a young supervisor with a poor record of solving disciplinary problems was assigned the task of making a proposal to a supervisory development group in which he was a participant. His task was to study various methods of handling disciplinary problems, evaluate them, and make a written and oral presentation on the merits of different methods.

The second case involves a middle manager with an outstanding background in sales but a notable weakness in accounting and finance. In addition to recommending that this manager take correspondence courses in the areas of accounting and finance, her superior placed her on a committee assigned to study the budgeting procedure and to recommend improvements. The assumption was that this experience would increase her awareness of and appreciation for the importance of financial controls.

Goal Setting. Although goal setting is ordinarily associated with an organization's planning and motivational systems, it is also related to management development. Given that the organization's primary objective in developing managers is goal-oriented behavior change, it is logical to believe that goal clarification might be helpful. Critics of management development often raise questions about the relevance of the changes that occur within managers, especially in the case of attitude change programs. Goal clarification helps a manager to know when an attitude or behavior change is relevant to improved effectiveness and when it is relevant only to the limited objectives of the development program itself. A program may be eminently successful in teaching a given skill, but unless the skill is needed for improved present or future performance, the development investment is not justified.

When managers become increasingly goal oriented, certain changes occur in their perceptual and thought processes as well as in the results they achieve. For example, goal setting broadens a manager's perspective, focuses attention on relevant problems, enhances leadership ability, and improves the quality of decisions. Since these and other changes associated with goal setting are sought in management development programs, it follows that an effective goals program, normally established to increase productivity, may serve as an outstanding development method. We will examine the merits of goal setting in greater detail in Chapter 20.

Understudy Positions. In many organizations, managers are given assignments as assistants or assistants-to, primarily for the developmental value of the positions. Ordinarily an *assistant* (say, assistant general manager) occupies a line position while an *assistant-to* is considered to be staff. Thus, the assistant-to may be a young trainee, but an assistant is normally next in line for the superior's position or one that is comparable.

The assistant position has the advantage of allowing the understudy to assume responsibility, make decisions, and take risks. The main advantage of the assistant-to position is that the young manager has an opportunity to learn through involvement as an understudy long before he or she is capable of assuming heavy responsibility. Both provide an opportunity to study the behavior of a manager with more experience, to observe organizational life at a higher level, and to form personal identification with superiors that will potentially facilitate the acquisition of managerial skills. The effectiveness of understudy positions, however, depends greatly upon the concern of the superior for the understudy's development and the suitability of the superior as a managerial model.

Off-the-Job Development Programs

If all development programs had to be of one type, either on- or off-the-job, on-the-job would be preferable. Fortunately the two are complementary. At times managers need to get away from the job in order to gain perspective. It is important that they exchange ideas with managers from other organizations and learn from behavioral scientists, technical specialists, and others whose viewpoints differ from their own.

Development Sites. Off-the-job development programs ordinarily take place in one of three sites: (1) the organization's own facilities, (2) a university continuing education center, or (3) a location selected by a private management development firm. Most large organizations have a staff of professionals who do nothing but conduct development programs for first line supervisors and middle managers. Organizations that have extensive in-house programs are also the best clients of university programs and private development firms.

Universities offer a variety of programs tailored to the needs of operating managers and ranging in length from a few hours to several months. Most of these programs avoid traditional testing and grading. Although a wide variety of methods are employed, most university programs take advantage of the broad experience of participants by providing time for information sharing.

During the past 25 years, a number of private organizations have been formed to offer seminars and laboratories on subjects of current interest to managers. Several of these advertise nationally through direct mail and locate their seminars in major cities across the country. Small firms, sometimes consisting of only an individual, offer courses within a limited geographical area. Some firms periodically offer seminars in which managers from different companies participate, while others tailor programs to meet the needs of selected groups within a single organization. The largest private organization in the development field is the American Management Association (AMA). In addition to providing seminars in its home office in New York City and in large cities across the United States, the AMA is a major publisher of management literature.

Conference Method. The conference or discussion format is intended to provide maximum opportunity for participants to test their ideas, ask questions, exchange information, and challenge concepts which are presented in lectures or printed materials. The conference method holds the attention of participants over long periods of time and elicits a high degree of emotional involvement. If poorly managed, however, it can be a disaster. Unless a means is provided for injecting a core of valid and challenging information into the conference, it sometimes degenerates into an unorganized discussion session in which participants share their collective ignorance.

Although widely differing conference leadership styles may be effective, the skill of the leader is a major factor in the success of a conference. Some leaders play a **content role**; that is, they become involved in the content of the discussion by supplying information, questioning, challenging, and persuading. They also keep the discussion on track, making sure all conference members have an opportunity to participate, summarizing points of view, minimizing the unhealthy effects of arguments, and making sure the subject matter is covered. Leaders who play the **process role** limit their involvement to the latter functions (that is, keeping the discussion on track and the like).

It takes greater skill to be successful in the content role. The possibility is always present that the content leader will dominate the conference and elicit too little participation. On the other hand, it is wasteful for a leader's expertise to be suppressed because of a commitment to the process role.

Case Study and Role Playing. Case studies have been used extensively in management development programs in many settings. Although many variations of the method are used, the essentials are the same. Participants are presented with the details of a management problem (in human relations, finance, production, or marketing, for example) to which each arrives at a solution. The solutions are then discussed, along with the assumptions, methods of analysis, and the logic upon which they are based. In some treatments of case studies, participants may receive additional information upon request. Out of the total experience, they gain insights into their own biases, strengths and weaknesses, and typical modes of solving problems. They also learn through observation how others interpret and solve those same problems.

A major advantage of the case method is that it focuses attention on problem situations rather than on theory and principles. Supposedly, insights gained in this way are more likely to be applied on the job than are those acquired through more abstract methods. Managers are often frustrated by the fact that no "correct" solutions are provided to case problems. Real-life problems offer the same frustration, however. The case study method is more concerned with the process through which solutions are reached than with the solutions themselves.

Role playing is often used in conjunction with case studies. In a case involving disciplinary action, for example, two managers may act out a proposed solution and then switch roles so that each can experience the feelings elicited by the proposed action. Role playing can be highly realistic or so phony as to be embarrassing to participants. The skill of the leader and the pyschological climate within the development group are critical determinants of its success.

Case studies and role playing are used extensively. They are not ideal for every situation, but they have been proven to be valuable techniques when used properly.

Business Games. Like case studies and role playing, business games are simulated or reconstructed representations of some aspect of organizational life to which participants are asked to react. Business games describe a situation in case study form but go further to describe a set of rules and relationships concerning the relevant aspects of the problem.

For example, participants may be supplied with information concerning product costs, company goals, finances, market conditions, and the actions of competitors.

The objectives of business games are to familiarize participants with the complex, interacting factors involved in a functioning organization and to develop decision-making skills. Participants play the game by making decisions concerning investments, expenditures, production, inventory, and so on. Computers provide rapid feedback on the result of each decision, and competing teams continue to make decisions for a specified period or until a trend develops. Then the results and decision processes are discussed, and the critical points are highlighted.

Some business games are quite realistic, but they are no substitute for actual decision making because the risk factors are different. Participants who are the most analytical and scholarly perform well in business games, but they may or may not have the quality of toughness required to perform in the real world. Also, some participants are able to make good decisions in a business game by deciphering a simplistic decision strategy that would not be effective in real organizations. All things considered, however, business games are an excellent and extensively used development technique.

In-Basket Problems. The manner in which managers handle their in-basket items (such as routine correspondence, grievances, directives, customer complaints, reports, and requests for information or action) reveals much about their leadership and decision styles, human relations skills, personal organization, ability to communicate, and other characteristics. In-basket simulations provide development specialists with valuable insights in diagnosing a manager's development needs and serve as a point of reference for developmental counseling.

A professionally designed in-basket problem comes close to providing an actual job sample. Although, at this point in the method's evolution, it is more often used as a selection than a development tool, its potential for the latter is high.

Behavior Modification. The human relations movement made the point that external control through fear has serious limitations. Specifically, control through fear requires close supervision, causes resentment, and is less effective than control that results from internalized goals and favorable attitudes. Thus, the primary target of the human relations movement was attitude change.

In recent years, however, it has become obvious that favorable attitudes do not automatically lead to improved performance. High job satisfaction may result in a country-club atmosphere rather than in increased productivity. These facts, together with a predisposition to think in behavioral terms, led some researchers to conclude that if behavior change is the ultimate goal of development it may as well be the immediate target. Further research disclosed that attitude change often follows behavior change—that once behavior is changed, attitude changes tend to follow in order to remove the cognitive dissonance and restore an internal equilibrium.

There are many ways to approach development from a behavioral point of view, but they have in common the application of learning principles. In particular they focus on reinforcement theory. People learn to repeat those behaviors that are rewarded and to drop from use those which are not rewarded or which are punished.[13]

A number of organizations, including the American Telephone & Telegraph Co., have successfully used this technique called **behavior modification**. The principles are simple but sound. They are, however, more appropriate for teaching specific skills (for example, handling grievances and conducting postappraisal interviews) than they are for developing complex abilities such as decision making. In terms of the way training and development were defined earlier, behavior modification is more a training than a development technique.

Behavior technology is improving, however, and is now being applied in "self-shaping" programs with middle managers. In such programs, the participants establish their own target behaviors, methods of measuring and recording behavior change, schedules of reinforcement, and means of receiving feedback on performance. In other words, they decide on certain desired behavior changes and follow a systematic approach to achieving them.

Laboratory Training. Since the late 1940s, when **laboratory training** (also called **T-group** and **sensitivity training**) was first used as a management development method, it has been the subject of continual controversy. Although there are many variations and applications of laboratory training, the outcomes most often sought are (1) increased self-awareness, (2) the development of sensitivity to the needs and behavior of others, (3) the clarification of personal values and goals, (4) insight into the nature of group forces on individual growth and decision-making processes, and (5) the resolution of conflict.

The leader of a T-group always plays the process role. The group members are usually from different organizations and thus constitute a "stranger group." The sessions are often begun with a minimum of structure and without explicit goals. From a relatively innocuous beginning in which group members introduce themselves, there is a gradual deepening of relationships until members disclose their normally hidden feelings, attitudes, beliefs, and self-perceptions. Feedback provides participants with a unique opportunity to view themselves through the eyes of others to whom their inner selves have been laid bare.

One of the strongest criticisms of sensitivity training is that the outcome is unpredictable. In rare instances, the trauma of self-disclosure and feedback has even lead to a psychotic break. In other instances, managers have decided that the pressures of business life are too great and have returned to their organizations only to turn in their resignations. For some managers, no doubt, the objectives of sensitivity training have been fully realized and expressed in constructive on-the-job behavioral changes. Many of those for whom sensitivity training was a waste of time should never have become involved in it. Especially for some of the early programs, participant screening was poor or nonexistent. In addition, group leaders have sometimes shown little awareness of the objectives of management development.

Sensitivity training reached its crest of popularity in the 1960s. A 1974 mail survey conducted in 300 business firms throughout the United States led University of Cincinnati researchers William Kearney and Desmond Martin to conclude:

> At present this development tool is not an important part of the corporate development programs surveyed, nor does it emerge as being a significant part of future plans. Rather, it appears to be a tool created and refined by a few behavioral scientists to achieve ends that are difficult to measure and evaluate. Some comments from the respondents lean favorably to the T-group approach, but they reflect improvements within the organization that are hard to define. This fact could be sensitivity training's greatest liability. Although behavioral scientists may like to experiment with this tool in the research setting, the pragmatic training director has difficulty concluding that it is an effective means for developing managers.[14]

Sensitivity training fell under increasingly heavy criticism during the 1970s. It is, nevertheless, a method that has been extensively used to develop managers. Had it been used only with managers who needed it and by competent professionals rather than amateurs exploiting its commercial potential, its reputation today would, no doubt, be more favorable. There is a place for sensitivity training, but it is more limited than it first appeared to be.

THE ORGANIZATION DEVELOPMENT (OD) APPROACH TO CHANGE

> An organization development approach to change is committed to a Theory Y view of people, to the notion that strategies for change should involve the total organization rather than be focused on individual managers, and to a belief that planned change should be a continual process. At this stage of its development, OD is making a significant contribution but is falling short of its potential and professed ideals.

Organization development began in 1946 through the work of Gestalt psychologist Kurt Lewin and his associates at The Research Center for Group Dynamics (Massachusetts Institute of Technology), although the phrase *organization development* did not appear in published literature until ten years later. In addition to the impetus given by Lewin and associates, organization development grew out of the laboratory training movement and the development of survey research and feedback methodology.[15]

OD: Definition and Values

Warner Burke, of the National Training Laboratory for Applied Behavioral Science, defines OD as ". . . a planned, sustained effort to change an organization's culture."[16] In this context, an organization's **culture** refers to the norms which regulate member behavior; the organization's purpose, policies, and values; its channels of communication; centers and modes of influence; and the psychological climate which determines the roles and relationships of organizational members.

Although there is no universally accepted definition of organization development, Burke's definition may be deficient in omitting reference to an objective of satisfying the needs of the organization's members. Like the human relations movement to which OD is closely related, organization development is strongly committed to the individual, to collaboration between employees and management, and specifically to employee participation through group involvement.

An OD **change agent** (OD process leader), unlike the typical management development specialist, is identified with a specific value system. Margulies and Raia state the OD values as

1. Providing opportunities for people to function as human beings rather than as resources in the productive process.

2. Providing opportunities for each organization member, as well as for the organization itself, to develop to his or her full potential.

3. Seeking to increase the effectiveness of the organization in terms of *all* of its goals.

4. Attempting to create an environment in which it is possible to find exciting and challenging work.

5. Providing opportunities for people in organizations to influence the way in which they relate to work, the organization, and the environment.

6. Treating each human being as a person with a complex set of needs, *all* of which are important in his or her work and life.[17]

Since some organizations are not committed to all these values, OD specialists are unable to function effectively in all organizations. Management must be strongly committed to a Theory Y view of human nature and to the philosophy of management that generally characterized the human relations movement. In spite of protestations to the contrary, OD specialists often seem to be excessively concerned with employee need satisfaction and too little concerned with productivity.

OD Interventions

Because organization development is concerned with improvement of the total organizational culture, OD authors are apt to refer to virtually any means of influencing the organization as an *OD intervention*. Recent literature makes reference to management by objectives and job enrichment as OD interventions. They would qualify under the above definition, but neither has historically been identified exclusively with the OD movement.

Sensitivity training is the intervention with the longest history of identification with OD. Other interventions, most of which involve sensitivity training, are briefly described below.

1. *The Grid OD Method.* The Managerial Grid®, described and illustrated in Chapter 16, is used to identify the degrees of concern participating managers have for people and for production. The Grid OD method is not, however, limited to the use of this one instrument as the name would seem to imply. Other instruments used for analysis are in-baskets and organizational simulations. Analyses are also conducted of the team effectiveness of work groups, long-range planning, union-management relations, incentive systems, and other organizational variables. Over a three- to five-year period, a six-phased program, including such interventions as sensitivity training, goal set-

ting, and team development, are used to bring about the desired changes in individuals and the organization.

2. *Team Building.* The purpose of team building is to improve the effectiveness and performance of people who work together on a daily basis. Unlike traditional staff meetings, the sessions may last from two to five days and attention is focused on personal relationships within the group as well as upon group goals, work distribution, and how the group functions in order to reach its objectives (that is, procedures, processes, and norms). The group is led by an OD change agent, and the sessions themselves are likely to involve a T-group format.

3. *Confrontation Meetings.* The purpose of confrontation meetings is to resolve conflict between individuals and/or groups. In one version of this technique, the OD specialist obtains written descriptions from each group member of his or her perceptions of the members of the other group. These are exchanged for study and are followed by T-group meetings to clarify problems and find solutions.

4. *Survey and Feedback Technique.* Data concerning attitudes and perceptions of personnel toward various aspects of the organization are obtained through questionnaires, interviews, direct observation, and other means. The information is presented to the individuals from whom it was obtained in a variety of ways; and T-group interventions are used to change attitudes, improve communication, and plan organizational changes.

Evaluation of OD

Organization development specialists make no claim that their discipline has fully matured. They are, in fact, quite introspective and aware of the many discrepancies between their ideals and their performance. The following criticisms are offered by researchers and theorists who are identified with OD.

1. Although OD claims to take a systems approach, in practice OD specialists are most often involved in localized, fragmented studies such as reducing the conflict between two work groups. OD projects theoretically consist of long-term, continuing, and coordinated interventions; but to date most have been short term.

2. OD practitioners do not have sufficient knowledge of and appreciation for the role power plays in the functioning of an organization.

3. Specialists in OD should expand their knowledge and skills to include a broad base of management theory and practice and should avoid overreliance on sensitivity training as an intervention.

4. Although OD authors sometimes imply that the contrary is true, organization development is not a clearly defined discipline in terms of theory or practice.

5. The education available for OD practitioners leaves something to be desired. Most universities have been reluctant to institute professional degree programs in the area.

6. OD practitioners tend to limit themselves to a few techniques such as laboratory training, surveys, and team building. In reality, there are many other ways to change organizations. Change may be effected, for example, through modifying the work flow or organizational structure.

7. OD change agents usually content themselves with expressing their humanistic values in areas of job satisfaction, motivation, and productivity without becoming involved in resource allocation, availability of equipment, choice of supervisors, content of jobs, allocation of rewards, and so on.

8. OD has gained a reputation with managers for being so committed to human relations that organizational objectives are neglected. It may, therefore, be developing healthier individuals who work in progressively less productive and less economically viable organizations.

9. OD is lacking in political sophistication and insight.[18] It does not yet fully appreciate the impact of organizational politics on change programs, and it has not developed the knowledge and tools that represent a sophisticated political orientation.

Although OD has earned a place for itself, these criticisms lead to the conclusion that OD is a poorly delineated, fledgling discipline which purports to take a systems approach to organizational change but actually operates on the periphery. If and when OD specialists become sophisticated in their understanding of the role of power in organizations, greatly expand their methodologies, and begin to operate at the center rather than on the periphery of organizations, they will no longer be OD specialists. They will have become integrated into a large group of eclectic, systems-oriented behavioral science practitioners concerned with management development and organizational effectiveness.

Probably the most serious problem with OD is the narrowness it must maintain in order to continue its identification as an independent discipline. If it continues on its present course, organization development's greatest contribution will lie in the techniques it contributes to management specialists whose horizons are not limited by an identification with OD.

IMPORTANT TERMS AND CONCEPTS

the critical incidents technique	T-group
content role	sensitivity training
process role	culture
behavior modification	change agent
laboratory training	

STUDY AND DISCUSSION QUESTIONS

1. At all levels of an organization there are employees who resist change. What are the positive and the negative implications of this?

2. What experiences were most instrumental in convincing management that the power approach to instituting organizational change should be limited?

3. What relationships exist between the development of managers and effecting change in organizations?

4. How is management development most directly influenced by an organization's (a) power structure, (b) methods of management selection, and (c) motivational systems?

5. Evaluate the following statement as it applies to management development: Experience is the best teacher.

6. What are the similarities and differences between management coaching and counseling?

7. What are the relative merits of on-the-job and off-the-job management development programs?

8. What arguments can be made for concentrating management development efforts on behavior rather than attitudes?

9. How might an objective observer have been able to predict the criticisms of OD from the statement of its values?

10. How do you account for the fact that sensitivity training has lost favor with management in recent years?

11. In what sense do OD practitioners limit their own effectiveness by their insistence on developing OD into an independent discipline?

CRITICAL INCIDENT

TIME TO CHANGE

The Polyplastics Manufacturing Company in 1985 was much like the one Charles Champaign founded in 1947 when he completed his military service. It was still family owned, had no union, and was conservatively and paternalistically managed. The company adapted to changes slowly, but it remained a profitable operation.

In 1950 the company sent five of its first line supervisors to a human relations training program, but the liberal ideas with which the supervisors were indoctrinated made a negative impression on Polyplastic's upper management. As a result, all supervisory training was conducted in-house for the next 35 years. In 1985, labor problems and conflicts between the supervisors and the human resource department led management to enroll the company's 17 supervisors in a 5-day management development seminar taught by an outside management consultant. This change of policy was initiated by the new general superintendent, Carla Duran. To avoid having too many supervisors away from the factory at once, two were sent to each monthly seminar.

Roberta Fusako, a young supervisor who had received two years of community college education before joining the company, returned from the seminar excited about what she had learned, especially about delegating decision making downward, giving employees the opportunity to assume the maximum possible responsibility, and establishing channels of open communication with employees.

After the Friday afternoon session, Roberta discussed some of these ideas with her immediate superior and Duran. Both seemed genuinely pleased to learn that she felt she had profited.

When Roberta returned to work on Monday morning, she discovered that several quality-control problems had to be dealt with, a report was due, and several employees needed to talk with her about work schedule problems. It was Friday afternoon before she realized that she had not yet been able to take any of the actions about which she had become so enthusiastic. By this time, the frustrations of the week had taken the edge off her enthusiasm, and she became preoccupied with the pleasant thought of a relaxed weekend with her fiancé. Monday morning would be a good time to begin the new approaches.

1. What is the probability that the "outstanding" training program will change behavior?

2. What factors in this organization function as a deterrent to change?

3. What, if any, OD interventions do you recommend in this situation?

4. What two or three first steps do you recommend to stimulate lasting changes in supervisory behavior?

5. What might be the consequences of involving only one organizational level in such a training program?

REFERENCES

1. Toffler, Alvin. *The Third Wave*. New York: William Morrow and Co., Inc., 1980.

2. Naisbitt, John. *Megatrends: Ten New Directions Transforming Our Lives*. New York: Warner Books, 1983.

3. Huber, George P. "The Nature and Design of Post-Industrial Organizations," *Management Science*, Vol. 30, No. 8, August, 1984, pp. 928–951.

4. Powell, Gary, and Barry Z. Posner. "Resistance to Change Reconsidered: Implications for Managers," *Human Resource Management*, Vol. 17, No. 1, Spring, 1978, pp. 29–34.

5. Kotter, John P., and Leonard A. Schlesinger. "Choosing Strategies for Change," *Harvard Business Review*, Vol. 57, No. 2, March-April, 1979, p. 112.

6. Ouchi, William G. *Theory Z: How American Business Can Meet the Japanese Challenge*. Reading, Mass.: Addison-Wesley Publishing Co., 1981.

7. English, Jon, and Anthony R. Marchione. "Nine Steps in Management Development," *Business Horizons*, Vol. 20, No. 3, June, 1977, pp. 88–94.

8. Livingston, J. Sterling. "Myth of the Well-Educated Manager," *Harvard Business Review*, Vol. 49, No. 1, January-February, 1971, p. 87.

9. Livingston. "Myth of the Well-Educated Manager," p. 85.

10. Zeira, Yoram. "Introduction of On-the-Job Management Development," *Personnel Journal*, Vol. 52, No. 12, December, 1973, pp. 1,049–1,055.

11. Mintzberg, Henry. "The Manager's Job: Folklore and Fact," *Harvard Business Review*, Vol. 53, No. 4, July-August, 1975, pp. 49–61.

12. Kurke, Lance B., and Howard E. Aldrich. "Mintzberg was Right! A Replication and Extension of 'The Nature of Managerial Work,'" *Management Science*, Vol. 29, No. 8, August, 1983, pp. 975–984.

13. Luthans, Fred, and Mark J. Martinko. *The Power of Positive Reinforcement: A Workbook in O.B. Mod.* New York: McGraw-Hill Book Company, 1978.

14. Kearney, William J., and Desmond D. Martin. "Sensitivity Training: An Established Management Development Tool?" *Academy of Management Journal*, Vol. 17, No. 4, December, 1974, pp. 755–759.

15. French, Wendell, and Cecil Bell. "A Brief History of Organization Development," *Journal of Contemporary Business*, Vol. 1, No. 3, Summer, 1972, pp. 1–3.

16. Burke, W. Warner. "The Demise of Organizational Development," *Journal of Contemporary Business*, Vol. 1, No. 3, Summer, 1972, p. 57.

17. Margulies, Newton, and Anthony P. Raia. *Organization Development:*

Values, Process, and Technology. New York: McGraw-Hill Book Company, 1972, p. 3.

18. Cobb, Anthony T., and Newton Margulies. "Organization Development: A Political Perspective," *Academy of Management Review*, Vol. 6, No. 1, January, 1981, pp. 49–59.

SUGGESTED READINGS

Allan, Peter. "Managers at Work: A Large-Scale Study of the Managerial Job in New York City Government," *Academy of Management Journal*, Vol. 24, No. 3, September, 1981, pp. 613–619.

Beckhard, Richard, and Reuben T. Harris. *Organizational Transitions: Managing Complex Change.* Reading, Mass.: Addison-Wesley Publishing Co., 1978.

Babb, Harold W., and Daniel G. Kopp. "Applications of Behavioral Modification in Organizations: A Review and Critique," *Academy of Management Review*, Vol. 3, No. 2, April, 1978, pp. 281–292.

Burke, W. Warner, ed. *Current Issues and Strategies in Organization Development.* New York: Human Sciences Press, Inc., 1977.

Franklin, William H., Jr. "Six Critical Issues for the Eighties," *Administrative Management*, Vol. XLIII, No. 1, January, 1982, pp. 24–54.

Guay, Claude G., and James A. Waters. "Start with Results: A Bottom-Line Strategy for Management Development," *Management Review*, Vol. 68, No. 2, February, 1980, pp. 25–42.

Kanter, Rosabeth Moss. *The Change Masters: Innovations for Productivity in the American Corporation.* New York: Simon and Shuster, 1984.

Kotter, John P., and Leonard A. Schlesinger. "Choosing Strategies for Change," *Harvard Business Review*, Vol. 57, No. 2, March-April, 1979, pp. 106–114.

Marchione, Anthony R., and Jon English. "Managing the Unpredictable . . . A Rational Plan for Coping with Change," *Management Review*, Vol. 71, No. 2, February, 1982, pp. 52–58.

Michael, Stephen R. "Organizational Change Techniques: Their Present, Their Future," *Organizational Dynamics*, Vol. 11, No. 1, Summer, 1982, pp. 67–80.

Nadler, David A. "Managing Transitions to Uncertain Future States," *Organizational Dynamics*, Vol. 11, No. 1, Summer, 1982, pp. 37–45.

Nicholas, John M. "The Comparative Impact of Organization Development Interventions on Hard Criteria Measures," *Academy of Management Review*, Vol. 7, No. 4, October, 1982, pp. 531–542.

Pavett, Cynthia M., and Alan W. Lau. "Managerial Work: The Influence of Hierarchical Level and Functional Specialty," *Academy of Management Journal*, Vol. 26, No. 1, March, 1983, pp. 170–177.

Powell, Gary, and Barry Z. Posner. "Resistance to Change Reconsidered: Implications for Managers," *Human Resource Management*, Vol. 17, No. 1, Spring, 1978, pp. 29–34.

White, Louis P., and Kevin C. Wooten. "Ethical Dilemmas in Various Stages of Organizational Development," *Academy of Management Review*, Vol. 8, No. 4, October, 1983, pp. 690–697.

LEADERSHIP IN ORGANIZATIONS

Leadership can and should be viewed from many perspectives. Classical management theory thought of it in terms of authority—the right of a manager to influence the behavior of subordinates. From that perspective, when managers lack the ability to influence effectively, one logically asks whether their authority is commensurate with their responsibility. But the concept of authority is more complex than classical theorists recognized, and its meaning continues to change as the influence of specialists increases. Authority and power, the subject matter of Chapter 15, introduce this section on leadership in organizations.

Chapter 16, "Leadership Theory and Practice," discusses various leadership styles used by managers. Although no single style is universally superior, a strictly authoritarian style is increasingly less effective than a more participative one. Chapter 17, "Personal Characteristics, Managerial Effectiveness, and Organizational Culture," deals with the long-debated question of the extent to which personal characteristics of managers affect managerial performance and organizational culture. Research does not support the existence of a definable managerial personality, but it does indicate that certain characteristics are more likely than others to contribute to managerial success. The first line supervisor, who plays a unique, often demanding, and complicated role among managers, is the subject of Chapter 18.

Chapter 19 deals with "Participation," an effective and increasingly used managerial tool. A number of practical guidelines and techniques are included in this chapter. "Goal Setting in Organizations" (Chapter

20) is concerned with a single dimension of leadership behavior; and because it deals with the objectives of organizational leaders, it is an important topic. The leadership theory of the human relations movement put too little emphasis on achieving organizational goals (in contrast to classical theory, which was preoccupied with it). Today we recognize that neither goal achievement nor the satisfaction of human needs can be neglected without undermining organizational effectiveness.

15

Authority and Power

> *In the situations that have been discussed, a subordinate accepts commands in the absence of a determinate choice of his own. But a subordinate may also accept commands in opposition to a determinate choice of his own. In such a case, the element of authority in the behavior pattern is unequivocal. When there is a disagreement between two persons, and when the disagreement is not resolved by discussion, persuasion, or other means of conviction, then it must be decided by the authority of one or the other participant. It is this "right to the last word" which is usually meant in speaking of "lines of authority" in an administrative organization. Too often, however, the element of disagreement in obedience is overemphasized at the expense of the other elements of the situation. The term "authority" would be too narrowly employed if it were restricted to such instances of disagreement.*
>
> *A final complication must be added to the notion of authority. If authority were evidenced entirely in the acceptance of explicit commands, or in the resolution of disagreements, its presence or absence in any relationship could be sought in the presence or absence of these tangible concomitants. But it is equally possible for obedience to anticipate commands. The subordinate may, and is expected to, ask himself "How would my superior wish me to behave under these circumstances?" Under such circumstances, authority is implemented by a subsequent review of completed actions, rather than a prior command. Further, the more obedient the subordinate, the less tangible will be the evidences of authority.*
>
> *Herbert Simon[1]*

As Herbert Simon suggests in the introductory paragraphs, authority is a complex phenomenon that interacts in complex ways with other forms of managerial influence. At times managers must exercise their right to the last word, and at such times subordinates may have to act contrary to their own best judgment. Since the individual members of organizations act out of private interests, perceive the world in different ways, and behave emotionally as well as rationally, managers need power to buttress their leadership skills and ensure the achievement of organizational objectives. In complex, modern organizations it is virtually impossible for managers to achieve their ends through personal leadership, persuasion, or even formal authority. They increasingly need a broad power base from which to influence other people on whom they are dependent. In this chapter we focus on the important concepts of managerial authority and power. The chapter objectives are

TO UNDERSTAND:

1. The distinction between authority and power

2. The uses and limitations of formal authority

3. Alternatives to the use of formal authority

4. The legitimacy of power

5. How managers acquire power

FORMAL AUTHORITY

A manager's position within an organization conveys certain rights to use power. This authority may be viewed as a contingent grant, received initially as part of a formal position but standing in need of reinforcement from other power sources.

Formal authority is the institutionalized right to employ power. It is a delegated right that accompanies a manager's formal position. If it could be isolated from other forms of authority (and it cannot be), it would be independent of any particular individual and available equally to anyone who might occupy a given position. Formal authority is a *contingent* (conditional) *grant* in that the absolute amount of functional authority a manager possesses depends on a number of variables, most of which are related to managerial behavior.

In real life the authority associated with a position is never totally defined and perhaps should not be, since different occupants have different needs for power and are capable of handling different degrees of responsibility. Clues about a position's formal authority may be picked up from position descriptions; observation of the behavior of previous occupants of the position; observation of persons in comparable positions; statements made by one's superior; the size and nature of budgets managed; and the difficulty of assigned tasks and other such factors. These clues are sometimes vague and subject to much interpretation on the part of all members of the organization, including the power holder in question. Thus, much of the initial authority grant may be subject to question at the outset.

Position Power

Position power, as used here, may be defined as that ability to influence the behavior of others which is derived primarily from a manager's position within the organization—that is, from a manager's formal authority. This is not a static and constant quantity. Rather, it continually fluctuates, typically following a general tendency either to increase or decrease systematically from the initial, ill-defined authority grant. In a sense it is a potential for influence that may or may not become actualized in the experience of a particular manager.

Many a bright, ambitious manager has clashed head-on with the position power of an immediate superior. The superior may, relatively speaking, be ineffective and yet still possess a considerable amount of position power. Here are seven of the major sources of such power:

1. *Reward power.* Managers have a certain ability to reward performance: through raises, promotions, and praise, for example, or through withholding punishment that normally would be justified.

2. *Coercive power.* The manager may apply sanctions of various sorts: suspension, layoff, discharge, demotion, and so on.

3. *Control of critical information.* Power with reference to subordinates, peers, and even superiors may result from a manager's ability to control access to information needed by others in order to perform well or deal with the political aspects of their jobs. Research shows that a manager's power is greatest where others depend on his or her expertise in their own jobs and, more specifically, where others have a need for reducing uncertainty in decision making.[2] In times of material shortages, for example, the power of purchasing agents increases because they know which materials are available and where they can be bought. Because of this knowledge they participate in managerial decisions from which they would otherwise be excluded. Lower level employees often possess power over managers because they have information the manager needs access to but does not possess.[3]

4. *Control over resources.* Control over money, materials, or personnel may give tremendous power. A financial executive often exerts a high

degree of control over peers as well as subordinates. Even the human resource manager, who is normally thought of as being in a relatively weak position, may wield power through the ability to influence the personnel resources available to line managers. Control over resources is usually different from control over information, although the purchasing agent in the example just presented exerts control over both, giving power to a person normally considered to have relatively little.

5. *Status and prestige.* The position itself may open doors that would otherwise be closed. For example, a given officeholder has access to high-level executives on an informal, social basis that would not be available to a lower level manager.

6. *Ability to delegate.* Position power conveys the right to make subordinates more powerful or less powerful through delegation. Delegable power also enables a manager to delegate tasks in a manner that may offset a personal weakness.

7. *Control over policy and rules.* At a given organizational level a manager is able to set policy, make rules, and otherwise take action that will both serve the organization and be personally enhancing. For example, one newly appointed operating manager very effectively increased her own power by systematically restructuring the vaguely defined positions of her subordinates. By taking the initiative to clarify the duties and authority of others, she underscored her own authority and power to act.

Limitations of Position Power

Professional observers of organizational behavior are not altogether in agreement concerning the effectiveness of position power. Sometimes, in order to make a point, an author takes an extreme position and in the process presents a distorted picture of the facts. One such position is a reaction against the classical emphasis on formal authority. It is expressed in this well-known statement by Herbert Simon:

> Theoreticians of history have often questioned the extent to which "leaders" really lead. How broad is the area of indifference within which a group will continue to follow its leadership? In a very real sense, the leader, or the superior, is merely a bus driver whose passengers will leave him unless he takes them in the direction they wish to go. They leave him only minor discretion as to the road to be followed.[4]

This is obviously a strong statement of the fact that a manager's authority must be accepted to be effective, and it is important that we avoid carrying the analogy too far. It presents a limited view of the facts in that it fails to take into consideration the impact of the position power that is often available to a manager. It is true that when a manager gives an order subordinates are free to disobey, but they are not free to disobey without having to face the consequences. One could, depending on the situation, just as easily take the position that the awesome power of the organization, as expressed through formal authority, leaves followers with little choice but to follow. Either position is extreme and unrealistic.

The notion that a leader's task is to take followers where they want to go was characteristic of the human relations literature of the late 1940s and early 1950s. Most of these studies stressed the power of informal groups but tended to ignore altogether the organizational power structure. It is not too surprising that such a movement would spawn the anarchistic viewpoint that followers rather than the leader have the last word about their goals and objectives.

Managers should recognize the considerable power of their subordinates without being excessively awed by it. In the real world, managers who are too impressed with the power of subordinates sacrifice their initial grant of position power only to find that subordinates have neither the authority to provide them with a monthly paycheck nor the inclination to assume the responsibility that should be associated with such authority. It cannot be said that managers who believe they have the power to take a given action always do, but it is generally true that managers who believe they do not have power are limited by that belief.

EXPERTISE AND THE AUTHORITY OF COMPETENCE

Managers who are endowed with relevant knowledge, analytical skills, and other abilities that are in high demand can draw upon these abilities to increase their power. This type of power is often more effective than position power in getting results without negative repercussions from subordinates.

We generally refer to individuals with outstanding knowledge or expertise in a field as **authorities**. Even when such persons have no formal authority within an organization they have great power to influence organizational behavior. For example, line managers often take the advice of consultants on major policy and operating decisions. By their very nature consultants rely heavily on their **authority of competence**—the right of a person to influence others by virtue of recognized ability and expertise.

In the absence of evidence to the contrary, it is normally assumed that a manager possesses the technical and/or managerial expertise required to perform assigned duties satisfactorily. Superiors, peers, and subordinates cautiously confer on the new officeholder a contingent grant of authority of competence which carries with it certain rights and behavioral expectations. For example, other organizational members tend to accept without serious question certain authoritative opinions and judgments within the area of the manager's expertise. The grant is *contingent* in that it will be withdrawn if the manager's subsequent behavior proves that it was unjustified.

From a practical point of view this means that a manager must ultimately earn the initial authority grant. At times others greet a new officeholder with exceptionally high competence expectations, but in the final analysis all assumptions must be tested on the firing line. Thus, the power of managers to influence behavior depends on performance as well as position. So it is that an experienced top sergeant may have more influence on the decisions of a field commander than a crowd of young officers of superior rank, and a manager at a given organizational level may be more powerful than one or more managers higher up the line.

Success-oriented managers typically place a high value on the opportunity an organization provides for personal growth. They continually expand their authority by increasing their expertise rather than by being content with the official power expansion provided by promotions. Since expertise has no value unless it is expressed, they volunteer to assume additional responsibility—taking on the undesirable jobs and complex problems passed over by less ambitious managers—until their expertise is recognized and their power is felt within the organization.

Once a manager's **expert power** is recognized and accepted by others, no distinction is made between it and position power. However, for purposes of understanding, it is helpful to note the bases on which expert power is attributed to an individual. The following are among the most often observed contributors to expert power:

1. Formal education (degrees, specialized courses, academic honors).

2. Depth of relevant knowledge (without reference to formal education).

3. Successful on-the-job experience.

4. A history of successful problem solving and decision making.

5. A willingness to tackle difficult problems which others have avoided or failed to observe.

6. Formal status as an expert (for example, appointment to a position normally held by an expert or designation by one's superior as the person to consult on certain problems).

Managers acquire expert power in different ways and to different degrees. Possession of expertise alone does not ensure that a manager will gain expert power. To be expressed as a power, expertise must be recognized and valued.

AUTHORITY OF THE PERSON

Without reference to their competence or formal authority, managers differ greatly in their ability to influence others. Each manager possesses attitudes, personality characteristics, and behavior patterns that interact to produce a uniquely personal form of influence. This constitutes an accepted and important source of power.

Classical organization theory made little allowance for the impact of personal influences on organizational life. One such influence that throws askew the most rationally contrived theories of formal authority is **authority of the person** or the recognized right of a manager to influence others—a right based on previously established personal relations, personal leadership skills, and charisma. For purposes of discussion, this topic is subdivided into personality factors and motivational factors.

Personality Factors

There are undoubtedly a great many factors related to personality that directly affect an individual's personal power. The three discussed here—social ascendancy, domination, and identification—are closely intertwined.

Social Ascendancy. A socially ascendant personality tends to be dominant in interpersonal relations, and more often than not social ascendancy contributes to identification of subordinates with their superiors. *Power*, as we have used the term, is a social concept; that is, it refers to relationships between people. The term **social ascendancy** is a personal concept. It refers to certain characteristics of an individual which are, in turn, expressed as social power. Socially ascendant individuals tend to assert themselves in the presence of other people. They feel free to say what they think and are relatively unconcerned about the approval of others. Everything else being equal, the socially ascendant manager is more powerful—has a greater influence on the behavior of others—than the manager who is restrained. In recent years much has been written about the importance of standing up for your rights and learning to behave assertively rather than passively, at one extreme, or aggressively at the other. Socially ascendant persons do not usually need assertiveness training. Assertive behavior flows naturally from a socially ascendant personality.

Domination. Although all forms of personal power are present in formal organizations and interact with other forms of power, **domination** can best be understood by reference to informal relations. It occurs any time one individual gives a command or makes a request and another complies because of the personal qualities (other than expertise) of the one making the request. Thus, within an informal group of friends, one or more individuals may tend to make the decisions; influence the behavior, attitudes, and life-styles of the group; and, in general, behave as though formal superior-subordinate relationships prevail.

It is the nature of some individuals to cower before a person who is self-confident and assertive. Sometimes the unassertive person becomes submissive to a specific manager even though the latter is not particularly forceful and has no motivation to dominate. Because people differ in the dominance-submissive personality characteristic, it is inevitable that when they are continually thrown together in any form of social interaction a "pecking order" (superior-subordinate relationship) will develop. It should be noted that this status and power hierarchy often serves to meet the needs of followers as well as leaders. The unassertive role is preferred by many persons since it typically involves a minimum of responsibility and risk taking.

Identification. The term **referent power** refers to the power superiors sometimes enjoy because their subordinates identify with them. **Identification** in this sense typically involves the three elements described here:

1. The superior-subordinate relationship provides the subordinate with certain important need satisfactions (for example, security, status, and a sense of belonging).

2. The subordinate strives to be acceptable to the superior (sometimes expressed in attempts to be like the superior). The subordinate often admires and has affection for the superior.

3. The subordinate typically accepts the superior's goals and salient values.

Referent power is a singularly valuable type of managerial power. It usually grows out of a manager's deep and consistent concern for people and exists in significant amounts only when a manager is unusually successful in meeting the needs of others.

Identification is facilitated when the superior is gifted with charisma or personal charm. Any behavior that is generally accepted as favorable (friendliness, intellectual brilliance, sense of humor, or an interest in others) may contribute to the leader's charisma.

The qualities that make a leader charismatic and facilitate identification need not be consciously identifiable by the follower to be effective. The recognition of charisma in an individual is to some extent a matter of personal opinion; it exists in the eye of the beholder. This being true, the factors that contribute to identification are more likely to be emotional than rational. Nevertheless, charisma is an undeniable source of personal power and is a significant aspect of the stuff of which relationships among people are formed.

Motivational Factors

David McClelland, a psychologist who has spent much of his life studying the motivation of managers, assumed that the heads of achievement-oriented organizations would be persons with a high need to achieve; however, he was confronted with the fact that the president of one of the most achievement-oriented firms in his studies scored exactly zero on his need-for-achievement scale.[5] From this and other observations McClelland concluded that managers are primarily concerned with influencing others to achieve and that they are more likely to have a high need for power than a need for achievement.

Most of us are somewhat suspicious of others who seek power. We cannot help but question the power seeker's motives and wonder whether the power will be used wisely. Even managers who themselves seek additional power tend to question their own motives. Actually, power in and of itself is morally neutral; but it may be employed to achieve either good or evil ends by means which do or do not respect the rights of others. Likewise, people who have a high need for power are not in themselves more or less honorable than those who have a high need for, say, achievement, or affiliation (the need to belong and be accepted by others).

Although the motives of managers differ, there are four primary reasons why successful managers seek power:

1. Management positions tend to attract individuals with a high need for power. They derive satisfaction from directing the activities of

others, making decisions, and having others defer to them. Such persons may react favorably to interpersonal conflict and to the risks associated with assuming responsibility.

2. Managers need power in order to accomplish their organizational objectives. They cannot succeed without power because they must constantly deal with powerful individuals and groups.

3. Managers need power as a means of reducing the insecurity and frustration that are a result of having to get work done through other people.

4. Power contributes to a manager's self-esteem and sense of personal worth. Power is valued in its own right, apart from its utility. Semantic studies indicate that being powerful is identified with goodness, health, and beauty while its polar opposite, weakness, is identified with evil, sickness, and ugliness. Persons who do not seek power are no less interested in ego enhancement than those who do; they have simply learned to satisfy their needs in other ways.

DETERMINANTS OF LEGITIMACY

The use of power is legitimate when it is right and proper in a moral sense. Unfortunately, individuals and groups within organizations often perceive rights and morals differently. As a result, the question of who has the right to make certain decisions and to take certain actions is debatable.

Authority was implied early in this chapter as the *right* of one individual to influence another, in contrast to power which is the *ability* to influence. Obviously, there are times when an individual has the power to influence another without having the right. For example, the mugger influences behavior by offering two unacceptable choices: your money or your life. The right of one person to manipulate another is also questionable. The manipulator influences through deception: The person being influenced is ignorant of the manipulator's motives and intent. These behaviors are not considered legitimate because the power holder violates the rights of the persons influenced. We look now at some of the variables that determine whether a power act is perceived as legitimate.

Weber's View of Legitimacy

The most widely publicized view of legitimacy, called **acceptance theory**, follows a line of thought developed by Max Weber (and later, in

America, by Chester I. Barnard and Herbert Simon). For Weber, a power act is legitimate only when acknowledged as such by the subordinated individual. Subordinates voluntarily accept authority because they believe that the superior has a right to command and they have an obligation to obey. In situations where the superior gains compliance without this type of willing cooperation (for example, when disciplinary action is threatened), the employee has submitted to coercion, not authority, in the same sense that a slave chooses to obey rather than be beaten or killed. Coercion is a form of social control, but it should not be associated with legitimate power according to Weber. He visualized three forms of legitimate power:[6,7]

1. *Legal or rational power.* **Legal** or **rational power** is based on the individual's commitment to the organization and its purposes, policies, and rules. The superior is perceived to have been objectively selected on the basis of leadership ability; and the best interest of everyone is served by working within the rational, impersonal organizational framework.

2. *Traditional power.* The legitimacy of **traditional power** is based on the subordinate's belief that the power holder has a right to command because of a preordained right (without reference to the power holder's personal qualities). For example, a king, priest, or member of an elite caste holds legitimate power over persons who believe in the particular political, religious, or social system in which the leader is endowed with authority.

3. *Charismatic power.* Legitimacy is based on a belief in and commitment to the power holder as an individual. **Charismatic power** is legitimate because followers freely choose to obey and are in a personal way compensated by their association with the leader. The charismatic leader wields power through the ability to inspire and to solicit the loyalty of devoted followers.

The Question of Rights

Although Weber's concept of legitimacy is widely accepted, it is not altogether satisfactory to the individual who is interested in understanding the power relationships that exist in real organizations. The following statement by Peter Blau pinpoints the major problem with Weber's viewpoint:

> The power to sanction formally invested in the bureaucratic official has paradoxical implications for authority. In terms of the concept advanced, the direct use of sanctions by a manager to compel subordinates

to carry out his orders does not constitute the exercise of authority. Quite the contrary, it shows that his directives do not command their unconditional compliance. It is this official power of sanction, on the other hand, that makes subordinates dependent on the bureaucratic superior, and this dependence, in turn, is the ultimate source of his authority over them.[8]

Expressed another way, when a manager must resort to coercion because subordinates refuse to obey otherwise, by definition (Weber's definition) that manager's power act is not legitimate. Weber's concept of legitimacy makes interesting theory, but it is too limited to be fully acceptable to most managers.

Most managers would seriously question the value judgment in the notion that an action has legitimacy only when subordinates comply in a spirit of unconditional, willing obedience. The failure of subordinates to comply or to comply willingly obviously indicates something about the *effectiveness* of a power act, but it does not necessarily indicate anything about its moral or ethical rightness.

If we are to think of legitimacy in terms of an individual's right to influence the behavior of others, we must deal realistically with the fact that the question of rights always involves value judgments. Management and labor (or superior and subordinate at any level) often perceive a situation differently, and the most morally qualified panel of jurists would often have difficulty deciding who has the right to take authoritative action. For example, does management have the right to require longshoremen to load wheat into foreign ships bound for Russia? In 1979 a significant number of longshoremen thought that management had no such right and therefore engaged in a wildcat strike. Even though the labor contract provided what appeared to be clearly an affirmative answer, the question of rights was still debatable in the opinion of the parties involved. Considering the possibilities for perceptual bias, it would be simplistic to define our terms in such a way that management's command automatically lacks legitimacy merely because subordinates refuse to obey.

Although there is no one best way to interpret legitimacy, we may, within the framework established to this point, draw three practical conclusions:

1. The refusal of subordinates to obey, even when severe sanctions are threatened or applied, does not negate management's right to command or the subordinates' obligation to obey.

2. Management may have the authority and the right to influence the behavior of subordinates without having the ability to do so.

3. We should not expect authority in organizations always to be rationally discernible and incontestable. By their very nature, rights are subject to question and the object of contest. The perception of rights will necessarily remain in a state of flux, and the question of who has the authority to command will often be decided on the basis of who has the power to influence behavior rather than who has the right to influence it.

The Rights of Ownership

Most managers, past and present, would probably be willing to accept the following as a statement of the source of their authority:

> Under our democratic form of government the right upon which managerial authority is based has its source in the Constitution of the United States through the guarantee of private property. Since the Constitution is a creature of the people, subject to amendment and modification by the will of the people, it follows that society, through government, is the source from which authority flows to ownership and thence to management.[9]

Although this represents an early view of the rights of management, it is still a strong and valid statement as far as it goes. Its primary limitations as a statement of managerial authority are that (1) it pertains only to formal authority, omitting any reference to the earned authority of competence and authority of the person, and (2) it fails to take into consideration nonmanagerial sources of authority within the organization which are also grounded in the Constitution and will of the people. It is, nevertheless, a valuable statement of one major source of managerial authority.

Bottom-Up Authority

Traditionally the subject of authority within organizations has been dealt with as if its flow were only downward from the top. Although this condition is the one most managers would prefer, it is a distorted view of the authority and power relationships that actually exist. There are in fact sources of authority other than ownership. These are often in conflict with the power of management and dilute it to some extent.

The Authority of Organized Labor. The National Labor Relations Act of 1935 (the Wagner Act) for the first time clearly legitimized at the national level the authority of organized labor. Workers were given the right to organize with some degree of immunity from the power of management, to bargain collectively, and to use their collective power (through the strike, for example) to challenge the authority of employers. In a deliberate move to reduce the imbalance of power between an organization and an individual worker, the federal government created an environment in which industrial warfare—the power of management pitted against the power of organized labor—became national policy.

The labor-management competition, endorsed by law, presents some interesting implications in the area of rights. Granted that each party has an initial right to employ power to protect its own interests, many of the so-called rights of each are thereafter determined by which of the two is more powerful. Who has the right to decide on wages, hours, and general personnel policies? The answer: whoever has the most power. Although, in practice, elements of personal morality, reason, and human relations are involved in the bargaining process, it remains the rule that might makes right. Incongruous as it may be, the legitimacy, the ethical sanctification, of authority is often decided on the basis of trial by combat.

The labor-management power struggle is a never-ending process in unionized companies, sometimes involving extreme bitterness and hostility. This, of course, is not always the case. The mood is often that of two powerful football teams that fight with all possible force, aggressiveness, and cunning on the field and then socialize at a friendly after-game party or that of opposing trial lawyers who do their best to win in the courtroom but remain friends afterward.

The Authority of Individual Rights. Each employee, from the floor sweeper to the president, lays claim to certain rights and powers by virtue of being a human being in a free society. Each maintains an area of privacy and self-rule which remains inviolate and beyond the legitimate reach of the organization's power. The manager who fails to respect this private domain is usually confronted with a noteworthy contest of power.

The basis for what is here called the authority of individual rights lies partially in broadly accepted moral and ethical values, some of which are expressed as constitutional and legal rights. For example, regardless of our commitment to an organization or an individual leader, most of us would feel a sense of moral indignation if a supervisor were to attempt to use personal power to influence our religious beliefs or require us to act contrary to those beliefs. Such behavior is perceived as a violation of our rights—an encroachment into that area over which we reserve the right to rule.

Each of us has a slightly different way of defining just what this area of privacy is, depending on our values, self-concepts, and learned expectations. Most employees would probably agree that supervisors have no right to physically abuse them (push and shove them, for example) or to touch them (say, through an act of intimacy or affection). Some would say that a supervisor has no right to verbally abuse a subordinate—by a "bawling out," for example. One research engineer put it this way to a superior who had just delivered a reprimand for the way the engineer had handled a project:

> Let's get something straight. You have the authority to do a lot of different things to me when I foul up. Perhaps you can even fire me. But one thing you have no right to do is talk to me as if I were a dog, or a naughty child, or somebody who is inferior to you as a human being. I'm as much a human being as you are; so don't talk down to me!

Because people have different expectations, managers must know their subordinates as individuals in order to be maximally effective. Supervisors who are insensitive or disrespectful of the rights of subordinates are perceived as using their power in illegitimate ways. The resulting conflict tends to erode the supervisor's future ability to influence behavior, even in legitimate areas.

It should be noted that management, in its official role, is confronted with the individual authority of its own members as well as that of nonmanagerial personnel. Thus, the power of management is never totally consolidated; and the roles which managers must play are often in conflict. At one point in time a manager is a defender of the organization; at another, that same manager is motivated strictly by self-interest, often at the expense of the organization. It is obvious from a study of the summary of managerial and employee authority presented in Figure 15-1 that much of a manager's power is individual rather than organizational and can therefore be used in dealing with superiors as well as with subordinates.

EXTERNAL SOURCES OF AUTHORITY

> As society becomes more complex, management power diminishes. Although the wealth controlled by management has increased, its power has been greatly reduced by the involvement of federal, state, and local governments in all areas of business life.

To some extent, the challenge to the power of management that organized labor presents is from within the organization. When bargaining takes place at the local level, at least the organization is dealing with

MANAGERIAL AUTHORITY		
CLASSIFICATION	**SOURCE OF RIGHTS**	**EXAMPLES OF POWER**
Formal authority	Ownership-delegation	Rewarding subordinates Control over budgets
Authority of competence	Demonstrated expertise	Solving complex problems Services in demand
Authority of person	Personal qualities	Persuasiveness Ability to win loyalties

Authority of individual
    rights[1]
	Accepted morality	Refusal to be owned
		    Requiring fair treatment

EMPLOYEE AUTHORITY		
CLASSIFICATION	**SOURCE OF RIGHTS**	**EXAMPLES OF POWER**
Formal authority	Ownership-delegation	Control over a machine Control over information
Authority of competence	Demonstrated expertise	Problem solving Withholding productivity
Authority of the person	Personal qualities	Persuasiveness Trouble-making

Authority of individual
    rights
	Accepted morality	Refusal to be owned
		    Demanding constitutional rights

Authority of organized
    labor [2]
	Legislation	The strike
		    Picketing and boycotting

[1] In one sense a manager's authority of individual rights relates more to his or her role as an employee than as a manager. However, since this power contributes to the manager's dignity and self-respect, it is also a positive image builder and is therefore a contributor to managerial power.

[2] Although there is no form of managerial authority which is directly parallel to the employees' authority of organized labor, managers do, of course, unite to meet specific power confrontations from below, and by virtue of their formal authority relationships they continually function more or less collectively.

FIGURE 15-1   Managerial and Employee Authority

its own employees. There are, however, outside challenges to management's authority that may be even more demanding than those from within the organization. The most important of these challenges is the influence of government.

There was a time when a business owner's greatest complaint about government interference was the requirement of detailed records for tax purposes. Today even the owner of a relatively small business must spend endless hours studying government regulations, complying with them, making reports, and defending whatever action is taken. As society becomes more complex, federal government, in particular, continues to reduce the authority of management and to substitute its own.

The areas in which the power of government limits organizational power are too numerous to list completely; but examples include the right to make decisions concerning employment, promotion, wages, prices, employee safety, product safety, product design, advertising, transportation, borrowing and lending, competitive practices, and a host of other areas which were once generally believed to lie solely within the legitimate domain of managerial authority. The point should be clear that the so-called rights of management are constantly in a state of flux and are gradually diminishing.

There are, of course, other institutions in the organization's external environment that limit the effective power of management. Public opinion, for example, is important to most organizations because of the public's power to regulate (as in the case of transportation and public utilities), and because the general public consists of customers. At times management's freedom of movement is almost totally limited by the actions of competitors, lending institutions, or major customers or suppliers. Although the power of management remains substantial, only those managers who are skilled in its acquisition and use are able to manage effectively. There is now concrete evidence that managers who understand power are able to influence government policy—to slow down the proliferation of government controls, for example—but counteracting government power requires a sophistication few managers have.[10] It may be necessary for managers to develop that sophistication in order to retain the right and ability to manage.

GENERALIZED DEFERENCE TO AUTHORITY

The acceptance of managerial authority is in part dependent upon beliefs, perceptions, and attitudes which are deeply imbued in our society. Generally speaking, Americans are suspicious of authority and repelled by the notion of blind obedience. These qualities tend to limit the power of management.

The United States was in part founded by individuals who sought to escape the tyranny of unbridled power. The freedoms spelled out in our Constitution and the system of checks and balances designed to prevent any one branch of government from becoming too powerful reflect their consciousness of the dangers of power and their determination not to be excessively controlled by it. The concept of democratic government (or democratic leadership) represents an antiauthority philosophy which is deeply ingrained in the people of most freedom-loving countries of the world; and our general commitment to it is in itself sufficient to create some problems with authority of any sort.

The lack of respect that many Americans have for authority greatly diminishes the power of managers. This point should not, however, obscure the fact that a vast majority of our population does respect the law and honors our institutions. Because a democracy permits citizen in-volvement in the legal process, most of our institutions are perceived as legitimate.

Thus, in spite of all the obvious antiauthority sentiment, the man-agers of most organizations still have the authority to manage as long as they use discretion and avoid overreliance on formal authority. Since most people still show a degree of deference to authority, managers who are sophisticated in the acquisition and use of power need not suffer from lack of it.

DELEGATION AND POWER

> Delegation is one of the most effective ways for a manager to acquire power. The manager who attempts to hoard power loses it, while the one who develops powerful subordinates through delegation generates the maximum amount of power available for the achievement of or-ganizational objectives.

It is common for managers to refuse to delegate for fear they will lose power in the process. This is especially characteristic of weak or insecure managers who sense that delegation may further weaken their positions. The presence of powerful subordinates may pose a threat in two interrelated ways: first, through a fear that the subordinate will take the superior's job; second, through a fear that the superior's ineffective-ness will be accented in contrast with a powerful and effective subor-dinate.

In some situations it may be realistic for a manager to fear the pres-ence of powerful subordinates. However, assuming that a manager is rea-sonably competent, the development of powerful subordinates through delegation usually has the effect of strengthening the superior. The man-ager of a unit composed of individually powerful subordinates is able to coordinate and control their collective power in the interest of achieving organizational objectives. The poor delegator has no such power avail-able.

It is noteworthy that delegation does not reduce a manager's initial grant of power. Theoretically the delegator's power and responsibility remain constant even when the power of subordinates is dramatically increased. Thus, the effective delegator optimizes both the absolute amount of power controlled and the total responsibility assumed by members of the organization. The delegator's powerful subordinate man-agers have less need to use power directly than do weak managers in comparable positions. Consequently, the former have more potential for using such forms of influence as persuasion and suggestion. These less obvious power acts, in turn, increase the managers' personal power and decrease the likelihood that countervailing power will develop (such as the personal power of hostile subordinates or the power of a union).

A mature attitude toward the power of subordinates was expressed to a supervisor by an immediate superior in the General Tire and Rubber Company:

> In the past 30 years I've helped train more supervisors who became plant managers than any other person in this company. Considering my education, I've probably gone as far as I can go; but I'm proud to say I've never held anyone back. I can call any one of 50 people in the home office who know me by my first name. I've never thrown my weight around, even when I could have. If I ever need help, I'm sure they will go to bat for me.

Managers who try to maintain power at the expense of subordinates undermine their own positions. Managers who help and develop their subordinates by delegating power are recognized for this and consequently gain both respect and future allies.

AN EFFECTIVE NONUSE OF FORMAL AUTHORITY

The most effective use of authority is usually the least obvious one. Although formal authority must at times be expressed directly and bluntly, it serves best to increase a manager's potential for using unobtrusive forms of power such as persuasion and suggestion.

Managers who rely heavily on their formal authority place themselves in an untenable position with reference to their subordinates. When compared with other managers who depend more on their expertise, persuasiveness, or personal relationships with subordinates, the authority-oriented manager appears to be weak. Nothing symbolizes the possession of power better than a power holder's ability to avoid its use in situations where it could be legitimately applied. When a manager who is perceived as weak refrains from the direct use of power, the act is perceived by subordinates to be motivated by fear; but when a powerful manager does the same thing, the act is perceived to be a result of choice behavior and is therefore seen as magnanimous.

The most perfect power act is often the least obvious one. This is best exemplified when subordinates perform an act, or refrain from performing it, because they anticipate the reaction of a superior. For example, commission sales representatives for a certain printing company do not accept single orders under $500 (even though company policy allows them to do so) because they know their superior thinks such orders are unprofitable. In this particular case the sales representatives do not agree fully with their supervisor's judgment, but authority controls their behavior. In such cases subordinates are not likely to make a conscious distinction between formal authority, authority of competence, and personal authority. Ideally all three function simultaneously; but when competence and personal authority fail, formal authority provides an effective backup.

Persuasion

In certain work environments subordinates have learned to expect and respond favorably to direct, unequivocal commands. Combat soldiers must obey commands or endanger their own lives and the lives of others. Construction bosses often use direct commands, especially where noise levels are high and immediate obedience is sometimes necessary to coordinate the activities of a work group and to avoid accidents. There is a time and place for direct commands in the experience of any supervisor, and subordinates typically recognize and accept this fact.

On the other hand, effective managers can often more easily solicit the active cooperation of subordinates by convincing them that a particular task needs to be performed or that it should be performed in a certain way. The manager who *persuades*—who influences subordinates by providing them with convincing reasons for behaving in a specific way—communicates a degree of respect for their mentality which leads to a strengthening of the superior-subordinate bond. The use of persuasion also contributes to the growth and understanding of the subordinate, thus reducing the need in the future for commands and external controls.

Although persuasion tends to substitute reason for a formal power act, it would be erroneous to assume that persuasion is independent of formal organizational power. As a matter of fact, the subordinate may be incapable of drawing a distinction between the power and the reasoning of a superior.

Power holders have a unique ability to gain and hold the attention of subordinates and are often given the benefit of the doubt because of their access to privileged information and their presumed competence. When relating to a superior, subordinates often withhold critical judgment and avoid decisions without being aware that they are doing so. Of course, managers who gain a reputation for faulty reasoning and illogical conclusions may undermine their potential for using persuasion and thereafter have to resort excessively to formal authority.

Two very practical warnings are in order with reference to the attempted use of persuasion with subordinates. They are exemplified by the behavior of these two managers:

> Jane Morris, a production superintendent in an automotive parts remanufacturing plant, had spent most of her career as a staff engineer and had a strong aversion to issuing any sort of a direct order. Actually she felt quite uncomfortable as a formal power holder. Because she was obsessed with the virtues of persuasion over formal power, she wasted endless hours arguing with subordinates who had only a fraction of her expertise. She finally learned with the help of a management counselor simply to tell a subordinate, "I'm sorry you don't agree, but that's the way we're going to do it." Unknowingly she had taught her subordinates to be inappropriately argumentative.

The second manager was entirely different from Morris, but he too had a problem with the use of persuasion.

> Jim Cullen, a highly successful entrepreneur, did not dislike having to use power; in fact, he was sometimes too authoritarian. His problem was that he could not simply issue an order, have it obeyed, and then let the matter drop. He wanted his subordinates to agree with his thinking when from their viewpoint he was often incorrect and illogical. His need for their approval caused his subordinates to view him as domineering and overbearing. As one of his two vice-presidents expressed it, "I'm perfectly willing to follow his orders, but I will not pretend to agree with him. I respect his right to influence my actions, but I resent his attempts to control my thoughts."

These two cases suggest two practical conclusions for the practicing manager:

1. Since attempts to persuade are not always successful, managers who rely heavily on persuasion to gain the compliance of subordinates may undermine their own ability to be persuasive. When persuasion fails, a manager must often fall back on the right to the last word, and this should not be done apologetically.

2. The person who is forced to agree—overtly, at least—has not been persuaded. It is typically less objectionable to comply with orders with which one disagrees when one is not also called on to endorse them.

Suggestion

Effective supervisors are sensitive to the fact that the issuance of commands draws heavily on one's formal authority and may in time undermine it. The use of persuasion provides an alternative form of influence, but even this may at times be unnecessarily directive. An even less offensive alternative is the use of suggestion. The supervisor who uses suggestion sets an example, proposes a course of action, hints that a course of action may be appropriate, or calls to the subordinate's attention a possibility for action which might otherwise be overlooked. For example, instead of saying, "I would like you to follow last year's format when you write your report," a manager suggests, "Before you finalize the format of your report you might want to see if last year's report has something to offer."

The substitution of suggestions for direct commands permits subordinates to experience a greater sense of self-esteem and dignity than is ordinarily possible when continuous submission to a superior's direct orders is required. Even when the suggestion is synonymous with a command, they can appreciate their supervisor's preference for using suggestion and respond accordingly.

The use of suggestion by a power holder must be considered a power act, but it is an *indirect power act* and more acceptable to subordinates than is a direct order. It somehow communicates to the subordinate: You are not the sort of person who has to be commanded. Because you are an intelligent and responsible person, you are capable of deciding for yourself the best course of action. Even when the suggestion is obviously a veiled command, the subordinate is given an opportunity to rationalize and interpret the communication in a way that is self-enhancing.

HOW MANAGERS ACQUIRE POWER

Managers differ greatly in the means by which they acquire and use power. Each possesses a unique power style based on a combination of position power, personal characteristics, competencies, and power tactics.

In our discussion of the nature and legitimacy of power, the point has been made that managers need power to function effectively. Since they are called on to achieve objectives through other people in an environment controlled by power centers, they must at times depend on one form or other of power in order to be successful. Figure 15-2 presents a summary of some of the interacting conditions and behaviors that ordinarily contribute to the acquisition of managerial power.

A FAVORABLE ENVIRONMENT FOR THE ACQUISITION OF POWER

1. A profitable organization; availability of vast resources
2. Minimal external controls (from government, banks, etc.)
3. Minimal countervailing powers (unions, hostile employees, etc.)
4. An organization characterized by growth and change
5. Decentralization and delegation as organizational policy
6. General rather than close supervision; maximum autonomy

EXPANSION OF AN INITIAL GRANT OF POSITION POWER

1. Directly seeking additional power grants when appropriate
2. Obtaining control of critical resources (money, materials, etc.)
3. Discreetly using rewards and punishment
4. Making optimal use of policies, regulations, and controls
5. Upgrading the technology and processes controlled
6. Selecting strong subordinates; delegating maximally

A POWER-ORIENTED PERSONALITY

1. A high motivation to obtain power
2. Expression of socially ascendant behavior
3. Demonstration of self-confidence in social relations
4. Skillful use of the power of persuasion
5. Taking calculated risks versus inhibited, cautious behavior
6. Charismatic behavior; development of loyal followers
7. Mastery of a body of valuable and scarce information

THE ACHIEVEMENT OF A HIGH LEVEL OF PERFORMANCE

1. The achievement of impressive results; overfilling one's position
2. Working hard and long; making personal sacrifices
3. Seeking out rather than avoiding problems
4. Skillfully solving difficult problems
5. Making decisions that are right most of the time
6. Initiating action rather than accepting the status quo

THE USE OF TACTICAL BEHAVIORS WHICH INCREASE POWER

1. Making friends; forming alliances
2. Avoiding antagonisms and the development of opposition power
3. When in doubt, exceeding authority rather than underrating it
4. Directly using formal authority only when necessary
5. Avoiding power acts that are likely not to succeed
6. Occasionally (and discreetly) demonstrating power
7. Constantly doing favors; creating obligations; earning credits
8. Using skill in compromising and making trade-offs
9. Being willing to lose small battles in order to win big ones
10. Seeking wise counsel; developing trust; behaving with integrity

FIGURE 15-2 Some Factors That Contribute to the Acquisition of Power

It should be obvious that no two managers acquire or use power in exactly the same manner. One relies heavily on formal authority and somehow maintains a high level of effectiveness, another depends more on personal persuasiveness, while still another maintains power primarily because of unusual ability to solve complex problems. The many contributors to the development of power constantly interact within the individual and the external environment to produce a unique managerial **power style** (defined as the manner in which a manager acquires and uses power).

The uniqueness of a manager's power style is demonstrated in the life of a regional vice-president of a major oil company. He is unusually quiet and unassertive in social situations, is apparently not a seeker of power, and is in no sense charismatic, but his power within the company is unmistakable. He explained his success and his rather awesome influence in this way:

> I started to work for this company during the depression. Although I had a degree in petroleum engineering, I worked as a laborer in the oil fields for three years and did practically every dirty job in the production division. Early in my career I earned a reputation for making good decisions. It became a challenge to me to do my homework better than anybody else—regardless of the cost to me—and to be right most of the time. Of course, it was easier to be an expert when my education and experience were far beyond what my job required, but I've tried to keep from losing that early reputation. I'm a very nonpolitical, nonsocial manager, but it's my way—the only one I feel comfortable with.

A body of literature directly related to managerial power is gradually developing under the topic of organizational politics. It seeks to describe this important but neglected aspect of organizational behavior by recognizing that "power struggles, alliance formation, strategic maneuvering, and 'cutthroat' actions may be as endemic to organizational life as planning, organizing, directing, and controlling."[11,12] A few of these tactical behaviors that increase a manager's power are listed in the last section of Figure 15-2.

IMPORTANT TERMS AND CONCEPTS

formal authority	expert power
position power	authority of the person
authorities	social ascendancy
authority of competence	domination

referent power   traditional power
identification   charismatic power
acceptance theory   power style
legal/rational power

STUDY AND DISCUSSION QUESTIONS

1. Should a manager with outstanding leadership skills really need position power in order to be effective? Explain.

2. Why can a manager's authority not be clearly and absolutely defined? How does a newly appointed manager know how much authority he or she has?

3. In what sense is a manager's position power a contingent grant?

4. In what way does a manager's perception of the amount of power possessed by subordinates affect the manager's power?

5. Why would a manager who usually gives subordinates the same raise probably have less power than one who gives merit raises?

6. What personal qualities contribute to the ability of an informal leader to influence followers?

7. Are persons with a strong need for power more likely to abuse their power than those who have little need for power? Explain.

8. Explain and evaluate acceptance theory.

9. From what different sources does one individual derive the right to influence another?

10. After an extended strike the XYZ company granted its employees, along with other concessions, the right individually to decide whether to work overtime when asked to do so. Relate this method of establishing rights to the concept of legitimacy as moral rightness.

11. Why do Americans as a group respond less favorably to authority than do people in some other countries?

12. How is delegation related to power?

13. What justification can there be for treating persuasion and suggestion as forms of power?

14. Evaluate the following statement: Power tends to corrupt, and absolute power corrupts absolutely.

THE OLMSTEAD COMPANY

The headquarters of the Olmstead Company, a manufacturer of men's work clothes and casual slacks, is located in a North Carolina city of 40,000 people where Joseph Olmstead founded the organization in 1947. The company consists of 17 plants, all located within a 200-mile radius of the home office. Company sales run about $65 million a year. All the company's products are sold to six large retailing chains which have national outlets and which also buy similar products from other manufacturers.

Seven years ago, when the company was unionized, Olmstead resigned from the presidency and has since been primarily involved in other businesses while still serving as board chairman of the Olmstead Company. With 25 percent ownership of the stock, Olmstead is the largest single stockholder. He and four close associates, whose companies were acquired through stock trades, control about 60 percent of the stock. The remainder is widely dispersed. Primarily because of foreign competition and high union wages, company profits and stock prices have declined steadily; and the principal stockholders now feel that some action should be taken. They are considering several alternatives, including closing down the least profitable plants, accepting an acquisition offer by another company (basically a stock trade), and selling the company to its union employees. Although the latter possibility is looked upon with disfavor by most of the company's executives, it remains a serious possibility in the thinking of the major stockholders. Accordingly, they have established a committee to study the union's proposal and make a recommendation. The committee consists of the following persons:

Julia Mercado, age 58, president since Olmstead resigned. She owns little stock and recently has been under considerable stockholder pressure because of the profit situation. Her relations with the union are good—too good, according to Olmstead. She also maintains close personal ties with key executives in the customer organizations. Her managerial and technical skills are generally respected throughout the company.

Terry Boyce, age 28, production superintendent of the home office plant, a nephew of Joseph Olmstead. He is described as a dependable plodder—the stable kind of individual who effectively keeps the routine operations running. Boyce evidences no ambition to become a corporate executive.

Sarah Shils, age 50, controller, and eight-year employee. She is one of the highest paid executives in the company and is respected by everyone who knows her for her genius in the financial area. Before entering the business world, Mrs. Shils was the financial officer for several large charitable and social organizations.

Lewis Woodfin, age 35, a union steward who played a major role in the company's unionization. Woodfin is poorly educated but highly intelligent, articulate, and possesses qualities that make others listen and identify with him even when they disagree with his point of view. On several occasions he has turned down opportunities for promotion to supervisor and for a full-time position with the union. Because of his position as a senior mechanic, he has broad contact with plant employees, and he values highly his close personal relations with them.

Leo Ballentine, age 38, a middle manager with direct responsibility for sales and customer relations. He is also responsible for the general supervision of personnel, warehousing, and shipping. Although no one seems to know just how it happened, Ballentine has continued to acquire responsibility. His relations with Woodfin and the labor force in general have always been excellent, and he does not attempt to hide the fact that he would some day like to be the company president. He is independently wealthy, but this does not seem to affect his ambition or productivity.

Olmstead's primary goal in establishing the study committee was to get a feel for the political implications of selling the company to the union. He wonders whether the sale itself will destroy the company, and he does not want that to happen. It appears to him that the action of this committee may help determine the likelihood of the company's success under union ownership.

1. What are the sources of the power each individual possesses?

2. What external conditions affect the power structure of the company?

3. What tactical behaviors for influencing others are likely to be used by the individuals involved in this incident?

4. What motives of the committee members are likely to influence the position each takes on the issue under consideration?

5. Is the committee recommendation more likely to be influenced by logic or power? Why?

6. What additional information is needed to understand this incident adequately?

REFERENCES

1. Simon, Herbert A. *Administrative Behavior*, 3rd ed. New York: The Free Press, 1976, p. 129.
2. Spekman, Robert E. "Influence and Information: An Exploratory Investigation of the Boundary Role Person's Basis of Power," *Academy of Management Journal*, Vol. 22, No. 1, March, 1979, pp. 104–117.
3. Blackburn, Richard S. "Lower Participant Power: Toward a Conceptual Integration," *Academy of Management Review*, Vol. 6, No. 1, January, 1981, pp. 127–131.
4. Simon. *Administrative Behavior*, p. 134.
5. McClelland, David C. "The Two Faces of Power," *Journal of International Affairs*, Vol. XXIV, No. 1, 1970, pp. 29–47.
6. Weber, Max. *The Theory of Social and Economic Organization*, ed. Talcott Parsons, trans. A. M. Henderson. New York: Oxford University Press, Inc., 1947, pp. 56–77.
7. Weber, Max. *Basic Concepts in Sociology*, trans. H. P. Secher. New York: Citadel Press, 1962, pp. 71–84.
8. Blau, Peter M. "Critical Remarks on Weber's Theory of Authority," *The American Political Science Review*, Vol. LVII, No. 2, June, 1963, p. 313.
9. Peterson, Elmore, and E. G. Plowman. *Business Organization and Management*. Homewood, Ill.: Richard D. Irwin, Inc., 1949, p. 62.
10. Fenn, Dan H., Jr. "Finding Where the Power Lies in Government," *Harvard Business Review*, Vol. 57, No. 5, September–October, 1979, pp. 144–153.
11. Schein, Virginia E. "Individual Power and Political Behaviors in Organizations: An Inadequately Explored Reality," *Academy of Management Review*, Vol. 2, No. 1, January, 1977, pp. 64–72.
12. Bacharach, Samuel B., and Edward J. Lawler. *Power and Politics in Organizations: The Social Psychology of Conflict, Coalitions, and Bargaining*. San Francisco: Jossey-Bass, Inc., Publishers, 1980.

SUGGESTED READINGS

Cobb, Anthony T. "An Episodic Model of Power: Toward an Integration of Theory and Research," *Academy of Management Review*, Vol. 9, No. 3, 1984, pp. 482–493.
Hambrick, Donald C. "Environment, Strategy, and Power Within Top Management Teams," *Administrative Science Quarterly*, Vol. 26, No. 2, June, 1981, pp. 253–275.

Mitton, Daryl G., and Betty Lilligren-Mitton. *Managerial Clout*. Englewood Cliffs, N.J.: Prentice-Hall, Inc., 1980.

Newman, William H. "Company Politics: Unexplored Dimensions of Management," *Journal of General Management*, Autumn, 1979, pp. 3–11.

Pfeffer, Jeffrey. *Power in Organizations*. Marshfield, Mass.: Pitman Publishing, Inc., 1981.

Shukla, Ramesh K. "Influence of Power Bases in Organizational Decision Making: A Contingency Model," *Decision Sciences*, Vol. 13, 1982, pp. 450–470.

16

Leadership Theory and Practice

Life provides many opportunities to achieve a sense of satisfaction for "having made a difference" such as parenting, team sports, counseling co-workers, and so on. One of the most gratifying of these opportunities may be successfully leading a group of people through a challenging experience.

The intrinsic rewards associated with leadership must not be underemphasized, but it is the extrinsic rewards—the status, power, and financial compensation accorded to repeatedly successful leaders—that are most noticeable and perhaps notable. For whatever personal reasons, many people attempt to exert some degree of leadership at certain times in their lives. This chapter is the first of five chapters that make clear how leadership can be exerted to some degree by anyone who is willing to regard it, at least in part, as a learnable skill.

The success of an organization depends on many factors, none more important than the impact of its leaders. They make the decisions that determine both organizational purpose and the means by which that purpose is fulfilled. Their actions determine whether the potential of the organization's members will be actualized or lie dormant and whether the emotional tone of the organization will be warm, cooperative, and goal oriented or cold, hostile, and self-defensive.

Leadership, as the term is used here, is behavior by which one person motivates another to work toward the achievement of specific objectives. This definition is by no means the only one in use. There is, in fact, little agreement about the meaning of leadership or even about the advisability of using a concept encompassing such varied behaviors. Nevertheless, it continues to be functional and is an important aspect of managerial behavior about which our insights are steadily increasing. The objectives of this chapter are

TO UNDERSTAND:

1. The meaning of leadership in organizations
2. The major styles of leadership
3. Some techniques of participative leadership
4. The most frequently used theoretical models of leadership

LEADERSHIP IN ORGANIZATIONS

> All managers are leaders because they influence, to varying degrees, the behavior of other persons within the organization. Some are poor leaders; they have little influence except that which their formal authority permits them to exercise. Others combine personal leadership qualities with position power and prestige to produce a powerful influence on subordinates, peers, and superiors alike.

The concept of leadership is ambiguous for several reasons. For example, it may be argued that leadership acts, unlike power acts, require compatability of superior and subordinate goals. Once that distinction between leadership and power is accepted, however, problems arise with the concept of leadership. Not only must the leader motivate the subordinate (by whatever means) to achieve certain goals, but part of the subordinate's motivation must be a personal commitment to those goals. Within that context, what we usually mean by autocratic or authoritarian leadership styles probably would not qualify as leadership at all. Furthermore, if leadership necessarily requires that goal commitment be a motivator, the superior would not be leading when subordinate compliance is motivated primarily by leader charisma, or by pay, security, and other payoffs exchanged for the subordinate's services. Actually there are many kinds of leaders who lead in greatly differing situations through using a variety of motivational appeals.

Jeffrey Pfeffer correctly notes that few meaningful distinctions exist between leadership and other forms of social influence and that the concept of leadership may not be necessary to explain the phenomena collectively classified as leadership behaviors.[1] The concept does, however, provide a convenient classification for those behaviors in which one person motivates another to achieve specific objectives. It is irrelevant that those behaviors can be further subclassified (for example, into persuasion, suggestion, charismatic influence, social dominance, and so on). In real life an action usually results from a complex set of interacting motives, and in leadership situations we should expect that power will often be intertwined with other motivational factors. The influence of power, though often imperceptible, is expressed in varying degrees in most leadership styles. However, effective leadership increasingly requires that formal power be subordinated to other forms of influence; and, as we use the term, an act of leadership goes beyond the influence of power.

The notion that leadership involves an ability to influence that transcends authority underscores an important aspect of leadership—namely, that the quality of leadership must, in part, be judged in terms of leader-follower relationships. Positions are structured in such a way that a new manager can lead subordinates—can motivate them to behave in ways that contribute to the achievement of organizational objectives—before he or she has an opportunity to establish personal relationships with them. A position of leadership also enables a manager to get a job done even after negative relationships have been formed (for example, after subordinates have become hostile because of an unpopular management decision). Because these possibilities exist, leadership in organizations is not always the fragile and friendly relationship it is often pictured to be. Nevertheless, managers who rely too heavily on formal authority are in danger of losing some or all of their ability to lead.

Leadership in organizations is complicated by the many factors that affect behavior and limit leader influence on followers. Classical thought treated leadership as a simple matter of downward influence; but, as shown in Figure 16-1, the most effective leadership styles involve a leader-follower exchange with each influencing the other.[2,3] Figure 16-1 also shows that the behaviors of a given manager and subordinate are influenced by

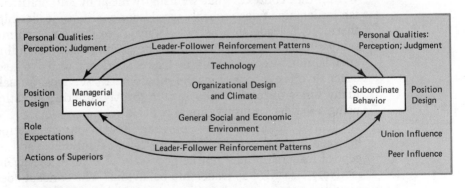

FIGURE 16-1 Influences on the Behavior of Leader and Followers

other variables that reduce personal influences in both directions. So impressed have some researchers become with these environmental constraints that they minimize the fact that in many situations leaders do have a strong impact on both their followers and on environmental factors that less effective leaders would view as insurmountable constraints.

STYLES OF LEADERSHIP

Leadership style refers to the pattern or constellation of leadership behaviors that characterize a given leader. Because each leader feels most comfortable with a particular style and tends to be relatively consistent in its use, the effectiveness of a specific leader will vary from one situation to another.

Some leaders tend to be **authoritarian**, relying heavily on the power of their formal positions, while others are more **participative** (inclined to involve subordinates in organizational planning and decision making). Highly authoritarian leaders usually place a high value on completing assigned tasks while neglecting the needs of subordinates. Participative leaders show more concern for the needs of subordinates, often at the expense of achieving organizational objectives. A leader may, of course, exhibit a strong concern for both task and people. The two emphases are not incompatible.

Sometimes style is expressed in terms of *closeness of supervision*. Managers often have the option of **close supervision**, keeping themselves informed concerning the details of their subordinates' work and exercising close personal control at all times, or of **general supervision**, delegating freely and concentrating attention more on results than on the means by which the results are achieved. While close supervision tends to be associated with authoritarian leadership and centralized organizations, general supervision is more likely to be associated with some form of participative leadership and decentralized organizations.

One extreme form of general supervision is **laissez-faire** or **free-reign** leadership. A leader using this style almost abdicates the leadership role, allowing subordinates more or less to lead themselves. Although such a style could lead to total disaster, there are a few situations in which it appears to be reasonably effective (for example, the supervision of highly responsible research scientists or college professors). Figure 16-2 shows the interaction patterns of three major leadership styles.

Since these and other elements of leadership style can be applied in varying degrees and combinations and must be integrated with the unique

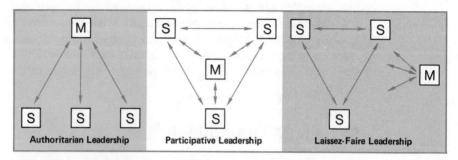

FIGURE 16-2 The Primary Manager-Subordinate Interaction
Patterns of Three Leadership Styles

personality makeup of a given manager as it interacts with a specific
environment, no two leadership styles are exactly alike. Among the many
other elements of leadership style we might consider are (1) the leader's
approach to motivating subordinates (such as the use of coercion or incentives); (2) the leader's unique approach to making decisions; (3) the
extent to which the leader's personal charisma and authority of personality influence relationships with subordinates; and (4) the leader's ability to vary his or her leadership behavior to meet the unique demands
of different situations.

AUTHORITARIAN LEADERSHIP

Authority is a valuable and necessary aspect of organizational life, but
a strictly authoritarian leadership style is inappropriate in today's organizations.

People with organizational power choose to use varying degrees of
authoritarian control. Although many understand the need for the support and cooperation of subordinates, the temptation for a power holder
to rely on position power rather than on an alternative form of influence
is sometimes overwhelming. The Caesars of Rome moved progressively
from a relatively democratic form of government to a totally autocratic
one. Ultimately they proclaimed themselves gods and demanded to be
treated as such.

The temptation to place excessive reliance on formal authority is
no less real for a manager than for a totalitarian ruler. When opportunities arise for choosing between persuasion and command or personal
influence and authority, the power-based alternatives are often preferred

for their simplicity, efficiency, and immediate effectiveness. Machiavelli's words express the sentiments of a true autocrat:

> Is it better to be loved than feared, or the reverse? The answer is that it is desirable to be both; but, because it is difficult to join them together, it is much safer for a prince to be feared than loved, if he is to fail in one of the two. . . . Men have less hesitation in injuring one who makes himself loved than one who makes himself feared, for love is held by a chain of duty which, since men are bad, they break at every chance for their own profit; but fear is held by a dread of punishment that never fails you.[4]

Leadership in Classical Theory

Authoritarian leadership has its theoretical basis in classical organization theory and in capitalistic doctrines concerning the rights inherent in private ownership of property. Historically managers, especially owner-managers, have understandably believed that management has a right to make organizational decisions and to issue commands and expect them to be obeyed. From the classical viewpoint, leadership as personal influence is considered unnecessary since the primary basis for influence is organizational authority.

The authoritarian approach to leadership is logical and rational, given the assumptions of classical organization theory. The problem lies in the fact that people are not as simple and rational as the model implies. Human behavior is controlled as much by emotions as by logic, and perceptions of rights change as the values of society change. Although classical theory provides an invaluable point of departure for understanding organizations, it is in many ways naive and unrealistic. It simply does not take all the facts into consideration.

The Authoritarian Personality

Sometimes a leader develops an authoritarian style by imitating other managers. Another tries a variety of leadership behaviors and finds that in a specific setting the authoritarian approach works best. If an authoritarian style is based on one of these simple forms of learning, a manager can learn to use other styles when they are appropriate.

There exists, however, an individual whose authoritarian leadership style is based on deeply ingrained personality characteristics. This person we describe as an **authoritarian personality**. In many cases the parents of this leader were highly authoritarian, and their leadership approach was successful; that is, the child submitted to the authority rather than rebel and refuse to accept it. As a result, the adult behavior of this individual follows the parents' authoritarian style. Because leaders with authoritarian personalities learned in early life to believe in the rights of superiors to dominate their subordinates, they are submissive toward superiors while dominating their subordinates.

It might at first appear that people with authoritarian personalities would have difficulty relating to superiors, and in one sense they do. If they feel hostility or resentment toward superiors, they repress or bottle it up lest it be expressed and jeopardize the relationship. Usually, however, they vent these feelings through relationships with subordinates, causing the subordinates to develop hostile feelings in return.

The superior and subordinate of an authoritarian personality see two entirely different persons. The subordinate sees one who is strong, powerful, and dominant; and the superior sees one who is weak and submissive. Actually the paradoxical behavior of authoritarian personalities is quite consistent. When their background and personality development are considered, they can hardly be expected to behave otherwise.

It should be noted that the submissiveness before superiors is almost as undesirable as domination of subordinates. Mature leaders, even those who are relatively authoritarian, are not submissive. They are not passively dependent individuals who grovel before the controlling power of a superior. Rather, they identify with and assume a comfortable working relationship with their superiors.

The Antiauthoritarian Personality

A close relative of the authoritarian personality is exemplified by an individual we will call George:

> George had authoritarian parents, but he reacted by rebelling instead of submitting. Just the thought of someone telling him what to do makes him bristle. Although he occupies a formal position in management, his real identification is with the underdog subordinate whom he perceives as being pushed around by management. Although he resents authority, he too is often attracted to an authoritarian management style—doing to others as others did to him. George may look to subordinates like an authoritarian personality, but he differs in one important aspect: He is not submissive to his superiors. He may, in fact, be openly aggressive; and this usually ensures his demise in the management hierarchy.

It is interesting to note that where an authoritarian style is an outgrowth of deeply ingrained personality characteristics there may be considerable inconsistency between what the leader believes and does. The professor with a total intellectual commitment to participative techniques may be a model of authoritarian leadership in the classroom. The corporate manager whose formal education has provided an arsenal of prepackaged, ready-to-use participative techniques may intellectually proclaim their virtues but emotionally reject them as just so much theoretical garbage. Behavior is more often influenced by long-standing habits and gut-level feelings than by what one rationally holds to be true and good.

THE CHARISMATIC LEADER

Although charismatic leaders are rare, they are not an extinct species in business organizations, and elements of the charismatic style are found in many managers. The greatest weakness in this style is that the superior-subordinate relationship is presumed to be between a superior leader and an inferior subordinate.

One variation of the authoritarian style is what Max Weber called **charismatic leadership** (based on charisma, the "gift of grace"). Such leaders differ from the typical autocrat primarily in the extent to which leadership style is calculated to focus attention on their own "superhuman" qualities and the extent to which their authority is personality based as well as position based. Like kings or feudal lords, charismatic leaders think of themselves as having certain attributes that make them superior to and better than their subordinates. Subordinates are expected not merely to obey but also to show reverence and personal loyalty.

Employees who do not respond to the lord-vassal treatment typically leave the organization, by choice or otherwise, and those who remain are ideally suited for reinforcing the leader's self-deceptive, ego-enhancing behavior. Charismatic leaders are often found among entrepreneurs who have somehow succeeded beyond all expectations and lack the insight to know that their success is not solely the result of their own genius. Managers who are talented and powerful, but unduly egotistical, may have an especially difficult time avoiding the undesirable elements of charismatic leadership in their relations with subordinates. When these qualities are combined with an unwillingness or inability to delegate, the stage is perfectly set for a charismatic style.

Managers who fail to delegate decision making to subordinates automatically increase their subordinates' dependence and place themselves in an unrealistically exalted position. Subordinates who must constantly seek advice, even with regard to trivia, are by definition placed in humble, demeaning, and inferior positions. In a real sense this leadership style creates a self-fulfilling prophecy. The prophecy of the leader's superiority relative to others is reinforced by the fact that the decisions made are often the right ones only because he or she is the judge and standard of rightness. The actual quality of the leader's decisions may well be inferior to the decisions many subordinates would make if they had the authority, but such a possibility is never put to the test.

Although a charismatic leader may be highly endowed with charisma (personal charm or magnetism that attracts others and establishes bonds of identification), it would be incorrect to assume that persons with charisma will necessarily adopt a charismatic style, as the term is used here. Adolph Hitler, whose generals were treated as though they were personal servants, and India's Mahatma Gandhi, whose political followers sought his personal blessing, were both charismatic leaders; and both possessed unusual personal charisma. To a limited extent, the same may be said for Franklin D. Roosevelt or John F. Kennedy, whose followers often spoke of them in hushed, messianic terms. On the other hand, large numbers of leaders who possess a relatively high level of personal charisma never make it the focal point for their leadership behavior. Although charisma is obviously a desirable quality, especially for someone in a leadership position, it is not in itself a sufficient basis on which to develop a leadership pattern.

PATERNALISM

> Paternalism was one of management's great mistakes. From it management learned that employees will not willingly tolerate a relationship in which they are made to feel dependent and in which they are expected to work out of feelings of gratitude.

Of the many expressions of authoritarian leadership, paternalism ranks among the least successful. Although some company presidents still try to maintain the fiction that their employees constitute a family, attempts to recognize the company, its founder, or its president as a father who assumes responsibility for the welfare of his children have in their extreme forms been discontinued in America. It is noteworthy, however, that in some foreign countries, particularly in Japan, paternalism is still very much alive.

From its late nineteenth century beginning with company welfare programs, paternalism reached its heyday in the 1920s, mostly as management's attempt to stave off the rising tide of unionism. This fathering approach to leadership expressed itself primarily in two ways. First of all, management made a concerted effort to be good to its employees. In practice this meant the establishment of fringe benefits, cafeterias, company purchasing plans, recreation programs, and other programs intended to make employees happy and more productive.

The second expression of paternalism was somewhat more ominous. In many companies, among the more notable of which was the Ford Motor Company, organizational influence was not confined to the work situation. Company social workers were sent into the homes of employees to help them be more effective in handling their personal affairs. Employees were encouraged to practice financial budgeting, physical hygiene, and "high morality." (Divorce and drinking alcoholic beverages often topped the list of unacceptable behaviors.) Some organizations exercised additional controls over their employees through company-owned towns (company stores, housing, and recreational facilities). Owing one's soul to the company store was almost a reality for many employees in the 1920s and 1930s.

Whatever honorable motivation may have been involved in paternalism, the ultimate result was to reduce employees to the role of dependents. Since the fringe benefits and welfare programs were presented by management as though they were gifts rather than compensation, it became obvious that they could be withdrawn anytime employees failed to comply with company demands. The unacceptability of this crude use of power was increased by management's attempts to package it as goodness and concern for people, a tactic which was certain to provoke resentment and hostility. The long-range effect of paternalism apparently was to increase rather than decrease unionism.

PARTICIPATIVE LEADERSHIP

When compared with authoritarian leadership, participative leadership expresses greater confidence in the subordinates' willingness and ability to assume responsibility, involves subordinates in decision making to a greater extent, and accepts more fully the notion that management has a responsibility to subordinates as well as to superiors.

Although the terms *participative* and *democratic* leadership are used interchangeably, the latter is a less desirable term in that it tends to communicate the notion that managerial decision making is a matter of vote taking. Because of our popular use of the word *democracy*, we necessarily read meaning into it that ordinarily cannot be accepted by management. To be specific, the participation of subordinates in management decision making can never be taken so far that it undermines a manager's right to the last word. A purely democratic process would make accountability impossible. Since line managers remain accountable for results regardless of their leadership style, they cannot afford to abdicate the decision-making responsibility. The term *consultative* leadership is sometimes used in preference to participative leadership because it clearly avoids the connotation of pure democracy.

Participative Techniques

Managers have many opportunities for involving subordinates in organizational planning and decision making. Some companies, for example, have experimented with junior boards of directors composed of middle managers; others have formalized elaborate programs of employee representation on major planning and decision-making bodies of the organization.

Most OB theorists have long extolled the virtues of participative management, although more recent commitment to contingency management—which empirically studies the conditions under which different leadership styles should be used—has led many to rethink their positions. Practicing managers tend to make favorable comments about participative management, but most are cautious in their application of it. Perhaps their caution has been appropriate, since evidence is far from conclusive that participative leadership is always best. It certainly is not always best if one conceives of participation as having nothing to do with the extent to which authority is delegated and if it "is limited to cases where the decisions that are reached affect an entire group rather than only the individual(s) making the decision."[5] People with this view of participation identify it primarily with group dynamics and various methods of involving subordinates in group problem solving. The following examples and the earlier reference to the consultative nature of some participative methods make clear that this chapter is not using this narrow but popular interpretation.

Delegation. Delegation is not ordinarily classified as a participative technique. Yet, if the objective of participation is to involve subordinates in decision making, delegation should be high on the list. Since the determination of which decisions should be delegated is often difficult, a manager's leadership philosophy and degree of commitment to participative management certainly come into play. The manager who is committed to maximum participation will insist that decisions be made at the lowest possible level in the organization, while a more autocratic manager will prefer to centralize decision making.

Question Asking. Managers who respect the knowledge, opinions, and judgment of their subordinates may achieve a relatively high level of participation by simply asking questions. While authoritarian leaders are busy playing the role of oracle and telling others what to do, participative leaders are asking for information and insights that will improve the quality of their decisions and at the same time underscore the responsibility of their subordinates to think and solve problems. One manager formalized this practice and the philosophy by posting a small sign on the wall behind his desk. It read *DBMQ*, which he interpreted as *don't bring me questions.* Implied was the alternative: *Bring me recommendations.*

Many effective managers have learned not to be afraid that subordinates will think the manager's question asking is a reflection of ignorance, a form of buck passing, or an attempt to avoid responsibility. It is actually a form of tough-minded management, not recommended for leaders who are unable to relate effectively to strong subordinates or to live with the challenge of new ideas and creative change.

Committee Action. Committees are a vital means of continually gaining input from a large number of organizational members. Most companies have certain *standing committees* to deal with continuing or recurring problems. (For example, near the top of the management hierarchy an executive committee handles a variety of problems relating to corporate policy, goals, and operations.) Depending on the organizational structure, *special committees* may be established to deal with budgets, employment policies, grievances, disciplinary problems, and a variety of other organizational problems and activities.

The nature and function of committees vary according to the demands of the specific situation. Some are *permanent committees* with rotating membership, or membership determined by position within the organization, while others are ad hoc, special-purpose committees that are dissolved when their mission is completed. A decision may be delegated to a committee, or the committee may be asked to make a recommendation to a higher level governing body or to a specific manager. Ordinarily the latter course of action is followed, since it is difficult to fix responsibility for a committee decision, and a committee decision actually may be made by one or two of its dominant members.

Ad hoc committees of rank and file are sometimes used as a means of bypassing one or more levels of management in order to provide a middle or upper-level manager with information concerning special problems or attitudes toward pay, working conditions, supervision, and other work-related matters. Such committees provide management with insights into employee sentiments and attitudes which are essential for effective decision making.

Since committee members can be rationally selected, committees are ideally suited for handling situations in which coordination and interaction among members is important. Representatives from, say, sales, marketing, credit, and manufacturing may dynamically interact concerning a common problem to produce insights which could be gained only from such interaction. Committee action contributes significantly to the coordinative as well as the problem-solving function of an organization.

Shared Goals. Although MBO programs do exist in which all the planning is centralized and the objectives are authoritatively delegated, such programs miss the point of what MBO is all about. Ideally, an MBO program is highly participative, at least in the sense that each manager is able to exercise a degree of initiative and discretion in determining individual goals and the means for reaching them.

Authoritarian leaders are not prone to become involved in management by objectives (MBO) and similar goal-oriented programs. They often resist the loss of personal power that they fear will result from clear statements of goals. As organizational goals are clearly defined and the criteria against which decisions are to be made and evaluated are consequently clarified, differences between the roles of managers and their subordinates begin to diminish. Since effective goals programs involve a diffusion of responsibility throughout the organization, they require a concomitant increase in the authority of persons whose responsibilities have been increased. Authoritarian leaders often feel threatened by their subordinates' power, while the participative leader is more likely to view a high level of subordinate power and responsibility as an ideal to strive toward.

Advantages of Participative Leadership

Many advantages have been claimed for participative over authoritarian leadership. While recognizing that they do not apply in every situation, a manager should be aware of some of the major benefits to be derived from participative leadership.

Improved Decisions. Participation improves a manager's ability to make decisions. This point is especially convincing when we consider that the resources available through participation are above and beyond those available to the purely authoritarian decision maker. Since participation does not require managers to give up the ultimate right to choose between the available alternatives, managers lose few of the benefits of authoritarian decision making when participative methods are employed. Evidence does exist, however, that negative as well as positive elements occur when groups are involved in decision making. For example, Irving Janis has described what he calls **groupthink**, a group psychology that undermines critical analysis, legitimizes ignorance, reinforces collective biases, and promotes a group self-image of infallibility.[6]

Facilitation of Change. When employees, on any level, have had a voice in the formulation of a policy or course of action, they are less likely to resist its implementation. Because of their participation, they can understand the reasons behind the change and anticipate its positive as well as its possible negative consequences.

Identification with Leadership. Since participation affirms the value of subordinates by expressing the belief that they can make worthwhile contributions, it reduces defensiveness and increases the likelihood that a positive relationship will develop between superior and subordinate. Subordinates can more easily form a positive personal identification with a participative leader than with an authoritarian one.

A High Level of Achievement. To the extent that participation leads subordinates to accept organizational goals and to internalize the organization's standards and values, it should lead to increased productivity, fewer grievances, reduced turnover, and to the achievement of other objectives by which managerial success is typically measured.

Conditions Necessary for Participation

Managers are by no means universally successful in their attempts to use participative methods. In fact, for managers who are authoritarian because of deep-seated personality characteristics and, therefore, likely to be inept in their use of participative methods, a rapid shift to a high level of participation could be disastrous. Certain conditions must be present for participative management to be most effective.

1. *Adequate time.* Since participation ordinarily requires more time than authoritarian decision making, participative methods work best in situations where a manager is able to anticipate problems and plan ahead.

2. *Psychological preparation of subordinates.* Optimal participation requires that subordinates be psychologically prepared to contribute intelligently. They must have access to information that may typically

be withheld from them; they must believe that there is some personal benefit to be derived from participation and must not be too threatened by possible negative repercussions from it (for example, pressure from peers).

3. *Psychological preparation of management*. Managers must be convinced that participative leadership will pay off in terms of their own success. They must be psychologically prepared to deal with feelings, attitudes, and ideas from which an authoritarian leader may be relatively insulated. Only if they are highly motivated to change to participative methods will managers be willing to tolerate the frustrations involved in participative leadership.

4. *Belief in participative methods*. Managers who aspire to be successful using participative methods must have deep belief that their subordinates have a contribution to make. Insincere or token attempts at participative leadership on the part of persons who see participation only as a gimmick or manipulative technique will ordinarily be seen for what they are. Consequently, they will be resented and resisted by subordinates. Since participative management is based on an optimistic view of human nature, the manager who believes that people are inherently lazy and irresponsible is not likely to succeed with a participative style.

5. *Dual accountability*. Managers who employ participative methods must be willing to accept the idea that they have a responsibility and a form of accountability to subordinates as well as superiors. Participative leadership implies the existence of a partnership of sorts and a mutual respect that cannot be taken lightly when a conflict arises between the organization and a manager's subordinates. Managers must at times be their subordinates' advocate and representative to higher level management as well as the transmitter of commands from above.

(We will discuss approaches for using participation in considerable detail in Chapter 19.)

TWO-DIMENSIONAL MODELS

The two dimensions of leadership effectiveness that have received the most attention from researchers are (1) behaviors that are primarily concerned with achieving organizational objectives and (2) behaviors that are intended to meet the needs of followers or subordinates. Successful managers tend to place high emphasis on both.

Historically one school of thought stressed the achievement of organizational objectives while another focused attention on human needs. Traditional organization theory showed little concern for the individual. Achieving results was everything; the individual was often viewed as merely a means to an end. On the other hand, the human relations movement took the opposite approach. As the movement developed, the needs of the organization were de-emphasized, and the long-neglected needs and rights of the individual reigned supreme in the human relations literature.

In their reaction against the authority-oriented leadership of traditional theory, the leaders of the human relations movement interpreted the results of their experiments as though organizational authority were nonexistent or inherently evil. Placing all its hope on democratic leadership, narrowly conceived, the human relations movement lacked the realism and tough-mindedness to survive in its early form. It did, however, produce a major stream of thought that over a period of time was integrated with traditional concepts to produce a realistic and workable body of leadership theory.

Initiating Structure and Consideration

During the 1950s the two major dimensions of leadership behavior were first expressed as **initiating structure** and **consideration**, terms which became commonplace in leadership literature.[7] Initiating structure is intended to communicate the idea that task-oriented leaders rely heavily upon providing structure within which the behavior of subordinates is deemed acceptable. For example, they set goals, establish policies and procedures, issue directives, and otherwise limit the freedom of their subordinates. At the other extreme is consideration for people or concern for the needs of subordinates as individuals.

The two-dimensional view of leadership emphasizes the inadequacy of either initiating structure or consideration without the other. It suggests that a leader must be a mediator between the demands of the organization and the needs of the individuals upon whom the organization must depend for the achievement of its objectives.

The Managerial Grid

A variation of the two-dimensional approach was developed by Robert Blake and Jane Mouton. Beginning with a rather simple two-dimensional model called the Managerial Grid, they developed an elaborate system for evaluating and developing managers. As shown in Figure 16-3, leadership style is expressed in terms of concern for people and concern for production, corresponding roughly to consideration and initiating structure.

According to Blake and Mouton the 9,9 leadership style is always preferred. It is a goal-directed team approach that seeks a high level of productivity through involvement and redirection of potentially disruptive conflict. Managers with the 9,9 style believe that the best way to achieve organizational goals is by eliciting employee commitment to the

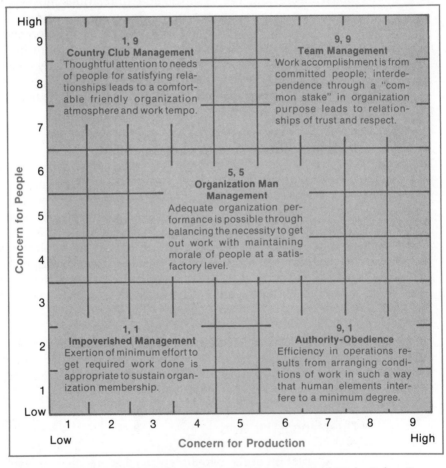

The Managerial Grid figure from *The Managerial Grid III*, by Robert R. Blake and Jane Srygley Mouton. Houston: Gulf Publishing Company, Book Division, Copyright © 1985, page 12. Reproduced with permission.

FIGURE 16-3 The Managerial Grid

values and goals of the organization.[8] Work motivation emerges from the fact that individual needs are met through the achievement of organizational objectives. Consistent with their commitment to the 9,9 style, Blake and Mouton object to a contingency approach in which a leader's style is selected on the basis of which behaviors are most likely to be effective in a given situation. They see situational leadership as void of positive concern for helping others, for contributing to the development of subordinates, and for changing the negative aspects of the leadership environment.

In spite of their commitment to the 9,9 leadership style, Blake and Mouton are not indifferent to the situation or leadership environment. Rather than accept the *flexibility* of shifting from one leadership style to another, however, they advocate a *versatility* in which commitment to certain principles remains constant while searches are made for solutions to problems arising in each situation. For example, if the transfer of a manager to another geographic area is called for, that individual is not ordered to go, nor is subtle leverage applied to produce the desired behavior. Rather, the subordinate is helped to see the costs and benefits of accepting the transfer in terms of career, family, and friends. Thus, the decision is based on free choice.

The 9,9 leadership style, as conceptualized by Blake and Mouton, is based on certain principles that are not to be sacrificed in the interest of short-term expediency. For example, a 9,9 style prefers freedom of choice to enforced compliance, active participation in problem solving and decision making over unilateral action, and self-direction guided by goal setting over external control. By consistently applying such principles the leader is perceived as developing relationships of trust and avoiding the image of being shifty or untrustworthy that could result from applying first one style and then another.

The concerns for productivity and people on which Grid theory is based are interactive rather than additive. Consider, for example, that thinking solely in terms of a high concern for production may suggest strong controls, jobs designed with only production in mind, and minimum opportunity for human choices. Adding to this a high concern for making employees happy produces a form of paternalism—not at all what Blake and Mouton mean by a 9,9 style. In the 1,9 style, the high concern for people is that they be happy; in the 9,9 style the concern for people, which interacts with a high concern for productivity, is a concern that employees grow, be maximally autonomous, be involved in their work, and find satisfaction in cooperative achievement. Distinctions such as these are based on important and practical insights.

Grid theory is criticized by contingency theorists because it advocates one best style, although its concept of versatility does permit shifts of tactics (within the 9,9 style) depending on the qualifications of one's subordinates and other situational variables. Grid theory has also been criticized because of its overemphasis on concern for productivity and people as though leadership contains only these variables. Why not, for example, consider the important leadership variable of decision style, as a Vroom/Yetton leadership model has done, or any one of several other variables such as bureaucratic tendency (commitment to a reign of rules)?[9,10] Some critics of Grid theory think it is unnecessarily complex—just the opposite of those who emphasize that too few variables are involved. One research study concludes that a simpler model that makes no assumptions about the interactions between concerns for people and productivity is just as predictive of leader behavior.[11]

Blake and Mouton have continued to refine the Managerial Grid in terms of theory and application. They have, for example, developed a third dimension: personal motivation.[12] Regardless of any criticism that may justifiably be raised about it, the Managerial Grid makes a contribution both to our understanding of leadership and to our ability to teach leadership behaviors.

CONTINGENCY THEORY

> From a contingency viewpoint there is no best leadership style. Leadership behaviors should be selected on the basis of research and experience that validate their appropriateness in a given situation.

During a business crisis or military campaign an authoritarian leadership style may be infinitely superior to other styles. A given leader should use a different approach when managing a little league baseball team, serving as a university department chairman, or commanding a military unit in the Marine Corps Reserves. Contingency theory also states that a given manager should lead the same people differently under different circumstances while always using good judgment (preferably guided by research data) in tailoring his or her behavior to the unique demands of the situation.

Fiedler's Contingency Model

In Fiedler's version of contingency theory, leadership style is defined as the extent to which a manager is "task oriented" versus "relationship oriented" (again, corresponding roughly to initiating structure and consideration). Style is measured by means of a least preferred co-worker (LPC scale).[13,14] The measuring instrument itself is a simple, bipolar adjective scale (for example, good-bad and strong-weak) which is commonly used in attitude measurement. According to Fiedler's studies, leaders who describe in favorable terms the co-workers with whom they have been least able to work are "relationship oriented," while leaders whose least preferred co-workers are described critically are "task oriented."

Situational favorableness is defined by Fiedler as the degree to which the situation itself provides the leader with power and influence over the behavior of subordinates. To be more specific, situational favorableness depends on (1) leader-member relations, (2) the extent to which the task is structured or clearly defined, and (3) the amount of formal organizational power the leader possesses (for example, the power to hire, fire, or give raises).

On the basis of a number of studies, conducted in different field and laboratory settings, Fiedler draws several conclusions about leadership and its development. Notable among these are the following:

1. Task-oriented leaders perform best in situations that are very favorable or unfavorable; while people-oriented leaders perform best in situations of intermediate favorableness.

2. Neither formal leadership training nor leadership experience contributes greatly to effectiveness in the leadership role. Because of the difficulty in changing the leader's behavior, leadership effectiveness can best be improved by changing the favorableness of the situation (for example, altering a leader's position power, selecting subordinates who fit the leader's style, restructuring the leader's job, or transferring the leader to a position that matches his or her style).

Fiedler's theory has been tested broadly, but it has received support primarily by researchers who use Fielder's methodology (the LPC scale) for determining whether a leader is task or relationship oriented. Actually the theory covers a narrow segment of all possible leadership behaviors, and there is no reason to believe that it has greatly influenced practicing managers in spite of the large number of published studies on it. Fiedler's emphasis on restructuring the environment to improve leadership is useful, but the idea of selecting subordinates to fit the manager is unrealistic in most organizations where managers change positions often.

Contingency Theory: Evaluation and Application

One strength of a contingency approach is that any number of variables can be related to other variables in field or experimental studies. That is also one of its weaknesses. A growing body of published studies relates various leadership behaviors to environmental conditions.[15]

PATH-GOAL THEORY OF LEADERSHIP

The path-goal theory of leadership, a form of contingency theory with great potential for explaining leadership behavior, is currently attracting the attention of serious researchers. Research findings to date, however, are conflicting. They do effectively demonstrate that a great number of variables, including individual leader characteristics, are required to explain the difference between effective and ineffective leadership.

Path-goal leadership theory is based on expectancy theory and the concepts of consideration and initiating structure.[16] According to this theory, leaders are effective in terms of their ability to motivate subordinates to reach organizational goals and to find satisfaction in their work. Although path-goal theory is rapidly evolving, at the present time it may be generally expressed as follows:

1. The leader may improve the motivation of subordinates by making the rewards for productivity more attractive to them (that is, by increasing the valence of goal achievement). For example, a manager has the potential for rewarding high productivity with raises, promotions, recognition, and praise, thereby increasing its attractiveness as a goal.

2. When the work of subordinates is poorly defined, a manager may increase motivation by providing structure (for example, through clarifying goals, giving supportive and helpful supervision, or training subordinates) which will reduce the job's vagueness and ambiguity and thereby increase the expectation of successful goal achievement. Since, as we saw in Chapter 5's discussion of expectancy theory, motivational force *equals* valence *times* instrumentality *times* expectancy, this increase in expectation should increase employee motivation and consequently increase leader effectiveness.

3. When the work of subordinates is already highly structured (for example, repetitive assembly-line or machine-tending work), this theory assumes that path-goal relationships are clear and that initiating

structure will be viewed by subordinates as unnecessary and too directive. Thus, it would lead to subordinate dissatisfaction. This highly structured situation calls for increased consideration for the personal needs of the individual (for example, understanding, praise, and related forms of support).

Path-goal theory appears to be quite logical, and there is some experimental evidence to support it.[17] There is, however, good research to show that in its original form the theory is too simple; that is, it does not take enough variables into consideration.[18,19] It applies to some people but not to others. In some unstructured situations, for example, when leaders take the initiative by clarifying goals and otherwise reducing ambiguity in the work environment, subordinates react unfavorably. Some employees either do not want their path-goal structured or believe in their own ability to provide whatever structure is needed without help from their superior. There is evidence that the reaction of subordinates to structure by a superior is related to a number of personal characteristics, including education, need for achievement, perceived ability, willingness to accept responsibility, and need for independence. A leader should not, therefore, assume that subordinate motivation will always be increased by giving structure to the path that leads to a goal, even when that path is very vague. There is, however, fairly strong evidence that increasing consideration for subordinates whose work is already highly structured does increase their job satisfaction.

The value of path-goal theory lies not so much in its proved ability to predict and interpret leadership effectiveness as in its use as a diagnostic aid to managers faced with the problem of low employee motivation. By reviewing the employee's situation in terms of valence, instrumentality, and expectancy, a manager can often identify the problem contributing to low motivation, and by taking actions to clear the "path," help the employee achieve his or her "goal."

LEAVING A MARK

Environmental favorableness is an important determinant of a leader's success, but managers are a part of that environment and capable of changing it. While one manager is submissive to an unfavorable organizational environment and conforms to all its demands, another manager acts to change it. Strong leaders leave their mark on the organization.

The leadership literature from Max Weber to Fred Fiedler is interesting and challenging, but it can hardly be described as inspiring. Its emphasis is on theories and leadership styles. Few of the many possible influences on leadership behavior are dealt with, and leader personality is conspicuously neglected—in part because earlier theories placed excessive emphasis on personal characteristics and in part because those characteristics are complex and hard to measure. Furthermore, many of the managers on whom empirical research is based are nominal leaders only: They hold positions of leadership but exhibit few personal leadership behaviors. On the basis of 100 published studies and AT&T experience with over 200,000 participants in management assessment centers, Joseph L. Moses concludes that less than 25 percent of all participants demonstrate "significant leadership skills" (defined as leadership ratings of four or five on AT&T's five-point scale). This led him to formulate "Moses' Commandment," which is "Thou shalt study leaders who are first *accurately identified* as leaders before attempting to build theories of leadership behavior."[20] Had Dr. Moses descended from the mountain earlier, our leadership theories might be more valid. By basing our understanding of leadership on the average behavior of masses of bureaucratic managers, many of whom operate in environments that require or permit only minimal leadership behavior, we tend to minimize the importance of a minority group of highly influential leaders.

Managers do exist who have the vision, the courage, and the influence to lift the expectations and performance of an organization from mediocrity to excellence. Bucking the odds, some managers do inspire individuals to heights of creative achievement and transform the members of aimless, traditional groups into value creators and tradition breakers. Burns describes how Franklin Roosevelt was committed to winning World War II and how, in certain circumstances at least, he was willing to give up the petty quest for esteem and prestige in order to make a moral impact that only a values-oriented leadership can make. "Clearly," Burns states, "the leader who commands compelling causes has an extraordinary potential influence over followers. Followers, armed by moral inspiration, mobilized and purposeful, become zealots and leaders in their own right." But he correctly notes that such moral leadership is purchased only at great cost. Leaders

> . . . must settle for far less than universal affection. They must be willing *to make enemies*—to deny themselves the affection of their adversaries. They must be willing and able to be unloved.[21]

Many managers, like their assembly-line subordinates who produce virtually unidentifiable fragments of a finished product, are only vaguely aware of their organization's purpose and goals; certainly they have no fervent identification with them. Lacking that commitment, they have problems with self-motivation—not just with motivating subordinates. Nevertheless, moral leaders can be found in business—managers who believe in their product and in making a contribution to their organization, to their employees, and to society; managers who care deeply about maintaining a vigorous private-enterprise economy; managers who are at least as committed to what they are building as to their own prestige and upward mobility. Certainly there is a need for such managers, but organizational behavior has had little to say about them.

Committed to studying the real world, organizational behavior (OB) researchers have understandably concentrated on the typical, bureaucratic manager and have often failed to make a distinction between *descriptive data* (that tell how managers typically behave) and *prescriptive data* (that tell how managers should behave). A purely descriptive approach to leadership continually directs attention to the influence of environmental constraints and to how little impact leaders have on their environments. It cannot, therefore, provide a complete basis for developing viable prescriptions for strong leadership. The theoretical foundations of prescriptive leadership theory must at least be influenced by empirical studies of that minority of managers who inspire through moral leadership; who call forth integrity, creativity, and high productivity from their followers; and who refuse to be intimidated by monolithic organizations, demanding subordinates, governmental controls, and pressures to be caretaker bureaucrats.

IMPORTANT TERMS AND CONCEPTS

leadership	authoritarian personality
authoritarian	charismatic leadership
participative	groupthink
close supervision	initiating structure
general supervision	consideration
laissez-faire	situational favorableness
free reign	

STUDY AND DISCUSSION QUESTIONS

1. In what limited sense is a manager always a leader? Must personal influence always extend beyond formal authority for a manager to lead?

2. What problems arise in defining leadership in such a way that leader and followers must hold mutual goals?

3. What facts cause some researchers to emphasize how little potential for influence managers have? Evaluate.

4. What problems are involved in using one best leadership style? What advantages accrue from consistently using one style?

5. In the absence of special training in participative leadership, why do managers tend to gravitate toward an authoritarian style?

6. Differentiate the leadership style of the authoritarian personality from that of the great mass of authoritarian leaders who have learned the style through imitation or trial and error.

7. What distinctions would you make between a charismatic leader and a leader who has charisma? Should a leader with charisma necessarily be classified as a charismatic leader, as the term is used here?

8. What are the primary shortcomings of paternalistic leadership?

9. In what sense is participative leadership not democratic?

10. In what ways are participative methods superior to authoritarian leadership as a general managerial style?

11. From one point of view, authoritarian leadership is the approach taken by the strong, tough-minded, and courageous manager. From another perspective, such a manager is more likely to use a participative style. Be prepared to support either point of view in classroom discussion.

12. How do Blake and Mouton meet the criticisms of persons who stress the importance of the situation? Evaluate their position.

13. What are the implications of "Moses' Commandment" for leadership research?

CRITICAL INCIDENT

THE TOO MOBILE MANAGER

Charles Batson gathered his personal belongings, turned in his keys, and prepared to leave for the day. It was his last day. He had been fired from the second highest paying position in the company after 14 months of outstanding achievement. It was not a new experience for Batson, who had averaged changing jobs every three years during his 20-year career in production management, but he was disappointed and did not feel that he was really ready for another job change.

At one point during the termination interview, Leslie Howard, president of Executive Mobile Homes, Inc., had made a statement that kept returning to Batson as he drove back to his apartment. Batson remembered it this way:

> Charles, I'm truly sorry it had to come to this. In slightly over a year you've changed this company from a mom-and-pop operation into a sound business. I give you credit for our success, but either you leave or a half dozen other key managers do. You're a great hatchet man, but the deadwood is gone now. Let's face it, you're a short-term operator.

In trying to ferret out the implications of Howard's statement, Batson thought back over the last 14 months. He had, indeed, started with something less than a business. In whipping the organization into shape he had conducted time and motion studies, set up a cost accounting system, instituted a quality-control program, and totally revised the manufacturing process. The production department was unquestionably efficient, and Batson was enormously proud of it.

He was not so proud of some of the steps he was forced to take to reach his goal. A number of skilled workers had to be discharged when their jobs were diluted to enable unskilled labor to perform them. Some supervisors were discharged, too. Batson worked closely with each of the six general supervisors until he knew every detail of their jobs. Three of the six were just too rigid to change their methods and were given an opportunity to resign. This statement by one of the three who left was characteristic of their inability to adapt to the new system:

> Batson, what do you care how we do the job as long as it gets done? I've been building mobile homes ever since the industry began, and I know what I'm doing. If you will just get off my back, I'll see to it that we make homes that meet all your standards, including costs.

Batson thought back over the insurance programs and retirement plan that he had installed and marveled that no one seemed to appreciate them. He also took note of the fact that everybody, including the stockholders and the president, was now making much more money than before he revolutionized the company; but this fact had not resulted in any warm feelings toward him.

Batson mused that he really would not have a great deal of difficulty getting another job. He had always been able to sell himself. In college he was everybody's candidate for the man most likely to succeed. During his senior year he was intramural tennis champion, leading man in a successful drama, and president of the student body. Today was a bad day; but he knew that his persuasiveness, superior ability, and willingness to work hard were still going for him; and he was determined not to make the same mistakes again.

1. How would you describe Batson's leadership style?
2. What should Batson have done differently?

REFERENCES

1. Pfeffer, Jeffrey. "The Ambiguity of Leadership," *Academy of Management Review*, Vol. 2., No. 1, January, 1977, pp. 104–112.
2. Fulk, Janet, and Eric R. Wendler. "Dimensionality of Leader-Subordinate Interactions: A Path-Goal Investigation," *Organizational Behavior and Human Performance*, Vol. 30, No. 2, October, 1982, pp. 241–264.
3. Wofford, J. C., and T. N. Srinivasan. "Experimental Tests of the Leader-Environment-Follower Interaction Theory of Leadership," *Organizational Behavior and Human Performance*, Vol. 32, No. 1, August, 1983, pp. 35–54.
4. Machiavelli, Niccolo. *Machiavelli: The Chief Works and Others*, ed. Allen Gilbert. Durham, N.C.: Duke University Press, 1964, p. 62.
5. Melcher, Arlyn J. "Participation: A Critical Review of Research Findings," *Human Resources Management*, Vol. 15, No. 2, Summer, 1976, p. 12.
6. Janis, Irving. *Victims of Groupthink*. Boston: Houghton Mifflin Company, 1972.
7. Fleishman, Edwin A., Edwin F. Harris, and Harold E. Burtt. *Leadership and Supervision in Industry: An Evaluation of a Supervisory Training Program*. Columbus: Ohio State University Press, 1955.
8. Blake, Robert R., and Jane S. Mouton. *The Managerial Grid III: A Key to Leadership Excellence*, 3rd ed. Houston: Gulf Publishing Company, Book Division, 1985, p. 12.
9. Jago, Arthur G., and Victor H. Vroom. "An Evaluation of Two Alternatives to the Vroom/Yetton Normative Model," *Academy of Management Journal*, Vol. 23, No. 2, June, 1980, pp. 347–355.
10. Howell, Jon P., and Peter W. Dorfman. "Substitutes for Leadership: Test of a Construct," *Academy of Management Journal*, Vol. 24, No. 4, December, 1981, pp. 714–728.
11. Larson, L. L., J. G. Hunt, and R. N. Osborn. "The Great High-High Leader Behavior Myth: A Lesson from Occam's Razor," *Academy of Management Journal*, Vol. 19, No. 4, December, 1976, pp. 628–641.

12. Blake and Mouton. *The Managerial Grid III: A Key to Leadership Excellence*, pp. ix–xi.

13. Fiedler, Fred E. "Validation and Extension of the Contingency Model of Leadership Effectiveness: A Review of Empirical Findings," *Psychological Bulletin*, Vol. 76, No. 2, 1971, pp. 129–148.

14. Fiedler, Fred E. "How Do You Make Leaders More Effective? New Answers to an Old Puzzle," *Organizational Dynamics*, Vol. 1, No. 1, Autumn, 1972, pp. 3–18.

15. Ford, Jeffrey D. "Departmental Context and Formal Structure as Constraints on Leader Behavior," *Academy of Management Journal*, Vol. 24, No. 2, June, 1981, pp. 274–288.

16. House, Robert J., and Terence R. Mitchell. "Path-Goal Theory of Leadership," *Journal of Contemporary Business*, Vol. 3, No. 4, Autumn, 1974, pp. 81–97.

17. House, Robert J., and G. Dressler. "The Path-Goal Theory of Leadership: Some Post Hoc and a Priori Tests" in *Contingency Approaches to Leadership*, eds. James G. Hunt and Lars L. Larson. Carbondale, Ill.: Southern Illinois University Press, 1974, pp. 29–55.

18. Stinson, John E., and Thomas W. Johnson. "The Path-Goal Theory of Leadership: A Partial Test and Suggested Refinement," *Academy of Management Journal*, Vol. 18, No. 2, June, 1975, pp. 242–252.

19. Downey, H. K., J. E. Sheridan, and J. W. Slocum, Jr. "Analysis of Relationships among Leader Behavior, Subordinate Job Performance and Satisfaction: A Path-Goal Approach," *Academy of Management Journal*, Vol. 18, No. 2, June, 1975, pp. 253–262.

20. Burack, Elmer H. "Leadership Findings and Applications: The Viewpoints of Four from the Real World—David Campbell, Joseph L. Moses, Paul J. Patinka, and Blanchard B. Smith" in *Crosscurrents in Leadership*, eds. James G. Hunt and Lars L. Larson. Carbondale, Ill.: Southern Illinois University Press, 1979, pp. 25–46.

21. Burns, James McGregor. *Leadership*. New York: Harper & Row Publishers, Inc., 1978, p. 34.

SUGGESTED READINGS

Adams, Jerome, Robert W. Rice, and Debra Instone. "Follower Attitudes Toward Women and Judgments Concerning Performance by Female and Male Leaders," *Academy of Management Journal*, Vol. 27, No. 3, 1984, pp. 636–643.

Griffin, Ricky W. "Task Design Determinants of Effective Leader Behavior," *Academy of Management Review*, Vol. 4, No. 2, April, 1979, pp. 215–224.

Hollander, Edwin P. *Leadership Dynamics: A Practical Guide to Effective Relationships*. New York: The Free Press, 1978.

Hunt, James G., and Lars L. Larson. *Leadership: The Cutting Edge*. Carbondale, Ill.: Southern Illinois University Press, 1977.

Jennings, Eugene Emerson. *An Anatomy of Leadership: Princes, Heroes, and Supermen.* New York: Harper & Row, Publishers, Inc., 1960.

Khandwalla, Pradip N. "Some Top Management Styles, Their Context and Performance," *Organization and Administrative Sciences,* Winter, 1976–1977, pp. 21–51.

McCall, Morgan W., Jr., and Michael M. Lombardo. *Leadership Where Else Can We Go?* Durham, N.C.: Duke University Press, 1978.

Miles, Robert H., and M. M. Petty. "Leader Effectiveness in Small Bureaucracies," *Academy of Management Journal,* June, 1977, pp. 238–250.

Peters, Thomas J. "Leadership: Sad Facts and Silver Linings," *Harvard Business Review,* November–December, 1979, pp. 164–172.

Podsakoff, Philip M., William D. Todor, and Randall S. Schuler. "Leader Expertise as a Moderator of the Effects of Instrumental and Supportive Leader Behaviors," *Journal of Management,* Vol. 9, No. 2, Fall–Winter, 1983, pp. 173–183.

Weihrich, Heinz. "How to Change a Leadership Pattern," *Management Review,* April, 1979, pp. 26–40.

17

Personal Characteristics, Managerial Effectiveness, and Organizational Culture

The great-man theory of leadership, a popular view of leadership throughout history, received new impetus during the psychological testing movement of the early twentieth century. In its simplest form, this theory states that effective leadership is best understood in terms of personal leadership traits—in terms of deep, enduring, relatively stable personality characteristics that collectively determine the extent of a person's influence on others.

The theory is, of course, incomplete. As we saw in the previous chapter, leadership effectiveness depends to a great extent on the compatibility between the leader's style and the situation's favorableness and between the leader's specific behaviors and the subordinate's specific perceptions of valence, instrumentality, and expectancy. The incompleteness of the great-man theory, however, does not negate its usefulness for all purposes. We will review in this chapter some personal characteristics that are conducive to managerial success across a broad range of situations and that may be useful in selecting and developing managers in these contexts. In addition, some characteristics of leaders affect the cultures of the organizations they lead, and cultures in turn affect performance.[1] For these reasons it is important to examine the personal dimensions of managerial effectiveness.

For several reasons it is important that individual characteristics be included in a study of managerial effectiveness. If certain personal characteristics (such as specific personality traits, aptitudes, acquired needs, attitudes and interests) enable some managers to be more effective than others, it is important that their impact in different environments be considered. To the extent that the personal characteristics of effective and ineffective leaders are different, they should be taken into consideration when selecting and promoting managers; and the implications of such differences for management development should be understood. Finally, if a leader's personal characteristics influence the behavior of subordinates and also other aspects of the organization's culture, it is important that we consider this in predicting and interpreting the behavior of people in organizations.

The specific objectives of Chapter 17 are

TO UNDERSTAND:

1. The importance of personal characteristics on leadership effectiveness

2. The problems involved in studying personal characteristics of leadership effectiveness

3. How certain personal characteristics relate to managerial effectiveness

4. The importance of the leader's creation of organizational culture

THE IMPORTANCE OF PERSONAL CHARACTERISTICS

Managerial effectiveness is contingent upon many variables; some are environmental, and some are personal. Although cautious interpretation is in order, research provides excellent insights into variables in both categories.

The contribution of personal characteristics to managerial effectiveness is strongly evidenced by research. After reviewing a number of published studies, John P. Campbell and his associates concluded that

Taken together, these studies provide good evidence that a fairly sizable portion (30 to 50 percent) of the variance in general managerial effectiveness can be expressed in terms of personal qualities measured by self-response tests and inventories and by predetermined rules or statistical equations.[2]

Ralph M. Stogdill, a recognized authority on leadership behavior, based the following statement on a thorough survey of published research studies in a variety of settings:

> It can be concluded that the clusters of characteristics listed above differentiate (1) leaders from followers, (2) effective from ineffective leaders, and (3) high-echelon from lower echelon leaders.[3]

Stogdill obviously goes beyond Fiedler by concluding that leadership, one of several complex behaviors of effective managers, can be partially accounted for by personal characteristics (for example, a strong drive for responsibility and task completion, self-confidence, willingness to tolerate frustration and delay, and so on).

Trait studies, while still conducted by reputable scholars, are only one of several ways of investigating the personal dimensions of leadership. One recent approach, concentrating solely on leadership traits or behaviors, focuses on how followers respond to leaders. Another new approach called **attribution theory** studies the explanations people give for why others behave as they do. It studies, for example, the motives that the followers attribute to leaders and the motives leaders attribute to followers. This attribution process is used as a basis for understanding leadership behavior and effectiveness.[4]

PERSONAL CHARACTERISTICS: PROBLEMS AND CONTINGENCIES

Personal characteristics influence managerial effectiveness in complex ways. They interact with one another and the situation to produce outcomes that lead to varying degrees of managerial effectiveness. It is only through an awareness of certain contingencies, certain "if-then" conditions, that the effect of personal characteristics can be understood.

An important issue in discussions of personal characteristics and managerial effectiveness is the extent to which the leadership of any one individual, even the chief executive, really makes a difference in the performance of large organizations. There is impressive evidence that the leadership of key individuals does make a difference in the performance of even large organizations, especially at critical points in the organization's life.[5,6]

It is useful to simplify burdensome and overly complicated theories and to avoid complex explanations when simple ones are effective. But oversimplification can be a problem, too. It can lead to shallow answers and to reliance upon rigidly held half-truths. Classical theorists erred in their quest for universally applicable principles of organization. Similarly, those who seek to enumerate the personal chracteristics of effective managers may generalize too far on the basis of too little knowledge. This section provides the background needed to avert such a possibility.

A Probability Frame of Reference

Although it would be convenient to specify the amount of a given characteristic (say, an IQ of 125) required for effectiveness in a particular managerial position, this is not possible. At best, we can define the position and make a statement concerning the probability that a given characteristic will contribute to a manager's effectiveness in it.

In the best studies of managerial effectiveness, a statistical relationship is established between a measurement of a characteristic (say, intelligence) and one or more criteria of success (performance evaluations or promotions, for example); that is, statistics are used to show what effect intelligence has on performance evaluations or promotions. Only in extreme cases, however, can a specific amount of a certain characteristic be regarded as necessary for effective performance. The more cautious and realistic approach is to conclude that individuals with a given characteristic have a higher probability of success than those who lack it.

The relationship between measurements of personal characteristics and measurements of success may be graphically expressed in the form of an expectancy chart (Figure 17-1). The ratings referred to in this illustration were obtained in off-the-job assessment centers designed to evaluate managerial potential.[7] On the basis of their combined ratings on a number of personal characteristics, the managers in this study were divided into four categories (see the left column of Figure 17-1). Note the tendency for managers with high ratings to rank high on the success criterion (managers receiving two or more promotions). Statistical tests indicate that the differences shown in Figure 17-1 would occur by chance less often than one time in 1,000. Individuals rated more than acceptable in terms of their personal characteristics are twice as likely to receive two or more promotions as those rated acceptable, and they are almost ten times more likely to meet the promotion criterion than those rated not acceptable. In the Bell System (AT&T), personal characteristics are clearly related to success.

One of the most extensive studies of the relationship between personal characteristics and managerial effectiveness was conducted by the

Composite Ratings of Personal Characteristics	Number of Assessees	Percentage Receiving Two or More Promotions								
		0	5	10	15	20	25	30	35	40	45
1. More than acceptable	410	40.5%								
2. Acceptable	1,466	21.9%								
3. Questionable	1,910	11.5%								
4. Not acceptable	2,157	4.2%								

Source: Joseph L. Moses, "Assessment Center Performance and Management Progress," *Studies in Personnel Psychology*, Vol. 4, No. 1, Spring, 1972, p. 9. (The data in this study were collected from 8,885 participants in the Bell System Personnel Assessment Center from 1961–1970.)

FIGURE 17-1 The Expectancy Chart Method of Relating Personal Characteristics to Managerial Success

Standard Oil Company of New Jersey.[8] The 443 managers who participated in the study held a variety of line and staff positions. Psychological test scores and background information were used as indicators of personal characteristics. These were correlated with three measures of managerial effectiveness: position level, salary history, and effectiveness rankings. When the composite personal characteristics scores were related to an overall success index, approximately half (49 percent) of the variation in managerial effectiveness was related to personal characteristics as measured in the study.

The Ambiguous Managerial Position

One way to increase the precision with which characteristics of effective managers are isolated is to single out a particular kind of manager for study. The president of General Motors is a manager, but so is the president-owner of Dameron's Delicatessen. It is unlikely that the ideal profile for the two managers is the same. The manufacturing supervisor, quality control superintendent, director of personnel, office supervisor, and chief engineer are all managers; and individuals who succeed in these positions may have certain characteristics in common. On the other hand, certain qualities are unique to each category. For example, successful office supervisors ordinarily need more detailed technical knowledge about processes and methods than do higher level line managers. The higher managers progress, the greater is their need for the ability to plan, organize, and make complex decisions.

Often managers are tritely defined as people who achieve objectives through the efforts of others. While this definition is appropriate in most cases, it does not allow for the fact that both line and staff managers spend much time performing nonmanagerial work. Because there are many different kinds of managers performing a variety of duties, one must be cautious in generalizing about managerial characteristics. The generalizations in this chapter will refer primarily to line managers above the supervisory level—to individuals who have responsibility for achieving organizational objectives through other people as well as for performing a variety of other tasks.

Problems in the Measurement of Managerial Effectiveness

One of the problems in isolating characteristics of effective managers is that research studies must somehow define and measure managerial effectiveness. Many measures of effectiveness have been used, such as performance evaluations, number of promotions during a specific period, level achieved in the management hierarchy, and salary. Virtually any criterion used is subject to some form of bias, although in recent years most researchers have made serious attempts to use meaningful and reliable criteria.

In discussing criteria, the terms *success* and *effectiveness* are used interchangeably. However, managers often succeed (that is, receive raises and promotions), because of political skills that may have little to do with their other abilities needed to perform effectively. Another factor that calls for caution in using promotion and salary as indicators of effectiveness is the element of luck. Successful managers create part of their so-called luck, but some of it is due to the chance factor of being in the right place at the right time. Managers who are fortunate enough to begin their careers under superiors who are highly promotable and excellent models and who are committed to the development of subordinate managers may succeed while other managers with comparable personal qualities fail or achieve only marginal success.

One study shows that managers considered promotable are significantly more aware of their superiors' views than are nonpromotable managers.[9] This could be the result of a manager's unusual empathy and perceptiveness, or it could result from a unique opportunity to observe one's superiors.

The Effect of Compensating Characteristics

Isolating the differentiating characteristics of effective managers is complicated by the fact that an individual always functions as a whole. Characteristics do not exist in isolation. Rather, they constantly interact with each other. Even though a manager lacks one desirable characteristic, strength in another area compensates for the deficiency and results in effective overall performance.

The effect of compensation is clearly operating in the following example taken from the senior author's assessment files (the name is, of course, fictitious):

Charles Clark functions effectively as the production manager of a manufacturing firm of about 300 employees despite the fact that his IQ is in a range where one would normally predict failure. His IQ is about average for the first line supervisors in that company and considerably below the average IQ of the other managers at Clark's level.

Although Clark is not known for his brilliance, he is respected, and he performs satisfactorily because of other outstanding qualities. He works extremely long hours, and through much effort he keeps abreast of advancements in his field. His common sense judgment is high, his human relations skills are outstanding, and he is methodical and organized. He is secure enough to hire technical advisers who are much better problem solvers than he is, and he delegates effectively. His predecessor, who had been a brilliant engineering student and a highly creative and analytical technical expert, failed miserably, in spite of his superior mental ability, because he related poorly to people. The intellectual abilities of Clark's predecessor failed to compensate for a lack of human relations skills.

Even though some compensation occurs, certain characteristics typically contribute to success. A success-related characteristic does not ensure success, nor does its absence always lead to failure. Its presence or absence does, however, affect the probability of success.

SELECTED CORRELATES OF MANAGERIAL EFFECTIVENESS

Since situational demands differ, it is not possible to describe personal characteristics that are critically important in all managerial positions. It is, however, possible to describe personal characteristics that significantly contribute to success in most managerial positions.

How many personal characteristics are related to managerial effectiveness? Too many factors are involved for this question to be answered definitively. For example, research studies show varying degrees of correlation between characteristics and effectiveness, and no one can say exactly how large a correlation must be to be considered important or practically significant. Another problem arises from the fact that researchers may use different terms to refer to essentially the same characteristic. Still another consideration is the fact that many of the personal characteristics which correlate with managerial effectiveness also correlate with one another. Decisiveness and self-confidence, for example, are overlapping concepts because self-confident managers are more likely to be decisive than are managers whose self-confidence is low. It is likely that studies which list more than, say, ten to twelve personal characteristics do so only because statistical analyses have not been performed to eliminate the inevitable overlapping of personal characteristics.

No attempt is made in this chapter to present an exhaustive discussion of personal characteristics of effective managers, nor is any claim made that those presented are independent of one another. They are, however, representative of the characteristics most often found to relate to managerial effectiveness.

Superior Mental Ability

Although mental ability (intelligence) does not always differentiate the various levels of effectiveness within management, research shows that effective managers are usually characterized by superior intelligence.[10,11] In addition, since it is virtually impossible today for a manager to succeed in most organizations without a college education, and since earning a degree typically screens out people who are average and below in intelligence, it is understandable that superior intelligence is required to compete within the ranks of management.[12]

Some studies have shown little correlation between managerial performance and the intelligence of present managers. The reason for this is usually obvious. If high intelligence is one criterion for selecting managers, all managers within an organization will be so much alike in this characteristic that differences are masked by differences in motivation, work habits, leadership behavior, and other success-related characteristics. If management were represented by the full spectrum of intellectual abilities, the correlation between intelligence and success would be extremely high. Those with below average intelligence would most certainly fail, those near the mean would very likely fail, and most of the successes would be considerably above the average category. As Figure

17-2 shows, within the relatively narrow spectrum of intelligence where most managers are found, other factors tend to mask out the average effect of intelligence on performance. However, all else being equal, higher intelligence gives a manager a competitive advantage, at least to a point.

Although space does not permit a detailed discussion of the nature of intelligence, it is noteworthy that it consists of a number of inter-related aptitudes such as ability to learn, practical judgment, and verbal, quantitative, and abstract reasoning. Because an overall IQ consists of different components, two managers with IQs of, say, 120 points are not necessarily equivalent; and different strengths are important in different managerial positions (for example, high quantitative reasoning is especially desirable for financial executives but is less important for personnel and sales executives). Because of the practical nature of business organizations, a high degree of practical judgment or common-sense reasoning is desirable in all managerial positions.

Emotional Maturity

Effective managers often have a fear of failure because they continue to accept challenges that require peak performance. However, since the fear is a natural and realistic function of the risk involved in such a life-style, they should not be considered fearful people. Effective managers are basically self-confident and free from fears, anxiety, and guilt feelings that are capable of interfering with performance. Self-confidence, viewed from the context of expectancy theory, is closely associated with the perceived probability of successfully exercising influence. It is an important component of motivation and a determinant of whether a manager will attempt to exercise influence in leadership and decision situations.[13]

Emotional maturity is expressed in many characteristics of effective managers. They tend to perceive themselves in a favorable light (to have a positive self-image), and their perceptions of reality have a minimum of distortion because of emotional needs and ego-defensiveness. Although their aspirations and self-expectations continue to increase as

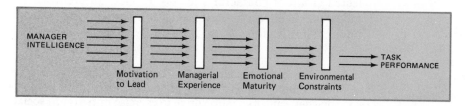

FIGURE 17-2 Factors Influencing the Application of Intelligence

goals are reached, effective managers generally have realistic expectations for themselves and others.

Characteristic of mature individuals, effective managers have a sense of purpose and meaning in life. They have sometimes been described as possessing a **strong self-structure**. This means that they know who they are, where they are going, and how they are going to get there. This appears to be more a function of decision making about oneself than a result of philosophizing, reasoning, and extensive self-analysis. It is associated with decisiveness, self-confidence, practicality, and with a desire to avoid excessive speculation and get on with the task of achievement.

Contrary to popular opinion, successful managers do not tend to be ulcer prone. This condition is more characteristic of the harried, frustrated manager whose career has been blocked by personal characteristics or external circumstances. Top managers tend to be highly resistant to the stresses of business life in spite of long hours of work and continual problem-solving activity. They are not prone to engage in escape activity, such as excessive drinking, drug use, problem avoidance, rationalization, and poorly planned job changing. The incidence of divorce and other family problems is no higher for successful managers than for the general population.

Leadership Characteristics

From the discussion to this point it should be obvious that the personal aspects of managerial effectiveness are not confined to leadership characteristics. Intelligence and emotional maturity, for example, may correlate just as highly with success in medicine and engineering as in business and for the same reasons. Managing, however, uniquely involves leading; and, despite the difficulties involved in personality measurement and trait theory, we have every reason to believe that personality characteristics do affect managerial effectiveness and, specifically, the manager's ability to influence others.

After comparing a 1948 survey of leadership characteristics with 163 studies conducted between 1948 and 1970, Stogdill concluded that a selected group of characteristics do, in fact, differentiate (1) leaders from followers, (2) effective from ineffective leaders, and (3) high-echelon from low-echelon leaders.

> The leader is characterized by a strong drive for responsibility and task completion, vigor and persistence in pursuit of goals, venturesomeness and originality, drive to exercise initiative in social situations, self-confidence and a sense of personal identity, willingness to accept

consequences of decisions and actions, readiness to absorb interpersonal stress, willingness to tolerate frustration and delay, ability to influence behavior, and capacity to structure social interaction systems to the purpose at hand.[14]

These characteristics are obviously intercorrelated; and they also overlap some of the other characteristics discussed in this chapter, particularly motivation. In view of the global nature of leadership, however, this should be expected. Some writers prefer to use the term *supervisory qualities* rather than leadership characteristics (or traits), presumably to avoid having to deal with the fact that leadership behavior is expressed in an unusually wide variety of situations, managerial and otherwise, and is therefore a difficult term to define.[15]

One personal quality that contributes to leadership skills is **empathy**. It relates to one's ability to understand the needs and motives of others—to place oneself in another's shoes and become aware of how he or she thinks, perceives, and feels. This is a quality in which people differ greatly, depending on early life experiences. **Impact**, or a term defined essentially the same way, is another leadership-related characteristic measured in many studies. Appearance, self-image, friendliness, the projection of a favorable self-image, and motivation to be attractive to others are all related to this characteristic. Too often an assumption is made that such qualities are inborn or that they are otherwise beyond the control of the individual manager. Neither assumption is altogether valid, and both are counterproductive for the manager who would like to be more effective.[16]

Problem-Solving Skills

Effective managers are problem solvers rather than problem avoiders. They accept problems as a challenge and as an opportunity to prove their superiority and worthiness for advancement. This ability is, first of all, related to motivation. Effective problem solvers have learned, often early in life, that solving problems is rewarding. Without this motivation, effectiveness is likely to be minimal because of the risk involved. Problem solving requires more than application of analytical skills, although this is important. For line managers, it also involves the high-risk behavior of making decisions and taking action (which may or may not be successful).

Problem solving may also involve the unpopular action of defining and attacking a problem at a time when other managers prefer to close their eyes to its existence or when they disagree concerning its nature and solution. This means that problem solvers are often irritants and boat rockers. To live with such an image, they must be self-confident and at times have an exceedingly thick skin.

Problem-solving ability is related to a number of other individual characteristics, among which are the possession of relevant knowledge, goal direction, creativity, decisiveness, intelligence, emotional maturity, and optimism regarding the likelihood that one's efforts will be successful. Relevant knowledge is not synonymous with formal education. At times it relates to information—about people, processes, products, and the like—that can be acquired only through practical experience over a long period of time. The higher managers progress, the broader their knowledge must be in order to obtain a grasp of overall organizational problems and to make decisions which will not have adverse, unforeseen implications for seemingly unrelated parts of the organization.

Decisiveness, an important aspect of problem-solving skills, has at least two major components: (1) the self-confidence to take reasonable and calculated risks and (2) a strong self-structure. The former is important to the problem solver because decisions sometimes result in failure, and a manager must be able to live with that ever-present possibility. The manager who experiences failure as defeat and humiliation will ordinarily value safety more highly than achievement and may therefore be controlled by excessive cautiousness in decision making. In contrast, the manager who views failure as an opportunity to learn from experience can afford to be decisive.

The role of a strong self-structure in decisiveness is associated with the fact that people who have made decisions about themselves possess internalized standards against which decisions may be made effortlessly. Consider, for example, two controllers who have an opportunity to embezzle a large sum of money. The one who has already made the firm decision not to be a thief can be decisive. The decision is made in an instant but without impulsiveness. In contrast, the controller with a poor commitment to standards of personal morality may struggle with the decision for months and, after making it, have serious questions about whether it was the right decision.

Personal Organization

People differ greatly in the extent to which they feel comfortable in a chaotic, disorderly environment. Some of these differences are deeply embedded in personality and are difficult to change; others are related more to habit or training and can be modified with relative ease. Managers with a deep need to impose order and system on chaotic situations are more likely than others to learn effective organizational techniques, to feel comfortable with the structure of complex organizations, and to systematize their work in ways which enable them to handle a wide variety of duties. Managers who prefer an unstructured life-style often feel boxed-in and overcontrolled by the employing organization and require special assistance in handling their organizing functions.

Personal organization involves more than the formalities of such activities as defining jobs, establishing procedures, and delegating authority. It affects one's ability to use time efficiently, to set priorities, to establish controls, and to manage by objectives. The issue of managerial effectiveness hinges on the question of whether a manager will organize with the aid of a sensitive, intuitive feel for the activity or whether dependency must be placed primarily on an intellectual understanding of when and how to organize. The so-called natural-born manager is a myth; but the nearest thing to such a manager is the individual whose early training and personality development provide an intuitive grasp of the managerial functions of organizing, deciding, and motivating subordinates to reach organizational goals.

Communication Skills

The ability to communicate orally and in writing is highly correlated with managerial success. Line managers spend most of their time in some kind of communication: directing, informing, report writing, listening, and attempting to persuade.

The practical nature of business students often detracts from the task of learning some of the basic skills of communication. Many think that such academic pursuits as learning to spell, to write grammatically correct sentences, or to perform as a fluent public speaker will contribute little to their success. This is far from realistic. Aside from the need to make one's ideas known and to be sensitive to what others are trying to say, communication ability is one of the primary means by which others decide whether a manager is educated or uneducated, knowledgeable or ignorant, brilliant or dull. To some extent these judgments may be unfair and unrealistic; but they are made, and they affect both the promotability and the effectiveness of the manager.

Students of management often play down the importance of spelling and grammar on the assumption (or rationalization) that as managers they will have secretaries to worry about such trivia. But in the real world there is always the question of who will catch the secretary's errors. In addition, the aspiring manager whose vocabulary is limited and whose grammar is poor cannot avoid displaying this limitation in conversations and meetings with superiors.

The ability to communicate is, of course, more complex than the mastery of speaking and writing skills. Empathy is an important dimension of communication in that it contributes a sensitivity to the needs and motives of the persons with whom one proposes to communicate.

Empathy provides cues concerning the appropriate times to speak and to listen; and it enables one to sense the meaning of nonverbal cues expressed in voice inflections, gestures, eye contact, and body movements. The empathic manager has an awareness of the importance of timing. Often it is when and how one speaks rather than what one says that determines the effectiveness of communication.

Finally, the ability to communicate involves trust. Whether a given communication is viewed with skepticism, doubt, interest, or acceptance may be more a result of who makes a statement than what is said or how it is said. This accounts in part for the fact that some managers whose language skills are minimal achieve a relatively high level of success. Because they are trusted and have a reputation for dependability, they succeed in spite of their inadequacy. There is always the possibility, however, that their success would be even greater were it not for the language deficiency.

Personal Integrity

In recent years many managers have been severely criticized for taking and giving bribes, making illegal political contributions, fixing prices, and a host of other behaviors which suggest a generalized character flaw. In many instances such behavior has led to sweeping attacks on the integrity of managers as a group, as though the role itself demands moral compromise, lack of concern for others, and a selfish, manipulative lifestyle.

Although there are obviously large numbers of business managers (as well as leaders in government, schools, churches, and other institutions) who lack personal integrity, such behavior is not typical of effective managers. In most organizations managers who tell the truth, operate within the law, and have a genuine sense of concern for the well-being of others are more likely to be effective and successful than are those whose word must be questioned, who are prone to behave unethically, and who are concerned only with self-gain.

To function effectively, organizations require a high degree of predictability. Managers must be able to trust one another and relate to employees in ways that create trust and respect. These qualities are equally important as managers relate to customers, suppliers, bankers, government, and the general public. If there were no more compelling reason than expediency, effectiveness in management would favor persons with character and integrity.

As a matter of fact, business managers often prove to be among the most responsible leaders in civic, religious, and charitable organizations, and evidence does not support the notion that such activities are motivated solely by business interests. Participation in such organizations is quite common among managers who are already successful, as well as among those who have humanitarian or religious values and seek a deeper level of expression than their work permits. It is significant that, when managers themselves describe the characteristics of effective managers, fairness and integrity are among the descriptive terms most often mentioned.[17]

Motivational Patterns

Effective managers are highly motivated and have a high activity level. Research shows that effective managers are motivated by achievement (i.e., by an intrinsic satisfaction in overcoming obstacles, achieving objectives, and seeing the fruits of their efforts) and by a need for power.[18]

The need for power may be fulfilled by the satisfaction a manager receives from controlling great amounts of wealth, making important and difficult decisions, and directing the activities of other people. It is also expressed in a seemingly insatiable desire for upward mobility and increased personal income. The latter are typically related to the manager's contribution to organizational growth and profits. It is not surprising that managers who contribute significantly to these goals are appropriately rewarded.

These motivations stand in sharp contrast to the motives of many who are less effective in the managerial role. Prominent among the latter are managers with a high affiliation need. This strong need for approval, nurturance, support, and friendship clashes with the necessity for making objective personnel decisions and for taking a courageous but unpopular stand on issues perceived as vital to organizational success. Effective managers need to have a genuine concern for people, but they cannot afford to be too dependent on the approval of others. Power gives independence and enables a manager to be effective in doing what must be done without being crushed by the pressures with which a decision maker must cope on a daily basis.

A high level of motivation and energy are vital to the manager with high aspirations because the work is often difficult, the hours are long, the pressures are intense, and the risks are great. Managers who cease to receive promotions before their full potential is reached often do so because they consciously or unconsciously prefer the relative comfort of a secure position to the conflict involved in the continuing struggle upward. In short, their success is less than it could be because of a lack of motivation. This is often a good choice for the individual and may benefit the organization since there is a limited number of positions at the top of the pyramid. Managers may function effectively long after their success, as measured by promotions, has leveled off.

Administrative Skills

Administrative skills is a catch-all term. Like leadership, it is correlated with other characteristics discussed in this chapter. As used here, it involves activities such as the following:

1. Developing techniques for paper flow, such as correspondence and interoffice memoranda, and for performing other routine office functions that cannot be delegated.

2. Developing organizational policies, procedures, and controls without introducing unnecessary red tape.

3. Organizing, planning, and clarifying organizational objectives.

4. Coordinating a variety of seemingly unrelated functions to enable the organization to function as a whole, integrated unit rather than as a conglomeration of disconnected parts.

5. Conducting meetings that efficiently achieve their objectives.

These skills can be learned and, therefore, are often related to the length and quality of a manager's experience. Yet there are great differences in the speed and thoroughness with which they are learned, and there is no guarantee that a manager will profit from experience. Some managers, for example, with long years of experience still cannot handle their correspondence. They shuffle papers back and forth from one side of their desk to the other, procrastinating, questioning, waiting, and hoping that problems—especially the morass of trivial problems—will somehow go away.

The manner in which one unusually effective executive handles correspondence illustrates how managers develop guidelines to ensure their own efficiency. After months of frustration over a mounting volume of incoming mail, the executive established a rule: Read a piece of correspondence only one time. Some exceptions must be made, but basically the rule is effective. Instead of placing a letter in a stack to be reread and answered later, the executive dictates a response, sends it to a subordinate for information or for answering, decides it is unworthy of an answer, or disposes of it in some other way. A "hold file" is used for items chosen to be ignored unless a further communication requires that action be taken. Periodically the bottom half of the file is destroyed.

This executive also leaves instructions not to be disturbed while correspondence is being answered except for genuine emergencies. These techniques may be unworkable for another manager, but they are a good example of the way an effective manager establishes mastery over one worrisome administrative problem. Simple as this problem appears to be, some managers never learn to handle it effectively.

THE DEVELOPMENT OF MANAGERIAL ABILITY

Personal characteristics that contribute to managerial effectiveness are, for the most part, subject to modification. One important attribute of effective managers is a motivation to develop themselves in ways that will contribute to increased personal effectiveness.

Scientists have long debated and researched the question of the relative contributions of heredity, environment, and individual initiative to the formation of personal characteristics. Actually all three are important.

Heredity establishes limits within which mental ability, for example, may develop. Some people lack the genetic background to learn and reason at a level necessary for managerial work or for the education it requires. Still, it is evident that a favorable environment influences the degree to which one's hereditary potential is actualized. Regardless of background, any normal person has the potential to become a more effective learner—for example, by learning how to concentrate more intensely, by developing better study habits, and by improving reading skills. People can learn how to think more analytically by using appropriate mathematical and qualitative decision models. Hereditary potential which has remained dormant during childhood and adolescence because of a lack of opportunity or motivation can often be actualized in adulthood as an individual experiences a strong need for abilities and skills in order to achieve career objectives and otherwise meet personal needs. The notion that mental abilities are unalterably fixed by heredity has long been rejected by competent researchers. This fact has far-reaching implications for the development of managerial abilities during adulthood, particularly abilities which relate to decision making.

Both mental abilities and personality characteristics are resistant to change. They are especially resistant when one person aspires to effect a change in another—when, for example, a manager wants to change a hypersensitive subordinate into one who can make tough decisions about people without worrying excessively about losing their approval. When, on the other hand, the subordinate with such a problem is intensely motivated to make the change, he or she can often find the means for doing so. The change may occur only after many painful experiences and a gradual process of densensitization through insight, perceptual modification, and growth in self-confidence. Nevertheless, changes in managers' personality and ability do occur, enabling them to assume increasing levels of responsibility as their careers unfold.

Since vocational decisions often are little more than chance happenings, many lower level managerial positions are filled by individuals whose personality characteristics are poorly suited for their work. This is especially true of managers with (1) an unusually strong need for the approval of others, (2) low tolerance for withstanding work pressures, (3) poor insight into the needs and motives of others, (4) a tendency to make poor decisions (for whatever reason), and (5) low motivation and/or ability to influence the behavior of others. Such individuals are handicapped and often find that the changes necessary for managerial effectiveness are too unnatural and painful to be worthwhile. In such cases, a switch to another career field is usually advisable. As noted in Chapter 14, many techniques are available through which management development can occur. A critical point in formulating a development plan is that, even when personality characteristics are the principal cause of ineffective behaviors, managers should concentrate on goal-directed behavior change rather than on personality change. Appropriate personality changes will follow if they are needed to give a subjective feeling of self-consistency.

LEADERSHIP AND ORGANIZATIONAL CULTURE

Organizational culture is the set of basic assumptions that a group has invented, discovered, or developed in working toward its goals and that have worked well enough to be considered valid and to be taught to new members as the correct way to perceive, think, and feel in relation to the group's goal-directed efforts.[19] The group's leaders exert an important influence on these assumptions through their communications and behaviors.

Importance of Organizational Culture

It seems reasonable to believe that an organization's culture is important. But important for what? One answer to this question is important for those who are choosing organizations in which to work. If organizational culture is a "set of basic assumptions," it seems important for job-seekers to consider whether these assumptions are congruent (or at least not in conflict) with their own values or perceptions. Some independent people might not want to be taught "the correct way to perceive, think, and feel" in relation to anything. On the other hand, the overall cultures of most organizations are compatible with the goals of the larger society;[20] and in fact they may differ from organization to organization much less than is commonly believed.[21] What does seem to vary is the intensity of the culture.

> The excellent companies are marked by very strong cultures, so strong that you either buy into their norms or get out. There's no halfway house for most people in the excellent companies. One very able consumer marketing executive told us, "You know, I deeply admire Procter & Gamble. They are the best in the business. But I don't think I could ever work there." She was making the same point that Adam Myerson at *The Wall Street Journal* had in mind when he urges us to write an editorial around the theme: "Why we wouldn't want to work for one of our excellent companies." The cultures that make meanings for so many repel others.[22]

Another response to the question of why organizational culture is important concerns organizational effectiveness. In their widely read book *In Search of Excellence*, Peters and Waterman state that

> Without exception, the dominance and coherence of culture proved to be an essential quality of the excellent companies. Moreover, the stronger the culture and the more it was directed toward the marketplace, the less need was there for policy manuals, organization charts, or detailed procedures and rules. In these companies, people way down the line know what they are supposed to do in most situations because the handful of guiding values is crystal clear. One of our colleagues is working with a big company recently thrown together out of a series of mergers. He says: "You know, the problem is every decision is being made for the first time. The top people are inundated with trivia because there are no cultural norms."
>
> By contrast, the shared values in the excellent companies are clear, in large measure, because the mythology is rich. Everyone at Hewlett-Packard knows that he or she is supposed to be innovative. Everyone at Procter & Gamble knows that product quality is the *sine qua non*. In his book about P&G, *Eyes on Tomorrow*, Oscar Schisgall observes: "They speak of business integrity, of fair treatment of employees. 'Right from the start,' said the late Richard R. Deupree when he was chief

executive officer, 'William Procter and James Gamble realized that the interests of the organization and its employees were inseparable. That has never been forgotten.' "[23]

On the other hand, Edgar Schein, one of the leading authorities on organizational culture, reminds us that

> It is very important to recognize that cultural strength may or may not be correlated with effectiveness. Though some current writers have argued that strength is desirable, it seems clear to me that the relationship is far more complex. The actual content of the culture and the degree to which its solutions fit the problems posed by the environment seem like the critical variables here, not strength. One can hypothesize that young groups strive for culture strength as a way of creating an identity for themselves, but older groups may be more effective with a weak total culture and diverse subcultures to enable them to be responsive to rapid environmental change.[24]

In addition:

> Poorer performing companies often have strong cultures, too, but dysfunctional ones. They are usually focused on internal politics rather than on the customer, or they focus on "the numbers" rather than on the product and the people who make and sell it. The top companies, on the other hand, always seem to recognize what the companies that set only financial targets don't know or don't deem important. The excellent companies seem to understand that every man seeks meaning (not just the top fifty who are "in the bonus pool").[25]

Clearly, organizational culture is important—important to us as individuals working in an organization and important to organizations seeking to create common and desirable perspectives among its members. These perspectives, of course, influence the behavior of the organization's members; and this in turn influences the organization's effectiveness.

Leadership and the Development of Organizational Culture

Organizational cultures, as noted in the opening sentences of this section, are learned. In small organizations, they appear to be heavily influenced by the interactive style of the manager, as this style influences the attitudes, beliefs, and behavior of subordinates.[26] In both small and large organizations they are also shaped by the imagery created by the leader:

> Andrew Pettigrew sees the process of shaping culture as the prime management role: "The (leader) not only creates the rational and tangible aspects of organisations, such as structure and technology, but also is the creator of symbols, ideologies, language, beliefs, rituals, and myths." Using strikingly similar language, Joanne Martin of Stanford thinks of organizations as "systems composed of ideas, the meaning of which must be managed." Martin has spurred a great deal of practical, specific research that indicates the degree to which rich networks of legends and parables of all sorts pervade top-performing institutions. Hewlett-Packard, IBM, and Digital Equipment Corporation are three of her favorite examples. The research also indicates that the poor performers are relatively barren in this dimension.[27]

The effect of the leader's interactive style and imagery is, of course, most pronounced if the leader is the organization's founder.[28]

One of the greatest challenges a leader can encounter is the need to make a radical change in an organization's culture, since by their very nature cultures are learned, basic assumptions and must therefore be unlearned. In what will undoubtedly be viewed as a historic event in the history of management, this challenge was successfully met by the top leaders of American Telephone and Telegraph (AT&T) during the early 1980s. Prior to the federal government's requirement for AT&T to separate its various companies (Bell Laboratories for research, Western Electric for manufacturing, and Bell Telephone for both local and long-distance service), and to enable other long-distance carriers to use its phone lines, AT&T had a clearly identifiable culture.

> To understand Bell's culture, one must understand that it evolved in a precise way to directly support the corporate mission: achieving universal service *in a regulated environment*. Everything related to culture was affected: the kind of people Bell companies hired, their shared value system, and the infrastructure of processes to run the business. For most of this century, Bell System people believed that the surest way to achieve universal service was to manage the entire telecommunications system "end-to-end" as a single entity, with both vertical and horizontal integration. (Within this context, universal service meant the design and implementation of a pricing structure that would enable everyone to afford a telephone.)
>
> These two driving forces—the goal of universal service and the concept of end-to-end responsibility—shaped the network, guided Bell Laboratories' technology, permeated Western Electric's manufacturing, forged

operational methods and practices, and even influenced the depreciation schedules. Equally important, these forces fashioned a corporate culture that was entirely congruent with the corporate mission.[29]

After AT&T was forced to compete for customers on a price basis, its long-time culture had to undergo a severe and rapid change. Clearly universal service and end-to-end responsibility could no longer be its driving forces. In addition, somehow the concept of a market-driven environment had to enter the thinking and therefore the culture of the organization. It appears that the cultural change is being achieved successfully, but in some instances managers themselves have been unable to adapt and have had to be replaced.[30] This highlights the interesting fact that the learning of an organizational culture often requires the unlearning of a previous culture.

IMPORTANT TERMS AND CONCEPTS

attribution theory   empathy
strong self-structure   impact

STUDY AND DISCUSSION QUESTIONS

1. Why is it less difficult to isolate characteristics of successful managers than characteristics of leaders?

2. Why is it important that a probability frame of reference be assumed in order to understand the relationship between personal characteristics and managerial effectiveness?

3. In the Standard Oil of New Jersey study, 49 percent of the variance in managerial effectiveness was accounted for by personal characteristics. What is most likely to account for the remaining 51 percent of the differences in effectiveness?

4. What is the meaning and significance of compensation as the term is used in this chapter?

5. Two managers are highly motivated to succeed, have excellent formal educations, are high in leadership abilities, and have equally favorable environments within which to manage. Their levels of effectiveness, however, differ greatly. What might account for these differences?

6. Why are differences in the intelligence of managers often not related to differences in performance?

7. Why do effective and successful managers experience less stress than do lower level managers of the same age and experience?

8. A high level of motivation to succeed is an important determinant of whether a manager will be successful. Why would this be especially true of managerial versus nonmanagerial employees?

9. Explain and evaluate the idea that managers whose personalities interfere with their success should concentrate on changing their behavior rather than their personalities.

10. Make a list of reasons that a strong organizational culture might not be associated with organizational success.

CRITICAL INCIDENT

VALUES, CULTURE, AND CREDIBILITY

Apollo Products, a computer software company with 100 employees, was founded by Jason Jenkins in 1976. Its early products met with a good market response, and the company prospered and grew rapidly.

Jenkins, as majority owner, had also prospered, but he had not lost sight of the values that were part of his Iowa farm background. These included a strong sense of "right and wrong," a firm adherence to the Protestant work ethic, and a belief that loyalty was an important virtue.

These values reflected themselves in his management style. Jenkins personally interviewed all prospective employees and questioned them concerning their values. He asked the employees whether or not they felt they "would be comfortable working in a company that goes beyond what is normal business practice in maintaining a reputation for personal and professional integrity, a concern for people and at the same time a concern for productivity, and a sense of loyalty to the company and its customers." Once hired, never fired was a slogan that Jenkins took to heart, and he was inevitably able to turn around employees whose performance or behavior was leading to conflict with their supervisors or co-workers. When at one point in the company's early history a major customer defaulted on a large, scheduled payment, Jenkins personally borrowed the necessary funds needed to maintain the wages and jobs of his employees, using his home as collateral for the loan.

Jenkins decided in 1984 to hire an experienced chief operating officer to run Apollo. "The company's gotten too big for a farm boy," he joked with friends, "and besides I'm ready to take on something new in life." After some months, he hired Karen Potter, a woman with a good record in mid-level positions in two medium-size software companies.

Potter had been on the job for two months when Jenkins dropped into her office looking a bit disturbed. After a few minutes of discussing sales and cash flows, Jenkins got to the point.

> Karen, overall I think you've been doing a good job, and other people think so, too. But a few things are bothering me, and I want to tell you what they are. One is that you've evidently decided not to interview the new people being brought in. I can understand that—we're looking at so many people you probably don't have time—but neither have you told the managers who are doing the interviewing to focus on the values of the new people as well as on their technical qualifications. The second concern I have follows from the company meeting you held on Monday. You gave a lot of facts and figures but made no mention of the company's character and how maintaining this character is essential to our long-term success in the marketplace. I know that you are a good person in every sense of that phrase, but I think it's important for a leader to send out clear and frequent messages about important values. Otherwise, people forget.

After a moment's reflection, Potter replied:

> I'd like to think about this and then have a talk with you about it. I can say one thing though—I'm simply not much good at preaching. If I try to say the things you've been saying all these years, they won't ring true. I won't sound credible, and we'd lose more than we'd gain.

1. What positive and negative results do you think Jenkins' value-related actions may have achieved in the early years of Apollo's life?

2. Besides the one he mentioned, what other reasons might account for Potter not communicating the ideas that Jenkins is suggesting she should have?

3. How can this issue be handled by the parties involved?

REFERENCES

1. Peters, Thomas J., and Robert H. Waterman. *In Search of Excellence: Lessons from America's Best-Run Companies.* New York: Harper & Row Publishers, Inc., 1982.

2. Campbell, John P. et al. *Managerial Behavior, Performance and Effectiveness.* New York: McGraw-Hill Book Company, 1970, p. 195.

3. Stogdill, Ralph M. *Handbook of Leadership: A Survey of Theory and Research.* New York: The Free Press, 1974, p. 81.

4. Green, Stephen G., and Terence R. Mitchell. "Attribution Process of Leaders in Leader-Member Interactions," *Organizational Behavior and Human Performance,* Vol. 23, No. 3, June, 1979, pp. 429–458.

5. Kimberly, John R. "Issues in the Creation of Organizations: Initiation, Innovation, and Institutionalization," *Academy of Management Journal,* Vol. 22, No. 3, September, 1979, pp. 437–457.

6. Weiner, Nan, and Thomas A. Mahoney. "A Model of Corporate Performance as a Function of Environmental, Organizational, and Leadership Influences," *Academy of Management Journal,* Vol. 24, No. 3, September, 1981, pp. 452–470.

7. Moses, Joseph L. "Assessment Center Performance and Management Progress," *Studies in Personal Psychology,* Vol. 4, No. 1, Spring, 1972, p. 9.

8. Laurent, H. "EIMP Applied to the International Petroleum Co.," *Standard Oil of New Jersey Technical Report,* 1966.

9. Labovitz, George H. "More on Subjective Executive Appraisal, an Empirical Study," *Academy of Management Journal,* Vol. 15, No. 3, September, 1972, pp. 289–302.

10. Campbell. *Managerial Behavior, Performance and Effectiveness.* See Chapters 8 and 9.

11. Moses. "Assessment Center Performance and Management Progress," p. 9.

12. Fiedler, Fred E., and Albert F. Leister. "Leader Intelligence and Task Performance: A Test of a Multiple Screen Model," *Organizational Behavior and Human Performance,* Vol. 20, No. 1, October, 1977, pp. 1–14.

13. Mowday, Richard. "Leader Characteristics, Self-Confidence, and Methods of Upward Influence in Organizational Decision Situations," *Academy of Management Journal,* Vol. 22, No. 4, December, 1979, p. 711.

14. Stogdill. *Handbook of Leadership: A Survey of Theory and Research,* p. 81.

15. Harrell, Thomas W., and Margaret S. Harrell. "The Personality of MBA's Who Reach General Management Early," *Personnel Psychology,* Vol. 26, No. 2, Spring, 1973, pp. 127–134.

16. Barrow, Jeffrey C. "The Variables of Leadership: A Review and Conceptual Framework," *Academy of Management Review,* Vol. 2, No. 2, April, 1977, pp. 231–251.

17. Sank, Lawrence I. "Effective and Ineffective Managerial Traits Obtained as Naturalistic Descriptions from Executive Members of a Super-Corporation," *Personnel Psychology*, Vol. 27, No. 3, Autumn, 1974, pp. 423–434.

18. McClelland, David C., and David H. Burnham. "Power is the Great Motivator," *Harvard Business Review*, Vol. 54, No. 2, March–April, 1976, pp. 100–110.

19. Schein, Edgar H. "Coming to a New Awareness of Organizational Culture," *Sloan Management Review*, Vol. 26, No. 2, Winter, 1984, pp. 3–16.

20. Wilkins, Alan L., and William G. Ouchi. "Efficient Cultures: Exploring the Relationship between Culture and Organizational Performance," *Administrative Science Quarterly*, Vol. 28, No. 3, September, 1983, pp. 468–481.

21. Martin, Joanne et al. "The Uniqueness Paradox in Organizational Stories," *Administrative Science Quarterly*, Vol. 28, No. 3, September, 1983, pp. 438–453.

22. Peters and Waterman. *In Search of Excellence*, p. 77.

23. Peters and Waterman. *In Search of Excellence*, p. 75.

24. Schein, Edgar H. "Coming to a New Awareness of Organizational Culture," p. 7.

25. Peters and Waterman. *In Search of Excellence*, p. 76.

26. Biggart, Nicole Woolsey. "Management Style as Strategic Interaction: The Case of Governor Ronald Reagan," *Journal of Applied Behavioral Science*, Vol. 17, No. 3, 1981, pp. 291–308.

27. Peters and Waterman. *In Search of Excellence*, p. 104.

28. Schein, Edgar H. "The Role of the Founder in Creating Organizational Culture," *Organizational Dynamics*, Vol. 12, No. 1, Summer, 1983, pp. 13–28.

29. Tunstall, W. Brooke. "Cultural Transition at AT&T," *Sloan Management Review*, Vol. 25, No. 1, Fall, 1983, p. 18.

30. Brown, Charles L. "A New Company, A New World, A New Culture." Presentation made at the 44th Annual Meeting of the Academy of Management, Boston, August, 1984.

SUGGESTED READINGS

Bass, Bernard M. et al. *Assessment of Managers: An International Comparison.* New York: The Free Press, 1979.

Birkman, Roger. "What Sets an Executive Apart from His Peers?" *S.A.M. Advanced Management Journal*, Vol. 43, No. 3, Summer, 1978, pp. 58–62.

Brenner, Otto C., and Jeffrey H. Greenhaus. "Managerial Status, Sex, and Selected Personality Characteristics," *Journal of Management*, Vol. 5, No. 1, Spring, 1979, pp. 107–113.

Business Week, "Who's Excellent Now?" November 5, 1984, pp. 76–86.

Drory, Amos, and Uri M. Gluskinos. "Machiavellianism and Leadership," *Journal of Applied Psychology*, Vol. 65, February, 1980, pp. 81–86.

Durand, Douglas E., and Walter R. Nord. "Perceived Leader Behavior as a Function of Personality Characteristics of Supervisors and Subordinates," *Academy of Management Journal*, Vol. 19, No. 3, September, 1976, pp. 427–437.

Frost, Peter J., Larry F. Moore, Meryl Reis Louis, Craig L. Lundberg, and Joanne Martin, eds. *Organizational Culture.* Beverly Hills, Calif.: Sage Publications, Inc., 1985.

Isenberg, Daniel J. "How Senior Managers Think," *Harvard Business Review*, Vol. 62, No. 6, November–December, 1984, pp. 81–90.

Pfeffer, Jeffrey. "Management as Symbolic Action: The Creation and Maintenance of Organizational Paradigms" in *Research in Organizational Behavior*, eds. L. L. Cummings and B. M. Staw. Greenwich, Conn.: JAI Press, Vol. 3, 1981, pp. 1–52.

18

The First Line Supervisor

*The position of **first line supervisor**, a person who supervises people who are not managers or supervisors, can be among the most gratifying or among the most frustrating of all occupations. Because the first line supervisor is close to the action, has relatively fast and specific feedback about his or her performance, and often has camaraderie with people who are actually doing the work, the job can provide a good deal of day-to-day satisfaction.*

On the other hand, the first line supervisor has relatively little control over many of the events that affect his or her work unit. In addition, the supervisor is held accountable by subordinates for decisions made at higher levels of management that affect their work and income. Finally, the first line supervisor is held accountable by higher levels of management for the performance of subordinates who may not have goals or attitudes that are highly congruent with those most useful to the organization. Thus, depending on the situation and the supervisor's goals and abilities, first line supervisor may be a position to be attained and retained or regarded as a stepping stone to another position.

Most managers hold the position of first line supervisor early in their careers. Performance in this first position often has an important impact on the remainder of a manager's career. If the manager is more than moderately successful in this first managerial assignment, the resulting positive reinforcement generally creates a hunger for more responsibility and greater managerial challenge. Success is also a critical signal to higher level managers who tend to label the new supervisor as a person on the way up and a person in whom they and the organization should invest developmental resources.

Many first line supervisors supervise professional employees—for example, the manager of a real-estate agency or of an industrial sales district. The problems, opportunities, satisfactions, and frustrations of all first line supervisors seem to have much in common whether their subordinates are clerks, factory workers, or professional staff. Consequently, in order to maintain a focus throughout the chapter (and also to recognize the especially critical role of the first line supervisor in manufacturing) our discussion will often be in the context of the supervisor of factory production workers. However, the reader should be able to easily generalize the discussion to apply to other supervisory contexts. The objectives of this chapter are

TO UNDERSTAND:

1. The supervisor's role conflicts

2. Changes in the supervisor's role and work

3. Methods of identifying supervisory talent

4. Possibilities for redesigning the supervisor's job

5. The nature of effective discipline

A CONFLICT OF ROLES

The important problems of first line supervisors center around the question of identity. Before supervisors can function effectively, they must answer the question, Who am I? in a manner that is satisfactory to themselves and to their superiors, subordinates, and peers.

The identity problem of first line supervisors arises from circumstances that are not present at higher management levels. Because supervisors are often promoted from the employee ranks, they may possess attitudes, modes of perception, and personal bonds that hamper their identification with management. The supervisor, furthermore, must look continually in two directions and be a buffer between the conflicting interests of labor and management. Success demands that the supervisor meet the needs of both parties while maintaining personal integrity and credibility.

Perceptions of the Supervisor's Role

The supervisory role lends itself to a variety of interpretations. From a legal viewpoint, at least, the supervisor is more than just another worker, although many supervisors feel a stronger identification with subordinates than with management. Who, in reality, are supervisors? What is their true identity? The answer varies between and within organizations, but one or both of the following role perceptions usually applies. First line supervisors are

1. A special class of *in-the-middle* managers.

2. Human relations specialists.

A Special Class of In-the-Middle Managers

In many organizations supervisors may be realistically described as caught in the middle—as lacking an adequate identity. They are no longer employees (technicians, programmers, salespeople, workers, or whatever they may have been called), but neither are they fully managers. New supervisors, at least, often find that their role falls short of their expectations concerning the nature of a managerial position.

The identity problem arises, in part, when the new supervisor encounters the fact that neither subordinates nor higher managers entirely trust the new supervisor. In this statement, a production supervisor reflects on her feelings soon after her promotion:

> I had been with the company for twelve years and knew all too well the derogatory kinds of things workers have to say about management—regardless of how good a job management is doing. It became painfully obvious that I was no longer one of them when they quit making such statements in my presence. They even cleaned up their language when they talked with me. They put on an act for me because I was now a supervisor.
>
> Unfortunately the other supervisors didn't really trust me either. I was too close to the employees, and they weren't sure whether I would keep my mouth shut. Perhaps they were right in being cautious with their conversation when I came around. I found it hard to resist passing along choice bits of inside information in order to regain some of the status I had lost with my old work group. I knew I had to have their cooperation to be a success.
>
> I had to lean heavily upon the other supervisors for advice just to survive, and they really came through. I soon felt a close kinship with them, especially after several occasions when we covered for one another to avoid getting in trouble with the production manager. We're a closely knit, self-help organization. We don't have a union; but don't kid yourself, we're organized.

Barriers to Upward Identification

The unique problem of keeping the goodwill of subordinates while relating to higher management tends to increase the cohesiveness of supervisory groups. Managers who supervise only other managers have little appreciation for the difficulties of relating to employees on a continuing basis—especially when those employees are hostile, resentful, and poorly motivated. Supervisors often believe that only peers who face similar pressures can know what they are experiencing. This, in turn, establishes a psychological barrier to identifying with their superiors.

The organizational environment poses still other barriers to the upward identification of supervisors promoted from the ranks. Their attitudes, values, interests, motivational patterns, education, and other important characteristics are often different from those of higher level managers who are usually college educated. On a superficial level these differences are seen in language, dress, and the subject matter of casual conversation. At a deeper level, a psychological barrier arises from the fact that college graduates anticipate future promotions. In contrast, first line supervisors promoted from the ranks often expect no more than one promotion, and they typically regard supervisory positions as dead-end jobs. It is no wonder that upward identification is often weak or nonexistent.

From one point of view, first line supervisors are perceived as important members of the management team. They should, therefore, be given the authority and prestige befitting such a position. They should be consulted on all technical or personnel decisions which affect their work or about which they have valuable information. Because of the importance of supervisors to the overall management of the organization, extreme care should be exercised in their selection and development. Special attention may be given to their potential for further education and for management development. Under no circumstances should managerial promotion policies discriminate against supervisors. Every effort should be made to break down barriers between supervisors and higher management, thus avoiding the popular notion that supervisors are a special, in-the-middle class of employee.

Making Peace with Subordinates

Supervisors must get results in order to succeed. To do this they must somehow come to terms with subordinates. While continuing to represent management, supervisors must understand the needs and motives of subordinates and solicit their cooperation. Supervisors interpret and administer management policy and must know when to compromise and when to stand firm.

Establishing sound relationships with subordinates requires supervisors to listen to their grievances and to alleviate them even when this requires taking an unpopular position with higher management. At this point, management is most likely to question the supervisor's loyalty—to suspect that the supervisor has not learned to think like a manager. Yet this in-between manager must take such risks in order to be effective.

Because of cultural and communication barriers the gap between upper level management and the worker would be at times insurmountable without the supervisor's mediating skills. Unfortunately this role permits supervisors who are either inept or manipulative to do great damage to the organization. Like double agents in international espionage, such individuals may serve only themselves while convincing both superiors and subordinates of their loyalty. There is little evidence, however, that successful supervisors choose this method of coping with their dilemma. The role can be, and often is, played with integrity and openness.

Human Relations Specialists

Since many functions previously performed by supervisors are now performed by others, such as engineers and human resource specialists, the one remaining specialty of the supervisor is human relations. From this perspective, human relations involves personal interaction with subordinates for the purpose of maintaining high motivation, morale, and job satisfaction. The supervisor counsels employees about job-related problems, adjusts grievances, takes disciplinary action, and assists subordinates in planning for personal development.

Both supervisors and their superiors are aware of the importance of good human relations to the achievement of organizational goals, including productivity. Management does acknowledge, however, that other specialists share in the responsibility for production. In some situations, the actions of these specialists may have a greater impact on production than do the actions of supervisors. Among such people are industrial engineers, machine design engineers, production planners and schedulers, and a host of others whose technical recommendations and decisions directly affect productivity.

To view the first line supervisor as a human relations specialist is more appropriate in some supervisory positions than in others. Nevertheless, more so than other managers, supervisors must be skilled in human relations.

SUPERVISORY RESPONSIBILITY AND AUTHORITY

Because specialists now perform duties once performed by supervisors, the range of supervisory duties has been reduced considerably. On the other hand, the organizational environment has become more complex—so much so that modern supervisors could not possibly perform all the functions performed by their predecessors. Thus today's supervisors must have greater ability than their predecessors. In addition, the increasing importance of technical expertise as a source of influence has contributed to the trend toward less authoritarian leadership in organizations. Superior ability is required, therefore, because supervisors must be effective with less authority than their predecessors and because they must deal with more complexity.

Factors Affecting the Supervisory Role

A number of environmental factors affect the supervisor's role and function. The most important of these are the organization's level of specialization, its size and complexity, and the influence of unions and government.

Specialization. Organizations facing many-faceted environments, such as companies serving many types of markets or working with many different technologies, tend to be highly specialized as they attempt to attain a variety in their competency that is congruent with the variety in the environment. The supervisory role in such organizations is different from the supervisory role in less specialized organizations and can require interaction with many types of individuals, as shown in Figure 18-1. In particular, the supervisory role in highly specialized organizations is affected by problems of coordination and accountability.

Specialization and Coordination. One approach to coordinating specialized work is the use of coordinating specialists such as production schedulers and expeditors. Even so, responsibility for coordination falls heavily on supervisors. When machine breakdowns occur, supervisors must contact the maintenance department to request repairs. Supervisors bring together employees, union stewards, and labor relations specialists to deal with complex grievances. They also serve as intermediaries between employees and other specialists to solve problems relating to product quality, safety, timekeeping, training, and raw materials. But this role is sometimes difficult to play. It is complicated by problems of authority and accountability.

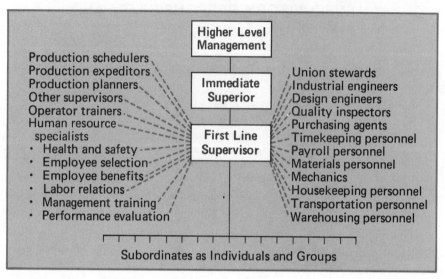

FIGURE 18-1 Personnel with Whom a Production Supervisor May Interact

Specialization and Accountability. Who is responsible when production falls behind schedule because of machine failure? The production supervisor reports a breakdown to the machine maintenance department but has no authority to establish repair priorities. A first-come-first-served rule may depersonalize the decision and treat all breakdowns as though they are equally important. If the maintenance supervisor sets priorities on a day-to-day basis, opportunities abound for this person to let favoritism or other inappropriate criteria influence his or her decisions.

An example of the accountability problem comes from an attitude survey conducted with the supervisors of a large manufacturer of apparel. One of the supervisors expressed the problem this way:

> I can't get the work out when the machines are down, and when they're down I have to wait forever to get them repaired. Whenever there's work to be done and I see a mechanic loafing, my blood boils, but there's nothing I can do about it. I know I'll catch it from the machine operator and from my boss, but my hands are tied. Our mechanics are prima donnas. Because they're in high demand, they work less and get paid more than any employees in the plant. Let's face it: The supervisors in this plant are held accountable for production, but we don't have the authority to obtain it.

Supervisors commonly experience frustrations of this kind. Subjectively the experience is one of being excessively dependent on others. For example, production supervisors depend on others for

1. Personnel who are able and willing to work.
2. Realistic production standards.
3. Efficient production methods.
4. Machine design and maintenance.
5. Motivational systems (such as financial incentives).
6. Quality raw materials or subassemblies.
7. Realistic production scheduling.

A breakdown in any one of these areas may seriously affect productivity. In some situations, productivity is so controlled by machine design, assembly-line processes, and company-wide motivational systems that the supervisor's actions have little effect on it. In such situations the supervisor logically has responsibility for little besides employee satisfaction, and even that is influenced by factors beyond the supervisor's control (such as the routine of jobs and company-wide morale factors).

Size and Complexity. In general more specialized organizations are larger, since additional specialities often require additional people. They also tend to be more complex structurally, as they organize their multiple specialties into multiple departments and as they create more levels of management to deal with their greater size.

Size and complexity create needs for control that are often satisfied through the use of policies and procedures. Thus supervisors in large and complex organizations have a role that is determined by organizational policies and procedures to a much greater extent than is the role of supervisors in smaller and less complex organizations.

The Influence of Unions. Union power significantly alters both the power and functions of supervisors in many factories and offices. In unionized companies, union stewards stand between supervisors and their subordinates in solving disciplinary and grievance problems. Stewards and other union representatives often become involved in minor disputes that would not even occur in nonunionized organizations. The following incident, which occurred in a unionized chemical plant, illustrates this point.

While a carpenter waited, two plumbers were called in to reroute a water line that interfered with the construction of a storage bin. Although they arrived about 9:00 a.m., the warehouse supervisor noticed that at 9:30 they had not begun to work. The plumbers explained that the lighting was poor and suggested that the supervisor call the electrical department about it. When the supervisor called and discovered that the electricians were busy, he personally set up two floodlights and wired them with extension cords which had been stored in the warehouse area. As he finished, the supervisor noticed that the plumbers were gone. They soon reappeared, however, with a union steward who protested that the union contract forbade supervisors to perform manual work.

The warehouse supervisor called the maintenance superintendent who agreed with him that his act was not a contract violation. The superintendent then ordered the plumbers to begin work. They refused and walked off the job. By late afternoon the issue was settled, but only after the local union president and company labor relations specialists entered the dispute.

The anticipation of incidents such as this can make supervisors in unionized companies extremely cautious about what they say and do. While the frequency of such incidents has declined in recent years—as unions and employees have become more aware of the need for productivity—they still occur and adversely affect supervisory authority and organizational performance.

Unions further limit the power of supervisors by reducing or eliminating supervisory authority to give promotions and wage increases based on merit. Instead promotions are based on seniority, and across-the-board pay raises are decided through collective bargaining. Reduction of the supervisor's power has the positive effect of reducing the incidence of unfair and arbitrary supervisory actions. On the other hand, it has often made supervisory positions so unattractive that they are difficult to fill. It is also difficult to clearly define objective standards for evaluating the performance of supervisors in such positions.

The Influence of Government. The controlling influence of government, like that of unions, limits the supervisor's autonomy and decision-making power (for example, federal laws specify minimum wages and outline conditions for the payment of overtime pay after forty hours of work per week). Since government controls affect most aspects of the supervisor's relations with subordinates, they increase the supervisor's dependence on staff specialists.

Both federal and state laws prohibit discrimination in hiring and in subsequent personnel decisions of all types (for example, pay, layoffs, promotions, and discharges) on the basis of race, color, religion, sex, national origin, or age. These antidiscrimination laws are designed to eliminate bias in personnel decisions—to ensure that only performance-related criteria are used in such decisions. Totally apart from morality and legality, the objectives of these laws are worthy organizational objectives. Sometimes, however, such laws cause supervisors to be overly cautious in making personnel decisions. For example, ineffective employees are occasionally allowed to remain on the payroll to avoid claims of discrimination. As other employees observe such abuses and realize that they will be tolerated, the abuses tend to increase.

Other laws specify in great detail what supervisors can and cannot do when employees attempt to unionize or after they are unionized. Numerous amendments and decisions of the National Labor Relations Board and federal courts have greatly increased the number of laws affecting organized labor. Still other federal, state, and municipal laws involve the supervisor in action designed to protect the health and safety of employees. The Occupational Safety and Health Act (OSHA) of 1970 goes further than most laws in giving government administrators the power to demand action and to impose heavy penalties for management's failure to respond immediately. Here, as elsewhere, government has become an ever-present, authoritarian superior of the first line supervisor.

The Work of the Supervisor

Because supervisory positions differ greatly from one organization to another, it is difficult to generalize concerning job requirements. In one study, 549 supervisors, representing a diversity of organizations, ranked 15 supervisory functions in order of perceived importance.[1] With a relatively high degree of consistency from one industry to another, the following rankings were given:

1. Setting goals
2. Improving present work methods
3. Delegating work
4. Allocating workers to jobs
5. Meeting deadlines
6. Controlling expenditures
7. Following progress of work
8. Evaluating employee performances

9. Forecasting work force requirements

10. Safety

11. Giving on-the-job instruction

12. Discussing performance with employees

13. Handling employee complaints

14. Enforcing rules

15. Conducting meetings

The supervisors in this study agreed that goal setting is the most important function because of its role in providing purpose, direction, and criteria for performance evaluations. This and other rankings, however, would have differed had the study focused on the amount of time spent in each activity. Goal setting, for example, requires relatively little time compared with a number of other activities.

Supervisors spend most of their time reacting to events and situations in the workplace: employee questions or complaints, production problems, and requests from superiors for information or action. Although most of the supervisor's time is spent in contact with subordinates, supervisors complain that they are unable to get the work out because of too much paperwork and too many meetings (with superiors, other supervisors, and specialists). Paperwork has in recent years been reduced somewhat by the actions of staff personnel and the use of computers for routine reporting; but legal problems require supervisors to prepare thorough reports on promotions, grievances, disciplinary matters, and accidents.

The following are among the supervisory functions on which the greatest differences in time usage exist:

1. *Personnel selection.* In some organizations selection is performed exclusively by the human resource department while in others the supervisor makes the employment decisions. In the latter case the supervisor may interview the applicants in addition to studying data prepared by the human resource department on one or more applicants.

2. *Grievance handling.* In unionized organizations and others with formal grievance procedures, more time is required than in organizations where the supervisor has the authority to dispose of grievances as they occur.

3. *Controlling expenditures.* Some supervisors have their own budgets and are able to make decisions which directly affect expenses (for example, purchasing and work methods). Others work within rigid structures where these functions are performed by staff personnel.

4. *Job training.* The training of subordinates is a major supervisory responsibility in some organizations. In others the function is performed exclusively by staff specialists.

As with any occupation, the nature of supervisory work affects satisfaction. One study of 12 organizations showed that first line supervisors experience less job satisfaction than do their superiors and subordinates, not a surprising fact in view of the role conflicts of supervisors.[2] The requirements for satisfaction fluctuate somewhat over time and according to the situation; but good wages, interesting work, chance for promotion, appreciation for work done, and job security usually rank high.[3]

THE IDENTIFICATION OF SUPERVISORY POTENTIAL

Many first line supervisors are promoted from a work group of the type they are to supervise, often on the basis of performance which bears little relationship to success in supervision. Knowledge and techniques are available, however, for selecting supervisors with a high probability of success.

For supervisors, higher level managers often select friendly, outgoing individuals who are top performers on nonsupervisory jobs. Although these qualities are admirable, they are relatively poor predictors of supervisory success.

Success-Related Characteristics

Because demands of supervisory positions differ widely, progressive organizations continually gather and analyze data concerning the characteristics of successful and unsuccessful supervisors in specific positions. These data are then used to improve the effectiveness of subsequent selection decisions.

Much of the information presented in Chapters 16 and 17 applies to the selection of first line supervisors. Emphasis should, for example, be placed on an applicant's leadership skills, motivation to become a supervisor, and ability to work under constant pressure. The applicant's mental ability, adaptability, and motivation to learn are also important characteristics since the new supervisor must often learn an entirely new set of skills. Although the supervisor's intelligence need not be as high as that of upper level management unless promotion into upper level management is likely, it should be above average and should contain a liberal amount of practical judgment.

Most supervisory positions require a relatively high level of empathy and skill in interpersonal relations. Although certain human relations skills can be learned, such as how to counsel employees or conduct disciplinary interviews, most managers try to promote only individuals whose background has already given them an intuitive understanding of people.

The Recruitment of Supervisors

Most companies promote some of their supervisors from within the organization. A few hire only college graduates as supervisors, reasoning that the position is the bottom rung of the management ladder and should be filled by someone who is promotable. This latter approach avoids certain problems that can occur if supervisors who were promoted from below identify more strongly with labor than with management and when employees resent supervision by someone who has recently been a peer.

There are, however, good reasons for maintaining a continuing flow of promotions into supervisory positions from employee ranks. Such a practice weakens the tendency for labor and management to form rigid, mutually exclusive, and antagonistic groups. It provides employees with possibilities for promotion that may reduce feelings of being hopelessly boxed in. It provides management with current, firsthand information about how employees think and feel. Employees can identify more easily with a management group that includes individuals who have come from their ranks, speak their language, and presumably understand their problems. Any organizational policy that blurs or eliminates the demarcation line between management and employees has the potential for reducing labor-management conflict.

Techniques for Selecting Supervisors

It is a common practice for human resource specialists to evaluate potential supervisors who are recommended for promotion. The specialist, in turn, recommends which, if any, of the applicants should be promoted. In addition to describing the candidate's strengths and weaknesses, the evaluation may also include recommendations for training and managing the new supervisor.

The methods used to evaluate supervisory applicants vary from a casual interview prompted by a recommendation for promotion from the applicant's current supervisor to an intensive psychological evaluation. Large companies with sophisticated human resource research departments are more likely than others to recognize the seriousness of the decision and to invest accordingly. Since assessments at this level often cost from $500 to $1,000 with many individuals being appraised but not selected, the investment is sizable indeed.

A thorough assessment of a supervisory applicant may require from one to three days, depending on the methods used. A one-day assessment may include a background study and evaluation and the administration of standardized psychological tests for mental ability, supervisory knowledge and attitudes, leadership style, personality characteristics, interests, and values. The assessment may also include one or more in-depth interviews to obtain general information and to probe for answers to specific questions which relate to the applicant's success potential. Other evaluation instruments may be administered which are clinically rather than statistically evaluated. The applicant may, for example, write a self-description essay, compose stories in response to picture stimuli, and respond to a wide variety of items in a simulated supervisor's in-basket (that is, handle the items typically found in a supervisor's incoming mail).

The longer evaluation process normally compares six applicants at one time by rating applicant behavior on **situational tests**—composed of standardized situations or problems similar to those which the prospective supervisor will face on the job—to which the applicants respond as individuals and groups. This **assessment center** method has been extensively validated and used by many large firms.[4]

RESHAPING THE SUPERVISOR'S ROLE

As presently constituted in many organizations, the supervisor's position is destined to cause unnecessary frustration and marginal effectiveness. Proven remedies for these conditions are available, however, to organizations that are willing to make the necessary investment.

The extensive unionization of supervisors between 1935 and 1947 stimulated a flurry of activity intended to bring supervisors back into the management fold. Although many such activities (human relations seminars, for example) failed to strike at the problems of role identity and role conflict, a variety of effective solutions have evolved. The appropriateness of each is dependent on current conditions in a particular organization. The management actions described here, among others, have proven effective in reducing the frustration of supervisors and increasing their ability to perform effectively.

Selection for Growth Potential

Extreme care is needed in the recruitment and selection of supervisors. This may even involve hiring employees with a view to having supervisory talent available several years hence. Supervisory selections should be made from those employees with superior mental ability, leadership potential, high motivation to lead, and potential for progressing into higher levels of management.

Motivation for Growth and Advancement

Where the opportunities are available, first line supervisors should be encouraged to move into higher management rather than to view themselves as an in-between special class. This begins with selecting supervisors who have the ability and motivation to continue their formal education. It also involves providing incentives for continued education and making promotions without prejudice toward managers who have risen from the ranks.

Upgrading the Position

Major changes in job design are sometimes used successfully to increase the authority, responsibility, and prestige of supervisors. One way to accomplish this with production supervisors is to flatten the organization—to eliminate some of the management levels between the first line supervisor and the production manager, as shown in Figure 18-2.[5]

The flat form of organization is possible only if the production manager and first line supervisors have ample staff support. The production manager is thus freed to interact directly with a large number of supervisors. The supervisors have an opportunity to participate in policy decisions, the authority to make operational decisions on their own, and the information needed to supervise effectively. It is important to make changes slowly from the traditional to the revised flat organization structure in order to avoid loss of control.

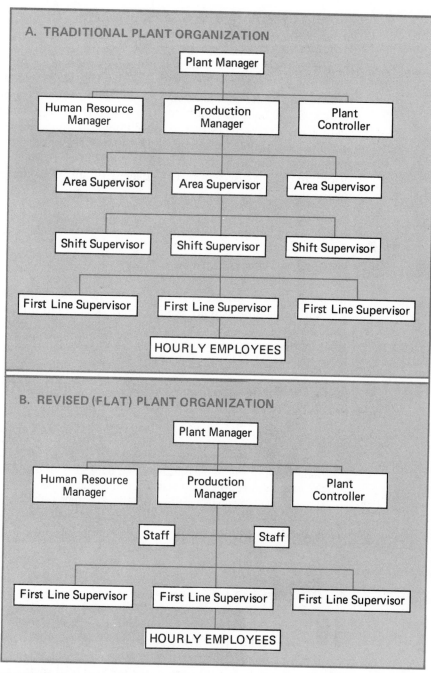

FIGURE 18-2 Traditional and Flat Organization of Plant Production Management

Facilitating the Transition to Supervisor

Professional guidance is typically needed to facilitate the transition from employee to supervisor. This involves more than supervisory training. Formal programs, both group and individual, enable the new supervisor to anticipate problems and to develop a repertoire of possible solutions. Some common problems include relating to former co-workers, dealing with the effects of the job change on one's family, learning to play a leadership role, adapting to the supervisory peer group, organizing and controlling time, coping with the pressures of the supervisory position, and managing feelings of insecurity and inadequacy in the new role.

Providing Career Guidance

It is important that the new supervisor understand that the first line supervisor's job is not the end of the line. To avoid this and provide motivation for personal growth and outstanding performance, the supervisor needs professional assistance in career planning. This should be made available on a continuing basis and is linked to planning for training in skills and general education.

SUPERVISION AND EFFECTIVE DISCIPLINARY ACTION

Supervisors are generally the first to detect the need for disciplinary action. Much of the unpleasantness and damage to the organization and the employee can be removed from disciplinary action by the use of appropriate methodology. Failure to take certain precautions, on the other hand, can lead to poor human relations, decreased productivity, serious legal action, and irreparable personal loss to the individuals involved.

Historically the management of disciplinary problems has been taken lightly. Discipline was one of many subjects included in training programs for first line supervisors, but it was hardly seen as worthy of serious consideration by higher levels of management. If a supervisor made a mistake or handled a disciplinary problem indiscreetly, the employee might be hurt, but the organization was not likely to suffer greatly.

Today things have changed. Perceptive managers recognize that the manner in which disciplinary cases are resolved may have a significant influence on job-related employee attitudes and behavior. But, beyond this, the many possibilities for claims of discrimination under federal and state law make it mandatory that disciplinary action be taken properly.[6] It is also significant that disciplinary problems are the single category of grievances most often referred to an arbitrator for a solution.

Guidelines for Disciplinary Action

As suggested earlier, the occasions for disciplinary action run the gamut from infrequent tardiness to smoking in the explosives storeroom; and the environments range from small, family-operated companies to international organizations dominated by militant unions. On one occasion the offender is a minimum wage laborer; on another occasion the offender is a $100,000-a-year executive. This variety makes generalizations about the disciplinary process difficult. Nevertheless, some generalizations are possible as long as intelligent adaptation is made for each unique situation.

Preparation. Impulsive disciplinary action is seldom advisable. Managers who are inclined to bawl out a subordinate immediately upon learning of an infraction may find satisfaction in expressing their own feelings and establishing their dominance over the subordinate, but their actions usually fall far short of achieving long-term behavior modification. Preparation for disciplinary action has a twofold purpose. It is needed to minimize the possibility of impulsive, ill-advised action—to make sure the action taken is fair and that it achieves its purpose. Preparation is also important because managers are called upon to defend their actions.

Although it is wise to avoid even the appearance of secretly and maliciously gathering evidence to use against an employee, it is often necessary for a manager to collect solid evidence over a period of time, meticulously keeping records of offenses, disciplinary actions, and warnings. Since cases are sometimes brought before the quasi-legal bodies involved in formal grievance or arbitration proceedings, a manager must be in the right and be able to prove it. In some situations where witnesses are likely to change their stories, it may even be necessary to obtain written statements or affidavits.

It is often advisable to avoid a highly legalistic approach to handling a disciplinary problem, but it is never advisable to be slovenly in record keeping. Even in companies where there is no union, there are always federal and state laws to be dealt with and the resulting prospect that one's actions may have to be defended in the courts.

One major benefit of thorough preparation for disciplinary action is that it may show that what at first appears to be a need for some form of punishment may turn out to be a need for training, motivation, or the removal of obstacles that prevent performance from matching the expectations of management. Even when the problem is an infraction of the rules rather than substandard performance, it can often be solved through positive action rather than punishment. Preparation for disciplinary action by reviewing employee records and asking appropriate questions, for example, may suggest the need for a sequence of actions designed to produce the desired employee behavior. It is particularly important that prior to taking disciplinary action a manager make sure the subordinate understood what was expected, was able to do it, and then elected not to do it.

Immediacy. Although preparation is important and impulsiveness is an invitation to disaster, punishment should follow as soon after the infraction as possible. Quick justice is more acceptable to the offender and is thus more effective. Immediately after the infraction, subordinates expect punishment and are less likely to view it as unjust than if they are led to believe they have escaped it. When the association between the infraction and punishment is strong, the probability of punishment makes repetition of the offense less likely.

In the case of a serious infraction possibly deserving termination, some companies prefer to lay off the employee for a short time (sometimes with pay in order to avoid union complications) until the needed information is gathered and a decision is made. Such a practice underscores the gravity of the situation. It permits swift action, gives the employee a brief time to reconsider the merits of abiding by the rules, and gives management enough time to make a deliberate decision.

Anticipation. Punishment is typically viewed as unjust by the offender, by arbitrators, and by the courts when it could not readily be anticipated (for example, when it represents a major change in policy without warning). The following case illustrates the point that even the relatively serious offense of stealing company property may be rationalized and justified when it is viewed as de facto company policy:

> Sure, I had a crescent wrench in my lunch box, but I'm no thief. Everybody does it. I could give you dozens of examples, but I won't. One thing I will say is that taking company property is not restricted to hourly employees. Look at the way management uses company cars and gasoline for personal trips. And in the shops, we're always fixing something for management—using company labor, tools, and parts. I'm always hearing stories from the front office about how managers combine vacations and company-paid business trips or use their expense

accounts for personal entertainment. I'm willing to live by the same rules everybody else does, but I won't sit still for being singled out. Let's face it: The way most employees think is that as long as you don't overdo it, taking company property is a form of employee benefit—like vacations and insurance.

Sometimes a new manager makes the mistake of reversing the lax policy of a predecessor without notifying subordinates of the change. A simple memo communicating the fact that certain enforcement changes are being made would avoid unnecessary problems and begin to establish a basis for trust. Strictly from a legalistic viewpoint, an employee has a good argument for claiming arbitrary and discriminatory action when it can be proved that the case in point is a not readily anticipated enforcement of a rule.

Certainty. Generally speaking, the certainty of punishment is more important than the severity. In a few cases, severe punishment is called for even on the first offense; but these are the exceptions. A large oil company, for example, has a firm policy of firing anyone caught smoking in an area of a refinery not specifically set aside for that purpose. The constant danger of explosions seems to justify this in the minds of employees as well as management.

Certainty of punishment means that there is a high probability that an offender will be caught and appropriately punished. To be more specific, it means that employees perceive that the probability of being caught and punished is high (that is, the subjective probability is high). To achieve this perceptual set, an offense should be punished every time it occurs rather than intermittently. Infractions are sometimes overlooked because they do little harm to the organization or simply because a manager wants to avoid the conflict, but this practice may give the offender and other employees the impression that such violations are sometimes acceptable.[7]

Consistency. Consistency of managerial action requires the enforcement of a given rule equally for all employees, but it also implies equal punishment for a given offense. To be perfectly consistent, different managers have to use the same standards and apply them in the same way. Obviously consistency is hard to come by.

Must identical punishment always be given for a certain offense in order to achieve consistency? Probably not. Consider the case of two individuals who are insubordinate. On different occasions, each of the workers refused to do a certain potentially dangerous task. However, one had extensive training in how to avoid all possibility of bodily harm while the other did not. Appropriate punishment for the trained worker might be a transfer to a less desirable job (depending on company policy and common practice). The worker who had not received safety training should not be punished. Certainly it would be inconsistent to treat the two employees identically.

In a second case, two employees are repeatedly late for work; but one employee is indifferent and surly while the other is penitent and makes an honest effort to improve. The employee who is making an effort to be on time may need counseling to provide insight that will help solve the problem; however, a strongly worded, written reprimand and warning would be more suitable for the other employee.

Consistency of punishment must also be related to an individual's unique needs and consequent reaction to punishment. Consider, for example, two employees who receive a one-week suspension without pay beginning on the first day of deer-hunting season. One employee has no financial problems and has been known to take vacation time to go deer hunting while the other employee has a pressing need for money and has no interest in hunting. Again, the inequity is obvious. Punishment should always be fair and should fit the offense, but to be so it must be tailored to the needs of the individual.

Objectivity. Difficult as it may be, close friends and well-liked subordinates should be disciplined as if bonds of affection are not a factor in determining punishment. Employees are generally aware of a manager's personal feelings for subordinates, either positive or negative, and they are highly sensitive to expressions of bias in either direction.

Because of the possibility for bias or the appearance of bias, first line supervisors, in particular, are well advised to avoid close emotional entanglements with subordinates. Subordinates can accept orders, criticism, and punishment more graciously when a degree of social distance exists between themselves and their superior than when their superior is perceived as a peer. Of course, where a manager is supervising persons in the work group from which he or she was promoted, attempts to break off close personal relationships and establish a social distance may be seriously damaging to interpersonal relations, at least in the short run.

Does the need for objectivity preclude the development of warm relationships between supervisor and subordinates in general? Definitely not, but those feelings should not be allowed to bias disciplinary decisions. As a matter of fact, research suggests that punishment works best if warm interpersonal relationships exist (although this certainly should not be the principal reason to develop such a relationship). The punishment should be impersonal—focused on the act rather than the person—but this in no sense suggests that all supervisor-subordinate relationships should be impersonal.

Confident Action. Disciplinary action should not be taken unless it is justified and procedurally correct (after preparation, with warning, immediate, consistent, and objective). However, when these conditions have been met, a manager has every reason to proceed with firmness and confidence. It is obviously inappropriate for a manager to exhibit arrogance or delight in taking disciplinary action; but an apologetic, self-doubting attitude is equally inappropriate. Firm, confident action reinforces the notion that what the manager is doing should be done. Apologetic action raises doubts about its propriety and consequently weakens its effectiveness.

The Disciplinary Interview

The disciplinary interview (or interviews) will necessarily reflect a manager's personality and leadership style depending on the nature of the offense, the characteristics of the offender, and the nature and history of the organization. Nevertheless, the following interview guidelines are generally applicable:

1. Enter the interview with as many facts as possible. Check the employee's personnel records for previous offenses or evidence of exemplary behavior and performance. It may be appropriate to contact the offender's previous supervisors.

2. Conduct the interview in a quiet, private place. This reduces defensiveness and emotionality and at the same time reduces the likelihood that other employees will identify with and become supportive of the offender. The tendency to identify with the underdog, especially if that individual is a friend, is sometimes irresistible, regardless of the facts.

3. Avoid aggressive accusations. State the facts in a simple and straightforward way: "I received a call from the human resources department this morning. They reported that you were again involved in a fight during work hours. I would like to hear your side of the story."

4. Make sure the employee understands the rule and the reason for its existence.

5. Allow the employee to make a full defense. Be a good listener. Ask probing questions, but do not attempt to use trickery or intimidation. Be straightforward and open. In some cases it is advisable to have a third person present to witness the employee's responses and

the fairness of the questioning. Statements made during a first interview are sometimes denied in later quasi-legal hearings (grievance and arbitration proceedings).

6. **Stay cool and calm.** Do not scold or behave as though the superior-subordinate relationship were that of parent and child. Never use foul language or touch the employee. Such behaviors are subject to gross misinterpretation, and the memory of them may be quite different from reality.

7. **Admit it if you made a mistake.** One of the practical advantages of avoiding accusations is that the manager is not placed on the defensive when it turns out that the situation is not what it appeared to be.

8. **Allow for honest mistakes on the part of the employee.** Consider extenuating circumstances and the unique perceptions of the offender. It is important that a balance be maintained between the extremes of being too soft and willing to rationalize for the offender and too hard and unwilling to view the situation from the other side.

9. **Even when punishment is required, try to express confidence in the employee's worth as a person and ability to perform acceptably in the future:** "Harry, you've really fouled up, and obviously you will not be getting the raise that we anticipated you would. But I believe you're the type person who will profit from your mistake and be more successful in the long run because of it. I want you to know that if I see you're really trying to do a good job, I will go out of my way to help you get a raise in the future."

10. **Avoid the temptation to continue to punish.** Prescribe the punishment and carry it out, but do not inject the additional punishment of being hostile or cool toward the offender. Keep in mind that the objective of disciplinary action is behavior change (rather than punishment as such) and that it can never take the place of positive motivation.

IMPORTANT TERMS AND CONCEPTS

first line supervisor   assessment center
situational tests

STUDY AND DISCUSSION QUESTIONS

1. What is the nature of the identity problem faced by first line supervisors?

2. Why is it important that first line supervisors have a strong identification with management?

3. In a situation where labor and management relations are in continual conflict, is it possible for a first line supervisor to relate to both sides without being two-faced in a hypocritical, deceitful sense? Explain.

4. Explain this statement: Today's first line supervisors perform a much narrower range of duties than did their predecessors. On the other hand, their job requires greater ability and skill.

5. What major problem does a supervisor face in coordinating the activities of others to achieve productivity goals?

6. A strictly behavioristic approach to dealing with disciplinary problems would primarily emphasize the importance of rewarding desirable behavior and punishing undesirable behavior. Is this an adequate approach to solving disciplinary problems? Why or why not?

7. Assume the position of a production superintendent searching for a new first line supervisor from a group of production workers. What behavior would provide helpful clues in making the selection?

8. What problems would likely result from consistently filling first line supervisory positions with recent college graduates who are expected to progress into higher management?

CRITICAL INCIDENT

PROMOTABLE PROBLEMS

Charles Gresham began his career at Mosley Electronics on the assembly line; but because of his two years of college and his Army experience in electronics, he was soon given a technician's job. As a technician, he was one of many who located problems in computer subsystems after they failed to pass quality control tests. Between 1972 and 1982 he received three promotions and gained a reputation for being a mature, highly analytical problem solver.

In June of 1982 Gresham received his first management assignment. He was promoted to supervisor over the 12 senior technicians with whom he had worked for several years, including two men, Ralph Corley and Mel Janek, who were his closest friends. In fact, the three families had developed close bonds of friendship because of mutual interest in camping. They had taken numerous trips together and in some ways felt a family kinship.

Gresham's promotion brought forth hearty congratulations from his two friends. After all, the position paid well and managers at Mosley Electronics were held in high esteem by the company's 3,000 nonunion employees. Soon after Gresham's promotion, however, problems began to arise. The first occurred when Gresham recommended another subordinate over Corley for a temporary duty assignment in Europe. Corley did not complain directly about the action, but his wife told Mrs. Gresham that Corley should have received the assignment. "We would be on our way to Amsterdam," she asserted, "if Charles wasn't afraid he would be accused of favoritism."

Because Gresham's new job required long hours, there was less time for camping trips; and, when the families did get together, the warm, relaxed, uninhibited relationships of the past were no longer present. On occasion, Gresham was forced to hedge when asked questions about company plans and to take an unpopular stand on controversial management issues, which, in turn, reinforced the fact that the friendships could no longer survive in their early form. Gradually the camping trips were dropped, and the old group seldom got together without other friends or department members present.

Gresham regretted the loss of his close friends; but, being deeply committed to his new career, he was also concerned that negative feelings on the part of Corley and Janek might cause difficulty on the job. The transition was softened somewhat by the fact that the wives of the three men continued to visit frequently. This was, however, a mixed blessing.

On one occasion, confidential information that Charles Gresham had shared with Mrs. Gresham was inadvertently passed on. Although the event caused no serious problems at work, Gresham unconsciously began talking less often with his wife about business problems. Her reaction was, "We're losing our friends. That's frustrating, but I can live with it. But perhaps you're leaving me behind, too. I miss knowing what you're doing and what's important to you. I'm happy for your success, but it is your success—not our success. You work too much, and you are too involved in it. You're moving into another world that I don't understand and don't like."

1. What is the underlying cause of Gresham's problems?

2. How should Gresham solve his problems?

3. What additional information is needed in order to answer Questions 1 and 2?

4. What potential problems associated with his promotion to supervisor has Gresham apparently avoided or at least not encountered?

REFERENCES

1. Lewis, Blake D., Jr. "The Supervisor in 1975," *Personnel Journal*, Vol. 52, No. 9, September, 1973, pp. 815–818.

2. Walton, Richard E., and Leonard A. Schlesinger. "Do Supervisors Thrive in Participative Work Systems?" *Organizational Dynamics*, Vol. 7, No. 3, Winter, 1979, pp. 25–38.

3. Abboud, Michael J., and Homer L. Richardson. "What Do Supervisors Want from Their Jobs?" *Personnel Journal*, Vol. 57, No. 6, June, 1978, pp. 308–334.

4. Moses, Joseph E. "The Development of an Assessment Center for the Early Identification of Supervisory Potential," *Personnel Psychology*, Vol. 26, No. 4, Winter, 1973, pp. 569–578.

5. Smiley, Laurence M., and Paul R. Westbrook. "The First-Line Supervisory Problem Redefined," *Personnel Journal*, Vol. 54, No. 12, December, 1975, pp. 621–622.

6. McAfee, R. Bruce, and Mark Lincoln Chadwin. "Evaluating an Organization's Disciplinary System," *Human Resource Management*, Vol. 20, No. 3, Fall, 1981, pp. 29–35.

7. Arvey, Richard D., and John M. Ivancevich. "Punishment in Organizations: A Review, Propositions, and Research Suggestions," *Monthly Labor Review*, Vol. 5, No. 1, January, 1980, pp. 127–132.

SUGGESTED READINGS

Krackhardt, David, John McKenna, Lyman W. Porter, and Richard M. Steers. "Supervisory Behavior and Employee Turnover: A Field Experiment," *Academy of Management Journal*, Vol. 24, No. 2, June, 1981, pp. 249–259.

Oberle, Rodney L. "Administering Disciplinary Actions," *Personnel Journal*, Vol. 57, No. 1, January, 1978, pp. 29–31.

O'Reilly, Charles A., III, and Barton A. Weitz. "Managing Marginal Employees: The Use of Warnings and Dismissals," *Administrative Science Quarterly*, Vol. 25, No. 3, September, 1980, pp. 467–484.

Preston, Paul, and Thomas W. Zimmerer. *Management for Supervisors*. Englewood Cliffs, N.J.: Prentice-Hall, Inc., 1978.

Sartain, Aaron Q., and Alton W. Baker. *The Supervisor and His Job*. New York: McGraw-Hill Book Company, 1978.

Sasser, W. Earl, Jr., and Frank S. Leonard. "Let First-Level Supervisors Do Their Job," *Harvard Business Review*, Vol. 58, No. 2, March–April, 1980, pp. 113–121.

Sims, Henry P., Jr. "Further Thoughts on Punishment in Organizations," *Academy of Management Review*, Vol. 5, No. 1, January, 1980, pp. 133–138.

Summers, Clyde W. "Protecting *All* Employees against Unjust Dismissal," *Harvard Business Review*, Vol. 58, No. 1, January-February, 1980, pp. 132–139.

Unterberger, Irene, and S. Herbert Unterberger. "Disciplining Professional Employees," *Industrial Relations*, Vol. 17, No. 8, October, 1978, pp. 353–359.

19

Participation

Managers generally know more facts about the workplace than any of the people they supervise, and about some things they know more than anyone else in their organization. But they never know all they wish to know. Subordinates and other organization members often have information, opinions, and ideas that managers can use to identify problems and opportunities, make better decisions, or motivate people. Given the increasing complexity of organizations, and thus of managerial jobs, gaining access to the knowledge of others is becoming increasingly important to managers at all levels.

In addition, increasing levels of education and increasing expectations concerning what their work environment should be are causing many employees to seek to influence their supervisors and their work environment. Thus "accepting" information, opinions, and ideas is becoming a more frequently observed behavior of managers at all levels. As a consequence of either or both of these trends, participation by subordinates in activities previously engaged in only by their managers is becoming commonplace.

Research and experience show that managers with participative leadership styles are better informed about (1) problems and opportunities in their work environment, and (2) the range of possible solutions to the problems they face and the nature of the consequences associated with these solutions.

Research and experience also make clear that people who have participated in a problem-solving process (1) tend to be more committed to implementing the solutions that evolve than are those who have not participated; and (2) tend to be more effective in implementing the solutions because they have a more in-depth understanding of the linkages among the problem, its causes, and the solution.

As a result, managers who practice participative leadership have fewer solution-implementation problems. Because they have fewer fires to fight, they have more time to build fire trails; because they have fewer implementation problems, they have more time to devote to decision making and implementation planning. Encouragement of participation is a pragmatic managerial behavior.

The objectives of this chapter are

TO UNDERSTAND:

1. The consequences of participation

2. How managers can keep themselves informed on an everyday basis

3. The nature of the behaviors that commonly interfere with effective meetings

4. The use of guidelines for managing participative meetings

5. How to use the Nominal Group Technique

OBTAINING PARTICIPATION ON AN EVERYDAY BASIS

Participation can be obtained in group or individual settings, either formally or informally. Because some people are reluctant to speak up about sensitive matters in group settings, and because formal participation is often scheduled for times other than when information is timely, a good deal of important information comes to the manager through informal conversations with individual subordinates.

What can managers do to encourage subordinates to pass on information, opinions, and ideas? The following guidelines have shown themselves to be effective. The challenge is for managers to remember to use them. In the manager's busy world, good managerial practices sometimes are forgotten. Their absence eventually has its negative effects—in this case, a lower average level of communications to the manager about workplace opportunities and problems.

Guideline 1—Be Responsive

Let your subordinates know that their information does influence your thinking and actions. If you do, they will know that they are participating in the planning and decision making that affects their work environment. This knowledge is an incentive for them to continue participating by providing useful information.

1a. *Let them know immediately.* Fast feedback is much more effective than delayed feedback.

1b. *Be as positive and as specific as possible about how subordinates' information will have its effect.* At the minimum say, "I'm glad you told me that. I hadn't realized it before." If possible, say something more definite such as "That is really useful to me. I'll act on it first thing in the morning."

1c. *Report back the eventual impact of subordinates' information.* Be as positive as possible. For example, you might say, "I've eliminated that problem you told me about Friday. Thanks very much. We would have had a real mess if you hadn't alerted me."

1d. *Make clear the nature of useful information.* If the subordinate begins to provide "junk information" to keep your attention, casually mention to him or her the difference between some specific useful information that the person provided in the past and the not-so-useful information now being given to you. Essentially this is teaching and coaching, and it will help the subordinate gain more insight into management's informational needs.

Guideline 2—Seek Out Bad News

It is common wisdom that people are reluctant to give their supervisors bad news, and research shows that people withhold bad news even when they're not responsible for the problem.[1] Evidently people want to avoid dealing with or even observing the emotional reaction that receivers of bad news generally display. Furthermore, people are reluctant to give bad news even to persons they will never see again and who can have no influence over their lives.[2] No wonder that in the workplace—where people see their supervisor every day and where their supervisor's opinions determine income, job security, and advancement—bad news often gets suppressed to the disadvantage of the manager who learns about problems too late to take effective action.

What can be done to get subordinates to pass on information about delays, defects, mistakes and other bad news? There are four good answers to this question—four useful and effective guidelines. The first one is primary. Without it, the others will have little effect.

2a. *Never display a negative emotional reaction to bad news.* Lapses from this guideline have a near-permanent adverse impact on the willingness of the observing subordinates to communicate anything but positive or bland information in the future. One way to accomplish this difficult task is to display a positive reaction, as described in Guideline 2b.

2b. *Always display a positive reaction to bad news.* This is not as difficult as it seems, once you realize that bad news is always information you can use even if it is used only to adjust your expectations. As bad as some news might be, about budget overruns, lost political battles, impending crises, and so forth, it helps the manager avoid making blunders based on incorrect assumptions about the future.

  The idea, then, is to tell the person who passes on bad news that the news will help you avoid acting on incorrect beliefs and that you can use it diagnostically. Say this right away. Speak positively about the usefulness of the information received. The bearer of bad tidings will feel relieved, even rewarded, for the risk he or she took.

2c. *Focus on dealing with the problem, not on fixing the blame.* The reason to find out who is responsible for a problem is to avoid having it happen again. This may even result in punishing the culprit (although more positive actions are to be preferred). But blame-fixing can wait. There is no rush. You will be better able to deal with the interpersonal aspects of culprit-confrontation after the problem has been dealt with constructively. Thus the first step is to attack the problem itself. This action is a positive reaction and it is positive feedback for the person who told you of the problem.

2d. *Let people know what you want to know.* People will feel more confident in communicating bad news if they know the kinds of information that you need and want. Informing subordinates about what's important helps them in many ways, one of which is easing into a difficult conversation with "I hate to tell you this, and I wouldn't except that you said you wanted to know, but I just learned that . . ."

Guideline 3—Create Communication Opportunities

  Our everyday observations show us that people communicate less, at least in any depth, when they are working at capacity. Research shows that they also communicate less to people whom they think are working hard. As a consequence, if you want subordinates or others to discuss complex or sensitive issues with you, you must create situations where both you and they have low perceived work loads. Garden variety examples include coffee breaks and prescheduled review sessions. Retreats, where a group of organization members meet at a site away from work for one, two, or several days to discuss matters in a more relaxed setting, are a more elaborate but useful approach to implementing this guideline. What is important is to be available at the time that your subordinates are in a position to be communicative—for example, when they are not busy and when other people are not around.

Managers who follow these guidelines tend to be better informed about opportunities and problems in the workplace. As a result, they tend to make better decisions. In addition, the increased satisfaction that subordinates obtain from personal interaction with their supervisor leads to a more pleasant work environment for both subordinates and managers. Everyone gains when participation in the manager's decision making takes place on an everyday basis.

PARTICIPATION IN MEETINGS

Many meetings are held so that participants, including the manager who calls the meeting, can exchange information and therefore obtain higher quality solutions to the problems addressed.

As we noted earlier, research and experience make clear that when people participate in a problem-solving meeting they (1) tend to be more committed to implementing the solutions that evolve than those who have not participated; and (2) tend to be more effective in implementing the solutions because they have a more in-depth understanding of the linkages among the problem, its causes, and the solution.

Given this, managers who involve their subordinates in the problem-solving process can be more confident that solutions will be implemented effectively because their subordinates will tend to be both more motivated and more capable.

Meeting Effectiveness

Most managers believe that most meetings, although necessary, are much less effective than they could be. Studies also show that these managers are right—most meetings are much less effective than they could be. Why is this so? Why are most meetings relatively ineffective? The answer requires that we define what we mean by an **effective meeting**. By effective we mean a meeting where the participants

1. accomplish their task (for example, a solution is evolved),

2. leave generally more satisfied than dissatisfied, and

3. suffer no reduction in their capacity to work together.

With this definition in mind, we can state that the *actual effectiveness* of a meeting is equal to the *potential effectiveness* that follows from the combined inputs of the members minus the losses in effectiveness that follow from group processes plus the gains in effectiveness that follow from the group processes. The process losses include, for example, the loss in solution quality or member acceptance resulting from some members not having the opportunity to participate and thus to contribute their knowledge or views or to learn the facts or opinions of others. The process gains might include the gain in solution quality resulting from one person thinking of a new and useful idea as a result of listening to the discussion of other participants or the gain in acceptance resulting from having had the opportunity to influence the meeting's outcome.

Meetings are opportunities for information exchange. The exchange occurs only through participation. If those attending a meeting do not get to participate, the potential benefits of the meeting do not occur. Information is not made available, errors in reasoning are not uncovered, enthusiasm and acceptance are not achieved, and the understanding of those attending is not increased. These are serious consequences. They motivate us to examine the behaviors that interfere with effective participation and that consequently reduce meeting effectiveness.

The management literature identifies several such behaviors. After reviewing these behaviors, we will review guidelines for dealing with them that may result in increased participation and meeting effectiveness.

Behaviors Interfering with Effective Participation

Most problem-solving meetings are relatively unstructured; people participate in various ways and to varying degrees in a relatively uncontrolled manner. Many of the behaviors in such meetings are useful in achieving group goals, but several common behaviors actually interfere with the effective participation that leads to meeting effectiveness. A list of some of these behaviors follows:

1. People with dominant personalities or intense interest in the situation tend to participate in the group discussion more than their contribution to the group's goal attainment merits. This in turn leads to lower quality solutions by suppressing the contributions of other people and thereby restricting the availability of information. It also leads to lower satisfaction among those whose participation is curtailed.

2. A willingness to persist stubbornly and thereby fatigue the opposition enables some participants to affect the solutions more than their information or knowledge justifies.

3. Low-status participants tend to defer to the opinions expressed by high-status participants, thus depriving the group of the potential contribution that justified the inclusion of the low-status members.

4. Group pressures for conformity suppress facts and opinions that are not in keeping with the direction in which the group is headed or are not in keeping with the values held by the majority of group members. This behavior leads to lower quality solutions in that it restricts the availability of information.

5. As time passes, groups lose sight of their immediate task; they get into ruts and pursue peripheral issues, conversations, and trains of thought. This not only slows the process down (with the consequent negative effect on decision timeliness and member satisfaction) but also causes some information that would be useful in completing the task to be set aside and eventually forgotten.

6. In order to reduce the tension created by the presence of their overall assignment, groups involved in problem solving frequently give insufficient attention to the problem-exploration and solution-generation steps. They move too quickly to the choice-making step and thus increase the likelihood that they will choose an inappropriate or low-quality solution. For example, such groups tend to consider only readily available solutions and tend to push toward closure by stifling, circumventing, or bargaining away dissent or disagreement— that is, by retarding participation.

As this listing indicates, there are strong social and psychological forces that work against participation. The prevalance and negative impact of the resulting behaviors have led organizational behavior researchers and management practitioners to develop guidelines that help to minimize their occurrence and impact.

GUIDELINES FOR MANAGING MEETINGS

The ability to manage meetings can be easily developed. Much of this ability is derived from the simple but consistent application of a few easily remembered guidelines.

The first two guidelines focus on achieving equitable participation. **Equitable participation** is the level of participation that is in keeping with the individual's information, knowledge, or other contribution to the group's efforts. Inequitable participation is participation to a degree that is either greater or less than that which is in keeping with the person's contribution. In most meetings, unmanaged or natural rates of participation are inequitable, with some people participating more than their contribution justifies and some participating less. Exactly equal or absolutely uniform participation is also generally inequitable. It is unlikely that on any given matter every person attending the meeting has equal information, ability to direct the discussion, or whatever contribution is required at the time.

In either case, whether the variation in participation is too great or too little, the effectiveness of the group will suffer. Performance will suffer for two reasons: (1) The time used by people with inequitably high participation levels will be unavailable to those who could have used it to make more valuable contributions; and (2) some people, who presumably are present because they have the potential to make a contribution, feel inhibited and do not contribute even when time is available. Research shows that satisfaction will also suffer as those who feel that their participation was curtailed will react negatively to the overall process. This is especially unfortunate when we realize that one of the potential payoffs from the use of participation is the increased enthusiasm and acceptance that accompanies the act of participating.

Guideline 1—Establish Fairness as a Standard

Establishing fairness as a standard can be accomplished through the use of guiding comments. For example, if one person continues to dominate the discussion with his view, we might say, "Okay, John, I think we understand your point of view. In all fairness, we should now give someone else the opportunity to be heard on the matter." Guiding comments can also be used to ensure equitable distribution between points of view, for example, by saying, "Well, we've just heard an argument for the proposal. Now I think it's only fair that we hear an argument against it."

In each of the above instances we were indicating to the speaker that it is only fair that he or she not participate for a while. We can be more aggressive but still tactful, such as "Ruth, we've heard your arguments in favor of the proposal. Maybe we ought to let someone else give their opinion." Also, in each of these instances we were not only closing the door, but with the second statement we were opening the door to another speaker and thus not shutting off discussion. You can state this explicitly as, "I don't mean to shorten the discussion—I just think that it's important that we share the opportunities to be heard."

Guiding comments can be used to increase the participation of certain members, as when saying, "Mr. Smith, we haven't heard from you on this proposal. What ideas do you have on the matter?" However, forcing people to speak can cause them to withdraw even further. In general, the better strategy is simply to provide openings in the discussion, as indicated above, and make general appeals to broaden participation, such as "I hope that before we close this discussion we get to hear from some of you who haven't yet made your contribution."

We have focused on the use of guiding comments to establish as standard behavior the maintenance of fairness with respect to opportunities to participate in the discussion. There is a second guideline for helping achieve equitable participation.

Guideline 2—Use the Round-Robin Technique

This is a very useful technique for attaining equitable participation when the purpose of the meeting is to identify and share key items. Examples of such items include nominees for a job opening or ideas for solving a problem. The procedure is to go around the table or other seating arrangement and ask for one item from one member at a time. As each item is put forth, the person leading the meeting writes it onto the chalkboard or flip chart and then asks for one item from the next participant. This elicitation and listing process continues around the table until the first person is reached. A second round then begins.

When participants whose turn it is have nothing to contribute, they simply say "pass." When their turn occurs again, on a subsequent round or cycle, they may have thought of another idea and are allowed to reenter the process, or they may pass again. The cycling is continued until all ideas are listed (that is, until everyone passes on the same round). In general, some participants will have fewer ideas and will therefore contribute in fewer rounds. At the same time, the structure of the process has provided the opportunity for equitable participation.

The **round-robin technique** is an excellent device for allowing everyone an equal opportunity to participate without forcing everyone to participate equally. In addition, it is quite useful for separating the generation of ideas from the evaluation of these ideas. In the application of the technique, the person leading the meeting usually asks that the idea simply be stated and not argued for or elaborated upon until all ideas have been elicited from all attending. Finally, the insistence that only one item be put forth during each participant's turn is useful in preventing the boredom and frustration that sets in when one person insists on enumerating all of his or her thoughts on a matter before anyone else gets to speak. A summary of the technique is shown in Figure 19-1.

The next four guidelines affect participation only indirectly but in important ways. Used individually or collectively they lead to increased information exchange, increased satisfaction, and consequently, in the long run, to increased participation. They are useful in the common situation where a series of meetings is held to address a complex problem or opportunity, but they are also useful in one-shot meetings.

As we see, the guidelines call for systematic application of common sense. The importance of formalizing them follows from the fact that if

THE ROUND-ROBIN TECHNIQUE

WHY USE IT?

1. Creates a public recognition of ideas.

2. Focuses the group's attention on the task.

3. Facilitates creation of ideas prompted by other ideas.

4. Leads to a larger number of ideas being shared.

5. Promotes equitable participation.

6. Provides task separation; that is, solution generation versus solution evaluation.

HOW TO USE IT

1. Record items as rapidly as possible (so the group's attention doesn't wander).

2. Record items in the words used by the participant, if at all possible (so that the person doesn't lose the sense of ownership).

3. Repeat each item aloud while recording it (so as to retain the attention of the participants).

4. Make the entire list visible by taping completed flip chart pages to the wall.

FIGURE 19-1 Whys and Hows of the Round-Robin Technique

they are not applied systematically the manager or other group leader may lose important opportunities for increasing the meeting's effectiveness.

Guideline 3—Establish the Task

At the beginning of each meeting, review the progress made to date and establish the task of the individual meeting. An example use of this guideline would be to say, "As you remember, at the end of the last meeting we had generated eight approaches for cutting costs in the department and had laid out a strategy for prioritizing them. Our schedule for today's meeting calls for prioritizing the approaches and then deciding who should take the lead on carrying each of them out." A more elaborate beginning, most useful with groups that meet more formally and less frequently, might also include overviewing the items on an agenda distributed for the meeting.

Use of this guideline accomplishes several goals. First, by reviewing the progress to date, we highlight the participants' past successes. This helps to increase satisfaction and the motivation to continue progressing. Second, by reviewing the progress, we identify where the group is with respect to carrying out its longer term task. This, combined with identifying the task of the current meeting, helps ensure that all of the participants have a common understanding of what needs to be done. Accomplishing these goals helps achieve the goal of minimizing confusion and misunderstanding and thus facilitates further progress.

Occasional reference to the particular task of the meeting can help keep the participants properly focused, and occasional reference to the progress being made at the meeting, such as "Well, we've successfully evaluated the first four alternatives, let's move on to number five," can help maintain interest and motivation.

The fourth guideline concerns reports from people with preassigned tasks. Whether these reports should be elicited just before or just after the progress review and task establishment mentioned above depends on the nature of the report and the preference of the person leading the meeting.

Guideline 4—Elicit Reports

At the beginning of each meeting, or as early as possible, get a report from each person with a preassigned task. For example, we might say, "Before we move on, let's hear what Sharon found out about the company's plans for upgrading its computing equipment." Use of this guideline accomplishes two goals. One is that it helps establish an atmosphere of accountability. If people learn through observation or experience that they will be held responsible for completing their assignments, they will be more inclined to complete them in the future.

The second goal accomplished is the providing of public recognition for the person reporting. On those occasions when the progress of the meeting causes the person leading the meeting to forget to elicit a report, the resulting nonrecognition invariably leads to dampened enthusiasm on the part of the member. To some extent, postponement of a report to subsequent meetings has the same effect. Similarly, people whose reports are put on hold generally do not contribute as effectively during their waiting period. In some instances they are concerned about whether or when they will receive credit for the completed assignment. In other instances they are concerned about making a good presentation.

There are, of course, some situations where reports may be premature and would require later repetition to be most useful. When this is the case, it is usually better to simply comment on the existence of the forthcoming report and the time when you will ask for it. The last two guidelines are applied at the end of the meeting.

Guideline 5—Summarize Group Accomplishments

At the end of each meeting, summarize what was accomplished, where this puts the group on its schedule, and what will be the group task at the next meeting. The goals accomplished through the use of this guideline are similar to those achieved by using the first guideline. By summarizing what was accomplished, we highlight the participants' success and progress and therefore increase their satisfaction with having participated in the meeting. This is especially helpful when not much measurable progress has been made—when all we can point to is the fact that we "exchanged views" or "examined alternatives." It is extremely important to highlight that something was accomplished, that information was shared, and that "we gained a better understanding of each other's views."

By noting where the participants are on the schedule and what the task of the next meeting will be, we minimize uncertainty and maximize the chances that the people will give some thought to forthcoming tasks. The sixth guideline also concerns the end of the meeting.

Guideline 6—Clarify the Assignments

At the end of each meeting, make public and clear who has what assignments to complete by the next meeting. If the assignments are simple and we expect that they will be fulfilled, we may restate them ourselves, as "Bill, now as I understand it, you're going to get the information about the cost of leasing the computer terminals." It is usually a good idea, however, to seek some sort of response or acknowledgement, for example, by continuing the above summary statement with "Is that right?" or "Do you need any help from me or anyone else to do that?" If the assignment is complex or if we are intent on ensuring that a commitment to carry through has been made, we might have members with assignments state the assignments. An example is "Now let's see what everyone's going to do between now and the next meeting. Mary, what will you be doing?"

This guideline serves several purposes. One is that it helps reduce misunderstandings about assignments. Another is that, since the group hears who is to do what, use of the guideline tends to create a feeling of being responsible to the group as well as to the manager. This tends to increase motivation. A third purpose that it serves is to highlight and recognize contributions that will be made by individual people. This also tends to increase motivation. The overall effect of this guideline is that the results and information needed at some subsequent time, usually the next meeting, are available. Few things are as detrimental as a meeting where no progress is made because someone did not bring a key piece of information.

These six guidelines are effective mechanisms for helping group members achieve equitable participation, accomplish their task, and feel genuinely satisfied about their participation in the group's efforts. The guidelines apply in a wide variety of situations.

We now turn to examining a more formal approach to managing participation that has become widely adopted by both private industry and public-sector organizations.

THE NOMINAL GROUP TECHNIQUE

Under some conditions it is necessary or appropriate to obtain the ideas of people in the context of a meeting and also to have the participants provide an evaluation of the ideas. The frequency and importance with which these conditions arise have led organizational behavior researchers and consultants to develop and test packaged techniques for accomplishing these ends. One of these is called the Nominal Group Technique (NGT).[3]

In many situations we know that we should obtain the ideas of a number of other people, and in some cases we should attempt to obtain some degree of public agreement on the value of these ideas. One example is the situation where a manager is looking for ways to increase sales and wants to be sure to obtain the ideas of the sales representatives on how this could best be accomplished. Another example is the situation where the president of the school board wants to obtain ideas on new programs or initiatives that the local school should undertake. Clearly such situations require that the opinions of the people affected should be obtained and, in some cases, considered publicly. Participation is necessary.

These are not easy situations to deal with. How can they best be managed? How can you control a meeting where you want everyone to hear the opinions or knowledge of participants who might have different goals, different beliefs about the best way to achieve common goals, or different information about the decision situation? A group management procedure that has been developed in response to this question, and that has proven itself effective in actual practice, is called the **Nominal Group Technique** (NGT). This technique is explicitly designed to obtain and review decision-related information in a group setting. For example, it is frequently used to identify concerns or worries that people might have about a proposed problem solution; or, more specifically, it is used to identify the criteria and constraints that people would use to evaluate a solution. As another example, the technique is also used to identify and define the problems that group members see in their present situation—it is used in the problem-exploration phase of the overall decision-making effort.

The Nominal Group Technique involves a structured group meeting which proceeds along the following format. Imagine a meeting room in which seven to ten individuals are seated around a table in full view of each other. At the beginning of the meeting they do not speak to one another. Instead, each individual writes ideas on a pad of paper. After five or ten minutes, a structured sharing of ideas takes place. Each individual, in round-robin fashion, presents one idea from his or her private list. The group leader writes the person's idea on a flip chart in full view of other members. There is still no discussion at this point of the meeting—only the recording of ideas. This round-robin listing continues until all participants indicate they have no further ideas to share.

The output of this **nominal group** phase of the meeting is a list of ideas, such as concerns or alternative solutions. Discussion of a structured nature occurs during the next, interactive phase of the meeting. The approach is to systematically ask for questions or comments about each item listed on the flip chart. When this process is complete, independent evaluation of the ideas takes place. Each participant privately indicates preferences by rank-ordering the subset of alternatives that he or she most favors. The initial group output is the mathematically pooled outcome of these two phases.

Turning now from this summary overview of the first two steps of the technique, let us examine the step-by-step procedure for using the technique in its entirety.

Step 1—Generate Ideas in a Nominal Group Setting

Have the participants generate their ideas or information in a nominal group setting. In this step you encourage people to work hard at the task of listing whatever you are seeking from them (for example, solutions, problems, or causes) and to work individually. For example, you might say, "During this ten minutes of independent thinking, please don't talk to other members, interrupt their thinking, or look at their work sheets." Your purpose in deliberately causing the participants to work in the presence of each other is to create some degree of task-oriented tension. When people are in a social environment where the objective of creating an extensive list is so clearly being striven for by others, they tend to be highly motivated to seek the same objective. Research shows that such nominal groups generate more and better ideas than conventional interacting groups.[4]

Notice that the participants are not assured that their ideas will not be shown to the other participants. Indeed, the next step in applying the technique is just the opposite; it involves the sharing of the ideas from all participants. The reasoning behind this procedure follows from research showing that when people know in advance that they will be sharing their ideas or information with other group members, they are motivated to work harder to develop more and better ideas. On the other hand, we also know that they will feel more inhibited because of possible criticism of their ideas. A procedure for dealing with these conflicting arguments is described under Step 2.

Experience shows that if you use the Nominal Group Technique to get at sensitive, political, or personal problems in the problem-exploration phase, you will be more effective if Step 1 is conducted twice. The first time, technical or operational (impersonal) items are elicited. The second time, political or emotional (personal) items are elicited. If this two-stage process is not used, these sensitive issues tend not to surface.

Step 2—Share Ideas with the Round-Robin Technique

Have the participants share their ideas using a round-robin recording procedure. In this step, the information the members have written down in Step 1 is recorded on a flip chart or chalkboard that is visible to the entire group. As we noted in our discussion of Guideline 2 for managing meetings, round-robin recording means going around the table where the participants are seated and asking for one idea from one member at a time. The group leader writes the idea of a group member on the flip chart and then proceeds to ask for one idea from the next group member in turn.

The fact that a list is written is of particular importance. A written idea is more objective and less personal than a verbal statement. If the idea is in writing, individuals are better able to separate it from the personality or position of the individual contributing it. People are also able to deal with a larger number of ideas if these ideas are written down and displayed.

If there is a concern that the participants may be inhibited in generating ideas if they know that these ideas will be made public to the other group members, the group can be asked to pass in the written lists anonymously. The group leader then writes down an item from the first list, then an item from the next list, and so forth, in round-robin fashion. In either case, applying the round-robin technique to the written lists maintains participant interest more effectively than would listing all the items from one person's list before moving on to the next person's.

Step 3—Discuss Ideas in Sequence

Have the participants discuss the ideas in a predetermined sequence. This discussion gives the originators of the ideas, as well as other group members, an opportunity to clarify their meaning and intent. The members can also share their thoughts concerning the importance, feasibility, and merits of the idea. In other words, the discussion provides for the sharing of more detailed information.

In the early development and applications of the Nominal Group Technique, this step was carried out in a highly controlled manner—only explanations (rather than evaluation) were allowed. Recent research and experience with applications indicate that a more open discussion leads to greater member satisfaction; and because it facilitates information exchange, an open discussion also leads to improved decision quality. The continued requirement that some predetermined sequence be used to control the discussion helps ensure that the discussion of one idea is not curtailed by references to ideas still being discussed. It also ensures that all ideas do have a chance to get discussed. Occasionally, in order to be certain that all ideas are discussed within the time available, it is useful to limit the discussion time devoted to any one idea.

If the manager who will be receiving the group's output is interested in maintaining a great deal of personal latitude and flexibility in the particular decision situation, he or she can stop using the technique at this point. The manager will have acquired a good deal of information, and some participation will have taken place. However, Steps 4 and 5 allow the manager to sharpen his or her understanding of the group's views.

Step 4—Use Rank Voting to Rank Ideas

Have the participants use rank voting to indicate their feelings concerning the importance of the ideas. Then determine the group output by summing the ranked votes. The typical approach for implementing this step is for the group leader to ask each participant to (1) select the five ideas that he or she thinks are most important; (2) rank them in order of their importance; and (3) assign a score of five points to the first-ranked idea, four to the second, and so forth. The group's preference is determined by summing the point scores for each idea. Thus, the preferred idea is typically the one that received several five-point or four-point votes.

If it is felt that some members will not vote their true feelings if the individual votes are made public, the voting can be done with a secret ballot. In most cases, however, it is convenient to point to one of the recorded ideas and ask for those who assigned five points to the idea to raise their hands. The group leader then writes down next to the idea the "fives" that are indicated. The process is repeated for each of the remaining four rank values. This vote-elicitation cycle is repeated for each of the listed ideas. A good idea in a group of seven people will typically have written next to it "5, 5, 4, 2, 2," where two members did not include it in their preferred set of five. The use of rank voting allows all participants to influence the relative evaluation of several ideas and is more satisfying than allowing each participant to have only one vote to allocate across all ideas.

Step 5—Discuss the Voting Results

Once voting and tabulating are completed, it is often useful for the group to discuss the voting results. This helps achieve a sense of closure and accomplishment.

If Step 5 is included, it is most efficient to discuss those ideas that were ranked quite differently by different members of the group. For example, the group should be encouraged to talk about ideas that receive both point scores of five and scores of zero (where some members did not include the idea in their list of the best five ideas).

Step 6—Use Rank Voting to Rank Ideas

Have the participants use rank voting to indicate their feelings concerning the importance of the ideas. Then determine the group output by summing the ranked votes. Step 6 is a replication of Step 4 and is optional. It should be included if any of the participants would like to change their votes as a result of the discussion from Step 5.

The Nominal Group Technique can be used in each phase of the decision-making process—in problem exploration, in generating alternatives, and in choice making. Thus it can be used in place of the typical interactive group meeting with which we are all familiar. Its advantage is that it helps overcome most of the behaviors that diminish group effectiveness and that we discussed earlier. Its disadvantages are that, even though its nominal group phase is effective in surfacing information, the high level of control during the discussion phase may inhibit the full evaluation of this information. The technique has been especially effective in dealing with groups where wide differences in status or opinion were likely to lead to little generation or sharing of information or opinions. It is also useful when you want a preliminary and public evaluation of ideas or alternatives that you intend to draw upon more thoroughly at a later time.

The technique was developed around 1970 by two organizational behavior researchers, Andrew Van de Ven and Andre Delbecq, who were interested in minimizing the behaviors that interfere with effective participation. To a considerable extent the technique represents their creative synthesis of the scientific studies of other scholars.[5] It has been widely adopted by practitioners. A typical study of an application of the Nominal Group Technique resulted in the following report:

> Statistical analysis (based on participant questionnaires on a solar energy plan) compared NGT with traditional interacting groups (committees). Results were consistent with previous laboratory and field studies. The participants evaluated NGT as being superior to interacting groups in five specific areas: (1) balanced participation, (2) quantity of ideas, (3) quality of ideas, (4) efficiency of the NGT process, and (5) the overall sense of accomplishment felt by participants. NGT was also rated

superior on a composite index and on five general measures (would you use NGT again, expected quality of the solar plan, NGT versus conferences, NGT versus boards with citizen participation, and NGT versus boards with professional planners).[6]

Of the difficulties encountered in the study, training of the group leaders appeared to be the most serious. Group leaders must be well trained and comfortable with the mechanics and presentation of the technique if it is to be effective.

LABOR-MANAGEMENT COMMITTEES AND QUALITY CIRCLES

Given the complexity of the issues facing many organizations, it seems reasonable to believe that management could make better decisions if workers had an effective means of communicating their ideas on the issues—if they had an effective means of participating in the problem-solving process. This fact, plus the fact that participation tends to lead people to implement decisions more enthusiastically, has led to the development of formal means for worker participation.

Significant increases in formal participation by production workers in plant management have occurred several times in this century. The first occurred in the 1930s, when Joseph Scanlon, an accountant, steelworker, and local union president, led the development of what was to become known as the **Scanlon Plan**. The plan had two radical features. One was the establishment of shop-floor committees of supervisors and workers with the responsibility to generate and pass on worker suggestions for improving methods of doing the work. The other radical feature was a group-bonus, or gains-sharing plan, based on monthly performance and paid to the work groups monthly.[7]

The second significant experience with labor-management production committees took place during World War II, when industry was trying to increase output in the face of shortages of labor, materials, and energy. Over 5,000 joint committees were formed, about 1,000 of which concentrated on production problems. In the opinion of many employers and union leaders, these committees improved productivity and morale and enhanced mutual understanding of the broad problems of the common enterprise. When the war ended, most of the committees were discontinued.[8]

In the 1960s and 1970s, worker participation with a new thrust gained considerable momentum outside North America. As contrasted with the purpose of participation in the two earlier periods which was to increase productivity, the thrust of worker participation in Europe, South America, and elsewhere during this third period was **codetermination**, the equal sharing of decision making authority between labor and management.[9]

In the late 1970s and continuing into the 1980s, United States industry found itself competing with Japanese and other foreign firms that were able to produce products of similar or superior quality at a much lower cost. Again, as during World War II, American management began involving workers in production problem-solving and cost-reduction teams often called **quality circles**.[10]

There are no features of quality circles that distinguish them from the earlier labor-management efforts described previously, except perhaps the motivation for the workers to participate. The Scanlon Plan focused on financial incentives for the work group, the World War II committees were motivated at least in part by national security considerations, and the quality circles were formed in the face of potential loss of jobs due to foreign competition. In each of these three circumstances the need for worker participation became evident. Thus although the exact nature of quality circles varies somewhat from firm to firm, in all cases they involve workers and managers collectively determining ways to improve productivity.

IMPORTANT TERMS AND CONCEPTS

effective meeting
equitable participation
round-robin technique
Nominal Group Technique

nominal group
Scanlon Plan
codetermination
quality circles

STUDY AND DISCUSSION QUESTIONS

1. State four reasons why the encouragement of participation by employees is a pragmatic managerial behavior.

2. How can you display a positive reaction to bad news?

3. What, precisely, is meant by the guideline, "create communication opportunities"?

4. What is meant by the phrase "an effective meeting"?

5. What is meant by "equitable participation"?

6. How would you try to convince a group participant to go along with using the round-robin technique to collect and record ideas if he or she claimed that it was silly or unnecessary?

7. Why is it useful to have the participants discuss listed ideas in a predetermined sequence?

8. Why is it a good idea to have rank-voting participants allocate their 15 points in the amounts of 5, 4, 3, 2, and 1, instead of letting them allocate their points as they wish?

9. Do you think participation will increase or decrease in American businesses during the next decade? Why?

10. What possible disadvantages of participation can you think of and how could you minimize their likelihood or impact?

CRITICAL INCIDENT

SPRINGWOOD'S DECLINE

The Springwood Preschool and Day-Care Center is a for-profit day-care center for children from three to five years old. Founded in 1972, it was the first and only full-service day-care center in a medium-sized Sun-Belt city. The day-care center became quite profitable in just a few years, filling the rooms of the renovated Victorian home in which it was located with children and teachers throughout the workday.

In 1982 a similar business was opened by one of the former teachers, and in 1984 a third for-profit full-service child-care center (the Littlefolk School) opened. In spite of the city's fairly rapid growth, Springwood began to experience declining enrollments. This, combined with the increased property taxes and utility bills that followed from the city's attempts to cope with its growth, caused Springwood to lose money in 1985 for the first time ever.

To Eleanor Jordan, director and part owner of Springwood, 1986 and beyond looked like years of further financial losses, and undoubtedly the business would have to close unless something was done. Evidently some of the staff had the same concerns. Two of the eight full-time staff members took positions with the rival day-care centers at the end of 1985, explaining to Jordan that "While we like Springwood, job security seems better at the Littlefolk School." Two of the remaining full-time staff and two part-time staff members also expressed concern to Jordan about the enrollment trends.

Jordan was not at all confident that she had any really effective way to reverse Springwood's situation. Her training, she told people, was in child development, not business development. One evening, however, she attended a meeting of the newly founded Women's Business Association and heard a lecture expounding the advantages and methods of participative management. She became convinced that night that as a first step in addressing Springwood's problems she should call a meeting of the ten remaining staff members to discuss the situation and to identify actions that might be helpful. The next morning she was not as certain. "Maybe I should just go out and hire a consultant," she thought. "But I wonder what the staff would think of that."

1. What are the possible positive outcomes that might result from the meeting Jordan is considering?

2. What are the possible negative outcomes?

3. If Jordan does have the meeting, which Guidelines for Managing Meetings do you think she should use?

4. Briefly describe three tasks where the Nominal Group Technique might be useful to Jordan in managing the staff's efforts to address Springwood's problems.

REFERENCES

1. Rosen, S., and A. Tesser. "On Reluctance to Communicate Undesirable Information: The MUM Effect," *Sociometry*, Vol. 33, No. 3, 1970, pp. 253–263.

2. Rosen, S., and A. Tesser. "On Reluctance to Communicate Undesirable Information: The MUM Effect."

3. Delbecq, A. L., A. H. Van de Ven, and D. H. Gustafson. *Group Techniques for Program Planning: A Guide to Nominal Group and Delphi Processes.* Glenview, Ill.: Scott, Foresman and Company, 1975.

4. Van de Ven, A. H., and A. L. Delbecq. "Nominal Versus Interacting Group Processes for Committee Decision Making Effectiveness," *Academy of Management Journal*, Vol. 14, No. 2, June, 1971, pp. 203–212.

5. Van de Ven and Delbecq. "Nominal Versus Interacting Group Processes for Committee Decision Making Effectiveness."

6. Stephenson, Blair Y., and Stephen G. Franklin. "Better Decision-Making for a 'Real World' Environment," *Administrative Management*, Vol. 42, July, 1981, pp. 24–38.

7. Otis, Irvin. "Rx for Improving Productivity: Labor-Management Committees," *S.A.M. Advanced Management Journal*, Vol. 48, No. 2, Spring, 1983, pp. 53–59.

8. Otis. "Rx for Improving Productivity: Labor-Management Committees."

9. Cordova, E. "Workers' Participation in Decisions within Enterprises: Recent Trends and Problems," *International Labour Review*, Vol. 121, March–April, 1982, pp. 125–140.

10. Munchus, George, III. "Employer-Employee Based Quality Circles in Japan: Human Resource Policy Implications for American Firms," *Academy of Management Review*, Vol. 8, No. 2, April, 1983, pp. 255–261.

SUGGESTED READINGS

Boyle, Richard J. "Wrestling with Jellyfish," *Harvard Business Review*, Vol. 62, January-February, 1984, pp. 74–83.

Business Week, "Deep Sensing: A Pipeline to Employee Morale," January 29, 1979, pp. 124–128.

Dickson, John W. "Participatory Forums and Influence," *Academy of Management Journal*, Vol. 25, No. 4, December, 1982, pp. 915–920.

Erez, Miriam, P. Christopher Earley, and Charles L. Hulin. "The Impact of Participation on Goal Acceptance and Performance: A Two-Step Model," *Academy of Management Journal*, Vol. 28, No. 1, March, 1985, pp. 50–66.

Goldstein, S. G. "Organizational Dualism and Quality Circles," *Academy of Management Review*, Vol. 10, No. 3, July, 1985, pp. 504–517.

Halal, William E., and Bob S. Brown. "Participative Management: Myth and Reality," *California Management Review*, Vol. 23, No. 4, Summer, 1981, pp. 20–31.

Steel, Robert P., Anthony J. Mento, Benjamin L. Dilla, Nestor K. Ovalle, and Russell F. Lloyd. "Factors Influencing the Success and Failure of Two Quality Circle Programs," *Journal of Management*, Vol. II, No. 1, Spring, 1985, pp. 99–122.

White, Sam E., John E. Dittrich, and James R. Lang. "The Effects of Group Decision-Making Process and Problem-Situation Complexity on Implementation Attempts," *Administrative Science Quarterly*, Vol. 25, No. 3, September, 1980, pp. 428–440.

20

Goal Setting in Organizations

> It is no accident that the old story of the blind men meeting up with an elephant on the road is so popular among management people. For each level of management sees the same "elephant"—the business—from a different angle of vision. The production foreman, like the blind man who felt the elephant's leg and decided that a tree was in his way, tends to see only the immediate production problems. Top management—the blind man feeling the trunk and deciding a snake bars his way—tends to see only the enterprise as a whole; it sees stockholders, financial problems, altogether a host of highly abstract relations and figures. Operating management—the blind man feeling the elephant's belly and thinking himself up against a landslide—tends to see things functionally. Each level needs its particular vision; it could not do its job without it. Yet these visions are so different that people on different levels talking about the same thing often do not realize it—or, as frequently happens, believe that they are talking about the same thing when in reality they are poles apart.
>
> An effective management must direct the vision and efforts of all managers toward a common goal. It must insure that individual managers understand what results are demanded of them. It must insure that superiors understand what to expect of each of their subordinate managers. It must motivate each manager to maximum efforts in the right direction. And while encouraging high standards of workmanship, it must make them the means to the end of business performance rather than ends in themselves.
>
> *Peter F. Drucker[1]*

An organization is created to achieve certain objectives of its founders. It exists for a purpose, and the behavior of its members must make a contribution to the fulfillment of that purpose in order to have value and meaning in an organizational context.

The individual members of an organization have their own private objectives and, understandably, view employment as a means of achieving them. As a result, the possibility always exists that the objectives of the organization will be subordinated to the diverse private interests of its members. On occasion, jobs are created, expenditures are made, and projects are undertaken that serve no major organizational purpose and have meaning only in terms of the private goals of parasitic members who feed on the organization but do not significantly contribute to it. Because this is an ever-present danger, an organization must constantly make its objectives explicit and exert a special effort to involve its members in those objectives.

Although the terms *objectives* and *goals* are popularly used as synonyms, writers in this field often make a distinction between the two. **Objectives** are desired outcomes, such as obtaining or retaining a dominant share of a product market. **Goals** are concrete and specific formulations of these objectives and include a completion schedule. For example, a goal may be set to increase market share by 10 percent each year for a specified time.

Chapter 20 takes a practical approach to a practical subject. Its specific objectives are

TO UNDERSTAND:

1. The benefits of goal setting

2. How to establish a successful management by objectives (MBO) program

3. How MBO programs relate to other systems of management and organization

THE BENEFITS OF GOAL SETTING

Goal setting may bring about significant changes in a manager's typical modes of thought, perception, and behavior. The occurrence of these changes, or lack of it, accounts in part for the success or failure of individual managers and of an organization's goals program.

Managers who have for the first time begun to set goals in a systematic way differ greatly in the value they place on goal setting and in their concept of what it involves. Because they think differently, they behave differently, and as shown in Figure 20-1, these changes are positively expressed in results. Although the organization benefits directly when its objectives are reached, it is not the only beneficiary. Each goal-directed manager also experiences personally the many tangible and intangible rewards of high achievement.

A Broader Perspective

Managers often need help to avoid becoming so preoccupied with one aspect of the business that other important areas are neglected. This was the case in a struggling plastics company whose young president, an aggressive marketer, pushed sales to the limit while giving so little attention to finances that the company was sold into receivership. The president seemed to believe that success was inevitable as long as sales continued to be strong at a price that would permit a reasonable profit. Because of inexperience in the financial area, however, the president failed to consider the enormous costs of manufacturing and shipping the company's products and the lag time between these expenditures and payment by the customers. In order to finance sales, the last of the company's assets, the accounts receivable (the presumably collectible debts of customers), were mortgaged. A short time later the bank took over the company when one of its large, slow-paying customers went out of business.

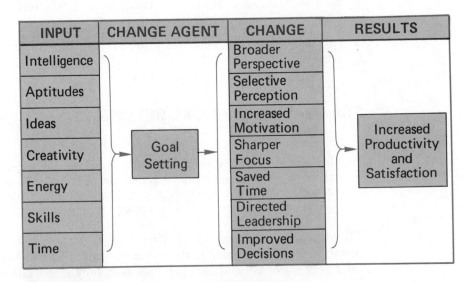

FIGURE 20-1 The Benefits of Goal Setting

The most serious problem in the example just stated is that the president had tunnel vision—he lacked the broad perspective needed to visualize all the important aspects of the business at one time. Goal setting encourages balanced achievement in all areas that are vital to an organization's success. It forces management to pull back from the pressures of day-to-day operations and systematically look at the different facets of current operations in terms of organizational purpose and long-term objectives.

Selective Perception

As we saw in Chapter 3, people with clearly defined goals are provided with a special set of filters which accent the part of the environment that contributes to goal achievement; these same filters suppress as irrelevant much that would otherwise clutter one's consciousness. Intensely goal-oriented managers selectively perceive their environment in terms of their needs. For example, managers who are deeply committed to achieving a specific level of production become preoccupied with that need and continually view their environment in terms of resources for achieving their objectives. Millions of stimuli constantly compete for their attention, but relatively few are admitted to consciousness. These are selectively filtered through the needs and desires with which the managers are most preoccupied.

The manner in which selective perception enables a manager to become aware of opportunities and resources which would otherwise be hidden is seen in this statement by a first line supervisor at General Tire and Rubber Company:

> I had 45 operators on my shift, but not one that I was willing to promote into the inspector position until the personnel director helped me spell out exactly what kind of person I needed. Then I discovered that the one to be promoted was right under my nose. I couldn't see her good qualities because I didn't know what I was looking for, and I didn't particularly like her. She was too strong, too efficient, and too willing to sound off when everything didn't go just right. She was exactly what the inspector job called for.

Increased Motivation

The process of goal setting emphasizes the importance of investing mental and physical resources in areas that have the highest potential for a payoff. To experience the attracting force of a goal is, in effect, to anticipate the rewards inherent in reaching it. Research by Ivancevich and McMahon suggests that persons whose higher order needs are strong (a need to do worthwhile work, to pace oneself, to make decisions about work methods, and so forth) are more motivated by goal challenge, clarity, and feedback than are persons whose higher order needs are weak.[2] The motivational implications of goal setting are also seen in the growing evidence that feelings of success, which are most likely to occur when one reaches a defined goal, are associated with increased self-esteem and work involvement. Thus, a cycle develops with success leading to involvement and involvement leading to higher motivation and success.[3] Edwin Locke makes the point that goal setting is now recognized, explicitly or implicitly, by virtually every major theory of work motivation.[4] Some evidence indicates that goal setting has a greater impact on motivation than does participation.[5]

Sharper Focus

When their normally diffused attention is focused on an important goal, managers tend to develop an intense concentration of thought and energy. This sharper focus increases the availability of the mental resources needed to think clearly and solve problems.

Saved Time

Goal setting itself is a time-consuming process, but the time invested is rapidly recovered through the efficiency that results from focusing on ends instead of means. The constant awareness that a specific result must be achieved by a specified time and that one's contribution will be measured in terms of that result inevitably motivates an individual to view time as a uniquely valuable resource.

Directed Leadership

Nobody wants to follow a leader who has no sense of direction. By contrast, people feel secure in following a purposeful, goal-directed leader. Commitment to goals suggests to others that a manager is knowledgeable, competent, and likely to succeed. Achievement-oriented people find it easy to identify with an achieving, purposeful supervisor. Furthermore, an increase in goal direction contributes to a high degree of self-confidence, a personal attribute found in most successful managers.

Improved Decisions

Goals serve as criteria against which decisions are made and evaluated. This is illustrated in the experience of a university sophomore whose first-year studies were almost a waste of time because of her lack of direction. When, during her second year, she set a goal to earn a BBA degree as a first step toward becoming an attorney, her decision processes changed abruptly. Realizing that high grades would be required to enter law school, her daily decisions for time allocation were made in the light of her ultimate career objective. The goal also influenced her decision not to pledge a time-consuming sorority and to back away from a relationship that could have led to marriage early in her educational career. Thus, her entire life-style became goal oriented.

Goal setting, like policy formation, is itself a decision-making process. Once a decision has been made to reach a particular corporate or individual goal, many other decisions can be made by reference to it. The role of goals in decision making is seen in this statement to a superior by a thoroughly frustrated and hostile production manager:

> How can you hold me accountable for anything? I don't know from one day to the next whether I'm supposed to be expanding production capacity or closing down operations. One day I read a memo that convinces me I should lay off workers, and the next day I get the feeling the president is going to be all over me because inventories are so low we can't fill our orders. Since I'm not sure what our objectives are, any decision I make around here is a shot in the dark.

This review of the benefits of goal setting strongly suggests that managers who set explicit goals will be more effective than those who do not. It also indicates that the manager's subordinates and employer will benefit from the manager's goal setting.

PERSONALITY AND GOAL SETTING

Because individual differences in goal-seeking behavior are deeply ingrained in personality, resistance to organizational goal setting can be expected in most organizations. Resistance may even be encountered in some individuals whose lives are generally goal directed but who choose to avoid the discipline and paperwork required by a formal goals program.

Goal seeking begins in infancy and by adulthood has matured into a highly complex mental activity. Children who are rewarded for high achievement tend to become goal-directed adults. On the other hand, children who encounter unrealistic expectations and low anticipation of reward are discouraged from goal setting and may develop a life-style almost void of conscious goal-setting activity. The personal influence of parents, teachers, and peers often combines with the impact of laws, rules, cultural expectations, and fixed schedules (school, sports, and music lessons) to externally guide an individual through school and into a career while requiring a minimum of purposive, self-directed behavior. This externally directed person learns to value the lack of conflict involved in drifting with the stream and waiting to see what happens rather than risk the possibility of failure involved in setting a goal to make something happen. In many organizations, even in some managerial positions, this externally directed behavior is rewarded. In practically all organizations, people who are not goal directed thrive in positions where opportunities for initiative and autonomy are limited.

As one might expect from the vast differences among people, many individuals are resistant to the goal setting involved in formal programs. Although the ranks of management are not free of goal-resistant personalities, effective managers do tend to be goal seekers. The goal-oriented manager is rewarded by opportunities for autonomy and self-direction. Among such persons success is perceived as a matter of deliberate, intentional action rather than luck. Events are perceived as occurring because of choice, not chance. The future is viewed as relatively predictable because of one's ability to learn from the past, anticipate future events, intelligently adapt to unforeseen circumstances, and overcome obstacles by force of will and rational action.

In view of the broad individual differences in goal directedness and everyone's natural resistance to change, it is unrealistic to expect goals programs to be equally effective at all organizational levels. The opportunity managers have to progress on the basis of merit and their consequent need to be responsive to the desires of their superiors are often incentives to become goal directed, even when it runs counter to deeply ingrained personality patterns. Resistance to goal setting is, however, sometimes strong and persistent among managers as well as lower level employees.

MANAGEMENT BY OBJECTIVES

Management by objectives (MBO) is a managerial philosophy and technique that has the potential for creating self-directed behavior change and for increasing productivity. The failure of MBO in specific settings does not detract from this potential.

The workday of a typical employee is defined in terms of hours on the job rather than results achieved. From the worker's point of view, acceptable performance often means being on time for work, keeping busy, and conforming to work rules. This is a normal response to supervision which attempts to achieve productivity exclusively by means of job design, lockstep procedures, close supervision, and other devices which divert the attention of employees from the objectives of the organization.

Definition

Management by objectives (MBO) or *management by results* de-emphasizes external controls and, to the greatest extent possible, focuses attention on ends rather than on means. Although the current theory and practice of MBO has evolved from the research, experience, and critical thought of many writers and practitioners, the contributions of Peter Drucker[6] and George Odiorne,[7] are especially notable. Odiorne defines the MBO process in these terms:

> In brief the system of management by objectives can be described as a process whereby superior and subordinate managers of an organization jointly identify its common goals, define each individual's major area of responsibility in terms of results expected of him, and use these measures as guides for operating the unit and assessing the contribution of each of its members.[8]

Evaluation

Since MBO programs differ greatly, there is a sense in which MBO must be understood and evaluated in terms of its application to each situation. For this reason it is difficult to make generalizations about either its nature or effectiveness. Nevertheless, from a strictly logical point of view, the system is defensible. Since it allows the individual maximum discretion in determining the means by which goals will be reached, it contributes to a supervisory style that respects the subordinate and provides an opportunity for meaningful work. Performance evaluation under MBO tends to be centered on results and behavior rather than personality and is consequently less likely to involve bias and irrelevant judgments. Furthermore, on the basis of theoretical considerations alone, one would predict that under MBO results would be better than under alternative management systems.

Research to date supports the hypothesis that goal direction such as that expressed in MBO does, in fact, increase productivity. Kolb and Boyatzis cite several studies that support the proposition that conscious goal setting leads to increased achievement, and they conclude from their own research that goal setting for personal development also yields favorable results:

> The experiment presents convincing evidence that conscious goal setting plays an important role in the process of self-directed behavior change. Individuals tend to change more in those areas of their self-concept that are related to their consciously set goals. These changes are independent of the difficulty of the change goal and thus do not appear to be a result of an initial choice of easy-to-achieve goals.[9]

Research by Latham and Baldes provides an example of the effectiveness of goals programs. Following up on previous research with 292 Southern pulpwood producers, the specific problem was to motivate truck drivers to more nearly approximate the legal weight limit of the logs they hauled from the woods to the mill. On the basis of data collected on the net weight of the logs hauled by 36 trucks over a 12-month period, Latham and Baldes noted that performance improved immediately when specific, hard goals were assigned. (The assigned goal was 94 percent of the legal limit, as opposed to "do your best to approximate the legal limit.") The following statement attests to the practical significance of the goal-setting program:

> Corporate policy prevents a detailed public discussion of the impact of this particular study on the company. However, it can be said that without the increase in efficiency due to goal setting it would have cost the company a quarter of a million dollars for the purchase of additional trucks in order to deliver the same quantity of logs to the mills. This figure does not include the cost for the additional diesel fuel that would have been consumed or the expenses for recruiting and hiring additional truck drivers.[10]

A number of studies conducted in different industries have produced similar results. Evidence exists, however, that early gains from MBO may sharply decline eight or nine months after initial goal setting.[11,12] Possibilities for offsetting this decline are found in periodic retraining programs and formal systems for directly linking rewards to the achievement of realistic but challenging goals.[13] The ongoing interest and participation of top management are also major determinants of continued payoffs from the use of MBO.

THE NATURE OF GOALS IN ORGANIZATIONS

> Goal setting, the heart of an MBO program, has always been an important aspect of effective management, but the goal setting of MBO is more than a restatement of common practices. Goal setting is gradually becoming less an intuitive art and more a scientific methodology.

Since the very existence of an organization is an expression of purposive behavior, it follows that organizational goal setting has historically been a part of the management process. MBO does, however, possess two unique characteristics which may potentially alter managerial behavior:

1. A strong emphasis on the importance of consciously formulating goals.
2. A body of information on which a workable goals system can be developed and integrated into the organization.

Managers differ greatly in goal-setting effectiveness, as do the methodologies they employ. In one sense the evolution of MBO as a management system has been a process of capturing the diverse experiences of those managers who have been most effective in setting and reaching goals and systematizing the results for use by others. There is currently no standardized MBO terminology or methodology in spite of the fact that much literature has been published on the subject, and increasing agreement is emerging on what constitutes effective MBO practice. Perhaps the most serious problem that exists for people who attempt to integrate and systematize the available information on MBO is that the process necessarily differs with the size and nature of the organization and the unique views of MBO held by the people involved. Although each writer selects for presentation what appears to represent the most advanced state of the art, it should be understood that the content presented is always a sample of a very heterogeneous body of information.

Strategic Objectives and Goals

In recent years managers have become increasingly aware of the importance of long-range corporate planning.[14] The complexities of modern business are such that effectiveness in making current operating decisions requires the broad perspective that long-range objectives and goals provide. In their most general form, long-range strategic objectives are broad statements of organizational purpose or reason for existence. In business organizations purpose is expressed primarily, but not exclusively, in terms of profitability. Some organizations have also found it meaningful to make explicit other purposes such as fulfilling specified responsibilities to customers, to the public, and to their own employees.

As shown in Figure 20-2, there are differences in the nature of the goals set by top management, middle management, supervisory management, and nonsupervisory employees. For purposes of communication, goals at different levels are assigned different names, beginning with strategic goals at the top, moving downward through tactical goals, and ending with projects or tasks. This should not be interpreted to mean that managers have no project-level goals. It does show, however, where each type of goal tends to originate.

Where MBO is practiced, organizational purpose is expressed by top management in the form of *strategic objectives* (formulations of desired outcomes). They provide an overall umbrella for goal setting at all management levels and may relate to any aspect of the organization such as profits, market standing, labor relations, technology, and management development. *Strategic goals* are concrete and specific statements of these objectives. In addition to their specificity, they differ from strategic objectives in that they are to be achieved within a designated period of time. Strategic goals may be long-range (extending several years into the future) or short range (one year or less). They are strategic in that their achievement is crucial to the organization's success, and they serve to communicate the meaning of success to the lower levels of the organization.

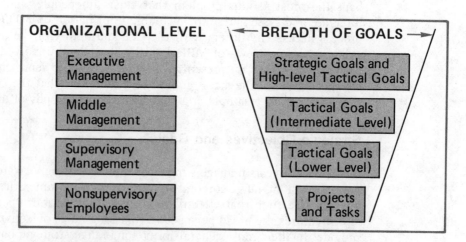

FIGURE 20-2 Relationship Between Level of Management and
Breadth and Type of Goals

Especially in medium and small organizations, there is a point at which top management may become excessively involved in the means of reaching strategic goals, although that point is difficult to define. The concept of goal levels is shown in the following goals statement:

> *Goal A.* During the 1986 fiscal year company profits will be increased from $500,000 to $650,000.
>
> *Goal B.* During the 1986 fiscal year employee turnover will be reduced from 4 percent per month to 3 percent.

Goal A is clearly a strategic goal and is, therefore, set by top management. Goal B, a subgoal or means of achieving Goal A, may also be set by top management if it applies to the entire organization. Still lower level goals may be set that will be a means to achieving the turnover goal, but such subgoals are not strategic goals. As shown in Figure 20-2, top managers should be primarily concerned with strategic goals, or the ends toward which the organization is striving. To the extent that they become involved in setting subgoals (tactical goals), they run a risk of minimizing the active participation of lower managers in goal setting.

Tactical Goals

Tactical goals are the subgoals that undergird and make possible the achievement of strategic goals. They are set throughout the organization, even at the employee level in unusual cases (as in the case of the logging industry example presented earlier). Ideally MBO should extend to the lowest organizational level, but such involvement is difficult to achieve.

Since goals must often be broken down into a series of successively smaller subgoals, there is a point at which the difficulty level of a given subgoal does not warrant the analytical treatment applied to strategic goals or relatively complex tactical goals. For example, tactical subgoals beneath the goal to reduce employee turnover by 1 percent a month within a year might include

1. Modification of the reward system in order to motivate supervisors to work at the task of reducing turnover and to motivate operators to become long-term employees.

2. Development of the human relations skills of first line supervisors to the point that they understand how to work on the turnover problem on a daily basis.

3. Determination of the causes of turnover by means of an attitude survey, interviews of present operators, and exit interviews.

4. Analysis of employment data in order to isolate variables that will predict turnover prior to employment.

5. Improvement of the physical environment by appropriate painting and by upgrading the heating and air-conditioning systems.

The first goal could turn out to be rather complex. The fifth goal, by contrast, may require little attention other than a written order and assignment of a target completion date. It is important that simple goals not be treated as though they are complex. Some companies become so enamored of their complicated systems and procedures that results are subordinated to goal-setting techniques.

Tactical goals are at times minor goals in the sense of being uncomplicated and easy to achieve, but they are critical to making a goals system function successfully. Unless they are established as goals in their own right, they may well be neglected and lead to a collapse of the entire goals system. They are a crucial link between strategic goals and daily behavior.

Official versus Operative Goals

Many studies of organizational behavior have been guided by an overrationalistic point of view in which goals are taken for granted or in which the assumption is made that the static, official goals of the organization are the real goals that control everyday decisions and behavior.

Official goals are found in corporate charters, annual reports, and similar publications designed primarily for public consumption. Such statements as "to make a profit," "to earn the maximum return on investment," or "to provide a specific service" are purposely vague. The **operative goals** are more concerned with the actual operation of the organization and, consequently, are more practical and specific. Where operative goals provide the specific content of official goals they reflect choices among competing values. They may be justified on the basis of one official goal even though they may subvert another official goal. In one sense they are a means to official goals, but since the latter are vague or highly abstract, the operative goals become ends in themselves when the organization is the object of close analysis. For example, where profit making is the announced official goal, operative goals will specify whether quality or quantity is to be emphasized; thus quality *or* quantity becomes an end to be pursued.

Performance versus Development Goals

Performance goals are related to achievement in an individual's official position and may relate to sales volume, production, services, profits, and the like. **Development goals**, on the other hand, refer to the growth of individuals in the organization. The contrast is seen in the following examples:

> A performance goal of a manufacturing supervisor: "Within the next six months the number of returns for reworking in my department will be reduced by 25 percent. Improvements will be evident the first month and will continue steadily until the 25 percent goal is reached."
>
> A development goal of a sales manager with aspirations to move into general management: "During the next 12 months I will improve my understanding of accounting and finance to the level of a university student with two years of study in these subjects."

Development goals are often neglected in part because of pressures to reach performance goals and in part because development is often intangible and difficult to measure. It is important to make the performance-development distinction, if for no other reason than to call attention to the vague, nonspecific manner in which most organizations treat development needs. Personal development serves a twofold purpose: to prepare the individual to perform at a higher level and to provide compensation for contributions to the organization. Its importance is sufficient to warrant consideration at the strategic goal level and at tactical levels throughout the organization.

PREREQUISITES FOR A SUCCESSFUL MBO PROGRAM

> Whether an MBO program will succeed depends on the nature of the program and the environment in which it is applied. Some organizations should move gradually toward MBO rather than take a chance that the organizational body will reject MBO as a "foreign element."

Although there is no guarantee that the most perfectly contrived MBO program will succeed in a given organization, there are certain precautions management may take to increase the likelihood of success. Any one of the following prerequisites may, under certain conditions, be absent to a degree without causing complete failure of an overall MBO program, but each is important and contributes to a program's success.

Participation by Top Management

Top management cannot limit its involvement in MBO to endorsement of the program. In addition to insisting that middle managers and first line supervisors take the program seriously, the president and other members of top management should become actively involved in formulating corporate objectives and high-level goals and should exhibit continuing support for the program.

Grass Roots Participation

As we ordinarily think of MBO, top corporate executives miss the point when they set goals without the participation of lower ranks of management and then authoritatively delegate the goals downward. The motivational and humanizing aspects of an MBO program are based on the assumption that each manager in the hierarchy has taken part in the goal-setting process and has made a commitment to reach specified goals. In a strictly top-down approach, neither of these elements is present. However, research does not show that participation necessarily leads to higher performance and goal acceptance. Latham and Saari, for example, found that participation is superior to the assignment of goals only to the extent that participation results in goals that are higher than those a superior would assign.[15] Similarly, Ivancevich found that in one study assigning goals got better results than participation (in terms of both satisfaction and performance).[16]

These surprising findings are made even more interesting by evidence that people who achieve assigned goals sometimes experience a greater sense of responsibility, success, and competence than do those who participate in setting their goals.[17] What conclusions can we draw then about the value of participation in goal setting? At least two points are noteworthy: (1) participation is not always best and (2) further research is needed to tell us when to elicit participation and when to assign goals.

Availability of Information

Effective goal setting requires extensive and accurate information. The manager who is kept in the dark about the goals of top-level managers is in no position to set realistic individual goals. In addition, a manager must have access to a broad spectrum of information pertaining to costs, availability of resources, willingness of peers and others to cooperate, market conditions, and the effect of one's actions on other units within the organization.

Control Over Means

The concept of MBO assumes that a manager has a degree of control over the means (processes, people, materials, and money) by which goals will be reached. If this is not the case, it is unrealistic to expect goal setting to alter managerial behavior and thereby affect results. A supervisor in a Texas cement plant that is closely controlled by its New York home office expressed well the predicament of a manager whose position is too narrow to permit a significant influence on results:

> I sometimes wonder why I'm even here. Productivity in this company has little to do with human effort. It's a matter of plant capability. As for my other management functions, personnel does the hiring, and it takes an act of Congress to get anybody fired. Raises are determined by collective bargaining between people I've never seen. A clock and a clerk do the timekeeping, payroll mails out the checks, maintenance does the housekeeping, mechanical keeps the equipment going, Q.C. oversees the product quality; and I'm supposed to supervise a department, but I can't say good morning without consulting the union contract. I'm not sure what I am, but don't call me a manager. Every union member in the plant has more freedom of action than I do!

Motivation to Take Risks

A manager who has always been evaluated on the basis of activities performed rather than results achieved is understandably threatened when required to set goals. A commitment to achieve specific objectives and an agreement on the standards by which performance will be evaluated inevitably involve a manager in risk-taking behavior. There is always the possibility of failure when an individual participates in MBO.

When an MBO program is installed, a manager's only motivation to participate may be a fear of the consequences of doing otherwise. The reluctant participant may give lip service to goal setting while subtly resisting and undermining the system. The goal-setting behavior of managers and nonmanagers alike may have much in common with that of machine operators who deliberately withhold valuable information about production methods and produce below their potential. Employees on any level who believe that a commitment to high productivity may entail a penalty, such as the threat of failure or harder work without more pay, will somehow subvert the system. From their point of view, it is the rational thing to do.

A Belief in People

Viewed as a participative system, MBO requires a Theory Y view of people (discussed in Chapter 3) and an experience-based trust in the individuals who are expected to set goals and assume responsibility for results. MBO assumes that it is the nature of people to be challenged by a goal and to respond favorably to responsibility, autonomy, and the opportunities for growth which are inherent in such a system.

Many MBO programs fail probably because historically the top corporate management has been oriented toward a Theory X viewpoint and simply cannot make the change MBO requires. It follows, too, that employees who have been selected and retained on the basis of their suitability for working in a Theory X environment may be unable to adapt rapidly enough to satisfy the demands of MBO.

Organizations change but, like the individuals of whom they are composed, they change slowly and grudgingly. Management should be cautious about trying to change the environment too rapidly in order to make it suitable for MBO. The successful installation of a fully developed crash program should be expected only if the environment is unusually favorable.

ESTABLISHING AN MBO PROGRAM

Goal setting in organizations is a long, technical process of serious planning and decision making. As such, it possesses the potential for influencing every major aspect of organizational life and should not be undertaken unless management is prepared to invest heavily in time and emotional involvement.

Because organizations differ greatly in the many aspects that affect the success of an MBO program, there can be no one best process for integrating it into the organization. Those responsible for its installation should always evaluate the total environment before deciding on a course of action. The adoption of a canned and supposedly universally applicable program is seldom advisable. While granting the need for tailoring MBO to each unique environment, the following is suggested as a very general model for establishing an MBO program.

Phase I: Preparation

All members of management and others who are expected to participate in the program are systematically informed about the nature and benefits of MBO. To the maximum extent possible, participants are made aware of the personal advantages of functioning within an MBO system. Participants should, if possible, have all their fears about the program allayed.

Phase II: Formulation of Strategic Objectives and Goals

It is top management's function to provide the purpose and criteria by which subsequent goal setting will be guided. In this regard three suggestions are in order:

1. Organizational purpose should be broad enough to allow flexibility as environmental changes occur. Some nineteenth century manufacturers would still be in business had they perceived their purpose in terms of providing transportation instead of making horse-drawn carriages.

2. Organizational purpose should be expressed in terms of as many strategic objectives as are needed to provide a meaningful statement of what the organization would like to become or achieve. For example,
   a. To maximize profits within the limits posed by ethical and legal behavior and other stated objectives.
   b. To contribute to the well-being of the organization's members by providing unusual opportunities for productivity, compensation, and challenge.
   c. To take affirmative action to include a reasonable portion of the area's disadvantaged and minority citizens in the company's employment, growth, and advancement opportunities.

3. The strategic goals for achieving the major corporate objectives should be established prior to the setting of organization-wide tactical goals. A knowledge of the former will give a quality of realism to the tactical goals which are subsequently set. The strategic goals should be stated concretely, specifically, and measurably; but they should be relatively free of statements of means that might unnecessarily restrict freedom of action at lower levels of management. For example, the statement "expansion of production capacity by 50 percent within the next 18 months" is preferable to "expansion of the production capacity *of present plants* by 50 percent during the next 18 months."

Phase III: Tentative Goal Setting at All Levels

Working within the parameters of broadly based corporate goals, middle and first line managers formulate a set of tactical goals for presentation to higher levels of management. Top management also formulates a set of high-level tactical goals it believes will best serve the purposes of the organization. Tactical goals, even those of top management, are at this point in time tentative because they have yet to be integrated and made consistent throughout the hierarchy.

At each management level this phase may be broken down into three steps:

Step 1. Goal Definition

Is the goal specific, measurable, and apparently achievable?

Step 2. Goal Analysis

A. Barriers to Achievement. What barriers will interfere with goal achievement?
  1. Personal barriers (attitudes, motivation, experience, education, and skills)
  2. Environmental barriers (actions of a competitor, inadequate technology, limited funds, or high interest rates)
  3. Conflict barriers (conflict with other goals for resources; mutually exclusive goals such as acquisition by a major corporation versus maintaining autonomy and independence)
B. Tactics and Resources. How will each barrier to achieving the goal be overcome?
C. Cost of Achievement. How much time, money, emotional involvement, and diversion from other worthy goals will be necessary?
D. Expected Payoff. Will the profits, growth, and opportunities be worth the necessary cost of achievement?
E. Risk Evaluation. Will possible losses warrant the risk involved in achieving the goal?

Step 3. Decision Making

Is the net return sufficient to warrant the investment required to reach this goal? If the answer is yes, proceed to Phase IV.

Phase IV: Proposal, Interaction, and Revision

In a series of meetings throughout the different levels of the organizational hierarchy, proposed goals are discussed and evaluated. Compromises and trade-offs result in a final set of goals with which everyone can live. Although conflicts must at times be settled by means of formal authority, by the time Phase IV is concluded all managers have a set of objectives that are in some sense personalized and to which each manager is willing to make a commitment.

Effective goal setting is necessarily an iterative process, often involving several cycles or repetitions of the working sessions within which goals are discussed, modified, and restated. This, of course, is time consuming. It is, however, a necessary process if goals are to be meaningful to the individuals involved and are to integrate the activities of the organization.

Phase V: Agreement on Goals and Standards of Evaluation

As an integral part of defining the goals on which agreement has been reached, the superior and subordinate jointly decide on the standards by which the latter's performance will be evaluated. To avoid future misunderstandings and to provide a means of crystallizing the subordinate's goal commitment, the agreement concerning frequency of evaluations and the standards for measuring results should be committed to writing with copies transmitted to the next higher level of management.

Phase VI: Daily Implementation

Far too many MBO programs make no systematic provision for translating goals into day-to-day planning and decision making. As a result, statements of goals gather dust and only in a general way influence organizational behavior.

One systematic way of bridging the gap between goals and everyday activity is to encourage all managers to begin each day with a brief but relatively formal planning session. Managers ask themselves: What specifically can I do today that will contribute to the achievement of my goals? It is often useful to go through a more detailed checklist such as the following:

1. *Initiation.* What projects should be started today?

2. *Continuation.* On what projects should progress be made today?

3. *Completion.* What projects should be completed today?

4. *Priorities.* In what sequence should today's tasks be done in order to make efficient use of resources and meet fixed deadlines or target dates?

5. *Follow-up.* What projects should be reviewed today to ensure successful completion within the allotted time?

Phase VII: Follow-Up and Performance Evaluation

As shown in Figure 20-3, the MBO process is incomplete without evaluation. General rather than close supervision is the style of the MBO manager, but this does not mean that the superior retires from the arena of action. As one manager put it, "I still inspect what I expect."

Assuming that a manager has a feedback system which provides adequate information about the subordinate's progress, monitoring of this system may be sufficient. Direct supervision becomes necessary primarily when there is reason to believe subordinates are falling behind schedule or utilizing unacceptable means to achieve their objectives. Of course, in addition to these interventions, the superior and subordinate will freely exchange information on an informal basis. However, as a means of stressing the seriousness of a goals commitment, mid-course

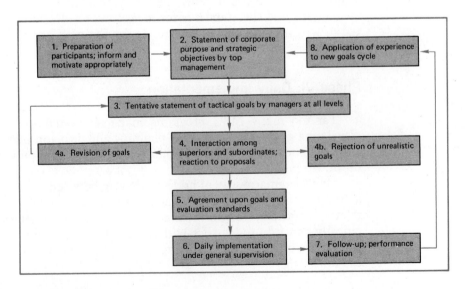

FIGURE 20-3 Prototype of an MBO Program

corrections in goals are preferably made only during regularly scheduled performance evaluation sessions. Since individual goals within an organization are interdependent, appropriate communications should be made when a major goal is changed.

SYSTEM IMPLICATIONS OF MBO

MBO is much more than a method for increasing productivity through goal setting. For goal setting to get maximum results, MBO must be integrated into the organization in such a way that it influences and is influenced by all major subsystems and processes.

MBO is not in itself an all-inclusive approach to managing, but its implications are broad for a number of subsystems within an organization. For example, where promotions have been strongly influenced by personality characteristics and political considerations, some reexamination of policy is called for. Where management compensation has been controlled by job classification and length of service, it may be necessary to make changes to permit a closer relationship between productivity and pay.

Management development practices will ordinarily be influenced by MBO. The behavior patterns of high- and low-achieving managers should be contrasted to determine whether management development efforts are being directed toward change that will improve results. Contrary to the assumption made in most development programs, it may be that the manager who has a strong desire to manage and is strongly committed to the achievement of clearly defined objectives will, with a minimum of help from formal programs, find the means. Under MBO, managers will be justifiably critical of programs that are expensive and time consuming but bear no demonstrable relationship to results.

While MBO is not intended to replace traditional managerial controls, it should to some extent move an organization in the direction of substituting internal for external controls. The more completely MBO becomes a reality, the greater the likelihood that the use of external controls will dampen the creativity, initiative, and sense of responsibility MBO tends to stimulate. This is consistent with the fact that MBO favors a high level of delegation, general rather than close supervision, and decentralization rather than centralized organizational structure.

Depending on the degree of delegation and goal setting practiced before its installation, MBO may drastically change the organization's patterns of communication. Since goal setting demands a high degree of information exchange and interaction between the different levels of management, MBO tends to change the quality of communication. Superior and subordinate typically move in the direction of a greater sense of shared responsibility, and status barriers give way to an increased awareness of mutual interdependence and common interests.

Depending on one's perspective, MBO will virtually replace or add a significant dimension to organizational planning as it is practiced in most organizations. The critical difference between MBO and traditional organizational planning is that MBO involves the entire organization in certain aspects of the planning process and provides a much needed framework for translating plans into day-to-day behavior.

THE FUTURE OF MBO

The brief history of MBO leaves much to be desired. Enough showcase examples exist in organizations of all sizes to demonstrate its value, but the many more examples of failure have seriously damaged its reputation. Any fair and objective evaluation of MBO must deal with the fact that there are many MBO methods applied in a variety of organizations by persons with greatly differing levels of commitment and expertise.

For the most part the MBO programs that have failed have been characterized by one or more of the following:

1. *Authoritarian leadership.* MBO requires a high level of participation by a large number of individuals. It is not a quick route to increased productivity. There is a price to pay.

2. *Hasty implementation without organizational preparation.* Outside MBO "specialists" skillfully sell and hastily install canned programs without reference to whether the organizational climate is favorable (the attitudes, motivation, leadership styles, and the like).

3. *Excessive paperwork.* MBO is equated in the minds of participants with the completion of large numbers of elaborate forms. Managers go through the motions of goal setting but only to satisfy the demands of their superiors.

MBO is not likely to pass from the scene as fads do. If it does lose its identity, the process will be one of maturation and integration with the accepted managerial practices of strategic planning, goal setting, and participative management. Some companies will continue to reject MBO, but its name and specific techniques are unimportant when compared with the philosophy and fundamental practices which are its essence. Companies would do well not to reject MBO based on the objectionable procedures of one particular program. An inappropriate or poor implementation of an MBO program does not negate the basic value of MBO practices and philosophy.

IMPORTANT TERMS AND CONCEPTS

objectives	official goals
goals	operative goals
management by objectives	performance goals
tactical goals	development goals

STUDY AND DISCUSSION QUESTIONS

1. Prior to the human relations movement, management philosophy and practice tended to emphasize productivity at the expense of people. What is to prevent MBO from doing the same?

2. In what ways does the goal setting of MBO typically differ from goal setting in an organization that has no MBO program? Is the difference of any importance?

3. Review your own experiences in organizations and identify an instance where goal setting would most likely have led to some of the benefits described in the chapter. Briefly describe this situation and explain how goal setting could have resulted in the benefits you have in mind.

4. Develop a rationale to support participation in goal setting. Under what circumstances would it not apply?

5. Why are development goals more often neglected than performance goals? Just how important are development goals?

6. In what significant ways does goal setting affect a manager's thought processes?

7. Why do managers sometimes resist goal setting? What do you think superiors should do about such resistance by a subordinate manager when a corporate decision has been made to institute MBO?

8. Describe an organization in which MBO will probably fail.

9. Describe what you think a company president should do in an ideal MBO program. Would you recommend that the president's role differ depending on the size of the organization?

10. Evaluate this statement by a manager in terms of what you know about MBO: "MBO is a waste of time. We need more people with their heads in today's ball game instead of spending so much time thinking about what's going to happen in the future."

11. Why do you think goal setting tends to work best at the management level?

12. MBO and general supervision, as contrasted with close supervision, are often found in the same organization. Why is this true?

13. Planning has long been accepted as an important part of a manager's work. How does it relate to MBO?

CRITICAL INCIDENT

MANAGING BY OBJECTIVES*

Doris Schwaller, president of the Schwaller Corporation, believed in MBO. Since MBO had worked well for her in the past, she believed, as many managers do, that people are more highly motivated to reach objectives they have helped formulate.

To initiate the planning process for the forthcoming year, Schwaller called a meeting of her sales manager, controller, and plant manager. During the meeting, basic objectives, consistent with the firm's five-year plan, were established. Schwaller then asked each manager to submit his or her individual goals to her in a follow-up conference.

Lee Davidson, the sales manager, was scheduled for the first meeting since the sales forecast provided a basis for establishing the production schedule and for absorbing overhead into the cost system.

---

*This critical incident was prepared by Donald L. Sexton, Ph.D., Caruth Professor of Entrepreneurship, Baylor University, Waco, Texas.

Schwaller developed a sales forecast of her own prior to meeting with Davidson. She arrived at an $11 million figure based on the following facts:

Sales for the last year were $10 million.

Sales for the firm had been increasing at a rate of 6 percent to 7 percent each year.

Sales for the industry had increased at an annual rate of 10 percent for the last three years, and industry experts predicted they would increase by 12 percent to 14 percent during each of the next three years.

Economists generally agreed that economic conditions would remain relatively stable for the next two years.

The firm's inventory policy was to stock only 20 percent of the items that made up 80 percent of its sales. Schwaller believed that her forecast could be easily achieved and would probably not require increases in the promotion or advertising budget.

Davidson came into the meeting with reports showing sales information for the past three years. After discussing those reports and the economy in general, he presented his sales projection for the next year— $9 million. Schwaller was surprised at the low figure—even more surprised when Davidson presented a sales budget with a 25 percent increase in promotion and advertising. Obviously dissatisfied with the proposal, Schwaller asked Davidson how he had arrived at his estimate, considering the stable economy and projected growth rate of the industry.

Davidson's reply was, "I don't pay any attention to those numbers. They don't mean a thing." Adding that his own forecasts were based on personal judgment, he expressed some "bad feelings" about the forthcoming year. He had had "similar feelings five years earlier and, sure enough, sales were down that year." After much discussion Davidson was still unwilling to change his forecast and reiterated that he considered the industry and general economic data to be irrelevant.

Schwaller then presented her own forecast of $11 million, expressing her conviction that "it should be a cakewalk and should not require additional expenditures for advertising and promotion." Davidson assertively countered with, "I'm not even sure I can get the $9 million, and I sure can't do it without the additional 25 percent in the budget. Your goal is unrealistic. You're asking for too much."

At this point the discussion became more heated. Schwaller held to the $11 million figure, thinking it would be easy, while Davidson believed the $9 million would be difficult with the budget increase and nearly impossible without it. Finally, Schwaller stated emphatically, "I think it can be done! It's your responsibility to make sure we reach the $11 million goal."

Davidson stood up and started for the door. He hesitated and then offered a parting remark: "Since you had your mind made up before I came in, why did you bother to ask for my sales estimate? Do you really call this management by objectives?"

1. Was Schwaller using an MBO approach?

2. Should Schwaller suggest a compromise goal of $10 million?

3. What action should Schwaller take now? What should she have done originally?

4. What problems are associated with participative goal setting?

5. What assumptions are inherent in MBO?

REFERENCES

1. Drucker, Peter F. *People and Performance: The Best of Peter Drucker on Management.* New York: Harper & Row Publishers, Inc., 1977, pp. 63–64.

2. Ivancevich, John M., and J. Timothy McMahon. "A Study of Task-Goal Attributes, Higher Order Need Strength, and Performance," *Academy of Management Journal,* Vol. 20, No. 4, December, 1977, pp. 552–563.

3. Hall, Douglas T., and Lawrence W. Foster. "A Psychological Success Cycle and Goal Setting: Goals, Performance, and Attitudes," *Academy of Management Journal,* Vol. 20, No. 2, June, 1977, pp. 282–290.

4. Locke, Edwin A. "The Ubiquity of the Technique of Goal Setting in Theories of and Approaches to Employee Motivation," *Academy of Management Review,* Vol. 3, No. 3, July, 1978, pp. 594–601.

5. Latham, Gary P., and Timothy P. Steele. "The Motivational Effects of Participation Versus Goal Setting on Performance," *Academy of Management Journal,* Vol. 26, No. 3, September, 1983, pp. 406–417.

6. Drucker, Peter F. "What Results Should You Expect? A User's Guide to MBO," *Public Administration Review,* Vol. 36, No. 1, January–February, 1976, pp. 12–19.

7. Odiorne, George S. *Management by Objectives: A System of Managerial Leadership.* New York: Pitman Learning, Inc., 1965.

8. Odiorne. *Management by Objectives: A System of Managerial Leadership,* pp. 55–56.

9. Kolb, David A., and Richard E. Boyatzis. "Goal-Setting and Self-Directed Behavior Change," *Organizational Psychology—A Book of Readings*, 2d ed. Englewood Cliffs, N.J.: Prentice-Hall, Inc., 1974, p. 363.

10. Latham, Gary P., and James J. Baldes. "The Practical Significance of Locke's Theory of Goal Setting," *Journal of Applied Psychology*, Vol. 60, No. 1, February, 1975, p. 124.

11. Ivancevich, John M. "Different Goal Setting Treatments and Their Effects on Performance and Job Satisfaction," *Academy of Management Journal*, Vol. 20, No. 3, September, 1977, pp. 406–419.

12. Quick, James C. "Dyadic Goal Setting and Role Stress: A Field Study," *Academy of Management Journal*, Vol. 22, No. 2, June, 1979, pp. 241–248.

13. Quick. "Dyadic Goal Setting and Role Stress: A Field Study," p. 248.

14. Steiner, George A., and Harry and Elsa Kunin. "Formal Strategic Planning in the United States Today," *Long Range Planning*, Vol. 16, No. 3, June, 1983, pp. 12–17.

15. Latham, Gary P., and Lise M. Saari. "The Effect of Holding Goal Difficulty Constant on Assigned and Participative Goals," *Academy of Management Journal*, Vol. 22, No. 1, March, 1979, pp. 163–168.

16. Ivancevich. "Different Goal Setting Treatments and Their Effects on Performance and Job Satisfaction," pp. 406–419.

17. Chacko, Thomas I., Thomas H. Stone, and Arthur P. Brief. "Participation in Goal-Setting Programs: An Attributional Analysis," *Academy of Management Review*, Vol. 4, No. 3, July, 1979, pp. 433–437.

SUGGESTED READINGS

Abelson, Michael A. "The Impact of Goal Change on Prominent Perceptions and Behaviors of Employees," *Journal of Management*, Vol. 9, No. 1, 1983, pp. 65–79.

Cosgrove, Don J., and Robert L. Dinerman. "There is No Motivational Magic," *Management Review*, Vol. 71, No. 8, August, 1982, pp. 58–61.

Erez, Miriam, and Frederick H. Kanfer. "The Role of Goal Acceptance in Goal Setting and Task Performance," *Academy of Management Review*, Vol. 8, No. 3, July, 1983, pp. 454–463.

Ivancevich, John M., and J. Timothy McMahon. "The Effects of Goal Setting, External Feedback, and Self-Generated Feedback on Outcome Variables: A Field Experiment," *Academy of Management Journal*, Vol. 25, No. 2, June, 1982, pp. 359–372.

King, William R., and David J. Cleland. *Strategic Planning and Policy*. New York: Van Nostrand Reinhold Company, 1978.

Kondrasuk, Jack N. "Studies in MBO Effectiveness," *Academy of Management Review*, Vol. 6, No. 3, 1981, pp. 419–430.

Linneman, Robert E. *Shirt-Sleeve Approach to Long-Range Planning for the Smaller, Growing Corporation*. Englewood Cliffs, N.J.: Prentice-Hall, Inc., 1980.

McConkie, Mark L. "A Clarification of the Goal Setting and Appraisal Processes in MBO," *Academy of Management Review*, Vol. 4, No. 1, January, 1979, pp. 29–40.

Muczyk, Jan P. "A Controlled Field Experiment Measuring the Impact of MBO on Performance Data," *Journal of Management Studies*, Vol. 15, No. 3, October, 1978, pp. 318–329.

Pringle, Charles D. "The Ethics of MBO," *Academy of Management Review*, Vol. 7, No. 2, April, 1982, pp. 305–312.

Salton, Gary J. "The Focused Web—Goal Setting in the MBO Process," *Management Review*, Vol. 67, No. 1, January, 1978, pp. 46–50.

SUBJECT INDEX